T0310767

Handbook of Research on Advancements in AI and IoT Convergence Technologies

Jingyuan Zhao
University of Toronto, Canada

V. Vinoth Kumar
Jain University, India

Rajesh Natarajan
University of Applied Science and Technology, Shinas, Oman

T.R. Mahesh
Jain University, India

A volume in the Advances in Computational Intelligence and Robotics (ACIR) Book Series

Published in the United States of America by
   IGI Global
   Engineering Science Reference (an imprint of IGI Global)
   701 E. Chocolate Avenue
   Hershey PA, USA 17033
   Tel: 717-533-8845
   Fax: 717-533-8661
   E-mail: cust@igi-global.com
   Web site: http://www.igi-global.com

Copyright © 2023 by IGI Global. All rights reserved. No part of this publication may be reproduced, stored or distributed in any form or by any means, electronic or mechanical, including photocopying, without written permission from the publisher. Product or company names used in this set are for identification purposes only. Inclusion of the names of the products or companies does not indicate a claim of ownership by IGI Global of the trademark or registered trademark.

Library of Congress Cataloging-in-Publication Data

Names: Zhao, Jingyuan, 1968- editor. | Kumar, V. Vinoth, 1988- editor. |
  Natarajan, Rajesh, 1983- editor. | Mahesh, T. R., 1978- editor.
Title: Handbook of research on advancements in AI and IoT convergence
  technologies / Jingyuan Zhao, V. Vinoth Kumar, Rajesh Natarajan, and
  T.R. Mahesh, editors.
Description: Hershey, PA : Engineering Science Reference, [2023] | Includes
  bibliographical references and index. | Summary: "This book presents a
  fully understanding on recent advancements in AI and IoT convergence
  technologies, with a focus on state-of-the-art approaches,
  methodologies, and systems for the design, development, deployment, and
  innovative use of those convergence technologies"-- Provided by
  publisher.
Identifiers: LCCN 2022038158 | ISBN 9781668469712 (h/c) | ISBN
  9781668469729 (eISBN)
Subjects: LCSH: Internet of things. | Convergence (Telecommunication) |
  Artificial intelligence.
Classification: LCC TK5105.8857 .H349 2023 | DDC
  004.67/8--dc23/eng/20221019
LC record available at https://lccn.loc.gov/2022038158

This book is published in the IGI Global book series Advances in Computational Intelligence and Robotics (ACIR) (ISSN: 2327-0411; eISSN: 2327-042X)

British Cataloguing in Publication Data
A Cataloguing in Publication record for this book is available from the British Library.

All work contributed to this book is new, previously-unpublished material. The views expressed in this book are those of the authors, but not necessarily of the publisher.

For electronic access to this publication, please contact: eresources@igi-global.com.

Advances in Computational Intelligence and Robotics (ACIR) Book Series

Ivan Giannoccaro
University of Salento, Italy

ISSN:2327-0411
EISSN:2327-042X

MISSION

While intelligence is traditionally a term applied to humans and human cognition, technology has progressed in such a way to allow for the development of intelligent systems able to simulate many human traits. With this new era of simulated and artificial intelligence, much research is needed in order to continue to advance the field and also to evaluate the ethical and societal concerns of the existence of artificial life and machine learning.

The **Advances in Computational Intelligence and Robotics (ACIR) Book Series** encourages scholarly discourse on all topics pertaining to evolutionary computing, artificial life, computational intelligence, machine learning, and robotics. ACIR presents the latest research being conducted on diverse topics in intelligence technologies with the goal of advancing knowledge and applications in this rapidly evolving field.

COVERAGE

- Automated Reasoning
- Evolutionary Computing
- Artificial Intelligence
- Agent technologies
- Artificial Life
- Cyborgs
- Computational Intelligence
- Computer Vision
- Heuristics
- Machine Learning

IGI Global is currently accepting manuscripts for publication within this series. To submit a proposal for a volume in this series, please contact our Acquisition Editors at Acquisitions@igi-global.com or visit: http://www.igi-global.com/publish/.

The Advances in Computational Intelligence and Robotics (ACIR) Book Series (ISSN 2327-0411) is published by IGI Global, 701 E. Chocolate Avenue, Hershey, PA 17033-1240, USA, www.igi-global.com. This series is composed of titles available for purchase individually; each title is edited to be contextually exclusive from any other title within the series. For pricing and ordering information please visit http://www.igi-global.com/book-series/advances-computational-intelligence-robotics/73674. Postmaster: Send all address changes to above address. Copyright © 2023 IGI Global. All rights, including translation in other languages reserved by the publisher. No part of this series may be reproduced or used in any form or by any means – graphics, electronic, or mechanical, including photocopying, recording, taping, or information and retrieval systems – without written permission from the publisher, except for non commercial, educational use, including classroom teaching purposes. The views expressed in this series are those of the authors, but not necessarily of IGI Global.

Titles in this Series

For a list of additional titles in this series, please visit: www.igi-global.com/book-series

Scalable and Distributed Machine Learning and Deep Learning Patterns
J. Joshua Thomas (UOW Malaysia KDU Penang University College, Malaysia) S. Harini (Vellore Institute of Technology, India) and V. Pattabiraman (Vellore Institute of Technology, ndia)
Engineering Science Reference • © 2023 • 286pp • H/C (ISBN: 9781668498040) • US $270.00

Handbook of Research on Thrust Technologies' Effect on Image Processing
Binay Kumar Pandey (Department of Information Technology, College of Technology, Govind Ballabh Pant University of Agriculture and Technology, India) Digvijay Pandey (Department of Technical Education, Government of Uttar Pradesh, India) Rohit Anand (G.B. Pant DSEU Okhla-1 Campus, India & Government of NCT of Delhi, New Delhi, India) Deepak S. Mane (Performance Engineering Lab, Tata Research, Development, and Design Center, Australia) and Vinay Kumar Nassa (Rajarambapu Institute of Technology, ndia)
Engineering Science Reference • © 2023 • 542pp • H/C (ISBN: 9781668486184) • US $350.00

Multi-Disciplinary Applications of Fog Computing Responsiveness in Real-Time
Debi Prasanna Acharjya (Vellore Institute of Technology, India) and Kauser Ahmed P. (Vellore Institute of Technology, India)
Engineering Science Reference • © 2023 • 280pp • H/C (ISBN: 9781668444665) • US $270.00

Global Perspectives on Robotics and Autonomous Systems Development and Applications
Maki K. Habib (The American University in Cairo, Egypt)
Engineering Science Reference • © 2023 • 405pp • H/C (ISBN: 9781668477915) • US $360.00

Stochastic Processes and Their Applications in Artificial Intelligence
Christo Ananth (Samarkand State University, Uzbekistan) N. Anbazhagan (Alagappa University, India) and Mark Goh (National University of Singapore, Singapore)
Engineering Science Reference • © 2023 • 220pp • H/C (ISBN: 9781668476796) • US $270.00

Handbook of Research on Deep Learning Techniques for Cloud-Based Industrial IoT
P. Swarnalatha (Department of Information Security, School of Computer Science and Engineering, Vellore Institute of Technology, India) and S. Prabu (Department Banking Technology, Pondicherry University, India)
Engineering Science Reference • © 2023 • 432pp • H/C (ISBN: 9781668480984) • US $335.00

701 East Chocolate Avenue, Hershey, PA 17033, USA
Tel: 717-533-8845 x100 • Fax: 717-533-8661
E-Mail: cust@igi-global.com • www.igi-global.com

List of Contributors

Table of Contents

Detailed Table of Contents

Chapter 1

    H. K. Shashikala, Jain University, India
    T. R. Mahesh, Jain University, India
    V. Vinoth Kimar, Jain University, India
    K. Chanchani Keerthana, Jain University, India
    S. Priyanka, Jain University, India
    Rangareddygari H. Meghana, Jain University, India
    Yarragunta Thanmai, Publicis Sapient, India

In the standard direction of business, continuously tracking and dealing with the fitness of a person is a tough task. Humans of all ages ought to have their fitness examined on an everyday basis. The aim is to notify the victim's household of the twist of fate through predetermined contacts and locate the nearest hospital, telling them of the twist of fate in order that assistance may be dispatched. This prototype uses the gyroscope, accelerometer, GPS, and GSM. The aim of these studies is to create a device that may come across the presence of a twist of fate even as additionally reminding continual sufferers and the aged in their prescription obligations. The MPU6050 sensor detects the presence of a twist of fate through the use of a 3-axis gyroscope and a 3-axis accelerometer. The GPS module locates the twist of fate scene and contacts emergency responders in addition to guardians who've been stored with the aid of the users.

Chapter 2

    Kamalendu Pal, University of London, UK

Wireless sensor data communication networks (WSNs) based on the Internet of Things (IoT) technology have many potential applications for the industrial world. The IoT paradigm encompasses ubiquitous computing, pervasive computing, data communication protocols, sensing technologies, and embedded devices, and they merge selectively to form an information system where the physical and digital worlds meet. They can serve different categories of business services through continuous symbiotic interactions. In this way, the formed interconnected information system, through the Internet, exchanges data and information to create services that bring tangible benefits to the industrial world and its supply chain operations. This chapter presents a system architecture (i.e., Apparel Business Decentralized Data Integration (ABDDI)) and its knowledge representation scheme, based on formal languages – Description Logics (DLs), to address the needs of formal information modeling and reasoning for web-based services provision using ontology. Finally, the chapter presents an example of the experimental result of service composition ontology's similarity assessment.

Chapter 3

Prasanna Ranjith Christodoss, University of Technology and Applied Science, Shinas, Oman
Rajesh Natarajan, University of Technology and Applied Sciences, Shinas, Oman
Syed Khaja Mohideen, University of Applied Science and Technology, Salalah, Oman
Justus Selwyn, John Brown University, USA
B. Anandapriya, Patrician College of Arts and Science, India

Machine learning (ML) is one of the most popular fields in medical research. Correct identification of the presence of diabetes is essential for providing efficient treatment. Numerous machine learning models were developed to predict diabetes. However, many ML models suffer from misclassification due to a lack of proper feature selection methods. How to select the best features is still a significant problem in the classification domain. To address the problem, an ensemble-based feature selection is proposed. The proposed feature selection is then evaluated in five machine learning models. The experimental results show that the proposed feature selection is 36% more efficient than existing feature selection methods.

Chapter 4

Reepu, Chandigarh University, India
Sushil Kumar, Dhanauri PG College, India
Megha Gupta Chaudhary, SRM Institute of Science and Technology, India
K. Gurnadha Gupta, KL University (Deemed), India
Sabyasachi Pramanik, Haldia Institute of Technology, India
Ankur Gupta, Vaish College of Engineering, India

Internet of Things (IoT) is a fast-growing idea that aims to connect billions of objects (such as smartphones, sensors, and potential networking equipment) and allow them to communicate with one another. The IoT is a network of interconnected devices which utilises sensor to use technology communicate relating to one another across without the necessity for human contact, a wireless communication medium is used to exchange, alter, and move data. This interconnectedness is important in a variety of ways, including well-timed coordination with a variety of simple devices such as sensors, thermostats, fitbits, routers, and so on. These networks may be particularly vulnerable to prone assaults due to their open and heterogeneous nature. Aside from the advantages of IoT development, there may be significant concerns regarding security and privacy, which is likely to be one of the most frustrating aspects of IoT design adaptation and development.

Chapter 5

K. S. Archana, SRM Institute of Science and Technology, India
B. Sivakumar, SRM Institute of Science and Technology, India
B. Ebenezer Abishek, VelTech Multitech Engineering College, India
Shaik Ghouhar Taj, JNTUA College of Engineering, India
V. Kavitha Reddy, JNTUA College of Engineering, India
A. Vijayalakshmi, VISTAS, India

In the current scenario, one of the recent research works is stock prediction in the future using machine learning techniques. Today, the stock market is one of the greatest investments to retail their current shares to get profit. This necessity forces everyone to turn back to predict the future stock price market using the efficient techniques in machine learning. However, the latest market analysis and prediction is one of the most complicated tasks to decide the value. This article proposed stock price prediction using an improved algorithm in machine learning. Machine learning uses different types of models to identify the prediction easier and accurately. This chapter presents the use of LSTM based machine learning to predict stocks and factors considered are date, time, closing price and opening price of the stocks. Finally, this machine learning model was trained with numerous data, and the results were compared with existing algorithms. These performance results show the maximum prediction accuracies of 92.10% and 84.10% were attained using improved LSTM model.

Chapter 6

S. Nagini, VNR VJIET, India
Sravani Nalluri, VNR VJIET, India
Manik Soni, VNR VJIET, India
Ramasubbareddy Somula, VNR VJIET, India

In this chapter, the authors present a novel approach to detect illegal wildlife trade online using deep learning. The purpose here is to implement a deep convolutional neural network for the detection of illegal wildlife trade on the web. For this research, data consists of two types of images, legal and illegal. The illegal images, such as tiger skin and elephant tusks, are collected using web-scraping techniques from social media websites and legal images are collected from Kaggle. The outcomes of our research and experiments show that usage of deep CNN pre-trained on image-net achieves testing accuracy of 92.26% with an f1 score of 0.8234 with very low inference time.

Chapter 7

Thangarasu Nainan, Karpagam Academy of Higher Education (Deemed), India
Ramaraj Muniappan, Rathinam College of Arts and Science, India
V. Vijayalakshmi, Christ College of Science and Management, Malur, India
R. Rajalakshmi, Arignar Anna College, India
Sabareeswaran Dhandapani, Rathinam College of Arts and Science, India
Murugadass Muthaiyan, Arignar Anna College, India

Image mining is tantamount to data mining concept. It is most imperative to understand the data mining concept to the prior knowledge of image mining. Data mining is an assemblage of methods that are used to automated approach to exhaustively explore and create associations in very large datasets. Image mining process is an analyzing large set of domain-specific data and consequently extracting information and knowledge in a form of new relationships, patterns, or clusters for the decision-making process. This research article mainly focuses on color pixel-based image segmentation to infer the age of the tiger and also applied several reasonable and applicable filters, enhancement processes in the speculative real-time images. The objective of the research work is to be done on assessing the age of the tiger using the color pixel based image classification and clustering is the main of the research work. To optimization of reduce the processing Time, Retrieval Time, Accuracy and Error Rate by generating the better results is to real time tiger image database.

K. Uday Kiran, Koneru Lakshmaiah Education Foundation, India
Ella Kalpana, TTWRDC, India
Prabha Shreeraj Nair, S. B. Jain Institute of Technology Management and Research, India
S. K. Hasane Ahammad, Koneru Lakshmaiah Education Foundation, India
K. Saikumar, Koneru Lakshmaiah Education Foundation, India

The MRI spinal cord image-based injury detection is very complex in the current world. In this research, an advanced deep learning-based spinal injury detection algorithm has been proposed. The segmentation was performed with the Otsu technique. The feature extraction and training were performed with shape-based intensity parameters of nothing but standard deviation, variance, mean, and kurtosis. The testing can be possible with ResNet CNN technology. The classification has been performed through 167 layers of architecture. Finally, with confusion matrix accuracy of 98.43%, Recall97.34%, F 1 measure of 95.23%, and throughput of 96.76%.

Antoine Toni Trad, IBISTM, France

This chapter presents the fundaments of the cloud transformation concept (CTC), and this concept is a basic component of the author's framework. The implementation of the CTC compute system (CTC-CS) is supported the author's applied holistic mathematical model (AHMM) for CTC (AHMM4CTC) and many research works on compute systems (CS), mathematical models, artificial intelligence (AI), and business/financial/organizational transformations projects. The AHMM is based on cross-functional research on an authentic and proprietary mixed research method that is supported by his own version of an AI search tree, which is combined with an internal heuristic's algorithm. The main focus is on CTC-CS requirements and transformation strategy. The proposed AHMM4CTC based CTC-CS is a virtual secured computing environment which uses an integrated empiric decision-making process. The CTC-CS is supported by a real-life case of business transformation project, which needs a Cloud infrastructure that is supported by the alignment of various existing Cloud standards.

Ravi Kiran Kumar Meduri, Government Degree Colleges of Andhra Pradesh, India
Sreeram Gutha, Vignana Bharathi Institute of Technology, India
Vijay Chandra Jadala, KL University, India

Cloud computing has become a popular ingredient in the information management of enterprises cutting across the globe and size. Its popularity lies in its ability to provide resources – infrastructure, platform, and software – as services on demand without compromising much on the quality of service. On-demand resource provisioning is possible by sharing the resources across multiple users or multiple tenants. Among all the three (IaaS, PaaS, and SaaS) deployments, SaaS offers more cost benefit to enterprises and users as compared to its predecessors because of its ability to share both hardware and software across multiple tenants with very minimal data sharing. The feature of sharing resources among multiple users known as multi tenancy is essential in achieving the objectives of cloud computing. This paper gives a detailed account of multi tenancy in cloud computing with special focus on SaaS applications and its associated problems followed by solution approaches.

Chapter 11

M. Rajani Shree, BNM Institue of Technology, India
Abhinav Ram Bhatta, Jain University, India
M. R. Sarveshvar, Jain University, India
Kritika Jain, Jain University, India

The various methods which have been adopted in processing and segmentation of medical images using deep learning and machine learning techniques are examined and analyzed in this article. Medical images analysis and their methods have been swiftly evolved into deep learning techniques and especially in convolutional neural networks. Deep learning concepts that may be used for the image classification, detection, and logging of medical related pictures and objects have been examined. Medical applications include: research and investigations into neuro, retinal and pulmonary, digital pathologies, breast, heart and musculoskeletal diseases and their corresponding analysis. Deep learning has already been used to accurately diagnose diseases and classify image samples, and it has the potential to revolutionise the entire landscape of healthcare. These uses are only expected to expand in the future. The most recent developments, including a critical analysis of the current problems have been summarized, and made plans for additional research in medical imaging.

Chapter 12

B. Swapna, Dr. M.G.R. Educational and Research Institute, India
P. Amudhan, Dr. M.G.R. Educational and Research Institute, India
S. Gayathri, Dr. M.G.R. Educational and Research Institute, India
E. Kavitha, Dr. M.G.R. Educational and Research Institute, India
M. Kamalahasan, Dr. M.G.R. Educational and Research Institute, India
K. Saravanan, Dr. M.G.R. Educational and Research Institute, India
M. Sujitha, Dr. M.G.R. Educational and Research Institute, India

Satellite tracking and control module in charge of maintenance is the subsystem. Monitoring and control of satellite locations affect the environment. Satellites are subjected to torque. This causes alignment and satellite angle instability while it is in space. The project involves the implementation of a satellite system and a test tool technology platform able to have it for lunch in the near future. It is also aimed towards them. Investigate the use of low-cost cube sats in the realm of remote sensing. In the original iteration of their design, the cube satellite utilized Picosat passive attitude control. However, a new version has been released to fulfil the accuracy standards of Picosat, the primary payload, which was supposed to be active attitude control. New posture determination and control the subsystem is in charge of successfully de-tumbling Picosat after booting and keeping it pointed in the right direction. As much as feasible, the desired alignment. This chapter describes the concept and execution of strong decision-making.

    K. Vanitha, Jain University, India
    M. Mohamed Musthafa, Al-Ameen Engineering College, India
    A. M. J. Md Zubair Rahman, Al-Ameen Engineering College, India
    K. Anitha, Al-Ameen Engineering College, India
    T. R. Mahesh, Jain University, India
    V. Vinoth Kumar, Jain University, India

In recent times, cyber security offers a significant advancement in smart grid technologies for its availability and functionality. The potential intrusion in smart grids marks the system to behave in a vulnerable way all the private data. Smart grids are often prone to data integrity attacks at its physical layer, which is been a critical issue presently. This attack alters the measurement of compromised meter set by the attacker(s). It misleads the decision making by the operators at the control center and thereby the reliability of the measurement is affected. In this chapter, the authors present a deep learning ensemble (DLE) model that possibly detects the potential data integrity attacks in the physical layer. The deep learning model uses ensemble learning to make decisions and combines the classified results to improve the classification on test data. The experiments are conducted on the proposed DLE model to find the accuracy of classifier the malicious and benign measurements.

    Janani Chennupati, Velagapudi Ramakrishna Siddhartha Engineering College, India
    Mounika Susarla, Velagapudi Ramakrishna Siddhartha Engineering College, India
    Vani K. Suvarna, Velagapudi Ramakrishna Siddhartha Engineering College, India
    K. S. Vijaya Lakshmi, Velagapudi Ramakrishna Siddhartha Engineering College, India
    Chennu Nandini Priyanka, Velagapudi Ramakrishna Siddhartha Engineering College, India

Bamboo is a natural air purifier that helps to keep the surroundings clean. Bamboo forests, an essential source of socioeconomic life for rural communities and an integral part of the ecosystem, are undergoing substantial changes. In the mapping and identification of natural resources, space technology has been beneficial. The objective of classification is to divide a large subject into fewer, more manageable fractions. For land use and land cover, four supervised learning methods, namely Naive Bayes, random forest, support vector machine, and decision tree, are used. Their overall accuracies will be compared to obtain the best algorithm. Land cover mapping and monitoring were carried out to preserve current natural resources and better understand the causative factors of land use in the study region, i.e., East Garo Hills, a district of Meghalaya, for the 2018 data. The application performance was measured in terms of Accuracy 97.23%, Recall 89.23%, F1 measure 97.23%, and Throughput 96.34%, which were improved and competed with future-level applications.

    V. R. Niveditha, Sathyabama Institute of Science and Technology, India
    Santhiya Parivallal, Sathyabama Institute of Science and Technology, India
    Maria Jones, Sathyabama Institute of Science and Technology, India
    Amandeep Singh K., Sathyabama Institute of Science and Technology, India
    P. Rajasekar, Sathyabama Institute of Science and Technology, India

Due to the smoothness and various other characteristics, the Android OS is familiar among all kinds of mobile users. Traditionally signature-based techniques are applied to identify malware. But this technique is not able to identify the latest malware. Classification algorithms can support huge datasets needed to protect Android-based platforms. At the same time, a huge dataset needs scalability for detecting and classifying automatically at the malicious identification stage and feature retrieval. In this chapter, enhanced CNN (ECNN) classifier is used for identifying malware in smart devices. The outcome of this suggested classifier is compared with the existing models like XGBoost, random forest, and CNN. The performance of the proposed work is assessed based on their accuracy, precision, and recall values. From the results it is proved that proposed enhanced CNN (ECNN) produces accuracy of 95.8%, precision of 0.96, and recall of 0.92, which is high compared to other algorithms. The tool used for execution is python.

    S. Satheesh Kumar, REVA University, India
    V. Muthukumaran, College of Engineering and Technology, SRM Institute of Science and
        Technology, India
    A. Devi, REVA University, India
    V. Geetha, REVA University, India
    Poonam Nilesh Yadav, REVA University, India

The internet of things (IoT) offers several benefits to the healthcare industry, including the ability to actively monitor patients and use data for analytics. For medical device integration, the focus has moved to the consumer end of the IoT, that captures data on patient vital signs. Unfortunately, when healthcare centers link these devices to the internet, they typically overlook security concerns. Short-term monitoring and emergency alerting of healthcare signals are becoming increasingly accessible thanks to the Internet of Things (IoT). Data secrecy is critical hence, encryption is required out of real concern. In this book chapter, we explore the privacy and security issues of Internet of Things (IoT) healthcare applications for special needs users. IoT enables health-related enterprises to lift necessary data from diverse sources in real-time and this helps in accurate decision-making to reducing data vulnerability and therefore creating opportunities for secure patient data, particularly for special needs patients.

Chapter 17

Vinaya Babu M., Sri Venkateswara University, India

Sreedevi Mooramreddy, Sri Venkateswara University, India

Data processing technique of data mining has the power to identify patterns and relationships in huge volumes of data from multiple sources to make decisions to drive the world in the current scenario. Association rule mining (ARM) is the most significant method used in data mining. This approach is employed to find trends in the database that are typical. The field of ARM has seen a lot of activities. ARM remains a source of concern for various experts. There are algorithms that assess fundamental factors like precision, algorithm speed, and data assistance. The ARM algorithms, namely AprioriHybrid, AIS, AprioriTID, and Apriori, as well as FP-Growth, are examined in this work. This chapter provides a comparison of different algorithms utilized for association rules mining against several performance factors.

Chapter 18

Vinu Sherimon, University of Technology and Applied Sciences, Muscat, Oman

Sherimon Puliprathu Cherian, Arab Open University, Muscat, Oman

Rahul V. Nair, Royal Oman Police Hospital, Muscat, Oman

Khalid Shaikh, Royal Oman Police Hospital, Muscat, Oman

Natasha Renchi Mathew, Sri Ramachandra Institute of Higher Education and Research, Chennai, India

Alzheimer's disease is a universal medical challenge. A timely identification of this ailment can reduce expenses and enhance the patient's quality of life. Alzheimer's diagnosis includes a critical component called cognitive assessment. These examinations have been carried out by neurologists, utilizing paper-and-pencil ever since the development of neurological tests. But it's obvious that integrating digital technologies into such assessments has many advantages. This chapter describes the design of an Android application, GanglioNav WithYou, for conducting cognitive assessments in Alzheimer's patients. The researchers have built a 3D virtual neurologist to conduct this assessment for Alzheimer patients. The virtual neurologist will ask questions that test the different mental abilities of patients such as time orientation, ability to recall things, concentration skills, language skills, visual interpretation skills, etc. At the end of the assessment, the total score is calculated, and the virtual neurologist will generate a detailed assessment report.

Preface

Recently, the Internet of Things (IoT) has brought the vision of a smarter world into reality with a massive amount of data and numerous services. With the outbreak of COVID-19, Artificial Intelligence (AI) has gained significant attention by utilizing its machine learning algorithms for quality patient care. The integration of IoT with AI, on the other hand, may open up new possibilities for both technologies. AI-powered IoT can play a big part in smart healthcare by providing improved insight into healthcare data and allowing for more inexpensive personalized care. It can also offer strong processing and storage facilities for large IoT data streams (big data) that go beyond the capabilities of individual "things", as well as provide real-time automated decision-making. While academics have made progress in their individual studies of AI and IoT for health services, there has been little focus on establishing cost-effective and affordable smart healthcare services. The AI-driven Internet of Things (AIIoT) for smart healthcare has the potential to transform many aspects of our industry; however, many technological difficulties must be overcome before this potential can be realized.

Technologies are all about the creation of tools to achieve goals in more efficient ways. Convergence is the combination of two or more different technologies in a single device. Technology able to focus on multiple streams allows for a more diverse approach and convergence technologies mean more pathways for today's economic and social issues. COVID-19, the most recent pandemic that is ravaging in many parts of the world with untold human loss and suffering has resulted in an unprecedented global economic upheaval and social issues. The COVID-19 pandemic has put a major emphasis on the essential impact that AI and IoT convergence technologies play in smart healthcare services. The *Handbook of Research on Advancements in AI and IoT Convergence Technologies* aims to explore advanced convergence technologies in the pandemic and post-pandemic era. This book is a collection of high-quality research on recent advancements in AI and IoT convergence technologies, with a focus on state-of-the-art approaches, methodologies, and systems for the design, development, deployment, and innovative use of those convergence technologies to provide insight into smart healthcare service demands. Furthermore, this book assesses the importance of AI and IoT convergence technologies in dealing with emerging crises such as unpredicted pandemic diseases like COVID-19.

The book is organized into 18 chapters that provide insights on AI and IoT Convergence Technologies as a whole, covering topics such as AI-enabled contact tracing for preventing the spread of the COVID-19, AI and IoT convergence for pandemic management and monitoring, AI-empowered big data analytics and cognitive computing for smart health monitoring, IoT cloud-based predictive analysis for personalized healthcare, AIIoT convergent services, systems, infrastructure and techniques, security, privacy, and trust of AI-IoT convergent smart healthcare system. A synopsis of each chapter is given below.

Chapter 1, "Smart Medicine Reminder System and SOS Device," presents a device that may come across the presence of a twist of fate even as additionally reminding continual sufferers and the aged in their prescription obligations. The MPU6050 sensor detects the presence of a twist of fate the use of a 3-axis gyroscope and a 3-axis accelerometer. The GPS module locates the twist of fate scene and indicators emergency responders in addition to guardians who've been stored with the aid of using the users.

Chapter 2, "Internet of Things Applications Architecture for Industrial Interoperability Business Service," describes new methods with grounded knowledge representation techniques to address the needs of formal information modelling and reasoning for web-based services. The chapter presents a framework, Apparel Business Decentralized Data Integration (ABDDI), which uses knowledge representation methods and formal languages (e.g., Description Logics – DLs) to annotate necessary business activities. This type of web service requires increased interoperability in service management operations.

Chapter 3, "An Efficient Feature Selection in Classifying Diabetes Mellitus," claims that many ML models suffer from misclassification due to a lack of proper feature selection methods. How to select the best features is still a significant problem in the classification domain. To address the problem, an ensemble-based feature selection is proposed. The proposed feature selection is then evaluated in five machine learning models. The experimental results show that the proposed feature selection is 36% more efficient than existing feature selection methods.

Chapter 4, "Information Security and Privacy in IoT," presents the importance of interconnectedness in a variety of ways, including well-timed coordination with a variety of simple devices such as sensors, thermostats, fitbits, routers, and so on. These networks may be particularly vulnerable to prone assaults due to their open and heterogeneous nature. Aside from the advantages of IoT development, there may be significant concerns regarding security and privacy, which is likely to be one of the most frustrating aspects of IoT design adaptation and development.

Chapter 5, "A Novel Long Short-Term Memory Method for Model for Stock Price Prediction," proposes the stock price prediction using an improved algorithm in machine learning. Machine learning uses different types of models to identify the prediction easier and accurately. This study presents the use of LSTM based machine learning to predict stocks and factors considered are date, time, closing price and opening price of the stocks. Finally, this machine learning model was trained with numerous data, and the results were compared with existing algorithms.

Chapter 6, "Artificial Intelligence to Protect Wildlife," presents a novel approach to detect illegal wildlife trade online using deep learning. The purpose of this chapter is to implement a Deep Convolutional Neural Network for the detection of illegal wildlife trade on the web. In this research, data consists of two types of images, legal and illegal. The outcomes of the research and experiments shows that usage of Deep CNN pre-trained on image-net achieves testing accuracy of 92.26% with an f1 score of 0.8234 with very low inference time.

Chapter 7, "A Sophisticate Image Filtering and Enhancement Method With Worn Speculative Segmentation Process," mainly focuses on color pixel-based image segmentation to infer the age of the tiger and also applied several reasonable and applicable filters, enhancement processes in the speculative real-time images. The objective of the research work is to assess the age of the tiger using the color pixel-based image classification and clustering is the main of the research work.

Chapter 8, "MRI High-Dimensional Data and Statistical Analysis on Spinal Cord Injury Detection," introduces an advanced deep learning-based spinal injury detection algorithm. The segmentation was performed with the Otsu technique. The feature extraction and training were performed with shape-based intensity parameters of nothing but standard deviation, variance, mean, and kurtosis. The testing can be possible with ResNet CNN technology.

Chapter 9, "Enterprise Transformation Projects/Cloud Transformation Concept: The Compute System," presents the fundaments of the Cloud Transformation Concept (CTC) and the implementation of the CTC Compute System (CTC-CS). The proposed AHMM4CTC based CTC-CS is a virtual secured computing environment which uses an integrated empiric decision-making process. The CTC-CS is supported by a real-life case of business transformation project, which needs a Cloud infrastructure that is supported by the alignment of various existing Cloud standards.

Chapter 10, "An Architectural Review of Multi-Tenancy in Cloud Computing," claims that among IaaS, PaaS and SaaS, SaaS offers more cost benefit to enterprises and users as compared to its predecessors because of its ability to share both hardware and software across multiple tenants with very minimal data sharing. The feature of sharing resources among multiple users known as multi tenancy is essential in achieving the objectives of cloud computing. This chapter gives a detailed account of multi tenancy in cloud computing with special focus on SaaS applications and its associated problems followed by solution approaches.

Chapter 11, "An Analysis of Deep Learning Techniques Adopted in Medical Imaging," claims that Deep Learning has already been used to accurately diagnose diseases and classify image samples, and it has the potential to revolutionize the entire landscape of healthcare. These uses are only expected to expand in the future. The most recent developments, including a critical analysis of the current problems have been summarized, and made plans for additional research in medical imaging.

Chapter 12, "Design and Implementation of an On-Board Computer Sub-System for Picosat," investigates the use of low-cost Cube sats in the realm of remote sensing. In the original iteration of their design, the Cube satellite utilized Picosat Passive attitude control. However, a new version has been released to fulfil the accuracy standards of Picosat, the primary payload, which was supposed to be active attitude control. New posture determination and control the subsystem is in charge of successfully de-tumbling Picosat after booting and keeping it pointed in the right direction.

Chapter 13, "Analysis on Detecting Cyber Security Attacks Using Deep Ensemble Learning on Smart Grids," presents a deep learning ensemble (DLE) model that possibly detects the potential data integrity attacks in the physical layer. The deep learning model uses ensemble learning to make decisions and combines the classified results to improve the classification on test data. The experiments are conducted on the proposed DLE model to find the accuracy of classifier the malicious and benign measurements.

Chapter 14, "Algorithm-Based Spatio-Temporal Study on Identification of Pure Bamboo Vegetation Using LULC Classification," claims that in the mapping and identification of natural resources, space technology has been beneficial. The objective of classification is to divide a large subject into fewer, more manageable fractions. For Land use and Land cover, four Supervised Learning methods, namely Naive Bayes, Random Forest, Support Vector Machine, and Decision Tree, are used. Their overall accuracies will be compared to obtain the best algorithm.

Chapter 15, "Malware Detection in Android Systems Using Deep Learning Techniques," explores the Enhanced CNN (ECNN) classifier used for identifying malware in smart devices. The outcome of this suggested classifier is compared with the existing models like XGBoost, Random Forest, and CNN. The performance of the proposed work is assessed based on their Accuracy, Precision, And Recall values.

Chapter 16, "A Quantitative Approach of Purposive Sampling Technique for Security and Privacy Issues in IoT Healthcare Applications," discusses the privacy and security issues of Internet of Things (IoT) healthcare applications for special needs users. IoT enables health-related enterprises to lift necessary data from diverse sources in real-time and this helps in accurate decision-making to reducing data vulnerability and therefore creating opportunities for secure patient data, particularly for special needs patients.

Chapter 17, "Performance Evaluation and Analysis of Different Association Rule Mining Algorithms," provides a comparison of different algorithms utilized for association rules mining against several performance factors. Association rule mining (ARM) is the most significant method used in data mining. The field of ARM has seen a lot of activities. The ARM algorithms namely AprioriHybrid, AIS, AprioriTID and Apriori, as well as FP-Growth are examined in this work.

Chapter 18, "GanglioNav WithYou: Design and Implementation of Artificial Intelligence-Enabled Cognitive Assessment Application for Alzheimer Patients," describes the design of an android application, GanglioNav WithYou, for conducting cognitive assessments in Alzheimer patients. The researchers have built a 3D virtual neurologist to conduct this assessment for Alzheimer patients. The virtual neurologist will ask questions, which tests the different mental abilities of patients. At the end of the assessment, the total score is calculated, and the virtual neurologist will generate a detailed assessment report.

Jingyuan Zhao
University of Toronto, Canada

V. Vinoth Kumar
Jain University, India

Rajesh Natarajan
University of Technology and Applied Science, Shinas, Oman

T. R. Mahesh
Jain University, India

Chapter 1
Smart Medicine Reminder System and SOS Device

H. K. Shashikala
Jain University, India

T. R. Mahesh
Jain University, India

V. Vinoth Kimar
Jain University, India

K. Chanchani Keerthana
Jain University, India

S. Priyanka
Jain University, India

Rangareddygari H. Meghana
Jain University, India

Yarragunta Thanmai
Publicis Sapient, India

ABSTRACT

In the standard direction of business, continuously tracking and dealing with the fitness of a person is a tough task. Humans of all ages ought to have their fitness examined on an everyday basis. The aim is to notify the victim's household of the twist of fate through predetermined contacts and locate the nearest hospital, telling them of the twist of fate in order that assistance may be dispatched. This prototype uses the gyroscope, accelerometer, GPS, and GSM. The aim of these studies is to create a device that may come across the presence of a twist of fate even as additionally reminding continual sufferers and the aged in their prescription obligations. The MPU6050 sensor detects the presence of a twist of fate through the use of a 3-axis gyroscope and a 3-axis accelerometer. The GPS module locates the twist of fate scene and contacts emergency responders in addition to guardians who've been stored with the aid of the users.

DOI: 10.4018/978-1-6684-6971-2.ch001

Copyright © 2023, IGI Global. Copying or distributing in print or electronic forms without written permission of IGI Global is prohibited.

INTRODUCTION

People's living standards are continuing to rise as economic development accelerates. Road traffic accidents are prevalent, resulting in major human and property losses for the country and its residents. Traffic has become a key event in the national interest. When traffic develops, it will have far-reaching consequences if individuals are unable to communicate with the outside world for help. The design is for a device that can detect accidents, search for the location of the accident, and automatically send a rescue alert. Our main motivation is to assist injured persons on the scene of an accident at the appropriate moment. If correct treatment is not delivered, the consequences can be devastating. These kinds of mishaps sparked our interest in writing this study. Accounting for 71% of all deaths worldwide. Every year, 18 million people aged 31 to 69 die from chronic diseases, with 85 percent of these deaths occurring early in some countries. A chronic condition is one that lasts a year or longer and involves continuing medical care (CDC). A chronic illness affects six out of ten adults, and four out of ten people have two or more chronic illnesses. Cardiovascular disease, diabetes, chronic respiratory, cancer, and other chronic conditions require long-term treatment to stabilize their status. As a result, medicines have become the most .It is estimated that a significant component in the treatment approach that proper drug use alone can reduce chronic disease patients' burden by up to 80% in various nations.

The proposed approach is beneficial in both chronic patient and accident detection situations. This device comes into action in the event of chronic patients or elderly individuals who need to take medications on a regular basis. It reminds people to take medications by displaying the prescription name, time, and buzzing them. It also keeps track of the user's temperature and informs them if the temperature rises. The medicine and user data are stored on a Raspberry Pi pico processor in the suggested system. The temperature is kept track of by the MPU6050 CPU. On a 12-pin LCD panel, the device displays the medicine name and time. In the event of an accident, the user is given a list of pre-defined contacts. Whenever a collision or accident occurs, the system recognizes the event and sends the users' precise longitude and latitude to predefined contacts as well as the nearby hospital. It is really essential in preserving the lives of people who have been injured, as well as reducing the state's and citizens' losses of lives and property, by reducing road traffic threats. Road accidents can be caused by poor road construction and maintenance, overcrowding. Aside from that, drivers' and other road users' lack of road sense has aggravated the situation. The majority of young people die on the roadways due to rash driving, inebriated driving, and other circumstances, which is a significant loss for our country.

In the standard direction of business, continuously tracking and dealing with the fitness of a domestic affected person is a tough task. In order to store their lives in life-threatening situations, humans of all ages, mainly the aged, ought to have their fitness examined and knowledgeable on a everyday basis. Notifies the victim's household of the twist of fate through predetermined contacts, and locates the nearest hospital, telling them of the twist of fate in order that scientific assist may be dispatched proper away. This prototype uses the gyroscope, accelerometer, GPS, and GSM. The aim of these studies is to create a device that may come across the presence of an twist of fate even as additionally reminding continual sufferers and the aged in their prescription obligations. The MPU6050 sensor detects the presence of an twist of fate the use of a 3-axis gyroscope and a 3-axis accelerometer. The GPS module locates the twist of fate scene and indicators emergency responders in addition to guardians who've been stored with the aid of using the users. This approach has benefited in lowering the time it takes to reply to an twist of fate with the aid of using effectively reporting to hospitals. This becomes important in saving the lives of the victims.

LITERATURE SURVEY

Ali Gunawan presented an emergency call system in which he used five ways to focus on the scope of the member: direct observation, digital marketing, previous study in the form of journals, data collecting, and the SDLC process, which consists of three steps. planning, analysis, and design for SDLC Maintaining the Integrity of the Specifications (Abhishek Madankar, 2021). Benjamin Kommey and Sethkotey proposed a system which uses a microcontroller module, and some sensors, an LED and an LCD. The user's pulse is read by the pulse sensor, and the user's body temperature is read by the temperature sensor. These data are displayed on the LCD, and when these values are abnormal, the Bluetooth module sends an alert to the user's phone, which is then transmitted to the confidants. When the temperature or pulse values are abnormal, the buzzer sounds and the LED lights up to inform the user. There is also a push button that allows the user to send the alarm manually (G. Karthy, 2021).

Durgesh Kumay Yadav suggested the Accident Detection using Deep Learning method, which is concerned with many crashes in the event of a road traffic accident. They used OpenCV, Keras, and Tensor Flow to build this system. Two layers of short-term memory are used in the algorithm. The temporal dependency of each video is controlled using NN.LSTM (long Short-Term Memory) (Ruhul Amin, 2020). Harsh Agarwal and Smitipoddar proposed the methodology used in the suggested system is as follows: The vibration caused by the vehicle's impact is measured using a vibration sensor. The presence of a person inside the car will be detected by an ultrasonic sensor. If the sensor does not identify the presence of a person, the entire system will not be activated. The GPS module will be activated by a microprocessor that reads vibration frequencies to determine the location of the incident. The GPS component gives the coordinates to the microcontroller, which utilizes the GSM module to send them to the emergency contacts via SMS as a Google Maps URL (Rajvardhan Rishi, 2020).

PlacideShabisha and Chamara Sandeepa this proposed work utilizes 3rd party mobile relays and also supplied a novel secure symmetric key agreement that can create a shared common key among end devices and is secure in emergency scenarios, providing protection against security issues (LuhKesuma Wardhani, 2021). Hyunho Park presented a fusion analysis-based emergency system that analyses 119 emergency calls. This approach assists people in understanding crisis situations and responding to disasters in order to minimize harm. The proposed solution utilized artificial intelligence (AI) to assist call recipients, as well as with the expanded 119 emergency call data, machine learning was used (Arnav Chaudhari, 2021). Parag Parmar, The suggested car collision detection and reporting system can identify the existence of a vehicle collision, whether it's a collision or a rollover, and send a text message to the family members or relatives, as well as to a nearby hospital, saving time in providing medical assistance to the injured passengers. The system is based on a microprocessor and is connected to a MEMS sensor that includes an accelerometer and gyroscope, (GSM) as well as (GPS) (Md. Motaharul Islam, 2020).

S. Mohana Gowri planned a framework using the Arduino Uno microcontroller. The suggested framework's hardware component will be situated near the vehicle's dashboard. This device will include an eye flicker sensor, a vibration sensor, a beat rate sensor, GPS, GSM, a buzzer, a battery, a switch, a power supply, and a bell switch. The microcontroller is linked with GSM. Whether or not to send a message is determined by the sensor values. The location's latitude and longitude are determined using GPS, and the link to the location is supplied via Google (Chaudhari, 2021). Keshav Korde and Anand Nagde proposed a system called Automation System in Accidental Case; first they collect the user information at beginning and create a QR code for each person. User snaps a photo after an accident and sends the location information and the nearest hospital's address to the closest police station that the system has advised (H K Shashikala, 2022). After With the police station's approval, the system immediately creates an accident report and sends it to the hospital. the hospital feedback to the user, and when the nurse arrives at the scene of the accident, she scans the user's QR code to rapidly obtain user information. and offer giving the user treatment.

The Arduino uno, which serves as the controller, is connected to the GPS module, GSM module, and accelerometer to form a system that can alert the appropriate people about the disaster. By detecting a change in the vehicle's preset value of orientation, the accelerometer detects an accident and sends the location via GPS module to the registered sim card via GSM module without the driver or passengers' knowledge. The proposed approach promises to reduce the number of people killed in car accidents by about 90% (Hyunho Park, 2021). The suggested system uses sensors to measure body temperature and heart rate, as well as reminding users to take their medications on time. The Node MCU, sensors, GSM module, Blynk, and other components are used to do all of this. Users benefit from this initiative since it sends out timely updates. Various firms are employing digital world concepts that connect various sensors and LPUs for data sharing (P. Ghosh, 2016).

Figure 1. System architecture

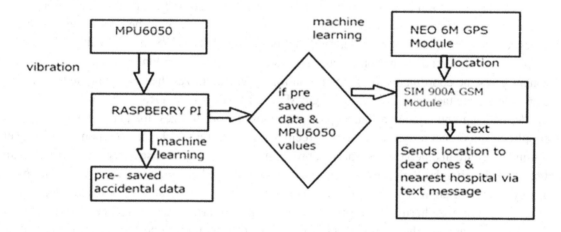

METHODOLOGY

The following are the methods:

Feature 1 and Step 1: First feature of this prototype is reminding medicine name along with the timings displaying on the LCD screen with a buzzer as shown in the figure 2.

Feature 2 and Step 2: On the device, we also have an SOS button that is used for the emergency cases. When it is pressed emergency text message will be sent to the pre saved contacts using SIM900A GSM GPRS module and locating accurate longitude and latitude details using NEO6M GPS module

Feature 3 and Step 1: The device is equipped with MPU6050 Accelerometers, which continuously gather any vibration data that happens to the device.

Feature 3 and Step 2: The vibration data is continually reviewed, compared, and matched against a pre-saved Machine Learning Model of typical unintentional vibrations.

Feature 3 and Step 3: If a match is detected between the vibration data being gathered and also the pre-saved model, matters are classed as a collision or accident. During this case an SMS is sent to pre-saved contacts and also the city's featured nearest hospitals.

Feature 4 and Step 4: Within the event that another vehicle or pedestrian has attempted to help the victim by transporting him to a different nearby site or hospital, an eternal track of the victim's whereabouts is taken using NEO6M GPS module.

The MPU6050 detects the vibration and delivers it to the Raspberry Pi Zero Processor. The Raspberry Pi zero processor then checks to see if the vibration data matches the accident data and if they do immediately informs the SIM900ANEO6M GSM module, which sends the location in text to loved ones or hospitals, indicating whether the person has collided or been involved in an accident, to which the NEO6MGPS module adds the latitude, longitude, and exact location of the person with an accuracy of up to 2 meters.

RESULTS

Figure 2. Displaying medicine name and time

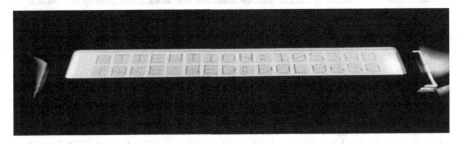

HARDWARE REQUIREMENTS

Raspberry pi Zero W

Raspberry Pi Zero W is credit card sized computer which acts as a micro-controller. It stores all the data that are required and we should connect raspberry pi to our personnel computer through USB B cable.

MPU6050

MPU6050 is basically a 3-axis accelerometer and 3-axis gyroscope which measures both linear and angular movements. It has 7 pins which includes VCC, GND, SCL, SDA. VCC pin is used to supply power and GND also known as ground pin which is used to connect to the computer, SCL known as serial clock which is used for setting clock rate and SDA known as serial data it is used for transferring data through I2C communication.

Figure 3. This reminds the patients to take DOLO 650

M:Dolo650
T:2121

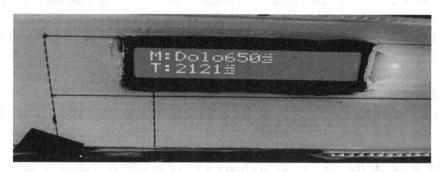

Figure 4. Alert message when there is increase in temperature

!!FIRE!!
!!FIRE!!

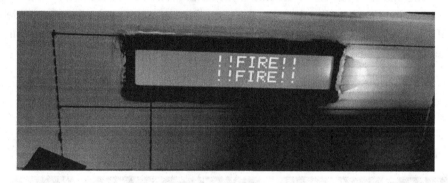

Figure 5. Sample message format received from the device when accident occurred

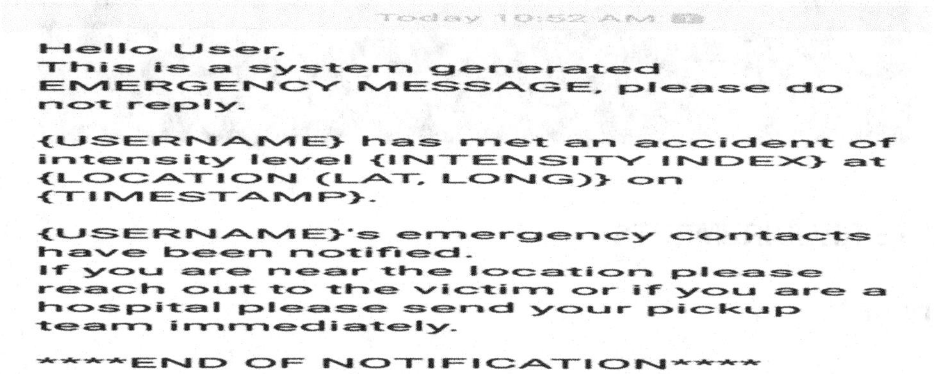

Today 10:52 AM
Hello User,
This is a system generated EMERGENCY MESSAGE, please do not reply.
{USERNAME} has met an accident of intensity level {INTENSITY INDEX} at {LOCATION (LAT, LONG)} on {TIMESTAMP}.
{USERNAME}'s emergency contacts have been notified.
If you are near the location please reach out to the victim or if you are a hospital please send your pickup team immediately.
****END OF NOTIFICATION****

Figure 6. Original message generated from device

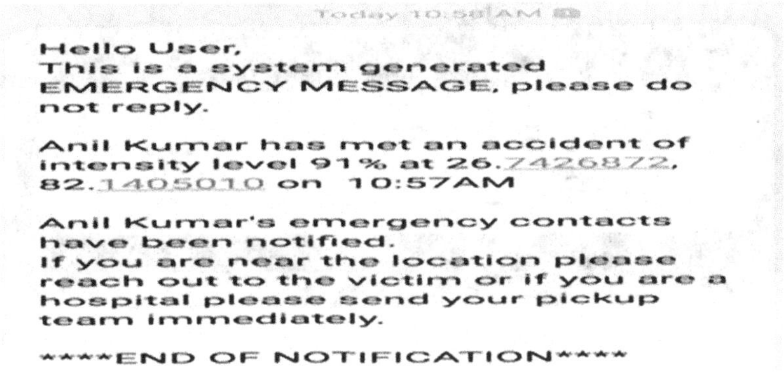

Today 10:58 AM

Hello User,
This is a system generated
EMERGENCY MESSAGE, please do
not reply.

Anil Kumar has met an accident of
intensity level 91% at 26.7426872,
82.1405010 on 10:57AM

Anil Kumar's emergency contacts
have been notified.
If you are near the location please
reach out to the victim or if you are a
hospital please send your pickup
team immediately.

****END OF NOTIFICATION****

Figure 7. Image of Raspberry Pi Zero W

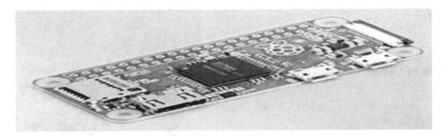

Figure 8. Image of MPU6050

LCD Screen

When the time is remembered, the LCD screen displays the time and the names of the medicines.

Figure 9. LCD screen

UBLOX Neo 6M GPS Module

It is a GPS module which is used to locate the accurate longitude and latitude details whenever a collision is occurred.

Figure 10. Image of Ublox Neo 6M GPS module

SIM 900A GSM Module

It is a GSM module which is used to send message to the presaved contacts and nearest hospital when accident occurred.

Figure 11. SIM 900A GSM module

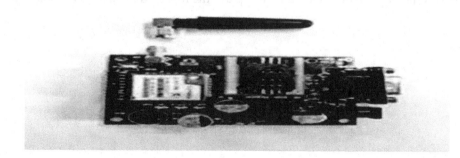

CONCLUSION

The proposed paper mainly focused on Accident detection and Prevention system. Simulation and Prototype results were discussed in detail. The proposed system could be helpful for the user's dear ones (pre saved contacts) to track the accidents through receiving SMS and Locations to aid before leading to any disaster to the lives of people. With an increasing number of vehicles, the number of accidents is increasing. The main factor for accidents is Consumption of alcohol, drowsiness, and badly designed speed bumpers. Our proposed system provides the efficient, cost-effective and real-time solution to all these problems. Our Model provides the efficient way to minimize the increasing number of accidents. As we wanted to design a multipurpose device, the other two features were added (i.e, Medicine reminder system and SOS button).

REFERENCES

Arun Kumar, K., Rajalakshmi, R., & Shashikala, H. K. (2022). Gestational Diabetes Detection Using Machine Learning Algorithm: Research Challenges of Big Data and Data Mining. *International Journal of Intelligent Systems And Applications In Engineering, 10*(2s), 260–263.

Chaudhari, A. (2021). Smart Accident Detection and Alert System. Academic Press.

Deshmukh, Dubal, TR, & Chauhan. (2012). Data Security Analysis And Security Extension For Smart Cards Using Java Card. *International Journal of Advanced Information Technology, 2*(2).

Ghosh, P., & Mahesh, T. R. (2016). A privacy preserving mutual authentication protocol for RFID based automated toll collection system. *2016 International Conference on ICT in Business Industry & Government (ICTBIG),* 1-5. 10.1109/ICTBIG.2016.7892668

Gowramma, G. S., Mahesh, T. R., & Gowda, G. (2017). An automatic system for IVF data classification by utilizing multilayer perceptron algorithm. *ICCTEST, 2017*(2), 667–672. doi:10.21647/ICCTEST/2017/49043

Karthy, G., Surya Kumar, M., & Gudipadu Bhargav, K. (2021). Medication Alerts and Supervisory of Health Using IOT. *2021 Second International Conference on Electronics and Sustainable Communication Systems (ICESC),* 4-6.

Madankar, A., & Agrawal, A. (2021). IoT based Advance Pill Reminder System for Distinct Patients. *2021 Fifth International Conference on I-SMAC (IoT in Social, Mobile, Analytics and Cloud) (I-SMAC),* 11-13.

Mahesh, Vinoth Kumar, Muthukumaran, Shashikala, Swapna, & Guluwadi. (2022). Performance Analysis of XGBoost Ensemble Methods for Survivability with the Classification of Breast Cancer. *Journal of Sensors.* doi:10.1155/2022/4649510

Mahesh, S., Mahesh, T. R., & Vinayababu, M. (2010). Using Data Mining Techniques For Detecting Terror-Related Activities On The Web. *Journal of Theoretical and Applied Information Technology,* 16.

Mahesh, T. R., Dhilip Kumar, V., & Vinoth Kumar, V. (2022). AdaBoost Ensemble Methods Using K-Fold Cross Validation for Survivability with the Early Detection of Heart Disease. *Computational Intelligence and Neuroscience.*

Mahesh, T. R., Prabhanjan, S., & Vinayababu, M. (2010). Noise Reduction By Using Fuzzy Image Filtering. *Journal of Theoretical and Applied Information Technology*, 15.

Mhetre, M., & Kumar, L. M. (2021). MedicalEmergency System. *2021 International Conference on Communication information and Computing Technology (ICCICT)*, 25-27.

Motaharul Islam, Ridwan, Mary, Siam, Mumu, & Rana. (2020). Design and Implementation of a Smart Bike Accident Detection System. *IEEE Region 10 Symposium (TENSYMP).*

Park, H., Kwon, E., & Byon, S. (2021). Emergency Call Fusion Analysis System for Disaster Response. *2021 International Conference on Information and Communication Technology Convergence (ICTC)*, 20-22. 10.1109/ICTC52510.2021.9621071

Pinaki, G., & Mahesh, T. R. (2015). Smart city: Concept and challenges. *International Journal on Advances in Engineering Technology and Science*, *1*, 1.

Rishi, Yede, Kunal, & Bansode. (2020). Automatic Messaging System for Vehicle Tracking and Accident Detection. *2020 International Conference on Electronics and Sustainable Communication Systems (ICESC)*, 2-4.

Shashikala, H. K., Madhumala, R. B., Keerthana, C., Priyanka, S., & Meghana, R. (2022). Smart Reminder SOS & Emergency Detection Device. *IEEE International Conference on Distributed Computing and Electrical Circuits and Electronics (ICDCECE).* 10.1109/ICDCECE53908.2022.9793171

Shashikala, H. K., & Madhuri, G. S. (2021). Image Pre-processing Techniques for X-Ray Medical Images: A Survey. *International Journal of Creative Research Thoughts, 9*(1).

Shashikala, H. K., Mahesh, T. R., Vivek, V., Sindhu, M. G., Saravanan, C., & Baig, T. Z. (2021). Early detection of spondylosis using point-based image processing techniques. *Proceedings of the 2021 International Conference on Recent Trends on Electronics, Information, Communication & Technology (RTEICT)*, 655–659. 10.1109/RTEICT52294.2021.9573604

Sindhu, M. G., & Shashikala, H. K. (2021). Image Processing Techniques for detecting Extra Growth of Teeth in Medical Images. *Solid State Technology*, *64*(2).

Sindhu Madhuri, G., & Shashikala, H. K. (2022). Analysis of Medical Images using Image Registration Feature-based Segmentation Techniques. *2nd International Conference on Technological Advancements in Computational Sciences (ICTACS).* 10.1109/ICTACS56270.2022.9987895

TroyeeSharmisthaSaha, Bin Hassan, Anjum, & IshfakTahmid. (2020). IoT Based Medical Assistant for Efficient Monitoring of Patients in Response to COVID-19. *2020 2nd International Conference on Advanced Information and Communication Technology (ICAICT)*, 28-29.

Wardhani, Anggraini, Anggraini, Hakiem, Shofi, & Rosyadi. (2021). Medicine Box Reminder for Patients with Chronic Disease with IoT-Based Database Monitoring. *2021 9th International Conference on Cyber and IT Service Management (CITSM)*, 22-23.

Chapter 2
Internet of Things Applications Architecture for Industrial Interoperability Business Service

Kamalendu Pal

iD https://orcid.org/0000-0001-7158-6481

University of London, UK

ABSTRACT

Wireless sensor data communication networks (WSNs) based on the Internet of Things (IoT) technology have many potential applications for the industrial world. The IoT paradigm encompasses ubiquitous computing, pervasive computing, data communication protocols, sensing technologies, and embedded devices, and they merge selectively to form an information system where the physical and digital worlds meet. They can serve different categories of business services through continuous symbiotic interactions. In this way, the formed interconnected information system, through the Internet, exchanges data and information to create services that bring tangible benefits to the industrial world and its supply chain operations. This chapter presents a system architecture (i.e., Apparel Business Decentralized Data Integration (ABDDI)) and its knowledge representation scheme, based on formal languages – Description Logics (DLs), to address the needs of formal information modeling and reasoning for web-based services provision using ontology. Finally, the chapter presents an example of the experimental result of service composition ontology's similarity assessment.

INTRODUCTION

Humanity dwells on earth with ambitious goals to manage and mitigate unprecedented social, economic, and environmental challenges. Science, technology, and innovation play an enormous role in realizing these ambitious goals to improve human living conditions. The process of creative destruction started by technological progress can help change economies and improve living conditions by increasing productivity, reducing production costs and produced goods prices, and helping to raise real wages. One of the essential ingredients to create a better world is using technology to move forward and unprecedented change in its scope and pace of daily life.

DOI: 10.4018/978-1-6684-6971-2.ch002

Copyright © 2023, IGI Global. Copying or distributing in print or electronic forms without written permission of IGI Global is prohibited.

Harnessing the frontier of technologies helps to mitigate the persistent gaps between developing and developed nations in getting and using existing technologies. It also creates and delivers innovations (including non-technological and new forms of social innovation), which could be transformative in creating sustainable development goals and producing more prosperous, inclusive, and healthy human societies. In this way, society gets required solutions and opportunities for sustainable development that are better, cheaper, faster, scalable, and easy to use. The extent of technological development impact has already ushered in the transformative implications of information and communication technologies (ICTs) in many countries worldwide. However, these new technologies are often threatening to outpace the capability of societies and policymakers to adapt to the changes they can create, giving rise to wide-spread anxiety and ambivalence or hostility to some technological advances.

One of the central questions of where ideas come from is on the mind of researchers visiting a research laboratory, a painter's workshop, or an inventor's experimental laboratory. It is the secret human society hopes to see – the magic that happens when new things are born. This way, it is possible to provide creativity, like the discovery of *millimeter radio waves* by Professor Jagadish Chandra Bose (Sarkar, 2006). Today the world is witnessing the tremendous influence of wireless communication technology on daily working activities. Three great scientific minds heavily influence modern wireless telecommunications - James Clerk Maxwell (Mahon, 2004), Jagadish Chandra Bose (Sarkar et al., 2006), and Tim Berners-Lee (Berners-Lee, 2000). James Clerk Maxwell provided the theoretical foundation of electromagnetic wave propagation; Jagadish Chandra Bose showed his colleagues the transmission of millimeter waves by transmitting this new type of waves in Presidency College (Kolkata, India) laboratory; and Tim Berners-Lee created the World Wide Web at CERN (Geneva, Switzerland). Today's computer data communication network is at once intangible and constantly mutated, growing larger and more complex with each passing second. Many of the world's business community uses this incredible network of networks for day-to-day work.

The advent of development and adoption of new technologies in recent decades is continuing, and this continuation is driven by: (i) the cumulative nature of technological change; (ii) the exponential nature of technologies such as microchips that are doubled in power every two years for more than half a century; (iii) the convergence of technologies into new combinations; (iv) drastic reduction in costs of production; (v) the emergence of digital "platforms of platforms" – most prominently the Internet; and (v) adoption of artificial intelligence (AI) techniques, the Internet of Things (IoT), and cognitive technologies have successfully been applied to various industrial applications (Zhao & Kumar, 2021). In addition, IoT has paved the way for many industrial application domains while posing several challenges as many devices, protocols, communication channels, architectures, and middleware exist. Big data generated by these devices calls for advanced machine learning (ML) and data mining techniques to understand, learn effectively, and reason with this volume of information, such as cognitive technologies. Cognitive technologies play a significant role in developing successful cognitive systems which mimic "cognitive" functions associated with human intelligence, such as "learning" and "problem-solving".

AI-based applications now help to solve real-world problems, it includes image recognition, problem-solving, and logical reasoning that sometimes exceed human performance. AI applications, particularly robotics, can transform production processes and business activities, especially manufacturing. Big data technologies are opening new opportunities and enabling breakthroughs related to, among others, manufacturing data analytics addressing different perspectives: (i) descriptive to answer what happened, (ii) diagnostic to answer the reason why it happened, (iii) predictive to understand what will happen and (iv) prescriptive to detect how human operators can make it happen.

Without any doubt, the potential impact of big data technology can bring huge changes, the economy, and society is relevant, boosting innovations in organizations and improving business models. Besides, today the Internet has become ubiquitous, has influenced almost every corner of the world, and affects human life unimaginably. However, the journey is far from over. Human society is entering an era of even more pervasive connectivity where many service applications will be connected to the Web. Human society is entering an era of the IoT. Different academics and practitioners have defined this term in many ways. The IoT is a things-connected network wirelessly connected via smart sensors; IoT can interact without human intervention. Some preliminary IoT applications have already been developed in the manufacturing, transportation, and automotive industries (He et al., 2014) (Pretz, 2013). The evolution of IoT involves many development issues, such as infrastructure, communications, interfaces, protocols, and standards. The IoT refers to a new world where almost all devices and appliances are connected to a network. In addition, industrial application service providers can use them collaboratively to achieve complex tasks requiring high intelligence.

IoT devices are geared with embedded sensors, actuators, processors, and transceivers for this intelligence and interconnection. IoT is not a single technology but an agglomeration of various technologies that work together. In simple terms, sensors and actuators help interact with the physical environment. The data collected by the sensors must be stored and processed intelligently to derive valuable inferences from it. This chapter broadly defines the term *sensor*; a handheld mobile phone or even a microwave oven can be a sensor if it provides inputs about its current state (internal state + environment). An *actuator* is a device used to effect a change in the environment, such as the temperature controller of an air conditioner.

Data storage and processing can be done on the network's edge or a server located in a different place. If any data preprocessing is done, it simply happens at some other proximate device or sensor. In the end, data is then typically sent to a remote server after processing. An IoT object's storage and processing capabilities are also restricted by the available resources, which are often very constrained due to size, energy, power, and computational capability limitations. Consequently, the central research challenge is ensuring that users can get the appropriate data type at the desired level of correctness.

In addition to data collection and handling challenges, there are also challenges in processed data communication to the relevant service entities. The collaboration and communication between IoT devices are generally wireless because these devices are simply installed at different work locations. Wireless communication channels are often suffering from high rates of disturbance. This way, reliably communicating data without too many retransmissions is a central research issue. Moreover, actions must be taken based on the derived inferences after processing the received data. The nature of action can be diverse. One can directly modify the physical world through actuators. Alternatively, one may do something virtually. For example, one may send raw data and information to other smart objects. Creating a change in the physical world depends on its state now, called *context awareness*. Each action is taken, considering the context and why an application can behave differently in separate business contexts. For example, an office member may not like messages from office colleagues to interrupt when that individual is on vacation.

Sensors, actuators, data storage, and the communication network form the central infrastructure of an IoT framework. However, many software aspects need to be considered. First, one needs middleware that can be used to interconnect and manage all these heterogeneous components. This way, the IoT industry needs much standardization to connect many different devices. However, the conceptual realization of IoT is far from achieving a full deployment of converged IoT services and technology. Current information technology and communication (ITC) research focuses on providing integrated solutions, primarily on the feature that enables convergence or "*interoperability*". Interoperability can be simplified as the feature for providing a seamless exchange of information to personalize services automatically or simply exchanging information so that other systems can use it to improve performance, enable and create services, and control operations information processing. This type of scenario requires increased interoperability in service management operations.

This chapter reviews the recent trends and challenges on interoperability in the IoT applications domain, discuss physical versus virtual sensors, and, while addressing technology interoperability challenges in parallel, discusses how, with the growing importance of data understanding and processing, semantic web technologies, frameworks, and information models can support interoperability in the design of services in the industrial information system design. Finally, this chapter aims to identify relevant issues and challenges that need to be considered in the coming and future information system projects.

The remainder of this chapter is described as follows. Section 2 presents the background of IoT-based industrial applications. Section 3 reviews representative research on semantic modelling methods for general IoT-based applications. Section 4 describes the background knowledge about the proposed system. Section 5 presents the knowledge representation and reasoning approach. Section 6 explains some mathematical concepts using a business case and includes a concept similarity assessment. Finally, section 7 puts the ideas of future research work forwards. Finally, section 8 concludes the chapter by discussing relevant research issues.

BACKGROUND KNOWLEDGE OF IoT ARCHITECTURE

Reviewing Industrial IoT applications combines many emerging technologies, from sensing and actuating to networking and application-specific service provisions. In this way, the paradigm of industrial IoT application covers a broad range of technological issues (e.g., protocol, architecture, and hardware), network and connectivity technologies (e.g., cellular and Wi-Fi), infrastructure and platform technologies (e.g., standards, and gateway), and users' application-specific technologies (e.g., predictive maintenance, and extended reality). Moreover, there is no unique consensus on architecture for IoT, which is agreed upon universally. Different research groups have proposed different architectures. From the broad scope, this chapter discusses two critical aspects of an industrial IoT ecosystem: (i) architecture and (ii) interoperability of service provision. In the following subsections, the chapter explains these concepts.

ARCHITECTURAL ISSUES

Three-Layer and Five-Layer Architectures

The most straightforward architecture is a three-layer architecture (Mashal et al., 2015) (Said & Masud, 2013) (Wu et al., 2010), as shown in Figure 1. The presented layered IoT system is initially applied to the Mobile Business Architecture (MBA) entities, and Mobile Internet Technical Architecture (MITA) fundamentals are mapped to these principles and concept models for MIBA and MITA.

Figure 1. Layered architectures of IoT system

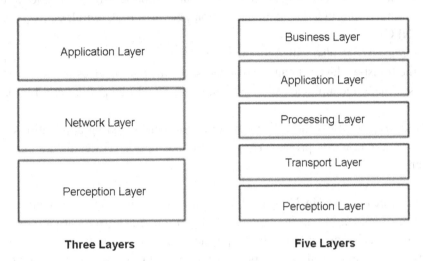

The middleware layer in digital Mobile Internet Technical Architecture has been named the Network Layer, as illustrated in Figure 1 (Three Layers) model. The above three-element layers are used for each of the MIBA segments and their elements. In addition, an interaction between the elements is provided with protocols and content delivery within the payloads of the protocols.

This three-layer architecture was introduced in the early research stage in this area. It has got three layers, namely, the perception, network, and finally, application layers.

1. The *perception layer* is the physical layer, with sensors for sensing, gathering data, and creating information about the business operating environment. It senses physical arguments or identifies other smart objects in the business environment.
2. The *network layer* is the sole authority for making other smart objects (e.g., servers, network devices, and physical servers). Its characteristics are also used for transmitting and processing sensor data.
3. The *application layer* is responsible for providing business-specific services to the user. However, there are different applications in which the IoT can be deployed, such as smart cities, factories, smart health, and smart homes.

A three-layer architecture defines the main idea of the IoT. However, this is not enough for research on IoT due to its focus on more delicate aspects of the IoT. That is why many more layered architectures are presented in the academic article. One is the five-layer architecture that includes the processing and business layers (Mashal et al., 2015) (Said & Masud, 2013) (Wu et al., 2010) (Khan et el., 2012). The five-layers architecture includes perception, transport, processing, application, and business layers (see Figure 1). The purpose of the perception and application layers is the same as the architecture with three layers. This chapter outlines the function of the remaining three layers.

- The *transport layer* transfers the gathered sensor data from the perception layer to the processing layer and vice versa through data communication networks (e.g., wireless, 3G, LAN, Bluetooth, RFID, and NFC).

- The *processing layer* is also called the middleware layer. It stores, analyses, and processes vast data from the transport layer. It can control and serve diverse services to the lower layers. In addition, it uses many technologies such as databases, cloud computing, and big data processing modules.

- The *business layer* controls the IoT system environment, including applications, profit models, and business and end-users' privacy. However, the business layer details are out of the scope of this chapter.

Another architecture proposed by Ning and Wang (Ning & Wang, 2011) is influenced by the processing layers in a typical human brain. The human intelligence characteristics also inspire it (e.g., think, feel, remember, make decisions, and react to the physical environment). It is constituted of three parts. First is the human brain, analogous to the processing and data management unit or the data centre. The second is the spinal cord, analogous to the distributed network of data processing nodes and smart gateways. The third is the network of nerves, corresponding to the networking components and sensors.

Figure 2. Fog architecture of an innovative IoT gateway

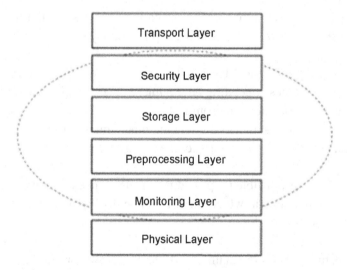

Cloud and Fog Based Architectures

Cloud and fog computing architectures have played a significant role in recent years. In some system architectures, cloud computers do the data processing in a significant, centralized fashion. Such a cloud-centric architecture keeps the cloud at the centre, applications above it, and the network of smart things below it (Gubbi et al., 2013). Cloud computing is given main importance because it gives enormous scalability and flexibility. It provides services (e.g., platform, core infrastructure, storage, and software). Developers can use their storage tools, software tools, data mining, machine learning, and visualization tools through the cloud.

Lately, there has been a move towards another system architecture, namely, *fog computing* (Bonomi et al., 2014) (Bonomi et al., 2012) (Stojmenovic & Wen, 2014), where the sensors and network gateways do a part of the data processing and analytics. A fog architecture (Aazam & Huh, 2014)is shown in Figure 2, including storage, monitoring, pre-processing, and security layers between the transport and physical layers. The monitoring layer looks after power, resources, responses, and services. The processing layer does sensor data filtering, processing, and analytics. The short-time storage layer provides storage functionalities (e.g., data replication, distribution, and storage). Lastly, the security layer uses encryption/decryption to ensure data integrity and privacy. Controlling and pre-processing are done on the edge of the data communication network before sending data to service-oriented computing.

Moreover, "fog computing" and "edge computing" are used interchangeably in different business contexts. The latter term relates to the former and is constructed to be more generic. Fog computing, originally called Cisco, refers to smart gateways and smart sensors, whereas edge computing is slightly more penetrative. This paradigm envisions smart data pre-processing capabilities for physical devices such as motors, pumps, or lights. The aim is to do data processing on these devices located at the *edge* of the network. The diagram is not appreciably different from Figure 2, and this chapter does not describe edge computing details separately.

Interoperability and Related Issues for Business Applications

IoT-based service oriented architecture plays an essential role in modern industrial systems automation. Two central factors, (i) interoperability of business services, and (ii) quality of service (QoS), lay the foundation for system automation. Different ways industrial systems interoperability are contextualized (e.g., technical interoperability, syntactical interoperability, semantic interoperability, pragmatic interoperability, platform interoperability, and conceptual interoperability) for system development purpose. Moreover, academic literature states that the interoperability between IoT devices and computing servers depends on different operational characteristics (e.g., business models, hardware and software composition, communication protocols, and business policies). A research group (Pal & Karakostas, 2014) tried to introduce a hardware and software interoperability issue with an ontology-based system architecture. In this chapter, interoperability represents the capability of heterogeneous things or devices to connect and exchange meaningful information among themselves (Pal, 2023).

The QoS values of a composite service are determined by the QoS values of its component services and by the composition structure used (e.g., sequential, parallel, conditional and/or loops). Here, we focus on the sequential composition model. Other models may be reduced or transformed to the sequential model, using for example techniques for handling multiple execution paths and unfolding loops (Cardoso et al., 2004). Importance of business process orchestration and design patterns are highlighted by academics and practitioners (Courbis & Finkelstein, 2005) (Yoshioka et al., 2004) for service aggregation purpose. In a typical commercial IoT setting, this chapter treats the devices and services as bots to set up relationships between them and change them over time. This will allow the situation to let the devices cooperate and achieve a complex task seamlessly.

One needs to have many interoperating components to make such a model work. So let us look at some of the significant components of such a system.

- Object Identification (ID): One needs a unique way to identify an object. An ID can be allocated to an object based on traditional parameters such as the MAC ID, IPv6ID, a universal product code, or other custom methods.
- Metainformation: Along with an ID, one needs some extra information about the device that describes its

characteristics and operational methods.

- Security Controls: This way, an industrial owner of a device might restrict the kinds of devices that can connect to it. These are referred to as *owner control*.
- Service Discovery: Such a system is like a service cloud, where one needs to store details of devices providing certain kinds of services. It becomes essential to keep these directories updated so that devices can learn about other devices.
- Relationship management: This module manages relationship information. For example, it also stores the types of devices that a given device should connect with based on the services provided.
- Service Composition: This module takes the IoT model to a new level. The goal of having such a system is to provide better-integrated services to users.

The rest of the chapter presents a manufacturing service integration example with the help of an ontology-concept similarity assessment algorithm.

INDUSTRIAL MANUFACTURING APPLICATIONS

Today, all manufacturing businesses value the consequence of building an effective supply chain as part of enterprise proliferation and profitability (Pal, 2018). Different industry-specific supply chain types (e.g., automotive, pharmaceutical, apparel, agriculture), and a supply chain consists of a system with organization, people, technology, activity, information, and resource involved in delivering a service or product from suppliers to customers.

Supply chain business activities transform resources into ultimate products and deliver them to customers. The supply chain network comprises the enterprises and departments involved in this process. The essential requirements of supply chain operation are minimizing the inventory, creating seamless material and information flow, effective communication among the business partners, market, sale, purchase, manufacturing plan, and control, customer delivery service, and after-sales service. Therefore, a supply chain is a network of facilities and distribution options that performs material procurement functions, transforming these materials into intermediate and finished products and delivering these finished products to customers. This definition, or a modified version of it, has been used by several researchers (e.g. (Lee & Billington, 1993) (Swaminathan, 2001a) (Keskinocak & Tayur, 2001) (Pal, 2017)). Supply Chain Management (SCM) aims to improve logistical resource allocation, management, and control. In this way, manufacturing SCM is a set of synchronized activities for integrating suppliers, manufacturers, transporters, and efficient customer service so that the right product or service is delivered in the right quantities, at the right time, to the right places (Pal, 2020) (Pal & Ul-Haque, 2020).

The ultimate objective of SCM is the efficient management of the end-to-end process, which starts with the design of the product or service and ends with the time when it has been sold, consumed, and, finally, discarded by the consumer. This process includes product design, procurement, planning and forecasting, production, distribution, fulfillment, after-sales support, and end-of-life disposal. Supply chain management issues can be classified into two broad categories: configuration (design-oriented) issues that relate to the basic infrastructure on which the supply chain executes and coordination (execution-oriented) issues that relate to the actual execution of the supply chain. Configuration-level issues include the following topics:

1. Procurement and Supplier Decisions: Procurement involves making buying decisions under conditions of scarcity. At the same time, the requirements criteria for selecting suppliers and the number of suppliers need to be decided. If sound data is available, using economic analysis methods such as cost-benefit or cost-utility analysis is good practice. Procurement ensures the buyer receives goods, services, or works at the best possible price when aspects such as quality, quantity, time, and location are compared.

2. Production Decisions: This is a multi-criteria decision activity. Does it include the decisions regarding production network design (e.g., Where, and how many manufacturing sites should be used for production purposes? How much capacity should be installed at each of these sites? What kind of products and services will be supported through the supply chain network?).

3. Distribution Decisions: It is based on infrastructure design decisions (e.g., What kind of distribution channels should a manufacturing company have? How many and where should the distribution centers and retail outlets be situated? What types of transportation services and routes should be used? What types of environmental issues does the distribution infrastructure need to be considered?).

4. Information Support Decisions: Managing a manufacturing supply chain involves numerous decisions about the flow of information, product, funds, and coordination. SCM has been instrumental in connecting and smoothing business activities and forming various kinds of business relationships (e.g., Customer Relationship Management, Supplier Relationship Management) among supply chain stakeholders.

Coordination-level issues include the following topics:

1. Material Flow Decisions: These decisions include – How much inventory of different product types should be stored to provide the target service levels? Should inventory be carried in finished form or semi-finished form? How often should inventory be replenished? And so many other issues need to be considered.

2. Information Flow Decisions: SCM systems utilize modern Information and Communication Technologies (ICT) to acquire, interpret, retain, and distribute information. The software applications are ready-made packages, usually targeting a set of tasks, e.g., tracking product-related information during the transportation process. These ready-made package-software applications are mass-customized products that ignore the specific requirements of a particular business sector, so they are problematic. However, the problem of the appropriate IT solutions for supporting collaboration between supply chain business partners is not new, and it has been approached with several standards and protocols implemented in numerous enterprise information systems.

Application like ERP (Enterprise Resource Planning), CRM (Customer Relationship Management), and WMS (Warehouse Management System) contains valuable data that can be utilized by the decision support systems (DSS). Moreover, the digital transformation of business and society presents enormous growth opportunities offered by technologies such as the Internet of Things (IoT), Big Data, advanced manufacturing, blockchain technologies, and artificial intelligence. This digital transformation is characterized by a fusion of advanced technologies and the integration of physical and digital systems, the predominance of innovative business models and new processes, and intelligent products and services.

The main goal was to reduce inventory levels drastically and regulate the suppliers' interaction with the production line more effectively. It consisted of material and information flow through the supply chain organizations. The scope of the supply chain begins with the source of supply and ends at the point of consumption. It extends beyond simply a concern with the physical movement of materials. Equal emphasis is given to supplier management, purchasing, inventory management, manufacturing management, facilities planning, customer service, information flow, transport, and physical distribution. Some of the critical business processes along the supply chain are shown in Figure 3.

Also, the critical challenges in supporting massive heterogeneous data integration in global supply networks are: (i) increasing number of business alliance partners due to the globalization of business processes, (ii) different business practice and infrastructure facilities within participating business partners, and (iii) differences in data exchange formats and standards among business-partners. Moreover, data capture and transmission mechanisms (e.g., barcoding, radio frequency identification technique, electronic data interchange, wireless networking infrastructure and protocols, global positioning system's capability) produce vast amounts of supply chain transportation data that, if properly controlled and shared, can enhance performance and agility of global supply chain networks. A single representation data format is essential to harness the value-added service.

Figure 3. Diagrammatic representation of the supply chain business process

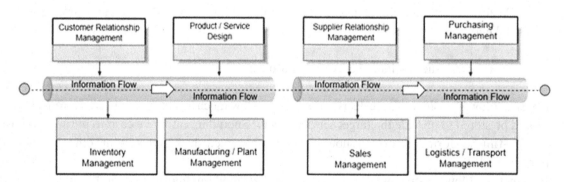

As a result, much global manufacturing (e.g., textile and clothing) businesses invest in new ICT to harness smooth information-sharing ability in their supply chain operations (Monteneggro et al., 2007). With the recent progress in Radio Frequency Identification (RFID) technology, low-cost wireless sensor hardwires, and world comprehensive web technologies, the Internet of Things (IoT) advance has attracted attention in connecting global apparel business activities and sharing operational business information. In this context, IoT technology supports connecting and integrating both digital and physical business entities, enabling the provision of a new type of information system (IS) applications and services. Also, the Semantic Web of Things (SWoT) is ushering in a new opportunity in the business community by integrating the Semantic Web and IoT technologies. It aims to associate semantically rich and easily accessible information with real-world objects, locations, and events using inexpensive, disposable, and unobtrusive micro-devices, such as RFID tags and wireless sensors. This opportunity provides new IS applications and services in many apparel business areas (e.g., manufacturing, inventory, and transportation management).

In order to facilitate this vision, information technologies and software system frameworks must mitigate typical pervasive computing application-related issues: platform heterogeneity, appropriate resource utilization, intelligent intractability of the user, device volatility, dependence on context, and limitation of device-specific computation power. Hence, the SWoT vision requires pervasive knowledge-based systems with higher degrees of automatic capability in information storage, management, and discovery and transparent access to information sources for processing.

Most IoT technology solutions inherit support from stable data communication infrastructures and assistance from centralized brokers for service management and information discovery. Also, optimization of alternative information provision has been recently getting prominence, for example, 6LoWPAN (IPv6 over Low Power Wireless Personal Area Networks) (Monteneggro et al., 2007) and the Constrained Application Protocol (CoAP) (Colitti et al., 2011). In parallel attempts, device and data annotation ontologies were presented, for example - OntoSensor (Russomanno et al., 2005) and the SSN-XG ontology of the World Wide Web Consortium for semantic sensor networks (Lefort et al., 2005). Current research projects, such as UBIWARE (Katasonov et al., 2008), and Sense2Web (Barnaghi et al., 2010), integrate data communication networking and semantic technologies to make software frameworks for semantically enriched IoT application services.

These services are composed of different data sources from real-world objects related to apparel business processes. With many devices in the textile and clothing world, many physical parameters and real-world entities can collaborate in a business service through data communication networks or the Internet. Thus, there is a need for seamless integration of the physical world with the digital world in IoT. Also, the progress in IoT-enabled device abstraction and integrating different data sources in the apparel business is challenging. The traditional web service discovery mechanisms are incapable of producing the appropriate result. Also, the heterogeneous nature of IoT-generated data requires semantic modelling. Thus, IoT entities must be formally represented and managed to achieve interoperability.

An essential step towards the vision of IoT-based information systems interoperability is reusing data collected from widely distributed sensor-enabled devices. Ontology-based semantic modelling helps capture entities' capability to represent information and its relationships among other entities to enable efficient information exchange. In this way, semantic modelling in conjunction with service-oriented computing and ontology, ushers a scalable means of accessing IoT entities. An ontology describes a vocabulary modelling a domain of interest and specifying the meaning of terms in that vocabulary. Depending on the accuracy of this specification, the notion of ontology encompasses different data or conceptual models (e.g., classifications). In other words, ontology is a shared conceptualization, and it is used to represent knowledge as a set of concepts related to each other. The structural part comprises four key components: *classes*, *relations*, *attributes*, and *individuals*. Classes represent the concepts in ontology design, and individuals are the basic, '*ground level*' components or instances of an ontology. Attributes or characteristics represent the features of the classes, and relations describe how the classes and individuals are related to one another.

This chapter presents semantic knowledge-based on IoT-related entities in an apparel manufacturing business. Since most of the IoT data in a textile and clothing industry setting needs to be made available homogeneously to allow integration from various sources. A unified machine-understandable representation of world knowledge must put things into an everyday semantic context. The integrated Apparel Business Decentralised Data Integration (ABDDI) framework uses semantic modelling. Ontologies are used to form a unified knowledge base to support: (a) semantic definition and representation of IoT entities; (b) dynamic service discovery and matching based on user request; and (c) service composition and orchestration in dynamic environments. This chapter considers ontologies as the vital component for automatic service representation, composition, discovery, and orchestration for IoT in dynamic environments. The proposed knowledge base hides the heterogeneity of entities and consequently enables semantic searching and querying capabilities. Finally, the presented knowledge base integrates several existing ontologies related to sensor resources and web services and extends them for IoT.

RELATED RESEARCH WORKS

In recent decades automatic identification technologies are gaining more attraction for industrial applications. These applications are combined with RFID, Electronic Product Code (EPC) technologies, and sensor-based data communication networks to share application-specific data. Advances in ICT are bringing into reality the vision of many uniquely identifiable, interconnected objects and things that gather data from diverse physical environments and deliver the information to various innovative applications and services. In this way, the network of objects (e.g., devices, vehicles, machines, containers), embedded with sensors and software can collect and communicate data over the Internet. The inter-and intra-organizational communication and information exchange are perceived to be facilitated by IoT capability. This, IoT-based technology adoption can be viewed as an additional capability that may add value to the supply chain industries.

While IoT's many applications are used in different supply chain industries (Jandl et el., 2019), industrial IoT (IIoT) focuses primarily on the industrial usage of IoT devices (Jakl et al., 2018) (Jeschke et al., 2017). Thomas Moser's research group recently presented an overview of industrial IoT applications (Jandl·et al., 2019) for the smart industry (also known as Industry 4.0). With the advent of the IoT, new opportunities and capabilities emerge in real-time monitoring, management, and optimizing goods distribution and supply chain. As more physical objects in supply chain industries are equipped with barcodes, RFID tags, or sensors, transport, and logistics companies can monitor the movement of physical objects from one location to another. The goal is to track a product along the entire supply chain, including material management, production, transportation, and distribution (Karakostas, 2013).

Manufacturing companies are changing their IT infrastructure towards the fourth industrial revolution (Lasi et al., 2014). The utilization of artificial intelligence (AI) techniques in cyber-physical systems (CPSs) (Broy et al., 2012) is a typical characteristic of this change (Lee et al., 2014). In this context, flexibility is one of the essential criteria for manufacturing companies, mainly because of ever-shorter market launch times and increasing customer demands for individualization (Cheng et al., 2017; Lasi et al., 2014). To conduct industry 4.0 research, researchers use the factory simulation model because companies are often unwilling to provide data from and access to their production lines for research purposes.

More researchers have started concentrating on techniques enabling machines to understand IoT data better intelligently from various sources. In order to use AI applications, contextual operational knowledge must be available in formal and machine-readable representation (Humm et al., 2020). Semantic web services address the issues of automatic discovering, composing, and executing by providing a declarative, ontological framework for describing them. Using AI methods (e.g., automated planning such as (Marrella, 2018) (Marrella & Mecella, 2018), multi-agent systems for decentralized manufacturing control such as (Ciortea et al., 2018), Case-Based Reasoning (CBR) such as Minor et al., 2014) (Muller, 2018)) to enhance flexibility in cyber-physical production workflows (Bordel Sanchez et al., 2018) (Seiger et al., 2018)) inevitably require such semantic annotations.

Much related research work (Puttonen et al., 2010) (Puttonen et al., 2013) exists that already highlights these issues by using semantic web services (SWS). Moreover, the currently available approaches that use semantic web services in the context of Industry 4.0 focus only on specific aspects and do not consider the entire context of a manufacturing environment. Also, the complex reasoning within the knowledge base makes real-time execution and monitoring of manufacturing processes difficult. In this way, managing interoperable industrial applications is the key to success. One of the key components of interoperability is the specific information system's architecture. A reference architecture (RA) represents a robust and ground-level understanding of the scenarios that help recognize problems and difficulties. The key idea of designing a RA (e.g., service-oriented architecture (SOA)) is to highlight modularity, scalability, adaptiveness, and interoperability among the connected heterogeneous devices in a real-time environment (Sarkar et al., 2021) (Schneider, 2018) (Hazra et al., 2021) (Nagarajan et al., 2021).

Several research works propose using SWSs for smart manufacturing in Industry 4.0 but focus only on partial aspects and do not consider the entire shop floor context. For instance, Puttonen et al. (2013) present an approach to using SWSs for executing manufacturing processes using three software agents represented as web services. One of these agents, Service Monitor, is a specialized web service that performs semantic web service composition by using planning techniques concerning a given production goal and the current state of the world provided by a domain ontology. Therefore, they use OWL to describe the state of the production system and OWL-S and SPARQL expressions for semantically describing the available web services that offer production capabilities.

Since modern Cyber-Physical Production Systems (CPPSs) (Monostori, 2014) consist of many different components and therefore, many stakeholders are involved in their development process up to the later use in the manufacturing of products, Lobov et al. (2008) investigated the application of SWSs for orchestration of flexible control. They propose OWL for modelling a Process Taxonomy, Product Ontology, Equipment Ontology, and Service Ontology and discuss the responsibilities of involved persons for knowledge acquisition and maintenance rather than present their detailed semantic specification.

Many academics and practitioners, work-like Henson et al. (Cory et al., 2009), experiment a semantically enhanced sensor service application, known as SemSOS, having the capability to query both high-level knowledge and low-level environmental reading by sensors. Concerning the classical sematic-matchmaking approach, different research groups distinguish among full (subsume), potential (intersection-satisðable), and partial (disjoint) match types to represent the relevant knowledge of different types of entities (Colucci et al., 2007) and (Li & Horrocks, 2004) respectively. Similarly, queries in ubiquitous infrastructure allow only exact matches with facts derived from a support knowledge base. Non-standard inferences like abduction and contraction are needed to support approximate matches, semantic ranking, and explanations of outcomes (Colucci et al., 2007).

This chapter highlights the requirement for a unified semantic knowledge base for automatic service representation, discovery, modelling, and composition in dynamic environments. Different research projects try to address these issues using ontologies in prototype system design. For example, semantic commonalities in the RFID semantic streams project use DLs for system modelling (Ruta et al., 2011). This work is of considerable interest, but so far, it is sui generis.

All these schemes are worthy of considerable study, and together they represent the wealthiest characterization of a knowledge-based approach in pervasive service computing so far produced. Moreover, the systems are implemented and can be shown to generate relevant services using appropriate data streams.

OVERVIEW OF THE FRAMEWORK

The proposed framework uses model-theoretic semantics modelled in ontologies for IoT-generated data modelling purposes. It helps to gather detailed information regarding the characteristics of IoT devices based on their technical requirements. The advantages of this encoding are – (i) interconnecting different classification systems to represent capabilities and properties of constituent parts, (ii) translating characteristics or properties among compound constituent parts, and (iii) aggregating basic properties into complex properties based on the constituents of a superordinate system. Those concepts can be used and adapted for the IoT to enhance the uses of IoT devices in connecting them as a group, create coordination between IoT devices, and improve their interoperability.

One of the main objectives of this framework is to define an IoT architecture, which can also be used for other applications. The design principle in Apparel Business Semantic Data Management (ABDDI) is that any physical/real-world object in the global textile and clothing business can have a virtual representation through a Virtual Object (VO). AVO uses a semantic representation of the functionality and conceals the varied identity of the real-world object. Multiple VOs can be combined to form a Composite Virtual Object (CVO) that provides more compact and reliable services. In simple, CVOs are combined to form a service request. Thus, the ABDDI architecture has three layers: VO, CVO, and Service, as shown in Figure 4.

The functionalities of the three layers are presented below:

1. VO layer: Real-world objects are represented in the digital format as VO. End-users can search semantically and retrieve information from any existing VO. Also, actuation can be done through the VO.
2. CVO layer: In this layer, VOs are combined to form a service request. This layer caters functionality to search and query categories of CVOs for service provision semantically.
3. Service layer: This layer gets the request from a user and analyses the service requests to determine the categories of CVOs needed for service accomplishment. This layer also performs service composition and orchestration in a dynamic cloth and textile business environment.

The ABDDI system also has got other components: *a registry* and a *control unit*. Every layer in this framework has a registry referencing the available VOs, CVOs, and services. These registries provide methods to semantically search and query existing VOs, CVOs, and services. In addition, the control unit regulates access to the VOs, CVOs, and services based on the level of the end-user requirements.

Figure 4. RFID tagging level at different stages in the apparel manufacturing network

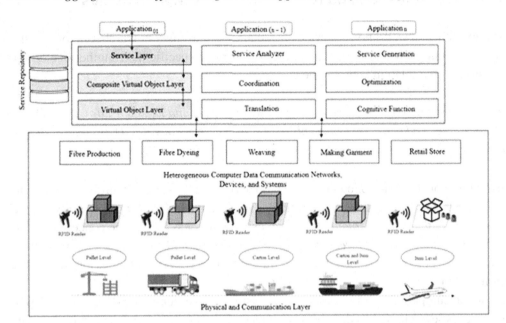

KNOWLEDGE REPRESENTATION AND REASONING APPROACH

One of the motivations for this chapter stems from the Description Logics (DL) [1] based knowledge representation approach in pervasive computing applications along the global apparel supply chain. This DL-based knowledge representation systems play a role very much like Database Management Systems (DBMS). In DL, elementary descriptions are *atomic concepts* and *atomic roles*. Complex descriptions can be built from them inductively with *concept constructors*. In abstract notation, one can use the letters A and B for atomic concepts, R for atomic roles, and C and D for concept descriptions. Possible DL constructors and the related examples are shown in Table 1, and these constructors are used in the DLs investigated in this chapter.

Table 1. DLs set of constructors

Constructor Name	Syntax	Explanation
Top concept	$\top$	Universal concept. All the objects in the domain.
Bottom concept	$\perp$	The empty set.
Atomic concept	A	All objects belong to set A.
Atomic negation	$\neg A$	All the objects are not belonging to set A.
Conjunction	$C \sqcap D$	The objects belong to both C and D sets.
Disjunction	$C \sqcup D$	The objects that are in the extension of either C or D or both
Value restriction	$\forall RC$	All the objects are participating in the R relation, whose range is all the objects belonging to the C set.
Existential restriction	$\exists RC$	At least one object participating in the relation R.
Concept definition	$A \equiv C$	Concepts represent sets of elements and can be viewed as unary predicates.

Resource Representation and Reasoning in Description Logics

The most important and well-known service characterizing reasoning in DL checks for specificity hierarchies by determining whether a concept description is more specific than another one or, formally, if there is a *subsumption* relation between them.

Definition 1 (Subsumption): Give two concept descriptions, C and D, and a TBox τ in a DL L; one can say that D subsumes Cτ ($C \sqsubseteq_\tau D$) concerning if for every model of τ, $C^I \subset D^I$. In a particular case, two concepts are equivalent if they subsume each other.

For example, consider the following concept descriptions, referring to different garment types in an apparel supply chain network: G_1 = *SweaterBodyGarment* ⊓ ∀ *hasMain.Colour.Red,* and G_2 = *UpperBodyGarment* ⊓ ∀ *hasMain.Colour.Red.* Then using TBox reasoning – the concept inclusion can be achieved, and the output will be *Sweater* $\sqsubseteq_T$ *UpperBodyGarment.* Hence, given the model, knowledge expressed by G_1 is more specific than the one required by G2 concerning the reasoning mechanism and the definition of G_2 subsumes G_1.

Based on subsumption, new reasoning mechanisms can be defined in DLs. The ABDDI system development uses several non-standard reasoning mechanisms (e.g., Least Common Subsumer – LCS).

Definition 2 (Least Common Subsumer): Let C_1, ..., C_p be p concept descriptions in a DL L. A Least Common Subsumer (LCS) of C_1, ..., C_p, denoted by LCS (C_1, ..., C_p) is a concept description E in L. state that the following conditions hold: (i) $C_h \sqsubseteq E$ for h = 1, ..., p; (ii) E is the least L–concept description satisfying (iii), i.e., if E' is an L–concept satisfying $C_i \sqsubseteq E'$ for all i = 1, ..., n, then $E \sqsubseteq E'$.

It is worth showing how to model concept collections formalized in ALN (D) according to a compact lossless representation. Such modelling allows for finding commonalities in resource annotations formalized in DL.

Definition 3 (Concept Components): Let C be a concept described in a DL L, with C formalized as C^1 ⊓ ... C^m. The Concept Components of C are defined as follows: if C^j, with j = 1,..., m is either a concept name, a negated concept name, or a concrete feature or a number restriction, then C^j is a Concept Component of C; if C^j=∀R.E, with j = 1 ..., m, then $∀R.E^k$ is a Concept Component of C, for each E^k Concept Component of E.

Definition 4 (Subsumption): Give two concept descriptions C and D, and a TBox τ in a DL L; one can say that D subsumes Cτ ($C \sqsubseteq_\tau D$) concerning if for every model of τ, $C^I \subset D^I$. In a particular case, two concepts are equivalent if they subsume each other.

Definition 5 (Least Common Subsumer): Let C_1, ..., C_p be p concept descriptions in a DL L. A Least Common Subsumer (LCS) of C_1, ..., C_p, denoted by LCS (C_1, ..., C_p) is a concept description E in L. state that the following conditions hold: (i) $C_h \sqsubseteq E$ for h = 1, ..., p; (ii) E is the least L–concept description satisfying (iii), i.e., if E' is an L–concept satisfying $Ci \sqsubseteq E'$ for all i = 1, ..., n, then $E \sqsubseteq E'$.

Definition 6 (r-Common Subsumer, Informative r-Common Subsumers): Let C_1, ..., C_p be p concept descriptions in a DL L, and let be $k \leq p$. An r-Common Subsumer (r-CS) of C_1, ..., C_p is a concept D $\neq$ $\top$ such that D is an LCS of at least $r = k/p$ concepts among C_1, ..., C_p. One can define a particular case as Informative r-Common Subsumers (IrCS) that specific r-CSS for which r < 1.

It is worth showing how to model concept collections formalized in ALN (D) according to a compact lossless representation. Such a modelling framework allows for finding commonalities in resource annotations formalized in DL.

Definition 7 (Concept Components): Let C be a concept described in a DL L, with C formalized as C^1 $\sqcap$ ... C^m. The Concept Components of C are defined as follows: if C^j, with j = 1,..., m is either a concept name, a negated concept name, or a concrete feature or a number restriction, then C^j is a Concept Component of C; if $C^j = \forall R.E$, with j = 1 ..., m, then $\forall R.E^k$ is a Concept Component of C, for each E^k Concept Component of E.

Definition 8 (Aggregate Collection Matrix): Let S_1, ..., S_n be an aggregate collection, with $S_j = C_{1}$, .., C_{pi} for i = 1 ... n. Let D $\in \{D_1, ..., D_m\}$ be the Concept Components deriving from all the concepts in the aggregate collection. The Aggregate Subsumers Matrix is defined as A = (a_{ij}), with i = 1 ... n and j = 1 ... m, such that for each i, $a_{ij} = v$, with $0 \leq v \leq p_i$, where v is the number of concept descriptions in Si subsumed by the component D_j.

Definition 9 (Aggregate Model): Let S_1, ..., S_n be an aggregate of concept collections; for i = 1 ... n, Si is a concept collection descriptions Ski with k = 1 ... p_i. An Aggregate Model for S_1, ..., S_n and each of this element consists of the pair of items - <E, G> with the following characteristics: (i) E represents the subsumers matrix deriving from the collection $C_1, .., C_p = \cup(C_{ki})$, with i = 1 ... n and k = 1 ... p_i, whose elements e_{kj} are calculated by using prognostications to subsumption; and (ii) G is the collection subsumers matrix deriving from the input collection $S_1, .., S_n$, whose elements a_{ij} are calculated by using information stored in E. In this computation, each row i in G is related to an aggregate collection S_i, defined as a collection of description C_{ki} whose subsumption relationship with components deriving from $S_1, .., S_n$ is stored in E. To this modelling, values a_{ij} for each component D_j are determined as Concept Component Relative Cardinality $RC_{D_j}^{S_i}$.

Semantic Similarity Assessment

Before describing the proposed approach's theoretical framework, the employed reasoning services will be shortly recalled in the following subsection to make the chapter self-contained. Furthermore, the proposed algorithmic concept of similarity measurement is presented in this section.

In ABSDM, the similarity between concepts C_i, C_j can be expressed by a number, and its values can fall between 0 and 1. It may be viewed as a one-directional relation, and its larger values imply a higher similarity between the concepts. The concept similarity is described as follows:

Definition 10 (Concept Similarity): *An ontological concept (C) similarity (∂) is considered a relation, and it can be defined as $\partial C \; x \; C \rightarrow [0, 1]$. In simple, it is a function from a pair of concepts to a real number between zero and one, expressing the degree of similarity between two concepts such that:*

1. $\forall C_1 \in G, \; \partial(C_1, C_1) = 1$
2. $\forall C_1, C_2 \in G, \; 0 \leq \partial(C_1, C_2) \leq 1$
3. $\forall C_1, C_2, C_3 \in G,$ IF $Sim_d(C_1, C_2) > Sim_d(C_1, C_3)$ THEN $\partial(C_1, C_2) < \partial(C_1, C_3)$

The above properties provide the range of semantic similarity functions $\partial(C_i, C_j)$. For exactly similar concepts, the similarity is $\partial(C_1, C_1) = 1$; when two concepts have nothing in common, their similarity is $\partial(C_1, C_2) = 0$. In this way, the output of the similarity function should be in the closed interval [0, 1]. Here Sim_d represents the semantic distance, and (C_1, C_2, C_3) represent three concepts of graph G. In CSIA, the following semantic similarity (∂) function has been used for computation purposes:

$$\partial(C_1, C_2) = \frac{1}{deg * Sim_d(C_1, C_2) + 1}$$

Where C_1 and C_2 represent two concepts, and 'deg' represents the impact of semantic distance on semantic similarity, it should be between $0 < deg \leq 1$. A weight allocation function is used, as shown below, to compute the semantic similarity between concepts:

$$w(C_m, C_n) = \left[\max(depth(C_m)) + \frac{OrderNumber(C_n)}{TNodes(G) + 1} + 1 \right]^{-1}$$

Where C_m and C_n represents two nodes directly connected, $\max(depth(C_m))$ represents the maximum depth of the node C_m (the depth of the root node is equal to 0 and 1 for the nodes directly connected to the root node and so on), TNodes(G) and OrderNumber(C_n) represent the total number of nodes in concept graph G and the order number of the node (C_n) between their siblings. The detailed description of these mathematical formalizations is beyond the scope of this chapter.

Semantic Similarity Assessment

In ABDDI, the similarity between two concepts C_i, a number can express C_j, and its values can fall between 0 and 1. It may be viewed as a one-directional relation, and its larger values imply a higher similarity between the concepts. The concept similarity is described as follows:

EXAMPLE OF A BUSINESS SCENARIO

A simple apparel manufacturing scenario is used to present a part of ABDDI algorithmic computation. Semantic IoT-based product flow in a retail outlet is considered. Each product is described using semantic-enhanced IoT as an ALN (D) concept expression in OWL language. As the retail apparel product arrive or depart the shop, they are scanned by the gate RFID readers; reading events, including semantic annotation extracted from tags, are fed to a semantic Data Service Management Service (DSMS), which computes Concept Components and subsumption test through a reasoning mechanism.

Let us consider a situation that allows a user to purchase a sweater from an online business. This example considers how a request is matched with the service advertised for wool garments selling service. An algorithm (i.e., ALGORITHM 1) tries to perform semantic matching for a relevant sweater.

Algorithm 1. Algorithm for semantic similarity computation

input: two concepts (C_1, C_2), the root node (root), concepts graph (G)
output: semantic similarity value between two concepts
1: begin
2: if C_1 and C_2 are same concept then Sim_d = 0
3: else
4:     if C_1 and C_2 are directly connected then Sim_d = w (C_1 , C_2)
5:     else
6:         if idirect path connection exist then
7:             S_{path01} = ShortestPath (G, C_1, Roots)
8:             S_{path02} = ShortestPath (G, C_2, Roots)
9:             Sim_d = w(S_{path01}) + w(S_{path02}) − 2*w(CSPath]
10:        end if
11:            $\partial(C_1, C_2) = \frac{1}{deg \cdot Sim_d + 1}$
12:    end if
13: end if
14: return ∂
15: end

The algorithm takes two ontological concepts, the root node (root), and the concepts graph (G), as input and computes a semantic similarity between the concepts as output.

The part of the concept hierarchy used in this example is shown in Figure 5. Each node of this hierarchy represents a concept. The experimental comparison considers semantic similarity among Wool, Shirt, Sweater, Trousers, Cardigan, Pullover, and Jumper. The proposed algorithm (i.e., Algorithm-I) provides semantic similarity between concepts with a higher score than the path similarity algorithm.

In Table 2, (a) is the result of path similarity [18], and (b) tabulates the results of the proposed Algorithm-I used in ABDDI. In ABDDI, the similarity measure is flexible and customizable, allowing the consideration of user preferences. This refers to two aspects. Firstly, the user may determine some of the similarity assessment parameters' relative importance using the advanced search interface. Second, apart from presenting a single rank for each candidate service, more detailed results may also be provided (e.g., different values for recall, and the degree of match) to facilitate the user in identifying the timelier service.

Figure 5. The hierarchical concept relationships

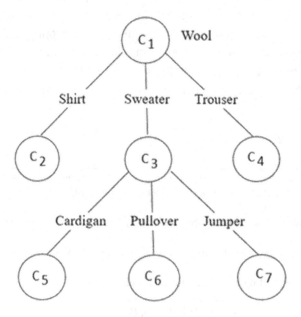

Table 2. The results of various similarity measures

	c_1	c_2	c_3	c_4	c_5
c_1	1.00	0.25	0.50	0.20	0.20
c_2	0.25	1.00	0.50	0.33	0.16
c_3	0.50	0.50	1.00	0.25	0.16
c_4	0.20	0.33	0.25	1.00	0.20
c_5	0.20	0.16	0.16	0.20	1.00

(a) Path similarity

	c_1	c_2	c_3	c_4	c_5
c_1	1.00	0.48	0.65	0.51	0.38
c_2	0.48	1.00	0.65	0.51	0.38
c_3	0.65	0.65	1.00	0.71	0.48
c_4	0.51	0.51	0.71	1.00	0.59
c_5	0.38	0.38	0.48	0.59	1.00

(b) The proposed method

FUTURE RESEARCH DIRECTIONS

Based on the findings, future studies, and experiments must be conducted on semantic reasoning with more diverse information content, complex scenarios, and more detailed contextual knowledge (e.g., rules and other forms). Reasoning engines certainly influence reasoning performance. Thus, different reasoning engines should be evaluated. For example, integrating real-time reasoned knowledge with background knowledge by utilizing federated RDF databases would be valuable, as they can provide background reasoning and knowledge integration services on specific platforms. In the future, the current research plans to use many context scenarios to evaluate the proposed approach's benefit more appropriately.

Although several academic and industry proposals address IoT-based information systems interoperability issues, no reasonable ground can cover some related research issues. The lack of standards and the absence of cutting-edge technologies slow the development of IoT. Proving semantically interoperable platforms across the different IoT domains requires research improvements. Hence, there is still significant room for future work on this topic.

CONCLUSION

This chapter presents some of the uses of IoT technologies (e.g., RFID tag-based technology, sensor) in the apparel industry. RFID technology can interact with items (i.e., transport carts, trolleys, keys, and valuable products) without physical contact in the textile and clothing retail industry. Thus, item-level IoT infrastructures provide item handling efficiency and offer a promising way to capture customers' in-store behavioural data and then gain insight into these data using data mining technology. In this way, these sensing objects and things form the Internet of Things (IoT), which are used to automate manufacturing business processes (e.g., material management, transportation management, and logistics management). In addition, ioT applications rely on real-time context data and allow sending information to drive users' behaviours in intelligent supply chain environments. These IoT-based solutions are mostly tailored for vertical applications and systems, utilizing knowledge only from business areas. However, to realize IoT's full potential, these specialized silo applications must be replaced with horizontal collaborative applications, including knowledge acquisition and sharing capabilities.

One of the main challenges in realizing an IoT system lies in dealing with device and data heterogeneities and fostering the interoperability between devices, information, and services built on top of it. Ontologies and semantic description frameworks play an essential role in the IoT. They operate on top of a standardized data interoperability infrastructure and enforce the concept of data uniformity that allows data and data semantics to be described in application-independent ways. Semantic technologies and ontologies decouple data semantics from application logic, facilitating information exchange, adaptability, and interoperability among tools and systems.

This chapter describes a unified semantic knowledge base (ABDDI) for IoT-related apparel supply chain management technologies. Semantic modelling is a critical component to address issues related to interoperability among different entities to realize the grand vision of IoT. ABDDI's knowledge base comprises ontologies to model different aspects of the apparel business (e.g., IoT resources, location information, contextual information, domain knowledge, policies for the dynamic environment, and IoT services). Most of the current work focuses on IoT resources and services; however, modelling contextual information in a dynamic environment assists in more accurate knowledge representation for IoT entities.

Real-time data gathering and processing are the main ingredients of current supply chain operations. To further enhance the potential of this promising application, in the future, this research will try to propose a unified framework for IoT-based path analytics, which uses both in-store shopping paths and IoT-based purchasing data for actionable navigation patterns. In the pre-processing data module, the critical problem of capturing the mainstream shopping path sequences while wiping out redundant and repeated details must be addressed in detail.

REFERENCES

Aazam, M., & Huh, E. N. (2014). Fog computing and smart gateway based communication for cloud of things. In *Proceedings of the 2nd IEEE International Conference on Future Internet of Things and Cloud (FiCloud' 14),* (pp. 464–470). IEEE. 10.1109/FiCloud.2014.83

Atzori, L., Iera, A., & Morabito, G. (2011). IoT: Giving a social structure to the internet of things. *IEEE Communications Letters, 15*(11), 1193–1195. doi:10.1109/LCOMM.2011.090911.111340

Baader, F., Calvanese, D., McGuinness, D., Nardi, D., & Patel-Schneider, P. (Eds.). (2002). *The Description Logic Handbook.* Cambridge University Press.

Barnaghi, P., Presser, M., & Moessner, K. (2010). Publishing Linked Sensor Data. In *Proceedings of the 3rd International Workshop on Semantic Sensor Networks.* IEEE.

Berners-Lee, T. (2000). *Weaving the Web: The Original Design and Ultimate Design of the World Wide Web by its inventor.* Harper Business.

Bonomi, F., Milito, R., Natarajan, P., & Zhu, J. (2014). Fog computing: a platform for internet of things and analytics. In Big Data and Internet of Things: A Road Map for Smart Environments. Springer.

Bonomi, F., Milito, R., Zhu, J., & Addepalli, S. (2012). Fog computing and its role in the internet of things. In *Proceedings of the 1st ACM MCC Workshop on Mobile Cloud Computing,* (pp. 13–16). ACM. 10.1145/2342509.2342513

Bordel Sánchez, B., Alcarria, R., Sánchez de Rivera, D., & Robles, T. (2018). Process execution in CyberPhysical Systems using cloud and Cyber-Physical Internet services. *The Journal of Supercomputing, 74*(8), 4127–4169. doi:10.100711227-018-2416-4

Broy, M., Cengarle, M. V., & Geisberger, E. (2012). Cyber-Physical Systems: Imminent Challenges. In *Large-Scale Complex IT Syst. Dev., Operat. and Manag.* Research Gate.

Cardoso, J., Sheth, A., Miller, J., Arnold, J., & Kochut, K. (2004). Quality of service for workflows and web service processes. *Journal of Web Semantics, 1*(3), 281–308. doi:10.1016/j.websem.2004.03.001

Cheng, H., Xue, L., Wang, P., Zeng, P., & Yu, H. (2017). Ontology-based web service integration for flexible manufacturing systems. In *15th Int. Conf. on Ind. Inf.,* (pp. 351–356). IEEE. 10.1109/INDIN.2017.8104797

Ciortea, A., Mayer, S., & Michahelles, F. (2018). Repurposing Manufacturing Lines on the Fly with Multi-agent Systems for the Web of Things. In *Proc. of the 17th Int. Conf. on Autonomous Agents and Multi-Agent Systems,* (pp. 813–822). Int. Found. for Autonomous Agents and Multiagent Systems / ACM.

Colitti, W., Steenhaut, K., Caro, N. De., (2011). *Integrating Wireless Sensor Networks with the Web.* Extending the Internet to Low power and Lossy Networks (IP+SN).

Colucci, S., Di Noia, T., Pinto, A., Ruta, M., Ragone, A., & Tinelli, E. (2007). A Nonmonotonic Approach to Semantic Matchmaking and Request Refinement in E-Marketplaces. *International Journal of Electronic Commerce, 12*(2), 127–154. doi:10.2753/JEC1086-4415120205

Cory, A., Henson, J., Pschorr, K., Sheth, A. P., & Thirunarayan, K. (2009). SemSOS: Semantic sensor Observation Service. In *Proceedings of the International Symposium on Collaborative Technologies and Systems*. IEEE.

Courbis, C., & Finkelstein, A. (2005). Weaving Aspects into Web Service Orchestrations. In *Proceeding of International Conference of Web Services (ICWS '05)*. IEEE. 10.1109/ICWS.2005.129

De Virgilio, R., Di Sciascio, E., Ruta, M., Scioscia, F., & Torlone, R. (2011). Semantic-based rfid data management. In *Unique Radio Innovation for the 21st Century* (pp. 111–141). Springer. doi:10.1007/978-3-642-03462-6_6

Gubbi, J., Buyya, R., Marusic, S., & Palaniswami, M. (2013). Internet of Things (IoT): A vision, architectural elements, and future directions. *Future Generation Computer Systems*, 29(7), 1645–1660. doi:10.1016/j.future.2013.01.010

Hazra, A., Adhikari, M., Amgoth, T., & Srirama, S. N. (2021, November). A Comprehensive Survey on Interoperability for IIoT: Taxonomy, Standards, and Future Directions. *ACM Computing Surveys*, 55(1), 1–35. doi:10.1145/3485130

Jakl, A., Schoffer, L., Husinsky, M., & Wagner, M. (2018), Augmented Reality for Industry 4.0: Architecture and User Experience. In *Proceeding of the 11th Forum Media Technology, CER-WS*, (pp. 38-42). ACM.

Jandl, C., Nurgazina, J., Schoffer, L., Reichl, C., Wagner, M., & Moser, T. (2019). SensiTrack – A Privacy by Design Concept for Industrial IoT Applications. In *Proceeding of the 24th IEEE International Conference on Emerging Technologies and Factory Automation*, (pp. 1782-1789). IEEE. 10.1109/ETFA.2019.8869186

Jeschke, S., Brecher, C., Meisen, T., Ozdemir, D., & Eschert, T. (2017). Industrial Internet of Things and Cyber Manufacturing Systems. In Industrial Internet of Things. Springer.

Karakostas, B. (2013). A DNS architecture for the Internet of things: A case study in transport logistics. *Procedia Computer Science*, 19, 594–601. doi:10.1016/j.procs.2013.06.079

Katasonov, A., Kaykova, O., Khriyenko, O., Nikitin, S., & Terziyan, V. (2008). Smart Semantic Middleware for the Internet of Things. In *Proceedings of the 5th International Conference of Informatics in Control, Automation and Robotics*, (pp. 11-15). IEEE.

Keskinock, P., & Tayur, S. (2001). Quantitive analysis of Internet-enabled supply chain. *Interfaces*, 31(2), 70–89. doi:10.1287/inte.31.2.70.10626

Khan, R., Khan, S. U., Zaheer, R., & Khan, S. (2012). Future internet: the internet of things architecture, possible applications and key challenges. In *Proceedings of the 10th International Conference on Frontiers of Information Technology (FIT '12)*, (pp. 257–260). IEEE. 10.1109/FIT.2012.53

Lasi, H., Fettke, P., Kemper, H.-G., Feld, T., & Hoffmann, M. (2014). Industry 4.0. BISE, 6(4):239–242.
Lastra, J. L. M. and Delamer, I. M. (2006). Semantic Web Services in Factory Automation: Fundamental Insights and Research Roadmap. *IEEE Transactions on Industrial Informatics*, 2(1), 1–11.

Lee, H. L., & Billington, C. (1992). Managing supply chain inventories: Pitfalls and opportunities. *Sloan Management Review*, 33(3), 65–77.

Lee, J., Kao, H.-A., & Yang, S. (2014). Service Innovation and Smart Analytics for Industry 4.0 and Big Data Environment. *Procedia CIRP*, *16*, 3–8. doi:10.1016/j.procir.2014.02.001

Lefort, L., Henson, C., Taylor, K., Barnaghi, P., Compton, M., Corcho, O., Garcia-Castro, R., Graybeal, J., Herzog, A., Janowicz, K. (2005). *Semantic Sensor Network XG Final Report*. W3C Incubator Group Report. https://www.w3.org/2005/Incubator/ssn/XGR-ssn/

Li, L., & Horrocks, I. (2004). A software framework for matchmaking based on semantic web technology. *International Journal of Electronic Commerce*, *8*(4), 39–60. doi:10.1080/10864415.2004.11044307

Lobov, A., Lopez, F. U., Herrera, V. V., Puttonen, J., & Lastra, J. L. M. (2008). Semantic Web Services framework for manufacturing industries. In *Int. Conf. on Rob. and Biomim.*, (pp. 2104–2108). IEEE.

Maass, W., Filler, A. (2006). Towards an infrastructure for semantically annotated physical products. *INFORMATIK 2006–Informatik für Menschen–Band 2, Beiträge der 36*. Jahrestagung der Gesellschaft für Informatik eV (GI).

Mahon, B. (2004). *The Man Who Changed Everything: The Life of James Clerk Maxwell*. John Wiley & Sons Ltd.

Marrella, A. (2018). *Automated Planning for Business Process Management*.

Mashal, I., Alsaryrah, O., Chung, T. Y., Yang, C. Z., Kuo, W. H., & Agrawal, D. P. (2015). Choices for interaction with things on Internet and underlying issues. *Ad Hoc Networks*, *28*, 68–90. doi:10.1016/j.adhoc.2014.12.006

Minor, M., Montani, S., & Recio-García, J. A. (2014). Process-oriented Case-based Reasoning. *Information Systems*, *40*, 103–105. doi:10.1016/j.is.2013.06.004

Monostori, L. (2014). Cyber-physical Production Systems: Roots, Expectations and R&D Challenges. *Procedia CIRP*, *17*, 9–13. doi:10.1016/j.procir.2014.03.115

Montenegro, G., Kushalnagar, N., Hui, J., & Culler, D. (2007). Transmission of IPv6 packets over IEEE 802.15.4 networks. Internet proposed standard RFC. IEEE.

Müller, G. (2018). Workflow Modeling Assistance by Casebased Reasoning. Springer Fachmedien, Wiesbaden. .

Ocker, F., Kovalenko, I., Barton, K., & Tilbury, D., and VogelHeuser, B. (2019). A Framework for Automatic Initialization of Multi-Agent Production Systems Using Semantic Web Technologies. *IEEE Robotics and Automation Letters*, *4*(4), 4330–4337.

Nagarajan, S. M., Muthukumaran, V., Vinoth Kumar, V., Beschi, I. S., & Magesh, S. (2021). *Fine Tuning Smart Manufacturing Enterprise Systems: A Perspective of Internet of Things-Based Service-Oriented Architecture, Handbook of Research on Innovations and Applications of AI, IoT, and Cognitive Technologies, IGI Publication, September 2018, USA*. IGI Global Publication. doi:10.4018/978-1-7998-6870-5.ch006

Ning, H., & Wang, Z. (2011). Future internet of things architecture: Like mankind neural system or social organization framework? *IEEE Communications Letters*, *15*(4), 461–463. doi:10.1109/LCOMM.2011.022411.110120

Pal, K. (2017). Supply Chain Coordination Based on Web Services. In H. K. Chan, N. Subramanian, & M. D. Abdulrahman (Eds.), *Supply Chain Management in the Big Data Era* (pp. 137–171). IGI Global Publication. doi:10.4018/978-1-5225-0956-1.ch009

Pal, K. (2018). A Big Data Framework for Decision Making in Supply Chain. IGI Global.

Pal, K. (2020). Information Sharing for Manufacturing Supply Chain Management Based on Blockchain Technology. In I. Williams (Ed.), Cross-Industry Use of Blockchain Technology and Opportunities for the Future. IGI Global. doi:10.4018/978-1-7998-3632-2.ch001

Pal, K., & Karakostas, B. (2014). A Multi Agent-Based Service Framework for Supply Chain Management, In the proceeding of International Conference on Ambient Systems, Networks and Technology. *Procedia Computer Science*, *32*, 53–60. doi:10.1016/j.procs.2014.05.397

Pal, K., & Ul-Haque, A. (2000). *Internet of Things and Blockchain Technology in Apparel Manufacturing Supply Chain Data Management*. In 11th International Conference on Ambient Systems, Networks and Technologies (ANT-2020), Procedia Computer Science, Warsaw, Poland.

Pena-opez, I. (2005). *Internet Report 2005*. The Internet of Things.

Puttonen, J., Lobov, A., & Lastra, J. L. M. (2013). Semantics-Based Composition of Factory Automation Processes Encapsulated by Web Services. *IEEE Transactions on Industrial Informatics*, *9*(4), 2349–2359. doi:10.1109/TII.2012.2220554

Puttonen, J., Lobov, A., Soto, M. A. C., & Lastra, J. L. M. (2010). A Semantic Web Services-based approach for production systems control. *Advanced Engineering Informatics*, *24*(3), 285–299. doi:10.1016/j.aei.2010.05.012

Russomanno, D. J., Kothari, C. R., & Thomas, O. A. (2005). Building a Sensor Ontology: A Practical Approach Leveraging ISO and OGC Models. In *the 2005 International Conference on Artificial Intelligence*, (pp. 637-643). Research Gate.

Ruta, M., Colucci, S., Scioscia, F., Di Sciascio, E., & Donini, F. M. (2011). Finding commonalities in RFID semantic streams. *Procedia Computer Science*, *5*, 857–864. doi:10.1016/j.procs.2011.07.118

Said, O., & Masud, M. (2013). Towards internet of things: Survey and future vision. *International Journal of Computer Networks*, *5*(1), 1–17.

Sarkar, I., Adhikari, M., Kumar, N., & Kumar, S. (2021). Dynamic task placement for deadline-aware IoT applications in federated for networks. *IEEE Internet of Things Journal*, *1*, 2021.

Sarkar, T. K., Mailloux, R. J., Oliner, A. A., Salazar-Palma, M., & Sengupta, D. L. (2006). *History of Wireless*. John Wiley & Sons Inc. doi:10.1002/0471783021

Schneider, M., Hippchen, B., Abeck, S., Jacoby, M., & Herzog, R. (2018). Enabling IoT platform interoperability using a systematic development approach by example, In *Proceedings of the Global Internet of Things Summit (GIoTS'18)*, (pp. 1-6). IEEE. 10.1109/GIOTS.2018.8534549

Seiger, R., Huber, S., & Schlegel, T. (2018). Toward an execution system for self-healing workflows in cyber-physical systems. *Software & Systems Modeling*, *17*(2), 551–572. doi:10.100710270-016-0551-z

Stojmenovic, I., & Wen, S. (2014). The fog computing paradigm: scenarios and security issues. In *Proceedings of the Federated Conference on Computer Science and Information Systems (FedCSIS' 14)*, (pp. 1–8). IEEE. 10.15439/2014F503

Swaminathan, J. M. (2000). *Supply chain management*. International Encyclopedia of the Social and Behavioural Sciences, Elsevier Sciences.

Varelas, G., Voutsakist, E., Raftopoulout, P., Petrakis, E. G. M., & Milios, E. (2005). Semantic Similarity methods in WordNet and their application to information retrieval on the Web. In *Proceedings of the 7th annual ACM international workshop on web information and data management*. ACM. 10.1145/1097047.1097051

Vermesan, O., Friess, P., & Guillemin, P. (2011). Internet of things strategic research roadmap in Internet of Things. *Global Technological and Societal Trends*, *1*, 9–52.

Weyrich, M., & Ebert, C. (2016). Reference architectures for the internet of things. *IEEE Software*, *33*(1), 112–116. doi:10.1109/MS.2016.20

Wu, M., Lu, T. J., Ling, F. Y., Sun, J., & Du, H. Y. (2010) Research on the architecture of internet of things. In *Proceedings of the 3rd International Conference on Advanced Computer Theory and Engineering (ICACTE' 10)*. IEEE.

Yoshioka, N., Honiden, S., & Fnkelstein, A. (2004). Security Patterns: A Method for Constructing Secure and Efficient Inter-Company Coordination Systems. In *Proceedings of Enterprise Distributed Object Computing Conference 2004 (EDOC'04)*, (pp. 84–97). IEEE. 10.1109/EDOC.2004.1342507

Zhao, J., & Kumar, V. V. (2021). *Handbook of Research on Innovations and Applications of AI, IoT, and Cognitive Technologies*. IGI Global Publication. doi:10.4018/978-1-7998-6870-5

KEY TERMS AND DEFINITIONS

Description Logic: Description logics (DL) are a family of formal knowledge representation languages. Many DLs are more expressive than propositional logic, but less expressive than first-order logic.

EPC: Electronic Product Code (EPC), is a low-cost RFID tag designed for consumer products as a replacement for the universal product code (UPC).

Internet of Things: Internet of Things (IoT) means networks of things, software, sensors, network connectivity, and embedded 'things or physical objects. It collects or exchanges data. IoT makes objects sensed or controlled through a network infrastructure, supports integration between physical real world and automated information systems, and brings various effects such as improved productivity or economy in manufacturing industries.

Ontology: Information sharing among supply chain business partners using information systems is an important enabler for supply chain management. There are diverse types of data to be shared across the supply chain, namely – *order, inventory, shipment*, and *customer service*. Consequently, information about these issues needs to be shared to achieve efficiency and effectiveness in supply chain management. In this way, information-sharing activities require that human and / or machine agents agree on common and explicit business-related concepts (the shared conceptualization among hardware / software-agents, customers, and service providers) are known as explicit ontologies; and this help to exchange data and derived knowledge out of the data to achieve collaborative goals of business operations.

RFID Reader: An RFID transceiver, providing real and access to RFID tags information.

RFID Tag: An RFID tag (or transponder), typically consisting of an RF coupling element and a microchip that carries identifying data. Tag functionality may range from simple identification to being able to form an ad hoc network.

Semantic Web Service: A Semantic Web Service, like conventional web services, is the server end of a client-server system for machine-to-machine interaction via the Web. Semantic services are a component of the semantic Web because they use mark-up which makes data machine-readable in a detailed and sophisticated way (as compared with human-readable HTML which is usually not easily "understood" by computer programs).

Supply Chain Management: Supply chain management encompasses the planning and management of all activities involved in sourcing, procurement, manufacturing, and distribution. Importantly, it also includes coordination and collaboration with channel partners, which can be suppliers, intermediaries, third-party service providers, and customers. Supply chain management integrates supply and demand management within and across companies.

Web Ontology Language (OWL): The Web Ontology Language (OWL) is a semantic mark-up language for publishing and sharing ontologies on the Web. OWL is developed as a vocabulary extension of RDF (the Resource Description Framework) and is derived from the DAML + OIL Web Ontology Language.

Chapter 3
An Efficient Feature Selection in Classifying Diabetes Mellitus

Prasanna Ranjith Christodoss
ⓘ https://orcid.org/0000-0003-4778-7915
University of Technology and Applied Science, Shinas, Oman

Rajesh Natarajan
ⓘ https://orcid.org/0000-0003-1255-9621
University of Technology and Applied Sciences, Shinas, Oman

Syed Khaja Mohideen
University of Applied Science and Technology, Salalah, Oman

Justus Selwyn
John Brown University, USA

B. Anandapriya
Patrician College of Arts and Science, India

ABSTRACT

Machine learning (ML) is one of the most popular fields in medical research. Correct identification of the presence of diabetes is essential for providing efficient treatment. Numerous machine learning models were developed to predict diabetes. However, many ML models suffer from misclassification due to a lack of proper feature selection methods. How to select the best features is still a significant problem in the classification domain. To address the problem, an ensemble-based feature selection is proposed. The proposed feature selection is then evaluated in five machine learning models. The experimental results show that the proposed feature selection is 36% more efficient than existing feature selection methods.

DOI: 10.4018/978-1-6684-6971-2.ch003

Copyright © 2023, IGI Global. Copying or distributing in print or electronic forms without written permission of IGI Global is prohibited.

INTRODUCTION

Diabetes Mellitus (DM) is also called diabetes. It is one of the world's worst diseases. The main reason for diabetes is the pancreas does not produce a sufficient amount of insulin. This increases the level of blood sugar and creates many problems. There are two types of diabetes known as type 1 and type 2. T1DM (Type 1 Diabetes Mellitus) is caused when the pancreas fails to produce a sufficient amount of insulin as per Joe Abinas et al. (2021). This happens when there is a loss of beta cells. Most type 1 diabetes is developed at young ages, and the probability that an adult gets type 1 is very rare. Type 2 diabetes is very common. According to Abdulhadi and Al-Mousa (2021), around 77% of diabetes is type 2, and 10% of diabetes infections are type 1, this is shown in figure 1. This happens when the produced insulin is not able to enter the cells. Excessive weight and lack of proper exercise are one of the reasons to develop type 2 diabetes. Many factors such as age, and adiposity creates problem in classifying a patient as type 1 or type 2. It is estimated that around 465 million people are affected by diabetes and research shows that the number will rise to 700 million in 2045 as per Rawat et al. (2022). The graphical visualization of the types of diabetes is shown in figure 2.

Figure 1. Percentage of diabetes

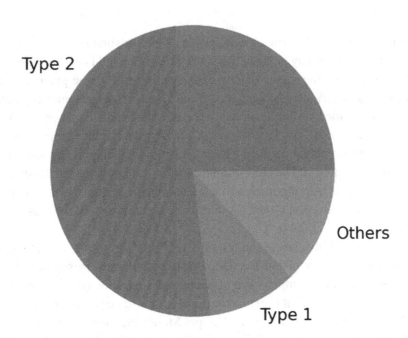

Figure 2. Types of diabetes

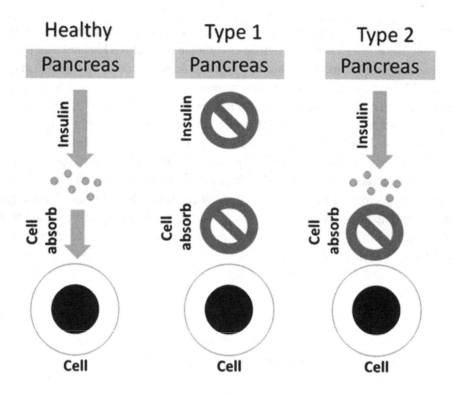

Machine learning is a type of artificial intelligence where the solutions of the real world are solved by learning without the need of any humans. As per Ashokkumar and Don (2019), right from 1952, the machine learning models are improving day by day from the small game playing to complex medical problems. Palanivinayagam, A., and Nagarajan, S. (2020) states that the majority of machine learning-based research focuses on medical applications from electronic health management, drug classification, recommendation systems, and so on. The main reason to develop machine learning models in the medical domain is to imitate the actual medical expert decisions and support. Classification is one of the categories of machine learning and has lots of applications. Ashour et al. (2020) states that, to increase the accuracy of the machine learning model, much research uses feature selection. This chapter uses a hybrid filter-based feature selection model for increasing the accuracy of the classification in the field of diabetes prediction.

Supervised classification involves training with a set of data from the dataset so that it can predict the target when new instances are given. The data used to train the supervised model consists of a set of instances (rows) and features (columns). The efficiency of a machine learning model is dependent on high instances and low features. That is, when the number of instances is huge, the model can learn better about the relationship between the input and output Moreover, when the number of features is more, then the model suffers from the curse of dimensionality as said by Zhou et al. (2021). So, the model requires fewer features. Removing features randomly will cause a negative impact on the performance, hence it is mandatory that a proper feature selection is used.

Nowadays, applying feature selection to the existing dataset is done to improve the performance of the classification. Thejas et al. (2021) mentions lots of advantages to applying feature selection before classification such as reducing dimensionality, removing redundancy, removing errors, and so on. Feature selection can be categorized into three types namely filter-based feature selection, wrapper-based feature selection, and embedded-based feature selection. Filter-based feature selection considers the statistical properties from the training data to rank the features or feature sets before performing the classification. These feature selection methods are the fastest when compared with other feature selection types. Haq et al. (2019) talks about the filter-based methods and they are classifier independent which means the selected features are the same irrespective of what classifier is used. Some examples of filter-based methods are information gain, correlation, and chi-square. Wrapper-based methods select a subset of features based on the performance of the classifier. These are classifiers dependent thus different sets of features are selected based on the classifier chosen. Wrapper methods are usually very computationally expensive because the iterative testing of the best feature selection subset needs to be found. The selected features are done either by a forward or backward selection strategy. Embedded-based feature selection combines both filter-based and wrapper-based methods. They are highly computation efficient according to Elhariri et al. (2020).

RELATED WORKS

A research work carried out by Meng et al. (2013) uses three models for diabetes classification. They used many classification models such as logistic regression, artificial neural networks, decision trees, and so on. The best classification performance was obtained by decision trees. A weighting scheme was proposed by ahan et al. (2005) in which the features are ranked based on their importance, by using 10-fold validation, an accuracy of 75.9% was obtained.

The kernel function determines how the SVM model works. Choosing the correct kernel is very important as it affects the overall performance of the classification. Rozi et al. (2018) proposes a radial-based kernel function with the SVM classifier to predict the presence of diabetes. The accuracy obtained was measured as 78%.

Diabetes prediction in childhood is studied by Achenbach et al. (2022). They aim to find any subtypes, endotypes, or thera types present in diabetes. CART trees are used for the prediction of diabetes. The number of samples they have considered is 1192, all of the patients are teenagers.

Identifying pathology is done by Tanabe et al. (2021) so that the treatment can be planned with appropriate therapeutic strategies. The authors have used cluster-based classification. Five clusters were considered to improve the performance of the classification.

The deep learning approach was used by Kannadasan et al. (2019) for diabetes prediction. They used a softmax layer and fine-tuning was performed through backpropagation with the training data to reduce the wrong predictions. The feature selection was done using stacked autoencoders and the accuracy of 86% was measured.

A questionnaire that consists of 18 questions was prepared by Tigga and Garg (2020) and 952 instances were created. Various machine learning models were considered and the same hyperparameters were used in the PIMA Indian dataset also. The authors found that random forest outperforms all other machine learning models in both the questionnaire dataset as well as in the PIMA Indian dataset.

EFFECTIVE FILTER-BASED FEATURE SELECTION (EFFS) FOR DIABETES CLASSIFICATION

This section briefs about the feature selection used in the diabetes classification. We have used the PIMA Indian dataset for the experiment. To measure the efficiency of the feature selection, four parameters should be considered.

1.   True Positive (TP): When a diabetes patient is classified as diabetes positive.
2.   True Negative (TN): When a healthy patient is classified as diabetes negative.
3.   False Positive (FP): When a healthy patient is classified as diabetes positive.
4.   False Negative (FN): when a diabetes patient is classified as diabetes negative.

Out of the above four metrics, the false negative is most dangerous as a false positive patient can take a second test to confirm the negativity, but the false negative will ignore the second test. Most health sector-based machine learning models aim to reduce the false negatives.

The simplest feature selection method is called an accuracy measure (ACC). This is calculated just by subtracting the true positive from the false positive. The drawback of this method is when the number of true positive and the false positive are the same, then a zero rank is observed and the respective feature can't be ranked for classification. The formula for calculating ACC is displayed in eq (1). However, few modifications are done to this method to improvise the ranking scheme, the second version of ACC is called a balanced accuracy score (ACC2). The ACC2 overcomes the limitation of ACC by introducing two new parameters called true positive rate and false positive rate. Eq (2) and Eq (3) explain how to calculate true positive and false positive rates. The ACC2 equation is displayed in Eq (4).

$$ACC = |TP - FP| \tag{1}$$

$$TPR = \frac{TP}{TP + FN} \tag{2}$$

$$FPR = \frac{FP}{TN + FP} \tag{3}$$

$$ACC2 = |TPR\text{-}FPR| \tag{4}$$

A balanced accuracy score solves a few problems of ACC, but when the differences are too low, then it is difficult for assigning a rank to a feature, in that case, a new feature selection method is known as the Normalized difference measure (NDM) is used. The NDM solves the problem of small differences by dividing the minimum of TPR and FPR as shown in eq (5)

$$NDM = \frac{|TPR - FPR|}{min(TPR, FPR)} \tag{5}$$

The od ratio (OR) is another feature selection method that picks based on the probability of appearance in the positive class. OR ranks the features present in positive class more than features that are not present in positive class. OR also shares the problem with ACC as it could not rank features when FP or FN is zero. OR is calculated as per eq (6).

$$OR = \frac{TP*TN}{FP*FN}$$ (6)

One of the criteria to judge a food feature is how to diverge the value. To check the diversity, a parameter is used to group values into bins. The algorithm that is used in the experiment uses the bin size as 3 and 5, but this can also be changed dynamically. The full working of the proposed feature selection is shown in Algorithm 1. After the feature values are grouped as bins, a frequency count is done to check how much diversity is present. Then the Information gain value is added to the score to increase the support. Finally, to break the tie if two more features share the same score, the correlation value is multiplied by the score. This step ensures that the more correlated a feature is with the target variable, the high score it receives.

Algorithm 1: EFFS

1	N <- Number of instances
2	M <- Number of instances considered for calculation of the score
3	S[] <- Scores of all features, initially 0
4	Y <- Target variable
4	For i=0 to M
5	$C1 = \dfrac{Covariance(i, Y)}{\sigma i\ \sigma Y}$
6	$C2 = -\sum_{i=1}^{m} P(c_i) logP(c_i) + P(t)\sum_{i=1}^{m} P(c_i \mid t)logP(c_i \mid t) + P(\bar{t})\sum_{i=1}^{m} P(c_i \mid \bar{t})logP(c_i \mid \bar{t})$
7	V=set(i) and convert to bins
8	V1=sort(list(V))
9	mid$= V1\left(\dfrac{|V1|}{2}\right)$
10	C3= number of instances <mid
11	C4=number of instances>mid
12	C5=C1*(|c3-c4|+C2)
13	S[i]=C5
14	Sort S
15	Return top values from S

The five classifiers that are used in the experiment are briefed below. SVMs are very powerful machine learning models which were developed by AT&T bell labs. SVM can be used for regression as well as classification. SVM is considered the most robust classifier. SVM works using the endpoints or are called support vectors. Given a set of training instances, the SVM model analyses the data and finds the support vectors. A support vector is present in the boundary of the class margin. Then the SVM picks a hyperplane that best fits between the support vectors. The target class is chosen based on which side the classification instance falls on.

Logistic regression is a statistical-based classification that considers the probability of one class by calculating the odds in a linear space. The model is developed for the linear space model but recent research optimizes the LR to work in non-linear space. The classifier is generally developed for binary classification, but by using multinomial classification, the LR can be used for the classification of any number of classes. The sigmoid function is used in the LR to maximize the performance of the classification.

Naïve Bayes classifier is one of the probabilistic classifiers. The working of this classifier is based on the concept of the Bayes theorem. Like other classifiers, this classifier also assumes that all the input features are independent of each other. Research is done to optimize kernels to increase accuracy. NB classifier is highly scalable.

K Nearest Neighbour (kNN) is a supervised classification model that relies on the concept of distances. kNN can be used as both classifier and regressor. The k closest instances are considered for classification or regression. The majority voting is performed to predict the class of the new samples. In the case of regression, the average of the k closest instances is calculated. The value of k is chosen as an odd number, it is usually a small number.

Random Forest is an ensemble classifier that is also used for both regression and classification. It generates lots of decision trees with many combinations. Each decision tree uses a subset of features/instances for its training process. The final predicted class is the class that is selected by most of the decision trees. If the random forest is used for regression, then the average of all the values returned by the decision tree is returned.

RESULTS AND DISCUSSION

The proposed feature selection method is tested and compared with existing feature selection methods by using five classifiers. The data set used in the experiment is the PIMA Indian dataset. The dataset contains eight input attributes and one target attribute which is described below.

1. Pregnant – the number of times the patient is pregnant
2. Glucose – measured blood glucose level during fasting (in mg/dl)
3. Blood Pressure – talks about the normal/high/low blood pressure
4. Skin Thickness – measures the fat level in the skin
5. Insulin – the level of insulin during fasting. 2-Hour serum insulin is measured as mu U/ml.
6. Body Mass Index – used to find the ratio between height and weight. Can be classified as many types such as underweight (<18.5 kg/mt) or Normal weight (between 18.5 kg/mt to 22.9 kg/mt) or average weight (between 23 kg/mt to 24.9 kg/mt) or obesity (> 25 kg/mt).

7. Diabetes Pedigree Function – describes the genetic history.
8. Age – The current age of the patient.
9. Diabetes (Target variable) – either 0 (health) or 1 (diabetes).

Table 1. Descriptions of the attributes

Sno	Attribute	Min	Max	Mean
1	Pregnant	0	17	3.845
2	Glucose	0	199	120.9
3	Blood Pressure	0	122	69.11
4	Skin Thickness	0	99	20.54
5	Insulin	0	846	79.8
6	Body Mass Index	0	67	31.99
7	Diabetes Pedigree Function	0.07	2.4	0.4719
8	Age	21	81	33.24

To measure the performance of the proposed feature selection method, three metrics are used which are described below

1. Accuracy: represents how many instances are correctly classified over the total number of instances
2. Precision: the ratio of true positives with the total number of instances that were classified as positives. Precision should be high for a good classifier.
3. Recall: the ratio of total positives predicted out of total positives in the dataset

The equations of accuracy, precision, and recall are shown in eq 7, 8, and 9 respectively.

$$\text{Accuracy} = \frac{TP + TN}{TP + TN + FP + FN} \tag{7}$$

$$\text{Precision} = \frac{TP}{TP + FP} \tag{8}$$

$$\text{Recall} = \frac{TP}{TP + FN} \tag{9}$$

The classifiers used in the experiment are Support Vector Machines (SVM), Naïve Bayes (NB), k Nearest Neighbour (kNN), Logistic Regression (LR), and Random Forest (RF). All these classifiers are used with five feature selection methods which are ACC, ACC2, NDM, OR, and the proposed EFFS feature selection method. Fig 3, 4, and 5 show the accuracy, precision, and recall of the classifiers when using the proposed feature selection method. The horizontal axis represents the number of features selected by EEFS. To compare the performance, the number of features that are considered are 3, 4, 5, and 6. It is found that when the number of features is 6, all the machine learning models have maximum performance. When the number of features is 7 or more, we observe a reducing performance hence we stopped the number of features still 6.

Figure 3. The accuracy of the classifiers when using the proposed feature selection method

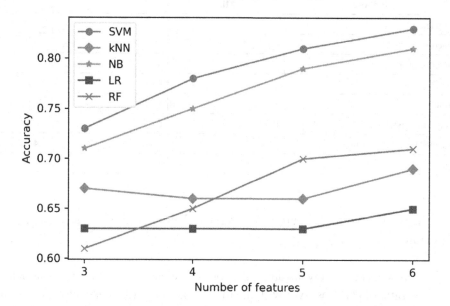

Figure 4. The precision of the classifiers when using the proposed feature selection method

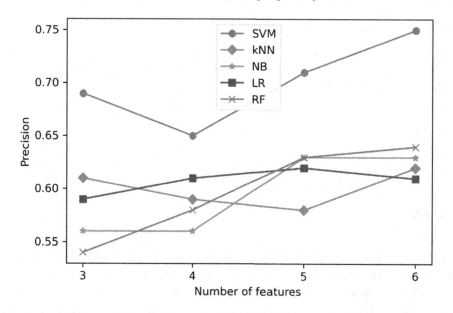

Figure 5. The recall of the classifiers when using the proposed feature selection method

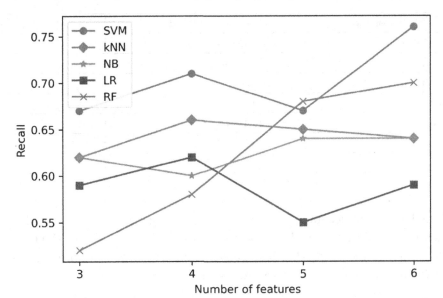

The EEFS feature selection method is compared with few existing research works in terms of accuracy. Six existing models were considered and fig 6 shows the comparison with EEFS. Table 2 displays the accuracy details. The main reason for the proposed method to have a higher performance is because of considering the diversity of the features across the data space.

Figure 6. The comparison of accuracies of existing models with the proposed feature selection method.

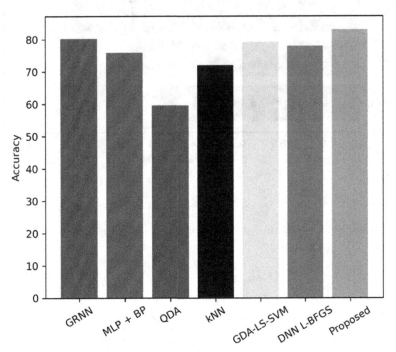

Table 2. The accuracy of existing models in diabetes classification

Reference	Model	Accuracy
Kayaer and Yldrm (2003)	GRNN	80.21
Polat and Gne (2007)	MLP + BP	75.8
Polat and Gne (2007)	QDA	59.5
Polat and Gne (2007)	kNN	71.9
Polat and Gne (2007)	GDA-LS-SVM	79.16
Caliskan et al. (2018)	DNN L-BFGS	77.9
Proposed	EFFS + SVM	83

Figure 7, 8, and 9 show the accurate comparison of the existing feature selection methods with EFFS. The classifiers used are SVM, NB, and RF respectively. It was noted that the SVM model is the highest performer in terms of accuracy with 83%. Naïve Bayes is the second best performing classifier with an accuracy of 81%. The accuracy of RF is measured as 71%.

Figure 7. The accuracy of SVM

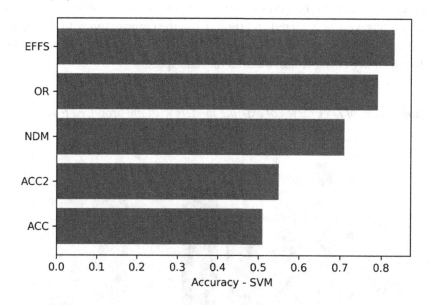

Figure 8. The accuracy of NB

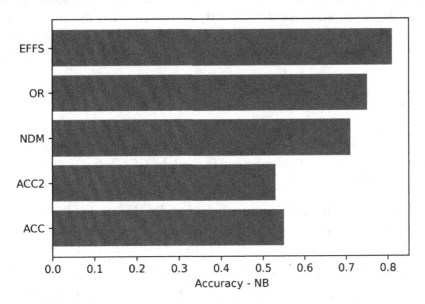

Figure 9. The accuracy of RF

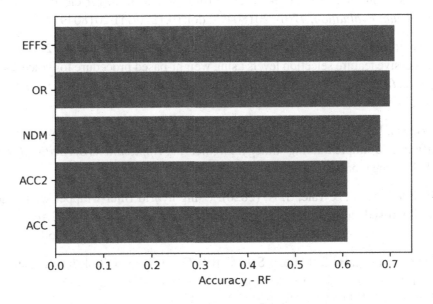

CONCLUSION

The number of diabetes cases is increasing day by day, proper diagnosis is required to prevent diabetes at an early stage. To improve diabetes prediction, machine learning models are used to detect diabetes at an early stage very efficiently. Moreover, still, there is a lot of room for improvement in the field of classification to improve performance. Feature selection is one of the methods to increase the performance of the machine learning model. In this chapter, a new filter-based feature selection method is introduced which ranks each feature based on the diversity ratio. Finally, the extracted features have been classified using five machine learning models SVM, kNN, NB, RF, and LR. Here the experimental analysis has been carried out on PIMA Indian dataset in terms of accuracy of 83%. In the future, the work will be extended by using more powerful ensemble classifiers to increase the accuracy of diabetes prediction.

REFERENCES

Abdulhadi, N., & Al-Mousa, A. (2021). Diabetes detection using machine learning classification methods. In 2021 International Conference on Information Technology (ICIT), (pp. 350–354). IEEE. 10.1109/ICIT52682.2021.9491788

Achenbach, P., Hippich, M., Zapardiel-Gonzalo, J., Karges, B., Holl, R. W., Petrera, A., Bonifacio, E., & Ziegler, A.-G. (2022). A classification and regression tree analysis identifies subgroups of childhood type 1 diabetes. *EBioMedicine*, *82*, 104118. doi:10.1016/j.ebiom.2022.104118 PMID:35803018

Ahan, S., Polat, K., Kodaz, H., & Gne, S. (2005). The medical applications of attribute weighted artificial immune system (awais): Diagnosis of heart and diabetes diseases. *Lecture Notes in Computer Science*, 456468.

Ashokkumar, P., & Don, S. (2019). Link-based clustering algorithm for clustering web documents. *Journal of Testing and Evaluation*, *47*(6), 20180497. doi:10.1520/JTE20180497

Ashour, A. S., Nour, M. K. A., Polat, K., Guo, Y., Alsaggaf, W., & El-Attar, A. (2020). A novel framework of two successive feature selection levels using weight-based procedure for voice-loss detection in parkinsons disease. *IEEE Access : Practical Innovations, Open Solutions*, *8*, 76193–76203. doi:10.1109/ACCESS.2020.2989032

Caliskan, A., Yuksel, M., Badem, H., & Basturk, A. (2018). Performance improvement of deep neural network classifiers by a simple training strategy. *Engineering Applications of Artificial Intelligence*, *67*, 1423. doi:10.1016/j.engappai.2017.09.002

Elhariri, E., El-Bendary, N., & Taie, S. A. (2020). Using hybrid filter-wrapper feature selection with multi-objective improved-salp optimization for crack severity recognition. *IEEE Access : Practical Innovations, Open Solutions*, *8*, 84290–84315. doi:10.1109/ACCESS.2020.2991968

Haq, A. U., Zhang, D., Peng, H., & Rahman, S. U. (2019). Combining multiple feature-ranking techniques and clustering of variables for feature selection. *IEEE Access : Practical Innovations, Open Solutions*, *7*, 151482–151492. doi:10.1109/ACCESS.2019.2947701

Joe Abinas, J., Chandolu, H. V. K., Nagabushanam, P., Radha, S., & Krishna, V. M. (2021), Analysis of diabetes patients using classification algorithms. In 2021 10th IEEE International Conference on Communication Systems and Network Technologies (CSNT), (pp. 810–814). IEEE. 10.1109/CSNT51715.2021.9509642

Kannadasan, K., Edla, D. R., & Kuppili, V. (2019). Type 2 diabetes data classification using stacked autoencoders in deep neural networks. *Clinical Epidemiology and Global Health*, *7*(4), 530–535. doi:10.1016/j.cegh.2018.12.004

Kayaer, K. & Yldrm, T. (2003). *Medical diagnosis on pima indian diabetes using general regression neural networks*.

Meng, X.-H., Huang, Y.-X., Rao, D.-P., Zhang, Q., & Liu, Q. (2013). Comparison of three data mining models for predicting diabetes or prediabetes by risk factors. *The Kaohsiung Journal of Medical Sciences*, *29*(2), 9399. doi:10.1016/j.kjms.2012.08.016 PMID:23347811

Palanivinayagam, A., & Nagarajan, S. (2020). An optimized iterative clustering framework for recognizing speech. *International Journal of Speech Technology*, *23*(4), 767–777. doi:10.100710772-020-09728-5

Polat, K., & Gne, S. (2007). An expert system approach based on principal component analysis and adaptive neuro-fuzzy inference system to diagnosis of diabetes disease. *Digital Signal Processing*, *17*(4), 702710. doi:10.1016/j.dsp.2006.09.005

Rawat, V., Joshi, S., Gupta, S., Singh, D. P., & Singh, N. (2022). Machine learning algorithms for early diagnosis of diabetes mellitus: A comparative study. *Materials Today: Proceedings*, *56*, 502–506. doi:10.1016/j.matpr.2022.02.172

Rozi, M. F., Novitasari, D. C., & Intan, P. K. (2018). Brain disease classification using different wavelet analysis for support vector machine (svm). *Proceedings of the International Conference on Mathematics and Islam*. Scite Press. 10.5220/0008523704600465

Tanabe, H., Masuzaki, H., & Shimabukuro, M. (2021). Novel strategies for glycaemic control and preventing diabetic complications applying the clustering-based classification of adult-onset diabetes mellitus: A perspective. *Diabetes Research and Clinical Practice*, *180*, 109067. doi:10.1016/j.diabres.2021.109067 PMID:34563587

Thejas, G. S., Garg, R., Iyengar, S. S., Sunitha, N. R., Badrinath, P., & Chennupati, S. (2021). Metric and accuracy ranked feature inclusion: Hybrids of filter and wrapper feature selection approaches. *IEEE Access: Practical Innovations, Open Solutions*, *9*, 128687–128701. doi:10.1109/ACCESS.2021.3112169

Tigga, N. P., & Garg, S. (2020). Prediction of type 2 diabetes using machine learning classification methods [International Conference on Computational Intelligence and Data Science.]. *Procedia Computer Science*, *167*, 706–716. doi:10.1016/j.procs.2020.03.336

Zhou, P., Li, P., Zhao, S., & Wu, X. (2021). Feature interaction for streaming feature selection. *IEEE Transactions on Neural Networks and Learning Systems*, *32*(10), 4691–4702. doi:10.1109/TNNLS.2020.3025922 PMID:33021946

Chapter 4
Information Security and Privacy in IoT

Reepu
Chandigarh University, India

Sushil Kumar
Dhanauri PG College, India

Megha Gupta Chaudhary
https://orcid.org/0000-0002-5950-361X
SRM Institute of Science and Technology, India

K. Gurnadha Gupta
https://orcid.org/0000-0003-0037-7572
KL University (Deemed), India

Sabyasachi Pramanik
https://orcid.org/0000-0002-9431-8751
Haldia Institute of Technology, India

Ankur Gupta
https://orcid.org/0000-0002-4651-5830
Vaish College of Engineering, India

ABSTRACT

Internet of Things (IoT) is a fast-growing idea that aims to connect billions of objects (such as smart-phones, sensors, and potential networking equipment) and allow them to communicate with one another. The IoT is a network of interconnected devices which utilises sensor to use technology communicate relating to one another across without the necessity for human contact, a wireless communication medium is used to exchange, alter, and move data. This interconnectedness is important in a variety of ways, including well-timed coordination with a variety of simple devices such as sensors, thermostats, fitbits, routers, and so on. These networks may be particularly vulnerable to prone assaults due to their open and heterogeneous nature. Aside from the advantages of IoT development, there may be significant concerns regarding security and privacy, which is likely to be one of the most frustrating aspects of IoT design adaptation and development.

DOI: 10.4018/978-1-6684-6971-2.ch004

Copyright © 2023, IGI Global. Copying or distributing in print or electronic forms without written permission of IGI Global is prohibited.

INTRODUCTION

IoT has undeniably changed how we think about connectivity. We have seen devices aside from private pc structures connect to the internet through IoT (Rahman, A., et al., 2021). IoT has made it viable to embed internet connectivity and relevant capabilities in masses of devices. Televisions, vehicles, refrigerators, air conditioners, hairbrushes, and a wide range of other devices now have internet access. At the equal time, as the arena recognizes the genuine capability of IoT, worries approximately safety and privateness in IoT have won prominence. Before delving into the troubles of privatized and safety in IoT, its miles crucial to first recognize IoT. In the broadest sense, IoT refers to a worldwide community of interconnected gadgets that trade statistics thru the internet. The gadgets talk with each other whilst additionally producing and gathering statistics to make sure most useful functionality. Indeed, IoT gadgets accumulate statistics approximately man or woman customer sand can comprise extraordinarily personal and touchy information. IoT is a network of physical elements or people that are categorised as "things" and are furnished with software, electronics, a network, and sensors for collecting and sharing data. IoT aims to extend internet connectivity (Dalsania, A.K., et al., 2022) from large equipment like computers, mobile phones, and medications to smaller devices like toasters. IoT makes nearly everything "smart" via way of means of improving components of our lives thru using records collection, AI algorithms (Tsamados, A., et al., 2022), and networks. In IoT, Someone with a diabetic display implant, an animal with monitoring devices, and so on are examples of elements.

Figure 1. IoT Works In Smart Devices

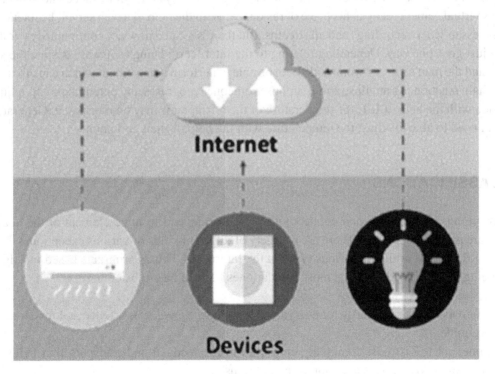

The IoT journey begins with the devices themselves, such as smartphones (Pronk, T., et al., 2022), smart watches, and virtual domestic equipment such as TVs and washing machines, which allow you to communicate with the IoT platform. There are four essential components of an IoT system.

Wearable sensor: Sensors or gadgets are an important detail that allows us to purchase real-time information from the environment. All of this information could also be complicated in a variety of ways. It's most likely a clean temperature monitoring sensor, or it could be hidden within the video feed's structure. A gadget may also contain a variety of sensors that perform many functions in addition to sensing. A smartphone, for example, is a gadget with various sensors such as GPS and a virtual camera, but your smartphone is unable to use these features.

Interconnection: All the accumulated statistics is transferred to a cloud-based infrastructure. The sensors should be cloud-connected using various Communications media. Mobile or satellite communications are represented by these communication mediums TV for pc television for laptop Bluetooth (Bansal, R. et al., 2021), Wi-Fi (Pramanik, S. 2022), WAN (Pradhan, D. et al., 2022), and other networks.

Data manipulation: After that, information amassed, and the software reaches the cloud program application performs during the processing the amassed information. Checking the temperature and analysing devices such as air conditioners and heaters are two examples of this method. But can on occasion more over identifying objects; for instance, can be quite difficult the usage of computer vision (Jayasingh, R. et al., 2022) filmed.

UI (user interface): Records desire to be accessible to the end user or woman someway as well as be carried out with the useful resource of the usage of sending them notifications or setting up alarms on their phones through electronic mailer send an SMS. Man or woman now and again might in all likelihood need a user interface that is active exams their Internet of Things system For instance, the man or woman possesses virtual camera set up at his place of residence. With the help of a web server, he intends to gain proper access to video recordings and all streams. But there's a catch now not continuously communication that just goes one way. Depending relating to the Internet of Things software despite the system's intricacy and the man's role, or woman also can be able to perform a movement which can also moreover create a chain reaction. As an illustration, suppose someone recognises any potential threats adjustments with inside with the help of IoT, the temperature of the refrigerator may be monitored. Generation man or woman need to able to adjust the temperature with the help of their cell phone.

IoT CLASSIFICATIONS

The networking, conversation and connectivity protocols depend in huge element at the appropriate IoT software program deployed. There are a variety of different kinds of various exceptional there are a variety of IoT devices available various types in the Internet of Things programs based mostly on how they're being used. A handful of the most popular ones in the area are listed here.

- IoT for consumers - primarily for everyday use appliances, voice assistance and moderate fixtures for example.
- Commercial IoT is most commonly employed in the medical and transportation fields. For instance, smart pacemakers and monitoring systems.
- Military Things (IoMT) - Mostly used within the navy for IoT creation software. For example, in combating, surveillance robots and biometrics those humans can wear it.

- IoT refers to the network of devices which are connected to industry is primarily utilised in manufacturing enterprise programs, together with inside the industries of manufacturing and energy. For example, enterprise big data (Pramanik, S. et al., 2022), smart agriculture, and digital control (Bansal, R. et al., 2022) systems.
- Infrastructure IoT is largely utilized for connecting smart cities. For instance, infrastructure sensors (Anand, R. et al., 2022) and manipulation systems.

ARCHITECTURE OF THE IoT

An IoT networking machine is made up of sensors (Choudhary, S. et al., 2022) actuators, protocols, cloud services, and layers, which when combined form an IoT architecture. It usually has distinct layers that allow directors to assess, monitor, and maintain the machine's consistency. As in any other situation, machine layout it is a strategy additionally calls for a approach for integration together along match the objectives of your company present Infrastructure and systems are important. IoT-enabled businesses structure appreciably extra a hit the ones without a few According to projections, it has a 34 percent chance of succeeding more danger For businesses with an architectural plan, IoT can be used to drive new sales or improve business procedures.

Figure 2. Architecture of the internet of things

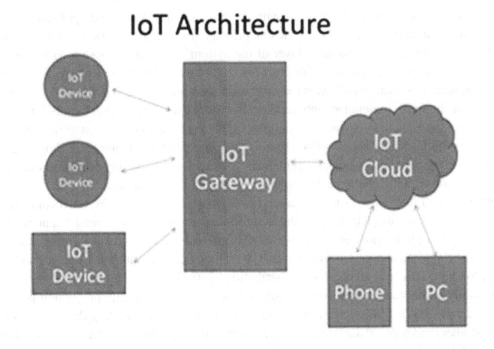

IoT Architecture Components

Basically, an IoT structure includes 4 additives: packages and infrastructure, as well as analytics (Bhattacharya, A. et al., 2021), integration, security, and protection. Packages and data analytics element techniques as well as displays facts accumulated through IoT consists of facts Tools for data analysis, artificial intelligence (AI), ML stands for machine learning, and visualisation. The integration component guarantees that all IoT venture packages, tools, security, and infrastructure work in tandem with the company's current ERP (Enterprise Resource Planning) and other control systems. Through firmware and inbuilt protection providers, the protection element manages bodily and cybersecurity for all device additives. Infrastructure is crucial element consists of the bodily gadgets which seize facts (Internet of Things sensors) and (Internet of Things actuators), which has the ability to control the surroundings. Is made up of a corporeal network where the sensors or actuators are genuinely placed (together with Wi-Fi, 4G, or 5G).Infrastructure is important additionally contains a mode of transport detail answerable for delivering information every IoT device zone to the platform where it'll be analysed and processed Because actuator and sensor infrastructure are often separate, the IoT infrastructure component also needs a control layer, complete with unique suppliers and packages.

Architecture Layers in IoT

There isn't a single IoT architecture that everyone agrees on, and one of a kind architectures having been proposed with the aid of using one of a kind researchers. The most common architectures are three, four, and five layers.

IoT Architecture on Three Layers: Along with the notion, community, and application layers, the most common configuration is a three-layer design primary structure for Internet of Things implementation. The perception layer is a physical layer of the system which includes sensors for sensing and collecting data about the surroundings. This layer has the ability to detect a few physical characteristics of the environment or determines different clever items within side the surroundings. The network layer is comprised of the following components accountable for IoT interconnection factors different clever Servers, network devices, and items are all examples of this Sensor data transmission and processing are also handled by this layer. The user interface layer is comprised with accountable for fortuning inutility-precise offerings user-friendly. Its design guidelines govern how the Internet of Things can be used in various applications (intelligent home, fitness care, business IoT, and so on).

Architecture with four layers: An application layer, a data processing layer, a network layer, and a perception or sensor layer are all included in the architecture this variant gives three-layer notion a slightly unique ordering. The application layer defines everything in four-layer IoT architecture. Packages in what type of IoT is being used and presents the method of communication among IoT devices and networks must come to a halt. This layer authorises the distribution of offerings to the recipients' diverse packages, primarily totally at the statistics amassed through sensors. The layer for data processing gets information acquired and is derived from a perceptual layer accountable to ensure that data is delivered from genuine customers and guarded dangers. Also referred to as transmission layer the network layer consists of made up of several layers. It serves as a link between two locations wearing as well as transmission records collected physical items through sensors, as well as connecting them to the rest of the system community gadgets and connects them to one another. The sensor layer, often known as the perception layer, accountable for spotting Gadgets for the Internet of Things and collecting statistics they're coming from. On a sensor community can have a variety of sorts, and the perception layer must have the ability to distinguish among them and accommodate their one-of-a-kindways for running.

IoT Architecture with Five Layers: The perceptual, network, and application levels of the three-layer model are not the only layers to consider structure, IoT with five layers structure consists of the treatment and commercial layers of a company. Perception and layers' of application function on this version is similar to the structure Three layers are present. The transport layer sends and receives data from IoT sensors between the perception layer and the processing layer are the two layers that make up the perception system. For this goals Wi-Fi, 3G, LAN (Local Area Network), Bluetooth, RFID (Radio Frequency ID) (Pramanik, S. et al., 2022), and NFC (Near-Field Communications) are some of the networks that are used. The layer of processing likewise referred to serves as a middleware layer in charge of storing, analysing, in addition to processing data big quantities. The delivery layer provides a set of facts. Databases, cloud computing, and massive amounts of data are all used in this process. It has processing modules which may manipulate as well as providing a diverse range of services offerings decreasing the layers. Commercial enterprise layer is responsible for the organisation whole System of the Internet of Things inclusive of applications of it, commercial enterprise and compensation mechanisms, as well as individual privacy (Gupta, A. et al., 2022)

Figure 3. IoT Architecture Layers

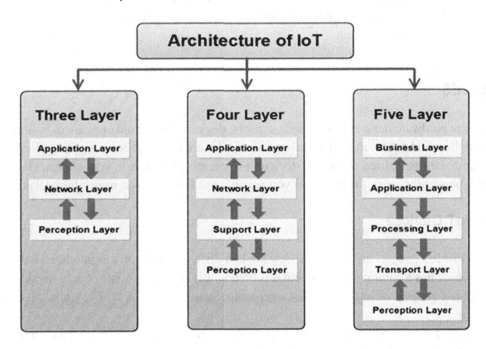

THE IoT DIFFICULTIES

Internet of Things is dealing with several issues, including:

- An insufficient amount of sorting and updating
- Concerns about privacy and the safeguarding of statistics
- The difficulty of software
- The amount of data and how it's interpreted
- AI and robotics integration
- Devices necessitate a regular power supply this a challenge
- Short-distance communication and interaction

The Consequences of IoT

The IoT does have made it feasible for physical worldwide to get to know the digital worldwide as well as working together. It offers several benefits companies thru manner of manner of letting them automate and streamline their day-to-day activities. As the IoT expands at such an increasing charge year after year agencies taking advantage of exceptional business enterprise it is highly regarded may provide. Some of the examples are as follows most crucial Internet of Things advantages:

- Develop new business concepts as well as sources of income
- Decorate business enterprise choices thru From IoT data, data-driven insights
- Boom productivity the overall performance of a company's operations
- Improve customer satisfaction

IoT DEVICES

IoT devices are hardware devices that include sensors, devices, household appliances, and special machines that collect and access this information. Those who are designed for positive applications and it can be integrated in specialised connected devices. For eg, an IoT system in your car can identify earlier visitors and robotically notify the character you are about to fulfil of your impending delay.

Types of IoT Devices

Various types of IoT gadgets are available. Few are less difficult to identify than others. But nearly any digital tool which has a community connection is both an IoT tool or consists of an embedded IoT tool. The forms of IoT gadgets variety range from easy temperature sensors to Wi-Fi (Sinha, M. et al., 2021) safety cameras.

The listing of forms of IoT gadgets is likewise always developing as greater methods to make use of the net of factors are developed. These are a number of forms of IoT gadgets:

Sensors: They are the oldest and maximum sorts of IoT gadgets. Optical sensors for computerized avenue lights, temperature sensors for clever thermostats, and the inner sensors embedded in business equipment are types of IoT sensors.

Security Devices: Smart domestic protection cameras and audio recording gadgets are already distinctly there in residential, commercial, and business locations. But IoT movement sensors also are frequently covered as a part of greater superior protection systems.

Smart Wearable Devices: Smart wearable era is one of the maximum recognized IoT gadgets. Currently, maximum wearable are watches and ear-buds. But smart glasses and different augmented fact gadgets are also being manufactured.

Intelligent Appliances: Smart thermostats, smart refrigerators, and linked TVs depend on IoT gadgets to acquire environmental facts and thus providing the proper adjustments.

Actuators: Nearly all of the IoT gadgets concentrate on collecting environmental information. Actuators concentrate on receiving commands from different IoT gadgets and are prepared with the mechanics had to make bodily adjustments primarily based totally at the information collected through different IoT gadgets.

Components of IoT Devices

The additives of IoT gadgets may be categorized into 2 types: data collection components and data transmission components. This same facts series specific is usually some kind of sensor. It could be an imaging or temp detector, Frequency identification as well as electronic sensor, and an electrical current sensor. Whatever the device detects, the sensing detail collects data and converts this into numerical measurement for processing data. An antenna is typically used for transmission of data. A data transmission sensor transmits collected data to an IoT device management framework, which handles the data gathered with the useful resource of the use of all IoT devices on the network. Few IoT gadgets can have facts garage additives. But those are normally very less. IoT gadgets simplest keep facts to manipulate network traffic, as IoT network data protocols are frequently designed simplest for lesser volumes of data.

Working Functions of IoT Devices

Various IoT gadgets have excellent features, but they all share approaches to how they work. To begin, IoT devices are physical devices that are interested in what is happening in the physical world. They typically include a Computer, network interface, and baseband and are linked to a Simple Network Management Protocol server. It also necessitates an Internet address to function on the network. The majority of Sensors are designed and managed to use a software system. For example, you could use an app on your smartphone to control the lights in your house. Some devices also include internet servers that also exclude these need external systems. For example, when you enter a room, the lights prompt you to go right away.

IoT Device Examples

Home Protection: The IoT is the main impetus beside 'intelligent as well as consistent residences. The Internet of Things attaches a set of equipment, lamps, warning lights, as well as webcams (that can all be monitored by a mobile phone) purpose of providing 24 * 7 protections.

Behaviour Monitors: Smart home control devices provide signs as well as peacefulness. Fitness trackers seem to be detector devices that can display and transmit important health symptoms in live time. Users can manage and analyze their pulse rate, desire to eat, physical activity, and respiration rate.

Figure 4. Working structure of IoT

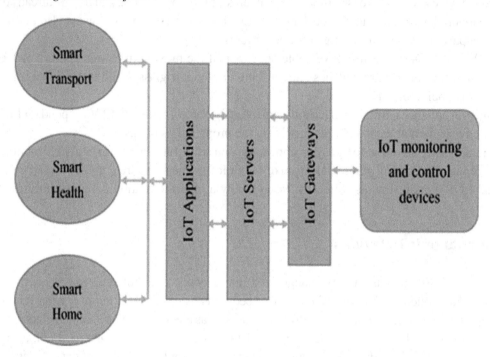

Commercial Safety and Security: To detect trespassers, IoT-enabled sensing devices, sensor systems, as well as webcams can be placed in restricted areas. They can also identify strain buildups and simple leakage of unstable industrial chemicals and join them before they become major issues.

IoT SECURITY

IoT safety refers back to the techniques of safety used to steady internet-related or network-primarily based totally gadgets. The time period IoT is notably broad, and with the generation persevering with to evolve, the time period has simplest emerge as broader. From watches to thermostats to online game consoles, almost each technological tool has the capacity to engage with the internet, or different gadgets, in a few capacities. IoT protection is the very own family of strategies, strategies and gadget used to guard the ones devices from becoming compromised. Ironically, it is the connectivity inherent to IoT that makes the ones devices more and more at risk of cyberattacks. IoT safety is the exercise that maintains your IoT structures safe. IoT safety equipment shield from threats and breaches, perceive and reveal dangers and may assist restoration vulnerabilities. IoT safety guarantees the availability, integrity, and confidentiality of your IoT solution. IoT safety is the safeguards and protections for cloud-related gadgets which include domestic automation, SCADA machines, safety cameras, and another generation that connects at once to the cloud. IoT generation is outstanding from cellular gadgets (e.g., smartphones and tablets) generation primarily based totally on its computerized cloud connectivity in gadgets. IoT safety entails securing historically poorly designed gadgets for information safety and cybersecurity. Recent information breaches have proven that IoT safety ought to be a concern for maximum producers and developers.

IIoT Privacy

The Internet of Things creates a variety of disturbing privacy conditions, many of which extend beyond the current information privacy issues. Much of this is due to the incorporation of gadgets into our surroundings that we do not consciously use which is becoming more popular through customer gadgets including such mobile and vehicle monitoring devices, and also intelligent TV screens. Speech prominence as well as perception abilities that can continuously be aware of conversations or appearances prior to hobby as well as differentially convey a certain information to the a web issuer for collection, that also occasionally contains a someone else, are included in this category. This data collection reveals crook as well as regulation troubling conditions dealing with information protection and privacy law.

Security Issues in IoT

With a smooth influence of an importance of security and safety through Connectivity, it's far critical to discover the issues. Enterprises should gain huge benefits as from IoT. Moreover, security concerns should pose significant barriers to mass acceptance of Sensor options. But at the other side, a smooth impact of the IoT security issues should aid in the development of appropriate mitigation strategies. Let us put some of the fantastic problems for IoT security to the test.

Insufficient Passcode Protection: The use of difficult as well as ingrained certifications through Internet of things allows attackers to straight negotiate with said gadgets. Access points also may make it easy for attackers to gain access to the device. One example of such an attack is the Mirai ransomware that infected IoT devices like routers, recording devices, and camcorders. Mirai ransomware could log in utilizing 61 stylish difficult login details.

IoT Manufacturers' Restricted Complies: Some other critical factor influencing this same safety element through privacy and safety in IoT is a lack of conformance from IoT manufacturers. As factories carry on with developing tools with restricted safety measures, considerations about safety in IoT may clearly rise. IoT device providers started to incorporate internet connection in their devices without taking into consideration the safety component during the product design procedure. Some of the notable IoT safety risks that can be attributed to manufacturers include,

- Hardware Requirements problems
- Insufficient data transmission and memory protection
- Usernames and passwords that is difficult, weak, or quickly cacheable

Hardware Upgrade Administration: Issues of security and privacy through IoT may also be related to security issues caused by tool replacement control. In most cases, insecure firmware or software programmes should result in IoT security threats. Even though a manufacturer produces a tool with the most current software programme update, you may face newer deficiencies.

Thus, updating is especially important for providing security on connected devices that must be updated when new fraud is detected. The utilization of IoT devices without critical updates should improve these same attacks to their own security. Furthermore, because devices will send backup systems towards the web, replace control may be unstable. Without appropriate cryptography for such relation and security for current documents, whatever suspicious entity could gain access to that information.

Inadequate Secure Interfaces: Most Devices are involved in data processing and verbal exchange. IoT devices require applications, procedures, as well as services to communicate, as well as non - secure devices seem to be responsible for many embedded device attack vectors.

Insecure interfaces can be found in internet, Web application, web, smartphone, as well as alertness connectors, only with potential to negotiate the tool and data. The most common challenge to safety in IoT connections is a lack of tool permission as well as strong authentication, as well as a vulnerable or non-existent encryption method.

IoT Privacy Concerns

Since security challenges are common in IoT, privacy concerns are also an important consideration. Let's take a look at some of the more common privacy concerns in IoT that you might come across today.

Privacy in Device: Personal information is spilled through unapproved manipulation as well as renovation of physical devices in Smart objects. For eg, by reconfiguring within a surveillance simulated webcam, this same documents recorded are not always sent out to legitimate customers, but are also sent to the intruder. As a result, here performs a critical function of maintaining the privacy of the tool for gathering sensitive data reliability and malicious attacks resistance. This will open the way for several other privacy issues, and it's far required to safeguard private information in the event of tool abuse.

Communication Privacy: The most common method for ensuring security protection at a certain moment during transmitting data is encoding. Encrypted data on elevated reflect the diversity records to packet header, which provides a way for identifying such as protection parameter measure, among many other things.

Storage Privacy: In order to maintain protective confidentiality of storing information, the following principles must be followed. It is most convenient to store as few records as possible. Only within extreme situations are first-rate personal data maintained. The information is then transmitted on the model based about whenever you want to realise it.

Handling Privacy: Even during pre-processing step this privacy of general facts is given special consideration. But first foremost, personal facts had to be handled in such a way that they could be considered in light of the ostensible motive. Following that, with no unique identification and the consent of the records owner, their personal information should no longer be revealed to the private entity. The data preparation pattern handles the privacy again for duration of the activity.

Figure 5. Conceptual model for data annotation

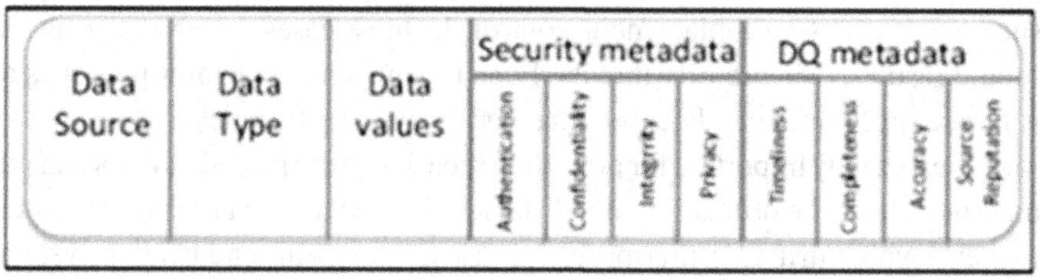

Data Source	Data Type	Data values	Security metadata				DQ metadata			
			Authentication	Confidentiality	Integrity	Privacy	Timeliness	Completeness	Accuracy	Source Reputation

Overcoming Protection Dificulties

IoT products are made strong simple stat the same time as protection is embedded within side the producing life cycle. Each building block of IoT solutions want to more over undergo a protection evaluation to stumble on vulnerabilities.

Countermeasures, which consist of the following, can be taken to cope with the protection challenges:

Analysis of the base device platform: Weak platform configuration might in all likelihood motive compromises which encompass privilege escalation. A platform for basic devices operating gadget so its safety assets, settings, as well as abilities need in being examined toward this same framework-protected information safety necessities. Proof must be completed to make sure that other test connections have been eliminated out from devices.

Congestion identification: Congestion (whether harassed as well as broadband) must be examined for interceptable, decrypted, as well as mutable information. Even though encryption is recommended, there is a trade-off between universal overall performance and safety. To meet universal overall performance requirements, portable cryptosystems can be used.

Proof of functional security requirements: Validation of high-level functional safety requirements is desired. They really want to be exposed to torturous checking (subversion or fuzzing). For authorization and authentication, IoT solutions can use Software as a Service (SaaS)-based completely identity manage solutions?

An evaluation of trust boundaries and testing: Everything receive as authentic with obstacles at some stage in the signal direction should be reviewed and problem to fault injection using horrible take a look at cases. Manual penetration techniques can be used to validate the receiver as authentic with obstacles. It is recommended to try out penetrations on a regular basis.

Validation of attack detection threat defence: Sometimes when component stream defences have been executed, whether in software systems, individuals should be tested using non-forestall absorption validation process. Constant absorption testing allows for the reduction of attacks (Apartments) for Software devices.

Audits of secure code: Initial adaptation methods are motivated by initial consistent code evaluations. Vulnerable as well as safety-impacting areas, such as the initialization phase, safety policing, as well as cryptographic components, require consistent code evaluations. While the safety vulnerability is discovered within the development cycle, this same rate of solving a safety disease has been greatly reduced.

Complete penetration testing: End-to-surrender penetration tests must be performed at some point in the signal path to identify each and every security problems within the net interaction, mobile connection, as well as web connection of Software devices. This same vulnerability assessment should provide the IoT solution's overall security for every one of the elements.

The IoT's Surface Attack Areas

As part of its Internet of Things Project, this same Open Web Application Security Project (OWASP) had also authored an extensive draught summary of Wireless sensor threat ground places, as well as areas through Wireless sensor applications and systems where threats and attacks may also exist. The list consists of Internet - of - things threat ground places:

Gadgets: Gadgets could be the primary means by which attacks are carried out. RAM, chipset, network adapter, and web applications all are susceptible elements of a gadget. Hackers can also take advantage of unsafe default options, preceding elements, and existing.

Communication channels: Threats may arise as a result of the communication channels that connect IoT elements. Procedures used throughout IoT applications may experience safety issues affecting the overall structure. IoT applications are indeed vulnerable to well-known cyberattacks including such provider inaction (Distributed denial of service) and intercepting.

Software or applications: Security problems through internet applications or related software for connected systems can find common ground systems. Application programs, for eg, could be used to steal user credentials or to distribute malware software updates.

Attacks Against IoT Devices

IoT gadgets are a giant chance to organization cybersecurity because of the recognition of those gadgets being deployed on enterprise networks. Unfortunately, those gadgets frequently comprise vulnerabilities that reveal them to exploitation. Cybercriminals have taken benefit of those vulnerabilities, and perform not unusual place assaults on those IoT gadgets which include:

Direct Exploitation: Printers (and different IoT gadgets) are a not unusual place get entry to factor to an organization's community. Attackers take benefit of this via way of means of gaining preliminary get entry to a community through the printer, then increasing their get entry to via the corporation community.

IoT Botnets: IoT devices are Internet-connected computers, making them ideal for carrying out automated attacks. When infected with botnet malware, an IoT device could be used to release Distributed Denial of Service (DDoS) (Pandey, B. K. et al., 2022) attack vectors, attempt to gain unauthorised access to person payments via compromised credentials, spaced malware or even other ransomware (Gupta, A. et al., 2022), as well as start taking other malicious actions against an organization's systems.

IoT-Based Data Breaches: IoT gadgets are generally designed to procedure touchy information, carry out vital actions, or are linked to cloud subscription services, making them a high goal for cybercriminals. For example, exploitation of Internet-linked cameras and/or the customers cloud provider may want to permit an attacker get admission to doubtlessly touchy information or different treasured information.

Functional Blocks of IoT Security

To meet the IoT scale, statistics security, device consider, and compliance requirements, IoT safety solutions must enforce the beneficial blocks listed beneath as changing systems, not in isolation.

- IoT Device Accept: Trying to establish as well as managing Gadget Integrity.
- IoT Data Trust: Strategy data protection and secrecy from formation to usage.
- Formalizing a Confidence: Automating and interconnects to requirements-based, proven technology solutions Cryptographic products, for example.

Security Requirements

Securing IoT structures and programs ought to start with know-how the maximum crucial protection necessities that emerge in such structures and programs. Hence, with inside the relaxation of this post, we enumerate the commonly taken into consideration protection necessities, and for each, we provide an explanation for how they may be relevant (or not) for the one-of-a-kind IoT utility domains. We additionally try and shed mild on how the usage of IoT makes it harder (or easier) to meet the ones protection necessities in comparison to pleasurable them in "traditional" IT structures.

Figure 6. IoT Security Factors

Confidentiality: This intrusion exposes touchy or exclusive information, such as the viewing of information with inside the real tool or the cloning of tool firmware itself.

Availability: This locations new necessities to the reliability of the products, networks, and cloud services, such that the fee created via way of means of the IoT machine is available, while the give up customers want it. Hence, availability is a key motive force for the IoT.

Authenticity: IoT (Internet of Things) Authentication refers to approaches to safely and without difficulty get right of entry to related gadgets together with clever homes, autos, transportation hubs, and workplaces.

Non-repudiation: Non-repudiation is the warranty that a person cannot deny the validity of something. Non-repudiation is a felony idea this is broadly utilized in records protection and refers to a service, which affords evidence of the beginning of records and the integrity of the records.

Access Control: Access manipulate is a fixed of permissions for a linked camera (or any IoT Device) that explain which customers are granted get admission to and the operations they're accredited to perform. Each access in an Access Control List (ACL) specifies a camera, a user, and a related get admission to level.

Authentication: Authentication is the process of which to just an authentication method individuality. Users grant privileges for using IoT Cloud Fundamental and Backend policies in Cloud Service. This topic is about Amazon Web services Major policies. For further information on Backup and recovery guidelines, view Identity management control for Amazon Web services and then how IoT Technology appears to work with Information security.

Privacy: Internet of Things privacy refers to the issues required to protect people's records from public disclosure within the IoT environment, for which nearly every software or hardware element or item could be assigned a completely identifiers and the ability to communicate autonomously over Web as well as comparable connection.

DoS protection: Denial of provider safety or DoS safety is a tactic applied via way of means of groups to defend their content material community in opposition to DoS attacks, which flood a community with server requests, slowing typical site visitor's capability and subsequently inflicting long time interruptions.

IoT SECURITY MODEL BASED ON BLOCKCHAIN

Here, the blockchain-dependent IoT security model's concepts and operations are explained. The blockchain-dependent IoT security framework is shown in Figure 7 based on the properties of the blockchain and conventional IoT architecture. 3 components—IoT devices, blockchain nodes, and service providers—are included in the paradigm.

Figure 7. Model for IoT security dependent on blockchain

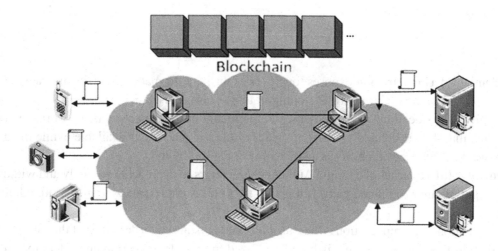

IoT gadgets, blockchain nodes, and service providers all authenticate themselves in the model using their own public keys. Figure 8 displays a blockchain-dependent IoT service flow. First, an Internet of Things device starts a transaction and signs it with a private key. The service request information, the service provider public key, the device public key, and the signature are all included in the signed transaction. The transaction is then packed and transmitted to the blockchain via the blockchain nodes. To accept service requests, the service provider first utilizes its public key for searching of relevant transaction records in the blockchain. Next, it uses the same method to generate the service answer. Four, the device utilizes its public key to get the service answer. The private key identifies who owns the data throughout the exchange, while the public key identifies the participants in the transaction.

Figure 8. IoT service flow using blockchain

For the public chain, POS, POW, PBFT, and combinations of these are the principal consensus algorithms now in use. This study unites the POS and PBFT mechanisms, supposing complete network node trust. The blockchain network receives the device-generated transactions. The public key and accompanying signature are used by the blockchain nodes to validate them. Verified transactions must either be completed or abandoned. When enough transactions have been processed, one blockchain node is chosen at random from all the others and is in charge of creating a new block. The public key, signature, and hash value of the chosen blockchain node are all included in the new block, just as when creating a transaction. The final chained block ensures that the information about the block creation technique is identifiable and that tampering is expensive since it includes both the hash values of the previous block and the new block. The IoT device delivering service requests is the basis for the mentioned case. The manner the service provider distributes service replies is consistent.

COMMON THREATS TO SECURITY AND PRIVACY OF IoT

We're going to move over the most important threats or, in different words, the reasons for records breaches and assaults on IoT devices.

Lack of Compliance from IoT Manufacturers or Developers: At this second in time, there's a loss of ordinary IoT safety requirements. As a result, a few IoT producers or builders don't prioritize tool or consumer safety. Furthermore, it leaves the door open to company spying. This will stay one in all the largest safety troubles inside the global of IoT till there are ordinary requirements and policies that producer sought to comply with. Make certain you're one of the accurate guys, and don't move down this path.

Users Lack Understanding and Knowledge of IoT Security: Over the years, the overall populace has come on top of things with threats at the internet. Whether that's studying a way to keep away from unsolicited mail or phishing emails or securing Wi-Fi connections with robust passwords (well, perhaps that might use a few practice). However, IoT remains a particularly new technology. You can infrequently accuse the common consumer of being reckless in the event that they recognise little approximately it. This places everybody at risk. IoT customers' lack of awareness and lack of understanding of IoT capability don't simply have an effect on them; it influences everybody who can also additionally have inadvertently or deliberately related to their device. This highlights the significance of IoT producers to defend customers from themselves and enforce excellent protection.

Poor Device Update Management: Insecure software program or firmware is greater safety and IoT privateness concerns. Of course, producers at the start promote gadgets with the cutting-edge software program update. That being said, with inside the fast-transferring on line world, it's inevitable that new vulnerabilities will floor over time. These may be prevented through frequently updating IoT gadgets whilst a new edition turns into available. However, that is frequently neglected. While smartphones and laptops can remind customers and perform computerized updates, a few IoT gadgets preserve jogging without the essential updates to fight new safety threats.

IoT APPLICATIONS

Internet which is a large improvement currently aided us in connecting to persons utilizing laptop and smartphones. The new generation of IoT, links gadgets with the things to recognize, manage and connect.

Residences and Office Intelligence

Smart home apps with the utilization of intelligent sensors have emerged as a well-known technology now. A smart device may be configured and linked to the internet and managed utilizing mobile application.

Figure 9. Residence as well as Office Intelligence

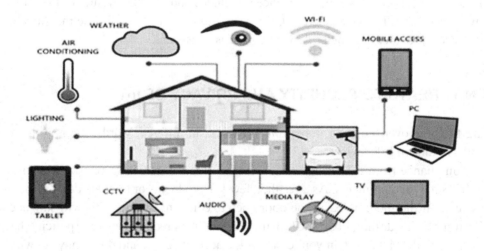

Access Control Framework for Smart Doors

Door devices as well as gate access systems were some of the most very well cost-effective Smart homes (Pramanik, S., 2022) solutions. Door devices seem to be simple to install but rather control via a web browser or mobile platform. Coordination with RDIF tags, intelligent door getting access to frameworks may be installed with security (K.aushik, D. et al., 2021). Users may offer entry to the entrances utilizing cell app and lock another time as quickly because the man or woman abandons the campus. For e.g. when a person tries to get in to your home during the time when you are not present, you can unlock the door for that man or woman utilizing a Smartphone application.

Home and Office Smart Lighting

Smart lighting fixtures are a smart domestic software program utilizing IoT. It saves electricity and moreover it lets in us to govern fruitfully. Light ecosystem may be altered utilizing smart hub devices or smart phone applications. Smart lighting fixtures may be configured for answering voice commands and motion detectors. The sensors can activate when anyone goes into the room or leaves the room. Further, it is able to be configured to reveal on at the same time as the ambient moderate is beneath superb threshold.

Gate Automation and Garage

Utilizing smart sensor generation and IoTs, gates and garages may be managed in a better manner. When you are trying to enter the house or leave the place, you can open or close the gate utilizing a mobile device.

Smart Thermostats and Humidity Regulators

Smart thermostats are cost-efficient and accessible smart domestic answers may be operated online and by using smart hub device (or utilizing a smartphone app).
Common sensors for domestic/administrative centre used for automation:

- Motion / proximity sensors
- Voice managed sensor
- Light sensor
- Humidity and Temperature sensors
- Smoke sensor
- Precipitation sensor

Smart Lighting on Streets

Smart lighting fixtures are a powerful way for shopping inside the cities. Smart sensors can discover affords of human beings or cars with inside the proximity and growth mild depth whilst a person skip by. Once the man or woman or car is far from that area, clever mild will robotically lessen mild depth to shop strength. During emergency situations, most mild depth may be activated to assist restoration activities. As the clever lighting fixtures structures are related for governing and tracking network, any defective mild gadgets may be robotically pronounced and essential preservation may be initiated.

CONCLUSION

The main reason for this paper has become to provide such a precise questionnaire among the most crucial components of Connectivity with such a special focus just on perception as well as protection traumatic accordance with common in IoT technology. The Internet of Things perspective will enable humans and topics to be associated with something and anyone at anytime, anywhere, and ideally to use any route and also any systems. Whereas Bluetooth and related technologies end up making this same theory of IoT feasible, there are numerous viable software programme areas for smart devices. Smart surroundings and identity devices, such as secure and timely, smart objects, transportation systems, smart well being, smart environments, and etc, are important IoT goals. However, innumerable troubles and distressful conditions are associated with IoT. Making sure connectivity, achieving a corporation framework during which tens of thousands of devices could be linked to something like a system, as well as privacy protection traumatic conditions are introduced as challenges, along with entity authenticated users. Attempting to address these traumatic conditions might very well continue to be the concentrate as well as fundamental endeavour of connectivity as well as verbal exchange studies in every academic and business laboratory in the coming years. Security and privacy are major factors of IoT networks.

REFERENCES

Anand, R., Singh, J., Pandey, D., Pandey, B. K., Nassa, V. K., & Pramanik, S. (2022). Modern Technique for Interactive Communication in LEACH-Based Ad Hoc Wireless Sensor Network. In M. M. Ghonge, S. Pramanik, & A. D. Potgantwar (Eds.), *Software Defined Networking for Ad Hoc Networks*. Springer. doi:10.1007/978-3-030-91149-2_3

Bansal, R., Jenipher, B., Nisha, V., Pramanik, S., Roy, S., & Gupta, A. (2022). Big Data Architecture for Network Security, in Cyber Security and Network Security. Wiley.

Bansal, R., Obaid, A. J., Gupta, A., Singh, R., & Pramanik, S. (2021). Impact of Big Data on Digital Transformation in 5G Era. *2nd International Conference on Physics and Applied Sciences (ICPAS 2021)*. IEEE. 10.1088/1742-6596/1963/1/012170

Bhattacharya, A., Ghosal, A., Obaid, A. J., Krit, S., Shukla, V. K., Mandal, K., & Pramanik, S. (2021). Unsupervised Summarization Approach with Computational Statistics of Microblog Data. In D. Samanta, R. R. Althar, S. Pramanik, & S. Dutta (Eds.), *Methodologies and Applications of Computational Statistics for Machine Learning* (pp. 23–37). IGI Global. doi:10.4018/978-1-7998-7701-1.ch002

Choudhary, S., Narayan, V., Faiz, M., & Pramanik, S. (2022). Fuzzy Approach-Based Stable Energy-Efficient AODV Routing Protocol in Mobile Ad hoc Networks. In M. M. Ghonge, S. Pramanik, & A. D. Potgantwar (Eds.), *Software Defined Networking for Ad Hoc Networks*. Springer. doi:10.1007/978-3-030-91149-2_6

Dalsania, A. K., Fastiggi, M. J., Kahlam, A., Shah, R., Patel, K., Shiau, S., Rokicki, S., & DallaPiazza, M. (2022). The Relationship Between Social Determinants of Health and Racial Disparities in COVID-19 Mortality. *Journal of Racial and Ethnic Health Disparities*, *9*(1), 288–295. doi:10.100740615-020-00952-y PMID:33403652

Gupta, A., Verma, A., & Pramanik, S. (2022). Security Aspects in Advanced Image Processing Techniques for COVID-19. In S. Pramanik, A. Sharma, S. Bhatia, & D. N. Le (Eds.), *An Interdisciplinary Approach to Modern Network Security*. CRC Press.

Gupta, A., Verma, A., & Pramanik, S. (2022). Advanced Security System in Video Surveillance for COVID-19. In *An Interdisciplinary Approach to Modern Network Security, S. Pramanik, A. Sharma, S. Bhatia and D. N. Le*. CRC Press. doi:10.1201/9781003147176-8

Jayasingh, R., Kumar, J., Telagathoti, D. B., Sagayam, K. M., & Pramanik, S. (2022). Speckle noise removal by SORAMA segmentation in Digital Image Processing to facilitate precise robotic surgery. *International Journal of Reliable and Quality E-Healthcare*, *11*(1), 1–19. Advance online publication. doi:10.4018/IJRQEH.295083

K.aushik, D., Garg, M., Annu, Gupta, A. & Pramanik, S. (2021). Application of Machine Learning and Deep Learning in Cyber security: An Innovative Approach. In M. Ghonge, S. Pramanik, R. Mangrulkar and D. N. Le (eds.) *Cybersecurity and Digital Forensics: Challenges and Future Trends*. Wiley.

Pandey, B. K., Pandey, D., Wairya, S., Agarwal, G., Dadeech, P., Dogiwal, S. R., & Pramanik, S. (2022). Application of Integrated Steganography and Image Compressing Techniques for Confidential Information Transmission. In Cyber Security and Network Security. Wiley. doi:10.1002/9781119812555.ch8

Pradhan, D., Sahu, P. K., Goje, N. S., Myo, H., Ghonge, M. M., Rajeswari, R., & Pramanik, S. (2022). Security, Privacy, Risk, and Safety Toward 5G Green Network (5G-GN). In Cyber Security and Network Security. Wiley.

Pramanik, S. (2022). An Effective Secured Privacy-Protecting Data Aggregation Method in IoT. In M. O. Odhiambo, W. Mwashita, & I. G. I. Global (Eds.), *Achieving Full Realization and Mitigating the Challenges of the Internet of Things*. doi:10.4018/978-1-7998-9312-7.ch008

Pramanik, S. (2022). Carpooling Solutions using Machine Learning Tools. In *Handbook of Research on Evolving Designs and Innovation in ICT and Intelligent Systems for Real-World Applications, K. K. Sarma, N. Saikia and M. Sharma*. IGI Global. doi:10.4018/978-1-7998-9795-8.ch002

Pramanik, S., & Bandyopadhyay, S. (2022). Analysis of Big Data. In J. Wang (Ed.), *Encyclopedia of Data Science and Machine Learning*. IGI Global. doi:10.4018/978-1-7998-9220-5.ch006

Pramanik, S., Galety, M. G., Samanta, D., & Joseph, N. P. (2022). Data Mining Approaches for Decision Support Systems. *3rd International Conference on Emerging Technologies in Data Mining and Information Security*.

Pronk, T., Hirst, R. J., & Wiers, R. W. (2022). *Can we measure individual differences in cognitive measures reliably via smartphones? A comparison of the flanker effect across device types and samples*. Behav Res. doi:10.375813428-022-01885-6

Rahman, A., Chakraborty, C., Anwar, A., Karim, M. R., Islam, M. J., Kundu, D., Rahman, Z., & Band, S. S. (2022). SDN–IoT empowered intelligent framework for industry 4.0 applications during COVID-19 pandemic. *Cluster Computing*, 25(4), 2351–2368. doi:10.100710586-021-03367-4 PMID:34341656

Sinha, M., Chacko, E., Makhija, P., & Pramanik, S. (2021). Energy Efficient Smart Cities with Green IoT. In C. Chakrabarty (Ed.), *Green Technological Innovation for Sustainable Smart Societies: Post Pandemic Era*. Springer. doi:10.1007/978-3-030-73295-0_16

Tsamados, A., Aggarwal, N., Cowls, J., Morley, J., Roberts, H., Taddeo, M., & Floridi, L. (2022). The ethics of algorithms: Key problems and solutions. *AI & Society*, 37(1), 215–230. doi:10.100700146-021-01154-8

Chapter 5
A Novel Long Short–Term Memory Method for Model for Stock Price Prediction

K. S. Archana
SRM Institute of Science and Technology, India

B. Sivakumar
SRM Institute of Science and Technology, India

B. Ebenezer Abishek
VelTech Multitech Engineering College, India

Shaik Ghouhar Taj
JNTUA College of Engineering, India

V. Kavitha Reddy
JNTUA College of Engineering, India

A. Vijayalakshmi
https://orcid.org/0000-0003-3594-6691
VISTAS, India

ABSTRACT

In the current scenario, one of the recent research works is stock prediction in the future using machine learning techniques. Today, the stock market is one of the greatest investments to retail their current shares to get profit. This necessity forces everyone to turn back to predict the future stock price market using the efficient techniques in machine learning. However, the latest market analysis and prediction is one of the most complicated tasks to decide the value. This article proposed stock price prediction using an improved algorithm in machine learning. Machine learning uses different types of models to identify the prediction easier and accurately. This chapter presents the use of LSTM based machine learning to predict stocks and factors considered are date, time, closing price and opening price of the stocks. Finally, this machine learning model was trained with numerous data, and the results were compared with existing algorithms. These performance results show the maximum prediction accuracies of 92.10% and 84.10% were attained using improved LSTM model.

DOI: 10.4018/978-1-6684-6971-2.ch005

Copyright © 2023, IGI Global. Copying or distributing in print or electronic forms without written permission of IGI Global is prohibited.

INTRODUCTION

The stock market plays a vital role in Indian economy. Today, the Indian economy highly depends on Stock market and agriculture. Agriculture and stock market is one of the back bones of today's income to Indian economy (Andersen, 2018) . It is one of the most significant investment opportunities for businesses and investors. When a firm expands its business through an Initial Public Offering, it can make a lot of money. It's a good moment to start something new an investor who wants to buy fresh stocks and make a profit dividend paid out as part of the company's bonus scheme for shareholders. An investor can also trade stocks as a trader in the stock exchange. Stock traders must be able to foresee stock market movements in order to make the best decisions on whether to sell, hold, or acquire other stocks. Stock traders who want to make money should acquire equities between raise and fall of stock market. Stock traders that properly predict stock price patterns can make significant profits. As a result, stock traders need to be able to foresee future stock market movements in order to make informed decisions. Investment in the stock market is dangerous, but when done correctly, it can be one of the most cost-effective ways to earn big profits (Altay E. &., 2005). To prevent buying dangerous stocks, investors assess a company's performance before deciding to purchase its stock. This assessment includes a look at how the company performs on social media and on financial news websites. Investors, on the other hand, cannot fully examine such many social media and financial news data. As a result, investors will need an automated decision support system, as this system will evaluate stock movements automatically utilising such enormous amounts of data. Machine learning techniques can be used to create this automated system (Nigussie, 2017) (Porshnev A. R., 2013). Artificial Intelligence research have taken a particular interest in this field since precise stock prediction based on external factors will boost investors' profits (Creamer, 2007) (Jammalamadaka, 2019).

The complexities of stock market prediction are anticipated with machine learning algorithms. Machine Learning, as stated in the introduction, requires the user to give a target values and label must be anticipated, as well as independent variables can be to identify the target variable's values (Xiao, 2014) (Obthong, 2020) . Machine learning is distinct from conventional predictive models. It employs optimization algorithms, cross-validation procedures, complex mathematical algorithms, and other advanced computing techniques to arrive at the result, which is highly accurate (but low in interpretability). Stock declaration made in advance that happen correct might influence meaningful rewards for traders. Prediction exists commonly recognised to be troublesome alternatively random, that mean possibly predicted by painstakingly examine the history of the appropriate stock exchange (Marcek, 2014). Machine learning is a good method to express these types of movement. It forecasts a package and sell goods value namely about the tangible value, reconstructing accuracy. Many human beings bear benefited from the request of image processing, machine intelligence to the field of stock declaration made in advance because of allure adept and accurate measures (Fischer, 2018).

By automatically pulling data from the higher dimension, a Deep Neural Network (DNN) can represent the lower dimension. Hierarchical neural networks are designed for integrating the bias of the respondent. Reinforcement learning does not express perception fully despite its use in decision-making processes (H. Srivastava, 2017).In order to achieve this, we have integrated Deep Learning with Reinforcement Learning because each of these methods complements the other (Selvin, 2017) (Mehtab, December 2019). A cognitive decision-making system of the sophisticated system can be created using an integrated approach. As a result, Deep Learning has excellent perception and feature extraction abilities (Murkute, 2015). The proposed work has three stages: Initial, Internal and Final Stage.

1. The initial stage has Data Collection, Data Preparation and Transformation

Data Preparation: Identify the incomplete, incorrect, inaccurate, or irrelevant parts of a record set, table, or database, and remove, modify, or replace the dirty or coarse data. This is called Data Cleaning.

Transformation: Transforming data from one format to another, usually from the format of a source system to the format of a destination system, involves converting the data before it can be read.

2. The Internal stage has data modelling

Data Modelling: The process of data modelling involves creating a diagram illustrating the relationships between types of information to be stored in a database. Creating a method of storing information that's efficient while still offering complete access and reporting is one of the objectives of data modelling (Masoud, 2017)

3. The Final stage has prediction using various modelling with comparisons of various existing algorithms

Prediction: Based on data from the train dataset, these are the results of the tests generated by the models. When the dataset has been processed, we'll be able to predict stock prices using the dataset

This work is notable for three main contributions:

1. a new dataset extracted and cleaned using data pre-processing method
2. a comprehensive feature analysis, and
3. a long short-term memory (LSTM) based deep learning model used.

RELATED WORK

On historical stock price data, researchers employed several machine learning approaches, such as deep learning and regression analysis, but it's also important to include in external elements, such as unexpected events communicated on social media and financial news (Sharma, 2019). Technical analysis, in which mathematics is used to examine data in order to predict future stock market trends, has used historical data. Individuals interested in investing in stock markets are frequently unfamiliar of market behaviour (Mnih V, 2015). As a result, they have no idea which stocks to buy and which to sell in order to maximise their earnings. These investors are aware that the stock market's growth is influenced by connected news. As a result, they require precise and timely information regarding stock exchange listings in order to make timely and correct trading decisions. Because financial news websites can provide this information, most of these websites have matured into valuable sources of information for traders (Mabu S, 2015).

The researchers improve on previously existing trading rules and delivers better results than previous studies. Multiple established market tactics are used in this study to motivate a real-time autonomous trader. This study concentrates on short-term gains, making it ideal for hands-off trading (M. Usmani, 2016) Trading in small time frames generates a lot of cash for their model (minutes). More features can be added, and the system can be made more adaptable. Another researcher published a study gives significant insight into how to properly conduct sentiment analysis. With each test, they recommend expanding the size of the corpus (training data). This is accomplished by including non-polarizing terms from the test data that aren't contained in the corpus. During each testing phase, the training data is adjusted using K-cross fold validation (Kolanovic, 2017).

The author used device learning to create an expectation based on social feelings in this paper. The assessment of the company conducted with the aid of humans. They are forecasting the economic exchange based on the positive and pessimistic observations of the public about the firm. We attempt to put together a framework that gauges the stock price improvement of distinct firms using presumption investigation at tweets obtained using the Twitter API and the give up estimations of various stocks (Patzelt, 2017).

(Kara Y, 2018) developed an algorithm to predict stock movement of stock price using ANN and SVM algorithm. Among this work's strongest points are the detailed records of the parameter adjustment procedures. This work has several weaknesses, including that neither the technical indicator nor the model structure is novel, and the authors fail to explain why their model performed better than other models. Additional validation across different datasets would be useful. As well as explaining how they work with stock market features, they documented the adjustments made to the parameters. This project will help for future research very well.

(Fischer T., 2018) proposed a method for financial market prediction using long short-term memory networks. The goal of this research work is the author applied new LSTM method for analyse the stock prediction. Because the LSTM technique did not have any background in finance, they had to rely on the LSTM technique. Even though the LSTM did better than DNNs and logistic regressions, the author neglected to mention how much effort was required to train an LSTM with long-term effects.

(Sirignano J, 2018) developed a method to predict the financial market using universal feature dataset. Generalizing beyond the data set that they used for training, the universal model was able to cover other stocks as well. Despite mentioning the advantages of implementing a universal model, their training was still quite expensive. Moreover, because there is no explicit programming behind the deep learning algorithm, it is unclear whether data is contaminated with useless features before the model is fed. According to the previous authors, it would have been more effective for them to perform the feature selection step before training the model, and they found it to be an effective way to reduce computational

MATERIALS AND METHODS

Stock market prediction appears to be a difficult problem to solve since there are so many variables involved, and it does not appear to be very productive at first. However, with the right use of machine learning techniques, one may link historical data to current data and train the system to learn from the present data and predict the future using that data as shown in Figure 1. Machine learning includes many models, but this paper focused on the two most significant ones and used them to make predictions.

Dataset

The input dataset is taken from Kaggle. The dataset represents data of National Stock Exchange of India for the years 2018 and 2019. There are certain differences in the size of individual data because of the large quantity of data contained in the dataset. Several stocks have been in existence for decades, whereas others have been listed for only a few months (W. Bao, Jul. 2017).Even though in the entire experiments

Figure 1. Architecture of stock market prediction

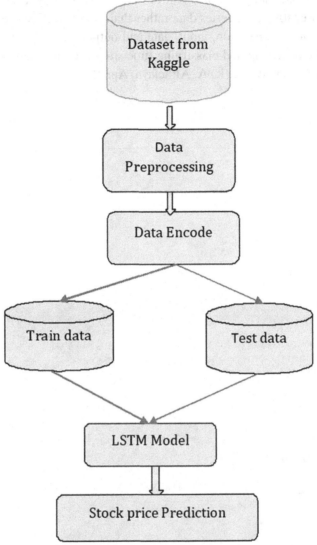

process, time is not taken into account as an input parameter that influences the experiment results, there will still be external influences in the actual market. After import dataset the data were in uncleaned such as missing valued. So that should be clean up with some advanced method (P. Liang, Apr. 2018). After the pre-processed, the data were analysed to ready format. As a result, various procedures must be followed prior to the construction of the model: 1. Dealing with missing data 2. One Quick Encode: It transforms categorical data into a quantitative variable because data in the form of a string or an object is useless for data analysis, as shown in Figure 2.

The first step is to change the data type of the columns to 'category.' The second stage is to use label encoding to turn the data into numerical values that may be used for analysis. The column is then converted to a binary value in the third phase (either 0 or 1with the agreed training data, the classifiers build a model. Similarly, the testing dataset also provided, and finally the model's accuracy is calculated.

This classifier employed in this study are as follows: Long Short-Term Memory (LSTM) is an artificial neural network with a feedback loop that allows it to function efficiently. LSTM has the advantage of being able to handle consecutive time series data rather than just a small value data point. It has three cells that control the network's operation, input, gate and output, as shown in Figure 3. This form of network is well suited for analysing and classifying time stamps issues, and we can use it to improve things that aren't testable by a network (K. A. Althelaya, Apr. 2018).

Figure 2. Close price history

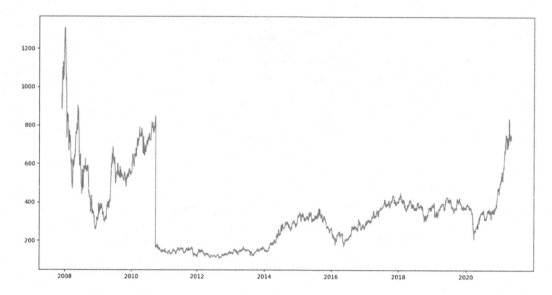

Figure 3. Open vs. close history

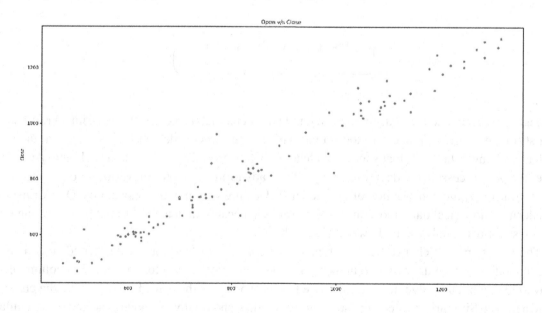

There are numerous LSTM topologies, but the most prevalent are three-cell architectures, which allow the network to work effectively and reliably anticipate values. There are three gates: an input, forget and output gate.

Data Pre-Processing

A data pre-processing step is necessary because good data is undoubtedly more important than good models, and a good data set is of utmost importance. The model uses the following features: Date, Open, High, Low, Close, adjclose, and Volume. Some attributes may not be relevant, and some may even contain incorrect or false values. As a result, companies and individuals spend significant amounts of time cleaning and preparing their data for modelling. Real-life data suffers from many quality issues, noises, and inaccuracies. The quality of the data pre-processing must be improved (W. Bao J. Y., Jul. 2017,) .During pre-processing, duplicates and irregularities in the data are eliminated, data is normalized for comparison, and results are more accurate.

Training and Testing Dataset

Step 1: Split the whole dataset into two different categories: Train data and Test data
   The size of the Spitted dataset is 70% and 30%.

Step 2: Build Model

   In Long Short-Term Memory (LSTM) tuned parameter is identified through the following scenario.

1.   Create a stationary time series by transforming the data. A lag=1 difference should be used to remove the increasing trend in the data.
2.   Create a supervised learning problem by transforming the time series. The main focus is on the organization of data into inputs and outputs. Observations from the previous step are used to predict observations in the current step using the observation from the previous step
3.   Based on certain assumptions. The LSTM activation function is defined as the hyperbolic tangent active function between -1 and 1.

   The final output is the last gate in the circuit, and it provides the value from output. It also has a critical role in determining which data should be hidden for the next time (Khalfay, 2017). First, the concealed data and input are transferred to the sigmoid function, which then multiplies the input value and sigmoid output to determine what should be stored for the next phase. The Forget Gate is the main gate that keeps track of past information for future use. The past and current data are fed into the sigmoid function, which returns a value of 0 or 1. These shows saving of data and zero shows else not saving, as shown in this Algorithm 1.

Algorithm 1. Stock prediction from LSTM method
Input: Dataset from Historic stock market
Output: An improved LSTM method is used to predict price
STEP 1: The first step is to import the historical stock market data and analyze it

STEP 2: The second step is to remove the missing values from the dataSTEP 3: Scaling the data with
  encoder
STEP 4: Encoding data for scaling
STEP 5: Creating the structure with a limit on timestamps
STEP 6: Separate data from the test and the train
STEP 7: Adding more input and output layers to the LSTM
STEP 8: Plot the values based on the prediction

COMPARISION

An evaluation of the models is conducted through a comparison of the two methods. The Proposed Model
is finally compared with Artificial neural network, Logistic regression and improved long short-term
memory (LSTM). The purpose of this work is built automatic financial modelling and completed with
better performance accuracy rate. A detailed comparisons data shown in Table 1. Here, in comparison
with previous works, our proposed solution has a different structure, and it would be difficult to compare
it naively. Since most of the studies related to price trend forecasting show the return on simulated investment rather than accuracy, it is hard to determine the exact accuracy of the prediction. It can sometimes
happen that a single accurate price trend prediction followed by a large trading volume will result in a
high gain rate due to mathematical processing based on simulated investment tests. Moreover, in our
proposed solution, we propose a heuristic method to extend the problem of predicting an exact price
straightforward to two sequential problems, namely, they are predicting the price trend first, building
an accurate binary classification model, then constructing a solid foundation for predicting the exact
price change in future works.In addition to the different result structures, previous research has also used
datasets that are different from ours.

Figure 4. Comparison of model evaluation

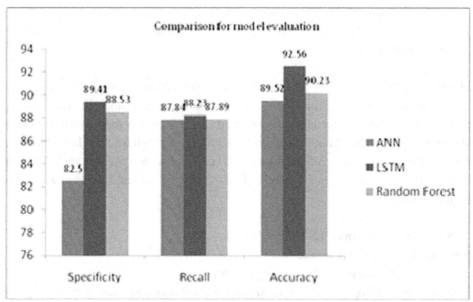

4.1 Artificial Neural Network

The artificial neural network is used for complex and challenging tasks. Artificial neural networks are used in data mining as a classification and clustering tool (Patel J, 2015). Typically, neural networks are made up of neuron-like processing units connected by weighted connections. There are two models. Two methods of activation transfer exist (Schulman J, 2015). In the activation transfer mode, the activation is transmitted throughout the whole network, and in the learning transfer mode, the network decides how to organize itself based on the most recent activation transfer. Learning Techniques are i) Supervised values and another one is ii) unsupervised values (Erhan D, 2010). Finally, the three layers of ANN are

1. Input Layer: In the input layer, bias values are received and passed to the hidden layer, where they are multiplied by a weight and added to the sum going into the neuron (shibata K, 1997).
2. Hidden Layer: A weight (wji) is added to each neuron's value in the hidden layer.The weighted values of each hidden layer neuron are then combined to find a combined value, uj.In turn, a transfer function * takes the weighted sum (uj) and produces the value hj from which hidden layer neurons receive outputs from the output layer neurons (Tsai C F, 2009)
3. Output Layer: Each hidden layer neuron's value (wkj) is multiplied with the resulting weighted value wkj, which is then added to generate vj (Yang., July 2009.).

Data is inputted, processed, and outputted from all layers to deeper layers. This neural network understands and learns complex things thanks to its layered interconnections (Porshnev, 2013).

4.2 Random Forest

Random Forest means data estimator. Based on the decision process it fits the number from the given data (Kunhuang, 2006). As a result, it controls the data of over fitting and improve the accuracy performance.

Algorithm:
STEP 1: N random records picked from the whole dataset.
STEP 2: Build random tree based on picked records.
STEP 3: the number trees are chooser and finally repeat step 2 and 3.
STEP 4: Finally for the regression problem, from the new record the decision analysed a values of Y.

Unlike decision trees or bagging classifiers, random forests have nearly the same hyper parameters. The best part is that you can easily use the classifier-class of random forests instead of combining a decision tree and a bagging classifier. In addition to handling regression tasks with random forest, the algorithm's regressed can be used (Che, 2009). Reliability is ensured with the random state hyper parameter. A model will always produce the same results if random state has a definite value, if its hyperparameters are the same and if it is trained with the same data.

4.3 Long Short-Term Memory (LSTM)

(Che, 2009) originally proposed long short-term memory (LSTM) in 1997. LSTM is generally used to problem extremely effective. Since LSTM can store important past information into the cell state and forgetting unimportant information, it is particularly suitable and successful in the time-series domain (Anandhavalli M, 2009). LSTMs have three gates that process input and store stored information in the state of the cell in order to accomplish these complex tasks (D. Rao, 2015) Finally, the parts of LSTM called gates. i) Input gate ii) Forget gate iii) Output gate.

1.   Input gate: it add information to the cell
2.   Forget gate: The model gets rid of information that it no longer requires
3.   Output gate: The selected important information shown in output.

LSTMs, just like RNNs, also have a hidden state, where H(t-1) represents the previous timestamp's hidden state, while Ht represents current timestamp's hidden state.

$$f_t = \sigma(x_t * u_i + H_{t-1} * w_f$$

Here,

xt = Current Timestamp
ui = Weight matrix
Ht = Hidden state
Wi = Weight matrix with hidden state

In this function finally sigmoid is applied. As a result, the timestamp will be 0 and 1

$$N_t = tanh(x_t * u_c + H_{t-1} * w_c$$

New information that must now be passed to a cell state is dependent on the hidden state at the previous timestamp t-1 and input x at the current timestamp t. The function is tanh. According to the tanh function, new information will have a value between -1 and 1. A value between -1 and 1 is assigned to new information using the tanh function. Whenever the value of Nt is negative, the current cell state is subtracted from the information, and whenever the value is positive, the current cell state is added to the information (Pei-Chann Chang, 2011).

RESULTS AND DISCUSSION

The objective of this module is to generate Stock Prediction values. It is a measure of a difference between opening and closing prices (P. D. Yoo, 2005) (Wymann B, July 2019). The factors that determine the strength of a difference between opening and closing prices are: Opening date, Minimum and maximum prediction day, average prediction day, opening and closing date, and highest and lowest prediction day. As a final step, the classifier model of the improved LSTM method is applied over Kaggle's dataset. The following is a plot of the closing amount of the model as predicted by the metrics in Figure 2. The timestamp limit used in our input and layer of improved LSTM method are used to increase the level of precision in our model. The timestamp limit used in the input and layer of improved LSTM method used to increase the accuracy level in our predicted model. Hence this could be thoroughly analysed and checked machine learning models gives better results

LSTM Based Model Results

Figure 5. Plot of price predication

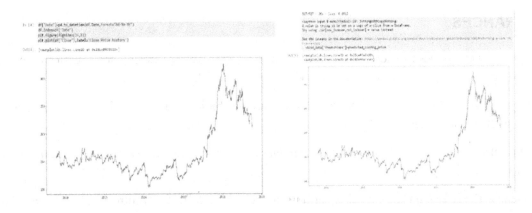

It is usually the sentiments of thousands of investors that determine the movement of the stock market. Investing in stocks requires the ability to predict the impact of recent events on investors. Investing in stocks requires the ability to predict the impact of recent events on investors. It can also be an international event, for example, a sharp movement in a currency or commodity. Corporate earnings are impacted by all of these events, which, in turn, affect the economy.

Based on these results, it appears that the deep reinforcement learning model can be applied to most stocks with sufficient information, but not all stocks. Therefore, practitioners should reduce the reliance on models when investing in order to reduce risk. Based on empirical results, deep learning is applied differently in the financial industry. The objective was to achieve accuracy and performance for computational financial modelling (Wang J, 2016). It was a subset of artificial intelligence. The algorithms can then better predict the movements once the trends are understood. The purpose of our Proposal is to facilitate stock market investments for stock brokers and investors. As a result of the dynamic nature of the stock market, prediction plays a vital role in the stock market business. The results of this work should be noted that by analysing the same data source with multiple models, it should be possible to compare the recognition accuracy to find the best predictive model based on a single data source (Choudhry R, 2008).

CONCLUSION

On the tata global dataset, two approaches were used in this paper: LSTM and Regression. Both strategies have shown an improvement in prediction accuracy, resulting in good outcomes. The use of recently announced machine learning algorithms and LSTM has resulted in better stock prediction. It has led to the conclusion that utilising machine learning techniques, it is concluded with greater accuracy and efficiency. The improve algorithm can be useful for stock price prediction in future with larger set of data. Once the trends have been identified, the algorithms can predict the movements more accurately. There are differences in the ways that each approach focuses, as well as its apparent strengths and suitability for different situations. When investors were familiar with stock, this novelty algorithm is familiar for investors. This contribution fit to interdisciplinary research direction of different deep learning applications.

REFERANCES

Altay, E. &. (2005). Stock market forecasting: Artificial neural networks and linear regression comparison in an emerging market *Journal of Financial Management and Analysis*.

Althelaya, K. A., E.-S.-M. E.-A. (Apr. 2018). Evaluation ofbidirectional LSTM for short-and longterm stock market prediction. *inProc. 9th Int. Conf. Inf. Commun. Syst. (ICICS)*. IEEE.

Anandhavalli, M. S. K. (2009). *Optimized association rule mining using genetic algorithm*. Advances in Information Mining.

Andersen, T. B. (2018). Intraday trading variance in the E-Mini S&P 500 futures market. *Social Science Research Network*.

Bao, W., Yue, J., & Rao, Y. (2017, July). A deep learning framework for financial timeseries using stacked autoencoders and long-short term memory. *PLoS One, 12*(7), e0180944. doi:10.1371/journal.pone.0180944 PMID:28708865

Bao, W., Yue, J., & Rao, Y. (2017, July). A deep learning framework for financial timeseries using stacked autoencoders and long-short term memor. *PLoS One, 12*(7), e0180944. doi:10.1371/journal.pone.0180944 PMID:28708865

Che, R. P. (2009). Textual analysis of stock market prediction using breaking financial news. *The AZF in text system" ACM Trans. Inf.*

Choudhry, R. G. K. (2008). A hybrid machine learning system for stock market forecasting. *World Academy of Science, Engineering and Technology*, 315–318.

Creamer, S. a. (2007). *Automated trading with boosting and expert weighting*. Quant.

Erhan, D. B. Y. (2010). Why does unsupervised pre-training help deep learning. *Journal of Machine Learning Research*.

Fischer, T., & Krauss, C. (2018). Deep learning with long short-term memory networks for financial market predictions. *European Journal of Operational Research, 270*(2), 654–669. doi:10.1016/j.ejor.2017.11.054

Fischer, T. e., & Krauss, C. (2018). Deep learning with long short-term memory networks for financial market predictions. *European Journal of Operational Research, 270*(2), 654–669. doi:10.1016/j.ejor.2017.11.054

Jammalamadaka, S. Q. (2019). Predicting a stock portfolio with multivariate Bayesian structural time series model: do news or emotions matter. *Int. J. Artif. Intell.*

Kara, Y. A. B. (2018). Predicting direction of stock price index movement using artificial neural networks and support vector machines: The sample of the Istanbul Stock Exchange. *Expert Systems with Applications.*

Khalfay, N. S. (2017). Stock Prediction using Machine Learning a Review Paper. *Int. J. Comput. Appl.*, 975–8887.

Kolanovic, M. a. (2017). Big data and AI strategies: Machine learning and alternative data approach to investing. *J.P. Morgan Global Quantitative & Derivatives Strategy Report.*

Kunhuang, H. &. (2006). The application of neural networks to forecast fuzzy time series. *Physical A: Statistical Mechanics and Its Applications.*

P. Liang, H.-D. Y.-S.-Y.-Z. (Apr. 2018). Transferlearning for aluminium extrusion electricity consumption anomaly detectionvia deep neural network. *Int. J. Comput. Integr. Manu.*

Mabu, S. O. M., Obayashi, M., & Kuremoto, T. (2015). Ensemble learning of rule-based evolutionary algorithm using multi-layer perceptron for supporting decisions in stock trading problem. *Applied Soft Computing*, *36*, 357–367. doi:10.1016/j.asoc.2015.07.020

Marcek, D. (2014). Forecasting high frequency data: An ARMA-soft RBF networkmodel for time series. *Applied Mechanics and Materials*, *596*, 160–163. doi:10.4028/www.scientific.net/AMM.596.160

Masoud, N. M. (2017). The impact of stock market performance upon economic growth. *International Journal of Economics and Financial Issue*, (pp. 788–798).

Mehtab, S. S. (December 2019). A robust predictive model for stock price prediction using deep learning and natural language processing. In: *Proceedings of the 7th International Conference on Business Analytics and Intelligence*, Bangalore, India. 10.2139srn.3502624

Mnih, V. K. K., Kavukcuoglu, K., Silver, D., Rusu, A. A., Veness, J., Bellemare, M. G., Graves, A., Riedmiller, M., Fidjeland, A. K., Ostrovski, G., Petersen, S., Beattie, C., Sadik, A., Antonoglou, I., King, H., Kumaran, D., Wierstra, D., Legg, S., & Hassabis, D. (2015). Human-level control through deep reinforcement learning. *Nature*, *518*(7540), 529–533. doi:10.1038/nature14236 PMID:25719670

Murkute, A., & Sarode, T. (2015). Forecasting market price of stock using artificial neural network. *International Journal of Computer Applications*, *124*(12), 11–15. doi:10.5120/ijca2015905681

Nigussie, A. a. (2017). J. Water Resour. Planning Manage. *Monthly water consumptionprediction using season algorithm and wavelet transform_based model.*

Obthong, M. T. (2020). *A survey on machine learning for stock price prediction: algorithms and techniques.* In: *Proceedings of the 2nd International Conference on Finance, Economics, Management and IT Business, FEMIB 2020*, Prague, Czech Republic. 10.5220/0009340700630071

Patel J, S. S. (2015). Predicting stock market index using fusion of machine learning techniques. *Expert Systems with Applications: An International Journal*, 2162--2172.

Patzelt, F. a. (2017). Universal scaling and nonlinearity of aggregate price impact in financial markets. *Physical Review*, 97(1), 012304. PMID:29448465

Pei-Chann Chang, C.-Y. F.-L. (2011). *Trend discovery in financial time series data using a case based fuzzy decision tree.* Elsevier Science Direct.

Porshnev, A. R. (2013). *Machine learning in prediction of stock market indicators based on historical data and data from Twitter sentiment analysis.* In *Proceedings of the IEEE International Conference on Data Mining Workshops*, Dallas, TX, USA. 10.1109/ICDMW.2013.111

Porshnev, I. R. (2013). Machine Learning in Prediction of Stock Market Indicators Based on Historical Data and Data from Twitter Sentiment Analysis. *IEEE 13th International Conference on Data Mining Workshops*. IEEE.

Rao, D., F. D. (2015). Qualitative Stock Market Predicting with Common Knowledge Based Nature Language Processing: A Unified View and Procedure. *7th International Conference on Intelligent Human-Machine Systems and Cybernetics*. IEEE. 10.1109/IHMSC.2015.114

Schulman, J. L. S. (2015). Trust region policy optimization. *International conference on machine learning*, (pp. 1889–1897). IEEE.

Selvin, S. V. (2017). Stock price prediction using LSTM, RNN, and CNN-sliding window model. In. *Proceedings of the IEEE International Conference on Advances in Computing, Communications, and Information*, (pp. 1643–1647). IEEE. 10.1109/ICACCI.2017.8126078

Sharma, V. K. (2019). Time series with sentiment analysis for stock price prediction. *In: Proceedings of the IEEE International Conference on Intelligent Communication and Computational Techniques (ICCT)*. IEEE. 10.1109/ICCT46177.2019.8969060

shibata K, O. Y. (1997). Reinforcement learning when visual sensory signals are directly given as inputs. *International conference on neural networks*, (pp. 1716–1720). IEEE.

SirignanoJ. C. R. (2018). Universal features of price formation in financial markets: perspectives from deep learning. Ssrn, doi:10.2139/ssrn.3141294

Srivastava, H. (2017). *What Is K-Fold Cross Validation? - Magoosh Data Science Blog*. Magoosh Data Science Blog.

Tsai, C. F., W. S. (2009). Stock price forecasting by hybrid machine learning techniques[. *Proceedings of the International MultiConference of Engineers and Computer Scientists*, (755). IEEE.

Usmani, M., S. H. (2016). Stock Market Prediction Using Machine Learning Techniques. *3rd International Conference On Computer And Information Sciences (ICCOINS)*. IEEE. 10.1109/ICCOINS.2016.7783235

Wang, J. H. R., Hou, R., Wang, C., & Shen, L. (2016). Improved v-support vector regression model based on variable selection and brain storm optimization for stock price forecasting. *Applied Soft Computing*, 49, 164–178. doi:10.1016/j.asoc.2016.07.024

Wymann, B. E. E. (July 2019). Torcs. *the open racing car simulator*. TORCS. http://torcs.sourceforge.net

Xiao, Y. X. (2014). *A multiscale modeling approach incorporating ARIMA and ANNs for financial market volatility forecasting*. J. Syst. Sci. doi:10.100711424-014-3305-4

Yang., W. (July 2009.). *Granule Based Knowledge Representation for Intra and Inter Transaction Association Mining*. Queensland University of Technology.

Yoo, P. D., M. H. (2005). Machine Learning Techniques and Use of Event Information for Stock Market Prediction: A Survey and Evaluation. *International Conference on Computational Intelligence for Modelling*, (pp. 835–841). IEEE. 10.1109/CIMCA.2005.1631572

Chapter 6
Artificial Intelligence to Protect Wildlife

S. Nagini
VNR VJIET, India

Manik Soni
VNR VJIET, India

Sravani Nalluri
VNR VJIET, India

Ramasubbareddy Somula
VNR VJIET, India

ABSTRACT

In this chapter, the authors present a novel approach to detect illegal wildlife trade online using deep learning. The purpose here is to implement a deep convolutional neural network for the detection of illegal wildlife trade on the web. For this research, data consists of two types of images, legal and illegal. The illegal images, such as tiger skin and elephant tusks, are collected using web-scraping techniques from social media websites and legal images are collected from Kaggle. The outcomes of our research and experiments show that usage of deep CNN pre-trained on image-net achieves testing accuracy of 92.26% with an f1 score of 0.8234 with very low inference time.

INTRODUCTION

Over the most recent 50 decades around 840+ species including passenger pigeon (Barnett, 2001), Tasmanian tiger, African Rhino and Javan Tiger (Van Uhm, 2018) – are known to have extinct and up to 16,000 others have been compromised. By 2025, 66% of turtles could be gone (Pickrell, 2006). Great apes have as of late reduced by more than 50% in various areas of the continent, Africa. Half of marsupials alongside one of every three creatures of land and water are in peril, and an astonishing 40% of Asia's flora and creatures may before long be vanished (Young, 2003). Untamed life the executives frameworks have gotten progressively famous in poaching avoidance systems. Modern, productive and financially savvy arrangements are present but humanity has little proof for showing that poaching is adequately controlled.

DOI: 10.4018/978-1-6684-6971-2.ch006

Copyright © 2023, IGI Global. Copying or distributing in print or electronic forms without written permission of IGI Global is prohibited.

The extinction of species has an increased rate which is 100 times (Ceballos et al., 2015) above normal where 1/4th of bio-diversity is currently endangered including species of mammals and birds which is about 25% and 14% respectively (United Nations., 2018). The Convention on International Trade in Endangered Species of Wild Fauna and Flora (CITES) addresses a vital agreement with the wildlife trafficking and also divides the species that are being threatened based on the protection they have. It also developed a system that needs to be implemented by each party at national level. Even after such efforts, trafficking of wild animals (Demeau et al., 2019; Angelici & Sollund, 2016) still remains prominent and it is known among all the illegal activities that are profitable behind drugs (Popper, 2017; Scammell & Bo, 2016), human trafficking, counterfeiting and so on. Social media has been extensively used for wildlife traffic (Eid & Handal, 2017).

Studies have been done to protect wildlife with Artificial Intelligence techniques like Support Vector Machines, deep Neural Networks and Fuzzy Logic (Chalmers et al., 2019). Since the past few years, CNNs have dominated the space of image classification due to its high accuracy to classify the images. CNNs (Krizhevsky et al., 2012) have been deeply used in Image classification and segmentation. We present a Deep Convolutional Neural Network Model, DenseNet121 (Huang & Liu, n.d) as a binary classifier to classify an image as legal or illegal activity. All images with parts of endangered animals will be classified as illegal.

RELATED WORK

Wildlife management systems have become more important and powerful to prevent trade of wildlife species and at the same time put an end to activities poaching and hunting. For the rest of this section, we'll show the exiting techniques used to prevent illegal wildlife trade and also discuss key limitations of each of them.

Current Solutions

Current solutions include an variety of tools and techniques to prevent wildlife trade. The most basic ones includes manually keeping an eye over the wildlife by rangers and preventing poachers and hunters from disturbing the wildlife. There are other solutions such as use of cameras (Norouzzadeh et al., 2018) which are fitted all over the forests or sanctuaries and are 24/7 monitored by the concerned department. The video recording is used to understand the most sensitive and poaching prone areas of forests. A lot of research is going in automating the task of manually monitoring the video footage via machine learning techniques (Minin et al., 2018; Di Minin et al., 2018). Reports have been presented on unprecedented species extinction rates(UN, 2019; Coscia & Rios, 2012). Social network data analysis along has been tried to disrupt wildlife criminal networks (Haas & Ferreira, 2015) but challenges continue to occur while analysing big data (Tsou, 2017; Zook et al., 2017). (Hayes et al., 2018) includes developing a script using AppleScript to retrieve the account information for thousands of vendors and their respective marketplace listings. (Di Minin et al., 2015b) mentions and guides on usage of social media data to protect wildlife species.

Advancements have been done to increase accuracy of model but its usage at real-time for inference has always been a weak point . For example, Faster RCNN (Ren & He, n.d.) has been utilized to understand the video footage automatically. But Faster RCNN takes input at 5fps whereas live recording of the forests is at 25 fps. The video is upload to cloud after which it is passed to the model in cloud running with NVIDIA Tesla K40 GPU (Chalmers et al., 2019). The model in turn returns the output. The bottleneck is because of time frames difference which makes the inference time of the model very high and suffers issues with video synchronisation. It is also found that low resolution images are not suitable for inference and the model can make wrong predictions with low resolution images due to the inability to capture important parameters during training an testing time. Faster RCNN models are very efficient in objection detection, and they have high computational requirements at inference time which are very costly(Chalmers et al., 2019).

Many approaches use models with few parameters such as MobileNet (Andrew, 2017) or You Only Look Once (YOLO) (Redmon et al., n.d) which are easy to train. Such models are used in addition with an drone (Chalmers et al., 2019) where the AI model can detect the animals live but only when the video is of 2 fps. Such approach may not provide desired results practically as the video fps is very low.

Limitations

Many existing approaches discussed in 2.1.1 have been suggested by researchers. The approach with Faster RCNN (Ren & He, n.d.) is very powerful but cannot be used practically because of its high power consumption. In particular, all the studies mentioned above lacks the presence of an lightweight model which is fast at inference time and at the same time detects the not just the illegal activities but also the sources which are used to sell the wildlife parts It has been generally detailed that YOLO (Redmon et al., n.d) experiences spatial imperatives and this thus restrains the quantity of close by objects that can be identified. Many important issues have been addressed by Faster-RCNN (Ren & He, n.d.) by using Region-based proposals but such approach also increase the inference time significantly. Plethora of changes have been made in improving Faster RCNNs, but they still suffer from high inference time.

Trading off between computation cost, inference time has been an challenge. Also, there has not been much success in detecting sources of illegal wildlife trade. In this paper, we present an solution with which an activity can be classified as legal/illegal and if confident, also output the source of such illegal trade.

RESEARCH METHODOLOGY

This part of the paper deals with strategies and methods used in this research. It is separated on Image Resizing, Dataset Description and Architecture of our Deep Learning Model. The description of dataset details a compact portrayal of procedure of collecting pictures with web scraping and description of complete data consumed with our research. In the Data pre-processing section, the process of image re-scaling and normalizing has been explained. The section 'Architecture' explains about the architecture of model along with the various values of hyperparameters uses to train the model.

Dataset Description

We collected images consist of parts of animals which are traded such as Rhino Horns, elephant tusks (Hernandez-Castro & Roberts, 2015), skin of tiger, skin of snake, reptiles(NatureServe, 2019), sharks (CITES, ; Government of Australia, 2004) etc using a python script. The script crawled on 10 websites and collected 2000 images of animal parts. Another part of data was collected from "iwildcam2019-

fgv6" dataset which consist of images of 21 different types of animals found in forest under various light conditions. This dataset consist of 196157 pictures taken from Southern California at 138 different locations. The final dataset we used is an collection of 2000 images scraped from web and 196,537 images from "iwildcam2019-fgv6" (FGCV, 2019). The training data contains 80%(156925) of images from "iwildcam2019-fgv6" and 80%(1600) images from web-scraped data, hence maintaining the class balance. The testing data contains 20%(39231) of images from "iwildcam2019-fgv6" and 20%(400) images from web-scraped data. While training the model 0.1% of training data is chosen at random as validation data. Sample images from dataset are shown below.

Figure 1. Images of animals in different lights (Kaggle, 12 images)

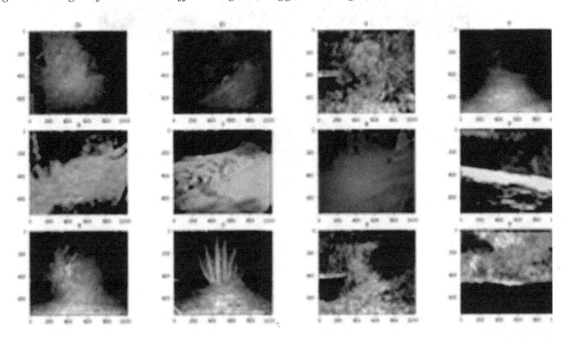

Data Pre-Processing

The dataset we collected has images of various sizes. Some of them were as big as 2380 x 3440 pixels and others as small as 50 x 50 pixels. We resized entire dataset to 32x32 using OpenCV and saved in .NPY format. In order to make the model converge faster, the images were scaled between 0 and 1 and normalised with image-net mean and standard deviation.

Architecture

We used 2 models, ResNet50 38 and DenseNet121 (Huang & Liu, n.d.) with hyperparameter configurations mentioned in Table 1. The aim of this was to find a model with fewer parameters and high accuracy. In this section, we'll compare and contrast Simple CNN, ResNet50 along with DenseNet121.

Figure 2. Tiger skin (web scraped)

Figure 3. Resizing each Image in dataset to 32 x 32

Conventional convolutional feed-forward neural networks connect the yield of the layer to the next layer subsequent to applying a set of operations. This incorporates a convolution operation or pooling layers, a cluster standardization and an activation function. Equation for that set of operations would be:

$x_l = H_l(x_l - 1)$

Equation 1 Equation of Simple CNN

Figure 4. Standard ConvNet

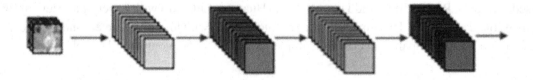

ResNets extended this behaviour including the skip connection, reformulating this equation into $x_l = H_l(x_l - 1) + x_{l-1}$. With this, all the information learned by n-1th convolution layer is present with n[th] convolution layer and hence the information propagates better and stays longer.

$$x_l = H_l(x_l - 1) + x_{l-1}$$

Equation 2 ResNet Equation

Figure 5. ResNet

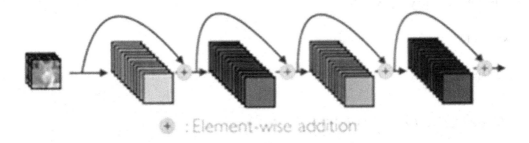

DenseNets make the first difference with ResNets (He et al., 2015) in the way information is passed. DenseNets concatenates feature maps of the output layer with the incoming feature maps instead of adding them. Hence, the equation turns to be:

$$x_l = H_l([x_0 + x_1 + \ldots + x_{l-1}])$$

Equation 2: DenseNet Equation

Figure 6. Dense block

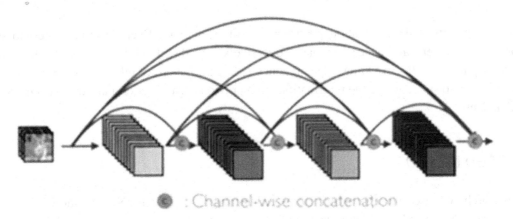

A similar issue we looked on our work on ResNets, this combining activity of feature maps is impossible when they are of different sizes. Regardless of the combining activity being an addition or a concatenation of feature maps. Therefore, and the same way we used for ResNets (He et al., 2015), DenseNets (Huang & Liu, n.d) are divided into dense blocks. Within a block, dimensions of the feature maps remains same, but the number of filters changes between them. These layers between the dense blocks are called ***Transition Layers.*** They are used for the down-sampling by applying a batch normalization, a 1x1 convolution and a 2x2 pooling layers. The channel dimension increase at every layer because of concatenation of feature maps.

'k' is the growth rate hyperparameter which maintains the amount of information stored in each layer to the network. If k feature maps are produced by H_1 then generalised equation for determining number of feature maps by l_{th} layer, is:

$$k_l = k_0 + k*(l - 1)$$

Equation 2 Rate of growth

Figure 7. Dense block in DenseNet with growth rate k

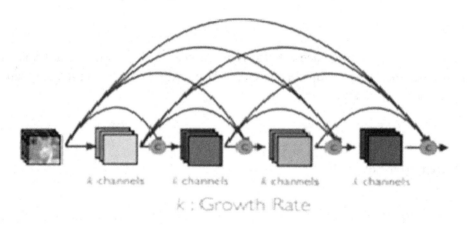

Feature maps acts as the information or learned data of the network. Every layer has access to feature maps of previous layers, and hence they have collective knowledge. Each layer adds new information or feature map to this collective knowledge, in concrete k feature maps of information. Because of this, DenseNet is able to save and use the information from previous layers better than ResNets and conventional ConvNets.

PROPOSED METHOD

In this research, We used the approach of transfer learning to train DenseNet121 and ResNet50 pre-trained on ImageNet. The ImageNet project is a large visual database, consisting of 1000 different types of objects' images, designed for research in visual object recognition software and technology. There are around 14 million images which are labelled manually to indicate the presence of various objects such as cats, dogs, cars, houses, including humans, present in the image. The architectures of DenseNet121 and ResNet50 are present below.

Figure 8. DenseNet121 architecture

Layers	Output Size	DenseNet-121	
Convolution	112 × 112		
Pooling	56 × 56		
Dense Block (1)	56 × 56	1 × 1 conv 3 × 3 conv	× 6
Transition Layer (1)	56 × 56 28 × 28		
Dense Block (2)	28 × 28	1 × 1 conv 3 × 3 conv	× 12
Transition Layer (2)	28 × 28 14 × 14		
Dense Block (3)	14 × 14	1 × 1 conv 3 × 3 conv	× 24
Transition Layer (3)	14 × 14 7 × 7		
Dense Block (4)	7 × 7	1 × 1 conv 3 × 3 conv	× 16
Classification Layer	1 × 1		

Transfer Learning

Transfer learning is the approach with which we can use an pre-trained model. Pre-trained models are trained on millions of images such as ImageNet. During the training process already learned parameters are fine-tuned using our own data. CNNs applied on small size datasets may lead to overfitting of the model and hence transfer learning is an robust solution to prevent such situations. The base models used in this research are DensetNet121 and ResNet50 pre-trained on ImageNet. The ResNet50 and DenseNet are trained on the following configurations.

Figure 9. ResNet50 architecture

stage	output	ResNet-50	
conv1	112×112	7×7, 64, stride 2	
		3×3 max pool, stride 2	
conv2	56×56	1×1, 64 3×3, 64 1×1, 256	×3
conv3	28×28	1×1, 128 3×3, 128 1×1, 512	×4
conv4	14×14	1×1, 256 3×3, 256 1×1, 1024	×6
conv5	7×7	1×1, 512 3×3, 512 1×1, 2048	×3
	1×1	global average pool 1000-d fc, softmax	

Table 1. Configurations of all five experiments

Experiment	Model	Optimizer	Batch Size
1	ResNet50	Adam	64
2	ResNet50	SGD	64
3	DenseNet121	SGD	64
4	DenseNet121	Adam	64
5	DenseNet121	SGD	32

Model Training

Model training is conducted on Amazon Deep Learning AMIs (Amazon Machine Images). The AMI is g3.16xlarge which consist of 188 EC2 Compute Units with 64 2.3 GHz Intel Xeon E5-2686 v4 CPUs. The AMI has 488 gigabytes of memory which was suitable to handle our large data. As mentioned above, we trained the models with configurations in Table 1, we used the following parameter values for Adam optimiser:

1. Stochastic Gradient Descent (SGD) persists only one learning rate which doesn't change while training whereas Adam adjusts learning rate dynamically during the training. To find the minima of the loss function, ResNet50 also implements Adam optimiser. Adam calculates the moving average of the gradient *mt*/squared gradients *vt* **and** the parameters *β*1 and *β*2 to a₁ter the rate of learning during the training.

$$m_t = \beta_1 m_t - 1 + (1 - \beta_1) g_t$$

$$v_t = \beta_2 v_t - 1 + (1 - \beta_2) g_t^2$$

m_t is the first moment of gradient
v_t is the second moment of gradient

In the above equation on the right, both m_t, v_t are initialised with 0's. Biases are changed to correct value by computing the first and second moment estimates (XuMay et al., 2016):

$$\widehat{m_t} = \frac{m_t}{1 - \beta_1^t} \quad \hat{v}_t = \frac{v_t}{1 - \beta_2^t}$$

Following Adam update rule equation is used to update the weights (θ): $\theta_{t+1} = \theta_t - \eta \dfrac{\widehat{m_t}}{\sqrt{\hat{v}_t} + \varepsilon}$

η: Eta is the learning rate hyperparameter. It is the rate at which model learns from the input. Very high learning rate could make the training unstable and very low learning rate could make the training process very slow.

β_1: is exponential decay rate for the first moment estimates.

β_2: is exponential decay rate for the second-moment estimates (e.g. 0.999).

ϵ: It's an small number to prevent DivisonByZero Exception (e.g. 10E-8).

We trained two variants of each model having different size of input and two different optimizers: Adam and SGD for 7 epochs. Alongside, as we observed that DenseNet121 with SGD as optimiser performs better compared to others, we also trained an variation of DenseNet121 with SGD and batch-size of 32.

Activation functions such as sigmoid and hyperbolic tangent experiences saturation near their input's middle point. Use of these activation functions can result in ineffective training and problems such as vanishing gradient (Xiao & Wang, 2015) and exploding gradient. To overcome these problems we use ReLU (Rectified Linear Unit) activation function defined as: g(x)=max(0,x).

EVALUATION METRICS AND ANALYSIS

In this section, we see the results of training the models with various configurations, experiments and evaluation metrics.

Evaluation Metrics

The dataset used in this research has class imbalance and hence to obtain the right comparison with existing models, we evaluated the model based on five different parameters which are Precision, recall, accuracy, F1 score, loss. Choosing these parameters for evaluation gives us an true picture of our model and testing results.

Experiment Analysis

- Config 1: ResNet50 trained with ADAM

Table 2. Evaluation metrics with config 1

Metric	Training	Testing
Accuracy	92.45%	90.764%
Precision	-	0.7966
Recall	-	0.7714
F1 score	-	0.7803
Loss	0.2228	0.2789

In configuration 1, ResNet50 is trained with Adam optimiser and with a batch size of 64. It took 35 minutes overall to train this model for 7 epochs. The validation accuracy of this model is 90.764% with F1 score 0.7803.

Figure 10. Config1 training and validation accuracy

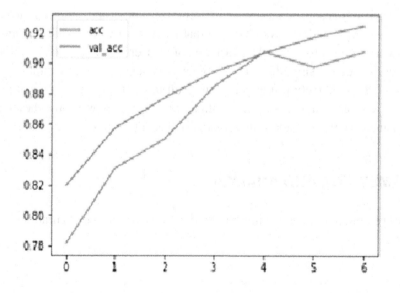

Figure 11. Config1 validation precision, recall, F1 score

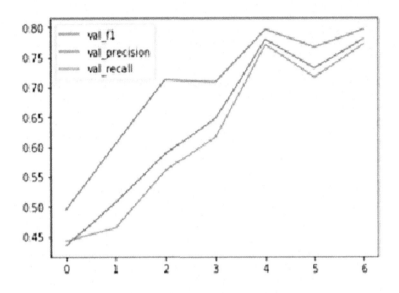

- Config 2: ResNet50 trained with SGD

Table 3. Evaluation metrics with config 2

Metric	Training	Testing
Accuracy	91.84%	91.1%
Precision	-	0.8027
Recall	-	0.7882
F1 score	-	0.7927
Loss	0.2425	0.2759

In configuration 2, ResNet50 is trained with SGD with same batch size as previously used. Surprisingly, ResNet50 with SGD got better accuracy than Adam. It took 24 minutes for the model to train and achieved better F1 score and validation accuracy compared to Configuration 1.

Figure 12. Config2 training and validation accuracy

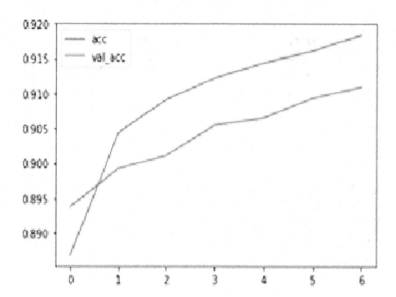

Figure 13. Config2 validation precision, recall, F1 score

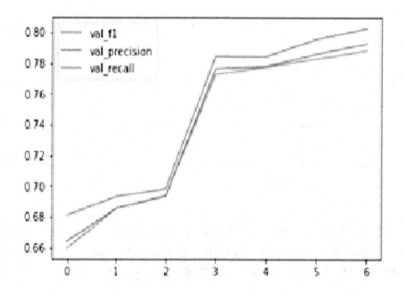

- Config 3: DenseNet121 trained with ADAM

In configuration 3, DenseNet121 is trained with Adam with batch size 64. DenseNet121 with Adam performed worse than ResNet50, also took 45 minutes to train which is more than training time taken by ResNet.

Table 4. Evaluation metrics with config 3

Metric	Training	Testing
Accuracy	88.59%	88.207%
Precision	-	0.7574
Recall	-	0.6982
F1 score	-	0.7170
Loss	0.2425	0.3516

Figure 14. Config 3 training and validation accuracy

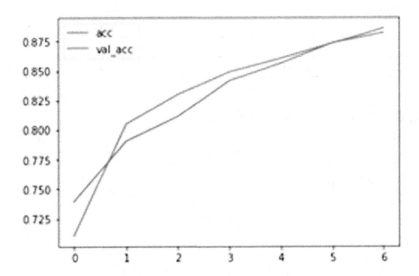

Figure 15. Config 3 validation precision, recall, F1 score

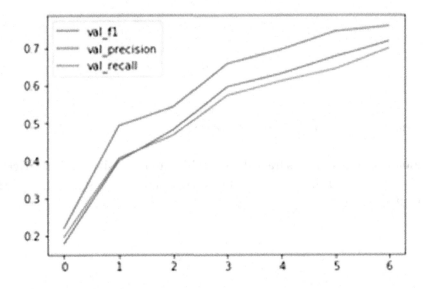

- Config 4: DenseNet121 trained with SGD

In configuration 4, DenseNet121 is trained with SGD with batch size 64. DenseNet121 with SGD performed better than all configurations of ResNet50 with an validation accuracy of 92.08%. This also portraits the state when SGD performs better than ADAM.

Table 5. Evaluation metrics with config 4

Metric	Training	Testing
Accuracy	94.08%	92.08%
Precision	-	0.8260
Recall	-	0.8124
F1 score	-	0.8164
Loss	0.1694	0.2458

Figure 16. Config 4 training and validation accuracy

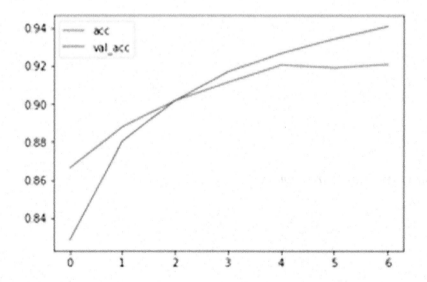

- Config 5: DenseNet121 with SGD on batch-size 32

In configuration 4, DenseNet121 is trained with SGD with batch size 32. DenseNet121 with SGD and batch-size 32 outperformed all the configurations and achieved highest accuracy of 92.26%. It took the model 72 minutes to train.

Figure 17. Validation precision, recall, and F1 score

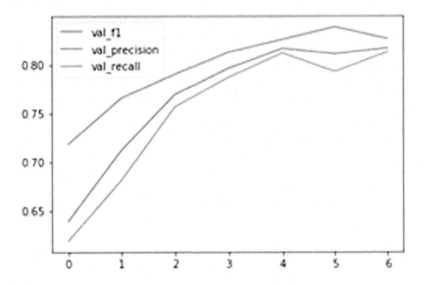

Table 6. Evaluation metrics with config 5

Metric	Training	Testing
Accuracy	93.31%	92.26%
Precision	-	0.8299
Recall	-	0.8182
F1 score	-	0.8234
Loss	0.1929	0.2370

Figure 18. Config 5 training and validation accuracy

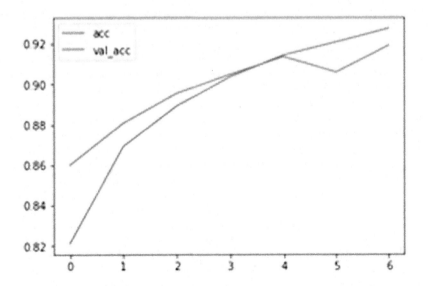

Figure 19. Config 5 validation, F1 score

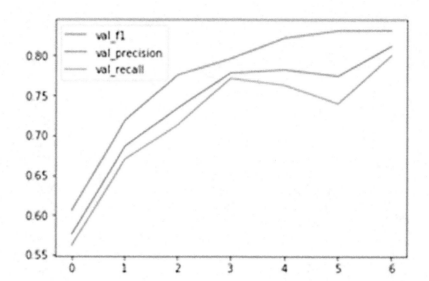

RESULT

As from section 4.2 'Experiment Analysis', we can observe that the model trained on DenseNet with optimiser as stochastic gradient descent and batch size 32 can detect the wildlife activity as legal/illegal most accurately. The model achieves an astounding f1_score of 0.8234 which means that the model is good in both precision and recall. As the model is pre-trained on image-net, it is fast during the inference time as it has very few parameters.

Figure 20. Config 5 validation F1 score

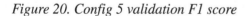

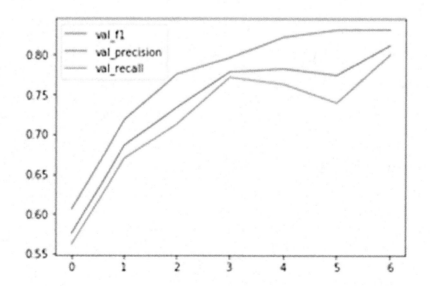

Table 7. Evaluation metrics of best configuration (Config 5)

Metric	Training	Testing
Accuracy	93.31%	92.26%
Precision	-	0.8299
Recall	-	0.8182
F1 score	-	0.8234
Loss	0.1929	0.2370

CONCLUSION AND FUTURE WORK

To detect illegal online wildlife trade (IEEE, 2010) and prevent species from going extinct, we proposed a novel approach using deep learning. We presented a Convolutional Neural Network model with less parameters and yet with high precision and recall. We leveraged transfer learning which helped us on comparing various models with different configurations. The precision and recall of the model is sufficiently encouraging. With this solution, the illegal wildlife trade through social media websites may come to an end.

The proposed base solution will be expanded in our upcoming research with new deep learning models and fine-tuning hyperparameters and activation functions. In addition, we will also extend this work to broad range of endangered species.

REFERENCES

Andrew, G. (2017). *MobileNets: Efficient Convolutional Neural Networks for Mobile Vision Applications*. Cornell University. https://arxiv.org/abs/1704.04861

Barnett, A. (2001). Safety in numbers may not be enough. *News Scientist*. https://www.newscientist.com/article/mg16922764-000-safety-in-numbers-may-not-be-enough/

Ceballos, G., Ehrlich, P. R., Barnosky, A. D., García, A., Pringle, R. M., & Palmer, T. M. (2015). Accelerated modern human-induced species losses: Entering the sixth mass extinction. *Science Advances*, *1*(5), 1–5. doi:10.1126ciadv.1400253 PMID:26601195

Chalmers, C., Fergus, P., Wich, S., & Montanez, A. (2019). *Conservation AI: Live Stream Analysis for the Detection of Endangered Species Using Convolutional Neural Networks and Drone Technology*. Academic Press.

CITES. (n.d.). History of CITES listing of sharks (Elasmobranchii). *Cites*. https://www.cites.org/eng/prog/shark/history.php

Coscia, M., & Rios, V. (2012). Knowing where and how criminal organizations operate using web content. *Proceedings of the 21st international conference on information and knowledge management* (pp.1412-1421). ACM. 10.1145/2396761.2398446

Demeau, E., Vargas, M., & Jeffrey, K. (2019). Wildlife trafficking on the internet: A virtual market similar to drug trafficking? *Criminality Magazine*, *61*(2), 101–112.

Di Minin, E., Fink, C., Tenkanen, H., & Hiippala, T. (2018). Machine learning for tracking illegal wildlife trade on social media. *Nature Ecology & Evolution*, *2*(3), 406–407. doi:10.103841559-018-0466-x PMID:29335570

Di Minin, E., Tenkanen, H., & Toivonen, T. (2015b). Prospects and challenges for social media data in conservation science. *Frontiers in Environmental Science*, *3*, 63. doi:10.3389/fenvs.2015.00063

Eid, E., & Handal, R. (2017). Illegal hunting in Jordan: Using social media to assess impacts on wildlife. *Oryx*. doi:10.1017/S0030605316001629

FGCV. (2019). *CVPR 2019 Fine-Grained Visual Categorization.* iWildCam - FGVC6. kaggle.com/c/iwildcam-2019-fgvc6

Government of Australia. (2004). *October 2, 2004: A Single Day Snapshot of the Trade in Great White Shark (Carcharadon carcharias).* CITES. https://cites.org/common/cop/13/inf/E13i51.pdf

Haas, T. C., & Ferreira, S. M. (2015). Federated databases and actionable intelligence: Using social networks analysis to disrupt transnational wildlife trafficking criminal networks. *Security Informatics*, *4*(2), 2. doi:10.118613388-015-0018-8

Hayes, D., Cappa, F., & Cardon, J. (2018). A Framework for More Effective Dark Web Marketplace Investigations. *Information, 9*(8), 186. https://doi.org/10.3390/info9080186

HeK.ZhangX.RenS.SunJ. (2015). Deep Residual Learning for Image Recognition https://arxiv.org/abs/1512.03385

Hernandez-Castro, J., & Roberts, D. (2015). Automatic detection of potentially illegal online sales of elephant ivory via data mining. *PeerJ. Computer Science*, *0*(0), 1–11. doi:10.7717/peerj-cs.10

Huang, G., Liu, Z., van der Maaten, L., & Weinberger, K. (n.d.). *Densely Connected Convolutional Networks.* https://arxiv.org/abs/1608.06993

IEEE. (2010). *Survey: Wildlife Trade and Related Criminal Activities Over the Internet.* IEEE.

Krishnasamy, K., & Stoner, S. (2016). *Trading Faces: A Rapid Assessment on the use of Facebook to Trade Wildlife in Peninsular Malaysia.* Traffic Facts. http://www.trafficj.org/publication/16_Trading_Faces.pdf

Krizhevsky A, Sutskever I, & Hinton, G.E. (2012). ImageNet classification with deep convolutional neural networks. *Advances in Neural Information Processing Systems, 1*, 1097–1105.

Minin, E., Fink, C., Hiippala, T., & Tenkanen, H. (2018). *A framework for investigating illegal wildlife trade on social media with machine learning.* NIH.

NatureServe. (2019). *Comprehensive Study of World's Reptiles: More Than One in Five Reptile Species are Threatened with Extinction.* IUCN.

Norouzzadeh, M.S., Nguyen, A., Kosmala, M., Swanson, A., Palmer, M., Packer, C., & Clune, J. (2018). Automatically identifying, counting, and describing wild animals in camera-trap images with deep learning. *Proceedings of the National Academy of Sciences of the United States of America.* National Academy. . doi:10.1073/pnas.1719367115

Pickrell, J. (2006). Introduction: Endangered Species. *News Scientist.* https://www.newscientist.com/article/dn9961-introduction-endangered-species/

Popper, N. (2017). AlphaBay, Biggest Online Drug Bazaar, Goes Dark, and Questions Swirl N Popper. *The New York Times.*

RedmonJ.DivvalaS.GirshickR.AliF. Y. O. L. O. (n.d.). Unified, Real-Time Object Detection. https://arxiv.org/abs/1506.02640

Ren, S., He, K., Girshick, R., & Sun, J. (n.d.). *Faster R-CNN: Towards Real-Time Object Detection with Region Proposal Networks.* https://arxiv.org/abs/1506.01497

Roberts, D. & Alfino, S. (2019). *Code word usage in the online ivory trade across four European Union member states.* University of Kent. https://kar.kent.ac.uk/67136/3/Alfino_%252526_Roberts_ivory_code_words_Oryx_revision.pdf

Roberts, D., & Hernandez-Castro, J. (2017). Bycatch and illegal wildlife trade on the dark web. *Oryx, 51*(3), 393–394. doi:10.1017/S0030605317000679

Scammell, L., & Bo, A. (2016). Online supply of medicines to illicit drug markets: situation and responses. In European Monitoring Centre for Drugs and Drug Addiction (Ed.), The internet and drug markets (Vol. 21). Luxembourg: Publications Office of the European Union.

Sollund, R. (2016). Wildlife Trafficking in a Globalized World: An Example of Motivations and Modus Operandi from a Norwegian Case Study. In F. M. Angelici (Ed.), *Problematic Wildlife: A crossdisciplinary Approach.* Springer International Publishing. doi:10.1007/978-3-319-22246-2_25

Tsou, M. (2017). Research challenges and opportunities in mapping social media and big data. *Cartography and Geographic Information Science, 42*(sup1), 70–74. doi:10.1080/15230406.2015.1059251

UN. (2019). *Nature Decline Unprecented Report. Sustainable Development.* https://www.un.org/sustainabledevelopment/blog/2019/05/nature-decline-unprecedented-report/

United Nations. (2018). *Nature's Dangerous Decline 'Unprecedented' Species Extinction Rates 'Accelerating': A Framework for More Effective Dark Web Marketplace Investigations.* MDPI. https://www.mdpi.com/2078-2489/9/8/186

Van Uhm, D.P. (2018). The social construction of the value of wildlife: A green cultural criminological perspective. *Theoritical Criminology, 22*(3), 384-401.

Xiao, Y., Wang, J. (2015). Moving Target: tracking online sales of illegal wildlife products in China. *TRAFFIC Briefing Paper.* TRAFFIC..

XuMay, L., Guan, J., & Xiao, Y. (2016). *Wildlife Cybercrime In China.* E-commerce and social media monitoring. (TRAFFIC)

Young, E. (2003). Biodiversity wipeout facing South East Asia. *News Scientist.* https://www.newscientist.com/article/dn3973-biodiversity-wipeout-facing-south-east-asia/

Zook, M., Barocas, S., boyd, Crawford, K., Keller, E., Gangadharan, S. P., Goodman, A., Hollander, R., Koenig, B. A., Metcalf, J., Narayanan, A., Nelson, A., & Pasquale, F. (2017). Ten simple rules for responsible big data research. *PLoS Computational Biology, 13*(3), e1005399. doi:10.1371/journal.pcbi.1005399 PMID:28358831

Chapter 7
A Sophisticated Image Filtering and Enhancement Method With Worn Speculative Segmentation Process

Thangarasu Nainan

(iD) https://orcid.org/0000-0001-6638-1262

*Karpagam Academy of Higher Education
(Deemed), India*

Ramaraj Muniappan

(iD) https://orcid.org/0000-0002-8821-3259

Rathinam College of Arts and Science, India

V. Vijayalakshmi

*Christ College of Science and Management,
Malur, India*

R. Rajalakshmi

Arignar Anna College, India

Sabareeswaran Dhandapani

Rathinam College of Arts and Science, India

Murugadass Muthaiyan

Arignar Anna College, India

ABSTRACT

Image mining is tantamount to data mining concept. It is most imperative to understand the data mining concept to the prior knowledge of image mining. Data mining is an assemblage of methods that are used to automated approach to exhaustively explore and create associations in very large datasets. Image mining process is an analyzing large set of domain-specific data and consequently extracting information and knowledge in a form of new relationships, patterns, or clusters for the decision-making process. This research article mainly focuses on color pixel-based image segmentation to infer the age of the tiger and also applied several reasonable and applicable filters, enhancement processes in the speculative real-time images. The objective of the research work is to be done on assessing the age of the tiger using the color pixel based image classification and clustering is the main of the research work. To optimization of reduce the processing Time, Retrieval Time, Accuracy and Error Rate by generating the better results is to real time tiger image database.

DOI: 10.4018/978-1-6684-6971-2.ch007

Copyright © 2023, IGI Global. Copying or distributing in print or electronic forms without written permission of IGI Global is prohibited.

1. INTRODUCTION

Image mining is an astonishing to data mining concept. Image processing is the process of image using mathematical operations. Images are the input of the processing that may be series of images, photograph, video etc. most of the techniques used the image as two-dimensional signal and applying standard signal processing methods to it (Jhala & Sadhu, 2017). First up all to understand the data mining concept in prior knowledge is more important to image mining. It is an interdisciplinary endeavor that draws upon expertise from computer vision, image processing, image acquisition, image retrieval, data mining, machine learning, database and artificial intelligence. Advances in image acquisition and storage technology have led to tremendous growth in very large and detailed image databases (Rani & Bhardwaj, 2016).

Analysis of images will reveal useful information to the human users. Image mining deals with the extraction of implicit knowledge, image data relationships or other patterns not explicitly stored in the images (Hassan et al., 2017). The objective of the image enhancement methods is to improve the information in images of human viewers or to provide better input for other automated image processing techniques. The next stage deals with the image segmentation method. Image segmentation deals with partitions an input image into its essential parts or objects (Sakthivel et al., 2014). In general ways, image segmentation is one of the most difficult tasks to perform the digital image processing. Segmentation stage usually is raw pixel data, constitution either the boundary of a region or all the points in the region itself (Wang & Liu, 2015).

It will be another stage for image processing also called image representation and description. Image representations of an image that can be take in various forms (Wang & Wu, 2014). Every time, it denotes the different ways that the transported information, such as color, is coded digitally and how the image is stored, for example, how is structured an image file. The goal of segmentation is to abridge and/or change the representation of an image into something that is more meaningful and easier to analyze (Wang & Wang, 2017). This is typically used to identify objects or other relevant information in digital images.

It can be used for different applications in computer vision in digital image processing. Many of the application require highly accurate and computationally faster image processing algorithms. The success of any application depends on reliability and accuracy of the image processing used (Das & Konar, 2009). Color image segmentation that is based on the color feature of image pixels assumes that homogeneous colors in the image correspond to separate the clusters and meaningful objects in the color image (Nida et al., 2015). In other words, each cluster explains a class of pixels that share parallel color properties. As the segmentation results depend on the used color space, there is no single color space, which can provide acceptable results for all kinds of images.

A segmentation of color images is tested with different classical color spaces, HSV, RGB, L*a*b, CMY, YUV and YCbCr to select the best color space for the considered kind of images (Oscar et al., 2010). Color is the most extensively used visual content for image retrieval. The color of each pixel in an image is characterized by three components R, G and B (Dubey et al., 2018). These color spaces have their own properties, which can be efficiently taken into account in order to make the final combined color spaces more reliable than the individual color space (Panwar & Gulati, 2013). Color model is to facilitate the specification of colors in some standard are generally accepted way.

The color model is a specification of three-D coordinated system and subspaces within that system, where each color is represented by a single color point. The most color model is uses of today are oriented either toward hardware such as color monitor and printers or where color manipulation is a goal of color animation and graphics (Napoleon et al., 2013). The color model is most often used for image processing are: RGB, CMY'K, Y'UV, YIQ, YCbCr, HSV, L*A*B. An image filter is a technique through which size, colors, shading and other characteristics of an image are altered (Ikonomakis et al., 2000). An image filter is used to transform the image using different graphical editing techniques. Image filters are usually done through graphic design and editing software (Noor et al., 2013).

Images are often corrupted by random variations in intensity, illumination, or have poor contrast and can't be used directly. Filtering is a transform pixel intensity values to reveal certain image characteristics (Hettiarachchi, 2016). There are several types of filtering and enhancement methods are available such as Mean, Median, Gaussian, conservative, unsharp filter and wiener filter, spatial domain filtering and frequency domain filtering concept (Ramani & Balasubramanian, 2015). Image enhancement is the process of adjusting digital images so that the results are more suitable for display or further image analysis. For example, you can remove noise, sharpen, or brighten an image, making it easier to identify key features (Eini & Einy, 2013).

The main aim of image enhancement is to improve the interpretability or perception of information in images for human viewers, or to provide `better' input for other automated image processing techniques. This first method is Spatial Domain direct manipulation of pixels of the image. The second methods for Frequency Domain is to modifying the Fourier Transform of an image. Image enhancement algorithms offer a wide variety of approaches for modifying images to achieve visually acceptable images (Khan et al., 2017). The choice of such techniques is a function of the specific task, image content, observer characteristics, and viewing conditions. The review of Image enhancement techniques in spatial domain have been successfully accomplished and is one of the most important and difficult component of digital image processing and the results for each method are also discussed.

Based on the type of image and type of noise with which it is corrupted, a slight change in individual method or combination of any methods further improves visual quality. Enhancement algorithms it may play a critical role in choosing an algorithm for real-time applications (##NO_NAME##, 2018). They have described recent developments methods of image enhancement and point out promising directions on research for image enhancement in spatial domain for future research (Tian et al., 2016). The future scope will be the development of adaptive algorithms for effective image enhancement using Fuzzy Logic and Neural Network.

2. LITERATURE REVIEW

Many works are published in the area of image segmentation by using innumerable methods and many of those literatures based on the different applications of image segmentation. A lot of researcher have been done in this domain, which gives better-segmented results. Some of the recent methodologies proposed are as follows: Y.V.Jhala et al. 2017, had described it gave details about how to predict the age of the tiger, which means to support for this article to the "field guide aging tigers" are discussed in this scenario(Jhala & Sadhu, 2017). Rakib Hassan et al. 2017, presented color image segmentation using automated k-means clustering with two common color spaces like RGB and HSV color spaces. Yongfu Wang et al. 2014, established a data mining approach for the noise filtering approaches and to propose a method for fuzzy filter design and improving the quality of noise corrupted images.

Imp denotes an image corrupted by mixed noise. Pixel xm:n is located at position (m*n) where the coordinate origin is assumed to be the left upper corner of the image. Then xm;n can be written as xm;n ¼ sm;n + nm;n where sm;n denotes the original image signal and nm;n denotes the noise. R.Geetha

Ramani et al. 2015, demonstrated manual segmentation of vessels requires expertise. Analyses, monitored the information about the PCA, filtering method and contrast enhancement which improves efficiency and performance to achieve higher accuracy, sensitivity, and specificity of 95.36%, 7.79%, and 97.78% respectively has been analyzed. Abder Elmoataz et al. 2005, had identified that the application of the FCM clustering algorithm to detect the skin color segmentation. The present work employed the skin color and adapted the spatial data mining procedures are integrated with segmentation tasks to perform and identify the significant skin color region in an image (Elmoataz & Chahir, 2005).

Swagatam Das et al. 2009, proposed an evolutionary Fuzzy clustering algorithm for robotically grouping the pixels of an image into different homogeneous regions. Arti Taneja et al. 2015 has described the performance study of image segmentation techniques. The paper had presented in different image segmentation techniques and it have been focused out that intensity and texture-based method based on level set function effectively segment the image (Taneja et al., 2015). E. A. Zanaty. 2012, presented that the number of cluster for kernelized Fuzzy C-Means algorithm for automatic medical image segmentation (Zanaty, 2012).

Loai AbedAllah et al. 2012, had proposed a K-Nearest Neighbor (K-NN) algorithm which depends critically good metric over the input space (Allah & Shimshoni, 2012). Poonam Panwar et al 2013, had proposed the image segmentation is a set of segments that collectively cover the entire image or a set of contours extracted from the image. Marta Mrak et al 2003, The quality of segmentation depends upon the quality of the image. The segmentation is mainly focused upon the measurement taken from the image and might be grey level, texture, color, depth or motion (Mrak, 2003). N. Ikonomakis et al. 2000, investigated the image segmentation is crucial parameter for multimedia application.

It revealed that the color image segmentation for multimedia application with databases can utilize segmentation for the storage and indexing of images and video. D. Napoleon et al. 2013, have described a segmentation based on the color features of an image. Noor A. Ibraheem et al. 2013. Had conducted a detailed study on skin color-based image segmentation techniques. The segmentation was based on the classification of the colored image into skin and non- skin color to derive pixels based on skin color information.

Preeti Rani et al. 2016, portrayed a color-based image segmentation methodology for partitioning the colors in the segments. The method gave PSNR values to calculate the segment in the images and to generate the output and accuracy in terms of color segmentation. K. Sakthivel et al. 2014, provided a color image segmentation using SVM pixel classification of the image. This paper is based on image segmentation that cluster pixels into salient image regions. Segmentation could be used for object recognition, constriction boundary approximation within motion or stereo systems, image compression, image editing, or image database lookup.

Lihua Tian et al. 2016, has presented, a new color image segmentation algorithm was introduced as MSHC (Mean Shift Hierarchical Clustering) are discussed in this scenario. Nida M. Zaitoun et al. 2015, had presented with different image segmentation techniques like 1). Reconstruction, 2). Transformation, 3). Classification.

A survey of literature showed an image segmentation processes are discussed . It described a comparative study of the basic Block-Based image segmentation techniques. Y. Q. Wang et al. 2015, used the improved support vector clustering algorithm for color image segmentation has been enticed gradually to deliberation with the many application fields during past few years. Propose algorithm to be a time complexity function is O ($m/_{\varepsilon^2} + 1/\varepsilon^3$) which is linear in the number of training samples m for a fixed, and space complexity of $(1/\varepsilon 2)$, which is independent of m for a fixed ε (Bethel, 1997). When compared with related algorithms, that has to be competitive performances of both on training time and accuracy.

Yongqing Wang et al. 2017, introduced that the new image segmentation algorithm is called Multi-Features Fusion techniques were applied for the high-resolution sensing image which contains richer information of spatial relation in-ground objects than low-resolution ones. R. Hettiarachchi et al. 2016, had introduced an adaptive and unsupervised clustering approach based on Voroni Regions, which could be applied to solve the color image segmentation problems. Zubair Khan et al. 2017, described the adaptive initial parameter estimate process for image segmentation using an enhanced k-means clustering algorithm. Zhiding Yu et al. 2010, introduced an adaptive unsupervised scheme for pixel clustering and color image segmentation . Kajal Gautam et al. 2018, demonstrated with several problems in the color image segmentation.

Solmaz EINI et al. 2013, have presented with a new clustering method for image segmentation by applying Gaussian mixture. RatchakitSakuldee et al. 2007, described the various applications which are used in the field of color image segmentation such as face recognition, object recognition, the real-time automatic road sign detection, segmenting acute, leukemia images, tree image, recognition, and feature extraction, etc (Sakuldee & Udomhunsakul, 2007). The main goal is to convert an image into a portrait using RGB color space are discussed in this scenario.

3. METHODOLOGY

Image noise occurs due to presence of errors during image acquisition, which is a random difference of color information produced by the scanner or sensor or digital camera. Noise in images is normally treated as undesirable by-product of image apprehension. These noises resulted in pixel values that do not reflect the true intensities of the original scene or images. While an image is acquired in a digital format directly, the technique used for collecting such data may introduce noise. If an image is scanned from photograph film, the grain of film is a cause of noise. While performing electronic transmission of image data can acquaint with noise. The few noises are show in below:

3.1. Filter Concept

3.1.1. Gaussian Noise

Gaussian Noise occurs due to image sensor's reading noise, there is a constant noise level in dark areas of the image. It is independent of signal intensity on an individual pixel.

3.1.2. Salt-and-Pepper Noise

The salt and pepper noise consist of dark pixels in bright regions and bright in dark regions. This kind of noise occurs due to analog to digital converter faults, dead pixels, and bit errors during transmission, etc. This can be eradicated in huge portion by overwhelming dark frame removal and by incorporating about dark/bright pixels.

3.1.3. Poisson Noise

It is also termed as shot noise, a kind of electronic noise which occurred when the determinate volume of particles, carrying energy like electrons or photons which rise to noticeable geometric variations in a dimension.

3.1.4. Speckle Noise

It is a granular noise which inherit and degrades the quality of radar images. It happens due to random fluctuations in the return signal from an object which rises the mean grey level of a limited area. The following images are examples for original image applied with particular salt and pepper noise

Figure 1. Applied salt and pepper noise on real time three-year tiger image

Figure 1 shows that salt and pepper noise applied in real time three years' tiger image. The above first image is an original one and second one is applied by the salt and pepper noise technique. In a second image of the tiger it can see the noise in some colors like Red dots, Green dots etc... The method of image de-noising is an essential task in image processing. There are various types of image de-noising. Image de-noising is an important image processing task. There are different techniques to detect de-noise an image or a set of data and methods that exists [Ganesh L. et al., 2012]. The significant property of a good image de-noising model is that it should completely remove noise as far as possible as well as preserve edges.

Average filter: Mean filter or average filter is a windowed filter of linear class, which smoothens the signal (image). The filter works as low-pass one. The fundamental idea can behind the filter is for any element of the signal (image) to take an average across its neighborhood.

3.1.5. Median Filter

It is a nonlinear method used to reduce impulsive or salt-and-pepper noise. It is also useful in processing edges in an image while overcoming random noise. Impulsive or salt-and-pepper noise can occur due to random bit errors in the communication channel. In the median filter, the window slides along the image, and the median intensity value of the pixels within the window displays the output intensity of the pixel is processed.

3.1.6. Rank Order Filter

Rank order filters have a certain size, but do not have any matrix values nor a gain factor. So, one value of the pixel values examined becomes the output value, without any calculation performed on the values itself. When a threshold is set, the value of the Centre pixel will only be replaced with the new value if the difference between the original and new value is smaller than or equal to the threshold.

3.1.7. Gaussian Filter

Gaussian filter is a filter which has the impulse response is the Gaussian function. When minimizing the rise and fall time these filters are developed to overshoot. The minimum possible group delay is connected closely with the Gaussian Filter. The process of image enhancement comprised of group of methods which are utilized to enhance the visual appearance of the image. It is a process which improves the visual quality and complete appearance of image to extract the spatial information of the image. It considers the number of pixels for every tonal value. The histogram of an image normally refers to a histogram of the pixel intensity values, and it's a graph displaying the number of pixels in an image at each distinct intensity value found in that image. The following co-occurrence matrix or distribution of co-occurrence matrix can be defined over an image to be the distribution of co-occurring pixel values of grayscale values or color values. The matrix equation is as following as,

$$C_{\Delta x.\Delta y}(i,j) = \sum_{x=1}^{n} \sum_{y=1}^{m} \begin{cases} 1, & if \ I(x,y) = i \\ 0, & otherwise \end{cases}$$

(1)

Where i and j are the pixel values. x and y are the spatial positions in the image I. the spatial relation for which matrix of Δx, Δy to be calculated. I(x, y) are indicated the pixel values of pixels is (x, y). The 'pixel value' of the image originally referred to the grayscale value of the specified pixel, but could be anything, from a binary on/off value to 32-bit color and beyond. 32-bit color will yield a 232×232 co-occurrence matrix. Co-occurrence matrices can also be parameterized in terms of a distance gp, and an angle of θ. Instated of an offset (Δx, Δy). In this method is the same as that of statistical pattern recognition. It considers a gray level values of pixels in particular image channels, their combination of local texture features and etc., it may be considering elements of a feature vector, one of which is assigned to each pixels. In the method understanding may be supervised or unsupervised process.

This method presented above work well with non-noisy data, and if the spectral properties determine classes sufficiently well. If noise or substantial variations in-class pixel properties are present, at the resulting image segmentation may have many small regions and which are misclassified. The following figure is shown in Figure 2.

$$\varepsilon = (f(x_0), f(x_i), \ldots\ldots, f(x_k))$$ (2)

$$x_i \in N(x_0) \; i=0,\ldots\ldots,k$$ (3)

Figure 2. Pixel neighborhood used in contextual image classification and 4&8-bit neighborhood

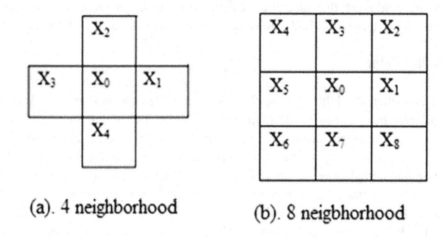

(a). 4 neighborhood   (b). 8 neigbhorhood

Contextual classification of image data is based on the Bayes minimum error classifier, for each pixel x0, a vector consisting of values is $f(x_i)$ of pixels in a specified neighborhood $N(x_0)$ is used as a feature representation of pixels x_0. The vector equation is 1 is followed.

Figure 3. Contextual image pixel classification algorithm

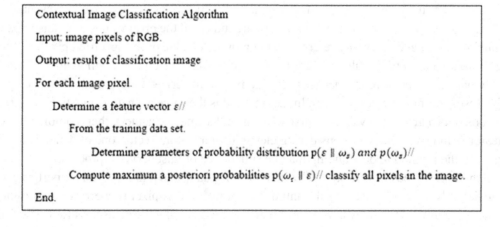

Contextual Image Classification Algorithm

Input: image pixels of RGB.

Output: result of classification image

For each image pixel.

    Determine a feature vector ε//

      From the training data set.

          Determine parameters of probability distribution $p(\varepsilon \parallel \omega_s)$ and $p(\omega_s)$//

          Compute maximum a posteriori probabilities $p(\omega_r \parallel \varepsilon)$// classify all pixels in the image.

End.

For each pixels of an image is classified using a corresponding vector ε from its neighborhood and so there are many vectors ε as there are pixels in an image. It based on spectral data of pixel x0 may classified into number of classes with similar probabilities distribution of p(ε||ωs), he information about labels in the neighborhood may increase confidence in one of those classes. If a majority of surrounding pixels are labeled as a members of a class ωr, the confidence that the pixel x0 should also be labeled ωi, increases. As shown in Figure 3.

Figure 4. Applied the histogram method for sample tiger image

Figure 4 shows that the histogram method applied for the two-year tiger image. The original color image is converted into gray scale image to a binary one of the thresholding. If the distribution is not like this, then it is unlikely that a better segmentation can be produced by thresholding. The performance of histogram equalization will increase the contrast and brightness p of dark and low contrast histogram equalization is implied to improve the contrast. A transformation $\mathcal{T}$ of the original brightness image p and q is given the formula.

$$q = \mathcal{T}\left(p\right) \tag{4}$$

The gray scale transformation for contrast enhancement is usually found automatically using the histogram equalization techniques. The following algorithm to perform the histogram equalization is follows:

This performance assumes that the intensity range of source and destination images is [0, G-1]. The results can be demonstrated on an image, applied on the histogram methods for a real time tiger image is as shown in Figure 5.

Figure 5. Algorithm for histogram equalization

Select the image from the image dataset.

Initialize the value G=0, length of I.

    For an m * n image of G gray scale levels.

        From the image histogram: scan every pixel and increment the relevant member of I -if the pixel p has intensity of g_p to perform.

        $I[g_p] = I[g_p] + 1$

    From the cumulative image histogram I_c

        $I_c[0] = I[0]$

        $I_c[p] = I_c[p-1] + I[p]$, p=1, 2... G-1.

Set

        $T[p] = round \left(\frac{G-1}{mn} Ic[p] \right)$

Rescan the image

Finally, output image with gray scale image g_p

        $g_p = T[g_p]$

3.2. Adaptive Histogram Equalization (AHE)

It may vary from simple histogram equalization in references to the adaptive method covers number of histograms, each similar to various section of the image, which is used to reorder the lightness value of the concern image. It is preferred for enhancing the local contrast of the image which results in more detailed picture. Normal histogram equalization customs the similar alteration resulting from the image histogram to modify all pixels. Adaptive histogram equalization technique recovers this singularity by altering each pixel with a conversion function consequent from a neighborhood region. The role of AHE method is used to improve the quality of the low contrast tiger image.

3.3. Color Pixel Pattern Matching

The color pixel pattern matching technique has to be used on every individual pixel to inter connect with other color pixel. They have every pixel of RGB color value starting and ending with 0 to 255. Color Pixel Pattern Matching is represented using multi-dimensional array and the value is calculated. Colors on the surface of the solid are fully saturated, i.e. pure colors, and the greyscale spectrum is on the axis of the solid. For these colors, hue is undefined. Conversion between the RGB model and the HSI model is quite complicated. The intensity is given by the equation:

$$i = \frac{R+G+B}{3} \tag{5}$$

Where i is an intensity value of RGB components, normalized to the range [0, 1]. The intensity is therefore just the average of the red, green and blue components.

$$s = 1 - \frac{\min(R,G,B)}{i} \tag{6}$$

$$1 - \frac{3}{(R+G+B)}\min(R,G,B) \tag{7}$$

where min(R,G,B), in the terms really just indicating the amount of white present. If any of R, G, and B value is zero, there is no white and they have a pure color. This technique of intensity is also called density, while color coding is one of the simplest examples for false color image processing.

$$f(x,y) = c_k \text{ if } f(x,y) \tag{8}$$

Intensity to color assignments are made according to the relation, where c_k is the color associate with the kth intensity interval of V_k defined by the partitioning planes at l=k-1 and l=k. the idea of planes is useful primarily for a geometric interpretation of the intensity technique and an alternative representation that defines the pixel range value is starting with 0 to 255 and grouping with each pixel has been representing with array value. Example R= [255 0 0] this is a red value, G= [0 255 0] and B= [0 0 255]. To change the RGB value in each array will be generate the different color in a pixels. At any color pixel can have a very unique value 0. The full color image is used often is to denote a 24-bit RGB color image. The total number of colors in a 24-bit RGB color image is (28)3=1, 67, 77, 216 as a possible colors in an RGB image. Megapixels refer to the total number of pixels in the captured image, an easier metric is raster dimensions which represent the number of horizontal and vertical samples in the sampling grid. An image with a 4:3 aspect ratio with dimension 2048x1536 pixels, contain a total of 2048x1535=3,145,728 pixels; approximately 3 million, thus it is a 3 megapixel image.

Figure 6. Image database is used to collect and store

Figure 6 is represented by the different collection of the real time tiger image database for different age group of tigers are stored in an image database. In the real time images of tiger are more helpful to identify the age of the individual tiger. And it based on the skin color, it is supposed to be RGB color pixels that is used to infer the age of the tiger.

3.4. Wiener Filter

A restoration method for deconvolution is inverse filtering, i.e., when the image is blurred by a known low pass filter, it is possible to recover the image by inverse filtering or generalized inverse filtering. The orthogonally theory of implies that the Wiener filter in Fourier domain can be expressed as follows:

$$W\left(f_1,f_2\right)=\frac{H^*\left(f_1,f_2\right)S_{xx}\left(f_1,f_2\right)}{\left|H\left(f_1,f_2\right)\right|^2 S_{xx}\left(f_1,f_2\right)+S_{\eta\eta}\left(f_1,f_2\right)} \tag{9}$$

Where $S_{xx}(f_1,f_2)$, $S_{\eta\eta}\left(f_1,f_2\right)$ power spectra of the original image and the additive are respectively noise, and $H(f_1,f_2)$ is the blurring filter. This filter is easy to divide into two parts, an inverse filtering part and noise smoothing part. It does not only perform the disconsolation by inverse filtering (high pass filtering), and it can remove the noise with a compression operation (low pass filtering). When the classical approach contains two separate steps like inverse filter and wavelet denoise. The algorithm for applying filtering in tiger image is as follows:

Figure 7. Classical wiener filter algorithm

✓ Load the image dataset.

✓ Initialize the process

✓ Add some noise to the original image.

✓ Noise image by Fourier transform used on the wavelet coefficient.

✓ Find the thresholding process for low and high pass frequency filter.

✓ To estimate the values of image signal with power spectrum of the original image.

$$S_{yy}^{per} = \frac{1}{N^2}[Y(k,l)Y(k,l)^*]$$

✓ Still another estimate which leads to a cascade implementation of the inverse filtering and the noise smoothing is

$$S_{xx} = \frac{S_{yy}-S_{\eta\eta}}{|H|^2}$$

✓ To estimate the vales of image or pixel with wiener filter formula. Equation

✓ Finally reconstruct the original image.

Figure 7 shows that the Wiener filtering and regularized inverse filtering that includes the estimation of the power spectrum of the original image inspires a new wavelet-based restoration procedure. Therefore, the wavelet coefficients of the image are better modeled to estimate the power spectrum, and they propose to exchange the order of the inverse filtering and wavelet transform. Wiener filtering techniques are applied to the original tiger image with a cascade implementation of the noise smoothing and inverse filtering. The images are listed as follows together with the PSNR, MSE, MNCC, AD, SC, and MD.

Figure 8. Image of tiger after applied Weiner filter technique

Figures 8 and 9 show that the output of the tiger image after applied wiener filter. The wiener filtering performs an optimal tradeoff between inverse filtering and noise smoothing, which produces more results that can compare with the Average filter, median filter, rank order, and Gaussian filter.

Sample Outputs on Filter Techniques

Figure 9. Applied four different noises filtering on sample tiger image

3.5. Contrast Limited Adaptive Histogram Equalization (CLAHE) Method

This technique does not require any predicted weather information to process the fogged image. Initially, it captures image by camera under foggy condition and then it is converted in to HSV color space from RGB color space. The images are altered since the human sense colors likewise as HSV signify colors. Furthermore, value component is treated by CLAHE deprived of completing hue and saturation (Noor et al., 2013). CLAHE is adopted for true color images and equalization is applied individually for all three colors space of RGB (Ikonomakis et al., 2000). The resultant components are combined together to produce equalized color image. CLAHE is mainly used for successfully enhancing low contrast tiger images. This technique divides the tiger images into related regions and determines equalization to each religion. The algorithm for applying CLAHE in tiger image feature enhancement is as follows:

Figure 10. Enhanced CLAHE algorithm

✓ Load the image dataset.
✓ Initialize the input parameters.

    Partition each tiger input image into number of equal size non-overlapping contextual regions, whose size is 8x8 blocks, each block corresponds to neighbor of 64 pixels.

    Compute the intensity histogram of each contextual regions of tiger.

✓ Clip limit is a threshold value which effectively alters image contrast.
✓ By applying transformation function each histogram is modified.
✓ Compute the histogram is transformed function to the CLAHE

$$gl=[glmax-glmin]*p(f)+glmin$$

✓ Compute the distribution gray level

$$gl=glmin-(1/a)*ln[1-p(f)]$$

✓ Find the neighboring tiles and combined by the bilinear interpolation of the image grayscale values
✓ Finally, to display the modified histogram images.

An example of the CLAHE enhanced image is shown in Figure 10 with non-uniform brightness. It is clear that the CLAHE method improves the information in the enhanced image by improving the contrast.

The AHE & CLAHE enhancement method is as show in Figure 11 respectively. Contrast enhancement is a process that makes the image features stand out more clearly by making optimal use of the color available on the display or output device. Contrast manipulations involve changing the range of values in an image in order to increase contrast. The following method, CLAHE is used to improve the visibility level of foggy image or pixels.

Figure 11. Applied enhancement method for AHE and CLAHE

a) Original Image   b) AHE Method   c) CLAHE Method

Sample Outputs for Enhancement Methods on AHE and CLAHE Methods and Histogram

The CLAHE enhancement method is employed to improve the quality level of the real time images of tiger. The histogram of an image normally refers to a histogram of the pixel intensity values and it's a graph showing the number pixels in an image at each different intensity value found in that image. To display the output result shown in Figure 12.

Figure 12. Comparison of different age of the tiger images with applied on CLAHE methods

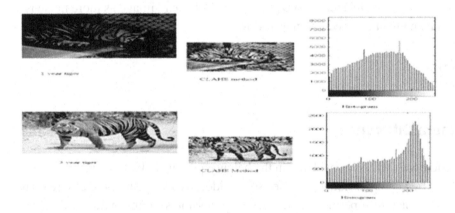

4. RESULTS AND DISCUSSIONS

The simulation for tiger image database pre-processing is done using MATLAB software. For comparing the performance of the noise removal peak signal to noise ratio metric is used.

4.1. Peak Signal-to-Noise Ratio

The value of higher SNR and PSNR specify a minor variance among the original and reassembled image. An imperative property of PSNR is that a minor three-dimensional shift of an image can source a large numerical misrepresentation but no visual distortion if all the mistake is intense in a trivial significant region (Sakuldee & Udomhunsakul, 2007). PSNR is computed using the following equation as follows:

$$PSNR = 10log_{10}\left(\frac{n}{MSE}\right)db \qquad (10)$$

4.2. Mean Square Error

In the field of image coding and computer vision works, the maximum recurrently used trials are eccentricities among the original and coded images of which the mean square error (MSE) or signal to noise ratio (SNR) being the most communal procedures (Bethel, 1997). MSE is calculated using the following equation as follows:

$$MSE = \frac{1}{n}\sum_{i=1}^{n}\left(Y_i - \widehat{Y}_i\right)^2 \qquad (11)$$

Where n is the number of data points, Y_i is the observed values of color pixels, $\widehat{Y}_i$ is the predicted pixel values of the image. The MSE value is shown in the table 2

4.3. Average Difference

A minor value of Average Difference (AD) stretches a "cleaner" image as more noise is condensed and it is calculated using the below equation as follows

$$AD = \frac{1}{n}\sum_{i=1}^{n}\left|Y_i - \widehat{Y}_i\right| \qquad (12)$$

4.4. Maximum Difference

Maximum difference (MD) is considered in the below equation and it has a respectable correlation with MOS for all verified compression techniques so it is ideal as a very simple measure by referring degree of the compressed picture superiority in diverse compression systems (Mrak, 2003).

$$\text{Maximum Difference (MD)} = Max\left(\left|Y_i - \widehat{Y}_i\right|\right) \qquad (13)$$

4.5. Normalized Correlation

The nearness among two digital images can also be enumerated in terms of association function. All the correlation-based procedures tend to 1, as the variance among two images incline to zero. As modification ration and correlation measures complement each other, lessening distance measures are make the most of correlation measure and Normalized Correlation is given as follows: Normalized Correlation

$$NK = \frac{\sum_{i=1}^{n} \left| Y_i . \widehat{Y}_i \right|}{\sum_{i=1}^{n} \left| Y_i \right|^2} \qquad (14)$$

4.6. Mean Absolutev Error

MAE is a measures the difference between two continuous variables. Adopt i and j are variables of paired observation that the express the same phenomenon.

$$MAE = \frac{\sum_{i=1}^{n} \left(Y_i - \widehat{Y}_i \right)}{n} \qquad (15)$$

MAE is computed in the above equation and large value of MAE resources that the image is of deprived quality. Where Y_i is the observed values and $\widehat{Y}_i$ is the predicted values and n is the number of objects.

4.7. Structural Correlation/Content

A familiar concept in image processing, that estimates the similarity of the structure of two signals is correlated. Then the decompressed image is of better quality and large value of SC means that the image is of poor quality.

$$SC = \frac{\sum_{i=1}^{n} \left(Y_i \right)^2}{\sum_{i=1}^{n} \left(\widehat{Y}_i \right)^2} \qquad (16)$$

Where Y_i is the observed values and $\widehat{Y}_i$ is the predicted values and n is the number of objects.

The above table 1 shows that the values of thresholding for color pixel classification with clustering is based on to infer the age of the tiger. This value is based on training dataset of the tiger image database and compared with real time captured camera trap image on tiger in the wild. The sample data are taken from the Berkeley Segmentation Dataset and Benchmark images were used. The table is denoted with individual age group of the tiger i.e., 1 to 15 years of the tiger images be collected in the Berkeley, to set the threshold values of each individual tiger and assuming that the age of the tiger is based on the range of the RGB and other color pixel values, the maximum seven color pixel values are tested for infer the age of the tiger. Example: R=40460, G=60450, B= 23020, Wh=493229, Bl=486656, Y=56132 these value is 1-year tiger and to check with real time camera trap tiger images to infer the age of the tiger.

Figure 13 is illustrated on analysis of thresholding values of each color pixels in the small precise to aged tiger image.

Table 1. Thresholding value for color pixels to infer the age of the tiger

Age	Red	Green	Blue	White	Black	Yellow
1	40460	60450	23020	493229	486656	56132
2	42304	64230	21045	697808	691235	89231
3	52134	53481	18963	1108946	1102373	84567
4	47589	56483	17586	500670	494107	74568
5	46589	52348	18456	705145	698575	86312
6	53245	64589	18576	764873	758302	87235
7	52356	66892	17589	745621	738324	85462
8	57468	65789	18456	883421	876851	72356
9	56487	54356	16578	612630	606060	56892
10 to 12	45681	47568	15689	747724	741154	45326
13 to 15	48956	49875	14782	805912	799340	56234

Figure 13. Analysis of thresholding value for the color pixels.

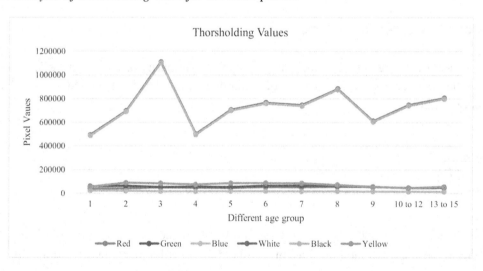

Table 2. Performance comparison on five different noise filters using Tiger Image

Methods	Selt and Pepper Noise					
	MSE	PSNR	MNCC	AD	SC	MD
AF	95.38	28.35	0.98	0.123	1.01	0.102
MF	70.2	19.6	0.95	0.178	1.04	0.183
WF	62.2	21.89	0.98	0.58	1.01	0.156
ROF	50.3	31.24	0.996	0.059	1.003	0.156
GF	95.38	28.35	0.98	0.123	1.01	0.102

The above table 2 shows that the performance comparison of five different Noise Filters (Average Filter or Mean Filter, Median Filter, Wiener Filter, Rank Order Filter, and Gaussian Filter) are applied on real time tiger images. As to calculate the MSE, PSNR, MNCC, AD, SD, and MD for the given images. These methods are compared taking into account both existing and proposed filtering techniques for the real time tiger image. When these techniques are compared with the other filter methods and much efficient result to be generated the Wiener Filter Method.

Figure 14. Analysis of five different noise filters applied in the real time tiger image dataset

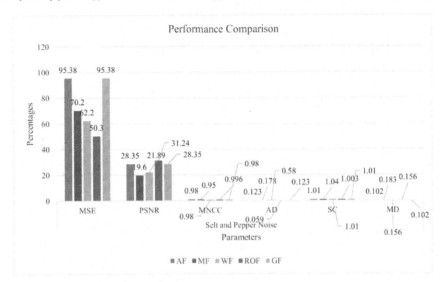

Figure 14 shows that the comparisons of noise parameters are compared with other proposed methods applied by real time tiger image dataset. It is observed that wiener filter is 21.89 db which is applied on salt and pepper noise presented tiger image. It is observed that MSE value of Rank order filter is very less value of 50.3 compared to other four filtering types. Weiner filter consist of 62.2 MSE value, Median filter consist of 70.2 MSE value and finally Gaussian and average filter consists of 95.38 MSE values which is very higher than other methods. the performance comparison of filter approaches using MNCC measure and it is observer that average filter, wiener filter and Gaussian filter scores same value of 0.98 whereas the Rank order obtains 0.996 of MNCC. The Average difference observed from the Figure 14 shows that average filter and Gaussian filter are similar with the value of 0.123. Whereas the wiener filter holds the value of 0.58 and median filter value is 0.178. The value of SC obtained by average, wiener and Gaussian filter are similar. Rank order filter holds the lowest value of SC. If the value of SC is high then it interprets poor quality of image.

Table 3. Performance comparison of AHE and CLAHE on tiger image database

Methods	MSE	PSNR	MNCC	AD	SC	MD
AHE	32.45	32.56	0.963	-6.42	0.095	128
CLAHE	20.31	35.2	1.30	-10.06	0.082	135

The above table 3 shows that the performance comparison different Enhancement Methods like (AHE and CLAHE Method) are applied on real time tiger images. As to calculate the MSE, PSNR, MNCC, AD, SD, and MD for the given images. These methods are compared taking into account both existing and proposed Enhancement techniques for the real time tiger image. When these methods are compared with the other techniques and much efficient result to be generated the CLAHE Method.

Figure 15 shows the feature enhancement of the tiger by applying CLAHE it produces sharpened image while comparing the existing approaches. The MSE value of CLAHE is low while comparing AHE. But PSNR value is high for CLAHE than AHE. Overall by applying CLAHE the process of age prediction using tiger image is greatly improvised.

Figure 15. Output of CLAHE based feature enhancement of tiger image

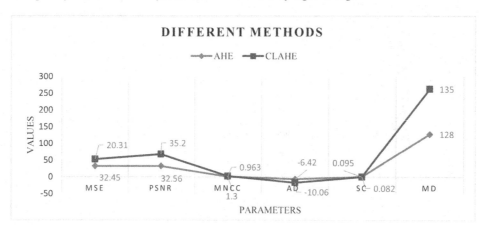

5. CONCLUSION

This article is mainly focuses on different filtering and enhancement methods like Mean, Median, Wiener filter and etc., and also applied for the Enhancement methods like AHE and CLAHE. The main goal of this article is to reduce the noise and improve the quality of the image or image pixels. This research work is to be done on assessing the age of the tiger using the color pixel based image classification and clustering is the main of the research work and to optimize the image filtering and enhancement methods that are used to remove the noise and to improve the quality of pixels or images and to optimization of reduce the noise level, processing performance measures in the result section, find the Accuracy and Error Rate by generating the better results is to real time tiger image database. The parameters are analyzing the real time tiger images and image dataset should be an effective result for comparison of these methods like PSNR values, MSE, MNCC, AD, SC, MD values are applied on salt and pepper noise filter image and also same parameters are used in the AHE and CLAHE methods. In the future, they have to applying on feature selection methods in the real time tiger image had to find the more accurate results.

REFERENCES

Allah, L. & Shimshoni, I. (2012). k Nearest Neighbor using Ensemble Clustering. In Data Warehousing and Knowledge Discovery. Springer Nature Switzerland AG.

Bethel, D. (1997). *Optimisation of still image compression techniques* [Ph.D. Thesis]. Bath University.

Das, S., & Konar, A. (2009). Automatic image pixel clustering with an improved differential evolution. *Applied Soft Computing, 9*(1), 226–236. doi:10.1016/j.asoc.2007.12.008

Dubey, S, Vijay, S., & Pratibha. (2018). A Review of Image Segmentation using Clustering Methods. *International Journal of Applied Engineering Research, Research India Publications, 13*(5).

Eini, SEiny, S. (2013). Image Segmentation using Gaussian Mixture Adaptive Fuzzy C-mean Clustering. *International Journal of Computer Science and Network Security, 13*(10), 114–118.

Elmoataz, A. & Chahir, Y. (2005). Skin-color detection using fuzzy clustering. *Proceedings in ISCCSP.*

Gautam, K., & Singhai, R. (2018). Color Image Segmentation Using Particle Swarm Optimization in Lab Color Space. *International Journal of Engineering Development and Research, 6*(1), 373-377.

Hassan, R. & Ema, R., & Islam, T. (2017). Color Image Segmentation using Automated K-Means Clustering with RGB and HSV Color Spaces. *Global Journal of Computer Science and Technology: F Graphics & Vision, 17*(2).

Hettiarachchi, R., & Peters, J. F. (2016). *Vorono I Region-Based Adaptive Unsupervised Color Image Segmentation.* Research Gate.

Ikonomakis, N., Plataniotis, K. N., & Venetsanopoulos, A. N. (2000). Color image segmentation for multimedia applications. *Journal of Intelligent & Robotic Systems, 28*(1/2), 5–20. doi:10.1023/A:1008163913937

Jhala, Y. V. & Sadhu, A. (2017). *Field Guide for Aging Tigers.* BMC Zoology.

Khan, Z., Ni, J., Fan, X., & Shi, P. (2017). An improved k-means clustering algorithm based on an adaptive initial parameter estimation procedure for image segmentation. *International Journal of Innovative Computing, Information and Control, 13*(5), 1509.

Mrak, M. (2003). Picture Quality Measures in Image Compression Systems. *EUROCON, 1*, 233–236.

Napoleon, D., Shameena, A., & Santhoshi, R. (2013). Color image segmentation using OTUS method and color space. *International Journal of Computer Applications.*

Nida, M., Zaitoun, Musbah, & Aqel. (2015). Survey on Image Segmentation Techniques. *Procedia Computer Science, 65*, 797 – 806.

Noor, A., Rafiqul I., Kha, Z., & Hasan, M. (2013). Comparative Study of Skin Color based Segmentation Techniques. *International Journal of Applied Information Systems, 5*(10).

Oscar Z., Au, C., Zou, R., Yu, W., & Tian, J. (2010). An adaptive unsupervised approach toward pixel clustering and color image segmentation. *Pattern Recognition, 43*, 1889–1906.

Panwar, P. & Gulati, N. (2013). Genetic Algorithms For Image Segmentation Using Active Contours. *Journal of Global Research in Computer Science, 4*(1), 34-37.

Ramani, RBalasubramanian, L. (2015, June). Retinal blood vessel segmentation employing image processing and data mining techniques for computerized retinal image analysis. *BBE, 85,* 1–17.

Rani, P., & Bhardwaj, R. (2016). An Approach of Colour Based Image Segmentation Technique for Differentiate Objects using MATLAB Simulation. *International Journal of Advanced Research in Computer and Communication Engineering, 5*(7), 553-556.

Sakthivel, K., Nallusamy, R., & Kavitha, C. (2014). Color Image Segmentation Using SVM Pixel Classification Image. *World Academy of Science, Engineering and Technology International Journal of Computer, Electrical, Automation, Control and Information Engineering, 8*(10), 1924–1930.

Sakuldee, RUdomhunsakul, S. (2007). Objective Performance of Compressed Image Quality Assessments. *PWASET, 26,* 434–443.

Taneja, A., Ranjan, P., & Ujjlayan, A. (2015). *A Performance Study of Image Segmentation Techniques, (ICRITO – 2015).* IEEE.

Tian, L., Han, L., & Yue, J. (2016). Research on Image Segmentation based on Clustering Algorithm. *International Journal of Signal Processing, Image Processing and Pattern Recognition, 9*(2), 1-12.

Wang, Y., & Wang, C. (2017). High Resolution Remote Sensing Image Segmentation Based On Multi-Features Fusion. *Engineering Review, 37*(3), 289–297.

Wang, Y., & Wu, G. (2014, June). Data mining base noise diagnosis and fuzzy filter design for image processing. *Computers & Electrical Engineering.* doi:10.1016/j.compeleceng.2014.06.010

Wang, Y. Q., & Liu, X. (2015). Improved support vector clustering algorithm for color image segmentation. *Engineering Review, 35*(2), 121–129.

Zanaty, E. A. (2012). Determining the number of clusters for Kernelized fuzzy c-means algorithms for automatic medical image segmentation. *Egyptian Informatics Journal, 13*(1), 39–58. doi:10.1016/j. eij.2012.01.004

Chapter 8
MRI High Dimensional Data and Statistical Analysis on Spinal Cord Injury Detection

K. Uday Kiran
Koneru Lakshmaiah Education Foundation, India

Ella Kalpana
TTWRDC, India

Prabha Shreeraj Nair
S. B. Jain Institute of Technology Management and Research, India

S. K. Hasane Ahammad
Koneru Lakshmaiah Education Foundation, India

K. Saikumar
 https://orcid.org/0000-0001-9836-3683
Koneru Lakshmaiah Education Foundation, India

ABSTRACT

The MRI spinal cord image-based injury detection is very complex in the current world. In this research, an advanced deep learning-based spinal injury detection algorithm has been proposed. The segmentation was performed with the Otsu technique. The feature extraction and training were performed with shape-based intensity parameters of nothing but standard deviation, variance, mean, and kurtosis. The testing can be possible with ResNet CNN technology. The classification has been performed through 167 layers of architecture. Finally, with confusion matrix accuracy of 98.43%, Recall97.34%, F 1 measure of 95.23%, and throughput of 96.76%.

DOI: 10.4018/978-1-6684-6971-2.ch008

Copyright © 2023, IGI Global. Copying or distributing in print or electronic forms without written permission of IGI Global is prohibited.

INTRODUCTION

With the exact coordinating for the treatment involved in the meaning of delimitation reasonable in claiming the pointless demonstration in the meaning of counteraction for the segmentation of which the tissue of ordinary kind has the space for organ in which associated for injury (Ahammad S K & Rajesh V, 2018). As a reason of the overexposure to the sunlight radiation, the radiosensitive structured organ can unequivocally differentiate for the prompt action provided with the inconvenience of the admitted person with illness and for instance causing the loss of motion or neuronal malfunction. To distinguish the pictures of CT in the spinal rope that exhibit the same properties as of the thorax with the information built in system. Moreover, a structure of anatomical based scheme is associated in keeping the assignment in combination to the delineate for the dependency in approach for the model designed further said to be the automatic SCI in merge to the techniques developed (Archip N et al., 2002). Nevertheless, a casing-oriented portrayal learned structure with full-scale capability is structured comprised to be as ASM (automatic spinal card injury finding mechanism) in the field of human thorax. Based on certain key parameters such as structure size, position decider in the oversees and the significant treatment for radiation (Peng Z et al., 2006). Based on several picture administration prepared for the arrangement of the solver to the treatment of the nuclear support in demand with the composite action of alleged structures, for instance snakes and thresholding of both kinds can be normalized for the standard action. The arrangement solver depends on various picture preparing administrators (Ahammad S H et al., 2020).

The PC with standard feature can withstand for the overall framework as per the investigations of the picture holding the material type of patient for bringing the approach to the acknowledgement for the rope spinal at the rate of accuracy in 92.5% in the trench of spinal exactly with 85% associated for standard actualized (Ahammad S H et al., 2019). The pictures for the therapeutic in parameter verification of the process in regard to the objects for the established data for the division of interest to the edges in over separating the information (Ahammad S K & Rajesh V, 2018). The system for over-division in which the articles are being subdivided for the components to be broke for constructing the cutoff limits in the evacuated reason of huge destruction. It is methodologically creating different points for the area in the respective undertaking for the insignificant problem of definition for the smooth structure in pre-separating organization in the prior database for the division making the inconvenience to the system (Ahammad S et al., 2019). The data acquired from the image is insinuated out of the issue in building the integral characteristics or attributes for the system in challenging the better outcome (Vijaykumar G et al., 2017).

The regions that are flanking are separated the moment the photograph has been made in order to less the division that is isolated in the concerned issue of closed loop system for the shape in which clear estimation is done. On the contrary, the estimation data for the division of interest to the edges in over separating the information (Inthiyaz S et al., 2019). The system for over-division in which the articles are being subdivided for the components to be broke for constructing the cutoff limits in the evacuated reason of huge destruction. It is methodologically creating different points for the area in the respective can be merged with the degree of functionality in similar frameworks of shade, surface, force, degree of shadiness, and many parameters involved for the high term creation of quantity builder suffered from the likelihood prompted in the technologies. The main strategy in controlling the pixel of the article in neighborhood (Kumar M S et al., 2019).

The numerical differentiation in consideration to the division of articles sweep for the enrolled schemed in small claim of the partition of the frameworks (Ahammad S H et al., (2019). The detachment of the framework is for the estimation went on the powers associated to the different existence of the curve fitting in almost near case to the objects that are usually capriciousness for employing the objects carrying lowest knowledge of power in the concerned challenges of photograph differentiates. To assess the contiguous issues of photograph for the aim to work the nearest part of structure a function is built named as (f) in a photograph (Kumar M S et la., 2019). The outcome produced is right away from the structured function in the scheme of the neighborhood product of the objects. The lines carrying the internal proportional score in which those points are settled at the farthest value of assembled with limitations of exactness with (F) in which the system symbolizes with the functional value (fn): Closeness Count = F (f1w1, f2w2, f3w3, ...) indicating with F as the work done at blended mode in enhancing the duplicated request for the most lesser count of the region from starting to weights at the range of wn for critically investigating the highlighted isolated in the concerned issue of closed loop system for the shape in which clear estimation is done (Myla S et al., 2019). On the contrary, the estimation data for the division of interest to the edges in over separating the information. The system for over-division in which the articles are being subdivided for the components to be broke for constructing the cutoff weights (Raj Kumar A et al., 2019).

Thus, the immediate action for the appropriate work in the field of division for the photograph created in underlining the application for the remedy casing to the picture for the strange technology in the transition states of low and high levels. The followed related studies are practically suggested about the distinct philosophies of the indication towards the work mostly being the estimation data for the division of interest to the edges in over separating the information (Gattim N K et al., 2019). The system for over-division in which the articles are being subdivided for the components to be broke for constructing the cutoff limits in the evacuated reason of huge destruction. It is methodologically creating different points for the area in the respective dealt with the surrounding estimations (Rajesh V et al., 2019). Overall, the approach proposed is presented in which the estimation caused with the breaking of blocks with the initial possibility of set of estimations inspiring the blueprint scheme for the division of photograph (Srinivasa Reddy K et al., 2019).

The theory demanded procedures related to division makes the photographs for the separation into various classes such as the acknowledgement towards the edge, low scale pictures, and extraction of territory (Narayana V Vet al., 2019). The assessment for the techniques that employed for the pictures for the therapeutic in parameter verification of the process regarding the objects for the established data for the division of interest to the edges in over separating the information. The system for over-division in which the articles are being subdivided for the components to be broke for constructing the cutoff limits in the evacuated reason of huge destruction additional division suggested for the kind of equipment in the feathery/non-fleecy the indication towards the work mostly being the estimation data for the division of interest to the edges in over separating the information (Reddy A P C et al., 2019). The system for over-division in which the articles are being subdivided for the components to be broke for devices, shading information, Markov Random Fields (MRFs) probabilistic models and additionally frameworks related to neural networks for the several picture administrations prepared for the arrangement of the solver to the treatment of the nuclear support in demand circumstances coming improvement (Xiao J R et al., 2007). Including important computations in the shading pictures for the centered exclusive data for division of expansion (Nagageetha M et al., 2017).

METHODOLOGY

The assessment made for the appeared study is figured for the foundation of particular analysis in the logical classification of low-level scheme of action (Stroman P W et al., 2014). Proportionally, the techniques related to the request for the division as depicted in figure 1 compose for the effort of the coordination made for the considering the composed photo, effort for the coordinated human level, the addressing of photo to start the process, the qualities sorted in the sequential number, and the natural movement for fundamental assessment (Fradet L et al., 2014). The computational division in which the isolation has begun for spatially created out the dependency rate in heed to the little pay in amusement (Rajesh V et al., 2019). Additionally, the characterization for the low-level reasonable proposed system has been depicted in the figure 1 for specially divided steps in the regions of property (Charan A S et al., (2019).

The division has assured the computation for vastly depended on the envisioned means of task in which the pictures for the MRI SCAN has the acknowledged between the sources of the diminished scale into the pictures of threshold limit for various applications (Saikumar K et al., 2019). The remote case of zones in SCI has predominantly made the features for the actional of infectious state in the patient data for the variability in the characteristics of data. One of the uninterrupted established data for the division of interest to the edges in over separating the information. The system for over-division in which the articles are being subdivided for the components to be broke for constructing the cutoff limits in the evacuated reason of huge destruction additional division suggested for the kind of equipment in the feathery/non-fleecy tests to learn the segmentation of image for the spinal cord MRI segmented for the remote identified or recognized zone of essential structures in the approach as shown in figure 1 represented with the blue squared shapes. Congregation based division calculates the frameworks debilitated in spatial manner of cloud for one-dimensional (1-D) scale of points in the center of the frame or structured shaded with the shape for the photo depending on the name of the structure collected in the technique (Kearney H et al., 2014).

In the essence of the approach so far collected, the best outlook favored in the ease of natural characteristics of execution in the part of concerned issue to be described feasibly (Saxton W O et al., 1979). Irrespective to the group of guidelines for the procedure built in the construction of the dimension at the high space possible appropriation is demonstrated. For instance, the procedure studied for the couple of divisions in packing designed strategy are dealing with several advanced machine learning techniques like fuzzy based network, neural systems, mean-shift division, tabu search, self-organizing map (SOM), and many others (Burger W et al., 2009). Out of which the most recognizing scheme is SOM. So far for the assessment of artificial based techniques, the applications dealing with the therapeutic descriptions to combinational work as the ANN does in stream to the Hopfield Network, and Multilayer Perceptron (MLP) are the selected networking systems. Moreover, the coordinated human level, the addressing of photo to start the process, the qualities sorted in the sequential number, and the natural movement for fundamental assessment. The computational division in which the isolation has begun for spatially rejoined system in uniting the subareas for conceivably separating the region of broad system to reduce the course of segments for the information associated to the picture. Instances of zone-based philosophies associated with remote distinguishing have been made here (Kang W X et al., 2009).

To Reduce the Segmentation of Certain Regions in the Complex Images of SCI by Employing MLS Algorithm

The crucial step in segmenting the image of SCI for analyzing the status of clinical action through the MLS is a predictable approach for dividing the picture. The medicinal utilization of the division associated to the picture for the constrained part of job in doing the task. Seeking for consideration the various attributes or parameters of the system involved in the extraction of feature of MRI image for the attractive reverberation of spinal line picture for the advancement in the proposed technique thereby, creating the downside loops of the system. The remote case of zones in SCI has predominantly made the features for the actional of infectious state in the patient data for the variability in the characteristics of data. One of the uninterrupted established data for the division of interest to the edges in over separating the information. The system for over-division in which the articles are being subdivided for the components to be broke for constructing the cutoff limits in the evacuated reason. Straight to the battle off period in exchanging the pictures at multi-scale for consecutive outcome reached for reproduction shifting in maintain the data in segmentation for the reason of loss in data over the period of interest.

The recommended procedure has been implemented and attempted on the MRI cerebrum picture material from diagnosis centers, healing center with cuts of 160 cuts for each person in adding to 3 people. The examining automated school assembly is Philips MR scanner and cut thickness is 1.5mm. To demonstrate the competence of the recommended strategy, a few and far between assessments have been achieved on the as of the thorax with the individual information built in system. Furthermore, a composition of anatomical based scheme is associated in preserving the assignment in combination to the delineate for the dependency in approach for the model designed further pictures with various attributes. Right off the bat, the examination is about the shape extraction of MRI spinal card picture. Thus, the SCI techniques for future programmed schemes are combined to the contemplate demyelination and deterioration in different spinal string sicknesses, for example, MS or cervical myelopathy.

Algorithm

The image in the context represents as the part of medical or others, whereas the monochrome represents the characteristics. GM and WM symbolize with the representation of color. In order to test the methodology for the idea creation to the change of the created cloud. Based on the methods comparison and pixel representation of image deprived of modules of single-scale and multiple-scale range for segmenting the images. Moreover, the attribution of image comprises of single and multiple attributes. As per the figure 1 depicted below the key functioning is divided based on the modules that are spatially blind and guided which represent the most important sections for segmenting the multi-level modules.

The wide range of intensities are depicted in the figure 2 vindicates the image, surface technological extraction of multi-level is employed over the clinical image and achieved better outcomes instead the comparison to the effects of segmentation. The following are the outcomes of the result analysis.

Figure 1. Multi-level segmentation block diagram

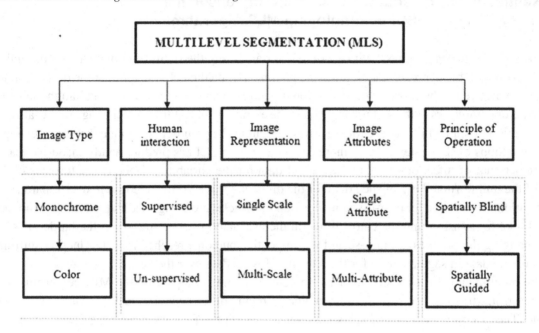

Figure 2. Multi-level functions

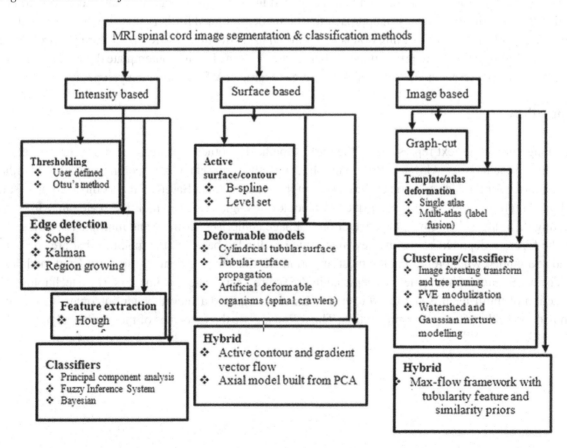

EXPERIMENTAL RESULTS

The major two nerves of spinal which certainly susceptible to the damage or infection that causes the problem for sciatic and radial for the methodology in the progress of MLS technique. Also, the cause for the paralysis into the improper modification in the reach of nerve compressed in the transfer of the structured parts in which the upper arm bone, underarm against the reaction of pain for the analysis made.

The automatic detection of SCCI image is depicted in the figure 3 for the problem in which MLS algorithm avoided in the detection of the image in segmenting for the information of patient listed in figure 4. Every image is obvious that SCI is displeased for clear bone structure in the observation, besides compared with the conventional methods resulting the better output. Therefore, the proposed method is compared with the existing and provided with the extraction rate at low level.

Figure 3. Human bodies focus on spinal card

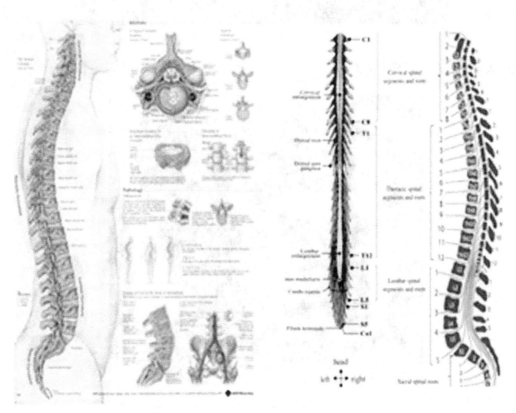

The employed method for the extraction of sub level for image selection of the patient for certain information is shown as the figure 5 and 6 demonstrates the train of echo in data of the length and rate of absorption. Finally, the data is chosen for the specified techniques in relative to the other techniques.

Figure 4. Patient -1 spinal cord

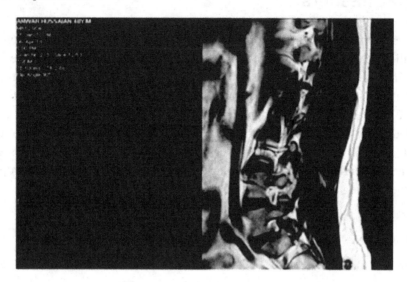

Figure 5. Detail images of Figure 3 sub

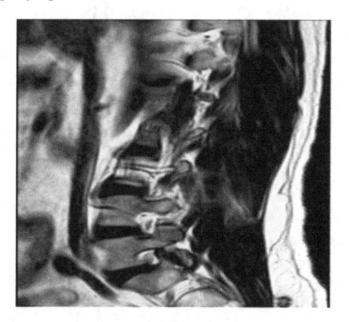

Figure 7 illustrates the segmentation of multi-level available dataset in the training period of image for the spinal cord information. The method of segmentation is further employed to the various types of disturbed noised for the aspect of eliminating the tracking for the noise in the regions of segmented section in the basis.

The segmentation of multi-level available dataset in the training period of image for the spinal cord information is depicted in figure 8 with the properties of statical analysis in attribute of each region of spinal line cord for the analysis of image.

Figure 6. Spinal cords of second patient

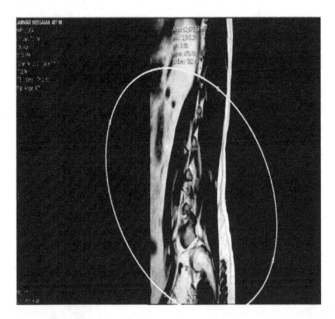

Figure 7. Evident multi-level segmentation process of patient-spinal

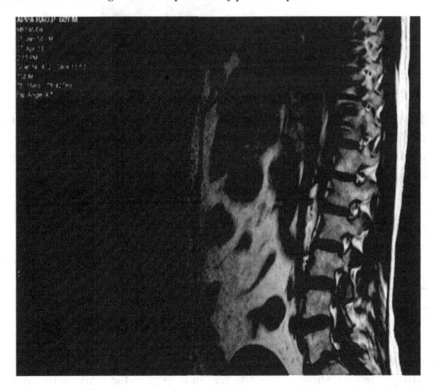

Figure 8. Spinal cord Injury data segments and its statistical properties.

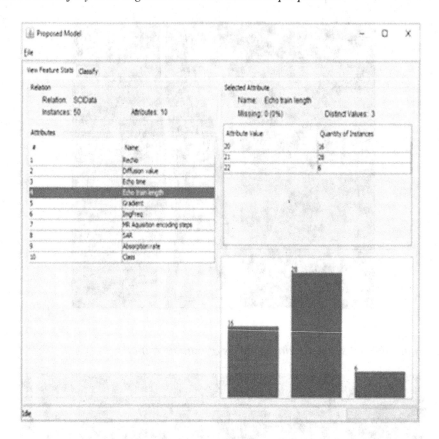

The segmentation of multi-level available dataset in the training period of image for the spinal cord information is depicted in figure 9 with the properties of statical analysis in attribute of each region of spinal line cord for the analysis of image for distinct values and missed value to associate with the validation to the regions of spinal cord.

Table 1. Comparison of proposed method to traditional methods

SNO	Parameter	Method	% Improvement
1	SCI	SVM	70
2	SCI-MLS	CT-MRI	90

The information of the suggested technology has been illustrated in table 1 for comparison with advanced and existing methods showing the progress in respect to the computational complexity and reliability.

Figure 9. SCI Training features and its sparsity values

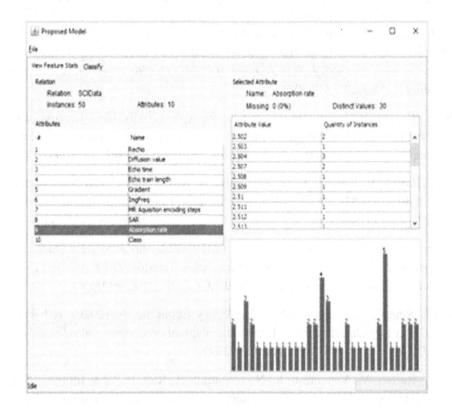

CONCLUSION

Ultimately, with the proposed mechanism the outcomes obtained achieve highest efficiency of 80% with exactness of increase 70%. Therefore, to locate the damages on the spinal cord the effective method is AUTOMATIC SCI-MLS technique.

FUTURE SCOPE

The particular importance in the estimation of CSA found to be the unique characteristics for the decade, eventually for investigating the inherent deception locations as (GM, WM tracts). Thus, the strategies built can suggestively support for reassuring longitudinal and multi- focus ponders, in addition considerate the way to spinal line composition to develop for the segmentation in hybrid manner as the measures to locate the improvement of subclinical medication to anticipate the potential prediction or accepting supervision.

REFERENCES

Ahammad, S. H., Rajesh, V., Hanumatsai, N., Venumadhav, A., Sasank, N. S. S., Gupta, K. B., & Inithiyaz, S. (2019). MRI image training and finding acute spine injury with the help of hemorrhagic and non hemorrhagic rope wounds method. *Indian Journal of Public Health Research & Development*, *10*(7), 404. doi:10.5958/0976-5506.2019.01603.6

Ahammad, S. H., Rajesh, V., Indumathi, U., & Charan, A. S. (2019). Identification of cervical spondylosis disease on spinal cord mri image using convolutional neural network-long short-term memory (Cnn-lstm) technique. *Journal of International Pharmaceutical Research*, *46*, 109–124.

Ahammad, S. H., Rajesh, V., Neetha, A., Sai Jeesmitha, B., & Srikanth, A. (2019). Automatic segmentation of spinal cord diffusion MR images for disease location finding. *Indonesian Journal of Electrical Engineering and Computer Science*, *15*(3), 1313–1321. doi:10.11591/ijeecs.v15.i3.pp1313-1321

Ahammad, S. H., Rajesh, V., & Rahman, M. Z. U. (2019). Fast and accurate feature extraction-based segmentation framework for spinal cord injury severity classification. *IEEE Access : Practical Innovations, Open Solutions*, *7*, 46092–46103. doi:10.1109/ACCESS.2019.2909583

Ahammad, S. H., Rajesh, V., Rahman, M. Z. U., & Lay-Ekuakille, A. (2020). A hybrid CNN-based segmentation and boosting classifier for real time sensor spinal cord injury data. *IEEE Sensors Journal*, *20*(17), 10092–10101. doi:10.1109/JSEN.2020.2992879

Ahammad, S. H., Rajesh, V., Venkatesh, K. N., Nagaraju, P., Rao, P. R., & Inthiyaz, S. (2019). Liver segmentation using abdominal CT scanning to detect liver disease area. *International Journal of Emerging Trends in Engineering Research*, *7*(11), 664–669. doi:10.30534/ijeter/2019/417112019

Ahammad, S. K., & Rajesh, V. (2018). Image processing based segmentation techniques for spinal cord in MRI. *Indian Journal of Public Health Research & Development*, *9*(6), 317. doi:10.5958/0976-5506.2018.00571.5

Ahammad, S. K., & Rajesh, V. (2018). Image processing based segmentation techniques for spinal cord in MRI. *Indian Journal of Public Health Research & Development*, *9*(6), 317. doi:10.5958/0976-5506.2018.00571.5

Archip, N., Erard, P. J., Egmont-Petersen, M., Haefliger, J. M., & Germond, J. F. (2002). A knowledge-based approach to automatic detection of the spinal cord in CT images. *IEEE Transactions on Medical Imaging*, *21*(12), 1504–1516. doi:10.1109/TMI.2002.806578 PMID:12588034

Burger, W., Burge, M. J., Burge, M. J., & Burge, M. J. (2009). *Principles of digital image processing* (Vol. 111). Springer.

Fradet, L., Arnoux, P. J., Ranjeva, J. P., Petit, Y., & Callot, V. (2014). Morphometrics of the entire human spinal cord and spinal canal measured from in vivo high-resolution anatomical magnetic resonance imaging. *Spine*, *39*(4), E262–E269. doi:10.1097/BRS.0000000000000125 PMID:24253776

Gattim, N. K., Pallerla, S. R., Bojja, P., Reddy, T. P. K., Chowdary, V. N., Dhiraj, V., & Ahammad, S. H. (2019). Plant leaf disease detection using SVM technique. *International Journal of Emerging Trends in Engineering Research*, *7*(11), 634–637. doi:10.30534/ijeter/2019/367112019

Inthiyaz, S., Prasad, M. V. D., Lakshmi, R. U. S., Sai, N. S., Kumar, P. P., & Ahammad, S. H. (2019). Agriculture based plant leaf health assessment tool: A deep learning perspective. *International Journal of Emerging Trends in Engineering Research*, 7(11), 690–694. doi:10.30534/ijeter/2019/457112019

Kang, W. X., Yang, Q. Q., & Liang, R. P. (2009, March). The comparative research on image segmentation algorithms. In *2009 First international workshop on education technology and computer science* (Vol. 2, pp. 703-707). IEEE. 10.1109/ETCS.2009.417

Kearney, H., Yiannakas, M. C., Abdel-Aziz, K., Wheeler-Kingshott, C. A., Altmann, D. R., Ciccarelli, O., & Miller, D. H. (2014). Improved MRI quantification of spinal cord atrophy in multiple sclerosis. *Journal of Magnetic Resonance Imaging*, 39(3), 617–623. doi:10.1002/jmri.24194 PMID:23633384

Kumar, M. S., Inthiyaz, S., Krishna, P. V., Ravali, C. J., Veenamadhuri, J., Reddy, Y. H., & Ahammad, S. H. (2019). Implementation of most appropriate leakage power techniques in vlsi circuits using nand and nor gate. *International Journal of Innovative Technology and Exploring Engineering*, 8(7), 797–801.

Kumar, M. S., Inthiyaz, S., Vamsi, C. K., Ahammad, S. H., Sai Lakshmi, K., Venu Gopal, P., & Bala Raghavendra, A. (2019). Power optimization using dual sram circuit. *International Journal of Innovative Technology and Exploring Engineering*, 8(8), 1032–1036.

Myla, S., Marella, S. T., Goud, A. S., Ahammad, S. H., Kumar, G. N. S., & Inthiyaz, S. (2019). Design decision taking system for student career selection for accurate academic system. *International Journal of Scientific and Technology Research*, 8(9), 2199–2206.

Myla, S., Marella, S. T., Goud, A. S., Ahammad, S. H., Kumar, G. N. S., & Inthiyaz, S. (2019). Design decision taking system for student career selection for accurate academic system. *International Journal of Scientific and Technology Research*, 8(9), 2199–2206.

Nagageetha, M., Mamilla, S. K., & Hasane Ahammad, S. (2017). Performance analysis of feedback based error control coding algorithm for video transmission on wireless multimedia networks. *Journal of Advanced Research in Dynamical and Control Systems, 9*(Special Issue 14), 626-660.

Narayana, V. V., Ahammad, S. H., Chandu, B. V., Rupesh, G., Naidu, G. A., & Gopal, G. P. (2019). Estimation of quality and intelligibility of a speech signal with varying forms of additive noise. *International Journal of Emerging Trends in Engineering Research*, 7(11), 430–433. doi:10.30534/ijeter/2019/057112019

Peng, Z., Zhong, J., Wee, W., & Lee, J. H. (2006, January). Automated vertebra detection and segmentation from the whole spine MR images. In *2005 IEEE Engineering in Medicine and Biology 27th Annual Conference* (pp. 2527-2530). IEEE.

Raj Kumar, A., Kumar, G. N. S., Chithanoori, J. K., Mallik, K. S. K., Srinivas, P., & Hasane Ahammad, S. (2019). Design and analysis of a heavy vehicle chassis by using E-glass epoxy & S-2 glass materials. *International Journal of Recent Technology and Engineering*, 7(6), 903–905.

Rajesh, V., Saikumar, K., & Ahammad, S. K. H. (2019). A telemedicine technology for cardiovascular patients diagnosis feature using knn-mpm algorithm. *Journal of International Pharmaceutical Research*, 46, 72–77.

Reddy, A. P. C., Kumar, M. S., Krishna, B. M., Inthiyaz, S., & Ahammad, S. H. (2019). Physical unclonable function based design for customized digital logic circuit. *International Journal of Advanced Science and Technology*, *28*(8), 206–221.

Saikumar, K., Rajesh, V., Ramya, N., Ahammad, S. H., & Kumar, G. N. S. (2019). A deep learning process for spine and heart segmentation using pixel-based convolutional networks. *Journal of International Pharmaceutical Research*, *46*(1), 278–282.

Saxton, W. O., Pitt, T., & Horner, M. (1979). Digital image processing: The Semper system. *Ultramicroscopy*, *4*(3), 343–353. doi:10.1016/S0304-3991(79)80044-3

Srinivasa Reddy, K., Suneela, B., Inthiyaz, S., Kumar, G. N. S., & Mallikarjuna Reddy, A. (2019). Texture filtration module under stabilization via random forest optimization methodology. *International Journal of Advanced Trends in Computer Science and Engineering*, *8*(3), 458–469. doi:10.30534/ijatcse/2019/20832019

Stroman, P. W., Wheeler-Kingshott, C., Bacon, M., Schwab, J. M., Bosma, R., Brooks, J., Cadotte, D., Carlstedt, T., Ciccarelli, O., Cohen-Adad, J., Curt, A., Evangelou, N., Fehlings, M. G., Filippi, M., Kelley, B. J., Kollias, S., Mackay, A., Porro, C. A., Smith, S., & Tracey, I. (2014). The current state-of-the-art of spinal cord imaging: Methods. *NeuroImage*, *84*, 1070–1081. doi:10.1016/j.neuroimage.2013.04.124 PMID:23685159

Vijaykumar, G., Gantala, A., Gade, M. S. L., Anjaneyulu, P., & Ahammad, S. H. (2017). Microcontroller based heartbeat monitoring and display on PC. *Journal of Advanced Research in Dynamical and Control Systems*, *9*(4), 250–260.

Xiao, J. R., Gama, B. A., & Gillespie, J. W. Jr. (2007). Progressive damage and delamination in plain weave S-2 glass/SC-15 composites under quasi-static punch-shear loading. *Composite Structures*, *78*(2), 182–196. doi:10.1016/j.compstruct.2005.09.001

Chapter 9
Enterprise Transformation Projects/Cloud Transformation Concept:
The Compute System (CTC–CS)

Antoine Toni Trad
iD https://orcid.org/0000-0002-4199-6970
IBISTM, France

ABSTRACT

This chapter presents the fundaments of the cloud transformation concept (CTC), and this concept is a basic component of the author's framework. The implementation of the CTC compute system (CTC-CS) is supported the author's applied holistic mathematical model (AHMM) for CTC (AHMM4CTC) and many research works on compute systems (CS), mathematical models, artificial intelligence (AI), and business/financial/organizational transformations projects. The AHMM is based on cross-functional research on an authentic and proprietary mixed research method that is supported by his own version of an AI search tree, which is combined with an internal heuristic's algorithm. The main focus is on CTC-CS requirements and transformation strategy. The proposed AHMM4CTC based CTC-CS is a virtual secured computing environment which uses an integrated empiric decision-making process. The CTC-CS is supported by a real-life case of business transformation project, which needs a Cloud infrastructure that is supported by the alignment of various existing Cloud standards.

INTRODUCTION

The CTC-CS is based on research resources related to Cloud CSs and Cloud security, in order to offer a set of transformation recommendations, which can be applied to enable Cloud based transformations. The CTC-CS strategy is a generic Cloud driven approach that uses Enterprise Architecture (EA) and any type of CP, like the GCP. The GCP includes various CS resources that offer different levels of controls, features, and Information and Communication Systems (ICS) management and design support. CS re-

DOI: 10.4018/978-1-6684-6971-2.ch009

Copyright © 2023, IGI Global. Copying or distributing in print or electronic forms without written permission of IGI Global is prohibited.

sources need different levels of provisioning, which depend on the used CS service. CS topics include: 1) Use of preemptible and standard Virtual Machines (VM) in Compute Engines (CE); 2) App Engine (AE) in two forms: Standard (AES) and AE Flexible (AEF); 3) Design of Kubernetes clusters; and 4) deploying cloud functions (CF). CSs use the infrastructure-as-code (IaC) for network configuration and infrastructure provisioning. The CTC-CS in the case of the GCP, includes the following activities and components: 1) Designing CSs; 2) relating CSs and use cases (UC); 3) CE's integration; 4) AE's integration; 5) Kubernetes engine (KE) integration; 6) CF's usage; 7) CS provisioning; 8) security and advanced design issues; 9) managing states in distributed CSs; 10) Data flows and pipelines; and 11) Monitoring and alerting. CE is Google's Infrastructure as a Service (IaaS) concept and the core functionality provided by CE is VMs. AE is a Platform as a Service (PaaS) concept, where AE users do not have to configure servers, but they use applications that run in AEs; where there are two types of AE: AES Standard and AEF. KE is a managed service offering cluster management and container orchestration. KE allocates cluster resources, manages containers, performs health checks, and manages VM lifecycles using CE's instance groups. CFs is a serverless compute service for event processing, and it is designed to execute code in response to events. Other CTC-CS aspects when designing the platform, are managing state in distributed systems, data flows, and monitoring and alerting; and above all the just-in-time AI requests (Sullivan, 2020).

Keywords: Cloud, Compute Systems, Artificial Intelligence, Enterprise Architecture, Mathematical Models, Development Cycles, Requirements, Strategic and Critical Business Systems, Business Transformation Projects, Critical Success Areas, Performance Indicators, Software (re)engineering and Strategic Vision.

BACKGROUND

This chapter's background combines: CTC-CS, AI, cloud security, development, and operations for CTC (DevOps4CTC) implementation strategy, knowledge management system for CTC (KMS4CTC), EA, heuristics/mathematical models, ICS management, and business transformation. The CTC-CS is a generic and cross-business that interacts with a reasoning method which manage sets of critical success factors (CSF) that can be used by an organizational transformation projects (or simply the *Project*). This chapter uses an insurance case (Jonkers et al., 2012a). This chapter is a continuation of many years of research and development project for CTC (RDP4CTC) on various *Project* aspects. The CTC-CS is business driven and is agnostic to any applied problem domain (APD). It is founded on a genuine research framework that in turn is based on many existing industry standards, like the architecture development method for CTC (ADM4CTC) (The Open Group, 2011a, 2011b). The Business Transformation Manager, Cloud architect or enterprise architect (or simply the *Manager*) can integrate CTC-CS in the *Entity's* architecture roadmap, where CTC-CS' must deliver the path for integrating the Cloud with the ADM4CTC, in all *Project's* activities. The RDP4CTC is based on literature review process for CTC (LRP4CTC), a qualitative analysis for CTC (QLA4CTC) methodology and on a proof of concept (PoC), used to solve the research question (RQ), in which the *Manager's* role is crucial and his decisions are aided by using the decision making system (DMS for CTC (DMS4CTC) (Agievich, 2014). Many CSFs influence CTC-CS's integration, like: 1) CS interface mechanisms; 2) Managing risks; 3) *Entity* resources mapping to CTC requirements; 4) CTC skills; 5) CTC security, infrastructure and requirements technological support; 6) Tests Capacities; and 7) Monitoring and control subsystem. A Cloud based systems approach is for the CTC-CS because the synchronizing of resources can be a problematic. There is extreme pressure to implementation CTC so the *Entity* becomes agile; that needs Cloud's high performances, security, availability, and AI capable. Exaggerated pressure is the main cause that *Projects* fail.

FOCUS OF THE ARTICLE

Cloud enabled EA methodologies, such as The Open Group's Architecture Framework's (TOGAF) and its ADM4CTC, which support is needed for the CTC. Actual Cloud techniques for *Project* focus on isolated tools, services, processes and CSs of the *Entity*. Minimal modelling technics is need for the CTC-CS which used standard CS and security frameworks to align with other CPs, AI based ADM4CTC, and atomic Building Blocks (aBB). This chapter also illustrates how *Projects* can benefit from using the CTC and proposes an adequate RDP4CTC.

THE RESEARCH AND DEVELOPMENT PROCESS FOR CTC

The TDP4CTC RQ is: "Which Cloud characteristics and support is needed for in the implementation of an *Entity* CP and CSs?". Where the kernel of this research is based on the Heuristics Decision Tree (HDT) and CSFs (and areas). A Critical Success Area (CSA) is a category (or set) of CSFs where in turn a CSF is a set of Key Performance Indicators (KPI), where a KPI maps (or corresponds) to a single CS requirement. For a given CTC-CS requirement or problem, the *Project* identifies sets of CSAs, CSFs and KPIs, for the DMS4CTC and map them to CTC-CS requirements. Hence the CSFs are important for the mapping between CTC-CS requirements, resources, and DMS4CTC (Peterson, 2011). Therefore, CSFs reflect CSAs that must meet the *Project's* goals and constraints. Measurements technics, which are provided by the Transformation, Research, Architecture, Development framework (*TRADf*), are used to evaluate performance in each CSA, where CSFs can be internal or externa. Once the initial sets of CSFs and CSAs have been identified, then the *Project* can use the DMS4CTC to deliver solutions for CTC-CS problems. The CSF-based RDP4CTC uses the AI/HDT based DMS4CTC, where in RDP4CTC's phase 1 (represented in automated tables), which form the empirical part of the RDP4CTC, checks the following CSAs: 1) RDP4CTC, synthesized in Table 1; 2) ICS, synthesized in Table 2; 3) ADM4CTC, synthesized in Table 3; 4) The DMS and KMS, synthesized in Table 4; 5) The APD; which is in this research chapter the CTC-CS, synthesized in Table 5; and 6) This chapter's outcome Table 6. The CTC-CS delivers recommendations on how to align *Project's* Cloud resources by using *TRADf*.

The Framework-TRADf and Related Works

The CTC-CS alignment strategies manage the *Entity's* Cloud resources and Microartefacts' which used various types of technologies. *TRADf*, supports various types of technologies. The CTC-CS is complex and is a risky approach, because: 1) Complex Cloud resources management; 2) Granularity level; 3) Processes synchronization; 4) Mapping mechanisms; and 5) Implementation of existing components. A system approach for CTC based *Projects* (Daellenbach & McNickle, 2005), and as mentioned, the focus is on the CS. CTC-CS is generic and can be applied to any CP. This chapter is a part of many years research cluster that has produced a large set of articles and *TRADf*; and parts of previous works are reused for the better understanding of this complex iterative research; like ; and related works are: 1) The Artificial Intelligence Services (CTC-AIS) (Trad, 2022b); 2) The CTC Holistic Security Integration (Trad, 2022c); 4) The CTC Business Process Management (Trad, 2022d); 5) The Business Transformation Framework and Enterprise Architecture Framework for Managers in Business Innovation-Knowledge and Intelligence Driven Development (Trad & Kalpić, 2019a); 6) The Business Transformation Enterprise Architecture Framework-intelligent Strategic Decision Making System (Trad & Kalpić, 2019b); 7) The Business Transformation Framework and Enterprise Architecture Framework for Managers in Business Innovation- Knowledge Management in Global Software Engineering (Trad & Kalpić, 2019c); and 8) Using Applied Mathematical Models for Business Transformation (Trad & Kalpić, 2020a), this book has to read to understand the AHMM, HDT and this RPD4CTC structures. If all facts are only referenced, it would have been tedious to understand this RDP4CTC which is based on an Empirical Engineering Research Model (EERM) (The Open Group, 2011a).

Empirical Engineering Research Model

The EERM is optimal for engineering projects and it uses an authentic mixed method that is a natural complement to Quantitative Analysis for CTC (QNA4CTC) and QLA4CTC research methods, to deliver empirical and &feasible concepts, which use a holistic approach for mixed methods. Such a mixed approach is needed because of the high failure rates in such transformations and that is why it is important to refer to the *Using Applied Mathematical Models for Business Transformation* (Trad & Kalpić, 2020a), to understand the underlying AHMM, HDT and this RPD4CTC structures and concepts. If all facts are to be explained in detail or only referenced, it would have been tedious to understand this RDP4CTC which is based on the EERM. The QNA4CTC and QLA4CTC methods are compatible and the difference is in the scope and depth of the research process. EERM's validity checks if the RDP4CTC is acceptable as a contribution to existing scientific (and engineering) knowledge. The author wants to convince the valuable reader(s) the proposed recommendations and the related PoC, are valid and applicable. In engineering, a PoC is a design and software engineering prototype of a testable RQ where one or more CSFs (or independent variables, in theoretical research) are processed to evaluate their influence on the EERM's dependent variables. The PoC permits to evaluate with precision the CSFs and if they are related, whether the cause–effect relationship exists between these CSFs and CSAs. The CTC-CS uses EA and ICS standards (The Open Group, 2011a).

RDP4CTC's CSFs

Based on the LRP4CTC, the most important CSFs are presented in Table 1. zzzz

The CSF-based RDP4CTC uses the DMS4CTC, for its Phase 1 (represented in automated decision tables), which forms its empirical, in which it checks the selected CSAs; and where Table 1 (and the chapter's tables) is the synthesis of all CSA's CSFs. The Tables' processing was influenced by the Object Management Group's (OMG) Decision Model and Notation (DMN), where the DMN can be used for the specification of business decisions and business rules. DMN is optimal for initial checking based on decision making (OMG, 2022).

Table 1. CSFs that have the average of rounded 9.2.

Critical Success Factors	KPIs		Weightings
CSF_RDP4CTC_Standards	Feasible	▾	From 1 to 10. **09 Selected**
CSF_RDP4CTC_CSF_CSA_Integration	Proven	▾	From 1 to 10. **10 Selected**
CSF_RDP4CTC_Complexity	High	▾	From 1 to 10. **08 Selected**
CSF_RDP4CTC_EERM	Proven	▾	From 1 to 10. **10 Selected**
CSF_RDP4CTC_TRADf	Possible	▾	From 1 to 10. **09 Selected**
CSF_RDP4CTC_LRP4CTC	Feasible	▾	From 1 to 10. **09 Selected**

valuation

ICS' ROLE

ICS Related Cloud Basics

ICS' evolution has enabled CTC to support distributed systems, where the integration of CSs is an important CS for the *Entity's* robustness, and sustainability. Therefore, the stability of an *Entity*, depends on the CTC, that includes a framework to manage distributed CSs, which are used to improve the *Entity*'s Time To Market (TTM) related activities. The CTC-CS can be used in all phases of a *Project* and is based on existing competitive Cloud concepts, best practices, agility, and aBB based services architecture. The CTC supports *Projects*, by applying the Cloud, to synchronize all its activities. The main problem for *Projects* is to unbundle its legacy ICS and use an aBB based Cloud. CP is the on-demand availability for transformed ICS and its aBBs/resources, like Cloud subsystem, and CSs' capacities, which can be interfaced by actors. *Entity* wide Clouds have business/technical operations and functions distributed over various locations (data centers). CP is based on sharing of resources to support business coherence and uses the *pay-as-you-go* business model; such a model reduces capital expenses but can also generate unexpected operating expenses, when wrongly used. As shown in Figure 1, CP includes a group of networked components providing services, which do not need to be individually located. The CTC-CS provides an entire managed suite of ICS platform components, which can be designed internally (Wikipedia, 2022a).

Entity's Private CP (PCP), enables the processing of its business activities, which include a large set of applications and resources. The *Entity's* set of applications and resources are managed by the PCP, where applications are used to serve end clients. The DMS4CTC is the base of the and CTC-CS to support the *Entity*'s business capabilities to operate in many PCP/ICS, financial and business fields, like, business data management, security management, business services, policy making, regulatory and governance activivies. The CTC uses central domains, like EA, CP, and services' coordination; where a PCP can built on existing patterns (Cloud Computing Patterns, 2022). This RDP will offer a set of recommendation to support the *Entity*'s evolution (Trad, 2022a).

Figure 1. The CP
(Wikipedia, 2022a)

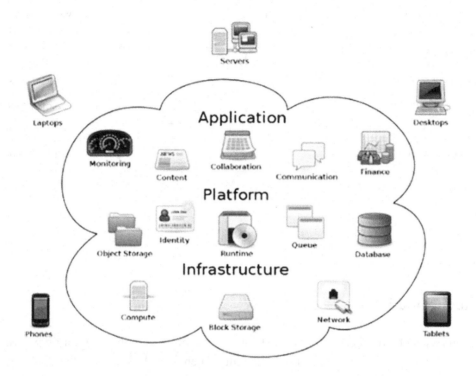

CP and CTC's Evolution

Entities have accelerated their use of Cloud providers, to become agile and the main differences between Cloud providers needs strategic *Project's* vision and decision. Where in the case of public Cloud IaaS can offer services under the following criteria(s) (Bala et al.,, 2021): 1) *If the cloud offering has publicly available for more than three years*; knowing that a minimum of $1 billion USD in the year 2020 was made in the public cloud by using IaaS and PaaS; and 2) *If the cloud solution offering has been openly available for less than three years*. The CTC-CS supports Business Process Management (BPM) usage in the context of a CP. There are many BPM solutions for CPs, whereas most BPM platforms are not optimally designed for the CP; and most used are *Appian, Pegasystems, and ProcessMaker*. CPs need to integrate BPMs that bring the *Entity* many tangible benefits, like: 1) Speed in development and design of business scenarios; 2) Provides reliable and available BPM environments; 3) Availability by using servers; and 4) *Pay-as-you-go* pricing concept, makes *Entities* pay for the resources they consumed.

By selecting a BPM platform with a optimal cloud support and *Project* architects (McClintock, 2020) 1) *Scalability and minimal maintenance*; 2) *Business automation for accessibility*; 3) *Agility and connectivity*, to enable BPM platforms; and 4) CP *Security*. CTC's structure must contain the following (Gupta, 2019): 1) Basic elements to support evolution; 2) Compatible with main CP providers, like Microsoft Azure, GCP... As shown in Figure 3; 3) Private CPs are accessible only to *Entity*'s employees; and Public CPs provide service to external clients and DevOps4CTC operations; 4) Benefits improvements; 4) Handles massive processing; 5) On demand strategies; and 6) The use of combined models: which combine PaaS, SaaS, IaaS, Services-based Application Programming Interface (API)… To support *Project's* readiness.

Figure 2. Magic Quadrant for the CTC
(Bala et al., 2021).

Figure 3. CP's evolution
(Gupta, 2019).

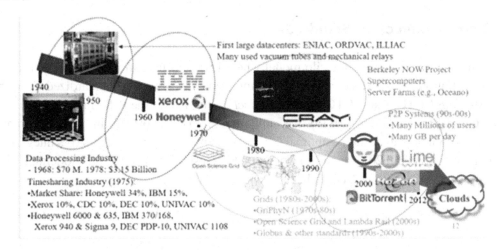

Business Transformation Readiness

The CTC supports all *Project* tasks, including the tools usage, processes, and CP management. Important advances in CPs' processes, discipline, skills, and methodologies to enhance *Enterprise Capacity to Execute*, which is the *Entity's* ability to perform all the tasks including decision making within time constraints. There exist non-ICS-specific processes, discipline, and skills to deal with this type of endeavor. The CTC can deal with *Project's* management issues (The Open Group, 2011a). Managing CP's infrastructure implies that the modeling the ICS that is based on: Resources sharing, High business availability, and Load-balancing. CP's security is important, and the *Project* defines how to design and implement security concepts and standards. Today there are many standards and they are applicable and help in the unbundling of legacy ICSs. An important CSF for *Projects* is to use aBBs based CTC strategy (The Open Group, 2011a); where such aBBs must respect standards. *Entity's* activities are achieved by combining various synchronized CSs to promote automation. There are no precise recommendations of such an aBB based CTC strategy, but there are some technics related to organizational services, and CP controls.

aBB Based CP

aBB based CP supports the interaction of *Project* resources, in a synchronized manner, by using the ADM4CTC to assist CTC-CS activities (The Open Group, 2011a). The CTC includes mapping mechanisms that use HDT based scenarios to support CP's integration and to avoid problems. The CTC-CS supports a *Project* by offering aBB mappings to handle various types of common and AI services. The author recommends using aBBs mapping construct, where the major set of aBBs are developed in portable code packages.

ICS's CSFs

Based on the LRP4CTC, the most important CSFs are presented in Table 2.

EA AND CTC'S INTEGRATION

The CTC and Architecture Standards

Legacy architecture layers represent a silo model where it is very hard to melt them down into a CP; in fact, it is a set of business and technology silo components. Moving to a standardized CP is the first step to a *just-enough* CTC. Using CTC-CS, the *Project* can transform the ICS platform into a dynamic aBB based CP (The Open Group, 2011a). EA supports the CTC-CS by offering: 1) The Architecture Capability Understanding to adapt the optimal CP; 2) As shown in Figure 4, TOGAF's integration with the CTC (The Open Group, 2011a); and 3) Tools for Business Architecture and Modeling, where the *Project* focuses on designing the CTC and delivering of PCP.

Table 2. CSFs that have the rounded average of 8.90.

Critical Success Factors	HMM enhances: KPIs	Weightings
CSF_ICS_CP_Basics	Proven	From 1 to 10. **10 Selected**
CSF_ICS_Standards	Proven	From 1 to 10. **10 Selected**
CSF_ICS_aBBs	Complex	From 1 to 10. **08 Selected**
CSF_ICS_CTC_Evolution	Complex	From 1 to 10. **08 Selected**
CSF_ICS_BTR	Possible	From 1 to 10. **09 Selected**
CSF_ICS_Development_Agility	Complex	From 1 to 10. **08 Selected**
CSF_ICS_Security	Complex	From 1 to 10. **08 Selected**
CSF_ICS_ADM4CTC_Automation	Proven	From 1 to 10. **10 Selected**

valuation

Figure 4. TOGAF's main phases
(The Open Group, 2011a).

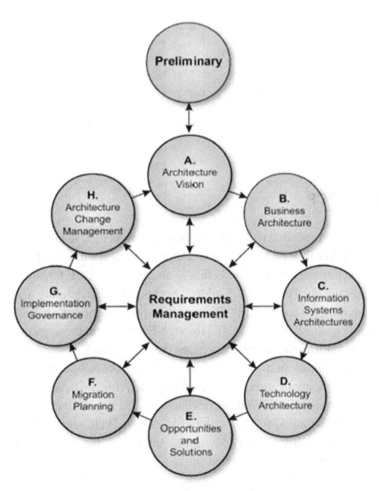

Designing the CTC Based PCP

The CTC based PCP is designed as a set of hosted CSs and Cloud models by using EA and the *On Premises Hosting Model*, as shown in Figure 5, where the *Entity* is responsible for its PCP (Charles, 2017).

The IaaS Hosting Model, represents hosting in both *On Premise* and in the *Cloud*, where the *Entity* manages its PCP and all its components like CSs and Operating System (OS), as shown in Figure 6.

Figure 5. On Premises Hosting Model
(Charles, 2017).

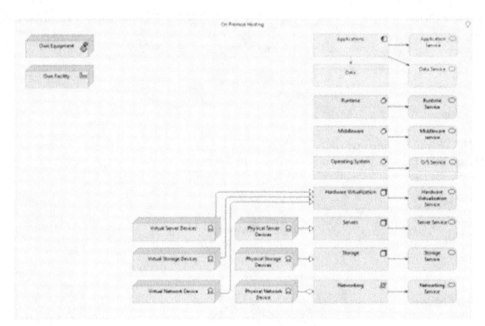

EA Based CTC and PCP

EA based CTC (EAI4CTC) is needed to transform *Entity's* fragmented legacy of processes (both semi-manual and automated) into a PCP that is agile and is supportive of the defined *Project* strategy. *Projects* need effective operation's management of CSs that is an important CSF for their successes and an to achieve competitive advantage. The CTC-CS addresses this need, by defining a strategic PCP context for the evolution of the *Entity*. To support PCP's architectural transformation, it is essential to develop an appropriate business capability for EAI4CTC, through *Entity's* structures, roles, responsibilities, and processes. EAI4CTC's maturity assessment, includes the following EAI4CTC's: 1) Governance processes, organization, roles, and responsibilities; 2) Architecture skills assessment; 3) Skills Framework for managing business, data, application, and technology activities; 4) Assess Business Transformation Readiness' (BTR) to quantify the *Entity's* readiness; 5) BTR's risks and mitigation activities, by identifying risks associated with EAI4CTC's vision; 6) Confirm BTR's feasibility, to review the results from the previous iteration; 7) Improves TTM; and 8) Impact on the *Architecture Roadmap and the Implementation, Migration Strategy*, and needed skills.

Figure 6. IaaS Hosting Model
(Charles, 2017).

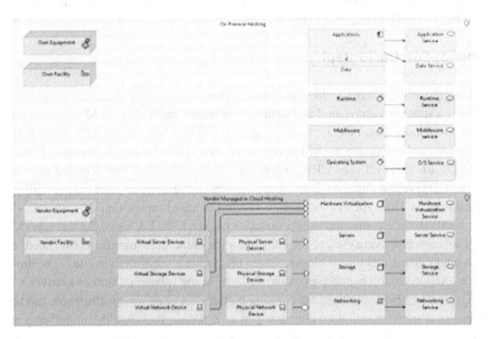

EAI4CTC Based CTC Skills

CTC and modeling strategy, comprise: PCP implementation, UC design, BPM integration, Strategic planning, services modeling, etc... The *Project team* must understand CTC requirements and to integrate business information, team members, facilitate consensus in the implementation phase, synthesizes and translates strategic goals into actionable tasks, etc.... *(TOGAF, Skills, 2011)*. The EAI4CTC skills, is another perspective of skills are the *Project*'s implementation, that typically comprises: Detailed system's modeling, Business building component design and Standardized ADM4CTC's integration, etc....

ADM4CTC's Integration

ADM4CTC's integration with the CTC-CS, enables the automation of the *Project's* aBBs/Microartefacts, throughout its phases. The ADM4CTC encloses cyclic iterations, where information about all its PCP operations. The CTC is business or technology agnostic platform and its integration with the ADM4CTC offers: 1) Strategic just-in-time Microartefact's management; 2) Performance improvements; and 3) Using EA tools for modelling. The ADM4CTC offers the control and monitoring of *Project's* Microartefacts' by using various types of tests and integration concepts like: 1) Test Driven Developments (TDD) that is an archaic manual concept where *Project* developers design the test first and then do the development. The TDD evaluate the design for a given set of PCP requirements and verifies its status; 2) The Acceptance Test Driven Development (ATDD) concept supports collaboration of *Project's* business clients, testers, and engineers (Koudelia, 2011). Based on TDD's and ATDD's concepts, PCP's requirement's behaviour can be checked; 3) The *Behavior-Driven Development* concept includes TDD, integration and ATDD tests that serve as a formalism for communication between the *Project* and the end business users; where PCP's application cartography is essential.

PCP's Application Cartography

Using EA4CTC modelling languages like Archimate, offers the following characteristics (Hosiaisluoma, 2021): 1) *Entity's* strategic behavioural and structural elements modelling; 2) Manages an optimal PCP infrastructure and landscapes. PCP applications can be classified as follows (Togaf-Modeling, 2020): 1) Classifications can be done the use of EA capacities like TOGAF's the Application Communication Diagram (ACD), to depict all used CP's models and applications; 2) Interfaces are associated to CP resources; 3) ACDs present either an *Entity's* application cartography of the existing configuration, or a transformed one; 3) This type of EA based CTC that is based on unbundled services; 4) Services' based components are interconnected using connectors; and 5) The EA based CTC is layered. *Project's* building and solution blocks are used to solve CP's implementation requirements that needs a set of EA principles to integrate the mentioned blocks, where blocks are a set of deliverables. The dimensions of applied EA are scoped to the boundaries of the *Project*. In the second edition of Gartner's hype cycle for CTC-CS, that describes aspirations are running high for *EA & modeling strategies* and their related applicable business transformation architecture patterns, it describes also the underlying avant-garde technologies; it concludes that business artifacts lag maturity and concrete market penetrations (Ylimäki, 2006; Schekkerman, 2004). EA based CTC supports CP's decision and knowledge systems.

The ADM4CTC and the CTC-CS CSFs

Based on the LRP4CTC, the most important CSFs are presented in Table 3.

Table 3. CSFs that have an average of 8.40.

Critical Success Factors	HMM enhances: KPIs	Weightings
CSF_ADM4CTC_CP_Standards	Feasible	From 1 to 10. 09 Selected
CSF_ADM4CTC_PCP_CTC	Complex	From 1 to 10. 08 Selected
CSF_ADM4CTC_Skills	Lack	From 1 to 10. 08 Selected
CSF_ADM4CTC_Integration_Requirements	Feasible	From 1 to 10. 08 Selected
CSF_ADM4CTC_ACD	Possible	From 1 to 10. 09 Selected

valuation

DECISION AND KNOWLEDGE FOR THE CTC

CTC's Risk Assessment

CTC's Risk Readiness Assessment and the CTC has the following characteristics (The Open Group, 2011a): 1) It integrates TOGAF's *Business Transformation Readiness Assessment*" that supports the *Capacity to Execute* all CP's tasks; 2) Includes the *Enterprise Capacity to Execute* the tasks needed for the *Project*; 3) Its assessment process checks CTC's readiness to implement defined requirements; 4) To assess the risks for each readiness CSF and identify improvement actions to mitigate risks; 5) Integrates *Business Transformation Risks and Mitigation Activities*; 5) Relates CSFs and *Risks Estimations* by an AI process (Ylimäki, 2006).

AI Usage

CTC can use GCP's AI Engine (GCPAIE), which is a suite of services used to build, deploy, and manage Machine Learning (ML) models. It is a hyper-accessible ML environment; where the GCPAIE is designed to support data scientists and data engineers to streamline ML workflows, and access AI modules; and is with AutoML (Google's ML engine). GCPAIE services are designed to support the activities seen in a typical ML workflow, as shown in Figure 6, these services are available for ML operations (Green, 2020):

- *Prepare*: Generally, data is first prepared that includes ingest, clean, feature engineer operations in *BigQuery Datasets*, which is a collection of tables in GCP hyper-scale data storage. *BigQuery* is an interface to the *Entity*'s data storage, and an AI service. But it's the backbone of ML workflows. GCP includes a *Data Labelling Service* for labeling experimental/training data; which uses human labelers to generate highly accurate labels for a collection of data that can be used in ML models; such a process is used for the classification of images, video, audio, and text. In the of images for example, labeling options may include: 1) Classification of images information; 2) Image box bounding; 3) Image segmentation; and 4) Data labeling characteristics.
- *Build*: Concerns AutoML, the zero-code platform for ML training models, where machines train machines. Cloud AutoML enables teams with limited ML skills to train high-quality ML models with an intuitive client. It uses transfer learning and neural architecture search technology; leveraging extensive research technology to support ML models to achieve faster performance and more accurate decisions.
- *Validate*: Explainable and manageable AI environment supports *Projects* to understand model's decisions, verify the model's behavior, recognize bias in models, and finding manners to improve models and related training data. This eliminates random decisions, activities, and recommends models' tuning. The *GCPAIE Vizier* has an advanced approach where it offers a black-box optimization service, to tune hyperparameters and optimize used model's output.
- *Deploy*: When a model was trained using no-code AutoML, or an advanced *Tensorflow* model built using *GCPAIE Notebooks*, *GCPAIE* offers a set of services to support the deployment of models and generate solutions, decisions and predictions. *GCPAIE Prediction* manages the *Entity*'s infrastructure needed to process the model and to make it available for of *Project* requests.

Figure 7. GCP's AI capacity
(Green, 2020).

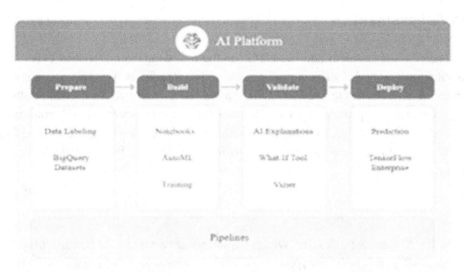

The previous operations support ML Pipelines (MLOps), which are important for the CTC-CS; where it is the practice of deploying robust, repeatable, and scalable MLOps to manage the pool of *Entity*'s models. The *GCPAIE* offers a set of services to support the *Entity*'s pipelines. The *GCPAIE Pipelines* support for creation of ML pipelines, using processors like, *Kubeflow* Pipelines or *TensorFlow Extended* (TFX). *Project*'s continuous evaluation supports the monitoring the performance of implemented models and provides continual return on how these models are performing in various *Project*'s phases. Deep Learning (DL) VM or image supports the provisioning of cloud VMs for ML applications. Finally, DL provides preconfigured and optimized containers for CP's (Green, 2020); and such a heterogenous needs a design strategy. The CTC supports complex intelligent systems and refers to classical operational research, systems analysis and global systems modelling. Complex systems management is an approach for building and deploying CPs and it replaces legacy distributed systems with a set of AHMM4CTC models that automate CP's Microartefact implementation. Complex system's management adapts to CP problems and requests by using CTC's mapping concept and intelligent scenarios (Daellenbach & McNickle, 2005).

Intelligent Scenarios

CP's use AI scenarios, where a scenario is an interaction of standard services; and a CP is an alignment of resources that is based on the 1:1 concept. A CP supports a variety of business actors including browsers, and mobile applications. A CP handles aBB requests by executing business processes (Richardson, 2014) which use MicroService Architecture (MSA) that differs from legacy architectures. The use of MSA provides autonomy, composability, scalability, and fault-tolerance. MSA is a promising architecture for intelligent scenarios. A *Project* delivers organizational design artifacts and a classification concept. This classification concept is used to classify the aBBs, intelligent scenarios, and business processes. Data models and related patterns, are agnostic to database types, but the diversity of data-sources generate major CP problems. Data services for CPs focuse on the encapsulation of the data schema (Pavel, 2011).

Using an AHMM4CTC Instance

The AHMM4CTC that is presented to the reader in a simplified form to be easily understandable on the cost of a holistic formulation of the architecture vision. The CTC uses the AHMM4CTC that is formalized as shown in Figure 8.

Figure 8. The AHMM4CTC nomenclature

Basic Mathematical Model's (BMM) Nomenclature

Iteration	= An integer variable *"i"* that denotes a *Project/ADM iteration*	
microRequirement	= (maps to) KPI	(B1)
CSF	= Σ KPI	(B2)
Requirement	= (maps to) CSF = $\cup$ microRequirement	(B3)
CSA	= Σ CSF	(B4)
microMapping microArtefact/Req	= microArtefact + (maps to) microRequirement	(B5)
microKnowledgeArtefact	= $\cup$ knowledgeItem(s)	(B6)
neuron	= action->data + microKnowledge.Artefact	(B7)
microArtefact / neural network	= $\cup$ neurons	(B8)
microArtefactScenario	= $\cup$ microartefact	(B9)
AI/Decision Making	= $\cup$ microArtefactScenario	(B10)
microEntity	= $\cup$ microArtefact	(B11)
Entity or Enterprise	= $\cup$ microEntity	(B12)
EnityIntelligence	= $\cup$ AI/Decision Making	(B13)
BMM(*Iteration*) as an instance	= EnityIntelligence(*Iteration*)	(B14)

Figure 9. The AHMM for a domain

The Generic AHMM's Formulation

AHMM	= $\cup$ ADMs + BMMs	(B15)

AHMM's Application and Instantiation for CTC

Domain	= CTC	(B16)
AHMM4(*Domain*)	= $\cup$ ADMs + BMMs(*Domain*)	(B17)

As shown in Figure 8, the symbol å indicates the summation of all the relevant named set members, while the indices and the set cardinality have been omitted. The summation should be understood in a broader sense, more like set unions. The *Project*'s development and mapping processes are a part of the CTC which uses the DMS4CTC. The DMS4CTC, as shown in Figure 9, is based on a light version of the ADM4CTC.

The enterprise AHMM4CTC is the combination of an EA and transformation methodologies. A transformation is the combination of an EA methodology like the TOGAF and the AHMM for a Domain, that can be modelled after the following formula for the CTC based Transformational Model (CTCTM):

CTCTM = EA + AHMM4CTC   (B18)

DMS4CTC's CSFs

Based on the LRP4CTC, the most important CSFs are presented in Table 4.

Table 4. CSFs that have an average of 9.0.

Critical Success Factors	AHMM enhances: KPIs	Weightings
CSF_KMS&DMS4CTC_AHMM4CTC_Support	Possible	From 1 to 10. 09 Selected
CSF_KMS&DMS4CTC_RiskAssessment	Complex	From 1 to 10. 08 Selected
CSF_KMS&DMS4CTC_AI_Support	Possible	From 1 to 10. 09 Selected
CSF_KMS&DMS4CTC_IntelligentScenarios	Possible	From 1 to 10. 09 Selected
CSF_KMS&DMS4CTC_ComplexSystems_Design	Proven	From 1 to 10. 10 Selected

valuation

CTC-CS' TRANSFORMATION AND INTEGRATION

Capacity and Competence Development

The ADM4CTC supports the CTC-CS by the creation of capacity building, best practices, and *Entity*-specific CP capabilities, which supports *Project* experts to avoid and evaluate CP risks. The CTC-CS is treated as a separate domain within the CTC, which is used to integrate CS resources. CTC-CS is the enforcement of the *Entity's* computing policies which includes the following domains (The Open Group, 2011b): 1) Services based methodology; 2) Management of viewpoints, where the CTC-CS is a separate one; 3) To design internal non-normative CTC-CS scenarios; 4) To design single-purpose CTC-CS instances; 5) To develop coordinated CTC-CS models; and 6) Defined security aspects.

Security Aspects

CTC-CS' Security (CTC-CSS) requirements are pervasive in all EA, ICS and business domains and to all ADM4CTC phases. The CTC-CSS focuses mainly on the infrastructure that is not visible to other functions; it also focuses on the protection of the CP resources. The CTC-CS manages single-purpose components and measures the quality of used artifacts, by: 1) Using AI modules and rules for handling of data/information resources; 2) Defined CTC-CSS policies, 3) Codify data/information management policies; 4) Enable CP risk analysis and evaluation scenarios; 5) Enable VM, load balancers and other artefacts management; 6) Support Internet of Things (IoT) artefacts management; and 7) Support Data classification policy documentation. The CTC-CSS has its types of unique building blocks, collaborations, and interfaces; these blocks must interface with the CP to support security policies and to avoid interfering with critical operations. CTC-CSS is effective to design and implement controls in the *Target Architecture* in the initial development cycle to support reengineering development and deployment. The CTC-CSS manages the services flow's fallout, abnormal flows, failure modes and the possibilities in which CP's applications can be interrupted or attacked. All *Entities* have security concerns and they should dedicate an CTC-CSS to support the CP (The Open Group, 2011b), which uses CP logs.

Security Monitoring and CP Logs

CP logging enables a central logging for all CTC-CS resources, where logged data is essential for t maintaining, measuring, and optimizing performance and security. It is complex to leverage logged data from heterogenous multi-CPs. Simplicity is critical for supporting CP logging and it is important to use multi-CP logging strategy that includes: tooling, organizational structure, and implementing CP logging processes. The CTC-CS supports in leveraging log-based insights to improve CP's performance and billing activities. CTC-CS logging is a practice that enables the CP to collect and correlate logged data from its applications, services, and platform/infrastructure. It supports CP's team to identify issues, measure performance, and optimize configurations. CP's logging relies on the management of log media, collections of data that document events occurring in the *Entity*. Log media can contain a wide variety of data, including requests, transactions, user information, and credible timestamps. Specific data sets that CTC-CS logs collect, depends CP's components which logging englobes various types of media. A log media includes: event logs, security logs, transaction logs, message logs, and audit logs. To achieve a cohesive collection and robust aggregation process, the CP implements a log management environment to ingest, process, and correlate logged data. The CTC-CS needs to build a *Multi-Cloud Logging Strategy* that includes where logging operations can be complex. *Multi-Cloud Logging Strategies* enable cohesive operations and unify incompatible services and data medias. The CTC-CSS is not dedicated to any specific CP and it offers to support: 1) Performance and availability; 2) Reliability and recovery; 3) Attack's tracing; 4) CP activities; and 5) Cybersecurity fundaments. The CP is controlled and monitored in real-time, using a unified logging system that supports distributed environments CTC-CS's main activity is to Consolidated Audit Trail (CAT), and to use regulatory reporting obligation(s), which will increase CP's power and storage requirements. While it's a complex undertaking, CAT supports the streamlining of older regulatory reporting systems like, the *Order Audit Trail System, Electronic Blue Sheet, Large Trader Reporting, CBOE* Rule 8.9 and *PHLX Rule* 1022,1; and also legacy systems used to support such requirements (Google, 2022a). CPs need strict governance and legal constraints to achieve this legal support, CSFs are selected and asserted, to monitor the used artefacts.

Business CPs

Entities need business CPs, which are complex, because of their technological heterogeneous structure and because of: 1) The development of virtualization; 2) The increasing capacity of IoT; and 3) The growing sophistication of IoT-based technologies. The CTC has five main characteristics: On-demand internal self-service, *Entity* wide network access, resources planning & pooling, rapid elasticity, and optimized services. CTC-CS has main backbone services models: IaaS, PaaS, and SaaS; and has four deployment models: PCP, public CP, community CP, and hybrid CP. CTC-CS type of cloud computing, has various forms and it can be implemented in various ways that can benefit the *Entity*'s evolution. To apply CTC-CS successfully, depends on the *Project*, where stakeholders must be involved and advised. Like in the case of classical/traditional outsourcing, needed CP skills may be required to replace legacy skills. The *Project* may imply a large change-management process. The *Project* must build a CTC common strategy and share practically the same understanding; because many of its units are affected, and there are *Project* strategic decisions to take. The strategic change to the CP requires a holistic corporate approach. *Entities* can use standard ICS methodologies, tools, and services to integrate a CP. Most *Entities* are using CPs, and some of them have internal PCP solutions; with time they are gaining experience needed for CPs. CPs have important potential, to confirm that potential, an *Entity* must use the form of CP that is the most suited to its needs, and in the way that will give it the best business advantage. As shown in Figure 9, main financial models presenting revenue, capital and operational expenditure, and costs are the models from which Return On Investment (ROI) is calculated. Using CTC, CSFs of the four ROI (or business advantages) are evaluated, these CSFs are: utilization, time compression, scale, and quality (The Open Group, 2021b).

Figure 10. The characteristics and models of CP computing
(The Open Group, 2021b).

Essential Characteristics	Service Models	Deployment Models
On-demand self-service	Infrastructure as a Service (IaaS)	Private cloud
Broad network access	Platform as a Service (PaaS)	Public cloud
Resource pooling	Software as a Service (SaaS)	Community cloud
Rapid elasticity		Hybrid cloud
Measured service		

The Business Advantages

CTC-CS is a mainstream technology for *Entities,* which want to eliminate the need for technological expertise; this is beneficial for Small and Medium sized Enterprises (SME), who need affordable, on-demand service that provides robust/secure data and storage solutions, and heavily improves overall business productivity. CP based services; *Entities'* PCP solutions are optimal for *Entities. Self-service* CP access means that *Entities* specialists can at any time retrieve and store data, in real time. These facts increase the collaboration between *Project* members and improves document handling, as all work files stored in one location. The flexibility and efficiency of CP extends to its instant ability to offer high bandwidth requests, without supplementary costs of standard PCP/ICS technology. For *Entities*, a CP is essential for disaster recovery, and without it, relying on complex disaster recovery scenarios plans is time consuming and lessens the reliability of business vital data backup. Changing to CP based services will enhance *Entity*'s performance, reduce costs and offer space for core business activities; it will also provide robustness for valuable business data and PCP's infrastructure, which have to be protected. The inception of PCP makes limitations of traditional ICS infrastructure, which are apparent. *Entities* are trying to adapt to marketplace innovative business models as their ICS are expensive and inefficient at sensing and responding complex situations. CP-based services offer scalable and reliable ICS infrastructure that is specifically implemented to streamline business performance, support development and growth; and PCP's main advantages are (LeadingEdge, 2022): Flexibility, Business continuity, Cost efficiency, Improved collaboration, Scalability and performance, Automatic software updates, Environmentally friendly, Automatic software integration, Usability and accessibility of information, Streamlining applications and processes, Compliance and security, and CP business models.

CP Business Models

The major and real disruptive power of CTC based platforms lies in its ability to manage innovative business and operating CP models. Applying rapid scaling of innovative capabilities and concepts, supported by the CTC that has made it an innovative operating CP model that an *Entity* wants to integrate. The development of such applications, has made the entrants in the ruthless environment possible for an *Entity* to provide new value propositions, and to allow them to disrupt the existing *value chain* in ways that was not done before, and which was impossible to do previously. *Entity's* new PCP enables the use of distributed services and tools. The major CSFs that can be mapped to innovative operating CP models, as shown in Figure 11, can support the *Project* by the use of CP (Digital Innovation Junction, 2020): *Business model,* O*perating model, Technology and enrichment of shopping experience, and artefacts.*

CP CS and Artefacts

The CP uses many standard artefacts like in the case of a GCP and they will be presented in this section that has the following CS types: 1) CE-VM that offer configured processors, memory, disk, and OS environments; 2) KE-Managed Kubernetes clusters, used to automate deployment, scaling, and management of containerized applications; 3) Cloud Run (CR), is a fully managed serverless platform that runs containers; 4) AE, is a fully managed serverless platform for web applications; where it handles the networking, application scaling, and database scaling; and 5) CF is an event-driven serverless function (Sullivan, 2020; Google, 2022b).

Figure 11. CP Models
(Digital Innovation Junction, 2020).

Figure 12. CS Types
(Google, 2022b).

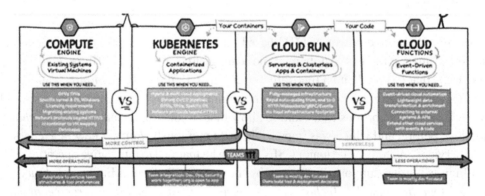

The Use of UCs

One of the most important CP's CSFs is the ability to access CS resources, like the ones discusses in UCs: 1) CPs provide access to VMs, where providers expanded the type of CSs offered; and a CP offers PaaS with AE; 2) The ability to execute functions in response to events without setting up servers for them, is useful for CP based applications; and 3) Capability is available with CF, in which containers are optimal to deploy MSA applications; managing many containers is a problem that needs GCP's container orchestration system or the GCP KE (GKE).

The Use of CEs and VMs

CE is an IaaS offering and is a building block for other services that run on top of CS resource, and its core functionality is a VM (or instances. VM's creation needs information: machine type, availability status, and enhanced security controls. *Machine Types and Service Accounts Instances* are provisioned by specifying machine types, which are differentiated by the number of processors and the amount of allocated memory to the instance. Machine types which have balanced processor and memory are called *standard instances*. But there are high (and mega) memory and high processor types, which differ from standard machine types. CP's can integrate machine types by specifying the configuration of processor and memory. VMs can be standard or preemptible, where standard VMs continue to run until their shut down or in the case of failure. If a standard VM fails, another instance will be started on another server. Preemptible VMs run up to 24 hours before their shutdown by the CP; in fact, they can be shutdown at any time. When a preemptible VM is shutdown, related processes are also shutdown. Shielded VMs are instances with enhanced security controls that includes: Secure boot, virtual Trusted Platform Module (vTPM), and Integrity monitoring. Secure boot runs only applications that are verified by digital signatures using *Unified Extensible Firmware Interface* features; and if an application cannot be authenticated, the boot process fails. vTPM is a VM for managing keys and other secrets. Integrity monitoring compares the boot measurements with a trusted baseline and returns true if the results match and false otherwise. VMs can be managed by CP like GCP's gcloud.

CE UCs

A CE provides flexible and customizable resources for CSs for the control of a VM, which includes the specification of: The OS, Enhanced security controls, and setting-up the storage. CE instances can be created using a container as a base image, where it uses a container-optimized OS. The GKE uses CE IGs to implement GKE clusters. To take advantage of advanced container-orchestration capacities, GKE can be used. AEF supports running custom containers in a PaaS. All VM aspects can managed by deploying CE instances and enables: The installation of additional software, changing access controls, setting-up users and groups, database management, configuration of persistent storage…

Instance Groups

Instance groups are VM clusters that are managed as a node and CPs have the following types of Instance Groups (IG): managed and unmanaged. Managed IGs (MIGs) contain identically configured instances, where the configuration is specified in IG's template. Unmanaged IGs which cannot be identical and they are not provisioned using an IG template. They are used only to support pre-existing cluster configurations for load balancing tasks. Unmanaged IGs are not recommended for new CP configurations. An instance template defines a machine type, book disk image or container image, network settings, and other properties of a VM. The instance template can be used to create a single instance or a managed group of instances. Instance templates are global resources which can be used in any region. The specification of zonal resources is done in a template.

AEs

AE is a serverless PaaS compute service that does not need to configure servers as it is a fully managed service. Applications run in an AE and there are two forms of AEs: 1) The AES s a PaaS that allows developers to run their applications in a serverless environment, and there are restrictions, on the development languages. AES provides the environments for: Go, JEE, PHP, Node.js, and Python. An application instance running in AES has an instance class that is determined by the processor's speed and available memory. The default instance class is *F1*, which has a 600 MHz processor limit and 256 MB of memory. The largest instance class, B8, provides a 4.8 GHz processor and 2048 MB of memory. AES is available in two forms: First generation and Second generation. Second-generation services offer more memory and more runtimes; and 2) The AEF allows engineers to customize their runtime environments by using Docker files. By default, the AEF supports JEE, Python, Node.js, Ruby, PHP, .NET, and Go. Engineers can specify how much processor and memory is allocated to each instance. AEF provides health checks and automatically patches the underlying OS. VMs are run in geographic regions specified by the CP project containing the AE application; and VMs are restarted on routine basis. And OS maintenance is performed at that time.

AE UCs

AES is optimal when: 1) An application that is implemented with a language and needs to rescale. Instance's start-up time is on the period of seconds; 2) Applications run in a Docker container; 3) An application uses MSA, when it depends on custom code, or when libraries are not available in AES. The following are the main differences between running containers in AEF and CE: 1) AEF containers are restarted once per week; 2) In AEF SSH access is disabled by default and SSH access is enabled by default in CEs; 3) Images in AEF are built by using the Cloud build service; and 4) Geographic location of AEF instances is determined by CP project's settings.

GKE

GKE is a managed service providing: 1) Kubernetes cluster management; and 2) Kubernetes container orchestration. KE allocates cluster resources, determines where to run containers, performs health checks, and manages VM lifecycles using CE instance groups. The Kubernetes Cluster Architecture (KCA) is a perspective of the VMs in the cluster (or in terms of how applications function in the cluster). Instances in Kubernetes have two types of instances: Cluster masters and Nodes; where: 1) The cluster master runs four core services that are part of the control plane: controller manager, API server, scheduler, and etcd; 2) The controller manager runs services that manage Kubernetes abstract components; 3) Applications interacting with the Kubernetes cluster make calls to the master using the API server. The API server also handles inter cluster interactions; 4) The scheduler is responsible for determining where to run pods, which are low-level compute abstractions that support containers; 5) The etcd is a consistent and highly-available key value store used as Kubernetes' backing store for all cluster's data; 6) Nodes are instances that execute workloads.

GKE UCs

GKE is a managed server that which of manages Kubernetes cluster and Kubernetes is used to allocate CS resources efficiently to a pool of containers running user applications. CP's applications and services are containerized before they run in Kubernetes. Kubernetes is optimal for MSA deployments to minimize CP's administration overhead, by using AEF.

CFs

CFs is a serverless compute service suited for events' processing and it is designed to respond to and execute functions in response to events in the CP; like in the case when an image file is uploaded to a CP storage, a CF can execute a function to transform the image or record metadata in a database. CF use three types of artefacts: Events, Triggers, and Functions. An event is an action that occurs in the CP. CFs cannot work with all possible events in the CP; but it is designed to respond to five kinds of events: Cloud Storage, Cloud Pub/Sub, HTTP, Firebase, Stackdriver Logging. CFs are used for event-driven processing and functions run in response to a triggering event, and other cases can be 1) When an image is uploaded to a storage bucket; 2) When a new version of an application is uploaded; 3) When a user of an Applica cation initiates an operation; 4) When a background process completes; 5) When a user authenticates to a database; .... CFs support AE's Cron Service, which executes Applications at specific times. With the use of the two mentioned services, CSs can execute applications without human assistance; and both services relieve *Project* teams from implementation of a service which runs as a daemon and checks if an event occurred and then may execute a CF; which needs CS provisioning.

CS Provisioning

A CP like GCP, provides an interactive console and a command-line interface for managing compute, storage, and network resources; and also provides the *Deployment Manager* (DM) service that supports the specification of IaC. IaC is optimal to allow *Project* teams reproduce CP environments rapidly. It also supports Application reviews, version control, and other implementation engineering practices. DM uses declarative templates that describe what is to be deployed; like specifying a template of an f1-micro instance that would be created in the us-west1 region using a project with the CP project ID of *gcp-arch-exam-project*, where a boot disk with the Centos OS installed, and an external network address on the network interface.

Managing State in CPs and Distributed Systems

Managing CP's state information is common when designing a CP (or a distributed system). Stateful CPs may present major challenges, when designing CP based Applications. Connecting a client to a server solves the problem of keeping state information available to an Application instance that uses it; as clients send data to the same instance, state information is persisted in that instance and all other instances do not have to be accessed to access client's state data. But this does not solve the problem of instance volatility an an instance (or container) may become unstable... That can generate a high availability problem and the need to switch to a redundant instance; that can become major problem as the number of instances increase. An optimal solution is to separate the storage of state data from volatile/unstable instances; and In-Memory Cache (IMC) and databases are viable options.

IMC

IMC like CP's *Memorystore*, which is a managed service, is optimal for Applications that need low-latency access to data in the cache, which can be persisted using snapshots. If the cache is corrupt, memory's memory can be restored by using the latest snapshot; the data modified between the time of the last snapshot and the cache corruption cannot be restored. If snapshots are configured to *once per minute*, the Time To Live (TTL) on messages in the queue is to be set to two minutes.

Databases

The second possibility to moving state data from volatile instances is to use a database, which is better than persisting data to durable storage. In the case of a database, the Application needs to define how to read and write data, and no additional actions are needed to snapshot caches (or manage message queues). Another possible issue is that database's latency may be higher than cache latency; and if latency is a major concern, then cache must be used to store database query results, so data that is repeatedly queried can be read from the

lower-latency cache instead of the higher-latency database. Another issue is that databases are complex Applications and can be difficult to manage. CPs (like the GCP) offer various managed databases, like: *Cloud SQL* and *Cloud Datastore*, which reduces operational barriers.

CP Dataflows and Pipelines

Applications contain a set of modules (or services) and monolithic (or legacy) Applications. Business operations need multiple steps of processing using Applications. These operations can be synchronous or asynchronous; the workflow uses a synchronous call to a service. Synchronous calls are calls to another service (or CF) that wait for the operation to complete before returning; asynchronous calls do not wait for an operation to complete. A CP Dataflow (CPD) is an implementation of the *Apache Beam* stream processing framework. CPD is fully managed and there is no need for provisioning and managing their instances to process data in stream. The service also operates in batch mode without changes to processing code. Team members can implement stream and batch processing code using JEE, Python, and SQL. CPD can be used in conjunction with Cloud Pub/Sub, with CPD being responsible for processing data and Cloud Pub/Sub being responsible for sending messages and buffering data. CPD pipelines often fit in Applications between data ingestion services, like Cloud Pub/Sub and CP IoT Core, and storage and analysis services, like Cloud Bigtable, BigQuery, or Cloud ML.

Monitoring and Alerting

Stackdriver is the service for collecting metrics, logs, and events; and it contains Applications for debugging and tracing. When designing a PCP architecture, types of metrics and events to collect, must be considered. Some metrics can support the utilization of CP resources, like the use of processor and memory use in sizing instances. Application specific events can inform on Application performance with respect to business constraints.

CTC Security

The Identity and Access Management (IAM) service is designed to allow a PCP specifies which operations can a user perform on resources. IAM elements are: Identities and groups, Resources, Permissions, Roles, and Policies.

Identities and Groups

Identities and groups are objects that are used to grant access permissions to users, where an identity is an object that represents an actor (person or other delimiter) that executes actions on a CP resource. There are various types of objects: Google account, Service account, and Cloud Identity domain. A Google account is used by an actor who interacts with the CP, like developers or administrators. These accounts are identified by an email address and a Cloud Identity is an IaaS offering. Groups have an associated email address and are useful for giving permissions to sets of users; and when a user is added to a group, he acquires the permissions granted to the group.

Resources

Resources are CP objects and can be accessed by users; there is a large category, like: Projects, VMs, AE applications, Cloud Storage buckets, Pub/Sub topics. A CP defines a set of permissions associated with each type of resource; and permissions vary according to the resource's functionality.

Permissions

A permission is the right to perform an action on a resource and permissions vary by the type of resource with which they are associated. Storage resources have permissions associated with creating, listing, and deleting data.

Roles

Roles are sets of permissions and by using the IAM is that administrators grant roles to identities, and not permissions. It is impossible to grant a permission directly to a user, and it is granted by assigning an identity. Roles can be granted to identities, where an identity can have multiple roles. Roles are granted for CP projects, folders, or organizations, and they apply to all resources under them. There are three types of roles: Predefined, Primitive, and Custom. Predefined roles are created and managed by a CP and the roles are organized around groups.

Policies

It is possible to associate a set of roles and permissions with resources by using policies. A policy is a set of statements that define a combination of users and associated roles. This combination of users and a role is called a *binding*.

Data Security

A CP provides multiple mechanisms for securing data in addition to IAM policies, which control access to data; and the essential services are encryption and key management. Encryption is the process of encoding data so it yields a coded version of data, which cannot be converted back to its original form without the key. There is a difference between encryption at rest and encryption in transit. Encryption at *Rest Google* encrypts data and there is no need to configure a policy to enable this operation, which is applied to Google data storage services, like: *Cloud Storage, Cloud SQL, and Cloud Bigtable*. Encryption occurs at multiple levels and there are various data encryption and key encryption keys in a CP.

Security Design Principles

A CP needs to enforce security design principles, like the Separation of Duties (SoD), least privileges, and defence in depth. SoD is the practice of limiting the responsibilities of a user to prevent malicious actions.

General Data Protection Regulation

The purpose of the General Data Protection Regulation (GDPR) is to standardize privacy protections across the European Union (EU), to grant controls to individuals over their private information, and to specify security controls required for *Entities* managing private information of EU citizens. GDPR distinguishes controllers and processors.

Supporting AI Scenarios

AI scenarios or workflows are interactions of aBBs; and a PCP is an alignment of resources that is based on the 1:1 concept. A PCP supports a variety of business actors including existing AI and generic Applications. A PCP handles aBB requests by executing business processes (Trad, 2015a). The use of services architecture, provides autonomy, composability, scalability, and fault-tolerance. aBB based architecture is the optimal platform for integrating AI scenarios. A *Project* delivers organizational design and an aBB classification concepts. The aBB classification concept is used to classify the aBBs and their related intelligent scenarios, workflows, and business processes. AI scenarios use aata models and other related patterns, and should be agnostic to database types, but the diversity of data-sources generate major CTC problems; where the Cloud Storage is a partial and a locked-in solution. Integrating AI scenarios in a PCP is a complex task, especially when using standard solutions and that can be a major locked-in burden. This just a subset of a long set of possible problems and it is recommended that the *Entity* builds its own PCP and its AI subsystem. The actual AI solutions like AutoML are primitive and the author considers it just one action in the complex learning process like Action Research (AR), which is real learning process. That is why he will present a more complex learning based on the AR based HDT, which is optimal for AI based PCP (Trad, 2022b).

CTC-CS's Development CSFs

Based on the LRP4CTC, the most important CSFs are presented in Table 5.

Table 5. CSFs that have an rounded average of 9.10.

Critical Success Factors	KPIs		Weightings
CSF_CTC_CS_Capacity_Competence	Possible	▾	From 1 to 10. 09 Selected
CSF_CTC_CS_Security	Feasible	▾	From 1 to 10. 09 Selected
CSF_CTC_CS_Business_CPs	Supported	▾	From 1 to 10. 09 Selected
CSF_CTC_CS_Business_Advantages	Feasible	▾	From 1 to 10. 09 Selected
CSF_CTC_CS_Business_Models	Supported	▾	From 1 to 10. 09 Selected
CSF_CTC_CS_Artefacts	Proven	▾	From 1 to 10. 10 Selected
CSF_CTC_CS_Instances	Possible	▾	From 1 to 10. 09 Selected
CSF_CTC_CS_Managing_States	Possible	▾	From 1 to 10. 09 Selected
CSF_CTC_CS_Dataflows_Pipelines	Possible	▾	From 1 to 10. 09 Selected
CSF_CTC_CS_Monitoring_Tracking	Supported	▾	From 1 to 10. 09 Selected
CSF_CTC_CS_Integration	Feasible	▾	From 1 to 10. 09 Selected

valuation

THE POC'S IMPLEMENTATION

This PoC uses a *Entity* using *CloudEcoSource* and the already presented UCs, which launches three separate transformation initiatives, or *Projects*, which use TOGAF and ADM phases, to apply the CTC-CS. *Entities* must have robust CP functions, therefore *CloudEcoSource and UCs*, which wants an CTC-CS-based solution, needs to engage several external *Cloud Service Providers and Partners,* to the transformation of its heterogeneous ICS and distributed infrastructure platform and software services; and also to support its critical business system's needs. The *Entity* intends to use the TOGAF standard for EA practices and aBBs, which are used to manage its CTC-CS based services as patterns. As already mentioned, *CloudEcoSource* has three distinct CTC-CS-specific initiatives which are based on the following sub-systems: IaaS, PaaS, and SaaS; these sub-systems are for basic *CloudEcoSource* operations. This PoC describes how *CloudEcoSource* plans to use EA and CTC-CS to create and evolve various business models. The following features present *CloudEcoSource*'s initiatives (The Open Group, 2021a): 1) The IaaS initiative, concerns the *Entity*'s infrastructure's modernization, optimization and consolidation; with the expectations on how to transform, manage and regulate dynamic resources consumption in a multi-tenant ICS infrastructure, with real-world effective management of security and privacy of its tenants, like for example the *Entity*'s clients; 2) The PaaS initiative, is related to the concept of Rapid Application Development (RAD) platform, where the PaaS-focused initiative is used to identify and describe EA based CTC-CS capabilities of a platform for *CloudEcoSource* business solutions. Dynamic instances of the CTC-CS platform(s) could be deployed and operated by a team, *Entity* or by partners of CTC-CS's Ecosystem; and 3) The SaaS initiative, concerns mainly an enhanced collaboration among multiple external service providers; where the CTC-CS assembles business capabilities for business collaborations that extend the *Entity*'s traditional applications' boundaries, to support extended users (both internal and external users). The PoC's development uses an adapted implementation environment.

The LRP4CTC's

The LRP4CTC (or Phase 1) outcome that supports the PoC's background, by the use of an archive of an important set of references and links that are analysed using a specific interface. After selecting the CSA/CSFs tag is linked to various CP Microartefacts scenarios; which is implemented as an item, in an Excel file; where all its details are defined; this concludes Phase 1. In this DMS4CTC related PoC (or Phase 2), the HDT to deliver solutions. The empirical part is based on the AHMM4CTC's instance and the CP Microartefacts mechanics', which uses the internal initial sets of CSFs' that are used in phases 1 and 2.

From Phase 1 to Phase 2

The *Project*'s enumeration of CSAs are: 1) The RDP4CTC; 2) The ACS4CTC Integration; 3) The Usage of the ADM4CTC; 4) The CP, CSs, and security; 5) The AHMM4CTC's Integration; and 6) The DMS4CTC and the KMS4CTC. Where Tables 1 to 5, where presented and evaluated in this chapter and they are this chapter's empirical part.

The PoC

The CTC-CS 's PoC was implemented using the research's *TRADf* that had been developed using: The GCP and its CS structure, *TRADf's* Natural Language Processing 4 CTC (NLP4CTC), Microsoft Visual Studio .NET, C/C++, and JEE. The PoC is based on the CTC-CS and the CSFs' binding, using a specific *Project* requirement and related resources, where the CTC-CS was designed using EA (like TOGAF) tools. The CTC-CS processing model represents the mapping relationships between CP's requirements, CP CSs, and the CSFs. As shown in Figure 13, the PoC sets-up the needed CSs.

The PoC was achieved using the development environment and the research framework; were in the frontend the mapping/linking actions are activated by: 1) Choosing an HDT node that contains the requirement; 2) Choosing the CS' Microartefact(s) to be linked; and 3) Choosing to a CS problem to be solved using an NLP4CTC scenario. When the setup is achieved, from the frontend the CS requirements development initiation interface that is shown in Figure 14, can be launched.

Figure 13. CSs configuration

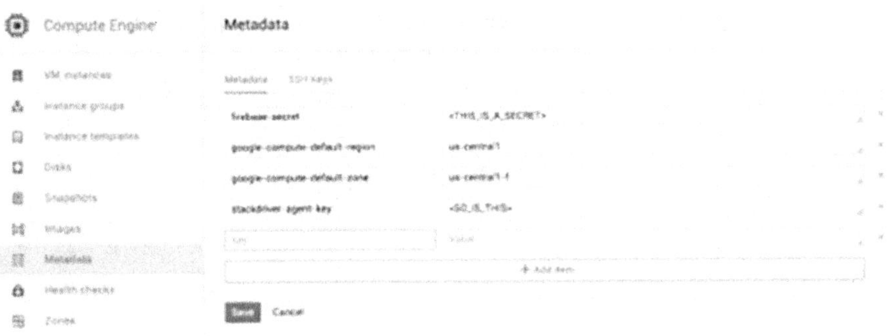

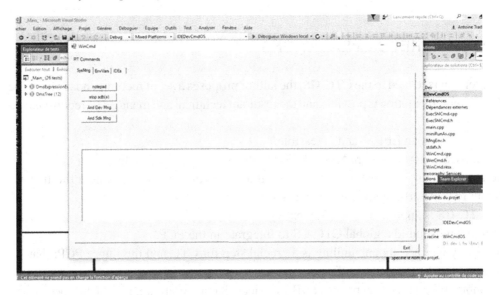

Figure 14. The TRADf's setup interface

The CTC-CS's uses the GCP database and the HDT makes calls to DMS4CTC to solve a concrete CS problems. Once the development setup interface is activated, the NLP4CTC interface can be launched to implement the needed CP Microartefact scripts. These NLP4CTC scripts that make up the DMS4CTC subsystem and the CTC-CS's relates set of actions. CTC-CS-related CSFs were also selected as demonstrated previously in this chapter's five tables and the result of the processing of the DMS4CTC, as illustrated in Table 6, shows clearly that the CTC-CS is not an independent component and in fact it is strongly bonded to the *Project*'s overall risk management approach.

RDP4CTC's constraint is that CSAs having an average result below 8.5 will be ignored. As shown in Table 6 (which average is 8.80), this fact keeps the CSAs (marked in green) that helps make this work's conclusion; and no ones in red. It means that such an CTC-CS integration will succeed and that the CTC-CS transformation must be done in multiple transformation sub-projects.

Table 6. The CTC-CS research's outcome is 8.80.

CSA Category of CSFs/KPIs	Influences transformation management	Average Result
RDP4CTC's Integration	Feasible ▾	From 1 to 10 9.20
ADM4CTC's Integration	Complex ▾	From 1 to 10 8.40
ICS' Integration	Complex ▾	From 1 to 10 8.90
KMS4CTC/DMC4CTC Integration	Feasible ▾	From 1 to 10 9.0
CTC-CS Transformation	Feasible ▾	From 1 to 10 9.10

Evaluate First Phase

SOLUTION AND RECOMMENDATIONS

In this chapter that is related to the CTC-CS, the author proposes a set of recommendations, table 6 shows that CTC-CS implementation is possible and the resultant technical and managerial recommendations are:

- The RDP4CT is an EERM and is feasible.
- An CTC-CS must be established and tried with a PoC for its feasibility.
- The *Project* must be separated in multiple transformation processes, where the first one should attempt to transform the ICS to be PCP's stub.
- The CTC-CS is applicable but complex.
- A *Project* must build a global CTC-CS to integrate in the PCP.
- The legacy ICS and its unbundling is a crucial step for CTC and the future PCP; that is the main condition for the Project's readiness.
- The unbundling process generates aBBs/services that are common to all CS types.
- EA and the ADM4CTC are the main methods for PCP's construction.
- After that the EA based CTC is ready the next step is to integrate the AHMM4CTC based KMS4CTC and DMS4CTC.
- CTC CS' include the main markets platform services for the PCP.
- The CTC-CS is CTC-AIS' infrastructure.
- An *Entity* can build its own CP or the PCP, there is no need for a specific product.
- A PCP must integrate various security aspects and it delivers major business advantages.
- Enormous efforts must be applied to integrate various existing standards and concepts because the main problem is alignment of existing silos.
- The PCP enables the automation of aBBs to support implementation activities.

FUTURE RESEARCH DIRECTIONS

The *TRADf* future research efforts will focus on the various strategy for CTC for AI.

CONCLUSION

The RDP4CTC is part of a series of publications related to *Projects* and CPs and is based on mixed action model the HDT, which uses QNA4CTC and QLA4CTC calls. Where CSFs are offered to help *Project* architects to diminish the chances for failure when building a PCP. In this article, the focus is on CTC-CS, where its formalism defines a structured inter-relationship of CP requirements, CSs, and *Entity's* resources. The CTC-CS is an important factor for the *Project's* evolution and the most important managerial recommendation that was generated by the previous research phases was that the *Manager* must be an architect of adaptive business systems. The PoC was based on the CSFs' binding to a specific RDP4CTC resource and HDT's reasoning model that represents the relationships between this RDP4CTC's concepts, requirements, aBBs, Cloud patterns, and CSFs. The final results prove that an CTC-CS supports the transformation process to deliver a PCP and to avoid commercial products. A PCP avoids that the *Entity* becomes locked-in.

REFERENCES

Agievich, V. (2014). *Mathematical model and multi-criteria analysis of designing large-scale enterprise roadmap.* IGI Global.

Bala, R., Gill, B., Smith, D., Wright, D., & Ji, K. (2021). *Magic Quadrant for Cloud Infrastructure and Platform Services.* Gartner Inc. https://www.gartner.com/doc/reprints?id=1-271SYZF2&ct=210802&st=sb

Charles (2017). *Hosting and Cloud Software Delivery modelled in Archimate.* Agile Enterprise Architecture. https://agileea.com/2017/04/hosting-and-cloud-software-delivery-modelled-in-archimate/

Cloud Computing Patterns. (2022). *Private Cloud.* Cloud Computing Patterns. https://www.cloudcomputingpatterns.org/private_cloud/

Daellenbach, H., & McNickle, D. (2012). *Management Science. Decision-making through systems thinking* (2nd ed.). Plagrave Macmillian.

Digital Innovation Junction. (2020). Cloud Innovative Model. *Digital Innovation Junction.* https://www.digitalinnovationjunction.com/cloud-innovative-model/

Google. (2022a). *Cloud for financial services.* Google. https://cloud.google.com/solutions/financial-services

Google. (2022b). *Where should I run my stuff? Choosing a Google Cloud compute option.* Google Cloud. https://cloud.google.com/blog/topics/developers-practitioners/where-should-i-run-my-stuff-choosing-google-cloud-compute-option

Green, J. (2020). *Google Cloud GCPAIE: Hyper-Accessible AI & Machine Learning*. Towards Data Science.

Gupta, I. (2019). *CS 425 / ECE 428 Distributed Systems-Introduction to Cloud Computing*. IG.

Hosiaisluoma, E. (2021). *ArchiMate Cookbook-Patterns & Examples*. Hosiaisluoma.

Jonkers, H., Band, I., & Quartel, D. (2012a). *ArchiSurance Case Study*. The Open Group.

Koudelia, N. (2011). *Acceptance test-driven development*. [Master Thesis, Uuniversity of Jyväskylä].

LeadingEdge. (2022). Advantages of Cloud Computing. *LeadingEdge*. https://www.leadingedgetech. co.uk/it-services/it-consultancy-services/cloud-computing/advantages-of-cloud-computing/

McClintock, M. (2020). *The Top 3 Cloud BPM Solutions-Exploring the Workflow Providers Who Think Cloud First*. ProcessMaker. https://www.processmaker.com/blog/top-3-cloud-based-bpm-solutions/

OMG. (2022). *DECISION MODEL AND NOTATION (DMN)*. OMG. https://www.omg.org/dmn/

Pavel, F. (2011). Grid Database—Management, OGSA and Integration. Academy of Economic Studies Romania Database Systems Journal, 2(2).

Peterson, S. (2011). Why it Worked: Critical Success Factors of a Financial Reform Project in Africa. *Faculty Research Working Paper Series*. Harvard Kennedy School.

Richardson, Ch. (2014). *Pattern: Microservices architecture*. Microservices. https://microservices.io/ patterns/microservices.html

Sullivan, D. (2020). *Official Google Professional Cloud Architect-Study Guide*. John Wiley & Sons, Inc.

The Open Group. (2011a). *Architecture Development Method*. The Open Group. https://pubs.opengroup. org/architecture/togaf9-doc/arch/chap05.html

The Open Group. (2011b). *TOGAF 9.1*. The Open Group. https://www.opengroup.org/subjectareas/ enterprise/togaf.

The Open Group. (2021a). *The Open Group Cloud Ecosystem Reference Model – Using the Cloud Ecosystem Reference Model with the TOGAF Standard (Informative)*. The Open Group. http://www. opengroup.org/cloud/cloud_ecosystem_rm/p5.htm

The Open Group. (2021b). *Cloud Computing for Business*. The Open Group. http://www.opengroup. org/cloud/cloud_for_business/index.htm

Togaf-Modeling. (2020). *Application communication diagrams*. Togaf-Modeling.org. https://www.togaf-modeling.org/models/application-architecture/application-communication-diagrams.html

Trad, A. (2022a). Business Transformation Projects: The Integration of Cloud Business Platforms (ICBP). *SCF International Conference on "ontemporary Issues in Social Sciences*. SCF.

Trad, A. (2022c). *Enterprise Transformation Projects-Cloud Transformation Concept–Holistic Security Integration (CTC-HSI)*. IGI Global. doi:10.37394/23205.2022.21.41

Trad, A., & Kalpić, D. (2017). *An Intelligent Neural Networks Micro Artefact Patterns' Based Enterprise Architecture Model*. IGI-Global.

Trad, A., & Kalpić, D. (2019a). *The Business Transformation Framework and Enterprise Architecture Framework for Managers in Business Innovation-Knowledge and Intelligence Driven Development (KIDD)*. *Encyclopedia*. IGI-Global.

Trad, A., & Kalpić, D. (2020a). *Using Applied Mathematical Models for Business Transformation. IGI Complete Author Book*. IGI Global. doi:10.4018/978-1-7998-1009-4

Wikipedia. (2022a). *Cloud computing*. The Wikipedia. https://en.wikipedia.org/wiki/Cloud_computing .

Ylimäki, T. (2006). Potential critical success factors for EA. *Journal of Enterprise Architecture*, 2(4), 29–40.

Chapter 10
An Architectural Review of Multi-Tenancy in Cloud Computing

Ravi Kiran Kumar Meduri

ⓘD https://orcid.org/0000-0003-2425-7233

Government Degree Colleges of Andhra Pradesh, India

Sreeram Gutha

Vignana Bharathi Institute of Technology, India

Vijay Chandra Jadala

ⓘD https://orcid.org/0000-0002-5149-5176

KL University, India

ABSTRACT

Cloud computing has become a popular ingredient in the information management of enterprises cutting across the globe and size. Its popularity lies in its ability to provide resources – infrastructure, platform, and software – as services on demand without compromising much on the quality of service. On-demand resource provisioning is possible by sharing the resources across multiple users or multiple tenants. Among all the three (IaaS, PaaS, and SaaS) deployments, SaaS offers more cost benefit to enterprises and users as compared to its predecessors because of its ability to share both hardware and software across multiple tenants with very minimal data sharing. The feature of sharing resources among multiple users known as multi tenancy is essential in achieving the objectives of cloud computing. This paper gives a detailed account of multi tenancy in cloud computing with special focus on SaaS applications and its associated problems followed by solution approaches.

DOI: 10.4018/978-1-6684-6971-2.ch010

Copyright © 2023, IGI Global. Copying or distributing in print or electronic forms without written permission of IGI Global is prohibited.

1. INTRODUCTION

Cloud computing has probably become the most successful computing techniques in the recent times. Having derived its name from the cloud-like diagrams of ARPANET the ancestor of Internet, cloud computing has made big strides since its inception (Miyachi, 2018). After being popularized by the advertisements of Amazon Web Services as opined by Miyachi, the word "Cloud" has become a buzz word and the idea of computing over cloud or cloud computing has made its presence felt in the world of computing.

Cloud computing is a pervasive computing paradigm which enables network access to a shared group of computing resources that can be dynamically provisioned or de-provisioned based on demand with minimal intervention from subscribers in a pay-per-use routine (Mell& Grance., 2011). The three major models of cloud computing are Infrastructure as a Service (*IaaS*), Platform as a Service (*PaaS*) and Software as a Service (*SaaS*) (Rashid & Chaturvedi, 2019). IaaS provides hardware computing resources such as processors, memory, storage, network, etc. through virtualization of physical resources. PaaS mainly aims at providing development environments to customers by deployment the frameworks on hardware resources. SaaS offers a great deal of cost benefit by providing access to a software application in a shared mode to end users. Any of these three computing models can be deployed either in a private cloud (on premise cloud). The resources are exclusively used in an organization, or in a public cloud (off premise cloud) where the resources are shared across users belonging to many organizations or in a hybrid cloud which uses a combination of the features garnered from private and public clouds. Community cloud is another cloud deployment model wherein several organizations pool and share their resources for a common cause (Aljahdali et al., 2013). These resources can be deployed either in a private or a in a public cloud while the resource management is taken care by one of the partnering organizations or by a third-party service provider. Analyzing these deployment models, we can understand that the most important aspect of cloud computing is to create an illusion of infinite resource capacity at the doorstep of customers while making the optimum utilization of customer-owned resources. Succinctly putting, cloud computing optimizes the capital expenditure and reduces the operational costs ensuring two-fold benefit to customers (Patel et al., 2009).

Having understood the rudimentary nomenclature and the attendant definitions of cloud computing, let us now succinctly look at the salient facets that enable the shift from the traditional computing to cloud computing models. ***On-demand resource provision through self-service*** is the first important characteristic of cloud computing wherein a customer gets access to the computing services individually without necessitating any administrative support from the service provider (Goralski, 2017) and it enables customers to request, access and release resources with the help of web services using a platform-agnostic and user-friendly interface (Rountree & Castrillo, 2014). The second characteristic in ***network-based access*** wherein resources are delivered and accessed through standard protocols available on different client platforms such as mobiles, desktop, laptops, etc. (Rountree & Castrillo, 2014). The third characteristic is ***resource pooling*** wherein a service provider pools a multitude of computing resources to serve the resource requests of multiple users dynamically based on demand (Rountree & Castrillo 2014). The fourth characteristic is ***elasticity*** wherein resources are almost automatically scaled up or scaled down based on demand without any intermission and with very little intervention from customers. The fifth characteristic is ***measured service*** wherein customers are charged based on the resource usage and the quality of service (QoS) being provided in a given time frame (Buyya et al., 2013).

In order to achieve the aforementioned characteristics, cloud computing employs certain key drivers such as virtualization, service-orientation, SLA driven service, reliability and multi-tenancy. Virtualization, as the name suggests, enables the emulation of physical computing resources to create multiple virtual copies and shares them among customers. Through virtualization, cloud computing can pool multiple physical resources to create virtual resources of larger capacity and can divide one physical resource into multiple virtual resources of smaller capacity. In other words, virtualization facilitates optimum resource utilization and achieves resource availability without losing its focus on power consumption (Aljahdali et al., 2013). Cloud computing realizes the benefits of service-orientation in the form of its service delivery through web services and simplifies the process of resource access across all kinds of networks and platforms. According to Raines and Tahvildari introduced, cloud computing essentially uses the foundations laid by service-oriented architecture (SOA) to enable integration and delivery of different resources independent of platforms and networks. Apart from service delivery, to achieve scalability and quality of service (QoS), cloud computing applies the standards adopted by SOA (Hamdaqa & Tahvildari, 2012). The adoption of service-oriented architecture enforces provision of quality service as a very important attribute in cloud computing. At the same time varying demands of consumers (customers) make it difficult for the service provider to determine the QoS attributes. Hence, in order to strike a healthy balance between consumers and service providers, cloud computing advocates a negotiable agreement process to monitor quality attributes and ensure QoS (Patel et al, 2009). This agreement process, also known as, service level agreement (SLA) plays a pivotal role in delivering services at optimum cost without deviating from the agreed-upon quality parameters (Jansen, 2011). In traditional computing, reliability is taken for granted as customers own all the resources while in cloud computing, ensuring guaranteed access to resources is of great importance. All the characteristics and the key drivers briefly explained thus far enable customers to appreciate the economic benefits of cloud computing only if multiple customers are allowed to share the resources without compromising on QoS and security. This feature is popularized as multi-tenancy as customers are the tenants of the cloud service being offered. In this paper, the first section presents the related work to describe how multi-tenancy is achieved in various cloud service models and the second section focusses on unleashing some of the key characteristics of multi tenancy while the third section describes the expectations from multi tenancy in Cloud Computing. The fourth section articulates various architectural models of multi tenancy along with a comparative analysis of these models. The final section concludes with a summary followed by a direction towards future scope of work (Ionita, 2012).

2. MULTI TENANCY

A tenant in terms of cloud computing is an instance sharing a resource to a community. It is analogous to a tenant sharing a building where the space of one tenant is separated and isolated from those occupying space in the same building. This idea of multiple tenants sharing resources is fundamental to Cloud Computing and achieves privacy and security to some extent while providing cost-effective services (Patel, 2009).

Multi tenancy is the process of enabling multiple tenants (customers) to share and use a common pool of resources (AlJahdali et al., 2014). It is a natural consequence of achieving economic gains through resource sharing (Jansen, 2011). Though multi tenancy is primarily defined as resource sharing, it is viewed differently in the context of different cloud models.

2.1 Multi Tenancy in Different Cloud Models

Infrastructure-as-a-Service (IaaS) achieves multi tenancy by sharing a single set of physical resources such as compute, storage, and network resources across multiple customers in the form of virtual resources. In other words, a single physical machine (PM) is shared by multiple virtual machines (VMs) (AlJahdali et al., 2014). The process of creating virtual version of a physical resource which can be a hardware resource, an operating system, a storage device, a network resource or a computing recourse (Venkatesan V.K et al, 2022). Intuitively, the real benefit if multi tenancy is realized in IaaS only if resources are shared through virtualization. If every tenant is provided with an exclusive set of physical resources, the economic benefit is compromised (Kanade & Manza, 2019).

In IaaS, multi-tenancy is a way to provide cloud computing resources to multiple customers on the same physical infrastructure. In multi-tenant IaaS, customers share the same pool of physical resources such as servers, storage, and networking infrastructure, but they have their own logical resources such as virtual machines, networks, and storage volumes. The IaaS provider ensures that each customer's logical resources are isolated from each other, so that one customer cannot access or interfere with another customer's resources (Maithili, K et al., 2018)

Multi-tenancy in IaaS provides several benefits:

a. Cost savings: Since multiple customers share the same physical infrastructure, the cost of hardware, software, and maintenance is distributed among them. This allows the IaaS provider to offer lower prices than traditional hosting models.
b. Scalability: IaaS providers can add more resources to the pool as needed, allowing customers to easily scale up or down their usage.
c. Resource optimization: Multi tenancy allows for better utilization of resources since the provider can dynamically allocate resources based on demand. This leads to better resource utilization and reduces wastage.
d. Security: Multi-tenancy can provide better security since each customer's logical resources are isolated from each other, reducing the risk of one customer's security breach affecting others.

However, multi-tenancy also poses some challenges such as ensuring resource allocation and performance guarantees for each tenant and preventing resource contention among tenants. To address these challenges, IaaS providers use various techniques such as resource allocation policies, network isolation, and monitoring and management tools.

Technically, multi tenancy in PaaS is not much different from the way multi tenancy works in IaaS as PaaS offerings only includes the system software and the libraries needed for setting up the platform for development and testing. Since PaaS also uses the same virtualization techniques for delivering the platforms to tenants on demand, it ensures security and isolation in the same way as IaaS does.

In PaaS, multi-tenancy allows multiple users to share a single application platform, development tools, and runtime environment, while providing each user with their own isolated space to develop, deploy, and run their applications. In a multi-tenant PaaS environment, each customer or tenant has their own application environment, data storage, and access to development tools and services. Tenants can customize and configure their own applications without affecting the other tenants on the platform. PaaS providers manage the underlying infrastructure, including hardware, software, and networking resources, while ensuring that each tenant's data and applications are securely isolated from each other.

Multi-tenancy in PaaS provides several benefits:

a.   Cost savings: PaaS providers can offer their services at a lower cost by sharing resources across multiple tenants. This enables smaller companies and startups to access powerful development tools and infrastructure that would otherwise be too expensive.

b.   Scalability: PaaS providers can easily scale resources up or down based on demand, which allows tenants to rapidly develop and deploy their applications without worrying about infrastructure.

c.   Flexibility: Multi-tenancy in PaaS allows tenants to use a range of programming languages, tools, and services to build and deploy their applications.

d.   Security: PaaS providers implement strict security measures to ensure that each tenant's data and applications are secure and isolated from each other.

However, multi-tenancy in PaaS can also present some challenges. For example, ensuring that each tenant's application and data is kept secure and isolated from others requires careful management and monitoring. Additionally, ensuring that each tenant has access to the resources they need without creating impact on the performance of other tenants can also be challenging (Ahmed, S. T et al, 2023). To address these challenges, PaaS providers use a range of techniques, including security measures such as data encryption and network isolation, resource allocation policies, and monitoring and management tools. They also provide tenants with visibility into their usage and performance metrics, enabling them to optimize their applications and usage of resources.

Multi tenancy is SaaS model is a crucial factor not only to ensure the cost benefit to tenants but also to guarantee security and isolation. SaaS applications achieve multi tenancy by sharing the hardware resources and using a single copy of the software while maintaining the isolation across different users to ensure security. Since a single copy of the application code is shared across multiple tenants, it makes maintenance activities such as backup and upgrade easier and avoids multiple dedicated servers for each tenant optimizing the resource utilization to the maximum possible extent (Kanade & Manza, 2019).

Multi-tenancy is an essential characteristic of SaaS applications where a single instance of the application serves multiple customers (or tenants) simultaneously. Each customer's data and configuration settings are kept separate and secure from other customers. In a multi-tenant SaaS application, a single codebase is used to serve multiple customers. This means that each customer is accessing the same software application, but with their own isolated data storage and customized settings (Rountree & Castrillo, 2013).

Multi-tenancy in SaaS provides several benefits:

a.   Scalability: Multi-tenancy allows for quick and easy scaling of the application to accommodate growing numbers of customers.

b.   Cost-effectiveness: By sharing resources across multiple customers, multi-tenant SaaS applications can be more cost-effective than other deployment models.

c.   Easy maintenance: With a single codebase, updates and maintenance are streamlined and can be applied to all customers simultaneously.

d.   Customization: Each customer can configure the application to their specific needs and requirements without affecting other customers up to a reasonable extent.

Despite having several benefits, multi tenancy SaaS applications suffer a few challenges as well. Following is a summary of the most common challenges that need to be addressed in SaaS applications:

a. Security: Security is a significant concern in SaaS applications since multiple customers share the same infrastructure, which increases the risk of data breaches and unauthorized access to sensitive data. Service providers must take measures to ensure the security of their applications and data, such as implementing data encryption, access control, and regular security audits.

b. Integration: Integrating SaaS applications with other enterprise systems can be challenging. Service providers must offer robust APIs and connectors to enable smooth integration with other applications.

c. Performance: Since multiple customers share the same infrastructure, the performance of SaaS applications can be affected by spikes in usage by other customers. Service providers must ensure that their applications can scale quickly to meet customer demands.

d. Customization: Customizing SaaS applications to meet specific business requirements can be difficult. Service providers must offer flexible and configurable solutions that allow customers to tailor the applications to their unique needs (Alex, D. S et al., 2022)

e. Availability: Service providers must ensure that their applications are always available and accessible to customers. Downtime can be costly and damaging to customer relationships.

f. Vendor lock-in: SaaS applications often require customers to rely on the service provider for ongoing support and maintenance. This can create a vendor lock-in situation where customers are unable to switch to another provider without significant disruption to their business processes.

g. Data ownership and portability: Customers may be concerned about the ownership and portability of their data stored in SaaS applications. Service providers must have clear data ownership policies and allow customers to export their data in a usable format if they decide to switch providers.

Overall, SaaS offers many benefits, but service providers and users must be aware of the challenges and take steps to mitigate risks and ensure a smooth and successful implementation.

2.2 Characteristics of Multi Tenancy

Now that we have had a look at the general features of multi tenancy, let us succinctly review the characteristics that accomplish multi tenancy in Cloud Computing (Odun-Ayo et al, 2017). According to Odun-Ayo et al concept to create, **Hardware and Software Resource Sharing** is fundamental to realize multi tenancy in Cloud based services. Virtualization of hardware resources enables the creation of several virtual resources out of a limited pool of physical resources and shares the same set of resources across multiple tenants. However, since virtualization does not alone achieve optimal resource utilization due to varying demands of different tenants, it is important to share the software resources as well to realize the cost benefits of Cloud Computing. Another important characteristic is **High Degree of Configurability**. A single tenant application is highly customized according to its tenant's needs, but a multi-tenant application invariably necessitates the configuration and customization capabilities based on varying requirements of different tenants. A multi-tenant Cloud application is supposed to include built-in features for configuration and customization based on changing needs. **Shared Application and**

Database Instance is another most important feature that makes multi tenancy scalable and optimal. While single tenant applications encompass dedicated instances of software and database to meet the fine-grained needs of customers, multi-tenant applications make use of shared instances of software and database to provide cost benefits. When software and database instances are shared, they are usually replicated to ensure high availability and scalability to achieve load balancing and performance.

2.3 Pros and Cons of Multi Tenancy

Multi tenancy offers multi-fold benefits to Cloud Service Providers (CSPs) and Customers while it has some drawbacks that need to be addressed. The key benefits to CSPs include economic benefits and easier maintenance due to a single set of resources being shared across multiple customers, better scope for mining data related to multiple customers to understand their needs, and cost savings due to reduced overhead per customer. The advantages meted out to customers are low total cost of ownership due to centralized maintenance of resources by the CSP, higher theoretical reliability and guaranteed scalability. When it comes to drawbacks pertaining to CSPs, any problem in the service provision impacts all the stakeholders. There is high degree of risk of data leaks among tenants due to sharing of resources. From the customers' point of view, the shortcomings include reduced flexibility due to limited scope for customizations, risk of data leaks and increased issues during upgrades.

2.4 Multi-tenancy as a Research Topic

Multi-tenancy fundamentally refers to the ability to share a computing resource across different users hosted on the same cloud platform. Though it is one of the foundational architectural pillars that make Cloud Computing practical and cost-effective, designing a robust multi-tenant model is key to success of realizing its benefits without compromising on possible vulnerabilities that are usually posed when resources are shared. It is considered one of the research topics in Cloud Computing for both its positive and negative impacts.

On the positive side, it provides the necessary food for thought on strategizing available resources for their effective and efficient utilization across different users. Resources should be so carefully maneuvered that they are utilized to their maximum extent while not being overloaded. The strategy must also consider the spikes in the usage of shared resources to address the supply-demand problem such that the resources can be augmented to meet higher demands and released when not needed.

On the contrary, if resource sharing strategies are not well-designed, it becomes more of a threat than an opportunity. Though the positive side of multi-tenancy see it as an opportunity in the sense that it makes the best utilization of available resources with a view to meeting any kind of demand, it can expose confidentiality to the outer world when multiple users co-exist in the same platform. Any multi-tenant model that does not consider the vulnerabilities and security concerns will prove to be futile and makes Cloud Computing a bane rather than a boon.

These two contradicting features of multi-tenancy will make the concept a choice for pursuing research.

3. OBJECTIVES OF MULTI TENANCY

When we have multiple tenants sharing resources, different tenants have different goals and needs. Though tenants usually do not concern about how a service provider implements multi tenancy, each tenant expects the resources being shared to behave as if they were exclusively allocated to the tenant. Based on the expectations of tenants, we can broadly classify the objectives of Multi Tenancy into following categories:

3.1 Isolation

It indicates that a tenant should not be impacted by the activities of other tenants who are accessing the same set of resources through sharing. Tenants want the resources to behave as if they were exclusively provided to them. It is one of the important quality attributes in cloud computing as tenants need their data and operations not to be exposed to other tenants. Neither do they want their activities to be interfered with activities of other tenants. Service oriented architecture plays a key role in managing isolation in cloud-based offerings as it ensures that each interaction with the cloud service happens in its entirety autonomously. Though operations can be executed in isolation in a multi-tenant model, data may not be fully presented in exclusive manner for each separate tenant. To harness the true sense of shared model, certain data, mostly the commonly accessible data elements, need to be maintained in a way that it is accessible to all the tenants while the tenant specific data is exclusively available to the individual tenants. Consequently, the level of isolation is one of the crucial elements to choose the appropriate multi-tenant model.

3.2 Availability

This is another important parameter which indicates that the resources are consistently available according to the limitations defined in the Service Level Agreement (SLA). Concurrent access of shared resources by multiple tenants should not affect the availability of the resources. Availability is compromised if the multi-tenant model is not properly chosen and implemented as it leads to DoS attacks and the distributed nature of cloud computing even poses DDoS attacks. At the same time, even usual spikes in demand also cause availability at stake and may lead to unnotified shutdown of cloud resources. Thus, multi-tenant model should espouse proper load balancing mechanism along with adequate resource pool to meet demand spikes and ensure availability. Inclusion of an intrusion detection system in the model is essential to prevent DoS and DDoS attacks.

3.3 Scalability

Even though multiple tenants access multi-tenant resources, it is not uncommon to expect the resources to be scalable according to their demand. In other words, each tenant expects the shared resources to perform according to the parameters defined in the SLA irrespective of the concurrent presence of other tenants. This quality attribute ensures availability and resource optimization. Success of a cloud offering depends on its ability to scale itself up during higher demand periods and scale down when demand subsides. Again, load balancing and auto scaling mechanism need to be included in multi-tenant models to avoid issues that may pop up due to supply-demand differences.

3.4 Cost

The most tangible expectation from a multi-tenant cloud offering is that the operational cost should be considerably less than those incurred with a dedicated single tenant offering. Tenants also expect the capital expenditure to be very minimal. This quality attribute is dependent on the other key quality attributes of cloud computing in the sense that a more stringent service level agreement invites higher costs. Since different users have different levels of financial implications, a common costing model may not suffice, and we usually have different financial plans to address different groups of users. Nevertheless, this quality parameter alone should not decide the design of the multi-tenant model as it may lead to compromise on other important quality attributes. The multi-model must strike the right balance between cost and the other quality attributes.

3.5 Configurability

Though configurability to a large extent is not possible in a multi-tenant cloud service due to its uniformity across multiple tenants, tenants usually expect some degree of customizability such as personalizing the environment, changing colors, and plugging in their own code to meet their requirements. In multi-tenant models, it is hard to achieve at times because of certain under-lying technical limitations. A fully configurable multi-tenant model will negatively impact the cost benefit that user may get due to the cloud switch over. A partially configurable model edges over the pricing over benefits but at the cost of minimizing the configurable ability to users. Depending on user demands, multi-tenant may come up with different plans to address varying user requirements pertaining to configurability.

3.6 Regulatory Compliance

Tenants of a multi-tenant cloud offering expect the service provider to adhere to the industrial and regulatory laws of a given geography. Storing personally identifiable information (PII) in securely and implementing local tax systems are some of the examples related to regulatory compliances. Adhering to regional laws and regulations are of paramount importance to ensure successful rollout of a cloud offering.

These objectives drive the architecture of the multi-tenant service provision and based on the quality of service needed, these parameters can be adjusted in the architectural modelling. The next section illustrates some of the possible candidate architectures and their capabilities in terms of the afore-mentioned parameters.

4. MULTI TENANCY - ARCHITECTURE

The architecture of a multi-tenant application determines how well the application achieves the afore-said objectives within in tolerable limits. We can categorize the candidate architectures into four levels. They are Customized Tenancy, Configurable Single Tenancy, Configurable Multi-Tenancy and Scalable Multi-Tenancy. Let us succinctly understand each of the architectures:

Figure 1. Ad-hoc Tenancy

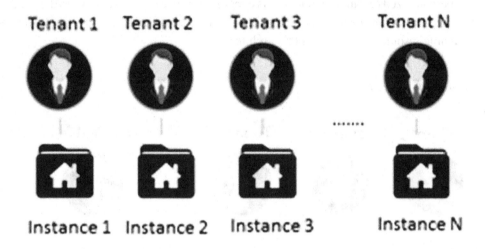

Figure 2. Configurable Single Tenancy

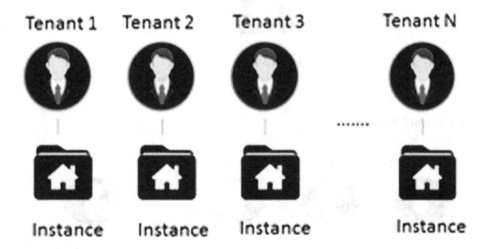

4.1 Ad-Hoc Tenancy

This architecture as shown in Figure 1 is built on the idea that tenants have their customized set of resources based on their needs. This warrants an enterprise data center that contains multiple instances and versions of both hardware and software resources that can cater to different customers according to their choice. In other words, each tenant will have access to a dedicated set of resources and processes tailored for their needs. This architecture performs well in terms of isolation, availability, configurability and regulatory compliance. On the other side, it does not give the cost benefit advantage as providing dedicated set of personalized resources per tenant is expensive. Since each tenant needs devoted resource management, it becomes extremely challenging for a service provider to manage multi-tenancy and implement a scalable resource provision in this architecture.

Figure 3. Configurable Multi Tenancy

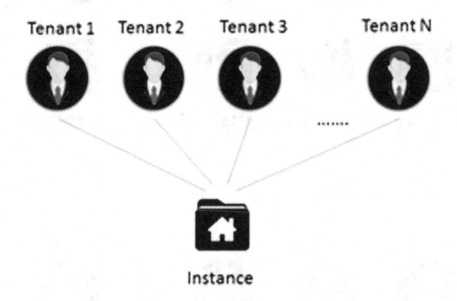

Figure 4. Scalable Multi Tenancy

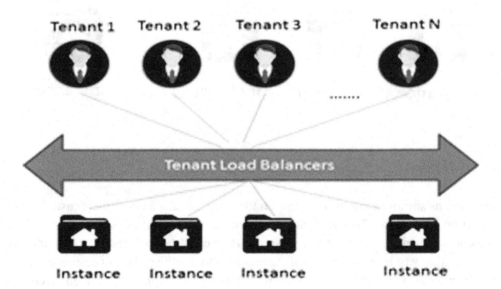

4.2 Configurable Single Tenancy

To overcome the challenges posed by the Ad-hoc Tenancy, we can define a new architecture wherein multiple tenants access the same set of resources duplicated for each instance. As shown in Figure 2, in this model, all the tenants will have access to identical copies of resources while the processes and business rules remain the same for each tenant. Each tenant can configure the standard resources offered to them according to their needs by adding new modules and deleting or modifying the existing modules. Though this architecture works well on all the parameters and provides easier management of resources, it poses a challenge in terms of finding skilled resources to configure an instance according to the business needs of a given tenant.

4.3 Configurable Multi Tenancy

In this model as shown in Figure 3, multiple tenants access the same set of resources through virtualization. A single physical set of resources are shared as virtual resources across multiple tenants. Since processes and modules are highly standardized, scope for customization is limited but it provides hooks for personalizing user interfaces and customizing reports. Management of resources is extremely easy as we have only a single instance and latest bug-free resources are available to all the hosted tenants. It offers excellent cost benefit to tenants as they will be charged only for accessing shared resources. On the flip side, any snag in a resource will bring the instance down for all the customers making availability a concern. Isolation may also be compromised if security is not properly injected in the service offerings. Customizability is less as compared to the previous two architectural models. Scalability is also an issue as we create multiple virtual copies of a single physical set of resources and creating multiple virtual resources to meet the demands may reduce the performance considerably making it unviable.

4.4 Scalable Multi Tenancy

To add scalability, we can introduce a load balancer per tenant as shown in Figure 4 in a Configurable Multi-Tenant Architectural model so that resources can be scaled up or scaled down from a dynamical pool of shared resources based on the demand. This offers a great flexibility both to tenants and service providers in terms of managing resources and meeting the individual goals of tenants. Though it carries a few challenges in managing physical resources and creating virtual resources dynamically, the benefits that we garner outperform these challenges making it the most practicable architecture in Cloud Computing for hosting multiple tenants.

4.5 Comparative Analysis

Analyzing the architectures hitherto discussed, we understand that each one has its own merits and demerits. Following table describes how each of the architectures performs on key indicators:

Table 1. Comparative analysis of multi tenancy architectures

Key Parameter/Architecture	Ad-hoc Tenancy	Configurable Single Tenancy	Configurable Multi Tenancy	Scalable Multi Tenancy
Isolation	High	High	Moderate	Moderate
Availability	High	High	Low	High
Scalability	Moderate	High	Low	High
Cost	High	Moderate	Low	Low
Configurability	High	Moderate	Moderate	Moderate
Regulatory Compliance	High	Moderate	Moderate	Moderate

4.6 Analysis on QoS Attributes

This section explains the analysis on various quality attributes that are paly a vital role in designing a multi-tenant architecture.

4.6.1. Isolation

Isolation is considered a very important characteristic in multi-tenancy and is thought as one of the difficult features to be implemented. To understand the possibility of implementing isolation without compromising on confidentiality threats, we need to assess it on a three-fold approach i.e., in terms of infrastructure, platform and software.

In infrastructure clouds, virtualization plays a vital role in creating multiple virtual copies of one or more physical resources and the virtualization software or hypervisor is built such that no two virtual copies of the same physical resources will infringe upon each other under any circumstances. In other words, achieving isolation in infrastructural clouds is achievable through hypervisors.

Platform clouds use a similar approach of virtualizing the physical resources in combination with the libraries and utilities through hypervisor which can provide isolation.

Providing isolation is software clouds is more challenging when compared to its lower-level counterparts as one copy of software may not be able to cater to the varying demands of its tenants. Based on the customizability and configurability requirements of different users, we need to choose the appropriate software provisioning mechanism. If tenants need uncompromising ability to configure their software application to meet their own unique needs, the possible option is to host them separate pieces of software with full license. This needs additional pooling of infrastructural resources to host multiple copies of the same software on the same physical platform. On the positive side, this architecture provides full isolation as each tenant is using his own software application. If tenants can compromise on their personalized experience, we can have single copy of software with minimal ability to personalize and customize their views and processes. This approach will provide partial isolation in the sense that all the global elements will be visible to all the tenants and only unique elements will be visible to the individual tenants according to their configurations. Isolation, in this architecture, may pose confidentiality threat if not implemented carefully in the sense that one tenant may get access to view the data of another tenant unauthorizedly which is a fundamental security threat.

4.6.2 Availability

Availability is so important that the success of a cloud offering solely depends on its availability metric. Most of the service level agreements need the availability to be at least 95%. In most of the multi-tenant architectures, availability is ensured to the highest level but in configurable multi-tenant architecture, the availability may not be fully guaranteed because the resource allocation may become difficult if scalability is not addressed. In scalable multi-tenant architectures, availability is fully guaranteed.

4.6.3 Scalability

Scalability in cloud offerings is possible with the help of a load balancer that can dynamically allocate resources from a shared resource pool to meet higher demand and release resources back to the shared pool when demand subsides. This offers a great flexibility both to tenants and service providers in terms of managing resources and meeting the individual goals of tenants. Though it carries a few challenges in managing physical resources and creating virtual resources dynamically, the benefits that we garner outperform these challenges making it the most practicable architecture in Cloud Computing for hosting multiple tenants. Scalability is highly available in scalable multi-tenant architecture with an automatic load balancer.

4.4.4 Cost

Financial benefit is one of the most pivotal reasons why many users are opting for cloud offerings over dedicated resources. Cloud offerings will not just eliminate the capital expenses but reduce operational expenses and this cost benefit is realized more when we go for a scalable multi-tenant architecture over any other types of cloud architectures.

4.6.5 Configurability

In a single tenant model, configurability is fully provided whereas in a multi-tenant model, configurability is minimal and sometimes, may not even be possible based on the implementation. In multi-tenant models, the common features are provided to all the users and version upgrades are available to all the tenants but addressing specific requirements of tenants may not be possible as a single piece of software is used by all the tenants.

4.6.6 Regulatory Compliance

Adhering to geographically enforced policies and regulations is of utmost importance if we want a cloud offering to be regulatory compliant. It is also known as cloud compliance which refers to the art and science of complying with regulatory standards of cloud usage in accordance with industry guidelines and local, national, and international laws. Cloud compliance is usually guaranteed in single tenant cloud offerings as separate licenses are issued to different user groups. On the other hand, multi-tenant cloud offerings may suffer the drawback of leaking sensitive data to other tenants if not designed properly.

5. SECURITY CONCERNS

As discussed in the previous sections of this paper, cloud computing offers scalable, flexible, and efficient service offerings and enables organizations to outsource their non-core data elements and operations to a service provider to reduce their capital expenditure and increase their operational efficiency. Despite these benefits, cloud computing is coupled with a few security and privacy concerns that need to be addressed to make it a viable option. In fact, these security concerns are causing organizations to refrain themselves from migrating to cloud offerings even for their non-core business activities.

Organizations are apprehensive of storing their data on physically inaccessible cloud services and running a software application on a platform owned by someone else. Some of the key concerns that arise while accessing cloud services are – data loss, data privacy issues, phishing, and hacking, DoS attacks, DDoS attacks and IP spoofing. These concerns are more conspicuous in multi-tenant models wherein hackers may provide reliable cloud services at relatively cheaper prices with a view to accessing sensitive information of its tenants. Cloud service providers must address how data loss can be prevented or how it can be compensated in the unlikely event of its happening. Data privacy is yet another security threat as data is hosted on infrastructure owned by a different party and there is not guarantee that it cannot be accessed by the owner of the infrastructure. Availability of cloud services is also a related security concern in the sense that it may be made unavailable intentionally causing damage to the organizational activities. DoS attacks prone to happen in cloud-based services as any kind of security compromise will give the leeway to potential hackers to seize the opportunity and flood the cloud system denying services to legitimate users. The distributed nature of cloud computing makes it more vulnerable to DDoS attacks and these threats must be carefully assessed and addressed. Since analyzing all possible security threats may not be possible, intrusion detection plays a paramount role in identifying possible security threats and preventing these attacks. Regulatory compliance is another key issue that many cloud service providers are grappling with as the cyber laws of different geographies may not support the hosting of institutional data on a third-party cloud storage service considering its security demerits. Succinctly speaking, we need address the key security concerns related to data privacy, data loss, resource availability and adherence to regulatory provisions to make multi-tenant cloud computing a practicable solution to organizations.

This argument lays the necessary foundation and provides the necessary impetus to come up with multi-tenant design approaches that are not only cost-effective but also secure. Further research should focus making multi-tenant architectures secure such that they meet the service level agreements without being detrimental to security provisions.

5.1 Security Concerns in IaaS

Though IaaS offerings provide major benefits like cost savings and scalability, they are associated with a few security concerns as listed:

a. Data Security: In a multi-tenant environment, data from different customers is stored on the same physical infrastructure. This means that there is a risk of data leakage or data breaches, which can compromise the confidentiality, integrity, and availability of the data.

b. Network Security: The shared network infrastructure can be a source of security concerns. One tenant's data traffic can be intercepted by another tenant if the network is not properly isolated. Also, if the network infrastructure is not secured properly, it can lead to unauthorized access, and in the worst case, a full-scale network breach.

c. Access Management: Multi-tenancy means that multiple users from different organizations access the same infrastructure. This makes access management a critical concern. If access control is not properly implemented, tenants may have unauthorized access to each other's data or even infrastructure.

d. Resource Allocation: In a multi-tenant environment, resources such as CPU, memory, storage, and network bandwidth are shared among multiple tenants. There is a risk that a resource-intensive tenant can hog resources and impact the performance of other tenants, leading to service disruption or denial of service.

e. Compliance: Different tenants may have different compliance requirements, and it is the responsibility of the IaaS provider to ensure that the infrastructure meets all applicable regulatory requirements.

f. Insider Threats: Insider threats are a major security concern in a multi-tenant environment. A rogue employee of the IaaS provider or a tenant can gain unauthorized access to sensitive data, exploit vulnerabilities, or disrupt services.

g. Inter-tenant Vulnerabilities: Multi-tenancy can lead to inter-tenant vulnerabilities, where a vulnerability in one tenant's application or infrastructure can be used to gain unauthorized access to another tenant's data or infrastructure.

Overall, these are some of the main security concerns that need to be addressed in a multi-tenant IaaS environment.

5.2 Security Concerns in PaaS

While PaaS provides many benefits, including scalability, flexibility, and cost savings, it also introduces a range of security concerns. Here are some of the key security concerns in PaaS:

a. Data security: PaaS providers may store sensitive data on their servers, such as user credentials, application data, and configuration information. The risk of data breaches and unauthorized access increases if the data is not adequately protected.

b. Access control: PaaS platforms may allow multiple users to access the same application, and this can pose a risk if proper access controls are not implemented. The lack of proper user authentication, authorization, and access controls may result in unauthorized users gaining access to the application or data.

c. Compliance: PaaS providers may be subject to various regulations and standards, such as PCI DSS, HIPAA, and GDPR. If the provider fails to comply with these regulations, it may result in data breaches, legal liability, and financial penalties.

d. Application security: Applications running on PaaS platforms may be vulnerable to various security threats, such as SQL injection, cross-site scripting (XSS), and session hijacking. These vulnerabilities can result in data breaches, application downtime, and loss of data.

e. Network security: PaaS platforms may use shared network infrastructure, and this can pose a risk if proper network security controls are not implemented. The lack of network segmentation and isolation may result in unauthorized access to other applications and data.

f. Identity and access management: Identity and access management (IAM) is critical for PaaS security. If IAM is not properly configured, it may result in unauthorized access to applications and data.

g. Business continuity and disaster recovery: PaaS providers must have robust business continuity and disaster recovery plans in place to ensure that applications and data remain available in the event of an outage or disaster.

Overall, PaaS providers must implement a comprehensive security program that includes regular security assessments, vulnerability management, incident response, and employee security awareness training to mitigate the risks associated with cloud computing.

5.3 Security Concerns in SaaS

SaaS provides many benefits, including scalability, flexibility, and cost savings, it also introduces a range of security concerns. Here are some of the key security concerns in SaaS applications:

a. Data security: SaaS providers may store sensitive data on their servers, such as user credentials, application data, and configuration information. The risk of data breaches and unauthorized access increases if the data is not adequately protected.

b. Access control: SaaS applications may allow multiple users to access the same data, and this can pose a risk if proper access controls are not implemented. The lack of proper user authentication, authorization, and access controls may result in unauthorized users gaining access to data.

c. Compliance: SaaS providers may be subject to various regulations and standards, such as PCI DSS, HIPAA, and GDPR. If the provider fails to comply with these regulations, it may result in data breaches, legal liability, and financial penalties.

d. Application security: SaaS applications may be vulnerable to various security threats, such as SQL injection, cross-site scripting (XSS), and session hijacking. These vulnerabilities can result in data breaches, application downtime, and loss of data.

e. Network security: SaaS providers may use shared network infrastructure, and this can pose a risk if proper network security controls are not implemented. The lack of network segmentation and isolation may result in unauthorized access to other applications and data.

f. Identity and access management: Identity and access management (IAM) is critical for SaaS security. If IAM is not properly configured, it may result in unauthorized access to applications and data.

g. Business continuity and disaster recovery: SaaS providers must have robust business continuity and disaster recovery plans in place to ensure that applications and data remain available in the event of an outage or disaster.

h. Third-party integrations: SaaS applications may integrate with third-party services, such as payment gateways and customer relationship management (CRM) systems. These integrations can introduce security risks if the third-party service is not adequately secured.

Overall, SaaS providers must implement a comprehensive security program that includes regular security assessments, vulnerability management, incident response, and employee security awareness training to mitigate the risks associated with cloud computing.

6. CONCLUSION

In this paper, we have laconically looked at various service offerings provided in Cloud Computing while emphasizing the importance of Multi Tenancy to realize the benefits of Cloud Computing. It is learnt that multi tenancy provides manifold benefits in SaaS offerings as compared to PaaS and IaaS. Isolation, configurability, cost, availability, scalability and regulatory compliance are some of the key objectivity functions that customers look at while going for a multi-tenant cloud service. Based on the parameters, different candidate architectures have been discussed and a comparison is also presented. This review provides us with the foundation to propose an algorithmic approach to suggest an architectural model based on the parametrized values assigned to each of the key performance indicators. We will also look at various vulnerabilities posed due to multi tenancy and the corresponding countenances as part of our future work.

REFERENCES

Ahmed, S. T., Kumar, V. V., & Kim, J. (2023). AITel: eHealth Augmented Intelligence based Telemedicine Resource Recommendation Framework for IoT devices in Smart cities. *IEEE Internet of Things Journal, 1*, 1. Advance online publication. doi:10.1109/JIOT.2023.3243784

Alex, D. S., Mahesh, T. R., Kumar, V. V., Aluvalu, R., Maheswari, V. U., & Shitharth, S. (2022). Cervical Cancer Diagnosis Using Intelligent Living Behavior of Artificial Jellyfish Optimized With Artificial Neural Network. *IEEE Access : Practical Innovations, Open Solutions, 10*, 126957–126968. doi:10.1109/ACCESS.2022.3221451

AlJahdali, H., Albatli, A., Garraghan, P., Townend, P., Lau, L., & Xu, J. (2014, April). Multi-tenancy in cloud computing. In *2014 IEEE 8th international symposium on service oriented system engineering* (pp. 344-351). IEEE. 10.1109/SOSE.2014.50

AlJahdali, H., Albatli, A., Garraghan, P., Townend, P., Lau, L., & Xu, J. (2014, April). Multi-tenancy in cloud computing. In *2014 IEEE 8th international symposium on service oriented system engineering* (pp. 344-351). IEEE. 10.1109/SOSE.2014.50

Aljahdali, H., Townend, P., & Xu, J. (2013, March). Enhancing multi-tenancy security in the cloud IaaS model over public deployment. In *2013 IEEE seventh international symposium on service-oriented system engineering* (pp. 385-390). IEEE. 10.1109/SOSE.2013.50

Buyya, R., Vecchiola, C., & Selvi, S. T. (2013). *Mastering cloud computing: foundations and applications programming*. Newnes.

Ding, W. M., Ghansah, B., & Wu, Y. Y. (2016). Research on the virtualization technology in cloud computing environment. In *International journal of engineering research in Africa* (Vol. 21, pp. 191–196). Trans Tech Publications Ltd.

Goralski, W. (2017). *The illustrated network: how TCP/IP works in a modern network*. Morgan Kaufmann.

Hamdaqa, M., & Tahvildari, L. (2012). Cloud computing uncovered: A research landscape. *Advances in Computers*, *86*, 41–85. doi:10.1016/B978-0-12-396535-6.00002-8

Ionita, A. D. (Ed.). (2012). *Migrating Legacy Applications: Challenges in Service Oriented Architecture and Cloud Computing Environments: Challenges in Service Oriented Architecture and Cloud Computing Environments*. IGI Global.

Jansen, W. A. (2011, January). Cloud hooks: Security and privacy issues in cloud computing. In *2011 44th Hawaii International Conference on System Sciences* (pp. 1-10). IEEE.

Kanade, S., & Manza, R. (2019). A Comprehensive Study on Multi Tenancy in SAAS Applications. *International Journal of Computer Applications*, *181*(44), 25–27. doi:10.5120/ijca2019918531

Maithili, K., Vinothkumar, V., & Latha, P. (2018). Analyzing the Security Mechanisms to Prevent Unauthorized Access in Cloud and Network Security. *Journal of Computational and Theoretical Nanoscience*, *15*(6), 2059–2063. doi:10.1166/jctn.2018.7407

Mell, P., & Grance, T. (2011). *NIST SP 800-145, The NIST definition of cloud computing. Nat. Inst. Standards Technol.* Tech. Rep.

Miyachi, C. (2018). What is "Cloud"? It is time to update the NIST definition?. *IEEE Cloud computing*, *5*(03), 6-11.

Patel, P., Ranabahu, A. H., & Sheth, A. P. (2009). *Service level agreement in cloud computing*. Wright State University.

Rashid, A., & Chaturvedi, A. (2019). Cloud computing characteristics and services: A brief review. *International Journal on Computer Science and Engineering*, *7*(2), 421–426.

Rountree, D., & Castrillo, I. (2013). *The basics of cloud computing: Understanding the fundamentals of cloud computing in theory and practice*. Newnes.

Venkatesan, V. K., Izonin, I., Periyasamy, J., Indirajithu, A., Batyuk, A., & Ramakrishna, M. T. (2022). Incorporation of Energy Efficient Computational Strategies for Clustering and Routing in Heterogeneous Networks of Smart City. [MDPI AG]. *Energies*, *15*(20), 7524. doi:10.3390/en15207524

Chapter 11
An Analysis of Deep Learning Techniques Adopted in Medical Imaging

M. Rajani Shree
BNM Institue of Technology, India

Abhinav Ram Bhatta
Jain University, India

M. R. Sarveshvar
Jain University, India

Kritika Jain
Jain University, India

ABSTRACT

The various methods which have been adopted in processing and segmentation of medical images using deep learning and machine learning techniques are examined and analyzed in this article. Medical images analysis and their methods have been swiftly evolved into deep learning techniques and especially in convolutional neural networks. Deep learning concepts that may be used for the image classification, detection, and logging of medical related pictures and objects have been examined. Medical applications include: research and investigations into neuro, retinal and pulmonary, digital pathologies, breast, heart and musculoskeletal diseases and their corresponding analysis. Deep learning has already been used to accurately diagnose diseases and classify image samples, and it has the potential to revolutionise the entire landscape of healthcare. These uses are only expected to expand in the future. The most recent developments, including a critical analysis of the current problems have been summarized, and made plans for additional research in medical imaging.

DOI: 10.4018/978-1-6684-6971-2.ch011

Copyright © 2023, IGI Global. Copying or distributing in print or electronic forms without written permission of IGI Global is prohibited.

INTRODUCTION

From the outset of medical imaging, only the patient and a skilled physician or doctor can produce the images for examination and diagnosis purposes. Over time, as technology evolves, medical picture quality has also grown considerably high and because of this, medical practitioners are able to carry out a more accurate diagnostic analysis. But, we still need to take human error and/or incomplete diagnosis into consideration. Because we have seen computers being faster and more accurate, the images taken by X-Rays, MRIs, CT scans, Position Emission Tomography (PET scan) and Ultrasound may be downloaded into the computer.

In order to foresee how special diagnosis will help the patient in future and how the proper treatment can be provided, the programmer would adopt various machine learning and profound learning methodologies, supervised, uncontrolled or regression analyses. Those major trends have been identified by members of the medical image analysis team. The move from hand-made to data-functional systems is extraordinarily slow. Before AlexNet's breakthrough many other alternative machine learning systems have become prevalent.

Known to be the Global Deep Learning Model Training, Researchers include primary component analysis, Medical image patcher clustering, Dictionary techniques and introduced CNNs that are only trained end-to-end after examination. In this paper, we focus on such profound models and discuss most prevalent functional learning methods for medical imaging. With great progress in this area, a considerable study has been made this a highest priority for the future of medical treatment and address the ultimate issue of how to win against different types of cancers like Skin cancer, Anal Cancer, Breast Cancer etc.

In medical imaging, the balance between protecting key diagnostic parts of the image and noise suppression must be emphasized. Denoising images is a difficult challenge that arises in many image processing and computer vision applications. The most important quality of a good picture denoising model is that it removes as much noise as possible while maintaining the edges. Thanks to significant improvements in computerized medical picture reconstruction and related discoveries in analytic approaches and computer-aided diagnosis. Medical imaging has risen to become one of the most important sub-fields in scientific imaging. Radiologists use medical procedures such as ultrasound, MRI, CT-Scan, and PET-Scan to visualize the interior structures of the human body without the need for surgery. These provide a lot of information on human soft tissue, which is helpful in determining the cause of illness *(N. Goel et. al., 2016)*.

LITERATURE SURVEY

To assess medical images, a large range of applications and algorithms have been proposed so far. Deep learning advances, particularly deep convolutional neural networks (CNN), have increased the performance of medical picture classification algorithms. However, training deep CNN using medical images from scratch is a difficult task that necessitates a substantial amount of annotated data.

Deep Learning Methods Used in Medical Image Processing

We begin by discussing the basic reasons for deep learning's popularity, which include numerous key achievements in computer science. Following that, we will go over the basics of perceptrons and neural networks, as well as some basic theory that is sometimes ignored. This allows us to better understand the reasons for deep learning's ascent in a range of industries. This rapid advancement has undoubtedly influenced medical image processing, notably image detection and recognition, image segmentation, image registration, and computer-aided diagnosis.

Learning Algorithms

Machine learning supervised and unsupervised are the two most frequently used techniques to develop high end applications. In order to build a prediction model, supervised approaches require a series of inputs and outputs to be "learned out." Supervised learning algorithms learn by refining a set of model parameters that work with the inputs of the model and best suits the output set of the model. The objective is to train a y-form model = f(x) so as to forecast output, y, from input, x.

Two primary types of supervised approaches are available. Classification is the first. Classification procedures anticipate categorical results, for example, if or not a certain object is a cat, a transaction is fraudulent or not and whether the customer is to return. Regression is the other type. Continuous variables, for example following week sales estimates, are calculated via regression methods.

Features are called inputs to machine learning algorithms. Mathematical modifications of data pieces essential to the learning task of machines can be included. Unlike supervised learning techniques, uncontrolled learning techniques function without known results or observations - i.e., these techniques do not strive to predict any specific results. Unattended approaches are instead trying to find patterns in data sets. Unattended learning is a feasible method to issues that do not have enough output or example data to train a supervised model. Unattended approaches include clustering algorithms that meaningfully group data. Clustering techniques are used to locate and identify similar clients in retail banking or equipment sensor data sources. Examples of clustering algorithms include k-means – a process for establishing subgroups of similar data points using 'distance' between data dots, based on characteristics – and Gaussian blend models – a method for identifying subgroups of similar data dots using statistical probability distributions.

Neural Networks

Most deep learning methods are based on a sort of learning algorithms. A neural network consists of neurons or units with certain initiations or features.

$$\Theta = \{W, B\}$$

W refers to a set of weights, while B refers to a series of biases. Activation, *a*, comprises of a linear grouping of the involvement of the neuron *x* with the learned parameters *w,b*, that are controlled by elemental non-linearity, $\sigma(\Delta)$ called as a transfer function:

$$a = \sigma(wT^x + b)$$

Typical transfer functions, $f(x,\theta)$, of traditional neural networks include ***sigma*** and ***hyperbolic*** tangent functions. This alteration is made via a multi-layer sensor (MLP), which is the leading classical network of neurons (*Geert Litjen et. al., 2017*)

$$f(x;\theta) = \sigma(w^T\sigma(w^T\ldots\ldots\sigma(w^Tx+b))+b$$

In this case, **w** is a matrix of $\mathbf{w}_k$ columns linked to the result's initiation **k**. The input-output layers are also known as 'hidden' layers. Deep learning is the output of a neural network with numerous hidden layers, which is referred to as a 'deep' neural network.

Convolutional Neural Networks

Convolutional neural networks (CNN) is a sort of deep-learning model for processing which has grid patterns, for example photographs, inspired by the organization and meant to analyse spatial hierarchies of low- and high-level patterns in a robotic and adaptive manner. CNN is a mathematical system made up of three different types of building blocks: convolution, consolidation, and fully linked layers. Convolution and pool layers are the first two, while the third, a completely linked layer, transforms the extracted features to their final output, as seen in Figure 1. CNN has a convolution component that consists of a series of mathematical operations, each of which is a unique linear operation. The pixel values are retained in a two-dimensional (2D) grid, a numerical array, and a tiny grid of parameters called kernel (a feature optimizer) are applied to each image point, making CNNs particularly resourceful at processing the image. The recovered characteristics can grow increasingly complicated hierarchically and progressively as one layer feeds its output into the next. Using a back propagation and gradient descent optimization approach, a training procedure is used to decrease the disparity between outputs and ground realities (*Yamashita et. al., 2018*). The CNN algorithm is a multi-dimensional array processing algorithm that may be used to analyze images.

In image processing, the first function is input standards (pixel standards) at a given place in the image, as well as the auxiliary function is a filter (kernel), both of which can be expressed as an array of numbers (*R. Buettner et. al, 2020 and J. Ker et. al. 2018*). The output is derived by multiplying the two functions by their dot product. The filter is then moved to the next place in the image, as indicated by the step span. The algorithm is repetitive until the complete picture has been spanned, resulting in a feature/characteristic (activation) map. This is a map that shows exactly where the filter is very active and sees things like a straight line, a dot, or a curved edge. The feature mappings gradually build up to higher features at successive layers, including eye, nose or ear, when they become input for next layer in the CNN architecture.

MEDICAL IMAGING AND DEEP LEARNING

Medical imagery has been available for quite a while and researchers improved it as the technology advanced. The researchers begin with the simple X-rays and go through advanced MRI and CT scans. The following sections look at methods in which deep learning can be used to analyze photos of various sorts of medical imagery.

Figure 1. General overview of a neural network

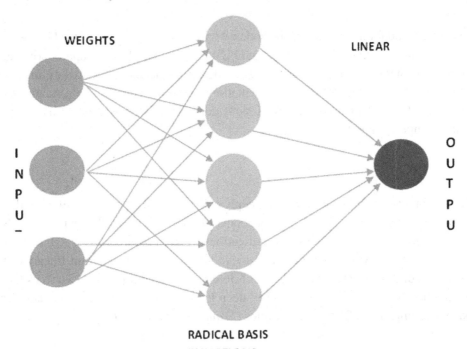

In medical field, machine learning has proven indispensable in the diagnosis and treatment of a wide range of disorders. With the advancement of new imaging techniques, the need to maximize the value of large amounts of data is becoming increasingly important. Machine learning, in particular deep learning, presents us with a new paradigm for learning and utilizing the massive amount of big image data intelligently. Machine learning in medicine is becoming one of the most hopeful and rapidly expanding areas of study. The primary objective is to progress scientific research in an extensive field of medical imaging using the concept of machine learning (*Wang, Q., Shi, Y., & Shen, 2019*). Deep Learning is not only beneficial in medical imaging field, but also it is more commonly adopted in Natural Language Processing (NLP) applications like POS tagger for Indian Languages using Deep learning concept using Keras (Rajani Shree M & Shambhavi B R, 2022).

It is critical that this study area contributes to better patient care. Machine learning tools are concerned about ensuring that they be used in the most effective way possible. Deep learning methods aid in categorizing, classifying, and enumerating illness characteristics from image processing in medical image analysis. It also allows for the expansion of analytical aims and the creation of therapy prediction models for patients. Deep learning is surviving and thriving in the health-care research sector, and medical imaging experts are looking into these issues. It is rapidly improving, much like deep learning in other fields outside of health care (*J. Latif, C. Xiao, A. Imran & S. Tu., 2019*)

X-Rays

X-rays have been around for a very lengthy period and with technology growth, we have witnessed a lot of progress not just in picture quality (Figure 2 and Figure 3), but also how computer advancement may increase and develop them further. By recognizing and detecting the features to make clinical judgments, Deep Learning can manage complex data representations and mimic qualified physicians. In medicine, Deep Learning architectures are used in medical X-ray detection as well as other domains such as image processing and computer vision.

Xception

Xception is neural network architecture with a deeply convolutional design that refers to the beginning modules that are replaced with profound, separate convolutions. When tested with the ImageNet dataset, which has 300 million pictures and 70,000 classifications, Xception outperforms V3. Hyperparameters may be used more efficiently with Xception V3. Convolutions with depth separation, linearity, and residual connections are used. The structure is made up of 36 convolutional layers that serve as the network's functional extraction foundation. With the aid of deep learning frameworks like Keras or Tensorflow, we can modify and implement 25 to 40 code lines (*Francois Chollet, 2017*).

Figure 2. Example of input x-ray images

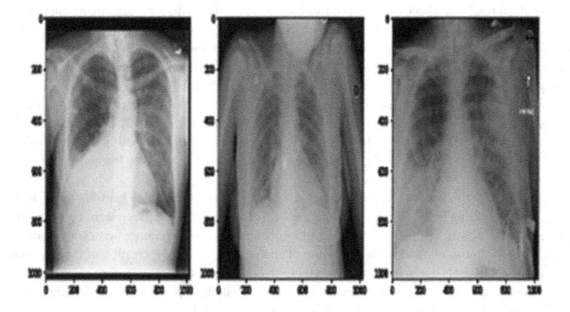

A Receiver Operating Characteristic curve (ROC) is indeed a diagram which shows a classification model's performance over all thresholds. On the basis of real positive rate or false positive rate, the curve plots. AUC (Area Under Curve) is a metric that aggregates performance across all thresholds.

Figure 3. X-ray image and image intensities depicted in a histogram

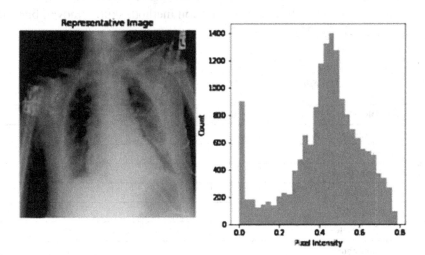

The results will be demonstrated using the area below the ROC curve (AUC – Area Under Curve) rating, which is used to estimate the model's capability in a multi-label classification of illness prediction. The ROC helps us evaluate the degree of separability, whereas the AUC helps us estimate the likelihood of illnesses. According to AUC, the higher the scores, the better the outcome in class discrimination *(Dmitriy Zinovev. 2011)*. This is depicted in the Table 1.

True Positive Rate (TPR) vs False Positive Rate (FPR) is presented on a graph.

- TPR= TP / (TP + FN)
- Specificity= TN / (TN + FP)
- Specificity = 1- FPR

For most diseases, the suggested model has generated improved AUC values and Hernia score is considered the best. Models were assessed on 75 percent training photos and 25 percent test images.

Magnetic Resonance Imaging

MRI is a non-invasive medical imaging method used by a radiologist to assist discovers and diagnose spinal problems. In contrast to an X-ray or CT scan (computed tomography), an MRI scan does not provide photos of the spinal cord structure.

Dynamic magnets and radio waves of the IRM interact with the water and fat molecules of your body to create detailed images of soft tissue and bone of the spine. Weak tissues are the spinal cord, nerve roots, blood vessel, ligaments, muscles, intervertebral discs and endplates. The bone tissue consists of the vertebral bodies and neighbouring components, for example, joints facet.

A MRI scan with or without contrast can be conducted, which is a medicinal tincture (e.g. gadolinium) injected into a vein, which improves image visibility. Tissues that collect more contrast seem brighter than tissues around them and can give more information on diseases such as bone cancer, infections (vertebral osteomyelitis) or inflammation. Due to their intensity, non-homogeneity and intensity variations, contrast, noise and signals, automatic interpretation of MR images is problematic. In order to process MR images, researchers followed a registration method, skull removal, bias correction, and intensity normalisation (*Akkus, 2017*).

Table 1. Diseases against their respective AUC scores

Disorder	AUC Scores
Effusion	.61
Pleural Thickening	.56
Emphysema	.52
Pneumonia	.58
Fibrosis	.69
Atelectasis	.57
Pneumothorax	.54
Infiltration	.54
Hernia	.83
Cardiomegaly	.30
Edema	.72
Mass	.56
Nodule	.57
Consolidation	.60

Registration is the anatomical spatial alignment of pictures. Image registration facilitates the stereotactic regulation of MR images (shown in Figure 4). Skull stripping involves removing the skull from the MR images that are obtained to draw the attention necessary to the brain and tissues. The bias field correction addresses the image contrast changes because of the magnets that interact with the final image. The most common approach for correcting this is the N4 field correction. In intensity normalisation, the intensities of all images in a reference scale are mapped. This is done manually by calculating the picture Z scores.

The quantitative investigations of brain damage include a large diameter, volume, count, and development of the reported imaging biomarkers for the measurement of treatment responses for related conditions like brain cancer, MS or stroke. The genuine production of these biomarkers requires preliminary segmentation. Despite major efforts in breakthrough segmentation and state-of-the-art imaging, accurate brain lesions segments remain a serious obstacle. Many automated approaches to lesion segmentation have been developed, including uncontrolled modeling methods aimed at automatically adapting to fresh picture data Supervised machine learning methods that learn textural and appearance attributes of lesions in a representative dataset and Atlas approaches that integrate supervised and unmonitored learning with a unified pipeline through the registration of labeled data or cohort data in a similar anatomical space (*Akkus, 2017*).. CNN based profound learning in MR imagery was applied in the detection of stroke, MS cerebral micro bleeds and therapeutic response prediction.

Figure 4. Stereotaxic apparatus for the human head to perform intricate procedures

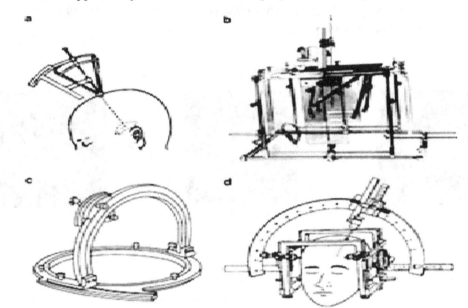

Patch by patch CNN Architecture is familiar and straightforward method for training a CNN algorithm for segmentation. A given image generates a N*N patch surrounding each pixel, on which the model is trained and provided class tags to effectively distinguish between classes such as regular, normal brain and a tumor. The intended networks incorporate many convolutional, activation, pooling, and fully linked layers in a sequential order. This is depicted in figure 5.

Two CNN architectures are linked together in a cascaded CNN design. To obtain categorization, the result of the primary CNN is used as an input to the secondary CNN. It is used to train the former CNN with primary class-label predictions, whereas the latter CNN is utilized to tweak the former CNN's results', as demonstrated in Figure 6.

Figure 5. An illustration of a patch-wise CNN architecture for the task of segmenting brain tumours

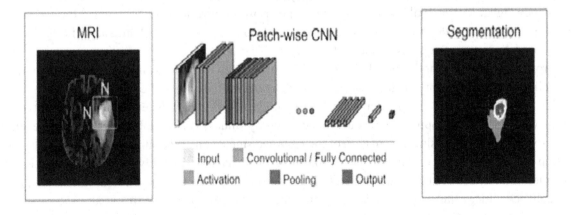

Figure 6. Visual display of a scheme that shows the CNN architecture for the brain tumor analysis problem where the initial network output (CNN-1) is used additional to picture information for refined input into the subsequent network (CNN-2)

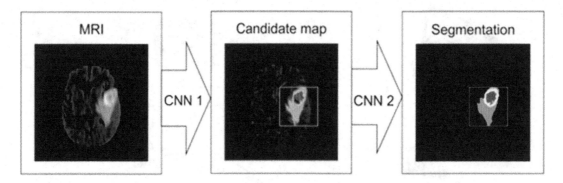

Ultrasound

Ultrasound scans, or sonography, are safe since they employ sound waves or echos to create a picture rather than radiation. Ultrasound scans are used to assess foetal growth and to diagnose liver, heart, kidney, or abdominal issues. They can also help with certain types of biopsies. The resulting image is termed a sonogram.

Sufficient front end radiation, signal extraction (for clutter suppression), compression and speed approximation determinate the success of ultrasonic imagery and its uses. It can be showed that neural networks are used as a universal function approximation to enhance resolution and contrast across the imaging chain as strong artificial agents and signal processors.

The high simplicity of the beam forming process has made it the conventional and industry standard approach for ultrasonic beam forming. Time-to-flight corrections which can affect the re-construction quality of native spatial filters are based mostly on the geometric sanctity of the scene and the assumption of the speed of the sound waves to be constant in the various media.

In the Fourier domain, they have neural networks to process channel data. For this purpose, discrete Fourier processing initially occurs in the axially delayed data sections of the channel. A separate, fully connected network will be used for each frequency silo array retorts. In order to create an emitted radio frequency signal at that axial point, a frequency spectrum is converted and aggregated throughout the array. Networks have deliberately removed off-axis responses from ULC (Ultrasound Lung Comets) data simulations for point goals (outside of the beam's first null).

From the Figure 7, adaptive weight beamforming using deep learning is shown, for both approaches, as well as exemplary reconstructed images of in-silico and in-vivo (*Ruud J.G, 2019*).

ULM (Ultrasound Location Microscopy) is a wonderful winning concept derived from fluoresce ultrasound microscopy optics. Ultrasounds and a highly diluted microbubble solution are generally used to perform ULM. Using information of the recorded signal construction, particularly its sparseness within a transforming zone, standard ULMs may be expanded to considerably loosen the restrictions on the micro-bubble concentration and therefore cover more vessels in less time (*R. J. G. van Sloun, 2017*). An enhanced image frame received can be represented as follows to achieve this goal:

Figure 7. Beamforming and In-silico and In-vivo images

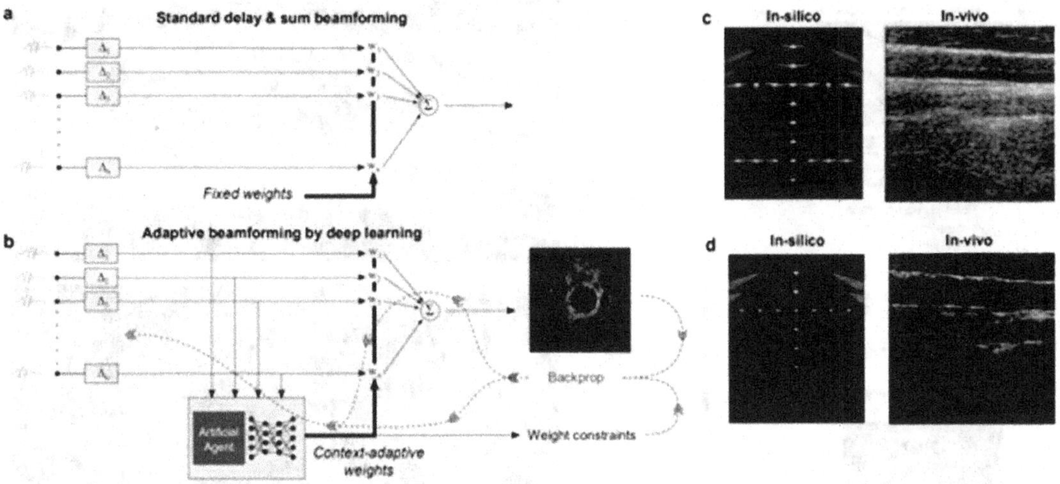

$$y = Ax + w$$

Where x denotes the microbubble's sparse dispersion on a high-resolution grid y. A is a matrix with a point dissemination function in each column and a noise vector w.

Assuming a sparse distribution on a high-resolution grid, the equation governing the creation of a final super-resolution picture is:

$$\hat{x} = \arg\min_{x} \left\| y - Ax \right\|_2^2 + \lambda \left\| x \right\| \tag{1}$$

In which 'λ' is a constraint that takes into account the influence of ‖x‖.

Figure 8 demonstrates a fast ultrasonic localization microscope using deep learning (deep-ULM) to map low-resolution, extremely resolute, sparse spots on an 8x thinner grid using a convolutional neural network. (a) Real simulations of the corresponding ultrasonic captures, including point spread estimation, modulation frequency, background noise and pixel spacing are used to train the network. (b) A continuous series of frames from the rat spinal cord with a conventional maximum intensity projection. (c) The deep-ULM matching to is reconstructed (*Ruud J.G, 2019*).

DEEP LEARNING FOR COMPUTER ASSISTED SURGERY WITH MINIMAL INVASIVENESS

Surgical device identification has been used in a marginally invasive computer assisted surgical setting but not properly detected desirable areas of the surgical instrument. The operational tool has been separated into two sections in a prior study: the termination effector and the shaft, not sufficient for the elements to be obviously detected. The accuracy and speed of processing of instrument detection can be improved using Deep Learning.

Figure 8. Fast Ultrasonic localization microscope

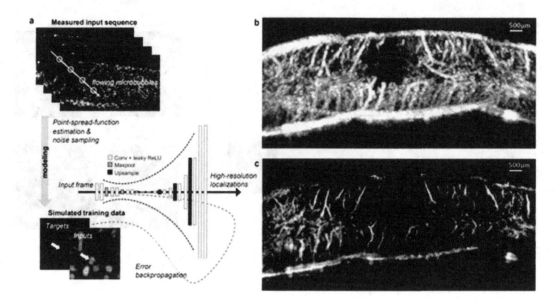

The CNN extracts functions by using the kernel. The extraction feature includes convolution, batch standardization, Rectified Linear Unit (ReLu), maximum grouping and decrease. Selected kernels also were used during convolution for the detection of surgical tools (*A. Sivarasa and O. D. Jerew, 2020*). The addition of ReLu to the convolution network and a 20% reduction in convolution output not only saves time but also enhances detection accuracy.

Slim surgical equipment which crosses the keyhole, endoscope, allows the least physical injury for patients during minimal invasive surgery (MIS). This type of surgery has also become a standard method for crucial procedures like colorectal cancer or other treatments. The detection of surgical devices such as forceps and endoscopes can give critical information for MIS surgery, especially for robotic minimal invasive surgery (RMIS) (*Zhao Z, 2017*).

Machine learning technologies are utilized to recognize device tips or shafts by providing appropriate training for distinctive classifiers/models. Machine learning algorithms are used to detect top-end, low-end and shaft forceps effectors in medical field.

The convolutional neural network model exploits the image data updating convolution kernel weights feeding back the kernel weights. The design of the CNN architecture and the training process of this network is done to learn attempting to predict the noise-free output from a given noisy MR image. A stack of noise filtering network kernels is added which include the dilated convolution filters, the batch normalization, and (ReLU) as an activation function (*R. Singh and L. Kaur, 2021*).

The CNN has the following computational elements:

1.   Convolution Element

$$Z_{r,s} = \frac{\sum_{i=1}^{M}\sum_{j=1}^{M} K_{(i,j)} {}^{*}SI_{(i+p,j+q)}}{M}$$

Where K is the intended output's matrix kernel, M is the kernel's width/height in pixels, SI is the source image's matrix, and (i,j) and (p,q) are the vertical and horizontal shift values of 'K' and 'SI', respectively. The formula's resultant matrix is Zr,s.

2.   ReLu:

$$ReZ_{r,s} = \max(0, Z_{r,s})$$

Where $\max(0, Z_{r,s})$, if value $Z_{r,s} < 0$ then, $Z_{r,s} = 0$.

3.   Max Pooling:

$$\text{Max } ReZ_{u,v} = \max Pool(ReZ_{u,v})$$

By employing the kernel's matrix size, maxPool gets the maximum value of ReZ (r,s). And u,v are the width and the height of the afresh produced matrix, respectively.

4.   DropOut 20%:

$$DRFC \text{ } Max \text{ } ReZ_b = drop \text{ } Out(FC \text{ } Max \text{ } ReZ_n)$$

DropOut drops the 'out' by 20% at random, and the given $\boldsymbol{DRFCMaxReZ_b}$ is the solution from dropout.

5.   Fully connected layer:

$$FC \text{ } MaxReZ_b = oneDiTrns(MaxReZ_{u,v})$$

Where, $n=u,v$ and *oneDiTrns* is altering the matrix into single dimension array (*A. Sivarasa and O. D. Jerew, 2020*).

Advantages of MRI Over Ultrasound, X-Ray, and CT-Scan

MRI is a non-invasive, non-radioactive procedure. RID reduces the risk of allergic reactions whenever iodine-based compounds are used for X-rays and CT scans. Other imaging technologies can't compete with the quality and detail of MRI soft tissue images (Figure 9).

Although MRI is more expensive than the other forms of medical imaging, we can safely assume that it has a higher scope for providing assistance and diagnosis to the patients that undergo this process of imaging for examinations. By adjusting the strength of the magnetic field, we can make the MRI behave like an X-ray machine or a CT scanner.

MRI may rapidly create hundreds of pictures from almost all directions. MRI tests may cover a wide section of the body, in contrast to procedures that evaluate limited portions of the body (e.g., mammography or ultrasound). MRI can evaluate the spread of disease and assist in determining the best treatment (*Barentsz J, 2006*)

With the advancement of technology in medical imaging practices and computer science disciplines, we can place out best interest in the machine predicted diagnosis for the coming future as human error can be avoided to a negligible length. By improving on deep learning techniques in the same field, we can help the greater community as the effective cost will also fall for the report diagnosis.

As we can see in Figure 9, MRI provides a much wider scope for analysis and provides a higher degree of clarity of the human body to minimize errors and give a healthy diagnosis. With the increased clarity of the MRI image, coupled with deep learning algorithms, we can help the betterment of judgment of the doctors by providing them with diagnosis to the patient. Since the algorithm detects various differences from a healthy image, the survival rate of patient's increases. In addition to MRI creating a clearer and more usable image, it is also much safer than a CT scan. The CT scan is harmful because they can include a small dosage of radiation and the dyes used in imaging can potentially cause unwanted reactions.

Figure 9. Different image scans of X-Ray, CT ,and MRI

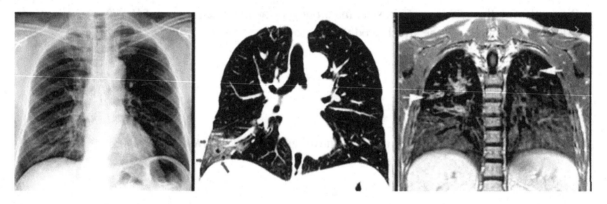

CONCLUSION

With the progress in technology, the process of applying deep learning techniques into the medical imaging process can only profit the community. Analysing medical images like CT scans, X-Rays, and MRIs is a challenging task due to the exponential growth of digital medical data each year. Deep learning is well-known for its extraordinary ability to sort images. We stress the use of deep learning techniques for medical imaging in this study. In addition, new structures that performed better for the patient's disease prognosis were discussed.

CNN models are also utilized to increase the model's capacity to forecast the model for improved cancer prediction. The clinical picture analysis includes transfer learning with well-adjusted parameters, which improves the efficiency of pre-trained models in order to better plan and decrease the time need for training. Uniform techniques aid in overcoming the challenge of filling and adjusting hyper parameters in order to increase DNN performance without introducing any architecture changes that are more effective and practicable. In compared to traditional imaging techniques, CNN models are more resourceful and operational at analyzing medical images. Finally, deep learning is revolutionizing health care because of its incredible powers to improve diagnosis accuracy and speed. All of these new medical science breakthroughs and upcoming technologies are helping to improve people's health.

REFERENCES

Barentsz, J., Takahashi, S., Oyen, W., Mus, R., De Mulder, P., Reznek, R., Oudkerk, M., & Mali, W. (2006). Commonly used imaging techniques for diagnosis and staging. *Journal of Clinical Oncology*, *24*(20), 3234–3244. doi:10.1200/JCO.2006.06.5946 PMID:16829647

Buettner, R., Bilo, M., Bay, N., & Zubac, T. (2020). A Systematic Literature Review of Medical Image Analysis Using Deep Learning. *2020 IEEE Symposium on Industrial Electronics & Applications (ISIEA)*, (pp. 1-4). IEEE. 10.1109/ISIEA49364.2020.9188131

Chollet, F. (2017). Xception: Deep Learning with Depth wise Separable Convolutions. *IEEE Conference on Computer Vision and Pattern Recognition (CVPR)*. IEEE. 10.48550/arXiv.1610.02357

Goel, N., Yadav, A., & Singh, B. M. (2016). *Medical image processing: A review. Second International Innovative Applications of Computational Intelligence on Power, Energy and Controls with their Impact on Humanity*. CIPECH. doi:10.1109/CIPECH.2016.7918737

Ker, J., Wang, L., Rao, J., & Lim, T. (2019). Deep Learning Applications in Medical Image Analysis. *IEEE Access: Practical Innovations, Open Solutions*, *6*, 9375–9389. doi:10.1109/ACCESS.2017.2788044

Latif, J., Xiao, C., Imran, A., & Tu, S. (2019). Medical Imaging using Machine Learning and Deep Learning Algorithms: A Review. *2nd International Conference on Computing, Mathematics and Engineering Technologies (iCoMET)*, (pp. 1-5). IEEE. 10.1109/ICOMET.2019.8673502

Litjens, G., Kooi, T., Bejnordi, B. E., Setio, A. A. A., Ciompi, F., Ghafoorian, M., van der Laak, J. A. W. M., van Ginneken, B., & Sánchez, C. I. (2017). Geert Litjens, Thijs Kooi, Babak Ehteshami Bejnordi, Arnaud Arindra Adiyoso Setio & Francesco Ciompi. (2017). A survey on deep learning in medical image analysis. *Medical Image Analysis*, *42*, 60–88. doi:10.1016/j.media.2017.07.005

Rajani Shree, M., & Shambhavi, B. R. (2022). POS Tagger Model for South Indian Language Using a Deep Learning Approach. In A. Kumar & S. Mozar (Eds.), *ICCCE 2021. Lecture Notes in Electrical Engineering* (Vol. 828). Springer. doi:10.1007/978-981-16-7985-8_16

Ruud, J. G. Van Sloun, Regev Cohen & Yonina C. Eldar. (2019). *Deep learning in Ultrasound Imaging*. arXiv: 1907.02994v2.

Singh, R., & Kaur, L. (2021). Magnetic Resonance Image Denoising using Patchwise Convolutional Neural Networks, *8th International Conference on Computing for Sustainable Global Development (INDIACom)*, (pp. 652-657). IEEE. doi: 10.1109/INDIACom51348.2021.00115

Sivarasa, A., & Jerew, O. D. (2020). Deep Learning For Minimally Invasive Computer Assisted Surgery. *5th International Conference on Innovative Technologies in Intelligent Systems and Industrial Applications (CITISIA)*, (pp. 1-5). IEEE. 10.1109/CITISIA50690.2020.9371813

van Sloun, R. J. G., Solomon, O., Eldar, Y. C., Wijkstra, H., & Mischi, M. (2017). Sparsity-driven super-resolution in clinical contrast-enhanced ultrasound. *IEEE International Ultrasonic Symposium (IUS)*, (pp. 1-4). IEEE. 10.1109/ULTSYM.2017.8092945

Wang, Q., & Shi, Y. (2019). Machine Learning in Medical Imaging. *IEEE Journal of Biomedical and Health Informatics*, 23(4), 1361–1362. doi:10.1109/JBHI.2019.2920801 PMID:30908957

Yamashita, R., Nishio, M., Do, R. K. G., & Togashi, K. (2018). Convolutional neural networks: An overview and application in radiology. *Insights Into Imaging*, 9(4), 611–629. doi:10.100713244-018-0639-9 PMID:29934920

Zeynettin, A., Alfiia, G., Assaf, H., Daniel, R., & Bradley, E. (2017). Deep Learning for Brain MRI Segmentation: State of the Art and Future Directions. *Journal of Digital Imaging*, 30(4), 449–459. doi:10.100710278-017-9983-4 PMID:28577131

Zhao Z, Voros S, Weng Y & Chang F Li R. (2017). Tracking-by-detection of surgical instruments in minimally invasive surgery via the convolutional neural network deep learning-based method. *Comput Assist Surg (Abingdon), 22.* . doi:10.1080/24699322.2017.1378777

Zinovev, D.,, Duo, Y.,, Raicu, D.,, & Furst, J., G, S., & Armato, G. (2011). Consensus Versus Disagreement in Imaging Research: A Case Study Using the LIDC Database. *Journal of Digital Imaging*, 423–436. PMID:22193755

Chapter 12
Design and Implementation of On-Board Computer Sub-System for Picosat

B. Swapna

https://orcid.org/0000-0002-7186-2842

Dr. M.G.R. Educational and Research Institute, India

P. Amudhan

Dr. M.G.R. Educational and Research Institute, India

S. Gayathri

https://orcid.org/0000-0002-1676-6284

Dr. M.G.R. Educational and Research Institute, India

E. Kavitha

Dr. M.G.R. Educational and Research Institute, India

M. Kamalahasan

Dr. M.G.R. Educational and Research Institute, India

K. Saravanan

Dr. M.G.R. Educational and Research Institute, India

M. Sujitha

Dr. M.G.R. Educational and Research Institute, India

ABSTRACT

Satellite tracking and control module in charge of maintenance is the subsystem. Monitoring and control of satellite locations affect the environment. Satellites are subjected to torque. This causes alignment and satellite angle instability while it is in space. The project involves the implementation of a satellite system and a test tool technology platform able to have it for lunch in the near future. It is also aimed towards them. Investigate the use of low-cost cube sats in the realm of remote sensing. In the original iteration of their design, the cube satellite utilized Picosat passive attitude control. However, a new version has been released to fulfil the accuracy standards of Picosat, the primary payload, which was supposed to be active attitude control. New posture determination and control the subsystem is in charge of successfully de-tumbling Picosat after booting and keeping it pointed in the right direction. As much as feasible, the desired alignment. This chapter describes the concept and execution of strong decision-making.

DOI: 10.4018/978-1-6684-6971-2.ch012

Copyright © 2023, IGI Global. Copying or distributing in print or electronic forms without written permission of IGI Global is prohibited.

INTRODUCTION

In this modern era, there is advancement of pico satellites to orbit masses of about 0.1 to 1 kg, although sometimes "it is used to refer to any satellite that is 1 kg" at lunch. Because actually has a decent option for enormous satellites in a few applications where low-cost and tiny size has arisen for their production.

Pico-Sat is the first pico-size satellite, developed for academic reasons by a student at "Dr MGR Educational and Research Institute" in Chennai. It is based on the concept of a cube satellite, which is described as the standard pico satellite, and it allows for the development of both the satellite's hardware and software architecture at a cheap cost.

This paper describes the Development and Operation of the AADCS for Pico-Sat. In Picosat, three subsystems are obtained and the most important subsystem in comparison to the others is OBCs. OBC is a bridge that connects other subsystems. It communicates with other subsystems using the I2C protocol. It performs many tasks that are performed by other subsystems, as well as housekeeping and monitoring the satellite's internal health. This is a final year research paper at Dr. MGR Educational and Research Institute for developing a cube satellite that sends an image and telemetry data it observes in the earth's atmosphere to a ground station.

Nano-satellites, which vary in mass between 1 to 50 kg, seem to be a huge trend in the development of space science and design research. Nano-satellites have emerged as an effective solution to large satellites within few applications, despite the small sample sizes and low costs, as the demand for their fabrication may have occurred. CubeSat's are compact, realistic satellites that enable companies entering orbit. Small satellites are usually 1U, 2U, 3U, 6U, or 12U, as depicted in the figure below by the standardized scale, 'U,' a square with segments of 10cm x 10cm x 10cm, 1.3kg. Every unit consists of fused equipment components, which have collectively chosen to complete the satellite's primary goal. Despite traditional space missions, Nano-satellites have functional properties and technology.

LITERATURE REVIEW

They proposed that a CubeSat makes it possible to demonstrate new technological advances at fraction of the cost of a typical large satellite initiative. This economic compromise has created many problems when trying to deploy components that enable important functions of large satellites in environments where size, weight, and performance are constrained (Junquan Li et al., 2013).

In general, CubeSats are nano satellites with dimensions ranging from 10 cm x 10 cm x 10 cm and higher, in 10 cm increments in length. It is made up of various subsystems that all work together to carry out the mission of the tiny satellites. In order for the mission to be successful, these subsystems, which include the communication system, power supply, and data handling, must be able to function together as one system (Pietruszewski et al., 2013).

A Proper system states that integration is required to ensure subsystem compatibility. In addition, depending on the CubeSat's mission, it may require some kind of stability mechanism. AADCS (Active Attitude Detection and Control Subsystem) is one of the subsystems needed to prevent CubeSat from rotating freely in orbit. It determines the orientation of the spacecraft relative to Earth or other reference systems and its position in a given direction (Markley, 2002).

The issues that CubeSat designers confront is determining and controlling the satellite's pointing. A smaller satellite means less space and mass for sensors and actuators, as well as less processing power for algorithms on a smaller and hence more constrained central processing unit. These issues have not yet been entirely resolved, since tiny satellites are still considered a fledgling industry (Mirghani et al., 2015).

The AADCS design includes a comprehensive test of the performance of small satellites operating in Low Earth Orbit (LEO). It is necessary to conduct a thorough investigation of the movement and stability of the satellite using a computer model. This includes research and testing to control spacecraft attitudes, as well as the development of a PicoSat attitude statistical model. The design process also includes sensors, actuators, and the development of all AADCS PicoSat software (Mirghani et al., 2015a).

The selection of hardware in two areas plays a key part in the AADCS design process: actuators, which are used to control the CubeSat, and sensors, which are used to determine the satellite's orientation of both the Sun and the Earth. Because the CubeSat has extremely precise dimensions and demands for power, the choice of sensors and actuators (Badawi and Seddig, 2016).

This white paper presents the PicoSat design prototype and CubeSat subsystem, focusing on the full AADCS specification and design requirements. It then describes the hardware selection criteria used, such as the sensor and processor selected for the PicoSat satellite, the drive design, the total power of the AADCS subsystem, and the budget size. All of these items have been carefully evaluated and built (Murphy et al., 2011).

To ensure subsystem compatibility, integration is necessary. Additionally, the CubeSat can need a stability device depending on its purpose. The OBC (on board computer subsystem) is one of the subsystems required to keep the CubeSat from rotating freely in orbit. It establishes the spacecraft's orientation with respect to the Earth or other reference systems as well as its position in relation to that direction (Lim et al., 2015).

Determining and managing the satellite's pointing is one of the challenges that CubeSat designers face. As a satellite gets smaller, there is less room and mass for sensors and actuators. There is also less computing capacity for algorithms on a smaller, and therefore more limited, central processing unit. Since microsatellites are still regarded as a developing industry, these issues have not yet been fully handled (Young et al., 2009).

The dimensions of CubeSats typically start at 10 cm x 10 cm x 10 cm and go up in 10 cm length increments. It is composed of numerous subsystems that all work together to complete the task assigned to the tiny satellites. These subsystems, which include the communication system, power supply, and data handling, must be prepared to operate as a cohesive unit in order for the mission to be successful (Kestila et al., 2013).

A CubeSat enables the demonstration of new technology improvements at a fraction of the expenditure of a traditional major satellite initiative. When attempting to deploy components that enable crucial tasks of huge satellites in circumstances where size, weight, and performance are constrained, this economic compromise has caused a number of issues (Matthew et al., 2011).

The performance of tiny satellites in Low Earth Orbit is thoroughly tested as part of the obc design (LEO). A 3d model should be used to carry out a detailed analysis into the satellite's movement and stability (Jeremy, 2010). In addition to the creation of a Picosat attitude statistical model, this also entails research and testing to regulate spacecraft attitudes. OBC Picosat software development and the design of sensors and actuators are also included. The choice of hardware for the CubeSat's actuators and sensors, which govern the satellite's position with respect to the Sun and the Earth, is crucial to the AADCS design process. The selection of sensors and actuators is based on the CubeSat's power requirements and exceptionally precise dimensions (Song et al., 2017). This white paper presents the Picosat design prototype and CubeSat subsystem, focusing on the full AADCS specification and design requirements. It then describes the hardware selection criteria used, such as the sensor and processor selected for the Picosat satellite, the drive design, the total power of the AADCS subsystem, and the budget size. All of these items have been carefully evaluated and built (Park et al., 2014).

METHODOLOGY

Pico-Sat Satellite

Pico-Sat is a cube satellite that measurement of 4cm in length, 4cm in width and 4cm in height, according to that one unit cube satellite. Pico-Sat is a satellite that is planned to launch at 350 kilometres in orbit. The purpose of the satellite is to monitor the environment and Capture the Geographical image of Tami Nadu. The Pico-Sat has contains four major subsystems: the On-board computer subsystems (OBC), the Communications subsystem (COMMS) and the Electrical power subsystems (EPS) and the Active Attitude determination and Control subsystem (AADCS) and the payloads subsystems and all the subsystems are working fine together to fulfil the mission of Pico-Sat.

On-Board Computer (OBC) Subsystems is the central processing unit of the satellite and it is responsible for processing the payload and monitoring the internal health of the satellite as well as housekeeping the data. OBCs synchronizes all the other subsystems and gathers data from other subsystems. The communication subsystems (COMMS) is responsible for sending data from OBCs to the ground station as well as receiving tele command from the ground station to the satellite. When the satellite has to be updated and recalibrated from the ground station, it will send a beacon to the ground station and capture the geographical image of Tamil Nadu and The payload system comprises a camera module that captures and saves pictures before transmitting them to the ground station through the communication subsystem.

The Electrical Power Subsystems (EPS), produce energy from the solar arrays, maintain, and transport power to the various subsystems and payloads, as well as using the generated voltage from the solar arrays to charge the internal power backup. Ultimately, the Active Attitude determination and Control subsystem (AADCS) stabilizes the Picosat satellite in orbit towards outside disturbances so one can orient it at the specified fixed nadir location.

Figure 1. Illustrates the 3D structures of Pico-Sat. "Picosat is made up of 4 outside frames and an inside stack made up of 5 printed circuit boards (PCB). It also has a camera (CAM), a GPS receiver, and a single battery. Furthermore, the Picosat enables deployable dipole antennas at the satellite's apex. The Picosat spacecraft also features four side panels that serve as support for the solar cells.

DEVELOPMENT AND OPERATION OF PICOSAT AADCS

This section details the development and operation of Picosat's active AADCS, which will be included in the Picosat cube satellite prototype's next version. That updated version works to add actuators to Picosat so that AADCS May function as an active ADCS. In addition to the AADCS algorithms, this Picosat AADCS version contains a set of sensors, actuators, and micro-controllers. AADCS may be divided into two types:

Figure 1. 3D Structure of Picosat

The Attitude Determinations System (ADS) calculates the current attitude and position of the Picosat cube satellite using a magnetometer, solar sensors, a gyroscope, accelerometer, altitude sensors, and GPS.

According to the data available from AD, the Attitude Control System (ACS) is responsible for dampening the first odd rotation and angular momentum following the deployment of a Pico-Sat, and sustaining its orientation following a de-tumbling. Figure 2. depicts the ACS block diagram

Figure 2. The ACS block diagram

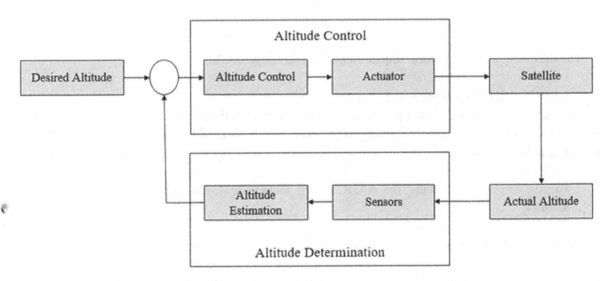

AADCS Design Rule

Picosat CubeSat needs to have the ability to correctly de-tumble itself and align the antenna to the ground station after deployment. This defines the AADCS number one obligations, which might be to de-tumble and guide the Pico-Sat satellite. Figure 3. Illustrate the flow chart of AADCS function and operation.

Figure 3. Flow chart of AADCS Function and Operation

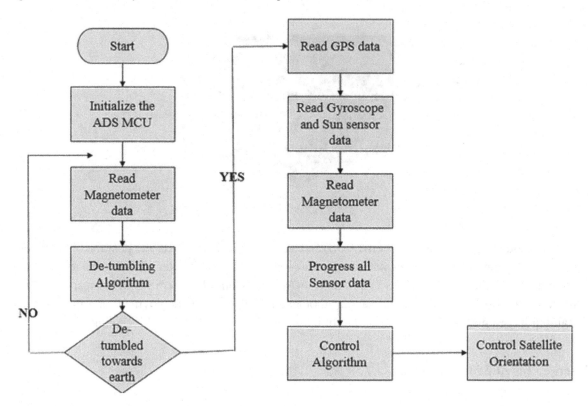

The following are the technical requirements for Picosat AADCS.

- AADCS will include a built-in microprocessor.
- In AADCS hardware, are not present in the movable part of the satellite.
- The system needs to employ memory to preserve data in AADCS itself.
- The AADCS must have a global positioning system (GPS) for data from locating the satellite using GPS.
- To give the current attitude, the AADCS must include a Magnetometer, Gyroscope, and Sun Sensors.

Picosat AADCS function requirements, on the other hand, are as follows.

- When the system is turned on, the software should initialize all sensor modules.
- The system software has to be capable of rebooting.
- GPS data processing requires system software to read GPS and analyse data such as the time, date, longitude, latitude, and altitude parameters.
- To calculate attitude, the system software must read and interpret sensor data (gyro sensor, magnetometer, and Sun sensor).
- The System software must store sensor data and system parameters in secondary storage.

Component Selection for the Pico-Sat

The selection step is one of the important stages that must be handled correctly in order to meet the Pico-Sat objectives and constraints. The AADCS component selection technique includes choosing sensors to determine and detect the PicoSat's orientation relative to Earth, suitable actuators to orient the Picosat in the desired orientation, and micro-controllers to run AADCS algorithms.

The sensors should be chosen based on their weight, design, and Energy requirements, as well as being precise, affordable, and simple to use. The actuators are chosen using the same criteria as the sensors, including dependability and acceptable pointing accuracy.

It is not essential to do complicated computations using the AADCS techniques used. The most challenging job may be measuring magnetic fields. As the system requires minimum two Pulse width Modulation (PWM), I2C protocol communication, and the ability to convert Analog to Digital signal for analog sensors. According to the system Requirement, Microchip Microcontroller is suitable for the Picosat AADCS. Table.1 shows the selected sensors of the AADCS system.

Table 1. Selected AADCS Sensors and Actuator for Picosat

Sensors / Actuators	Interface	Power requirement	Number Needed
Sun Sensor	Analog	No need	5
Magnetometer	I2C	0.25 mW	1
Gyroscope	I2C	30 mW	1
GPS	UART	1 mW	1
Magnetic Torquer	Analog	275 mW	3

Hardware and Software Design of Picosat AADCS

AADCS has two types ADS and ADC. The ADS has four-sensor GPS, Gyroscope, Magnetorquer and sun sensor. ADS to ADC has digital signals to physical energy. The ADC has three Magnetorquer. it creates a magnetic dipole that interfaces with the ambient magnetic field. The magnetic dipole generated by the magnetorquer. Figure 4. Illustrates the block diagram Active Attitude and Control Subsystem AACDS.

Software Design of Picosat AADCS

The AADCS software was written in C and was developed with the Arduino IDE and Proteus. The behaviour of the system was detailed. The overall system describes the AADCS system's major objectives. Table. 2 shows the Softwares for designing AADCS subsystem.

The attitude determination system (ADS) Microprocessor receives data from the various sensors and determines the attitude data. The ADS Micro controller communicates with other components through the Two Wire Interface (TWI). The TWI address for receiving was also given in ADS system communication. This address might originate from the COMM, ADC, or OBC subsystems. The ADS is comprised of four key procedures, which are listed below:

Figure 4. Block Diagram of AADCS

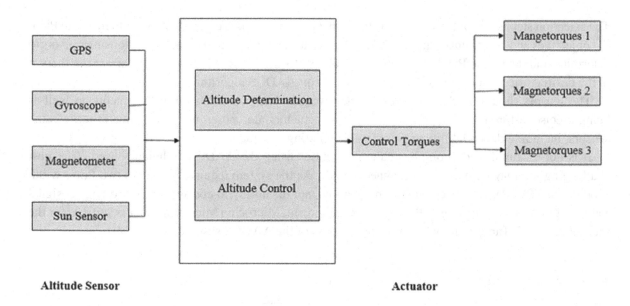

Altitude Sensor   **Actuator**

Table 2. The software's for designing the AADCS subsystem

Software	Version	Responsibility
Proteus	8.11	The AADCS circuit should be designed and simulated.
Arduino IDE	1.8.16	To write an AADCS code.

Waiting State

During the de-tumble phase wait operation, AADCS handles the whole system while waiting for an initiating message. The work begins at regular intervals.

Initialize the System

The initial step is to configure the sensors attached to the ADS microcontroller, as well as the micro-controller itself. The parameters for configuring the sensors are saved in the micro-controller's internal memory.

Condition of Estimation

Throughout this phase, the determination technique is used, and it gets information from external sensors as well as probable memory routes. In order to communicate with the ADC and COMM systems, the transmission will also be initiated.

State of Communication

The TWI is directed between isolated subsystems during the correspondence interaction. Messages are prepared to be sent and Incoming interchanges are interpreted. The information from the different sensors received by the mentality assurance framework ADS microchip, which decides the demeanour information. TWI handles correspondence between the ADS microcontroller and different parts.

RESULTS AND DISCUSSION

The AADCS microcontroller verifies the PicoSat's stability and reads the GPS sign over the UART interface. It parses GPS statistics to decide the vicinity of the Picosat dice satellite and sends it to the OBC and communique systems.

The satellite has five sun sensors. The output of the sensor converts analog to a digital sign through Atmega328P microcontroller pin1. Figure 5. depicts the sensor statistics utilized to pressure the solar direction from the PICOSAT. The sun on the (+x, axis) from the Pico-Sat is deflected at the digital Terminal.

Figure 5. Circuit Diagram of Sun Sensor and Direction

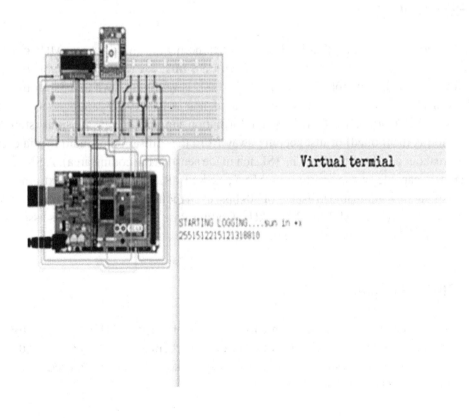

Operation Mode of OBC

There are two categories of modes:

- Normal Mode
- Safe mode Normal mode:

It is possible to disable the payload data that can be written into shared memory between the ADCS and the OBC by the OSBC. Temperature and minute-by-minute time data are read and stored by OBC. Every minute, the memory is updated.

Safe Mode

OBC disables the payload Subsystem. The OBC allows the payload to write data into Shared between it and the OBC. In order to transmit the temperature and time from OBC memory to the transceiver, the OBC sends them to the transceiver. The memory linked by the OBC and ADCS is being used to read the data from the ADCS. Data should be sent to Tran's receiver. OBC extracts the picture from the camera's memory and transmits it via the transceiver.

ON BOARD COMPUTER

The OBC is powered by an Atmega328P-AU 8 BitAVR microchip running at an 8MHz clock speed of 3.3V. To work on correspondence using a scaled-down USB link, use a locally available FT232R FTDI USBto Serial converter. The approaching 5V from the USB is ventured down to 3.3v for the framework installed. Two LED lights show TX and RX correspondence. A Micro-SD card peruse, ideal for social occasions, a lot of information, involving it as an information support for transmissions (store formation until transmission is mentioned) or just keeping away from the utilisation of radio media communications. Sensor breakout pins have this built in. (Sketch made sense in the coding area). A SX1278 100mW LoRa SPI handset capable of transmitting in AFSK, FSK, LoRa, and FM. Most extreme specialised information rates are now attainable in excess of 30kbps, even though Loa transmission is advised within the following indicated ranges: SF7-SF11, 125kHz, Coding Rate 4. The radio wire is associated with a U.FL port. 21 FORM N as shown in Figure 6.

OBC BLOCK DIAGRAM

The internal and external interactions between OBC components, as well as between the OBC and other subsystems, are represented in the OBC Block diagram. The schematic and simulation of the OBC, and also the data lines of cubesat, are shown in Figure 7. Easyeda software had been used to test the operation and algorithm of the OBC software.

Figure 6. Algorithm of OBCS

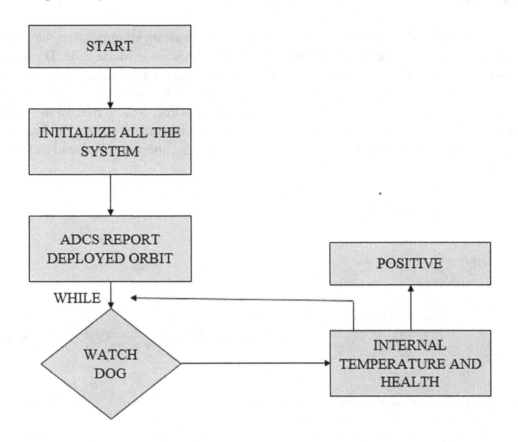

Figure 7. Block diagram of OBC

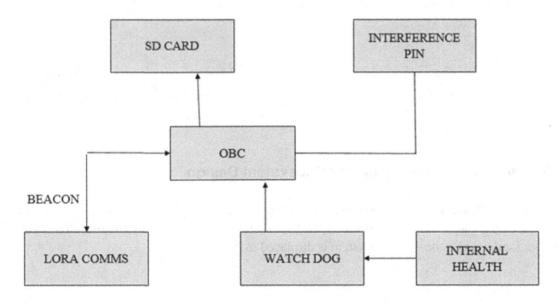

Beacon Subsystem

The estimation subsystem is a crucial component in all satellites, snaring information on the satellite's structure and status in the format of a Continuous Wave (CW) showing in Morse code. The reference point subsystem of MGRERI cube sat is completely insulated from the telemetry and communications transmitter and will function in the VHF band (128 MHz). The guide transmission timing was estimated based on two criteria: the amount of formation stored within Beacon rub and the reference point's authorized duty pattern in light of the MGRERI cubesat's transmitted power. The Beacon sign will be generated with an AVRMCU integrated in a sound loop and afterwards balanced including an FM modulator as shown in Figure 8 and Figure 9.

Figure 8. Block diagram of beacon

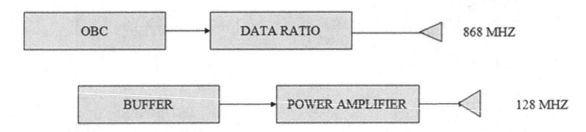

Figure 9. Block diagram of communication sub system

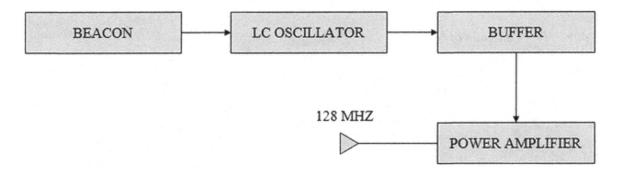

Software for On-Board Computer Subsystem Design

The Arduino IDE and Proteus were used to create the C-coded Obc software. The system's behaviour was explained in depth. The main goals of the Obc system are described by the overall system. The software for designing the OBC subsystem is displayed in Table 3.

Table 3. The software for designing the OBC subsystem

Software	Version	Responsibility
Proteus	8.11	The AADCS Circuit should be designed and simulated.
Arduino IDE	1.8.16	To write an AADCS code.

Required Components for On Boards Computer Subsystem

The transceiver will transmit mission and telemetry information to the earth stations as electronics. The OBC sends the temperature and time to the transceiver after receiving them from its used to communicate mission information (433 MHz). This gadget has numerous advantages, including: 1W is indeed the maximum transmission force. GFSK control method enables for a communication range of up to 10 miles from the nearest air to the ground. ISM band, 433 MHz transporter. The client has to choose between TTL/RS232/485 as an interface. This channel rate is4800 bps naturally, so long as that of the interaction point to send/get information is brief, the transformation of send and get information is accomplished. Time to transform the HFSS programming is being used to develop the COMM Transmitters. When the P-Pod is launched into orbit, dipole radio wires, which are already linked to the Structure, will be transferred. The dipole length of VHF radio wire is also 1.114m and 0.164m for UHF receive wire, as a response of the length of the radio wire. The receiver wire has to be deployable in terms of meeting the 3- dimensional 9uare satellite rule. The receiver cables were fabricated out of metallic estimating tape for all of this. The receiver wires will be sent into space later as components of the satellite setup; once EPS has begun, it will take care of the warmer to make the fish line warm. Furthermore, break it to deliver radio wires.

Add the required memory to our Arduino application to store data, media, etc. Compact SD Card Reader Module, commonly known as Micro SD Adaptor, is built to operate with two separate I/0 voltages. A primary response for transferring information to and from a standard SD card is the Module. The module (Micro SD card connector) is a smaller version of the existing SD card peruse module, and it utilizes the SPI interface to read and write to the SD card via the data structure driver, microcontroller system. A few features of SD are identical to the Compatible Micro SD Card (=2G) Power supply 4.SV 5.SV 32 GB Micro SDHC card (rapid card) A standard SPI interface serves as the communication connection point.

PCB FABRICATION

The Implementation of the On-Board Computer System of the MGRERI CubeSat has been extensively presented and analysed in this paper. The methodology used in the development of the On Board Computer (OBC) SubSystem for the MGRERI CubeSat was night lighted in the paper. The beacon subsystem is intended to have a microcontroller (MCU) that provides beacon signals.

Figure 10. OBC Fabricated board

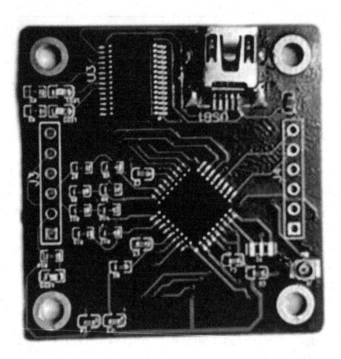

Figure 11. Communication result

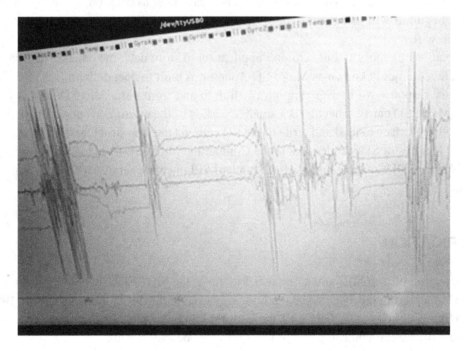

CONCLUSION

The Picosat Cube satellite control subsystem is comprehensive. It was presented and discussed. Various types of embedded software has been used to emulate a posture determination subsystem and controls those who have shown success. In PicoSat, three subsystems are obtained, and the most important subsystem in comparison to the others is OBCs. OBC is a bridge that connects other subsystems. It communicates with other subsystems using the I2C protocol. It performs many tasks that are performed by other subsystems, as well as housekeeping and monitoring the satellite's internal health. This is a research paper for developing a cube satellite that sends an image and telemetry data it observes in the earth's atmosphere to a ground station. The design and construction of an active attitude determination and control subsystem of the PicoSat cube satellite have been extensively shown and explored in this work. The interfacing of the PicoSat cube satellite subsystems' micro-controllers with sensors, actuators, and other components, as well as the software architecture for the entire AADCS subsystem, were discussed. To complete the AADCS system design, the micro-controller was programmed using Arduino IDE and Proteus packages in accordance with the completed circuit design

REFERENCES

Badawi, E., & Seddig, Y. (2016). Design and Implementation of ISRASAT1 Cube Satellite Structure. *Third International African CubeSat Workshop*, Cape Peninsula University of Technology, Cape Town.

Kestila, A., Tikka, T., Peitso, P., Kestila, A., Tikka, T., Peitso, P., Rantanen, J., Nasil, A., Nordling, K., Saari, H., Vainio, R., Janhunen, P., Praks, J., & Hallikainen, M. (2013). Aalto-1 nanosatellite – technical description and mission objectives. *Geoscientific Instrumentation, Methods and Data Systems*, 2(1), 121–130. doi:10.5194/gi-2-121-2013

Li, J., Post, M., Wright, T., & Lee, R. (2013). Design of Attitude Control Systems for Cubesat-class Nanosatellite. *Journal of Control Science and Engineering*, 1, 1–12. doi:10.1155/2013/657182

Lim, L. S., Bui, T. D. V., Lau, Z., Tissera, M. S. C., Soon, J. J., Lew, J. M., Aung, H., Ye, C., Low., K. S., Goh, S. T., & Chen, S. S. (2015). *Development and design challenges in VELOX-I nanosatellite.* International Conference on Space Science and Communication (IconSpace), Malaysia. 10.1109/IconSpace.2015.7283826

Markley, F. L. (2002). Fast Quaternion Attitude Estimation from Two Vector Measurements. *Journal of Guidance, Control, and Dynamics*, 25(2), 411–414. doi:10.2514/2.4897

Matthew, W., Smith, Sara Seager., Christopher, M., Pong, Matthew, W, Knutson. David W. Miller. (2011). The Exo planet sat mission to detect transiting exoplanets with a cubesat space telescope. *AIAA/USU Conference on Small Satellite,* USA.

Mirghani, M., TagElsir, A., & Saeed Kajo, A. (2015). Hardware selection for attitude determination and control subsystem of 1U cube satellite. *IEEE International Conference Computing, Control, Networking, Electronics and Embedded Systems Engineering (ICCNEEE).* IEEE.

Mirghani, M., Abobaker, H., Adel, E., & Saeed, A. (2015). Orbit Design of Cube Satellite, *The 10th Scientific Conference of National Center for Research*, Khartoum.

Murphy, T., Kanaber, J., & Koehler, C. (2011). PEZ: expanding CubeSat capabilities through innovative mechanism design. *AIAA/USU Conference on Small Satellite, SSC11-XII-5*, USU.

Park, T. Y., Chae, B. G., Jung, H. M., & Oh, H. U. (2014). Conceptual design of electrical power sub-system for cube satellite with permanent magnet attitude stabilization method. *Journal of Aerospace System Engineering*, 8, 42–47.

Pietruszewski, A. N., & David, A. (2013). Prox-1 Attitude Determination and Control. Center for Space Systems, 10, 25-36.

Song, S., Lee, S. Y., Kim, H. R., & Chang, Y. K. (2017). KAUSAT-5 development and verification based on 3U CubeSat standard platform. *Journal of the Korean Society for Aeronautical & Space Sciences*, 45(8), 686–696. doi:10.5139/JKSAS.2017.45.8.686

Young, Q., Burt, R., Watson, M., & Zollinger, L. (2009). *PEARL CubeSat bus building toward operational missions*. Small Satellites Conference from AIAA/Utah State University.

Chapter 13
Analysis on Detecting Cyber Security Attacks Using Deep Ensemble Learning on Smart Grids

K. Vanitha
ⓘ https://orcid.org/0000-0002-3447-3813
Jain University, India

M. Mohamed Musthafa
Al-Ameen Engineering College, India

A. M. J. Md Zubair Rahman
Al-Ameen Engineering College, India

K. Anitha
Al-Ameen Engineering College, India

T. R. Mahesh
Jain University, India

V. Vinoth Kumar
Jain University, India

ABSTRACT

In recent times, cyber security offers a significant advancement in smart grid technologies for its availability and functionality. The potential intrusion in smart grids marks the system to behave in a vulnerable way all the private data. Smart grids are often prone to data integrity attacks at its physical layer, which is been a critical issue presently. This attack alters the measurement of compromised meter set by the attacker(s). It misleads the decision making by the operators at the control center and thereby the reliability of the measurement is affected. In this chapter, the authors present a deep learning ensemble (DLE) model that possibly detects the potential data integrity attacks in the physical layer. The deep learning model uses ensemble learning to make decisions and combines the classified results to improve the classification on test data. The experiments are conducted on the proposed DLE model to find the accuracy of classifier the malicious and benign measurements.

DOI: 10.4018/978-1-6684-6971-2.ch013

Copyright © 2023, IGI Global. Copying or distributing in print or electronic forms without written permission of IGI Global is prohibited.

INTRODUCTION

In the modern era, the integration of power systems with communication technologies has improved the efficiency, reliability and consumption of electrical energy. The enabling of Advanced Metering Infrastructure (AMI) in smart grids offers transparency and reduces the consumption. However, it opens us the possibility of attacks in the form of cyber threats, where the entire system and it communication medium is highly prone to cyber-attacks .(Khanna, K.,et al., 2016).

These intrusions makes the smart grids susceptible to attacks that leads to serious degradation like leading of private information and system failures (Basodi, S.,et al., 2020). It further targets the confidentiality, data delivery and integrity, which may lead to financial, loses through theft, power grid instability or poor accessing of critical data (Farraj, A.,et al.,2017). In future, the Smart Grid may incorporate various other technologies and innovations like sensing, communication and distributed control for the accommodation of Electric Vehicle loads, renewable generation and storage (Giani, A.,et al., 2013). Hence, cyber security offers a significant role on smart grids by determining the possible potential intrusions.

In this study, we consider the attacks in smart grids occur due to the data integrity attack that alters the compromised power meter readings. The unobservable attack (power flow constraints on consistent compromised meter readings). A proper coordination is required by the unobservable attacks on the compromised meter readings and it should be orchestrated in a careful manner. Such that it operates on a low dimensional manifold to ensure that the attack is unobservable and it misleads the system operators by offering substantial errors in the state estimation algorithms. The vulnerability of grids is more prone to cyber-attacks, thus increasing the relevance and urgency on cyber security research (Giani, A.,et al., 2013).

There exist various efforts to analyze the data integrity attacks in smart grid environment that develops alternative strategies such that the damages can be reduced temporarily. The methods developed are accurate, quick and offers the detection in a cost-effective manner to mitigate the data integrity attacks and ensures improved security on smart grids(Ge, L.,et al., 2017).

Operation of smart grids under uncertainties leads to cyber-attacks, failures, poor quality of service, error in device synchronization, compromising the resources capacity, and so on. In addition, with increased and rapid communication across the communication channel, the existing methods tend to fail in processing large data while data integrity attack is on surge. Diagnosing these challenges finds that there are numerous concerns associated with smart grids that compromise on its resilience and security. To mitigate such challenges, we develop a deep learning ensemble classification model with a meta-heuristic feature extraction that process effectively the data in a larger scale basis and offers effective computations. The main contributions are stated below:

a) The author has developed a malicious classifier model that forms a series of framework including data pre-processing and normalisation, feature extraction using bee swarm optimisation (BSO) and ensemble classification.

b) The ensemble classifier is designed with a series of machine learning base classifier namely the neural network and the results of base classes are combined using ensemble technique and finally sent as input for deep neural network (DNN) classifiers to detect the malicious data samples from the input datasets.

c)   The input datasets are generated in massive on the IEEE bus systems including 30-bus and 57-bus and 118-bus systems. 70% of the input dataset is used as training data and the remaining data is used as testing datasets. The performance of the entire system under all the three bus systems is compared with existing classifiers against various performance metrics.

The outline of the paper is presented below: Section 2 offers the related works in the given field. Section 3 discusses the model and the deep learning classification model. Section 4 provides the dataset and section 5 provides the results and discussion of the present study. Finally, the section 6 concludes the entire work.

RELATED WORK

Various methods are used in past to mitigate the challenges of data integrity attack in smart grids that includes the following. In (Rawat, D. B., &Bajracharya C, 2015) cosine similarity matching algorithm is designed with Chi-square detector for the detection of attacks, where Kalman filter is used to measure the deviation from original smart grid measurements. In (Wang, D.,et al., 2014), extended distributed state estimation detects the attack, where decomposition of smart grids into subsystems exploits the use of graph based partition algorithm. The false data is detected using Chi-squares test in extended sub-system and in (Chen, P. Y.,et al., 2015) spatial-temporal correlations are used between the components in smart grids.

The extension of detecting the attacks is then carried out with optimization techniques (He, Y.,et al., 2017). An efficient greedy search algorithm (Hao, J.,et al., 2015) quickly finds the measurements (Li, S.,et al., 2014) against the stealth attack, which reports similar performance like brute-force method. In addition various game theoretical models are reported in (Sanjab, A., & Saad, W.,2016) to mitigate the adversaries by compromising its performance and resource usage. More recently, various machine learning (Esmalifalak, M,et al., 2014;Karimipour, H.,et al., 2019;Wang, Y.,et al.,2017) deep learning models (Ayad, A.,et al., 2018 ; Wei, J., & Mendis, G. J., 2016 ;Wei, L.,et al.,2018) are adopted to detect the data integrity attacks in the smart grids. There exist very few methods on deep learning that offers continuous learning on classification process in identifying the data integrity attacks in different ways from the given datasets. It continually learns the entire system and updates the infection profile in its control center to mitigate the attacks.

SYSTEM MODEL

State Estimation

The IEEE 30-bus and IEEE 57-bus but IEEE 118-bus systems uses deploys smart grid technology that entirely rely on its state estimation for the prediction of the system states and that helps in better determination of power generation in an optimal manner. It represents the relationship between the real recorded measurements and the system state variable in the power grid. Such measurements include voltage magnitude, power flow and phase angle, which is given in equation (1).

$$Z(k) = H(k)\, x(k) + \varepsilon(k) \tag{1}$$

Where

Z is the measurement vector,

H is the Jacobian matrix

x is the state variable vector and is the measurement error. k is the time step.

The estimation of states under the global observability is estimated using the least squares method, which is defined as shown in equation (2).

$$x(k+1) = x(k) + G-1(k)H(k)W-1[Z(k)-H(k)x(k)] \tag{2}$$

where

$G(k)$ - gain matrix, which is defined as $G(k) = HT(k)W\text{-}1H(k)$.

x' - estimated system state vector.

W- Covariance matrix.

The measurement data is measured for finding the malicious data for increasing the accurate estimation (Li, S.,et al., 2014). The detection is usually carried out using 2-norm residual test as shown in equation (3).

$$\|z\text{-}Hx\|2 < \varepsilon \tag{3}$$

where ε –malicious data detection threshold, where the measurement residual is above the threshold data, the malicious data tends to exist and it is then removed at next iteration.

Data Integrity Attack

Data integrity attacks, as one of the most dangerous threats to the smart grid, could disrupt the monitoring and control process by injecting false measurement reports through compromised components into the operating center. Such attacks consist of a number of compromised components including smart meters, substations and data channels. This attacks aim to stealthily inject or manipulate the transmitted data to disrupt the data exchange within the smart grid infrastructure. The target data can either be a user-side information or a utility-side status data. In order to bypass the detection algorithm, the data integrity attacks are normally unnoticeable and unobservable. As a result, data integrity attacks can cause substantial errors in estimating the state and damaging the grid.

In an IEEE bus system is represented in the form of a graph G with vertices as buses V and edge set as lines E, here n+1 buses are connected to each other through proper transmission lines. The injection buses connect the generators or loads and null buses connect the external power supply. We assume that each injection bus is connected to exactly one charge or generator. Also, some pairs of buses are connected by transmission lines, and no more than one line between any pair of buses. It is easy to relax those two assumptions. On selected lines there are m real power flow meters and power flow meters at all injection buses which measure real power from all generators/ injected loads. The IEEE power system is modeled as y = Hx, where line susceptance construct H and partition of y represents injection and null buses, and line meters. Consider the system to be observable, where the state x is deduced uniquely from y1observations. The range and null spaces are denoted as R(M) and N(M) over the matrix M. S, V, and A represents the sets of meter, bus and attacks, with total number of elements in S is represented as |S|.(Venkatesan, V.K.,et al., 2022)

An attack A = (S, a) is a set of |S| compromised meters S, and an attack vector 0 a = [0 a1a2]T∈Rm+n partitioned conformably with y = Hx. The nonzero components available in the attack vector a corresponds to the set of compromised meters S. The sparsely present in A is regarded as the total number of compromised meters |S|. Under the data integrity attack A, the attacker alters the meter readings with an uncompromised values yoin reference to the post-attack values yo + a. Let xo - current system state, and yo - uncompromised meter readings.

PROPOSED METHOD

The study use ensemble deep learning algorithm for classification in smart grid environment(Karthick Raghunath K. M.,et al., 2022). The feature extraction is carried out with BSO algorithm forming a hybrid model, which improves the attack classification on an IEEE bus system deployed in the smart grid. The architecture of the proposed data integrity attack classification system is given in Figure 1.

Figure 1.

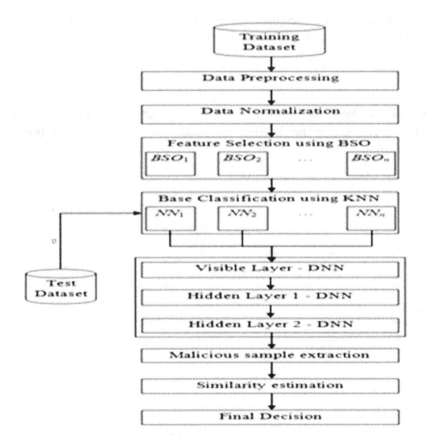

Feature Selection Using BSO

Bees are among the social insects which are well studied. The behaviour of the bees is divided into three categories: foraging, marriage, queen bee. First, a bee named InitBee is settling for a solution with good features. Using a certain strategy we determine a set of other search space solutions from this first solution called Sref. SA is the name for this set of solutions, where each bee considers a SA solution as its point of departure. The bees communicate with the best visited solution to all its neighbours through a table named dance after completing its search. During the next iteration (Djenouri, Y., et al., 2014) one of the solutions stored in this table will become the new reference solution.(T. R. Mahesh., et al., 2014). To avoid repeated iterations, the reference solution based on quality is kept in a taboo list at each iteration. However, if solution is not improved, a diversification criterion is used that prevents the solution being trapped in local solution. The diversification selects the most distant solutions in the taboo list. When the optimal solution is found, or the maximum number of iterations is reached, the algorithm stops (Djenouri, Y., et al., 2014 and Venkatesan, V.K.,et al., 2022).

A wrapper approach is used to select features with BSO algorithm to perform the subset search process (Sadeg, S.,et al., 2015). Applying BSO to selection of features requires the general algorithm to be adapted to the specifics of the problem. Selection of the reference solution and the bees performing local search. (Palanivinayagam, A.,et al.,2022)

Solution Encoding

A solution is represented by a binary length vector n, where n is the number of features originally used. If a corresponding function is selected, a vector position is set to 1 and to 0 otherwise.

Fitness

It represents the quality of the feature extracted from the smart grid data. This paper is equivalent to the classification accuracy returned by the classifier used, and is calculated using the formula i.e. accuracy = (tp+tn)/total population

Input: Smart grid dataset.   **Output**: K features extracted

Step 1. Sref ← solution from InitBee.
 Step 2. while $i<$Iter$_{max}$ do
 Step 3. Insert the value of updated S_{ref} in taboo list.
 Step 4. Search the swarm i.e. *SA* using S_{ref}
 Step 5. Assign a solution from *SA* to each bee.
 Step 6. for bee *K* do
    a. Build *SA(bee$_k$)*.
    b. Store result in table.
    c. end for
 Step 7. Choose the new S_{ref}.
 Step 8. end while

Ensemble Classification

Stacking is an ensemble technique in which predictions of a set of predictive models are combined to generate a final output through other learning models. In our stacking layer, base classifier predictions from the voting layer are combined with two Restricted Boltzmann Machine (RBM) as inputs into the KNN. RBM is a probabilistic model that models the distribution of observed data using hidden-layer variables. Typically, an RBM is trained to model the input distribution in an unsupervised manner. The strength of RBM is that, given the visible units, the hidden units are conditionally independent. (Bhargavi Mokashi., et al., 2022)

It can learn from the predictions of base classifiers to the abstract representation. We train the DNN which consists of 35 nodes in the input layer, which corresponds to the selected base classifiers with better performance, six nodes in the first hidden layer, and one node in the second hidden layer on base classifier predictions. The parameters of the trained DNN are used in the next layer to initialize three neural networks with the same structure which reduces the correlation effect from the predictions of base classifiers.S. (Roopashree., et al., 2022)

PERFORMANCE METRICS

A stratified 10-fold cross validation is carried out on the DEL classifier over its training and testing data. The cross validation on DEL finds its classification accuracy using its test datasets. The accuracy of classification is defined as the ratio of total number of training/testing samples predicted accurately against the total training/testing datasets. The classification accuracy is estimated as shown in equations (4) and (5).

$$Accuracy = \frac{No.\ of\ correct\ predictions}{Total\ number\ of\ test\ dataset} \qquad (4)$$

or

$$Accuracy = \frac{tp + tn}{tp + tn + fp + fn} \times 100 \qquad (5)$$

Secondly, the precision of a classifier is defined as the ratio of total number of training/testing samples predicted as malicious samples and labelled as benign samples against the positive samples. The precision of a classifier is estimated as shown in following equation (6)

$$precision = \frac{tp}{tp + fp} \times 100 \qquad (6)$$

Finally, the recall of a classifier defined as the ratio of total number of training/testing samples predicted as malicious samples. The recall rate of a classifier is estimated as shown in following equation (7).

Table 1. Estimation of Performance Metrics using a contingency table

	Attacked (Actual)	Secure (Actual)
Attacked (Predicted)	tp	fp
Secured (Predicted)	fn	tn

$$recall = \frac{tp}{tp + fn} \times 100 \qquad\qquad (7)$$

Where

tp is the true positive rate, which is the rate of total malicious samples classified as malicious.

tn is the true negative rate, which is the rate of total true samples classified as benign.

fp is the false positive rate, which is the rate of total malicious samples classified as benign.

fn is the false negative rate, which is the rate of total true samples classified as malicious.

This is illustrated in simple terms in the form of a contingency table in Table.1.

In this system, the input data $(s_i, y_i) \in S \times Y$ is normalized, feature extracted and classified (training and testing) to find the malicious data samples. The smart grid data is generated from three different IEEE buses namely 30-, 57-, and 118-bus system. The MATPOWER toolbox (Karimipour, H., et al., 2019) computes the Jacobian matrix H, where H is mapped with state variables and voltage bus, and power flow data of the input measurement data from the IEEE branches and buses, respectively. The operation state x of 30-, 57-, and 118-bus systems are then found and then the measurement z is computed by MATPOWER. Using this process, a total of 10-5data measurement is used as a training data that includes both true and malicious data measurements of data integrity attack at the physical layer. The extracted features from the normalised measurements are the inputs for classifiers, where its output layer logically predicts malicious or benign samples and presents it either as zeros or ones. Most of the data i.e. 10-4 measurement are used as training data instances that trains the classifiers.

The DLE is said to have both Ensemble and DNN classifier, which is implemented in Keas PAI with a backend library named Tensor flow in python. The Ensemble DNN learns the neurons with multiple parameters on hidden layers, loss function (integrated with distance metric), activation function (Exponential Linear Units at hidden layer and sigmoid function at output layer) and dropout factor. The sigmoid function on the output layer relates with the class label i.e. benign or malicious. The neurons are fixed on each classifier until the cross validation is carried out. With 100 hidden layers, the dropout factor is set as 0.5. Finally, the Scikit python library performs the grid search by the parametric space for finding the optimal parameter

RESULTS AND DISCUSSIONS

The result of accuracy is given in Table.1, where the DLE is compared with existing ANN models and over IEEE 30-bus, IEEE 57-bus, and IEEE 118-bus systems. At each bus, the number of features tends to vary w.r.t to the buses. In IEEE 30 bus system, we select 19, 32 and 51 features for evaluation. In

Table 2a. Accuracy of IEEE 30-bus with 15% of malicious data in training sets and 15% in testing sets

Selected Features	IEEE 30-bus		
	ANN	RNN	DLE
51	91.75	93.46	95.55
32	92.68	95.00	97.13
19	93.63	95.47	97.75

Table 2b. Accuracy of IEEE 57-bus with 15% of malicious data in training sets and 15% in testing sets

Selected Features	IEEE 57-bus		
	ANN	RNN	DLE
73	88.31	89.96	91.98
61	89.21	91.45	93.49
48	90.13	91.90	94.09

IEEE 57 bus system, we select 48, 61 and 73 features for evaluation. In IEEE 118 bus system, we select 60, 77 and 92 features for evaluation. A stratified 10-fold cross validation shows that the DLE model performs improved performance than other methods. With increasing features, the accuracy reduces; however, the performance of DLE is higher than ANN and RNN.

Similarly, the performance of DLE is reported in terms of precision and recall metrics over RNN and DNN in Table.2 and Table.3. When the number of attacks increases, DLE offers improved recall but a lesser precision than other two methods. The ANN has better recall with lower precision and RNN with good precision and lesser recall with increasing malicious features.

Certain buses like IEEE 30-bus and IEEE 57-bus used in the study reports highest accuracy with even two layers, however IEEE 118-bus system requires more layers to achieve higher accuracy and then the system stables. It nominally takes 50 hidden layers to achieve maximum accuracy by the IEEE 30-bus and IEEE 57-bus but IEEE 118-bus systems uses 93 layers to achieve maximum accuracy.

The accuracy varies w.r.t the increasing or decreasing attack features present in the dataset i.e. with increasing attack features, the accuracy reduces and vice versa. The optimal accuracy is reported by the IEEE 30-bus and IEEE 57-bus at the earlier stages of DLE hidden network, but a higher layers for IEEE 118-bus system. The IEEE 30-bus and IEEE 57-bus reaches its 90% accuracy at 2nd hidden layer of DLE but the accuracy of 80% is achieved by IEEE 118-bus at 30th hidden layer. The simulation results show the efficacy of proposed CRNN than other existing deep learning classifiers in terms of accuracy, precision and recall.

Figure 2a. Accuracy of IEEE 30-bus with 15% of malicious data in training sets and 15% in testing sets

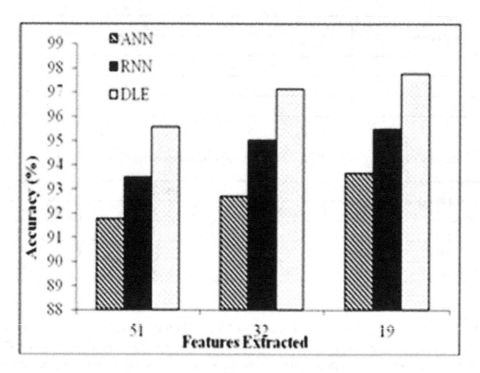

Figure 2b. Accuracy of IEEE 57-bus with 15% of malicious data in training sets and 15% in testing sets

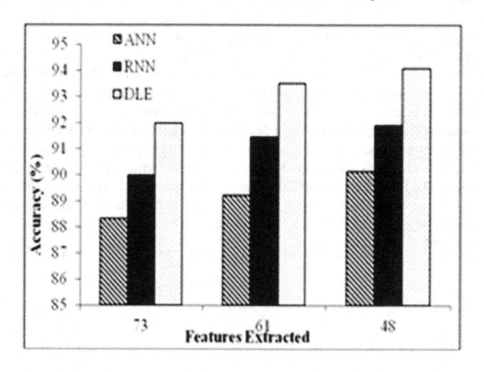

Table 2c. Accuracy of IEEE 118-bus with 15% of malicious data in training sets and 15% in testing sets

Selected Features	IEEE 118-bus		
	ANN	RNN	DLE
92	85.01	86.59	88.53
77	85.87	88.03	89.99
60	86.75	88.46	90.57

Figure 2c. Accuracy of IEEE 118-bus with 15% of malicious data in training sets and 15% in testing sets

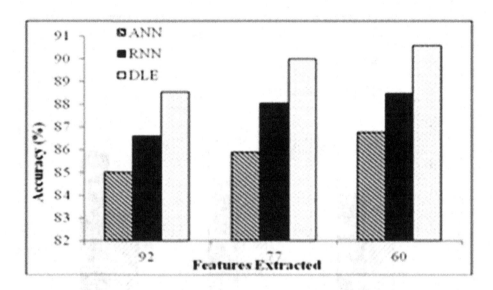

Table 3a. Precision of IEEE 30-bus with 15% of malicious data in training sets and 15% in testing sets

Selected Features	IEEE 30-bus		
	ANN	RNN	DLE
51	91.62	93.05	94.57
32	91.85	93.59	96.11
19	92.35	94.37	96.72

Table 3b. Precision of IEEE 57-bus with 15% of malicious data in training sets and 15% in testing sets

Selected Features	IEEE 57-bus		
	ANN	RNN	DLE
73	88.19	89.57	91.03
61	88.42	90.09	92.52
48	88.89	90.84	93.10

Table 3c. Precision of IEEE 118-bus with 15% of malicious data in training sets and 15% in testing sets

Selected Features	IEEE 118-bus		
	ANN	RNN	DLE
92	84.90	86.21	87.62
77	85.11	86.72	89.06
60	85.56	87.44	89.61

Figure 3a. Precision of IEEE 30-bus with 15% of malicious data in training sets and 15% in testing sets

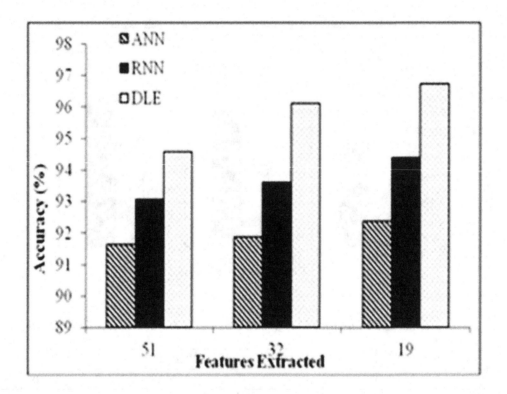

Figure 3b. Precision of IEEE 57-bus with 15% of malicious data in training sets and 15% in testing sets

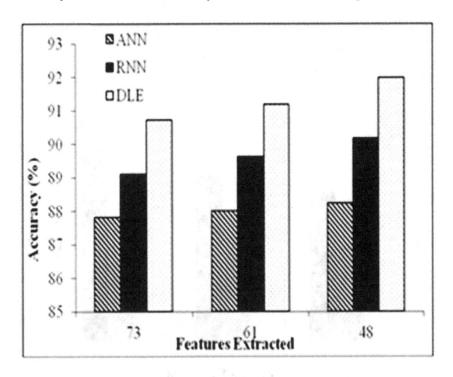

Figure 3c. Precision of IEEE 118-bus with 15% of malicious data in training sets and 15% in testing sets

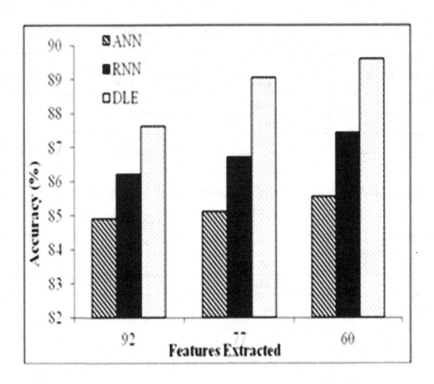

Figure 4a. Recall of IEEE 30-bus with 15% of malicious data in training sets and 15% in testing sets

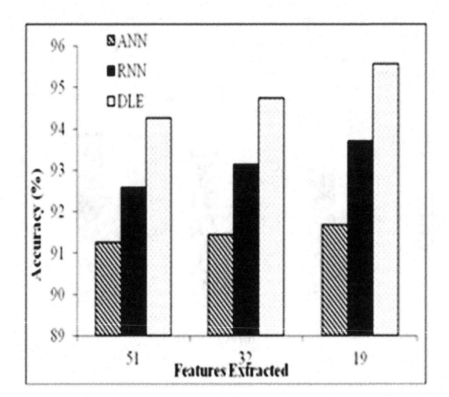

Table 4a. Recall of IEEE 30-bus with 15% of malicious data in training sets and 15% in testing sets

Selected Features	IEEE 30-bus		
	ANN	RNN	DLE
51	91.24	92.57	94.25
32	91.43	93.12	94.73
19	91.67	93.69	95.55

Table 4b. Recall of IEEE 57-bus with 15% of malicious data in training sets and 15% in testing sets

Selected Features	IEEE 57-bus		
	ANN	RNN	DLE
73	87.82	89.10	90.72
61	88.01	89.63	91.19
48	88.24	90.18	91.98

Figure 4c. Recall of IEEE 57-bus with 15% of malicious data in training sets and 15% in testing sets

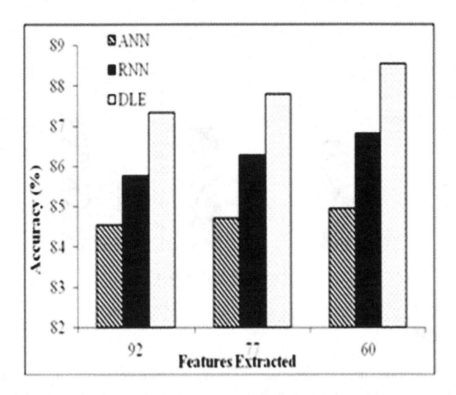

Table 4c. Recall of IEEE 118-bus with 15% of malicious data in training sets and 15% in testing sets

Selected Features	IEEE 118-bus		
	ANN	RNN	DLE
92	84.53	85.76	87.32
77	84.71	86.27	87.78
60	84.94	86.80	88.53

Figure 4b. Recall of IEEE 30-bus with 15% of malicious data in training sets and 15% in testing sets

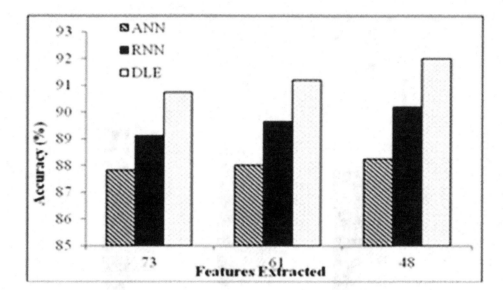

CONCLUSION

In this paper, we develop a deep ensemble learning model that mitigates the data integrity attacks at the physical layers of the smart grids. Since, the attacks on physical layer may pose leakage of user data on smart grids. The attack is thus classified using the DEL model that initially uses a series of steps, out of which BSO algorithm plays a major role in extracting the features. DEL algorithm then ensembles the base classification and sends the base classified results to the DNN to get the final accurate classified results. The fine-tuning of the results using the DEL model reduces the mean square error and the influence of base classifier correlation. The proposed model on integrity attack detection classifies the malicious samples from the input training dataset. The fine-tuning by the classifiers improves the results in such a way that it provides improves accuracy than the existing classifiers. The proposed model on detecting the data integrity attack at the physical layer achieves an accuracy of 98.52% than the other machine or deep learning algorithms.

REFERENCES

Ayad, A., Farag, H. E., Youssef, A., & El-Saadany, E. F. (2018). Detection of false data injection attacks in smart grids using recurrent neural networks. In 2018 IEEE Power & Energy Society Innovative Smart Grid Technologies Conference (ISGT). IEEE.

Basodi, S., Tan, S., Song, W., & Pan, Y. (2020). Data integrity attack detection in smart grid: A deep learning approach. *International Journal of Security and Networks*, *15*(1), 15–24. doi:10.1504/IJSN.2020.106506

Chen, P. Y., Yang, S., McCann, J. A., Lin, J., & Yang, X. (2015). Detection of false data injection attacks in smart-grid system. *IEEE Communications Magazine*, *53*(2), 206–213. doi:10.1109/MCOM.2015.7045410

Djenouri, Y., Drias, H., & Habbas, Z. (2014). Bees swarm optimisation using multiple strategies for association rule mining. *International Journal of Bio-inspired Computation*, 6(4), 239–249. doi:10.1504/IJBIC.2014.064990

Esmalifalak, M., Liu, L., Nguyen, N., Zheng, R., & Han, Z. (2014). Detecting stealthy false data injection using machine learning in smart grid. *IEEE Systems Journal*, 11(3), 1644–1652. doi:10.1109/JSYST.2014.2341597

Farraj, A., Hammad, E., & Kundur, D. (2017). On the impact of cyber attacks on data integrity in storage-based transient stability control. *IEEE Transactions on Industrial Informatics*, 13(6), 3322–3333. doi:10.1109/TII.2017.2720679

Ge, L., Yu, W., Moulema, P., Xu, G., Griffith, D., & Golmie, N. (2017). Detecting Data Integrity Attacks in Smart Grid. *Security and Privacy in Cyber-Physical Systems: Foundations, Principles and Applications,* 281-303.

Giani, A., Bitar, E., Garcia, M., McQueen, M., Khargonekar, P., & Poolla, K. (2013). Smart grid data integrity attacks. *IEEE Transactions on Smart Grid*, 4(3), 1244–1253. doi:10.1109/TSG.2013.2245155

Hao, J., Piechocki, R. J., Kaleshi, D., Chin, W. H., & Fan, Z. (2015). Sparse malicious false data injection attacks and defense mechanisms in smart grids. *IEEE Transactions on Industrial Informatics*, 11(5), 1–12. doi:10.1109/TII.2015.2475695

He, Y., Mendis, G. J., & Wei, J. (2017). Real-time detection of false data injection attacks in smart grid: A deep learning-based intelligent mechanism. *IEEE Transactions on Smart Grid*, 8(5), 2505–2516. doi:10.1109/TSG.2017.2703842

Karimipour, H., Dehghantanha, A., Parizi, R. M., Choo, K. K. R., & Leung, H. (2019). A deep and scalable unsupervised machine learning system for cyber-attack detection in large-scale smart grids. *IEEE Access : Practical Innovations, Open Solutions*, 7, 80778–80788. doi:10.1109/ACCESS.2019.2920326

Karthick Raghunath K. M, V. Vinoth Kumar, V.Muthukumaran, krishna kant singh, Mahesh T R, Akansha Singh, Raghunath, K., Kumar, V., Muthukumaran, V., Sing, K., Mahesh, T. R., & Singh, A., J. Detection And Classification Of Cyber Attacks Using Xgboost Regression And Inception V4. Journal of Web Engineering, *RIVER PUBLISHERS*, 21(4). doi:10.13052/jwe1540-9589.21413,2022

Khanna, K., Panigrahi, B. K., & Joshi, A. (2016). Data integrity attack in smart grid: Optimised attack to gain momentary economic profit. *IET Generation, Transmission & Distribution*, 10(16), 4032–4039. doi:10.1049/iet-gtd.2016.0350

Li, S., Yılmaz, Y., & Wang, X. (2014). Quickest detection of false data injection attack in wide-area smart grids. *IEEE Transactions on Smart Grid*, 6(6), 2725–2735. doi:10.1109/TSG.2014.2374577

Mahesh, T. R., Dhilip Kumar, V., & Vinoth Kumar, V. (2022). AdaBoost Ensemble Methods Using K-Fold Cross Validation for Survivability with the Early Detection of Heart Disease. Computational Intelligence and Neuroscience. doi:10.1155/2022/9005278,2022

Mahesh, T. R., Kumar, D., Vinoth Kumar, V., Asghar, J., Mekcha Bazezew, B., Natarajan, R., & Vivek, V., (2022). Blended Ensemble Learning Prediction Model for Strengthening Diagnosis and Treatment of Chronic Diabetes Disease. *Computational Intelligence and Neuroscience.*, 2022 doi:10.1155/2022/4451792

T. R. Mahesh, V. Vinoth Kumar, V. Muthukumaran, H. K. Shashikala, B. Swapna, Suresh Guluwadi, "Performance Analysis of XGBoost Ensemble Methods for Survivability with the Classification of Breast Cancer", Journal of Sensors, vol. 2022, Article ID 4649510, 8 pages,. . doi:10.1155/2022/4649510,2022

Mahesh, T. R., Kumar, D., Vinoth Kumar, V., Asghar, J., Mekcha Bazezew, B., Natarajan, R., & Vivek, V. (2022). Early predictive model for breast cancer classification using blended ensemble learning. *Int J Syst Assur Eng Manag.*. doi:10.1007/s13198-022-01696-0,2022

Mokashi, B., Bhat, V. S., & Pujari, J. D. S. (2022). Efficient Hybrid Blind Watermarking in DWT-DCT-SVD with Dual Biometric Features for Images. Contrast Media & Molecular Imaging. doi:10.1155/2022/2918126,2022

Rawat, D. B., & Bajracharya, C. (2015). Detection of false data injection attacks in smart grid communication systems. *IEEE Signal Processing Letters*, 22(10), 1652–1656. doi:10.1109/LSP.2015.2421935

Roopashree, S., Anitha, J., Mahesh, T. R., & Vinoth Kumar, V. (2022). An IoT based authentication system for therapeutic herbs measured by local descriptors using machine learning approach. *Measurement, 200.*. doi:10.1016/j.measurement.2022.111484

Sadeg, S., Hamdad, L., Benatchba, K., & Habbas, Z. (2015). BSO-FS: bee swarm optimization for feature selection in classification. In International Work-Conference on Artificial Neural Networks (pp. 387-399). Springer, Cham, Palanivinayagam. doi:10.1007/978-3-319-19258-1_33

Sanjab, A., & Saad, W. (2016). Data injection attacks on smart grids with multiple adversaries: A game-theoretic perspective. *IEEE Transactions on Smart Grid*, 7(4), 2038–2049. doi:10.1109/TSG.2016.2550218

Venkatesan, V.K., Izonin, I., Periyasamy, J., Indirajithu, A., Batyuk, A., & Ramakrishna, M.T. (2022). Incorporation of Energy Efficient Computational Strategies for Clustering and Routing in Heterogeneous Networks of Smart City. *Energies, 15*, 7524.. doi:10.3390/en15207524,2022

Wang, D., Guan, X., Liu, T., Gu, Y., Shen, C., & Xu, Z. (2014). Extended distributed state estimation: A detection method against tolerable false data injection attacks in smart grids. *Energies*, 7(3), 1517–1538. doi:10.3390/en7031517

Wang, Y., Amin, M. M., Fu, J., & Moussa, H. B. (2017). A novel data analytical approach for false data injection cyber-physical attack mitigation in smart grids. *IEEE Access : Practical Innovations, Open Solutions*, 5, 26022–26033. doi:10.1109/ACCESS.2017.2769099

Wei, J., & Mendis, G. J. A deep learning-based cyber-physical strategy to mitigate false data injection attack in smart grids. In *2016 Joint Workshop on Cyber-Physical Security and Resilience in Smart Grids (CPSR-SG)* (pp. 1-6). IEEE,2016 10.1109/CPSRSG.2016.7684102

Wei, L., Gao, D., & Luo, C. (2018). False data injection attacks detection with deep belief networks in smart grid. In *2018 Chinese Automation Congress (CAC)* (pp. 2621-2625). IEEE. 10.1109/CAC.2018.8623514

Chapter 14

Algorithm-Based Spatio-Temporal Study on Identification of Pure Bamboo Vegetation Using LULC Classification

Janani Chennupati

Velagapudi Ramakrishna Siddhartha Engineering College, India

Mounika Susarla

Velagapudi Ramakrishna Siddhartha Engineering College, India

Vani K. Suvarna

iD https://orcid.org/0000-0003-4608-6308

Velagapudi Ramakrishna Siddhartha Engineering College, India

K. S. Vijaya Lakshmi

Velagapudi Ramakrishna Siddhartha Engineering College, India

Chennu Nandini Priyanka

Velagapudi Ramakrishna Siddhartha Engineering College, India

ABSTRACT

Bamboo is a natural air purifier that helps to keep the surroundings clean. Bamboo forests, an essential source of socioeconomic life for rural communities and an integral part of the ecosystem, are undergoing substantial changes. In the mapping and identification of natural resources, space technology has been beneficial. The objective of classification is to divide a large subject into fewer, more manageable fractions. For land use and land cover, four supervised learning methods, namely Naive Bayes, random forest, support vector machine, and decision tree, are used. Their overall accuracies will be compared to obtain the best algorithm. Land cover mapping and monitoring were carried out to preserve current natural resources and better understand the causative factors of land use in the study region, i.e., East Garo Hills, a district of Meghalaya, for the 2018 data. The application performance was measured in terms of Accuracy 97.23%, Recall 89.23%, F1 measure 97.23%, and Throughput 96.34%, which were improved and competed with future-level applications.

DOI: 10.4018/978-1-6684-6971-2.ch014

Copyright © 2023, IGI Global. Copying or distributing in print or electronic forms without written permission of IGI Global is prohibited.

INTRODUCTION

Bamboo is an important material for the people in impoverished countries because of its uses in various industries like paper, cloth and also used for construction, furniture etc. bamboo forests are most commonly found in tropical, sub-tropical zones 9. In India, bamboo forests are most commonly found in north-eastern regions. Forests cover around 60% of the overall geography in these regions, with bamboo forests accounting for 7% of the total forest area. Classification of bamboo-growing areas is critical for effective resource planning and management (Bharadwaj S P et al., 2003). Traditional procedures like as monitoring and predicting growth stocks, which are expensive and complicated, make it difficult to determine bamboo forest areas. Space technology has played a critical role in the classification of natural resources in recent years. Using Google Earth Engine, one can identify and classify bamboo forests (Goswami J et al., (2010). Google Earth Engine is a cloud-based platform that gives customers instant access to advanced computer capabilities for analyzing large amounts of geographical data. Images are pre-processed before being fed into Earth Engine, allowing for quick and easy access (Gorelick N et al., 2017). To achieve excellent speed, the Earth Engine library's functions make use of a number of built-in parallelization and data distribution methods. Land cover and Land use classification, irrigation, urban management, environmental disasters, meteorological assessments, and image analysis are just a few of the uses for GEE (Amani M et al., 2020). Classification can be performed either by using supervised or unsupervised techniques. Land use and land cover change has now become a critical component of current natural resource management and environmental monitoring systems.

The East Garo Hills District present in Meghalaya which is rich in bamboo forests (Vivekananda G N et al., 2021). In the north-eastern side there is a plethora of vegetation ranging from temperate, sub-tropical and tropical types because of the varied topography and rainfall. The East Garo Hills data is imported into Google Earth Engine and the LULC-Land Use Land Cover classification is done on the imported dataset by considering different types of classifiers. The LULC-Land Use Land Cover Classification method is used to assign forest cover classes and categorize images (Alshari E A & Gawali B W, 2021). Land use and land cover change has been a crucial element of modern natural asset management and environmental surveillance systems. Land cover corresponds to how woodland, marshes, impenetrable surfaces, farmland, and other types of surface and groundwater resources cover the Planet's surface in the Land Use Land Cover categorization. The term "land use" relates to just how mankind use the land for evolution, preservation, wildlife habitats, and agricultural land (Friedl M A & Brodley C E, 1997).

The majority of land use and land cover categorization models were compared in order to discover the best models and their properties in order to identify aspects that will aid in the development of classification accuracy (Wang P et al., 2008). For attaining better accuracy the algorithm should be trained. Training is done by selecting a group of pixels for each classifier. For LULC-Land Use Land Cover classification different algorithms like SVM-Support vector machine, Decision Tree, Random Forest, Naïve Bayes can be used. A decision tree is a categorization method that recursively segments a range of data into fewer sections by using a series of tests defined at each branch. One of the main advantages of decision tree algorithms is the flexibility and simplicity with which they partition data as a combination of the input training dataset. It's a time-consuming procedure. Random forest (RF) is an effective predictive analysis classifier for land remote sensing (Gislason P O et al., 2006). However, the vegetation and the factors attempted at every division, have an impact on classification accuracy. Bayesian classification is a statistical approach that can categorize every pattern until none is left unclassified.

The use of color index descriptors in integration with a Naive Bayes classifier increases the separation of distinct plant types. When utilized with a limited set of training data, the support vector classifier outperforms both ML-Machine learning and NN-Neural network classifiers in terms of classification accuracy (Ming D et al., 2016).

After classification is done, the outputs of LULC classification using different algorithms of the given East Garo Hills data are saved (Pradhan R et al., 2010). The outputs are imported into ArcGIS platform for reclassification. ArcGIS is a geographic data framework (GIS) that allows you to work with maps and geographical data and it is a tool for doing geographical analysis on graphical and tabular data, editing and geocoding data, and creating maps. It includes the ArcGIS online program, which connects to a mapping platform to create intuitive web maps and applications (Sitthi A et al., 2016). ArcGIS functional capabilities are Geo-visualization, Geo-processing and Geo-data management. Geo-visualization is largely focused with the pictorial representation of geospatial information. The geographical analysis and modeling capabilities of ArcGIS are referred to as geo-processing. Geo-data Management is managing the geographic data (TAATI A et al., 2015). The output of LULC- Land Use Land Cover classification is masked and reclassification is done. Following reclassification, and a comparison of the accuracies of the algorithms Decision Tree, Random Forest, Naive Bayes and SVM, Support Vector Machine (SVM) seems to have the best accuracy among them (Khan S & Mohiuddin K, 2018).

Supervised learning: A kind of machine learning –ML known as "supervised learning" involves teaching a computer to make predictions based on input data that has been explicitly labelled. Because of the labelled data, we know that some of the inputs will lead to the desired results. The training data acts as a supervisor in supervised learning, ensuring that the system learns to accurately anticipate future results. It uses the same idea that a pupil does under the guidance of a teacher.

LITERATURE

The LULC- Land Use Land Cover classification based on different classifiers can be done by using various methods like Random Forest, Naive Bayes, Support Vector Machine and Decision Tree. Any algorithm will consider some factors like color, area etc (Ormsby T et al., 2010). LULC can represent the aspect of human land use in an area and is crucial for area, land, and water management. It also aids in the adaptation to global environment and sustainable development (Zubair A O, 2006, pp 176). Depending on the spatiotemporal images obtained from the satellite, LULC- Land Use Land Cover can estimate the rate of growth and decrease in the residential area, rate of aquatic bodies, and rate of forests bodies that may have a major influence on the natural environment. "Man's activities and multiple benefits, which are performed out on land (like farmland, communities, industries, and so on)" are referred to as "land use." The component present, such as plants, watersheds, rocks/soils, and other components arising from land changes, is referred to as land cover. There's really no single ideal classification for vegetation cover, and developing one would be improbable (Yu H et al., 2007). Even when using an objective numerical approach, the classification process has multiple perspectives, and the process itself is subjective. Land cover and land use activities are interrelated concepts that have been used interchangeably in several circumstances. Whether the area is being used for forest, agricultural, residential, or industrial purposes, there are typically connected forms of cover (Chaudhary B S et al., 2008). The activity is not immediately recorded by remote sensing image-forming equipment. The satellite sensors obtain a response depending on a range of land features, including ecological and man-made vegetation. Patterns, tones, textures, forms, and site associations are used by the interpreter to extrapolate information about land - uses from what is essentially land cover data. For LULC- Land Use Land Cover classification, approaches based mostly on pixel or object analysis have been used. As shown in, an object-based strategy frequently outperforms a pixel-based one (Pandey P C et al., 2021). In fact, unlike the pixel-based approach, which categorizes pixels based on their size, the object-based methods enclose semantic information that is not contained in the individual's spectral information. color, texture, brightness, and shape, but in pixels of an image with comparable qualities. In this scenario, both multispectral resolution are used to divide and then classify the image and transforms features into useful objects (Rajendran G B et al., 2020). SPOT and TM were used to improve LULC- Land Use Land Cover information and create a database, which was then merged with ground spectral feature information to create a decision tree model. Multiple levels of decision trees categorization were applied to complicated land cover types, using themed maps and the findings of non-supervised classification in analyzing (Jansen L J & Di Gregorio A, 2003). According to the approach, which is used as a component to retrieve modifications and categorization data from satellite photos, as well as concluding overview of the merging tiers, and to provide quick access to LULC- Land Use Land Cover information? A decision tree is a classification process that uses a series of tests provided at every level of the tree to recursively segment a data set into smaller subgroups (Wang P et al., 2008). The tree is made up of a root node, a collection of internal nodes, and a set of terminal nodes. Each node in a decision tree has one parent node and two or even more child nodes (Yang C et al., 2017). In this framework, a data set is classified by systematically partitioning as per the model developed provided by the tree, and each item is assigned a class label based on which branch node it falls into. Standard supervised classification algorithms employed in remotely sensed data, such as probabilistic classification, have significant advantages over decision trees (Adam E et al., 2014). Breiman (2001) developed RF, a supervised learning method for enhancing tree regression and classification tasks by combining multiple decision trees. Bagging and random subspace selection are two powerful techniques used in the process. First, RF creates a large number of binary classification trees (n-tree) using replacements derived from the original observations using many bootstrap samples. Second, for each node, a possible subset of the characteristics is used to select a number of input factors, and the appropriate partition is determined using only this feature subsets (Rodriguez-Galiano V F et al., 2012). There is no trimming, and all forests are maximally grown, ensuring lower resemblance between different trees and hence a limited performance. RF can be seen of as a black box classifier. RF includes a missing value estimation technique as well as the ability to do several forms of data analysis techniques, such as Regression, classification, survival analysis, and unsupervised learning (Eisavi V et al., 2015). To construct a prediction model with the RF classifier, just two parameters must be defined: the desired number of classification models (k) and the number of prediction factors (m) used per branch to generate the tree grow. To identify land cover, LST properties and spectral bands were compared in multiple configurations. The significant features produce the greatest rise in overall seperability, while the spectral and LST characteristics provide a much more significant increase in forest cover projection precision, according to a quantitative analysis of the data (Kamal M et la., 2019). Employing RFC to create forest cover maps, pick relevant multi-temporal spectral features and thermal characteristics to help overcome the challenge of differentiating between classes with identical spectral properties or seasonal variations. To identify mangroves from non-mangroves, wide areas, aquatic systems, and atmospheric objects, researchers used the region of interest (ROI) technique. The ROI of five classes was used to define the entire dataset for the data model. The results suggest that mangrove cover declined dramatically along the coastline and on various sides of fishponds from 2014 to 2015. However, it rose from

2016 to 2018, particularly on the south side. The creation of fishing or aquaculture ponds, as well as some coastal recovery attempts, have all contributed to the stability of forest cover in the study region. When there is a clear margin of distinction between classes, SVM-Support vector machine performs well. In an object-based approach, comparing the effectiveness of SVM with the random forest (RF) method in detecting tropical forests using Li-DAR data and aerial photographs (Campomanes F et al., 2016). The soil canopy height model (CHM) and concentration were among derivatives developed from the Li-DAR data. Several training object features were generated and used for classification using both the Li-DAR and orthophoto derivatives. The rest of the image was classified using SVM- SVM-Support vector machine with radial basis function, yielding a total accuracy of 95.83 percent. With the same features, Random Forest, another machine learning technique, achieved an accuracy of 99.1667 percent (Bhargavi P & Jyothi S, 2009).

The term "Naive Bayes classifier" is a simple classification technique based on Bayes' theorem and strict independent requirements in Bayesian statistics. Naive Bayes analyzers can be learned very quickly in a supervised learning approach, depending on the particular structure of the likelihood function. The method of probabilistic technique is employed to assess characteristics for Naive Bayes classifiers in real-world applications. Despite its simple design and simplified hypotheses, Naive Bayes models outperform in a wide range of difficult real-world circumstances (Juyal P et al., 2020). The Naive Bayes models has the advantage of just requiring a simple and inexpensive of training analysis to predict the classification features [29]. SVM-Support vector machine, Naive Bayes, Random Forest, CNN- CNN-Convolution neural network, and ResNet are all compared. The class label is identified by the classification technique. The following are the accuracies, 57 percent in Random Forest, Nave Bayes has 40 percent, 60 percent SVM, 75 percent Logistic Regression, 80 percent according to CNN-Convolution neural network and RESNET has shown86 percent.

METHODOLOGY

As the process flow started initially the research area is chosen and then various platforms and code editors are used for preparing the data, applying algorithms and obtaining results. This section methodology depicts the clear picture on how the overall procedure is performed.

The approach uses different indices to identify bamboo vegetation. The indices calculated are NDVI (Normalized Difference Vegetation Index) for estimating the density of green on an area of land, the estimation can be heild like, The NDVI always falls somewhere between -1 and +1. On the other hand, there is no delineated border between the various types of land cover. For instance, when you have negative values, its likely water. This is because water has negative values. On the other hand, if the NDVI value is near one, there's a good chance it's just a lot of green leaves packed together. However, when the NDVI is very close to zero, there are probably no green leaves, and the area might even be urbanized. SI(Stress Index) for detecting water content in the leaves, EVI(Enhanced Vegetation Index) an optimized vegetation index designed to improve vegetation monitoring by decoupling the canopy background signal and reducing atmospheric influences., The index value difference between bamboo and other land-use classes was smaller and the bamboo's leaf water content is also lower when compared to other forest types to increase it, EBVI (Enhanced Bamboo Vegetation Index-proposed name) was created using NDVI and SI. For calculating these indices following formula (1,2,3,4) are used.

Supervised Learning: "Supervised learning-SL" teaches a computer to predict depending on labelled input-i/p data. Due of the tagged data, we know that some of the inputs-I/P will contribute to the intended results. In supervised learning-SL, the training data helps the algorithm predict future results. It works like a student under a teacher.

Supervised learning-SL feeds its machine learning-ML model input and output-O/p data. A supervised learning-SL method finds a mapping function to map x to y. (y).Supervised learning-SL is used for risk assessment, image categorization, fraud detection, spam filtering, etc.

$$NDVI = \frac{NIR - RED}{NIR + RED} \tag{1}$$

$$SI = \frac{NIR - SWIR}{NIR + SWIR} \tag{2}$$

$$EVI = \frac{NIR - RED}{NIR + 6RED - 7.5BLUE + 1} \tag{3}$$

$$EBVI = \frac{NDVI - SI}{NDVI + SI} \tag{4}$$

All these are applied on the study area East Garo Hills using Google Earth Engine and based on Sentinel-2 data the results are obtained. In August 2020 Mayuri Sharma and Aniruddha Deka [31] proposed that the approximate threshold in Enhanced Bamboo Vegetation Index was considered as 0.7 or 0.8 and Thresholds in Stress Index were taken as 0.6 for vegetation class and 0.3 for non-vegetation class. In the present work the threshold values of Enhanced Bamboo Vegetation Index were observed in the range of 0.6 to 0.8. The major drawback of this study is that it cannot differentiate bamboo from other types of grass species. To extend this work an LULC classification method using various supervised learning algorithms based on the spectral signatures where ground truth points are used as a base is done and explained in the further sections of this work. The outputs obtained after applying various indices on East Garo Hills dataset are displayed below as Figure-1 NDVI Map NDVI is always in the range of -1 to +1. The dividing line between different land uses in blurry. Whenever the readings are negative, for instance, water is almost certainly the culprit. However, if the NDVI is near to +1, it's likely that the greenness is coming from leaves, Figure-2 SI Map It is possible to generate a time series of stress index (SI) maps for the R3 site by utilizing information from Landsat satellites, Figure-3 EVI Map The Enhanced Vegetation Index-EVI from Landsat can be utilized to quantify the amount of greenery in a given area, much like the NDVI, Figure-4 EBVI Map EBVI consider from 0.7 or 0.8, while Stress Index Thresholds is 0.6 for vegetation & 0.3 for non-vegetation. EBVI threshold values are 0.6 to 0.8 in this study respectively.

Figure 1. NDVI(Normalized Difference Vegetation Index) Map

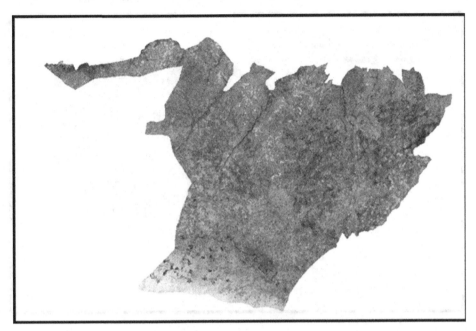

Figure 2. SI (Stress Index) Map

Figure 3. EVI (Enhanced Vegetation Index) Map

Figure 4. EBVI (Enhanced Bamboo Vegetation Index) Map

Research Area

East Garo Hills a district of Meghalaya which is a state in North-eastern India is selected as the study area. It is a district with approximately 2,603 km^2 and a population of about 317,917. Out of the total area 2217 km^2 is forest consists of very dense forest, moderate dense forest and open forest which is 85.17%, of district's geographical area, 9.88% of state's geographical area and 12.83% of state's total forest area.

Data Preparation

From the research region East Garo Hills some of the bamboo forests area truth points are collected and from those they are divided into mixed bamboo and pure bamboo for this study only pure bamboo data is used this separation is done with the help of QGIS tool. All the regions of forest area collected are in polygonal shapes. Also the district shape file of East Garo Hills is downloaded from ESRI website. The training is performed based on sentinel-2 data.

Algorithm Selection

The main purpose of this study is to classify the pure bamboo species from remaining vegetation. This can be done using either supervised learning techniques or unsupervised learning techniques with the former giving accurate results compared to latter so it is chosen for classification. Out of the many algorithms available in supervised learning techniques such as Logistic Regression, Naïve Bayes, Stochastic Gradient Descent, K-Nearest Neighbour, Decision Tree, Random Forest, and Support Vector Machine four algorithms are selected namely Naïve Bayes, Decision Tree, Random Forest, and Support Vector Machine. All the above 4 algorithms are used for LULC classification and compared for their accuracies.

Lulc Classification

A pixel-based LULC classification is performed on the study area East Garo Hills. Four classes were selected majorly they are water body, Pure bamboo, Built-up and other vegetation. Water body pointing all the ponds, lakes, rivers. Pure bamboo species are the bamboo forests in that region. Built-up consists of all the barren land and built-up area. Other vegetation representing all the remaining forest, crop lands, tundra, grasslands. Using the above mentioned classes training is given with the help of sentinel-2 data and Google satellite data. Based on the results of classification re-training is performed until the accurate results are obtained. In the same way, LULC classification is performed using all the four algorithms and the final results are exported from Google Earth Engine.

Re-Classification and Area Calculation

Reclassification is the method of re-assigning one or more values in a raster dataset to new output values. The raster data exported from Google earth engine is uploaded into the ArcGIS for re-classification. The masked raster is re-classified with the help of ArcGIS tools available for reclassifying the raster data. The classified data is used to calculate area occupied by each class. The area obtained is verified with data from literature and ESRI results and accuracy of each algorithm is obtained as depicted in the results section.

FLOW DIAGRAM

Following proposed system model Figure-5 represents the flow of project. The process starts from importing datasets and training it then by adding layers to the map. Later classifying the map using algorithms which are mentioned in the diagram following the image is exported into the drive. Next reclassification is performed by using ArcGIS on the exported image. Subsequently, the tabulate tool is used to calculate and classify the each area. By comparing existing and calculated area the accuracy is measured for each algorithm. By visually displaying the information in a flow diagram, we can quickly understand how the project is proceeding from the initial stage to the final step.

Figure 5. Process flow diagram of Classification

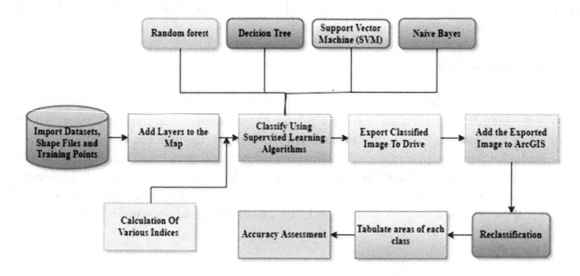

RESULTS

Lulc Classification

The complete area is classified into 4 different categories called classes namely water Body, Pure Bamboo, Other Vegetation and Built-Up area are represented with different colors and those colors are used for further map data identification as shown in Figure-6 respectively. Each class is differentiated by distinct colors which is shown in the below figure. This zone is classified by using 4 algorithms and for each algorithm, the area is divided into the 4 classes mentioned above. The respective areas covered based on classes may differ based on algorithm used. The LULC Classification results of each algorithm are depicted below in Figures. The Figures 7,8,9,10 uses the different algorithms they are. The Figure 7, represents the LULU Classification using Random Forest Algorithm representation on the selected zone. And the Figure 8, represents the LULC Classification using Decision Tree Algorithm on the selected zone. Figure 9 LULC Classification using Support Vector Machine Algorithm on the selected zone. Figure 10 LULC Classification using Naïve Bayes Algorithm on the selected zone.

Figure 6. Colors representing each class in LULC Classification

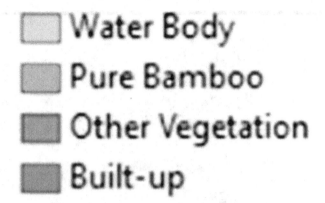

Figure 7. LULC Classification using Random Forest Algorithm on the selected zone

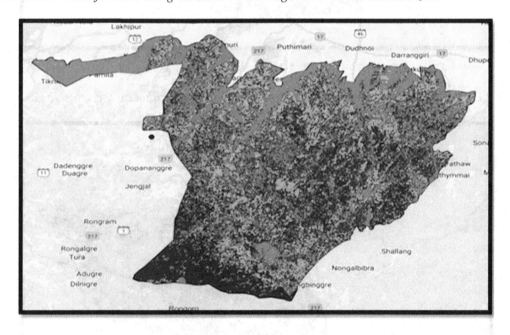

After the LULC classification algorithm is used on the selected zone, the exported classified image obtained is in the single-band format as in Figure-11 which is not understandable. This image is converted to multi-band image by doing re-classification using ArcGIS. This re-classification helps study the image by converting to human readable format.

Figure 8. LULC Classification using Decision Tree Algorithm on the selected zone

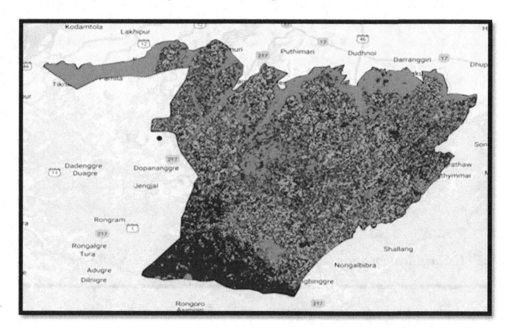

Figure 9. LULC Classification using Support Vector Machine Algorithm on the selected zone

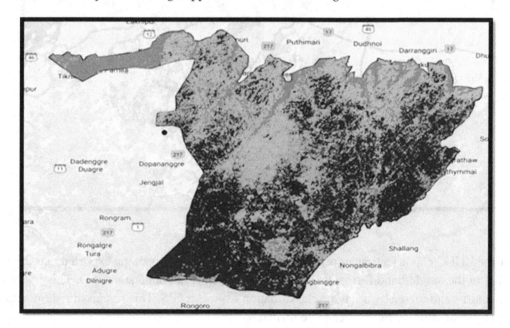

Figure 10. LULC Classification using Naïve Bayes Algorithm on the selected zone

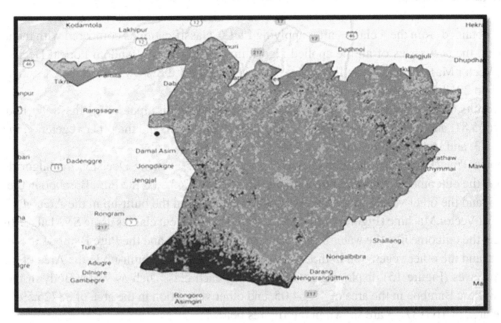

Figure 11. Exported classified image using Decision tree Algorithm from Google Earth Engine

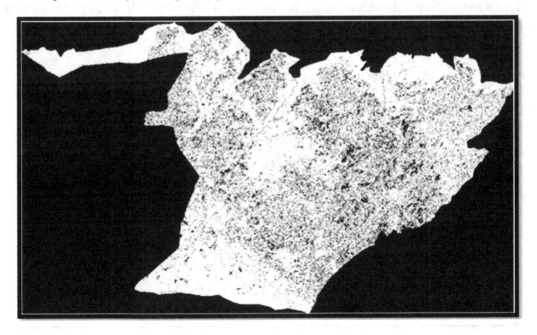

Performance Analysis

The area obtained from the 4 classes after applying LULC classification is compared with the literature data. Then, the accuracies of all the applied algorithms are obtained. Random Forest, Decision Tree, Support Vector Machine and Naïve Bayes gave accuracies of 89%, 98%, 98% and 57% respectively when analyzed on 2018 data of East Garo Hills.

The results of Random Forest (Figure-12) whenever we take an input image the water body in the area of 7665.81, and then the pure bamboo in the area of 39015.38, and the other vegetation in the area of 13095.43, and Built-up in the area of 87259.28.

Decision Tree (Figure-13) the area covered by various classes using Decision tree algorithm, then we can get the outcome like the water body in the Area of 8654.45, and the Pure Bamboo in the Area of 33668.55, and the other vegetation in the Area of 139518.85, and the built-up in the Area of 82156.82.

Support Vector Machine (Figure-14) the area covered by different classes using SVM algorithm, then we can get the outcome like the water body in the Area of 8712.86, and the Pure Bamboo in the Area of 33497.41, and the other vegetation in the Area of 139574.18, and the built-up in the Area of 82314.22.

Naïve Bayes (Figure-15) displaying area covered by each class such as Water Body in the area of 14771.18, Pure Bamboo in the area of 47364.05, and other vegetation in the area of 38725.59 and built-up in the area of 163137.13 are shown in the figures below.

The following Figure-16 depicts the bar chart plotted for the algorithm accuracies measured describing algorithms on x-axis and accuracy on y-axis. The decision tree algorithm can get the Accuracy of 98, and the Random Forest algorithm can get the Accuracy of 89, and the SVM can get the Accuracy of 98, and the Navies Bayes Algorithm can get the Accuracy of 57. As shown in the below graph.

Figure 12. Area covered by different classes using Random Forest algorithm

Class	Area(Ha)
Water body	7665.81
Pure bamboo	39015.38
Other vegetation	130957.43
Built-up	87259.28

Figure 13. Area covered by different classes using Decision Tree algorithm

class	Area(Ha)
Water body	8654.45
Pure bamboo	33668.55
Other vegetation	139518.85
Built-up	82156.82

Figure 14. Area covered by different classes using SVM algorithm

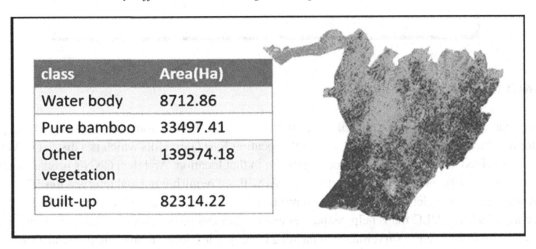

class	Area(Ha)
Water body	8712.86
Pure bamboo	33497.41
Other vegetation	139574.18
Built-up	82314.22

Figure 15. Area covered by different classes using Naïve Bayes algorithm

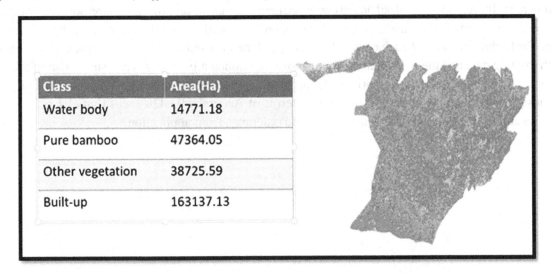

Class	Area(Ha)
Water body	14771.18
Pure bamboo	47364.05
Other vegetation	38725.59
Built-up	163137.13

Figure 16. Bar Chart representing accuracy of each algorithm

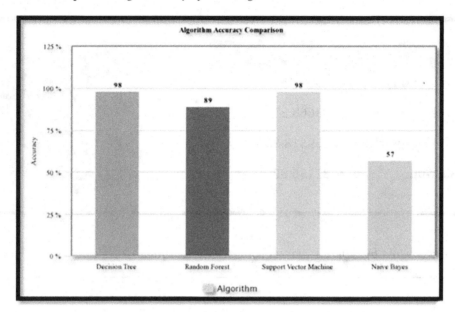

CONCLUSION

This research uses machine learning algorithms Random Forest, Decision Tree, Naive Bayes, Support Vector Machine is performed on 2018 data in the location East Garo Hills which is a district in Meghalaya. This helped in finding pure bamboo vegetation in that location. And then CNN's primary strength is that it can identify relevant features autonomously without requiring manual intervention. That's why Convolutional Neural Networks (CNNs) is so promising for fixing issues with computer vision and picture classification. LULC maps help people understand the landscape. Annual LULC data on national datasets would allow yearly surveillance of farming technologies, forest transformations, surface waters, etc. & the limitation is, the structural complexity of the areas, caused by regular vegetation continua in grasslands of varied densities and rural settlements' building materials of wood and grasses cut locally, hampered full-area coverage of sufficient classified data. The data is preprocessed to remove missing data, noisy data then the LULC classification is done on preprocessed dataset. Later, raster reclassification is done for finding the area of each class. This calculated area is used to compare and contrast the results with existing data and the performance of the above mentioned algorithms is measured. Out of the four algorithms decision tree and support vector machine provides 98% accuracy for the district data. The proposed method attains more improvement in terms of Accuracy 93.42%, sensitivity 94.32%, Recall 97.23% and F1 measure 94.34% which were good outcomes from application.

REFERENCES

Adam, E., Mutanga, O., Odindi, J., & Abdel-Rahman, E. M. (2014). Land-use/cover classification in a heterogeneous coastal landscape using RapidEye imagery: Evaluating the performance of random forest and support vector machines classifiers. *International Journal of Remote Sensing, 35*(10), 3440–3458. doi:10.1080/01431161.2014.903435

Alshari, E. A., & Gawali, B. W. (2021). Development of classification system for LULC using remote sensing and GIS. *Global Transitions Proceedings, 2*(1), 8–17. doi:10.1016/j.gltp.2021.01.002

Amani, M., Ghorbanian, A., Ahmadi, S. A., Kakooei, M., Moghimi, A., Mirmazloumi, S. M., Moghaddam, S. H. A., Mahdavi, S., Ghahremanloo, M., Parsian, S., Wu, Q., & Brisco, B. (2020). Google earth engine cloud computing platform for remote sensing big data applications: A comprehensive review. *IEEE Journal of Selected Topics in Applied Earth Observations and Remote Sensing, 13*, 5326–5350. doi:10.1109/JSTARS.2020.3021052

Bharadwaj, S. P., Subramanian, S., Manda, S., Ray, T. A. N. I. Y. A., Mukherjee, P. R. A. B. I. R., & Rao, I. R. (2003). Bamboo livelihood development planning, monitoring and analysis through GIS and remote sensing. *Journal of Bamboo and Rattan, 2*(4), 453–461. doi:10.1163/156915903322700476

Bhargavi, P., & Jyothi, S. (2009). Applying naive bayes data mining technique for classification of agricultural land soils. *International journal of computer science and network security, 9*(8), 117-122.

Campomanes, F., Pada, A. V., & Silapan, J. (2016). *Mangrove classification using support vector machines and random forest algorithm: a comparative study.*

Chaudhary, B. S., Saroha, G. P., & Yadav, M. (2008). Human induced land use/land cover changes in northern part of Gurgaon district, Haryana, India: Natural resources census concept. *Journal of Human Ecology (Delhi, India), 23*(3), 243–252. doi:10.1080/09709274.2008.11906077

Eisavi, V., Homayouni, S., Yazdi, A. M., & Alimohammadi, A. (2015). Land cover mapping based on random forest classification of multitemporal spectral and thermal images. *Environmental Monitoring and Assessment, 187*(5), 1–14. doi:10.100710661-015-4489-3 PMID:25910718

Friedl, M. A., & Brodley, C. E. (1997). Decision tree classification of land cover from remotely sensed data. *Remote Sensing of Environment, 61*(3), 399–409. doi:10.1016/S0034-4257(97)00049-7

Gislason, P. O., Benediktsson, J. A., & Sveinsson, J. R. (2006). Random forests for land cover classification. *Pattern Recognition Letters, 27*(4), 294–300. doi:10.1016/j.patrec.2005.08.011

Gorelick, N., Hancher, M., Dixon, M., Ilyushchenko, S., Thau, D., & Moore, R. (2017). Google Earth Engine: Planetary-scale geospatial analysis for everyone. *Remote Sensing of Environment, 202*, 18–27. doi:10.1016/j.rse.2017.06.031

Goswami, J., Tajo, L., & Sarma, K. K. (2010). Bamboo resources mapping using satellite technology. *Current Science*, 650–653.

Jansen, L. J., & Di Gregorio, A. (2003). Land-use data collection using the "land cover classification system": Results from a case study in Kenya. *Land Use Policy*, *20*(2), 131–148. doi:10.1016/S0264-8377(02)00081-9

Juyal, P., Kulshrestha, C., Sharma, S., & Ghanshala, T. (2020). Common bamboo species identification using machine learning and deep learning algorithms. [IJITEE]. *International Journal of Innovative Technology and Exploring Engineering*, *9*(4), 3012–3017. doi:10.35940/ijitee.D1609.029420

Kamal, M., Jamaluddin, I., Parela, A., & Farda, N. M. (2019). Comparison of Google Earth Engine (GEE)-based machine learning classifiers for mangrove mapping. In *Proceedings of the 40th Asian Conference Remote Sensing,* (pp. 1-8). ACRS.

Khan, S., & Mohiuddin, K. (2018). Evaluating the parameters of ArcGIS and QGIS for GIS Applications. *Int. J. Adv. Res. Sci. Eng*, *7*, 582–594.

Ming, D., Zhou, T., Wang, M., & Tan, T. (2016). Land cover classification using random forest with genetic algorithm-based parameter optimization. *Journal of Applied Remote Sensing*, *10*(3), 035021. doi:10.1117/1.JRS.10.035021

Ormsby, T., Napoleon, E., Burke, R., Groessl, C., & Bowden, L. (2010). *Getting to know ArcGIS desktop*. Esri Press.

Pandey, P. C., Koutsias, N., Petropoulos, G. P., Srivastava, P. K., & Ben Dor, E. (2021). Land use/land cover in view of earth observation: Data sources, input dimensions, and classifiers—a review of the state of the art. *Geocarto International*, *36*(9), 957–988. doi:10.1080/10106049.2019.1629647

Pradhan, R., Ghose, M. K., & Jeyaram, A. (2010). Land cover classification of remotely sensed satellite data using bayesian and hybrid classifier. *International Journal of Computer Applications*, *7*(11), 1–4. doi:10.5120/1295-1783

Rajendran, G. B., Kumarasamy, U. M., Zarro, C., Divakarachari, P. B., & Ullo, S. L. (2020). Land-use and land-cover classification using a human group-based particle swarm optimization algorithm with an LSTM Classifier on hybrid pre-processing remote-sensing images. *Remote Sensing (Basel)*, *12*(24), 4135. doi:10.3390/rs12244135

Rodriguez-Galiano, V. F., Ghimire, B., Rogan, J., Chica-Olmo, M., & Rigol-Sanchez, J. P. (2012). An assessment of the effectiveness of a random forest classifier for land-cover classification. *ISPRS journal of photogrammetry and remote sensing*, *67*, 93-104.

Sitthi, A., Nagai, M., Dailey, M., & Ninsawat, S. (2016). Exploring land use and land cover of geotagged social-sensing images using naive bayes classifier. *Sustainability (Basel)*, *8*(9), 921. doi:10.3390u8090921

Taati, A., Sarmadian, F., Mousavi, A., Pour, C. T. H., & Shahir, A. H. E. (2015). Land use classification using support vector machine and maximum likelihood algorithms by Landsat 5 TM images. [WJST]. *Walailak Journal of Science and Technology*, *12*(8), 681–687.

Vivekananda, G. N., Swathi, R., & Sujith, A. V. L. N. (2021). Multi-temporal image analysis for LULC classification and change detection. *European journal of remote sensing, 54*(sup2), 189-199.

Wang, P., Zhang, J. X., Jia, W. J., & Lin, Z. J. (2008, June). A study on decision tree classification method of land use/land cover-Taking tree counties in Hebei Province as an example. In *2008 International Workshop on Earth Observation and Remote Sensing Applications* (pp. 1-5). IEEE. 10.1109/EORSA.2008.4620331

Wang, P., Zhang, J. X., Jia, W. J., & Lin, Z. J. (2008, June). A study on decision tree classification method of land use/land cover-Taking tree counties in Hebei Province as an example. In *2008 International Workshop on Earth Observation and Remote Sensing Applications* (pp. 1-5). IEEE. 10.1109/EORSA.2008.4620331

Yang, C., Wu, G., Ding, K., Shi, T., Li, Q., & Wang, J. (2017). Improving land use/land cover classification by integrating pixel unmixing and decision tree methods. *Remote Sensing (Basel)*, *9*(12), 1222. doi:10.3390/rs9121222

Yu, H., Joshi, P. K., Das, K. K., Chauniyal, D. D., Melick, D. R., Yang, X. U. E. F. E. I., & Xu, J. (2007). Land use/cover change and environmental vulnerability analysis in Birahi Ganga sub-watershed of the Garhwal Himalaya, India. *Tropical Ecology*, *48*(2), 241.

Zubair, A. O. (2006). Change detection in land use and Land cover using remote sensing data and GIS (A case study of Ilorin and its environs in Kwara State). Department of Geography, University of Ibadan.

Chapter 15
Malware Detection in Android Systems Using Deep Learning Techniques

V. R. Niveditha

Sathyabama Institute of Science and Technology, India

Santhiya Parivallal

(iD) https://orcid.org/0000-0002-4818-3075

Sathyabama Institute of Science and Technology, India

Maria Jones

Sathyabama Institute of Science and Technology, India

Amandeep Singh K.

Sathyabama Institute of Science and Technology, India

P. Rajasekar

Sathyabama Institute of Science and Technology, India

ABSTRACT

Due to the smoothness and various other characteristics, the Android OS is familiar among all kinds of mobile users. Traditionally signature-based techniques are applied to identify malware. But this technique is not able to identify the latest malware. Classification algorithms can support huge datasets needed to protect Android-based platforms. At the same time, a huge dataset needs scalability for detecting and classifying automatically at the malicious identification stage and feature retrieval. In this chapter, enhanced CNN (ECNN) classifier is used for identifying malware in smart devices. The outcome of this suggested classifier is compared with the existing models like XGBoost, random forest, and CNN. The performance of the proposed work is assessed based on their accuracy, precision, and recall values. From the results it is proved that proposed enhanced CNN (ECNN) produces accuracy of 95.8%, precision of 0.96, and recall of 0.92, which is high compared to other algorithms. The tool used for execution is python.

DOI: 10.4018/978-1-6684-6971-2.ch015

Copyright © 2023, IGI Global. Copying or distributing in print or electronic forms without written permission of IGI Global is prohibited.

INTRODUCTION

In recent days, the number of smart devices is increased radically. More than 3.8 billion smart devices have reached people throughout the world in 2021. Among these smart devices, nearly 72% of the devices are executed based on the Android platform. Most of the Android platform users install security software on their devices for protecting them from unknown people and software. But most of the time security software also cannot identify the viruses in mobile devices. Many people stored their valuable data in their smart devices. Due to these reasons, attackers also show more interest to access Android-based devices. Particularly, once the familiar platform is used by more users automatically the attacker's numbers also increased.

With the enormous growth of smart devices, free Android-based applications have increased infinitely. This leads to a huge number of malicious activities, which break the security rules and the user's privacy. Malware identification on Android-based devices is one of the rising concerns due to the unwanted resemblance between malicious features and normal features. This leads to slow identification, and permits to preserve for a relatively long time in the affected devices. Android devices are the main target of the attackers because of the platform's popularity and the open nature features. Considering the development of the Android market, it is important to design efficient tools to identify the attacks on Android-based platforms.

Various solutions are already available to forecast the malware in Android systems. But most of the solutions are executed according to the signatures. Normally the signatures are retrieved and compared with the malware type signatures saved in the concerned database. But the major drawback of this signature-based prediction is, it is not able to identify the unfamiliar malware which is not available in the given dataset.

In 2019, 50% of attacks are increased in mobile phones. The number of malware is increasing day by day. It leads to creating a proper solution that will identify and recognize all kinds of attacks exactly with fewer amounts of resources and time. The major intention of this paper is to recommend a solution to identify the malware from different locations effectively and exactly with less time and resources.

Research Objectives

Researchers have suggested many dynamic analysis methods to identify Android malware. But, only few of the techniques are implied in real-life practice for monitoring the user devices as the Android OS doesn't render low-level data to the externally installed apps. In addition, some methodologies are used to ascertain some particular malware classes in an efficient way than others. Because of this reason, the end customers are profited with installation of multiple malware detection methods.

The earlier studies are proposed to identify the known and unknown samples of malware that are seen in the private and public datasets. Most of the public datasets used are gathered between the periods of 2010 to 2017. This raises a critical question about the process of detecting the recent application of malware whereas the behavior of the mobile malware is adaptable. Hence, a need is created to collect the updated application. Apart from that, some of the effective ways to identify the unknown malware understand the patterns of malware and categorization of patterns into families. The proposed study suggests a cost-effective and sustainable malware detection method based on the gathering of an updated dataset, categorizing malware families and iterating the behavior of the malware.

Main Contributions of the Proposed Study

The study resolves the various problems oriented with detection of Android malware. The contributions of the techniques are given below.

- A dataset is created using 7846 samples collected from present time, planned to enlarge and make it readily available for public
- An Android malware detection framework is recommended with the application of DL approaches based on sustainability metrics.
- Good Accuracy, Precision and Recall Rate should be the output.

LITERATURE SURVEY

Omar N. Elayan et al., (2021) presented a new approach for identifying malware in Android-based smart devices using GRU(Gated Recurrent Unit). It is a kind of RNN(Recurrent Neural Network). Here the authors extracted two fixed attributes, namely, API (Application Programming Interface) calls and credentials from Android-based applications. The proposed model is tested with CICAndMal2017 dataset. The outcome of the recommended system shows 98.2% accuracy.

Abdurrahman Pektaş et al., (2020) proposed a deep learning-based malware identification method for Android devices using extracted features from instruction type call graphs. The proposed technique observes all feasible paths and the remaining dataset increases the deep neural path against the spiteful path. Due to the unavailability of the public malware identification model, the authors train the networks from the initial stage. The grid searching technique was applied to find the best identifiers of the concerned network to identify the hyper-identifiers, which increases statistical type metric information. To assess the efficiency of the recommended technique, the authors calculate with the dataset 25,000 benign and 24,650 malicious samples. Here the authors assess the performance with different identifiers and statistical values are compared together with runtime. The investigational outcome shows 91.42% accuracy and 91.91% F-measure value.

Gianni D'Angelo et al., (2020) designed a work that illustrates the series of API calls raised by applications during execution as matrices like API images. They were used autoencoders to retrieve the major representative and selective attributes from the created matrices. Once the fewer amounts of samples for the training network, it exposes a valuable identifying malware. The final results describe the proposed framework can do better malware identification than traditional ML(Machine Learning) approaches.

Rahim Taheri et al., (2020) developed *four* malware identification techniques with the help of Hamming distance to get similarities among the samples. This proposed approach activates an alarm when malicious activities occurred on Android-based devices. Proposed system assists to keep away the malware from spreading. The recommended system is tested with three types of datasets such as Drebin, Contagio, and Genome. The outcome of the suggested system accuracy rate is 90% and it was compared with the existing solutions.

According to Xin Y et al., (2018), as new technology advance and more people use the internet, cyberattacks are on the rise, demanding the need of cyber security. In this article, we learn how ML and DL algorithms are used to investigate networks. We also receive a quick explanation of the many kinds of usable datasets.

To effectively detect android malware, Tianliang Lu et al., (2018) established the paradigm of malware detection. The expressed authorization is the basis for this model. It might have two layers. In the first layer, the analysis of the enhanced RF algorithm is employed, while in the second layer, the analysis of the fuzzy sets created by the recognition of sensitive permission constraint matching is used.

Mothanna Almahmouda et al., (2021) devised a new model that depends on the integration of four fixed features API calls, permission, rate of the permission, and system events. Particularly, the dataset contains 2,820 samples of benign and malware applications. Here the authors proposed a new structure of RNN (Recurrent Neural Network) that can be used to do the malware identification task. The investigational outcome says that the suggested model creates 98.58% accuracy and it is also capable of Android devices malware identification.

Many researchers have analyzed and published research works in this critical area that implies conventional desktop malware identifying approaches such as static and dynamic analysis methodologies to predict mobile malwares. Though various researches were conducted, none of them have conducted a thorough study based on the sensitivity computation of the attributes used. Samaneh Hosseini Moghaddam and Maghsood Abbaspour (2014) segregate the static attributes of classification-oriented malware identification techniques suggested in various research papers into some interlinked categories. It also studies the impact of making use of every category of attributes over the efficiency of classification-oriented Android malware detection technique with the help of static attributes.

Jordan Pattee and Byeong Kil Lee (2020) elaborated the multiple stages involved in investigating the critical problems of PMC based malware detection: Distribution-based attribute selection, Trade-off analysis of accuracy and complexity, Statistical characterization of malware and Design alternatives for PMC-related malware identification. The experimental result demonstrates that the suggested detection method renders a high accuracy in detection of malware. As structural implications, to get a more accurate detection of malware in practice, the hardware acceleration along with additional PMC registers are considered.

Shahrear Iqbaland Zulkernine (2018) proposed the sub-detectors are defined as the regular Android application which monitor and evaluate various information using monitoring module and it expose the detection module regarding the findings. The decision about considering an app as malware will be done by the detection module. App markets have become a place for publishing innovative techniques for the end users to detect malwares. The antivirus vendors and researchers enable the end users to install as many numbers of sub-detectors as per their need. Therefore, the researcher has executed SpyDroid embedded with AOSP and the experiment was done with a dataset of 4965 apps demonstrating the decisions extracted from multiple sub-detectors which increase the rate of malware detection on a real device.

As an equivalent to development in AI, the malware has also come out with new malware samples that differ in structure, size, and operation mode but it remains the same in performing the same functions in every metamorphic code production through suspicious code obfuscation methods. Therefore, they can surpass conventional signature-related malware recognition systems. (Necmettin Çarkacı et al., 2016) conducted a study on a pattern recognition-based method which identifies metamorphic malware with the help of the summary structure of MAIL that needs to be improved. In MAIL language code, the terms such as feature selection, classification algorithm, and feature extraction are researched concerning performance and accuracy. The designed system is examined using metamorphic malware development kits like G2, PSMPC, VCL32, and NGVCK and attains 100% accuracy using 2 of 26 MAIL attributes and install 93% reduction in attributes.

It is critical to select the architectural attributes from the images but it becomes difficult due to the restricted number of performance counters. This leads to a reduction in providing high-quality data while detecting malware. (Byeong Kil Lee et al., 2019) come out with a solution for the issue by setting up a metric named DoD as one of the criteria for malware detection. The experimental results demonstrate that the DoD is capable of differentiating malware software from benign software along with high accuracy in malware detection using the ML framework. In real-time, it is recommended to provide architectural implications such as hardware acceleration and additional PMC registers for getting accurate malware detection.

With the development of the web and the fast turn of activities, malware has grown into a major digital threat at present. Henceforth, the detection of malware is very much important in maintaining the security of computer networks. Nowadays, hackers commonly produce polymeric malware, which is a type of malware that changes its detectable attributes frequently to confuse the detection method based on signature. This gives rise to the utilization of ML in malware detection. (Sunita Choudhary et al., 2020) have derived a behavioral pattern that is achieved using static or dynamic analysis of the image. Further, with the application of dissimilar ML methods, the software is identified either as malware or benign. Behavioral-based techniques for malware detection get advanced with the implication of ML algorithms to frame the social-based malware detection and categorization model.

Due to the widespread of internet systems throughout the world in different areas, having a secured system is essential. As there is a continuous change in the variation of malware, it becomes a major threat to the security of computer systems. The key challenge faced in malware detection is the accurate detection of different types of malware. (Yongle Chen et al., 2018) have stated that a comparison of the nature of files leads to the identification of malware software and benign software. The static detection performed allows code obfuscation and file shelling, whereas dynamic detection is exposed to anti-virtual and anti-debugging ML technology. Hence, a combination of static and dynamic identification designed by the author outperforms the basic methods. Therefore, it is easy to analyze the malicious samples to segregate different destructive features with the help of the malicious detection method.

The complete size of IoT systems being employed at present shows an attack surface that imposes a significant security threat at a large scale that has been encountered before. To be specific, a single node/device used in a network that becomes affected by malware has the prospective to spread malware throughout the network, subsequently capturing the functions of the network. The simple steps carried out to identify and quarantine the malware found in IoT systems do not assure the prevention of malware propagation. Meanwhile, the utilization of conventional control theory used to confine malware is also not much effective due to the usage of existing methods that don't cope with real-time strategies of malware.

The strategies used for malware control are applied with the help of uncertain infection information rendered by specific nodes present in the network or holding the limitation issue decoupled from the performance of the network. (Sai Manoj Pudukotai Dinakarrao et al., 2019) have proposed a two-pronged framework, in which a runtime malware detection (HaRM) that engages HPC values is designed to identify benign and malware applications. The information is fed into the stochastic model predictive controllers during its runtime to trap the propagation of malware without hindering the performance of the network. The suggested solution is proved to provide an accuracy of 92.21% in the runtime of 10ns, which is an order of magnitude speedier than the prevailing malware detection solutions. The received outcome with the model predictive confinement strategy moves ahead to achieve an average network output of around 200% in IoT networks without any support from embedded defense.

PROPOSED METHODOLOGY

Android OS is one the well-known software among many software and it is the topmost OS in the market. Because of its adaptability, most organizations are creating various applications based on user requirements. Play store is one of the official websites but it supports unofficial layup and it does not force on developers in the time of publishing stage. These all features lead to the weakest platform for attackers, the common users are distressed from malicious software that destroy their phones and violate their security policy [6]. This research work uses DL(Deep Learning) methods like XGBoost, RF, CNN, and ECNN(Enhanced CNN) for detecting malware in Android-based devices. The above-mentioned algorithms are tested with an online UCI repository.

Following figure 1 illustrates the general structure of the malware detection system using deep learning algorithms.

Figure 1. Activities of malware classification in Android devices using deep learning

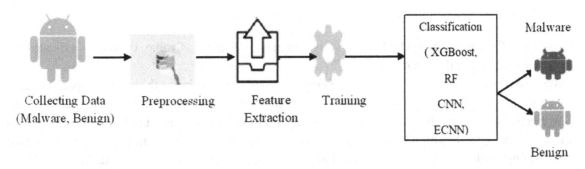

XGBoost classifier is developed for increasing the speed and the performance of the system. It uses less memory and effective computation time. XGBoost is one of the models used for the training dataset and it manages the missing values automatically. In RF(Random Forest) classifier, the given dataset is trained with extracted identifiers. Once the feature extraction is over the RF classifier is applied for the classification process. In the training time, a group of labels are identifying the type of application. RF contains a group of DTs(Decision Tree). Each DT is designed using the top-down technique. It means the process is initiated from the root node. When the training stage is over, the identifiers of RF at every node are situated and it has the capability of classifying android applications. Earlier research used CNN approach in malware identification due to their scalability. The success rate of CNN depends on the capability to spot out the malware activities and integrate the local patterns in an effective way. The existing research work uses unprocessed features from the decompiled applications. Here the CNN models are expanded by identifying opcode-based formats to find the positions that are malicious activity during recognition. This recommended system consists of various stages like data collection, preprocessing, feature extraction, training, and prediction. The performance of the proposed model is tested with the UCI Android malware dataset.

Convolutional Neural Network (CNN)

CNN is a feed forward neural network that includes gyration calculation and deep architecture. The capacity of the representation learning holds the performance translational shift-invariant categorization of input information with respect to its hierarchical structure.

The convolutional layer applies a sequence of learnable and learnable K filters to assess the image. Every CNN convolution layer is come after by a calculation type layer which aims at the local mean and secondary level extraction. Next, the pooling type layer is created to reduce the data that generated by the earlier convolutional layer and keep the most applicable attributes. This layer blows the filters one by one to create a new output information. Normally, the input information is described by the following attributes: h and w. Here, h denotes volume height and w indicates width. For every filter k, the convolutional layer put in a convolution described asthe following manner:

$$O_{i,j,k} = \sum_{h=0}^{h_k}\sum_{m=0}^{w_k}(w_{h,m}.x_{i+h,j+m}) + b_k, \tag{1}$$

Here the k filter is described by $h_k \times w_k$ weight matrix, b_k is the bias value, i and j are indicates the current pixel value x in the input data.

After every convolution type layer, use the pooling function to minimize the attribute space value of CNN classifier and filter based noises. The Max-Pooling method is to obtain the important delegate local attributes. The max-pooling method is described to remove the important significant attribute values of the input type vectors within a given window. The maximum rate of every attribute map is collected as the local optimal attribute. After the last flattening operation, get a one-dimensional vector value as input information for next level[24].

Enhanced CNN Procedure

The proposed methodology consists of CNN which will be optimized with SGD (Stochastic Gradient Descent optimizer). Initially our malware dataset will be loaded and it will be preprocessed. Then we will Initialize CNN and the training data will be load into the input layer followed by applying SGD optimizer in the pooling layer. Now we have to calculate the learning rate and with that learning rate check the over fitting data and error loss. We will give two conditions that is if Error loss is more adjust the learning rate and if Error loss is less proceed further to next classification process. The following Figure 2 represents the working of Enhanced CNN.

Smartphone with Android OS attracts most of the users due to its open-source nature and magnificent performance. Nevertheless, the comforts given by Android platform encourage the development of malware. The conventional techniques used to detect the malicious software with respect to the signature are not capable to identify unknown applications.

Figure 2. Working of enhanced CNN

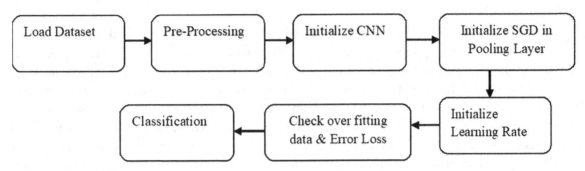

DL approaches has been useful in many security-oriented environments for securing applications. DL methods have been used for leading issues in cyber security like detecting intrusion, classification and malware detection, spam recognition and phishing finding. A CNN method concentrates on processing multidimensional data like images. This method is often used to process 2D matrices in the form of images or audio spectrograms. It is also rapidly used for 3D data such as videos, volumetric images, etc. The structure of a CNN is constructed with three types of layers namely the pooling layers, classification layer and the convolution layers.

Data Loading

The term Data loading means extraction of data from the available database and loading scheme. Generally, the data is fed into the destination application in a variant format besides the original source location. Extraction, transformation, and loading (ETL) is a three-step process in which data is retrieved, converted, and loaded into a data output container. Data can be gathered from one or maybe more sources and outputted with one or even more places.

Pre-Processing

In the Data pre-processing step, data mining and data analysis process are performed where the raw data is converted into a specific format that can be understood and investigated by computer system and ML.

The raw data available in real-world are in the form of videos, images, texts, etc. They are messy to handle. It not only comprises of inconsistencies and errors but also often retains incomplete and doesn't follow a uniform design.

Machines are well verse with processing information in a nice manner. They learn the data as 1s and 0s. Therefore, evaluating the structured data like percentages and whole numbers in an easy manner. The unstructured data present in the form of images and text need to be cleaned and formatted first before performing analysis.

Feature Selection

Feature selection infers to the procedure of minimizing inputs for investigation and processing, or for sorting out the most meaningful input variables. A relevant term, feature extraction or feature engineering infers to the operation of pulling out useful information or attributes from the available data. The process of feature selection is crucial to construct a good model for various purposes. The main reason for feature selection is to apply some grade of cardinality reduction, to propose a cut-off on the quantity of features which are most considered for construction of model. The dataset consists of more information than the information required building a model or it contains unnecessary kind of information. While performing feature selection the model gets trained and relevant information are picked out. With usage of some approaches in which feature selection methods are built-in makes the irrelevant columns of information to exclude and discovers the best attributes automatically. Every algorithm contains its own set of preselected techniques for applying attribute reduction in intelligent way.

CNN

In general, the basic framework of CNN includes two layers namely feature mapping layer and feature extraction layer. The feature extraction layer performs the function of connecting each neuron's input to the confined receptive area of the earlier layer and the normal characteristics are drawn out. After extracting the local attributes, the relationship among the different characteristics were established. In the feature mapping layer, every calculating layer in the network includes multiple attribute graphs that can be viewed as a plane. In the proposed model, the feature mapping framework utilizes the nonlinear activation function Relu.

$$f(x) = \max\{0, x\} \tag{2}$$

Figure 3. CNN architecture

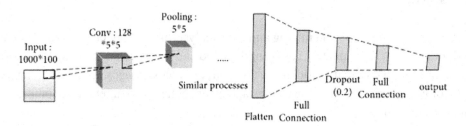

CNNs are typically composed of several layers of convolution layer and pooling layer. A non-linear operation is used in the convolution layer to exploit features from the input datasets by having to move the convolution filtration system in a predetermined window size. Discrete convolution with the K filter performs the subsequent change on the input *I* which is depicted in the following formula [4]:

$$\left(IXK\right)_{r.s} = \sum_{u=-h1}^{h1} \sum_{v=-h2}^{h2} K_{u.v} I_{r+u.s+v} \tag{4}$$

Here the K filter is written as:

$$K = \begin{pmatrix} K_{-h1,-h2} & \cdots & K_{-h1,h2} \\ \vdots & K_{0.0} & \vdots \\ K_{h1,-h2} & \cdots & K_{h1,h2} \end{pmatrix} \tag{5}$$

At last, the output value of the convolution layer (γ) contains a group of feature maps. The (γi) is calculated as follows.

$$Y_i = B_i \Sigma K_{i,j} \times X_j \tag{6}$$

Training Data

The most prime process in CNN training is convolution. The process of convolution is applied on an image as filter that is shown as a matrix. When the filter is applied to the images, it comes out with a set of small images which move through the pooling layer. This process series is repeated for several times using the network till it moves to the flattening layer. In the flattening layer, the vector carrying the conceptual characteristics will move to the dense layer. There are three ways to initialize filters.

Manual

In this method the filters are initialized manually. For example, the face parts are recognized with mouth filter, eye filter and so on. These filters make it easy to start with filters in manual manner as the parts of face are well known.

Random

This method is followed when conceptual objects or images that is tough to describe needs to be filtered. Here the users are forced to make use of randomly initialized filters.

Pre-Trained

The process of pre-training of filter is executed on some portions of the images. For example, when we need to learn about images of eye only, we need to implement filter related to eye.

SGD

Stochastic Gradient Descent (SGD) is a simple method but it is very much efficient for fitting linear regressors and classifiers performing under convex loss functions like Logistic Regression and linear SVM. Though SGD is working under ML for many years, it has recently received a considerable attention in the condition of large-scale learning.

SGD is applied successfully to sparse and large-scale ML issues often found in natural language processing and text classification. It is found that the given data is sparse and the classifiers present in the module easily measure the issues using more than 10^5 attributes and more than 10^5 training examples.

Learning Rate

While using statistics and ML, the rate of learning becomes a tuning parameter to obtain an optimized algorithm which establishes the step size at every iteration, when the loss function is minimized.

Over Fitting

One of the popular facts in data science is Overfitting that happens when a statistical algorithm fits appropriately to its corresponding training data. While performing this procedure, the model woefully cannot work accurately over the unknown data, making the purpose to fail. Generalization of an algorithm to new data is eventually what permits the system to make use of ML models in each day process in order to make predictions and to do classification of data.

Loss Function

Loss function is used to calculate the difference between the present outcome of the model and the anticipated outcome. In this method, the evaluation of model is done based on the provided data. The loss function is divided into two groups. The first one is classification which has discrete values like 0, 1, 2... and another is regression which has continuous values.

RESULT AND DISCUSSION

Android is one of the familiar operating systems among smartphone device users. Due to its flexibility and adaptability features most organizations are using this OS for their developing applications. Once the devices are affected by the malware it destroys the information available on the devices and it also tries to hack, alter steal, or encrypts the sensitive information. Recently DL models are also applied for predicting activities that occur in smart devices executed based on Android OS. In this research work XGBoost, RF, CNN, and ECNN models are used to predict the malware activities. The performances of the models are assessed based on their accuracy, precision, and recall. We have used the malware dataset which is been downloaded from the UCI repository. This dataset consists of 7846 Rows and 15 Columns and total we have 15 attributes.

The accuracy rate is a kind of metric that can describe the model performance across the entire class. Generally, precision is measured as the proportion among the total number of *Positive* type data exactly classified to the whole number of data classified as *Positive*. Recall metric is measured as the ratio among the correctly classified positive data to the entire positive data. Following equations are used to measure the accuracy, precision, and recall.

$$Accuracy = \frac{True\ Positive + True\ Negative}{True\ Positive + True\ Negative + False\ Positive + False\ Negative} \tag{7}$$

$$Precision = \frac{True\ Positive}{True\ Positive + False\ Positive} \tag{8}$$

$$Recall = \frac{True\ Positive}{True\ Positive + False\ Negative} \tag{9}$$

Accuracy Analysis

Now we are going to apply our proposed Enhanced CNN algorithm along with existing algorithms such as XGBoost, RF and CNN over Intrusion Dataset. The following Table 1 and Figure 4 represents Accuracy Analysis of proposed Enhanced CNN compared over XGBoost, RF and CNN. From the results its proved that proposed Enhanced CNN produces Accuracy of about 95.8% which is higher than X Gradient Boost Accuracy which is 84.8%, RF Accuracy which is 91% and CNN Accuracy which is 92.6% respectively.

Table 1. Accuracy of XGBoost, RF, CNN, and Enhanced CNN classifiers

Classifiers	Accuracy %
X Gradient Boost	84.8
Random Forest	91.0
Convolution Neural Network	92.6
Enhanced Convolution Neural Network	95.8

Figure 4 demonstrates the comparative chart of the accuracy rate of XGBoost, RF, CNN, and Enhanced CNN classifiers.

Figure 4. Comparison of Accuracy of XGBoost, RF, CNN, and Enhanced CNN classifiers

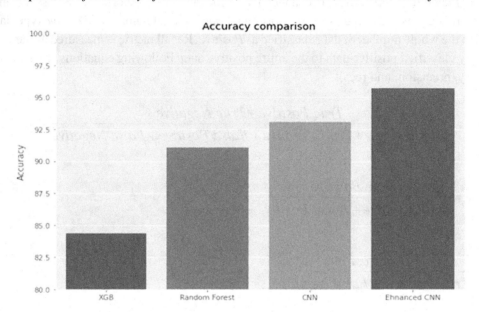

Precision and Recall Analysis

Now we are going to apply our proposed Enhanced CNN algorithm along with existing algorithms such as XGBoost, RF and CNN over Intrusion Dataset. The following Table 2 and Figure 5 represents Precision and Recall Analysis of proposed Enhanced CNN compared over XGBoost, RF and CNN. From the results its proved that proposed Enhanced CNN produces Precision of about 0.96 which is higher than XGB Precision which is 0.84, RF Precision which is 0.90 and CNN Precision which is 0.96 respectively. Proposed Enhanced CNN produces Recall of about 0.92 which is higher than XGB Recall which is 0.82, RF Recall which is 0.90 and CNN Recall which is 0.91 respectively.

Table 2. Precision and Recall value of XGBoost, RF, CNN, and Enhanced CNN classifiers

Classifiers	Precision	Recall
X Gradient Boost	0.84	0.82
Random Forest	0.90	0.90
Convolution Neural Network	0.94	0.91
Enhanced Convolution Neural network	0.96	0.92

Figure 5 demonstrates the comparison chart of precision and recall value of XGBoost, RF, CNN, and Enhanced CNN classifiers.

Among the above-mentioned four classifiers, Enhanced CNN produces a better result in terms of various metrics like accuracy, recall, and precision.

Figure 5. Comparison of Precision and Recall value of XGBoost, RF, CNN, and Enhanced CNN classifiers

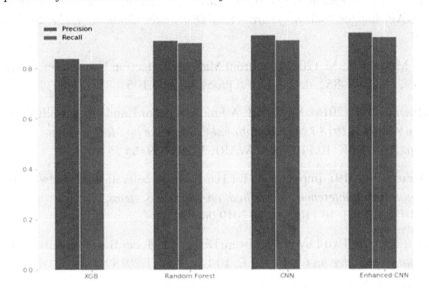

CONCLUSION

User friendly is one of the major benefits of the Android OS. Because of its s flexibility feature, much malware software also affects smart devices. The malware software tries to destroy, alter, or steal private information. So, malware detection is one of the major research areas in the computing domain. This research work uses XGBoost, RF, CNN, and Enhanced CNN for predicting malware from the UCI malware data set. The proposed work is developed and tested using Python software. It is one of the easiest tools for analyzing and predicting values from an online dataset. Enhanced CNN model predicts the malware in 98.5% accuracy rate. This suggested system is useful for Android system users.

REFERENCES

Almahmouda, M., Alzu'bib, D., & Yaseen, Q. (2021). "ReDroidDet: Android Malware Detection Based on Recurrent Neural Network", Science Direct, *The 2nd International Workshop on Data-Driven Security (DDSW 2021)*, Warsaw, Poland. *Procedia Computer Science*, *184*, 841–846. doi:10.1016/j.procs.2021.03.105

Chen, Y., Jin, B., Yu, D., & Chen, J. (2018). Malware Variants Detection Using Behavior Destructive Features. *2018 IEEE Symposium on Privacy-Aware Computing (PAC)*, (pp. 121-122). IEEE. 10.1109/PAC.2018.00020

Choudhary, S., & Sharma, A. (2020). Malware Detection & Classification using Machine Learning. *2020 International Conference on Emerging Trends in Communication, Control and Computing (ICONC3)*, (pp. 1-4). IEEE. 10.1109/ICONC345789.2020.9117547

D'Angelo, G., Ficco, M., & Palmieri, F. (2020). Malware detection in mobile environments based on Autoencoders and API-images. *Journal of Parallel and Distributed Computing, 137*, 26–33. doi:10.1016/j.jpdc.2019.11.001

Elayan, O. N., & Mustafa, A. M. (2021). Android Malware Detection Using Deep Learning. *Procedia Computer Science, 184*, 847–852. doi:10.1016/j.procs.2021.03.106

Iqbal, S., & Zulkernine, M. (2018). SpyDroid: A Framework for Employing Multiple Real-Time Malware Detectors on Android. *2018 13th International Conference on Malicious and Unwanted Software (MALWARE)*, (pp. 1-8). IEEE. 10.1109/MALWARE.2018.8659365

Lee, B. K., & Pattee, J. (2019). Implications for Hardware Acceleration of Malware Detection. *2019 IEEE 30th International Conference on Application-specific Systems, Architectures, and Processors (ASAP)*, (pp. 138-138). IEEE. 10.1109/ASAP.2019.00-14

Lu, T., & Hou, S. (2018). A Two-Layered Malware Detection Model Based on Permission for Android. *IEEE International Conference on Comp.* IEEE. 10.1109/CCET.2018.8542215

Moghaddam, S. H., & Abbaspour, M. (2014). Sensitivity analysis of static features for Android malware detection. *2014 22nd Iranian Conference on Electrical Engineering (ICEE)*, (pp. 920-924). IEEE. 10.1109/IranianCEE.2014.6999667

Çarkacı, N. & Sogukpına, I. (2016). Frequency-based metamorphic malware detection. *IEEE 2016 24th Signal Processing and Communication Application Conference (SIU)*. IEEE. doi:10.1109/SIU.2016.7495767

Pattee, J., & Lee, B. K. (2020). Design Alternatives for Performance Monitoring Counter based Malware Detection. *2020 IEEE 39th International Performance Computing and Communications Conference (IPCCC)*, (pp. 1-2). IEEE. 10.1109/IPCCC50635.2020.9391559

Pektaş, A., & Acarman, T. (2020). Learning to detect Android malware via opcode sequences. *Neurocomputing, 396*, 599–608. doi:10.1016/j.neucom.2018.09.102

Sai, M. P. D., Sayadi, H., Makrani, H. M., & Nowzari, C. (2019). "Lightweight Node-level Malware Detection and Network-level Malware Confinement in IoT Networks",*2019 Design* [DATE]. *Automation & Test in Europe Conference & Exhibition, 2019*, 776–781. doi:10.23919/DATE.2019.8715057

Taheri, R., Ghahramani, M., Javidan, R., Shojafar, M., Pooranian, Z., & Conti, M. (2020). Similarity-based Android malware detection using Hamming distance of static binary features. *Future Generation Computer Systems, 105*, 230–247. doi:10.1016/j.future.2019.11.034

Xin, Y., Kong, L., Liu, Z., Chen, Y., Li, Y., Zhu, H., Gao, M., Hou, H., & Wang, C. (2018). Machine learning and deep learning methods for cybersecurity. *IEEE Access : Practical Innovations, Open Solutions, 6*, 35365–35381. doi:10.1109/ACCESS.2018.2836950

Chapter 16
A Quantitative Approach of Purposive Sampling Techniques for Security and Privacy Issues in IoT Healthcare Applications

S. Satheesh Kumar
https://orcid.org/0000-0002-2635-4777
REVA University, India

V. Muthukumaran
College of Engineering and Technology, SRM Institute of Science and Technology, India

A. Devi
REVA University, India

V. Geetha
REVA University, India

Poonam Nilesh Yadav
https://orcid.org/0000-0001-9557-7459
REVA University, India

ABSTRACT

The internet of things (IoT) offers several benefits to the healthcare industry, including the ability to actively monitor patients and use data for analytics. For medical device integration, the focus has moved to the consumer end of the IoT, that captures data on patient vital signs. Unfortunately, when healthcare centers link these devices to the internet, they typically overlook security concerns. Short-term monitoring and emergency alerting of healthcare signals are becoming increasingly accessible thanks to the Internet of Things (IoT). Data secrecy is critical hence, encryption is required out of real concern. In this book chapter, we explore the privacy and security issues of Internet of Things (IoT) healthcare applications for special needs users. IoT enables health-related enterprises to lift necessary data from diverse sources in real-time and this helps in accurate decision-making to reducing data vulnerability and therefore creating opportunities for secure patient data, particularly for special needs patients.

DOI: 10.4018/978-1-6684-6971-2.ch016

Copyright © 2023, IGI Global. Copying or distributing in print or electronic forms without written permission of IGI Global is prohibited.

INTRODUCTION

The internet of things (IoT) is now widely used in various applications, and as a result, its significance in daily life is growing. For the purpose of effectively supplying patients with emergency services, IoT technology is also being developed in the healthcare monitoring (Ali, Z., et al.2018). Additionally, it is utilized as an E-health application for a variety of purposes, including the early identification of medical problems, emergency alerting, and computer-assisted rehabilitation. In order to track the subject's health, sensors are connected to smart phones, which have become an essential part of peoples' daily lives (Moses, J. C., et al. 2021) This sensing-based surveillance system collects various data from the wards and diagnostic tools and uses them to control healthcare effectively and automatically. The IoT healthcare system offers effective monitoring and tracking, which enhances the management of human resources. Healthcare data is handled through cloud computing, which offers resource-sharing features such flexibility, data service integration with scalable data storage, parallel processing, and early detection of security issues (Kumar, S. S., and Sanjay, M. 2018)). The IoT-based healthcare system uses wearables or sensors implanted in patients, both of which have relatively low battery life. The user experience is impacted by the regular charging of these gadgets and mobile devices, which can exhaust patients and involve the nurse (Amru, M., et al. 2020). Additionally, the cloud data center uses a lot of electricity, which raises the price of cloud computing. However, a health monitoring system truly needs low latency and energy-consuming cloud services. Security concerns in healthcare monitoring are another problem. The term "Internet of Things" (IoT) refers to a concept that connects everyone, everything, everywhere, at any time, with any service, over any network. The Internet of Things (IoT) is a megatrend in next-generation technologies that has the potential to have a significant impact on all business sectors. It can be conceptualized as the interconnection of individually identifiable smart objects and devices with extended benefits within the current internet infrastructure. Benefits frequently include these products' sophisticated connection, which goes beyond machine-to-machine (M2M) applications (Alsaadi, E. and Tubaishat, A. 2015).

Consequently, introducing in almost every industry, automation is a real possibility. Smart cities, traffic congestion, waste management, structural health, security, emergency services, logistics, retail, industrial control, and health care are just a few of the applications for which the IoT offers suitable solutions. One of the most alluring IoT application areas is the medical and health care sector. Numerous medical applications, including those for chronic diseases, exercise programs, and remote health monitoring, could emerge as a result of the Internet of Things. Senior care, too. Another significant potential use is ensuring that patients follow their healthcare providers' instructions regarding treatment and medication. As a result, several medical tools, sensors, and imaging and diagnostic tools can be seen. as intelligent objects or gadgets that form a crucial component of the IoT. Healthcare services powered by the internet of things are anticipated to lower costs, improve quality of life, and improve user experience. The Internet of Things has, in the eyes of healthcare professionals, the potential for remote provisioning to decrease device downtime (Muthukumaran, V., et al 2021). Internet of Things gadget uses sensors and actuators; the technology merges with cyber-physical systems shown in figure 1. These technologies include smart grids and smart homes, where lighting, heating, and cooling are controlled and automated using a smart thermostat like the Nest Thermostat. Appliances like refrigerators, stoves, washers, and dryers can use Wi-Fi for remote monitoring.

Figure 1. IoT healthcare trends

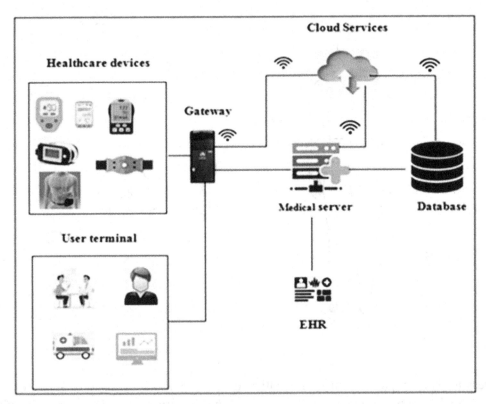

Health care providers may transform the way they diagnose illnesses and deliver novel treatment options by using Internet of Things (IoT) enabled technologies such as Wi-Fi and Bluetooth-LE. During a medical emergency, real-time monitoring using smart sensors has the potential to save many lives. Wireless Body Sensor Networks (WBSN) are commonly used to monitor psychological characteristics such as temperature, heart rate, electrocardiogram (ECG), brain activity, and other essential symptoms of a person (Gravina, R., et al. 2017). Smart Sensors are incorporated in a smart watch, which continually monitors the patient's vital signs and sends data in real time to a smart phone.

There are vehicles available that have sensors integrated in, as well as field operating tools, that can help firemen with search and rescue missions. The "Things," in the healthcare industry. The term "Internet of Things" can refer to a wide range of devices, including infusion pumps used in hospitals to administer a patient's prescribed number of fluids and cardiac monitoring implants. There are countless additional gadgets, including cochlear implants, insulin pumps, and pacemaker implants. While some of these gadgets, like pacemakers, can only transfer data wirelessly, others can send and receive data, there are also wearable's that can monitor important data, such as your daily activity data, including the number of steps you take, like the Apple watch or the Fitbit (Nagarajan, S. M., at al. 2022). Figure 2 shows the illustration of wireless body sensor network. Additionally, the IoT can accurately determine the best intervals for restocking supplies for specific devices. for their consistent and slick operation. The IoT also makes it possible to schedule scarce resources effectively by ensuring that they are used to serve more patients. Easy of an important trend is cost-effective exchanges between individuals, clinics, and healthcare organizations through smooth and secure communication.

Figure 2. Wireless body sensor network

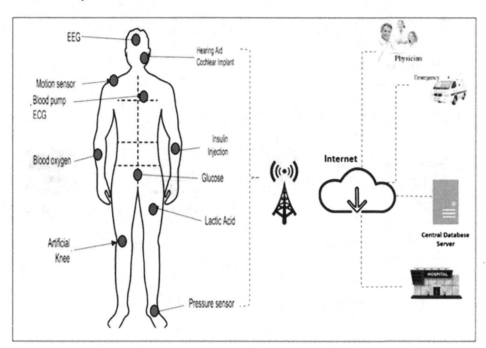

Wireless technology-powered modern healthcare networks are anticipated to support for chronic illnesses, early detection, continuous observation, and medical crises. In order to create health records and provide on-demand healthcare services to authorized stakeholders, gateways, medical servers, and health databases are essential tools. Researchers have been paying close attention to this area in recent years as they attempt to address the potential of the IoT in the healthcare industry by taking into account a variety of practical issues. As a result, there are currently many apps, services, and prototypes available (Kumar, S. S. and Koti, M. S. 2021). Network architectures and platforms, new services and applications, interoperability, and security are just a few of the research trends in IoT-based health care. In addition, several nations and organizations throughout the world have set laws and guidelines for the use of IoT technology in the medical industry. However, the IoT is still in its early stages in the healthcare industry.

- Categorizing current IoT-based healthcare networks studies into three trends, summarizing each one.
- Conducting a thorough analysis of IoT-based healthcare applications and services.
- Showcasing several commercial initiatives to adopt
- healthcare prototypes and products that are IoT compatible.
- Offering in-depth analyses of the security and privacy concerns related to IoT healthcare solutions and putting forth a security model.
- Talking about key technologies that can influence IoT-based healthcare technologies.

IoT HEALTHCARE NETWORKS

Cloud-based A framework for ensuring distributed-location based services to recurrently collect and broadcast has been made available by IoT. IoT has been extensively used in a variety of applications, including the medical healthcare system, as was previously mentioned. In contrast, CC provides a range of configurable, on-demand computing resources, including everything from mobile devices to super-computers, as a service. Healthcare actors must have a thorough awareness of the specific advantages and hazards in relation to the goal and scope of medical practice and healthcare delivery before deciding whether to utilize CC (Boufford, J. I., et al. 2002) enhancing case results while enhancing patient safety, as well as the affordability, efficacy, and efficiency of care and treatment the many types of service delivery, including infrastructure as a service, platform as a service, and software as a service, must also be taken into account. Different obligations and requirements are included in each model.

The private, public, and hybrid cloud deployment methods have an impact on strategic considerations. So, they must be carefully taken into account. Real-time connected objects and the Internet of Things (IoT) are two emerging internet-based technologies. It is well-liked across a wide range of businesses as a result of the convergence from the simple object to the smart object. This is a lengthy long-term effect on patient physiological data administration, health monitoring, and clinical services. Sensors are connected to the patients, and after the data has been linked to the control devices, it is sent to the health-monitoring unit. Data are occasionally kept in the cloud, which aids in managing the volume of data while maintaining security. Security is a crucial component of the Internet of Things since it might be difficult to encrypt data during its transfer from a sensor to a cloud computing facility while simultaneously posing a risk to its integrity and confidentiality. A critical issue in healthcare applications is how to build new effective solutions for next-generation mobile technologies with IoT-cloud convergence. Cloud-based IoT can be divided into static and mobile categories based on capabilities.

By gathering and disseminating passing service healthcare data, cloud-based IoT has created a platform to ensure distributed location-based services. in Figure. 3 (VANET - Vehicular ad hoc network). There are three layers in it: the application layer, the network layer, and the sensor layer. Since users of mobile IoT devices tend to move in similar directions and at similar speeds at particular times and locations, they are typically divided into social groups ((Roopashree, S., et al. 2022). One potential network paradigm for mobile cloud-based IoT is depicted in Fig.3. Resource limitations, mobility, self-organization, and short-range communication are its defining characteristics. Only when there is space for storing, packets are forwarded using the store-carry-and-forward technique. IoT nodes cannot handle computationally heavy tasks and must outsource both the storage and computing resources to the cloud. It is for this reason that resource-constrained properties necessitate efficient protocol design, particularly on the node of IoT users. It should be mentioned that moving Internet of Things (IoT) users are divided into several social groups based on their directions, velocities, and accelerations. One of the key components of the IoT in healthcare is the IoT healthcare network, also known as the IoT network for healthcare (Kruk, M. E., et al. 2018) It enables access to the IoT infrastructure, makes it easier to send and receive medical data, and this permits the use of healthcare-specific messaging.

Figure 3. Network architecture of Cloud Based IoT

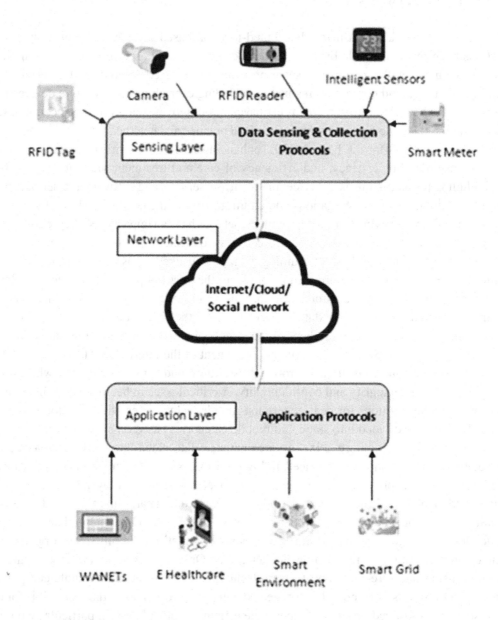

THE ROLE OF IOT IN HEALTHCARE

The Internet of Things (IoT) has consistently brought huge technical developments into our daily lives, consequently simplifying and making our lives more pleasant through its numerous uses. IoT has significant benefits in the realm of healthcare by lowering service costs and providing care to patients who require critical care or remote support. This opens up several potentials to improve healthcare quality while lowering healthcare costs. Due to a lack of medical services assets and growing clinical expenditures, IoT-based innovations must be adapted to solve the challenges in medical services. The Internet of Things enables remarkable breakthroughs in the realm of healthcare.

The act of performing preventative or essential procedures to enhance a person's wellbeing is referred to as healthcare. This can be accomplished through surgery, the use of medication, or other lifestyle changes. Usually, hospitals and doctors who make up a health care system provide these services.

IoT is crucial to the healthcare industry in a number of ways.

- Elder care, which entails keeping tabs on senior residents and hospital patients
- Real-time location is used to track people and assets at a cheaper cost.
- Data gathering, the most developed field in healthcare, involves several pieces of technology we see at the bedside in hospitals, such as the EKG monitor.

Both patients and healthcare professionals will gain from the growing use of IoT in the healthcare industry. Remote communication and monitoring, two areas where IoT can play a significant role, can improve the treatments that patients get. Mobile medical applications or wearable technology that enables patients to record their health data are another application of IoT in healthcare. The data revolution, which gives us the ability to live healthier lifestyles through linked gadgets like tablets, wearables, and handheld smart phones, is largely to blame for this. The decision-making abilities will be improved by the analysis of the data gathered through electronic medical records, diagnostic data gathered through imaging equipment, and hand-held personal gadgets. Patients will be able to manage their own health more actively as a result of this. This individualized, data-rich analysis of our health will eventually become the norm. Patients will receive individualized treatment plans to combat disease. We will learn how to improve our welfare from the data produced, and we will be inspired to take charge of our lives (Ahmad, M. O and Siddiqui, S. T. 2022).

A whole new market has emerged around clinical decision support software, an expanding IoT-related industry that strengthens the function of connected devices by more closely connecting their use to clinical judgments. The Food and Drug Administration (FDA) has already put in a significant amount of effort to create universal device identifiers for IoT applications that use medical equipment. Data should be able to be closely traced as it moves between connected devices or between connected devices and networks thanks to tagging of the metadata created by connected devices. Doctors don't need to question the data. They will be able to trust this information and be certain that their patient actually provided it. One of the industries that has embraced the Internet of Things the fastest is healthcare. For patients with chronic diseases, the elderly, and those who need ongoing care, integrating IoT capabilities into medical devices increases the quality and effectiveness of the services provided. For many years, hospitals have been implementing the Internet of Things. Inpatient rooms, electronic medical records, and other cloud-based services frequently contain IoT devices (Maktoubian, J. and Ansari, K. 2019). Networking new devices is a continuous effort at the majority of healthcare institutions. The interoperability of devices, which can expose a network to new security flaws and increased risk, represents the biggest problem. The BYOD (Bring Your Own Device) devices could be a problem since, without sufficient supervision, they could readily join a network and become a huge target for attack. Organizations must monitor the use of these devices, keep track of when they access or extract data, and manage the quality of the operating systems and programming that run on them. Healthcare systems are becoming more vulnerable as they are interconnected, especially when various wireless medical devices start linking to web-enabled IT systems. Malicious hackers are only one hazard to this weakness; other dangers include malware and computer viruses.

MEDICAL DEVICE INTEGRATION

Hospitals in our nation currently manage patient registration, care, and billing, among many other functions, using the HIS system, which has essentially been developed. Patients must frequently use medical equipment while receiving therapy in order to collect various inspection data. Currently, medical device output data are frequently manually entered into information systems, which make it simple for errors to occur or for patients and inspection reports to not match (Frehill, P., et al. 2007). The information produced by the devices is still delivered in the form of paper reports for some small hospitals where information creation is still comparatively weak. Doctors and patients are limited to looking at paper files when they need access to the information at a specific time again. Due to the exceptional variety of medical devices and the lack of obligatory unified global standards, data integration between medical devices has long been a challenging issue for the medical information system. Manufacturers employ particular protocols, among other things, to safeguard their own interests, leaving medical decisions as the "lonely island" of hospital information systems. Additionally, a disorganized application of the data will prevent a fair distribution of medical resources. On the assumption that there is reliable medical device integration (MDI) technology, medical information systems will inevitably grow towards mobile applications, intelligent analysis, and interconnection and interworking as IT building in hospitals progresses (Qin, Z., et al. 2015).

In order to accomplish intelligent identification and administration, the Internet of Things (IoT) technology refers to connecting all items by applying information sensing devices to the Internet for information exchange, which includes exchanging of physical objects. The Internet of Things (IoT) technology is used in this study to manage and identify medical devices. The cloud computing model is described by the U.S. National Institute of Standards and Technology (NIST) as a means of enabling universal, practical, on-demand network access to a pool of configurable computing resources (such as networks, servers, storage, applications, and services) that can be swiftly provisioned and released with little management work or service provider involvement. An efficient way to adapt software technology to the open Internet environment and consumers' evolving needs is through its dynamic evolution (Woskowski, C. 2014). Additionally, it serves as the foundational technology for adaptive software, grid computing, autonomous software, and network configuration software.

The integration of each group of medical devices while using this strategy creates a new need. Devices come from many manufacturers, and they have various output types, data standards, and data formats. Demand is continually changing for the model, which is a typical scenario for demand evolution. This model may dynamically evolve because to its hierarchical design. It is acceptable to simply add the device in the background, finish device adaptation thoroughly, and set the criteria for data filtering when there is adaptive demand for new devices (Karthick Raghunath, K. M., et al. 2022). The data filtering layer may filter the data in accordance with the defined rules at runtime, so there is no need to alter the system implementation codes. The cloud computing infrastructure, server, database, and storage used in this architecture are all supplied by cloud service providers. To economize on bandwidth and computer resources as well as significantly lowering system maintenance costs, the cloud services handle the model's data filtering chores, leaving the end MCU just responsible for sending the basic data to the cloud. Data provided by the system are accessible as long as it is in the connectivity state. The back-end expansions of the model are also made more convenient by a single data storage format. The system data is accessible from any device, including a computer terminal, a mobile app terminal, or a public WeChat account. The visit barrier is broken when the data are pushed to the users' closest terminal. Data can be easily sent between hospitals and clinicians, and patient data can be maintained indefinitely. Remote mobile medical care can be achieved by incorporating some video technology.

PRIVACY AND SECURITY ISSUES IN IOT HEALTHCARE

Special needs patients' sensed data is frequently wirelessly relayed to the appropriate careers (members of the family, nurses, or, doctors). The transmitted data could be followed even as it was travelling across the wireless channel (Das, S. and Namasudra, S. 2022). Unfortunately, the adversary may be able to intercept the wireless channel's data transmissions. Therefore, a work in presented a secure IoT transmission system based on PKI/CA and IBE to stop these attackers. To address the security concerns of data transmission within the wireless network, authors in suggested a chaotic synchronization framework. A public key infrastructure (PKI) is a technology or system that provides complete security services for diverse network applications. It employs public key encryption as well as digital signature services. offer consumers with a set of fundamental security platform technologies and requirements. With the PKI framework, users may create a secure network environment. The basic goal of PKI is to address the trust issue in the communications system space and to identify the uniqueness, authenticity, and validity of diverse participants in the informational cyberspace. To safeguard many subjects' security interests in cyberspace. PKI, as a technological system, may be used to enable authentication, integrity, secrecy, and non-repudiation. It is capable of resolving the security issues of identity verification, information integrity, and non-repudiation as well as providing trustworthy security for network applications.

The Public Key Infrastructure (PKI) is a set of CA identification, digital certificate, digital signature, and security related application modules. In reality, to achieve a thorough data recovery of any given encrypted signal, the suggested framework consists of two chaotic systems that are kept in sync. In order to improve the security of the Object Naming Service (ONS) querying procedure inside the tag, he also suggested a DNS protocol. This concept aided in the resolution of concerns regarding the security of plaintext data transmission difficulties. The authors in have presented end-to-end security procedures in addition to recommending peer-to-peer (P2P) systems to further strengthen the security of the transferred data. Additionally, it offers strong security for more effective data transmission at a lower cost. For gaining access to data stored in the cloud, authors in suggest using encryption and decryption methods (Bethencourt, J., et al. 2007). The security method in this case makes use of a Ciphertext-Policy-Attribute-Based Encryption (CPABE), which is based on Elliptic Curve Cryptography (ECC), Attribute-Based Encryption (ABE), and Bilinear Maps. Healthcare providers are necessary for the encryption of PHRs, but decrypting PHRs calls for a specific set of criteria in order to ensure proper access. Role-Based Access Control (RBAC) cryptographic ways have therefore been created thus far in order to incorporate the cryptographic nature of access control and approaches to safeguard and secure the protected data in the Cloud. In this way, RBAC makes it possible for data owners to share and administer unique data in the Cloud (Said, O. 2013). Most Internet of Things (IoT) devices are typically wirelessly connected and small. Therefore, it is crucial to provide safe storage tools within the context of the Internet of Things and to ensure that the stored data within IoT devices is protected to the fullest extent possible (IoT). This is due to the fact that expected patient information is communicated, as opposed to traditional systems, which have a higher chance of experiencing external attacks and, as a result, of allowing unauthorized access to important information in transit. The human, the technology ecosystem, the process, and the intelligent object are the four components that make up the system, according to these researchers. These elements communicate with one another via security considerations like identity, trust, privacy, accountability, and auto-immunity.

Edge technology layers can also be thought of as sublayers, and each layer has its own set of security requirements. Image, multimedia, and digital or text are examples of these sub-layers, according to Said (Lazarescu, M. T. 2013). Traditionally, the process of incorporating WSNs into an IoT system offers little energy for computational resources for intelligent applications. Because of this, they are more powerful and connected by lossy networks, making them more susceptible to attack from an enemy. In reality, an attacker can introduce a few malicious nodes that can work together to harm a specific network. For instance, a physical attack on a node can gain access to crucial information like the source code and other key data. The method for securing the link between the Internet host and Sensor node is a different problem. Since WSNs are now employed in a number of sensitive IoT for healthcare applications, if their security is hacked, it could result in both resource loss and human injury (Madakam, S., et al. 2015). As a result, there are many security criteria for WSNs that must be taken into account.

An increasing number of items, including sensor nodes, people, laptops, and many other crucial parts, are used in IoT applications to ensure the efficient use of resources. However, there are a number of identification techniques that are suggested for the IoT framework, such as IPv6, RFID item identifier, IPv4, and Near Field Communication Forum. By maintaining the items' identities and identifying them in a more distinctive fashion, this identification often contributes to the high scalability elements of the Internet of Things while also taking security awareness into account (Kumar, S. S. and Koti, M. S. 2022). propose a scalable physical object naming system (PONS) that may leverage both the URL-based semantic identities for signs and the current ontologies. The semantics are frequently constructed during the process and then assigned to the IoT objects by the PONS. The likelihood of security and privacy issues, such as those involving patient data, is subsequently reduced by these. As part of the verification process, the individual identity of the person claiming to be the information's source had to be corroborated. This is the precise information that was provided. In this context, authentication refers to identification verification. Prior to the creation of a communication channel between any two particular identities, it is crucial.

This frequently validates an already-existing mutual trust between different items and the users. This is accomplished by the authentication of their identities. The authors of suggest authentication and access methods for IoT applications. Typically, authentication is achieved by primarily defining the straightforward, effective key establishment based on the ECC. In addition, Role-based Access Control (RBAC) (Karunarathne, S. et al. 2021) which is based on authorization approach, is used to establish access control. In addition to the authentication based on the node's signal qualities that was proposed by the authors in a cluster-based authentication methodology was also put out by them in.

The nature of HIoT issues is related with many and networked devices. They are concerned with power sources and scalability, interoperability, dependability and security, biocompatibility, vulnerability, and the healthcare regulatory environment. integration, privacy, and security (Bandara, R., et al.2020).

METHODOLOGY

Through the use of Amazon Mechanical Turk (MTurk), we implemented a quantitative research methodology. The study was directed at medical staff members in various healthcare facilities who primarily care for people with special needs. A total of 88 respondents were obtained for the study by using a purposive sampling of four (4) medical professionals from each chosen facility. Multiple insights about IoT best practices were gleaned from the purposive sampling approach. To address the research questions, survey questionnaires were set out on Amazon MTurk. Every participant received an email encouraging them to take part in the study. The participants' quantitative survey data was cleaned, coded, transformed, and then analyzed using Minitab 19. The analyzed data was presented as percentages in charts to show the results. Methods of analysis in this sort of approach must also be tailored to the unique form of data provided as well as the study objectives. Social network analysis and categorization analysis, often known as cluster analysis, are two common types of ascending data analysis.

Comparative Analysis

To achieve our research objectives, we employ an exploratory qualitative approach. Exploratory research, in general, aims to comprehend the essence of an issue that has not been properly addressed, and so seeks to examine it at varied degrees of detail, identify clear avenues for additional research, and lead a topic of study in a new direction. "Exploratory research attempts to find out how individuals get along in the context in question, what meanings they attach to their activities, and what issues worry them" - the purpose is to comprehend, "what is going on here" Author discussed in (Campbell, S., et al.2020).

Probability sampling strategies are typically used in quantitative research, and may also be used in \ sthe quantitative phase of mixed methods research or what is referred to as triangulation. These \ssamples are useful when researchers want to generalize their findings to a larger population. The \sresults of studies that rely on probability sampling are typically statistical in nature. The following \ssubsections describe the main types of probability sampling strategies. Probability sampling provides assurance that the results are reliable and unbiased, as well as an indication of how precise the data is likely to be. Data from a properly drawn sample is preferable to data obtained from those who simply appear or show up at a meeting or even know the language.

Types of Sampling Methods

Disproportionate Stratified Sampling

This strategy is commonly used by social science researchers when they do not choose a sample representative of the full community to study. The aim is that persons representing specific subgroups will not have the same chances of getting included in the study sample. For example, the researcher requires 500 postgraduate students. The researcher does not require the male/female ratio in this procedure. Just s(he) requires 500 responses.

Cluster Sampling

When, how, and why should we use cluster sampling? It is a two-step process in which the entire population is organized into groups or clusters, usually villages, schools, wards, blocks, and other comparable sites. This sort of occurrence is more common in epidemiologic research than in clinical investigations. It is especially useful for surveys that cover a vast geographical area. A pool of respondents is used to choose clusters at random. The sample population includes each and every responder in the cluster. Larger sample sizes are usually necessary.

Multi-Stage Sampling Technique

When, how, and why not use multi-stage sampling techniques? Multi-stage sampling is sometimes known as multi-stage cluster sampling. It is a complicated type of cluster sampling that combines two or more sample selection phases into a single operation. In another sense, it is the act of breaking big populations into smaller clusters in order to make primary data collecting more successful and efficient. This strategy is typically used by researchers to circumvent the issues associated with random sampling from a big group of people.

Purposive Sampling Method

A variety of non-probability sampling strategies are included under the heading of "purposeful sampling." Purposive sampling, also known as judgmental, selective, or subjective sampling, depends on the researcher's judgement when choosing the units (such as persons, cases/organizations, events, or pieces of data) that are to be researched. When compared to probability sampling approaches, the sample under investigation is typically fairly small and method has been presented in Fig.4.

Figure 4. Illustration of Purposive sampling method

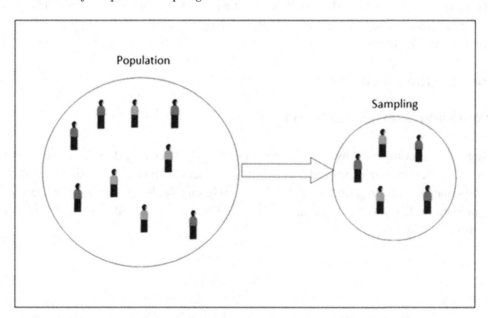

It is a type of non-probability sampling in which the researcher makes decisions about who should be included in the sample based on a range of factors, such as the person's competence and willingness to engage in the research or their expert understanding of the research problem. Purposive sampling's major objective is to concentrate on specific demographic features that are of interest since they will help you better address your research concerns. The population being investigated is not represented in the sample, however for researchers pursuing qualitative or mixed methods research designs, this is not seen as a limitation. Rather, it is a decision, the goal of which differs based on the kind of sampling procedure utilized for purpose. In homogeneous sampling, for instance, units are chosen based on their shared qualities because the researcher is particularly interested in these traits. Comparatively, exploratory qualitative research usually uses critical case sampling to determine whether the hypothesized phenomenon even occurs and the flow diagram of mixed method research shown in Fig.5.

Figure 5. Flow Diagram mixed method research

```
┌──────────────────────────┐        ┌──────────────────────────┐
│ Quantitative Data         │        │ Qualitative Data         │
│ Collection                │        │ Collection               │
└──────────────────────────┘        └──────────────────────────┘
             │                                    │
             ▼                                    ▼
┌──────────────────────────┐        ┌──────────────────────────┐
│ Analysis of quantitative  │        │ Analysis of Qualitative  │
│ Data                      │        │ Data                     │
└──────────────────────────┘        └──────────────────────────┘
                      │                    │
                      ▼                    ▼
              ┌──────────────────────────────────┐
              │          Interpretation          │
              └──────────────────────────────────┘
```

Steps Involved in Sampling Method

The following steps are involved in sampling method to explore the security and privacy issues of Internet of Things (IoT) healthcare applications illustrated in Fig.6.

Figure 6. Steps for Flow of Methodologies in sampling technique

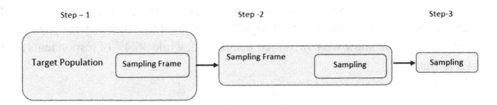

293

Advantages of Purposive Sampling

Many qualitative research approaches have been developed to assist: Purposive sampling can be used in a number of qualitative research. These designs frequently demand a one-of-a-kind sampling method and approach to acquire the necessary data to make a conclusion. The different approaches of the purposive sampling strategy make study planning more adaptable, allowing for the use of varied tactics as needed to get the desired result.

RESULT ANALYSIS

Eighty-eight (85) healthcare professionals make up the sample size for our research study, which examines security and privacy issues in IoT healthcare applications for users with special needs. Owing to the professionalism, we received a 100% response rate. Our research paper examines security and privacy challenges in IoT healthcare applications for users with special requirements, using a sample size of 85 medical professionals. We were able to receive a 100% response rate because to the researchers' professionalism in conducting the study. We examine the many IoT applications for patients with unique requirements, classifying them according to their identities. According to the study's findings, 40% of medical professionals agreed that they use IoT monitoring devices with the ability to detect falls or problems with vital signs for a special needs person living alone (whether they are in a homestead or not) in order to prevent the development of new illnesses or disabilities. According to the poll, 35.2% strongly agreed, 38.4 agreed, 14.4 were neutral, and 10.2% were not sure. According to the study's findings, 31.7% highly agreed, 32.8% agreed, 11.2% were neutral, 19.5% disagreed, and 18.5% strongly disagreed with the statement that the primary privacy and security concern is maintaining the confidentiality of the patients' PHRs. Fig.7. The study also revealed that 30.7% strongly opposed, 31.8 neutrally agreed, 10.2% strongly agreed, and 19.5% strongly disagreed that cyber-attacks inject misleading data into the system, seriously harming Internet of Things applications, and jeopardizing the security of individuals with special needs. The survey also showed that 18.3% of respondents disagreed with the study's findings, while 36.2% agreed that using public can increase data confidentiality. With 46.7% of respondents agreeing with the study's findings, it was clear from the study that people with special needs who reside in nursing homes, long-term care facilities, or hospital rooms benefit from the IoT healthcare monitoring application's ongoing monitoring of their health and vital signs. According to the study, 30.2% of respondents believed that the IoT's evolving model and its application to healthcare for people with special needs promised significantly better patient-friendly and highly individualized care as shown in Fig.8.

By enabling high levels of confidence for information exchange in a risky environment, key encryption (KPI) develops an efficient method for data encryption. The study's findings also showed that 46.7% agreed, compared to 11.2% who disagreed, that there is a higher possibility of attacks materializing and that unauthorized people may access the data being transmitted by an IoT application. The investigation into the privacy and security needs for IoT applications was the study's main objective. The results showed that 15.4% of respondents disagreed with the notion that they frequently encourage persons with special needs to know who owns their health data, while 36.4% of respondents agreed with it result shown in figure 6.

Figure 7. Confidentiality of the patients PHR

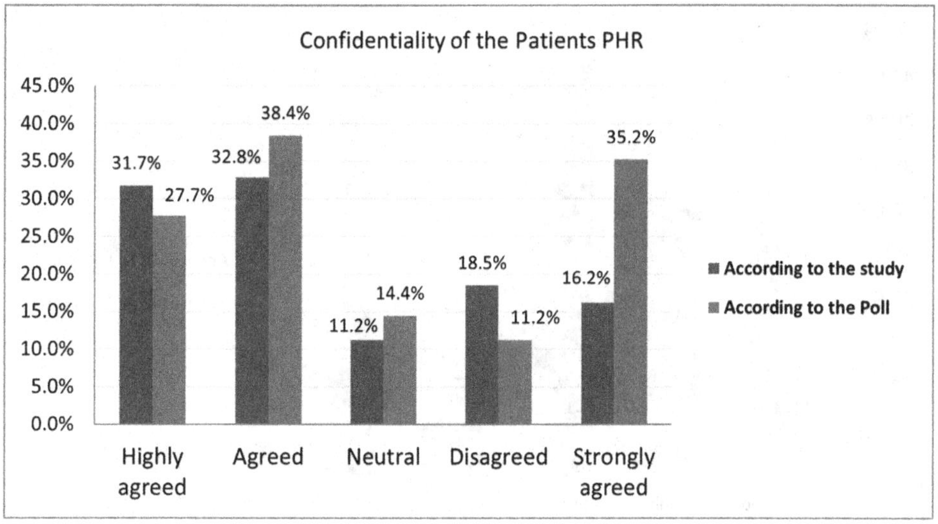

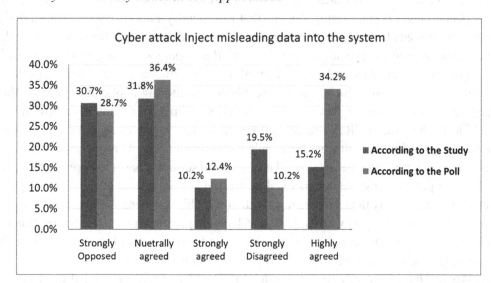

Furthermore, according to the study's findings, 36.4% of respondents agreed with the statement that they should get the proper special needs approval before using their health data, as opposed to 29.1% of respondents who disagreed. Furthermore, 46.7% agreed, while 11.2% disagreed, that they promote anonymity in order to conceal the true identities of individuals with special needs by breaking down their identities into sub-identities are analyzed and shown in Fig.9.

Figure 8. Privacy and security issues in IoT Applications

Figure 9. Privacy and security requirements for IoT applications

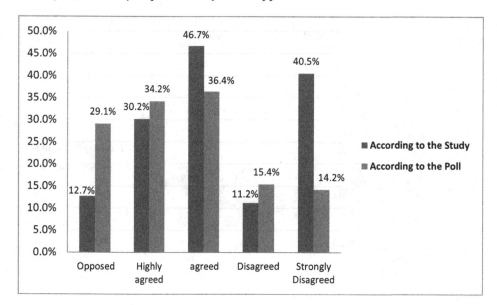

CONCLUSION

IoT can effectively monitor patients in remote locations and offer emergency care, particularly for people with cardiac conditions. This review work's main goal is to examine the numerous research initiatives connected to the IoT-based healthcare system. The majority of ongoing studies are effective at keeping tabs on the patient and sending information to the monitoring center. The study uses an ECG monitoring system that employs machine learning to accurately anticipate illness symptoms. To stop additional illnesses or disabilities, IoT monitoring devices that can identify falls or issues with vital signs in a person with special needs living alone (whether they live in a homestead or not) are employed. In fact, future illnesses or disabilities are being avoided by using the proper monitoring tools that allow for early prevention. The study reached a conclusion. The healthcare facilities questioned noted that the continuation of their status and vital signs by the IoT healthcare monitoring application benefits the people with special needs living in nursing homes, long-term care facilities, or remaining in hospitals. The use of Personal Health Records (PHRs) directly to e-health centers is one example of an IoT application milestone for the provision of healthcare for people with special needs. However, security issues, such as cyber-attacks that introduce false data into the system and seriously harm IoT applications, can arise. The results of our poll demonstrate that medical professionals take special needs patients' privacy and security much more seriously than was previously thought. This was demonstrated by the respondents' capacity to promote anonymity as well as the use of location privacy in keeping the location of people with special needs private, ask people with special needs for permission before using their data, and encourage people with special needs to know who owns their health data.

Future Work: Hybrid security framework for IoT Healthcare will be carried out to improve the security of EHR.

REFERENCES

Ahmad, M. O., & Siddiqui, S. T. (2022). The Internet of Things for Healthcare: Benefits, Applications, Challenges, Use Cases and Future Directions. In *Advances in Data and Information Sciences* (pp. 527–537). Springer. doi:10.1007/978-981-16-5689-7_46

Ali, Z., Hossain, M. S., Muhammad, G., & Sangaiah, A. K. (2018). An intelligent healthcare system for detection and classification to discriminate vocal fold disorders. *Future Generation Computer Systems*, *85*, 19–28. doi:10.1016/j.future.2018.02.021

Alsaadi, E., & Tubaishat, A. (2015). Internet of things: Features, challenges, and vulnerabilities. *International Journal of Advanced Computer Science and Information Technology*, *4*(1), 1–13.

Bandara, R., Fernando, M., & Akter, S. (2020). Addressing privacy predicaments in the digital marketplace: A power-relations perspective. *International Journal of Consumer Studies*, *44*(5), 423–434. doi:10.1111/ijcs.12576

Bethencourt, J., Sahai, A., & Waters, B. (2007, May). Ciphertext-policy attribute-based encryption. In 2007 IEEE symposium on security and privacy (SP'07) (pp. 321-334). IEEE. doi:10.1109/SP.2007.11

Campbell, S., Greenwood, M., Prior, S., Shearer, T., Walkem, K., Young, S., Bywaters, D., & Walker, K. (2020). Purposive sampling: Complex or simple? Research case examples. *Journal of Research in Nursing*, *25*(8), 652–661. doi:10.1177/1744987120927206 PMID:34394687

Das, S., & Namasudra, S. (2022). A Novel Hybrid Encryption Method to Secure Healthcare Data in IoT-enabled Healthcare Infrastructure. *Computers & Electrical Engineering*, *101*, 107991. doi:10.1016/j.compeleceng.2022.107991

Frehill, P., Chambers, D., & Rotariu, C. (2007, August). Using zigbee to integrate medical devices. In *2007 29th Annual International Conference of the IEEE Engineering in Medicine and Biology Society* (pp. 6717-6720). IEEE. 10.1109/IEMBS.2007.4353902

Gravina, R., Alinia, P., Ghasemzadeh, H., & Fortino, G. (2017). Multi-sensor fusion in body sensor networks: State-of-the-art and research challenges. *Information Fusion*, *35*, 68–80. doi:10.1016/j.inffus.2016.09.005

Karthick Raghunath, K. M., Koti, M. S., Sivakami, R., Vinoth Kumar, V., NagaJyothi, G., & Muthukumaran, V. (2022). Utilization of IoT-assisted computational strategies in wireless sensor networks for smart infrastructure management. *International Journal of System Assurance Engineering and Management*, 1-7.

Karunarathne, S. M., Saxena, N., & Khan, M. K. (2021). Security and privacy in IoT smart healthcare. *IEEE Internet Computing*, *25*(4), 37–48. doi:10.1109/MIC.2021.3051675

Kruk, M. E., Gage, A. D., Arsenault, C., Jordan, K., Leslie, H. H., Roder-DeWan, S., Adeyi, O., Barker, P., Daelmans, B., Doubova, S. V., English, M., García-Elorrio, E., Guanais, F., Gureje, O., Hirschhorn, L. R., Jiang, L., Kelley, E., Lemango, E. T., Liljestrand, J., & Pate, M. (2018). High-quality health systems in the Sustainable Development Goals era: Time for a revolution. *The Lancet. Global Health*, *6*(11), e1196–e1252. doi:10.1016/S2214-109X(18)30386-3 PMID:30196093

Kumar, S. S., & Koti, M. S. (2021, December). Efficient Authentication for Securing Electronic Health Records using Algebraic Structure. In *2021 5th International Conference on Electrical, Electronics, Communication, Computer Technologies and Optimization Techniques (ICEECCOT)* (pp. 366-370). IEEE. 10.1109/ICEECCOT52851.2021.9708050

Boufford, J. I., Cassel, C. K., Bender, K. W., Berkman, L., Bigby, J., & Burke, T. (2002). The Future of the Public's Health in the 21st Century. *Washington: Institute of Medicine of the National Academies, 6.* doi:10.1109/ICEECCOT52851.2021.9708050

Kumar, S. S., & Koti, M. S. (2022). Adaptive error approximate data reconciliation technique for health-care framework. *International Journal of System Assurance Engineering and Management*, 1-11.

Kumar, S. S., & Sanjay, M. (2018). Improved Quality of Patient Care and Data Security Using Cloud Crypto System in EHR. *International Journal of Advanced Studies of Scientific Research, 3*(10). Amru, M., Mahesh, A. V. N., & Ramesh, P. (2020, December). IoT-based Health Monitoring System with Medicine Remainder using Raspberry Pi. []. IOP Publishing.]. *IOP Conference Series. Materials Science and Engineering, 981*(4), 042081.

Lazarescu, M. T. (2013). Design of a WSN platform for long-term environmental monitoring for IoT applications. *IEEE Journal on Emerging and Selected Topics in Circuits and Systems, 3*(1), 45–54. doi:10.1109/JETCAS.2013.2243032

Madakam, S., Lake, V., Lake, V., & Lake, V. (2015). Internet of Things (IoT): A literature review. *Journal of Computer and Communications, 3*(05), 164–173. doi:10.4236/jcc.2015.35021

Maktoubian, J., & Ansari, K. (2019). An IoT architecture for preventive maintenance of medical devices in healthcare organizations. *Health and Technology, 9*(3), 233–243. doi:10.100712553-018-00286-0

Moses, J. C., Adibi, S., Shariful Islam, S. M., Wickramasinghe, N., & Nguyen, L. (2021, July). Application of smartphone technologies in disease monitoring: A systematic review. []. MDPI.]. *Health Care, 9*(7), 889. PMID:34356267

Muthukumaran, V., Arun, M., Kumar, S. S., Kumta, S. D., Kavitha, M. A., & Vijayaraghavan, R. (2021, July). Secure efficient signature for internet of things over near-ring. []. IOP Publishing.]. *Journal of Physics: Conference Series, 1964*(2), 022015. doi:10.1088/1742-6596/1964/2/022015

Nagarajan, S. M., Deverajan, G. G., Chatterjee, P., Alnumay, W., & Muthukumaran, V. (2022). Integration of IoT based routing process for food supply chain management in sustainable smart cities. *Sustainable Cities and Society, 76*, 103448. doi:10.1016/j.scs.2021.103448

Qin, Z., Denker, G., Giannelli, C., Bellavista, P., & Venkatasubramanian, N. (2014, May). A software defined networking architecture for the internet-of-things. In 2014 IEEE network operations and management symposium (NOMS) (pp. 1-9). IEEE. doi:10.1109/NOMS.2014.6838365

Roopashree, S., Anitha, J., Mahesh, T. R., Kumar, V. V., Viriyasitavat, W., & Kaur, A. (2022). An IoT based authentication system for therapeutic herbs measured by local descriptors using machine learning approach. *Measurement*, *200*, 111484. doi:10.1016/j.measurement.2022.111484

Said, O. (2013). *Development of an Innovative Internet of Things Security System*, *10*(6), 155–161.

Woskowski, C. (2014, September). A pragmatic approach towards safe and secure medical device integration. In *International Conference on Computer Safety, Reliability, and Security* (pp. 342-353). Springer, Cham. 10.1007/978-3-319-10506-2_23

Chapter 17
Performance Evaluation and Analysis of Different Association Rule Mining (ARM) Algorithms

Vinaya Babu M.
https://orcid.org/0000-0001-7647-5473
Sri Venkateswara University, India

Sreedevi Mooramreddy
Sri Venkateswara University, India

ABSTRACT

Data processing technique of data mining has the power to identify patterns and relationships in huge volumes of data from multiple sources to make decisions to drive the world in the current scenario. Association rule mining (ARM) is the most significant method used in data mining. This approach is employed to find trends in the database that are typical. The field of ARM has seen a lot of activities. ARM remains a source of concern for various experts. There are algorithms that assess fundamental factors like precision, algorithm speed, and data assistance. The ARM algorithms, namely AprioriHybrid, AIS, AprioriTID, and Apriori, as well as FP-Growth, are examined in this work. This chapter provides a comparison of different algorithms utilized for association rules mining against several performance factors.

INTRODUCTION

Data mining (DM) is the art of skillfully extracting hidden and valuable information from sizable heterogeneous data sources (Hegland, 2007). Knowledge from knowledge bases or data warehouses is revealed through data mining. Consequently, obtaining such expertise is essential. Several approaches are used in data mining including clustering, classification, association rule mining, regression, etc. Huge data is primarily used for analyzing in various ways which will help management to make good decision at

DOI: 10.4018/978-1-6684-6971-2.ch017

Copyright © 2023, IGI Global. Copying or distributing in print or electronic forms without written permission of IGI Global is prohibited.

right time (Yazgana, 2016). Usually, management data sets in various areas are huge and always growing as well as contain very complex features. For extracting information from such datasets require robust, simple and computationally efficient tools. To build and get familiar of such tools is the key application of DM (Witten, 2017). For these tools a highly efficient algorithms and vast computing resource is essential, which scale with data size and complexity. Branch of study in Information technology. Finding patterns, relations and summarizing them as simple data models from huge data sets is required and which is the main aim of Data mining (Peltier, 2002). Various applications of data mining include health industry, transport logistics, CRM, Machine learning and automation, IOT, economic forecast, etc. Mining of data involves business understanding in First phase, data understanding in second phase and next three phases are data preparation, modeling, and evaluation respectively (Kotsiantis, 2006).

Techniques of Data Mining

Descriptive mining and predictive mining are two categories into which data mining tasks can be divided as shown in Figure 1. The process of describing the fundamental features of database data is known as descriptive mining. The primary tasks involved in descriptive mining approaches are clustering, association, and sequential mining. Similar to predictions, predictive mining derives patterns from the data. Techniques for predictive mining include classification, regression, and deviation detection. A crucial challenge for numerous types of knowledge discovery, including association rules, sequential patterns, and classification, is mining Frequent Itemsets from transaction databases. A collection of sets of items is said to be frequent if its subsets occur frequently. To create association rules, frequent itemsets are typically used.

Figure 1. Data mining models

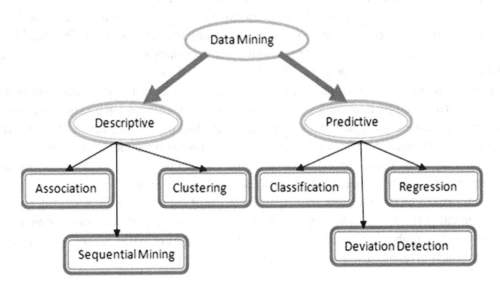

Database exploration uses a number of important DT approaches, including affiliation, rule classification, clustering, prediction, and measurement trends, among others, that have recently been developed and applied to DT projects (Shrestha, 2021).

- **Association:** It is a well-liked DM approach. We assess recurring trends and locate intriguing links inside data using this methodology.
- **Classification:** To locate an entity whose class label is unknown, it is necessary to look for interesting pattern that identifies and distinguishes the other data groups.
- **Clustering:** Clustering is the classification of particular things into groups according to their shared traits. Using a unique join technique, data mining splits the data into segments that are most appropriate for the required analysis. This analysis, known as the hard partitioning of this type, permits an object to not be strictly or entirely a part of a cluster. Smooth partitions, however, imply that each object in the same degree is a member of a cluster.
- **Prediction:** The categorization forecasts classified names and continuously priced prediction models. Instead of class labels, this is used to approximate lost or unavailable numerical data values.

ASSOCIATION RULE MINING (ARM)

Several approaches are used in data mining tasks, including clustering, classification, association rule mining, regression, etc. One of them that is of the biggest interest is association rule mining. With regard to performance variables, various strategies for association rule mining are taken into consideration, and a comparative analysis is reviewed. This review also takes into account a few privacy-related aspects that are appropriate for each association rule mining technique. By taking into account the available data set, association rule mining algorithms assist in extracting desirable association rules. In order to determine the relationship between a huge number of data objects, ARM is used (Sharma, 2021). Due to the enormous amount of data stored in repositories, many businesses are very much keen regarding their database mining associate in policies. The identification of the exciting connected links between vast quantities of transaction data might, for instance, support cross-marketing, catalogue design, and other commercial decision-making processes. The association rules generation is shown in Figure 2. The analysis of market baskets is a typical ARM application. By looking for connections between different things those customers pack in their packs, this strategy investigates consumer purchasing behaviors. By offering a summary of the things these partnerships typically purchase jointly, marketers will be able to expand their communication campaigns by identifying these partnerships.

Strong rules based on their interest are offered in terms of support as well as confidence in ARM as shown in equation (1) and (2). The support of ARM is the ratio of total transactions containing both items x and y to the number of total transactions D. If the support of ARM is 30%, then it means that 30% of the transactions contain both x and y using the equation (1).

$$Support(xy) = \frac{Transactional\ Support(xy)}{Total\ Number\ of\ Transactions\ in\ D} \tag{1}$$

Figure 2. Association rules generation

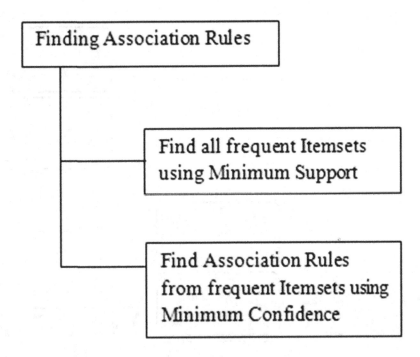

The degree of correlation between x and y in the database is indicated by the confidence of an association rule. It serves as a gauge for the power of a rule. The confidence of items x and y is the ratio of support of items a and y to the support of item x.

$$Confidence\left(xy\right) = \frac{Support\left(xy\right)}{Support\left(x\right)} \qquad (2)$$

As illustrated in Figure 3, there are various types of association rule mining, including multidimensional, frequent itemset, multilevel, Boolean, constraints-based, and quantitative association rule mining.

When it comes to support and confidence, association rule mining is offered, and if it doesn't meet the value criteria, it is biased (Johnson, 2021). Support measures the item's frequency, and confidence measures the number of transactions using the if/then pattern. For rule exploration, only an association rule that meets a predetermined threshold (breakeven) value for support and confidence is taken into account. In our study, we concentrate on numerous such methods for revealing robust association principles. The execution times for legacy Apriori and its upgraded versions, which aimed to increase the effectiveness of association rules, were briefly examined by the authors. By decreasing the unnecessary formation of sub-item sets while maintaining candidate item sets, this technique eliminates those subsets that are not frequently present there.

Figure 3. Different kinds of patterns to be mined

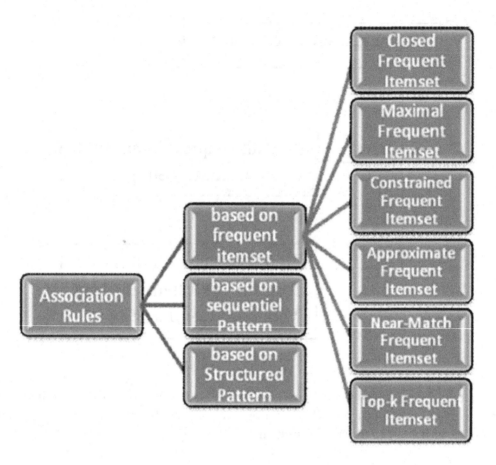

ARM is a major aspect in the data mining field. The mining rule of association is a method for developing mining technology advancements. Many different sorts of methodologies or algorithms are being developed for combination rule mining; however it is crucial to understand which strategy is most suitable for only combination rule. This article describes a novel technique called up growth that may help to simplify the high-dimensional details and temporal complexity (Subashini, 2012). The power monitoring equipment gathers a lot of information that is solely needed for alarms. Although there is a plethora of knowledge in this information, it has not been effectively unearthed. Consequently, in this research an advanced interaction law method based on an Upper-Triangular-Matrix(UTM) is built. The approach enables the database to be kept to a minimum and the total number of candidate sets to be simplified. The effectiveness of rules acquisition is thereby significantly increased. An analysis of association rule experiment is conducted to test the viability and validity of revised method. It offers a crucial route for both data extraction as well as the investigation of association rules.

The authors (Gowramma, 2017) examined frequent item set mining in transactional databases and found that there was an increased chance for information in scanning databases and a decrease in the size of itemsets. It seeks to cut down on the number of scans and thereby increase productivity. Comparative charts for several association rule mining algorithms' accuracy rates, applications, speeds, etc. were provided by the authors (Boghey, 2013). This information is open to in-depth analysis. The authors (Jha,

2021) examined a few special aspects as well as the inner workings of several mining algorithms, including all of the pros and downsides of algorithms like Apriori, DHP, partitioning, Eclat, and FP Growth. The author demonstrated why the merge and split (SaM) algorithm is superior to others. The authors (Kuramochi, 2004) thoroughly analyzed the impact of various rules of associations on the algorithms of e-commerce. The next section provides a methodology of different ARM algorithms.

METHODOLOGY OF VARIOUS ARM ALGORITHMS

Both supervised and uncontrolled association rule mining are possible. In order to find intriguing patterns, association rule mining was first applied in unsupervised situations. For instance, we may search through grocery store transaction data for recurring patterns and association rules. An example rule may be "milk, bread" -> "eggs," which would indicate that if someone bought milk and bread at the same time, they were probably also going to buy eggs. Later, a number of algorithms were created to classify data via association rule mining. You would do so in this situation. We would classify all of our data during the training phase, and then only mine the rules that had a class label on the right side. These rules serve as the classifier and are representative of the corresponding classes. When we receive a fresh (unlabelled) instance, we would evaluate it against all of the rules, and the class with the highest score would serve as the new instance's anticipated class label.

However, we can discretize any continuous attributes during the pre-processing stage. Association rule mining was initially intended to function with discrete (categorical) data. This section provides the methodologies of different ARM algorithms. The different ARM algorithms and the different performance factors are shown in Figure 4.

Apriori

Based on the principle or property that all subsets of frequent item sets must be frequent, R. Agarwal provided this approach for finding frequent item sets. (Mahesh, 2016). To generate candidates, this technique expands frequent subsets one at a time. We test these potential candidate groupings using data. The two steps of this algorithm's operation are join and prune. Apriori search is similar to a BFS that counts candidate item sets using a hash tree data structure.

Apriori TID

AprioriTID seeks to reveal frequently occurring item sets in a transaction database. It is a different application of Apriori that uses Apriori to identify candidate item sets prior to the start of the pass. The fact that the data base is not taken into account for support counts after the first pass is an intriguing aspect of AprioriTID. Candidate sets are always scanned for support counts using Apriori TID. When the problem grows in scope, it is not preferred (Ferreira, 2008).

Figure 4. Comparative study

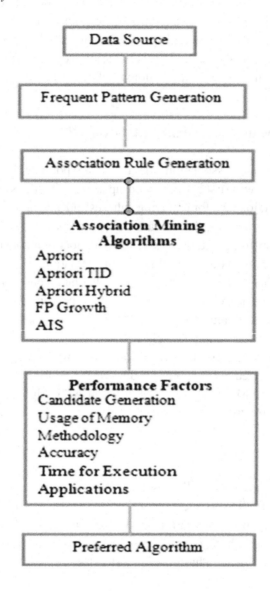

Apriori Hybrid

By combining Apriori and AprioriTID in the subsequent passes, Apriori TID glitters whereas the simple Apriori is used in the initial pass (Han, 2004). In many instances, this produces superior outcomes. When transitioning from Apriori to AprioriTID, this algorithm involves an additional penalty.

FP Growth

The compact structure known as the frequent pattern tree (FP-Tree) is used to store quantitative data on frequent patterns in databases. It uses the divide and conquer method (Dubal, 2011). It creates an FP-tree instance that represents frequent items after first compressing the input data. Then, the compressed database is split up into a number of condition databases and each one was connected to a typical pattern. At last, each such database is mined separately. In this manner, FP-growth reduces the search expense by recursively searching for patterns that are short and then concatenating those into long frequent patterns, and providing the best selectivity.

AIS

This algorithm enhances databases' appearance to facilitate improved decision-making. It only generates rules like $A \cup B \rightarrow C$, which are one item consequent association rules, Not $A \rightarrow C \cap B$. It has two stages: first, it generates frequent item sets; next, it investigates frequent and confident association rules (Srikant, 1996). It requires multiple iterations of scanning the data set for frequent item sets and then rules. Individual item support counts are taken into account during the first pass, and then minimum supported item sets are deleted or washed out based on the threshold value.

Association Rule Mining in Structured Data Patterns

Modern day data cannot be entirely represented in tabular datasets, which is the traditional way the software engineers mine data from these data using mining algorithms. But the growth and usage of semi-structured data has opened plenty of chances for data scientists. Association rule mining based on Structure mining or structured data mining depends on representation of structured data in specific format (Yan, 2002).

Frequent Sub-Graph (FSG)

Over the years, frequent Itemset discovery algorithms which are applied to traditional data domains cannot be used with non-traditional domains as these domains contains data cannot be modeled by the existing algorithms as the framework used in their design is not suitable for such data representation (Deshmukh, 2012). So one of the way of modeling such objects is to represent data sets using graphs to find sub-graphs frequently occurring in graph similar to frequent item sets in large data set. Structured data in graph representation uses topological ordering in order to find frequent patterns through frequent sub graphs over entire set of graphs. The main features of the algorithm is a) conserves storage and computation by representing graph in Sparse matrices b) moves level-by-level by adding each edge at a time to generate candidates efficiently c) employs various optimizations while generating candidates and frequency counting which can be scaled to large data sets also.

GSPAN

Frequent pattern finding in data sets or in subsets or substructure has been an emerging data mining problem used with many scientific and commercial applications (Shen et al., 2014; Shashikala, 2021; Mahesh, 2022). As FSG uses Apriori approach which has challenges such as generation k+1 sub graphs from k frequent sub graphs and sub graphs isomorphism test is a NP complete problem involves high complexity. GSPAN uses DFS approach to explore sub graphs for frequent sub graph mining (Roopashree et al., 2022; Pinaki, 2015; Sarveshvar, 2021; Mahesh, 2022).

WARMR

Scientific and technological applications generate complex structured data which becomes challenge for data scientists to extract meaningful knowledge. Inductive logical programming technique to find descriptive and expressive patterns which is used in WARMR algorithm (Reddy, 2021). These patterns are used to characterize the target mining pattern.

COMPARATIVE ANALYSIS

This section includes a comparative examination, with particular attention paid to the approaches for mining association rules, frequent itemsets, sequential rules, and sequential patterns. The majority of previously published papers focused on memory impressions and performance (Mahesh, 2022). The Comparison of ARM Algorithms against several features is depicted in Table 1 and the performance of ARM algorithms is depicted in Table 2.

Table 1. ARM algorithms: Comparative study

Features	Apriori	AprioriTID	Apriori Hybrid	FP-Growth	AIS
Accuracy	less	Medium, better than Apriori	Fast, better compare to Apriori TID	Super fast and very accurate	Very less
Data support	Medium	Often large	Very large	Very large	less
Speed during Initial Phase	high	slow	high	high	slow
Speed during later phase	slow	high	high	high	slow

Table 2. ARM algorithms: Comparative performance

Features	Apriori	AprioriTID	Apriori Hybrid	FP-Growth	AIS
Accuracy	1.45	2.46	4	5	0.5
Data support	2.5	4	5	5	1.5
Speed during Initial Phase	4.98	1.53	5	5	1.57
Speed during later phase	1.5	5	5	5	1.58

The Graphical Representation of performance of ARM Algorithms is shown in Figure 5.

Figure 5. Performance of ARM algorithms

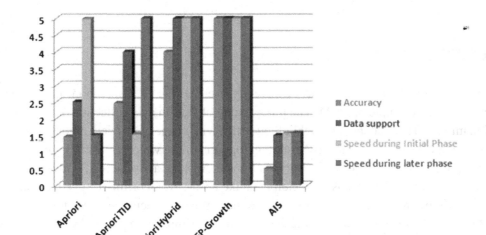

Comparisons representation of the ARM algorithm's execution time (in milliseconds) is depicted in Table 3 and the graphical representation is shown in Figure 6.

Apriori requires more time to run and is less effective with large datasets, but Frequent Pattern Growth is constrained by its complicated trees, which makes the technique more challenging.

Figure 6. Execution time of ARM algorithms

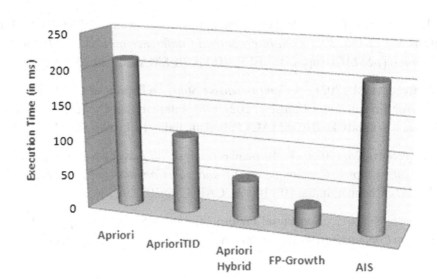

Table 3. ARM algorithms: Execution time in milliseconds

Apriori	AprioriTID	Apriori Hybrid	FP-Growth	AIS
212	109	55	28	205

CONCLUSION

Marketing professionals now particularly frequently use the rule of association mining. The market basket analysis is an example of ARM. The links among objects in data collection are part of the law of association mining. The best ones are highlighted with a wide range of efficient algorithms. This article, also offers a comparison of various ARM strategy options to see which algorithm will work best. The ARM algorithms AprioriHybrid, AIS, AprioriTID and Apriori, as well as FP-Growth are examined in this work. The comparison focuses on elements like accuracy, algorithmic speed, database support, etc. It was observed that every algorithm requires more time to execute, possess few advantages, and disadvantages. Fp-Growth is negatively impacted by an algorithm's complicated structure, which raises the complexity of an algorithm. Many applications are evolving day-by-day using various data mining algorithms. Different techniques has specific advantages and its drawbacks which gives the opportunity in this area to do more research and define new algorithms which will make applications efficient with respect to time, memory usage and calculation complexity.

Conflict of Interest: The authors declare that there is conflict of interest for the publication.

REFERENCES

Arathi, S., & Johnson, R. F. (2021). Predicting the number of new cases of COVID-19 in India using Survival Analysis and LSTM. *2021 Fifth International Conference on I-SMAC (IoT in Social, Mobile, Analytics and Cloud) (I-SMAC),* (pp. 1-4). IEEE. 10.1109/I-SMAC52330.2021.9640899

Babu, M. V., & Sreedevi, M. (2021). *A Comprehensive Study on Enhanced Clustering Technique of Association Rules over Transactional Datasets.* 2021 Fifth International Conference on I-SMAC (IoT in Social, Mobile, Analytics and Cloud) (I-SMAC), Palladam, India. 10.1109/I-SMAC52330.2021.9640681

Babu, M. V., & Sreedevi, M. (2022). Performance Analysis on Advances in Frequent Pattern Growth Algorithm. *2022 International Conference on Advances in Computing, Communication and Applied Informatics (ACCAI),* Chennai, India. 10.1109/ACCAI53970.2022.9752650

Boghey, R., & Singh, S. (2013). Sequential Pattern Mining: A Survey on Approaches. *2013 International Conference on Communication Systems and Network Technologies,* (pp. 670-674). IEEE. 10.1109/CSNT.2013.142

Chaitanya Reddy, P., Chandra, R. M. S., Vadiraj, P., Ayyappa Reddy, M., Mahesh, T. R., & Sindhu Madhuri, G. (2021). Detection of Plant Leaf-based Diseases Using Machine Learning Approach. *2021 IEEE International Conference on Computation System and Information Technology for Sustainable Solutions (CSITSS)*, (pp. 1-4). IEEE. 10.1109/CSITSS54238.2021.9683020

Ferreira, C. A., Gama, J., & Costa, V. S. (2008). RUSE-WARMR: Rule Selection for Classifier Induction in Multi-relational Data-Sets. *20th IEEE International Conference on Tools with Artificial Intelligence*, (pp. 379-386). IEEE. 10.1109/ICTAI.2008.73

Gunasekaran, K., Kumar, V. V., Kaladevi, A. C., Mahesh, T. R., Bhat, C. R., & Venkatesan, K. (2023). Smart Decision-Making and Communication Strategy in Industrial Internet of Things. *IEEE Access : Practical Innovations, Open Solutions, 11*, 28222–28235. doi:10.1109/ACCESS.2023.3258407

Han, J., Pei, J., & Yan, X.-F. (2004). From sequential pattern mining to structured pattern mining: A pattern-growth approach. *Journal of Computer Science and Technology, 19*(3), 257–279. doi:10.1007/BF02944897

Hegland, M. (2007). *The Apriori Algorithm*. CMA, Australian National University.

Ian, H. (2017). *Witten, EibeFrank,Christopher J. Pal, Data Mining Practical Machine Learning Tools and Techniques* (4th ed.). Willey publishers.

Jha, K. K., Jha, R., Jha, A. K., Hassan, M. A. M., Yadav, S. K., & Mahesh, T. (2021). A Brief Comparison On Machine Learning Algorithms Based On Various Applications: A Comprehensive Survey. *2021 IEEE International Conference on Computation System and Information Technology for Sustainable Solutions (CSITSS)*, (pp. 1-5). 10.1109/CSITSS54238.2021.9683524

Kotsiantis, S. (2006). DimitrisKanellopoulos,Association Rules Mining: A Recent Overview. *GESTS International Transactions on Computer Science and Engineering, 32*(1), 71–82.

Mahesh, T. R., Kumar, V. V., & Lim, S. J. (2023). UsCoTc: Improved Collaborative Filtering (CFL) recommendation methodology using user confidence, time context with impact factors for performance enhancement. *PLoS One, 18*(3), e0282904. doi:10.1371/journal.pone.0282904 PMID:36921014

Mahesh, T. R., Vivek, V., Kumar, V. V., Natarajan, R., Sathya, S., & Kanimozhi, S. (2022). A Comparative Performance Analysis of Machine Learning Approaches for the Early Prediction of Diabetes Disease. 2022 International Conference on Advances in Computing, Communication and Applied Informatics (ACCAI), (pp. 1-6). IEEE. 10.1109/ACCAI53970.2022.9752543

Mahesh, T. R., Vivek, V., Saravanan, C., & Vinay Kumar, K. (2022) Data Analytics: The Challenges and the Latest Trends to Flourish in the Post-COVID-19. In: Dua M., Jain A.K., Yadav A., Kumar N., Siarry P. (eds) *Proceedings of the International Conference on Paradigms of Communication, Computing and Data Sciences. Algorithms for Intelligent Systems*. Springer, Singapore. 10.1007/978-981-16-5747-4_43

Kuramochi, M. & Karypis, G. (2004). An Efficient Algorithm for Discovering Frequent Subgraphs. *IEEE Transactions On Knowledge And Data Engineering, 16*(9).

Peltier, J. W., Schibmwsky, J. A., & Schuhz, D. E. (2002). Interactive Psychographics:Cross-Selling in the Banking Industry". *Journal of Advertising Research*, *4*(2), 7–22. doi:10.2501/JAR-42-2-7-22

Ramakrishna, M. T., Venkatesan, V. K., Bhardwaj, R., Bhatia, S., Rahmani, M. K. I., Lashari, S. A., & Alabdali, A. M. (2023). HCoF: Hybrid Collaborative Filtering Using Social and Semantic Suggestions for Friend Recommendation. *Electronics (Basel)*, *12*(6), 1365. doi:10.3390/electronics12061365

Ramakrishna, M. T., Venkatesan, V. K., Izonin, I., Havryliuk, M., & Bhat, C. R. (2023). Homogeneous Adaboost Ensemble Machine Learning Algorithms with Reduced Entropy on Balanced Data. *Entropy (Basel, Switzerland)*, *25*(2), 245. doi:10.3390/e25020245 PMID:36832611

Roopashree, S., Anitha, J., Mahesh, T. R., Vinoth Kumar, V., Viriyasitavat, W., & Kaur, A. (2022). An IoT based authentication system for therapeutic herbs measured by local descriptors using machine learning approach. *Measurement, 200*. doi:10.1016/j.measurement.2022.111484

Sarveshvar, M. R., Gogoi, A., Chaubey, A. K., Rohit, S., & Mahesh, T. R. (2021, December). Performance of different machine learning techniques for the prediction of heart diseases. In *2021 International Conference on Forensics, Analytics, Big Data, Security (FABS)* (Vol. 1, pp. 1-4). IEEE. 10.1109/FABS52071.2021.9702566

Sharma, K., Mahesh, T. R., & Bhuvana, J. (2021). Big Data Technology for Developing Learning Resources. *Journal of Physics: Conference Series*, *1979*(May), 012019. doi:10.1088/1742-6596/1979/1/012019

Shashikala, H. K., Mahesh, T. R., Vivek, V., Sindhu, M. G., Saravanan, C., & Baig, T. Z. (2021). Early Detection of Spondylosis using Point-Based Image Processing Techniques. 2021 International Conference on Recent Trends on Electronics, Information, Communication & Technology (RTEICT), (pp. 655-659). IEEE. 10.1109/RTEICT52294.2021.9573604

Shen, W., Wang, J., & Han, J. (2014). Sequential Pattern Mining. In C. Aggarwal & J. Han (Eds.), *Frequent Pattern Mining*. Springer., doi:10.1007/978-3-319-07821-2_11

Shrestha, P., Singh, A., Garg, R., Sarraf, I., Mahesh, T. R., & Sindhu Madhuri, G. "Early Stage Detection of Scoliosis Using Machine Learning Algorithms," *2021 International Conference on Forensics, Analytics, Big Data, Security (FABS)*, 2021, pp. 1-4, 10.1109/FABS52071.2021.9702699

Srikant, R., & Agrawal, R. (1996). Mining sequential patterns: Generalizations and performance improvements. In *Proc. 5th Int. Conf. Extending Database Technology*. Springer-Verlag.

Venkatesan, V. K., Izonin, I., Periyasamy, J., Indirajithu, A., Batyuk, A., & Ramakrishna, M. T. (2022). Incorporation of Energy Efficient Computational Strategies for Clustering and Routing in Heterogeneous Networks of Smart City. *Energies*, *15*(20), 7524. doi:10.3390/en15207524

Venkatesan, V. K., Ramakrishna, M. T., Batyuk, A., Barna, A., & Havrysh, B. (2023). High-Performance Artificial Intelligence Recommendation of Quality Research Papers Using Effective Collaborative Approach. *Systems*, *11*(2), 81. doi:10.3390ystems11020081

Venkatesan, V. K., Ramakrishna, M. T., Izonin, I., Tkachenko, R., & Havryliuk, M. (2023). Efficient Data Preprocessing with Ensemble Machine Learning Technique for the Early Detection of Chronic Kidney Disease. *Applied Sciences (Basel, Switzerland)*, *13*(5), 2885. doi:10.3390/app13052885

Yan, X., & Han, J. (2002). gSpan: graph-based substructure pattern mining. 2002 IEEE International Conference on Data Mining, (pp. 721-724). IEEE. 10.1109/ICDM.2002.1184038

Yazgana, P. & Osman, A. (2016). A Literature Survey on Association Rule Mining Algorithms. *Southeast Europe Journal of Soft Computing*. doi:10.21533/scjournal.v5i1.102

Chapter 18

GanglioNav WithYou:
Design and Implementation of an Artificial Intelligence–Enabled Cognitive Assessment Application for Alzheimer's Patients

Vinu Sherimon
ⓘ https://orcid.org/0000-0003-4923-2841
University of Technology and Applied Sciences, Muscat, Oman

Sherimon Puliprathu Cherian
Arab Open University, Muscat, Oman

Rahul V. Nair
Royal Oman Police Hospital, Muscat, Oman

Khalid Shaikh
Royal Oman Police Hospital, Muscat, Oman

Natasha Renchi Mathew
Sri Ramachandra Institute of Higher Education and Research, Chennai, India

ABSTRACT

Alzheimer's disease is a universal medical challenge. A timely identification of this ailment can reduce expenses and enhance the patient's quality of life. Alzheimer's diagnosis includes a critical component called cognitive assessment. These examinations have been carried out by neurologists, utilizing paper-and-pencil ever since the development of neurological tests. But it's obvious that integrating digital technologies into such assessments has many advantages. This chapter describes the design of an Android application, GanglioNav WithYou, for conducting cognitive assessments in Alzheimer's patients. The researchers have built a 3D virtual neurologist to conduct this assessment for Alzheimer patients. The virtual neurologist will ask questions that test the different mental abilities of patients such as time orientation, ability to recall things, concentration skills, language skills, visual interpretation skills, etc. At the end of the assessment, the total score is calculated, and the virtual neurologist will generate a detailed assessment report.

DOI: 10.4018/978-1-6684-6971-2.ch018

Copyright © 2023, IGI Global. Copying or distributing in print or electronic forms without written permission of IGI Global is prohibited.

INTRODUCTION

Alzheimer's disease (AD) is a progressive, irreversible neurological illness that accounts for approximately 60 percent of all dementia cases (Qiao et al., 2022). More than 55 million individuals worldwide had dementia by the year 2020 (alzint.org, n.d.) and this number will roughly double every 20 years, reaching 78 million in 2030 and 139 million in 2050 (alzint.org, n.d.). Much of the increase will affect the developing globe. In low- and middle-income countries, 60 percent of adults suffer from dementia; by 2050, that percentage will rise to 71 percent (alzint.org, n.d.).

According to research, most people living with dementia do not have an official diagnosis. According to the study, around three-quarters of those with dementia have not been diagnosed (alzint.org, n.d.). The main clinical signs of Alzheimer's disease include cognitive impairment, memory impairment, speech disorders, and behavioral abnormalities (Arlt, 2013; Iodice et al., 2021; Jia et al., 2021; Lanzi et al., 2021; Martínez-Nicolás et al., 2021; Narasimhan et al., 2021). Magnetic resonance imaging (MRI) (Chen et al., 2022; Fathi et al., 2022; Saleem et al., 2022) has gained greater attention as a crucial tool for the early identification of some brain disorders and is an excellent measure to evaluate the stage of a subject, such as Normal Control (NC), mild cognitive impairment (MCI), and Alzheimer's disease (AD) (Orouskhani et al., 2022).

For neurodegenerative disorders in general, and specifically for dementia and its most common form, Alzheimer's disease (AD), age is a significant risk factor. The yearly prevalence of AD and its impact on society and the economy are rising along with rising life expectancy. As a result, it will be more crucial than ever to screen for dementia and cognitive impairment. Traditional paper-and-pencil cognitive tests and a series of neurological evaluations are often necessary for an AD diagnosis (Vos et al., n.d.). The problem is that many people wait until they or their loved ones notice a deterioration in memory before seeking a medical evaluation of cognitive functioning. There might already have been considerable, irreparable brain damage by then, along with fast worsening cognitive impairment (Vos et al., n.d.). Therefore, earlier diagnosis is significant and could aid clinical trial research in selecting the appropriate patients. So, tools that enable earlier diagnosis are necessary for earlier intervention so that a neurological workup can be taken into account.

Determining clinical scores such as the mini mental state examination (MMSE) of people now and in the future using MRI is also becoming a major topic in early Alzheimer's disease diagnosis (Tahami Monfared et al., 2022; Tian et al., 2022). The mini mental state exam is a simple 30-point questionnaire that can used to predict several neurodegenerative disorders such as Alzheimer's and dementia in the older generation (Hoops et al., 2009; Kang et al., 1997). It can be used to: (1) screen for cognitive impairment; (2) evaluate the degree of impairment at a particular time; (3) track an individual's progression of cognitive alterations over time; and (4) record an individual's response to therapy. It evaluates a variety of cognitive components, such as language, orientation, memory, and visuospatial ability. The total score across all items reflects the degree of cognitive impairment that is currently present. Reduced test scores over time reflect deterioration in cognitive.

Scores correspond with other mental tests, electroencephalography, computerized tomography, magnetic resonance imaging, single photon emission computed tomography (SPECT) scan, CSF proteins and enzymes, and brain biopsy synapse counts and are reliable between tests and between raters. Dementia, delirium, mental retardation, Parkinson's disease, stroke, and some forms of depression are all associated with lower test scores than healthy controls. (Counsell et al., 2022; Zhou et al., 2022).

Alzheimer's disease patients lose 3–4 points per year of illness after the onset of memory disturbance, although there is wide variability in this phenomenon (Jahn, 2013).

When interpreting the results of the mental status assessment, the patient's native language, educational level, and culture must be taken into account because these elements can alter performance. A score of less than 24 is thought to be symptomatic of dementia, although a score of 23 or less isn't enough for a diagnosis of such. A neurologist would combine this information with other findings, such as the results of a brain scan, a neurological assessment, review of the medical history, and possibly gene sequencing. So, a low MMSE score should not be interpreted as evidence of dementia; rather it is an indication that more testing is required (Dementia Care Central, n.d.).

MMSE is an extensively used clinical tool to evaluate cognitive function and impairment. However, it faces certain disadvantages, such as

- Bias against people with poor education due to elements of language and mathematical testing.
- Bias against visually impaired.
- Limited examination of visuospatial cognitive ability.
- Poor sensitivity at detecting mild/early dementia.

Technology and advances in artificial intelligence can be employed to overcome these drawbacks, creating the possibility of deploying clinical grade tools to patients that are cheap, quick, and noninvasive with higher sensitivity. Clinical decision support systems (CDSSs) are a new way of dealing with large amounts of data and presenting it to healthcare clinicians to enhance diagnosis and treatment (Mezzi et al., 2022).

When a doctor examines a patient, the history of the patient, details of physical examination, recommendations for lab tests, reports for referrals, etc., are either recorded using standard forms, in a doctor's prescription pad, or directly recorded in electronic health record (EHR) systems (Wang et al., 2022). These tasks are carried out while interacting with the patients during the consultation time (Wang et al., 2022). If forms or prescriptions are used for the recording of patient information, to subsequently covert to digital it must be either inserted into electronic health record (EHR) systems (Wang et al., 2022) or scanned. So, this is a duplicate task, and if the note of the doctor is not in a structured form, again it requires time to understand and record in computer-based systems. These strategies reduce efficiency and may lead to errors while entering the patient data.

Artificial intelligence (AI)-based efforts to address these issues have recently been developed, including the use of automated speech recognition (ASR) and natural language processing (NLP) technologies to transcribe patient-clinician discussions and generate clinical notes automatically. The application of speech recognition and natural language processing methods has brought about a revolutionary change in the medical field in many dimensions. AI allows for the creation of intelligent agents that can communicate with humans and improve flexibility and accuracy in virtual settings. In addition, patients can have a dialogue with you and even share their emotions (Mezzi et al., 2022). The purpose is to create a system that records patient replies to MMSE questions. A wide range of cognitive assessments, including measures of orientation, attention, memory, language, and visual-spatial skills, are included in the proposed system (Mezzi et al., 2022). It gives a complete diagnosis report of the patient's health and aids in the diagnosis of dementia, as well as the assessment of its development and intensity in people who have difficulty reasoning, communicating, understanding, or remembering things (Mezzi et al., 2022).

There are currently a variety of cognitive assessment instruments accessible, ranging from quick assessments to time-consuming, examiner-driven neuropsychological exams. The ability to take, score, and deliver screening tests remotely before seeing a doctor is another crucial factor. A cognitive test's self-administered component may be useful in a number of ways. Many people experience anxiety before to seeing a doctor and having their cognitive functioning evaluated by medical professionals. For patients who feel anxious answering questions or taking tests in front of others, the opportunity to self-administer exams eliminates several typical stressors. Digital technologies provide the possibility of remote medical condition monitoring in a setting that is comfortable for patients and might be utilized for both initial and ongoing assessments of cognitive impairment. So, in this research, we proposa a 3D virtual neurologist to conduct the cognitive assessment of Alzheimer suspected patients. The assessment is a self-administered one or can be conducted with the help of care-givers. Later, the item scores and interpretations are given to doctors so they can discuss the results with their patients. In addition to providing flexibility in an office setting by removing the need for a staff member to administer the exam, a self-administered test would also provide an objective cognitive assessment that could help establish whether additional neurological screening is necessary.

RELATED WORK ON COGNITIVE ASSESSMENTS USING MACHINE LEARNING AND DEEP LEARNING

The research (Souillard-Mandar et al., 2021) offers a novel method for testing cognitive function based on clock-drawing behavior analysis. The authors created DCTclock, an AI-based system that analyzes how individuals design a clock face using machine learning methods. The approach looks for details including the size, position, and shape of the clock face and numbers, as well as the placement of the clock hands. DCTclock calculates a score based on these characteristics that indicates the individual's cognitive function. The researchers tested DCTclock on 147 people, including healthy people and those with moderate cognitive impairment or dementia. The DCTclock score was found to be significantly linked with scores on known cognitive tests like the MMSE and the MoCA, as well as clinical diagnosis of cognitive impairment. DCTclock, according to the authors, might be utilized as a screening tool for cognitive impairment in clinical settings, as well as to track changes in cognitive performance over time.

AI-assisted CDT (Sato et al., 2022) was built by training the deep neural network (DNN) model with over 40,000 drawings gathered from a large cohort of older persons from the National Health and Aging Trends Study (NHATS). The results showed that identifying people with an impairment in executive function was roughly 90% accurate, and identifying those with probable dementia was up to 77% accurate. The authors propose that the automated clock-drawing test be utilized as a mass screening tool to detect persons with cognitive impairment, especially in contexts where cognitive tests may be difficult to get.

The researchers (Binaco et al., 2020) wanted to see how accurate machine learning algorithms were in classifying moderate cognitive impairment (MCI) subgroups and Alzheimer's disease (AD) using data from the digital Clock Drawing Test (dCDT). The dCDT was given to 163 patients, and 350 characteristics were assessed for maximum information/minimal redundancy. To train classification models, the best subset of features was employed. For 2-group classifications, the neural network attained accuracies of 83% or higher, with equivalent results for non-MCI versus all MCI patients study. According to the findings, applying machine learning to standard neuropsychological tests can be a useful screening approach for early detection of neurodegenerative disorders.

The study's (Ho et al., 2023) goal was to create an app that could automatically and accurately predict patient dementia classes (DCs) based on responses to the clinical dementia rating (CDR) instrument. A total of 366 outpatients in a Taiwanese hospital were evaluated using 25 and 49 items supported by patients and family members, respectively. Two models, convolutional neural networks (CNN) and artificial neural networks (ANN), were used to investigate the accuracy of prediction based on five types of cognitive decline. In all instances, the ANN model outperformed the CNN model in terms of accuracy. The accuracy rate of the ANN combo scenario was 93.72%. This work successfully created and presented a downloadable ANN-based software for predicting DC in patients, which could help physicians forecast DC.

This study (Javeed et al., 2023) proposes a novel strategy for predicting dementia 10 years ahead of time utilizing multivariate data with 75 components. Two automated diagnostic systems are deployed, one for feature selection and the other for dementia classification using genetic algorithms. Age, past smoking habit, history of infarct, depression, hip fracture, single leg standing test with right leg, score in the physical component summary, and history of TIA/RIND were identified as the best predictors by the model with genetic algorithm and deep neural network. It is critical to identify risk factors in order to prevent or delay the onset of dementia.

By analyzing brain magnetic resonance images, this study (Hazarika et al., 2023) examines the application of deep neural networks (DNN) to aid in the diagnosis of Alzheimer's disease (AD). According to the analysis, the DenseNet-121 model performs the best, with an accuracy of 86.55%. However, because this model is computationally expensive, the paper presents a lightweight hybrid technique that incorporates LeNet and AlexNet and has an overall performance rate of 93.58%. The suggested approach produces far fewer convolutional parameters, resulting in a more computationally efficient model.

To detect cognitive impairment, researchers (Lesoil et al., 2023) created the Santé-Cerveau digital tool (SCD-T), a computerized cognitive screening instrument. Validated questionnaires and neuropsychological tests for episodic memory, executive functioning, and overall intellectual efficiency are included in the application. The study assessed SCD-T's performance in detecting cognitive impairments as well as its usability. The tool was tested on three groups: controls, neurodegenerative disease patients, and post-COVID-19 patients. The SCD-T shows high accuracy and acceptability in patients with prodromal and mild dementia phases. It may be effective in primary care to refer people with considerable cognitive impairment to professional consultation, as well as to improve the Alzheimer's disease care pathway and pre-screening in clinical trials.

Researchers (Tasaki et al., 2023) created the PentaMind deep-learning model to detect cognitive impairment in older persons based on hand-drawn images of intersecting pentagons. The model explained 23.3% of the variance in global cognition scores after being trained on 13,777 pictures from 3,111 subjects in three aging cohorts. Because of its capacity to identify extra drawing traits linked with motor deficits and cerebrovascular diseases, PentaMind was 1.92 times more accurate than standard visual evaluation in diagnosing cognitive decline. Hand-drawn drawings, according to the study, can give rich cognitive information for quick assessment of cognitive decline and may have clinical consequences in dementia.

The purpose of this study (Yamada et al., 2023) was to investigate the utility of automatic speech analysis as a screening tool for the early diagnosis of Alzheimer's disease (AD) and moderate cognitive impairment (MCI). Speech data from 114 older participants was obtained using a mobile application during cognitive activities, and a machine-learning speech classifier incorporating acoustic, prosodic, and linguistic variables achieved 78.6% accuracy in categorizing AD, MCI, and cognitively normal (CN) groups. The findings show that automatic speech analysis could be a valuable and valid method for self-administered AD and MCI screening.

According to the analysis of the literature, there are no 3D tools accessible for cognitive testing in Alzheimer's patients. Although there have been studies on the use of virtual reality (VR) and avatars for cognitive assessment in other populations, such as stroke survivors and children with developmental disorders, there has been little research on Alzheimer's patients. Some studies have employed 2D avatars or video games to measure cognitive abilities, but the potential benefits of 3D avatars, such as improved realism and immersion, have yet to be investigated. As a result, more study on the development and usage of 3D tools for cognitive testing in Alzheimer's patients is required.

Apparently, the researchers did not come across any research that illustrates 3D virtual neurologists to conduct cognitive assessment tests. There have been some studies looking into the use of 3D virtual neurologists to do cognitive assessment exams, however this technology is still in its infancy and is not yet commonly used in clinical settings. So, the researchers believe this is novel research of its type.

The following are our contributions in this research: -

- Development of a 3D virtual neurologist.
- A deep learning model to assess the results of Pentagon Drawing Test (PDT) included in the assessment.
- Design and Implementation of Ganglio-Nav Cognitive Assessment Android application.

MATERIALS AND METHODS

Figure 1 illustrates the architecture of the proposed Ganglio-Nav Cognitive Assessment android application for conducting the cognitive test.

Figure 1. Architecture of Ganglio-Nav Cognitive Assessment application

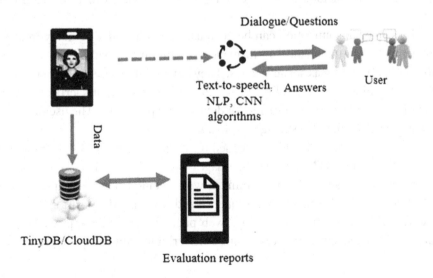

Development of the 3D Virtual Neurologist

The creation of a 3D virtual neurologist capable of performing cognitive exams necessitates a combination of technical expertise and cognitive testing understanding. At the beginning, we determine the scope of the 3D Virtual Neurologist. This comprises the exact cognitive tests that will be performed, the information that will be provided, and the functions that will be performed. We then developed a 3D virtual model of the neurologist. This entails creating the character's look, which includes facial features, body shape, and attire. Once the virtual model has been developed, we trained the model to perform cognitive tests. This entails creating algorithms that allow the virtual neurologist to interpret the instructions and accurately perform the cognitive tests. To administer cognitive tests, the virtual neurologist must have access to a cognitive testing knowledge base. So, the next step was to build a knowledge base which includes information on cognitive test administration, test interpretation, and standard data for different demographics. Once the virtual neurologist has been programmed, it was tested to ensure that it performs properly. This guarantees that the virtual neurologist is bug-free and functional testing. Later, the virtual neurologist was made available through a mobile application.

The 3D Virtual Neurologist was created using Blender, a free and open-source 3D design software. Blender is a powerful software that can be used for a range of tasks such as 3D modeling, animation, and rendering. Blender has grown in popularity as a tool for creating 3D visualizations and simulations due to its ease of use and vast feature set. 3D characters are then imported to iclone7 and various expressions, lip movement and the body movement are animated. iClone7 is an advanced 3D animation software that includes a variety of tools and capabilities for designing and animating 3D characters. iClone7 has a number of tools for modifying the character's joints, limbs, and body proportions to meet the intended animation.

The character's expressions and lip sync were added using iClone7's face animation tools from a library of pre-made expressions. The character's body movement was animated using iClone7's motion editing capabilities. Keyframes were designed to control the character's movements and to change the timing and speed of the animation. Multiple images are rendered from the animation created to extract the desired lip movement and body movement. iClone7 has several image rendering methods, including batch rendering and image sequence rendering. Selected images are then edited in Adobe Photoshop to create sprite images. Adobe include tools for evaluating photos and extracting specific movements or expressions.

The overall file size of the animation can be decreased by consolidating many images into a single sprite sheet, which can help to enhance performance and minimize loading times. Individual images cannot be rendered as efficiently as sprite images. They can aid in the creation of smooth and seamless animations. Sprite graphics may be readily scaled up and down without sacrificing quality, allowing you to design animations that work on a variety of devices and platforms. The use of sprites reduces the number of server requests while also saving the bandwidth.

Finally, the sprite images are animated as needed using JavaScript and the WebViewer of MIT App Inventor is used to display the HTML page. The images' speed, direction, and other properties, as well as the order of images in the sprite sheet to animate, were decided. The sprite pictures were then animated using JavaScript by displaying them in sequence and adjusting the position and size of the image as needed. The WebViewer component displays web pages in a mobile app and display the HTML page containing the animated sprite pictures. Using JavaScript to animate sprite graphics and MIT App

Inventor's WebViewer to display them results in entertaining and interactive animations that can be exhibited in mobile apps. MIT App Inventor and the designed HTML page in Web Viewer communicate with each other through WebView String. The WebViewString is used to transmit values between the application and the WebViewer.

Design and Implementation of Ganglio-Nav Cognitive Assessment Android Application

Speech recognition is an interdisciplinary subject of natural language processing (NLP) that creates approaches and technology that allow computers to recognize and translate oral language into text. Text-to-speech and speech-to-text functions of MIT App Inventor media extension is used in our application. The Media component extension in MIT App Inventor includes various important tools for interacting with audio and video content, such as text-to-speech and speech-to-text operations. The Media extension's TextToSpeech component converts text into spoken audio, which can be useful for providing audio tutorials, reading out text-based information, or adding voiceovers to a program. The pitch, tempo, and language of the voice can be altered and it can also create audio files that can be played afterwards. The Media extension's SpeechRecognizer component allows to turn spoken sounds into text. This can be helpful for developing voice-enabled apps or transcribing spoken content. The SpeechRecognizer recognizes spoken words and phrases in a variety of languages and can be configured with specific grammars or keyword lists.

Initial welcome texts coded in JavaScript works inside MIT App Inventor and outputs through WebViewer to the HTML page. JavaScript is used to code the behavior of the app and the interactions between the app and the HTML page. In MIT App Inventor, text-to-speech media extension will read the dialogues and questions and will convert to speech, then send to the HTML page of the WebViewer through WebViewString. Then the JavaScript of the HTML page will understand that the value of WebView string has changed, and it will split the individual letters of the words in the dialogue/question so that they can be displayed on the screen one by one as the text-to-speech audio is played. This can help to make the app more engaging and interactive for the user.

In sprite images, the lip-synch expression of each letter is already pre-defined. So, according to the letters in the question, the 3D virtual doctor will spell out the question. This approach is often used in animation and interactive media to generate the appearance of speech by playing back pre-defined animations or images in a sequence that matches the time and rhythm of the spoken words. A more realistic and engaging virtual persona is constructed here that responds to user interaction in a natural way by using sprite graphics with pre-defined lip-sync expressions. The answers given by the user will be recognized using MIT App Inventor media extension. The SpeechRecognizer component, in particular, can be used to detect spoken words or phrases and convert them to text, which can subsequently be used to initiate specified actions or reactions. The answers will be checked, and correspondingly, points will be awarded.

TinyDB is used for local storage and CloudDB for web storage. TinyDB is a small database that allows users to save data on their device. TinyDB allows to store and retrieve data in the form of key-value pairs, which is helpful for storing user preferences, game scores, and other little quantities of data that don't need to be shared between devices. CloudDB, on the other hand, is a cloud-based database that enables data storage and sharing between devices. CloudDB can be used to build programs that require data synchronization across numerous devices, such as multiplayer games and social networking apps.

Several open-source libraries and APIs are used in our application to check the answers of the assessment. For example, the tools in p5.js Javascript library are used to check the answer to a question where the user is required to say a sentence which contains a noun and a verb. p5.js is a JavaScript library popular for creative coding and visualization. An IP address's position can be determined using IP geolocation services geoPlugin, n.d.), which is a crucial tool for physically mapping cyberspace. This is accomplished by searching for the IP address in a database that has information about IP address ranges and their physical locations. One potential application for IP geolocation services is mapping the geographic distribution of website visits or online service customers. Using the JSON variables offered by geoPlugin, back-end JSON scripts can be easily programed to deliver dynamic geo-localized pages using the JSON Geolocation web service API. In the proposed application, this API is used to check the answer to the question where the user is required to say the name of the country and the name of the city where he/she resides.

Deep Learning Model for Assessing the Results of Pentagon Drawing Test (PDT)

The Pentagon Drawing Test (PDT) is a typical visuospatial function evaluation (Li et al., 2022). that assesses verbal comprehension, visual-spatial-constructional abilities, and executive functions (Cecato, 2016). It is a popular instrument for evaluating visuospatial skills and executive function in people with neurological diseases. The PDT is a useful tool for learning about a person's cognitive function, but scoring and interpreting the results might take a while and require specialist knowledge. A pattern of overlapping pentagons is shown in this test (Cecato, 2016). The PDT was described by Bourke et al. (1995) as having an easy scoring scale with a total of six points. The six points are awarded if the drawing is perfect, 5 points for an overlapping connection with one figure being a pentagon, 4 points for any two overlapping pictures, 3 points for two non-overlapping pictures, 2 points for each of the picture and 1 point is awarded for each line drawn or attempted figure. Table 1 illustrates the categories and scores of PDT.

Deep learning is a machine learning technique where a deep neural network architecture is employed (Krizhevsky et al., 2012). It has been found that the deep learning techniques using Convolutional Neural Networks (CNNs) give excellent results in many image recognition tasks (Charles Leek et al., 2022; Kumar et al., 2021; Sharma et al., 2022). The scoring and interpretation of the PDT might possibly be automated using a deep learning model, which would speed up the process and increase accuracy. So, for this test, a deep learning-based framework is developed which will automatically evaluate the drawing and calculate the score. The researchers created a dataset consisting of 676 images from different categories to train the machine learning model. The images were categorized into different groups such as normal, mild, mild-to-moderate, moderate, moderate-to-severe, and severe. The photos of the PDT drawings were pre-processed to make certain that they were all in the same format and quality. This entails standardizing image size, resolution, and color. The researchers prepared their own dataset because of the difficulty in collecting data from AD patients. All the images were verified by the medical expert in the team.

In this work, as the number of images available in the dataset is small, the researchers used a pre-trained deep CNN by the transfer learning approach to build the classification model. The PDT is a multiclass classification problem, with six classes – Normal, Mild, Mild-to-Moderate, Moderate, Moderate-to-Severe, and Severe. The researchers employed Google Teachable Machine, an online open-source platform to build the deep-learning classification model (*Image Classification Using Google's Teachable*

Machine - GeeksforGeeks, n.d.). Google Teachable Machine is a free and open-source online platform for training machine learning models for image, sound, and motion detection. It offers a simple web interface through which users may upload and label their own data, which is then used to train a bespoke machine learning model. The model attained an excellent classification performance with high values of Specificity (0.99), Sensitivity (0.99), Precision (0.99) and F1 – score (0.99).

Table 1. Categories and corresponding scores of the Pentagon Drawing Test

Normal-6 points	Mild AD – 5 points	Mild-to-Moderate AD – 4 points	Moderate AD – 3 points	Moderate-to-Severe AD – 2 points	Severe AD – 1 point

Figure 2. 3D Neurologist ready to start

RESULTS AND DISCUSSION

Figure 2 depicts the virtual 3D Neurologist in her office, ready to conduct the cognitive assessment. The virtual neurologist receives the speech input, analyzes the input, and provides a vocal response.

Twenty-two questions are included in the assessment. The assessment checks different mental abilities of patients such as time orientation, place orientation, ability to recall things, concentration skills, language skills, ability to follow written and oral instructions, visual interpretation skills, etc. A score is given for each correct answer. The assessment allows for a maximum score of 30. A normal score is higher than 24. A score of 24 or less 24 is typically seen as abnormal and indicative of possible cognitive impairment further subject to detailed analysis of a neurologist as the result may occasionally be impacted by certain physical impairments, language or speech barriers, education level, or cultural differences. Table 2 shows the selected questions included in the assessment.

Table 2. Selected questions included in the assessment and the corresponding screens of the 3D neurologist

Question	3D Neurologist screen	Question	3D Neurologist screen
Color of car		There are 3 buttons. Press buttons in the order – green, red, and blue	
Color of fish		Read the instructions and do as written.	
Name of object in the picture		Pentagon Drawing Test	

At the end, the total score is calculated, and the 3D Neurologist will suggest suitable recommendations. Figure 3 shows a sample assessment test report with the AI impression.

Figure 3. Cognitive Assessment Test report generated by GanglioNav WithYou application

GanglioNav Cognitive Assessment Test Report

Subject Name:	
Age:	
Test Conducted By:	Artificial Intelligence Neurologist Dr Natasha
Android App:	GanglioNav With You
Total Questions Asked:	21
Total Questions Answered Correctly:	15
Total Score:	21

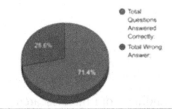

GanglioNav Cognitive Assessment Test Artificial Intelligence Impression:

Your Score Suggests that You Are Suffering From Mild Cognitive Impairment. Please Follow Up With Your Neurologist.

Scoring Criteria.

Score	Impression
Greater than 24	No Cognitive Impairment
20 to 24	Mild Cognitive Impairment
13 to 20	Moderate Cognitive Impairment
Less than 12	Severe Cognitive Impairment

Note:A low score is not a guarantee of dementia or Alzheimers Disease.

CONCLUSION

In summary, virtual assistants are interactive programs like Siri, Cortana, Amazon Alexa, and Google Assistant that communicate with users via text or audio. Instead of trying to replace clinicians, artificial intelligence aims to help them and make their tasks simpler. Also, there are various potential advantages of incorporating digital technologies into clinical practice and research. Digital evaluations may cut down on the time and expense of cognitive testing. There is also a chance that staffing costs will go down, if self-administered. If testing is carried out remotely as opposed to in an office, this benefit is further boosted. An automatic scoring mechanism is offered by many digital examinations, which can cut down on clinician time and the possibility of scoring mistakes. The key advantages of digital examinations include automated scoring and report generation.

The creation and development of GanglioNav – WithYou, the cognitive assessment application for Alzheimer patients is portrayed in this research article. A 3D virtual neurologist does the evaluation. To achieve this, the researchers created a custom 3D neurologist. Additionally, the researchers have shown how a deep learning model can be used to evaluate the Pentagon Drawing Test results, one of the test items in the evaluation. Our application will help human neurologists to evaluate Alzheimer patients' cognitive abilities. Our work may provide useful insights into how to develop health chatbots for greater user engagement and experience, in addition to its potential medicinal utility. Health chatbots have grown in popularity in recent years because they give patients with a quick and accessible way to communicate with healthcare practitioners and obtain individualized health information and recommendations.

Designing good health chatbots, on the other hand, can be a complex and difficult process, since they must combine the need for accuracy and reliability with the need for user-friendliness and engagement. The expected future contribution will include the evaluation of this application with Alzheimer patients in a hospital setting. By assessing our application's user engagement and experience, we may be able to find best practices and techniques for building effective health chatbots that can enhance patient outcomes and satisfaction.

ACKNOWLEDGMENT

The research leading to these results has received funding from the Research Council (TRC) of the Sultanate of Oman under the Block Funding Program BFP/ RGP/ ICT/ 19/ 229.

REFERENCES

ADI - Dementia statistics. (n.d.). Alzheimer's Disease International. https://www.alzint.org/about/dementia-facts-figures/dementia-statistics/

Arlt, S. (2013). Non-Alzheimer's disease—Related memory impairment and dementia. *Dialogues in Clinical Neuroscience*, *15*(4), 465–473. doi:10.31887/DCNS.2013.15.4arlt PMID:24459413

Binaco, R., Calzaretto, N., Epifano, J., McGuire, S., Umer, M., Emrani, S., Wasserman, V., Libon, D. J., & Polikar, R. (2020). Machine Learning Analysis of Digital Clock Drawing Test Performance for Differential Classification of Mild Cognitive Impairment Subtypes Versus Alzheimer's Disease. *Journal of the International Neuropsychological Society*, *26*(7), 690–700. doi:10.1017/S1355617720000144 PMID:32200771

Bourke, J., Castleden, C. M., Stephen, R., & Dennis, M. (1995). A comparison of clock and pentagon drawing in Alzheimer's disease. *International Journal of Geriatric Psychiatry*, *10*(8), 703–705. doi:10.1002/gps.930100811

Cecato, J. F. (2016). Pentagon Drawing Test: Some data from Alzheimer's disease, Paraphrenia and Obsessive compulsive disorder in elderly patients. *Perspectivas En Psicología: Revista de Psicología y Ciencias Afines*, *13*(2), 21–26.

Charles Leek, E., Leonardis, A., & Heinke, D. (2022). Deep neural networks and image classification in biological vision. *Vision Research*, *197*, 108058. doi:10.1016/j.visres.2022.108058 PMID:35487146

Chen, L., Qiao, H., & Zhu, F. (2022). Alzheimer's Disease Diagnosis With Brain Structural MRI Using Multiview-Slice Attention and 3D Convolution Neural Network. *Frontiers in Aging Neuroscience*, *14*, 871706. doi:10.3389/fnagi.2022.871706 PMID:35557839

Counsell, C., Giuntoli, C., Khan, Q. I., Maple-Grødem, J., & Macleod, A. D. (2022). The incidence, baseline predictors, and outcomes of dementia in an incident cohort of Parkinson's disease and controls. *Journal of Neurology*, *269*(8), 4288–4298. doi:10.100700415-022-11058-2 PMID:35307754

Fathi, S., Ahmadi, M., & Dehnad, A. (2022). Early diagnosis of Alzheimer's disease based on deep learning: A systematic review. *Computers in Biology and Medicine*, *146*, 105634. doi:10.1016/j.compbiomed.2022.105634 PMID:35605488

Hazarika, R. A., Maji, A. K., Kandar, D., Jasinska, E., Krejci, P., Leonowicz, Z., & Jasinski, M. (2023). An Approach for Classification of Alzheimer's Disease Using Deep Neural Network and Brain Magnetic Resonance Imaging (MRI). *Electronics (Basel)*, *12*(3), 3. doi:10.3390/electronics12030676

Ho, S. Y.-C., Chien, T.-W., Lin, M.-L., & Tsai, K.-T. (2023). An app for predicting patient dementia classes using convolutional neural networks (CNN) and artificial neural networks (ANN): Comparison of prediction accuracy in Microsoft Excel. *Medicine*, *102*(4), e32670. doi:10.1097/MD.0000000000032670 PMID:36705387

Hoops, S., Nazem, S., Siderowf, A. D., Duda, J. E., Xie, S. X., Stern, M. B., & Weintraub, D. (2009). Validity of the MoCA and MMSE in the detection of MCI and dementia in Parkinson disease. *Neurology*, *73*(21), 1738–1745. doi:10.1212/WNL.0b013e3181c34b47 PMID:19933974

Geeks for Geeks. (n.d.). *Image Classification using Google's Teachable Machine*. GeeksforGeeks. https://www.geeksforgeeks.org/image-classification-using-googles-teachable-machine/

Introduction—Free IP Geolocation by geoPlugin. (n.d.). Geoplugin. https://www.geoplugin.com/introduction

Iodice, F., Cassano, V., & Rossini, P. M. (2021). Direct and indirect neurological, cognitive, and behavioral effects of COVID-19 on the healthy elderly, mild-cognitive-impairment, and Alzheimer's disease populations. *Neurological Sciences*, *42*(2), 455–465. doi:10.100710072-020-04902-8 PMID:33409824

Jahn, H. (2013). Memory loss in Alzheimer's disease. *Dialogues in Clinical Neuroscience*, *15*(4), 445–454. doi:10.31887/DCNS.2013.15.4/hjahn PMID:24459411

Javeed, A., Moraes, A. L., Berglund, J., Ali, A., Anderberg, P., & Ali, L. (2023). Predicting Dementia Risk Factors Based on Feature Selection and Neural Networks. *Computers, Materials & Continua*, *75*(2), 2491–2508. doi:10.32604/cmc.2023.033783

Jia, J., Xu, J., Liu, J., Wang, Y., Wang, Y., Cao, Y., Guo, Q., Qu, Q., Wei, C., Wei, W., Zhang, J., & Yu, E. (2021). Comprehensive Management of Daily Living Activities, behavioral and Psychological Symptoms, and Cognitive Function in Patients with Alzheimer's Disease: A Chinese Consensus on the Comprehensive Management of Alzheimer's Disease. *Neuroscience Bulletin*, *37*(7), 1025–1038. doi:10.100712264-021-00701-z PMID:34050523

Kang, Y., Na, D.-L., & Hahn, S. (1997). A validity study on the Korean Mini-Mental State Examination (K-MMSE) in dementia patients. *Journal of the Korean Neurological Association*, 300–308.

Krizhevsky, A., Sutskever, I., & Hinton, G. E. (2012). Imagenet classification with deep convolutional neural networks. *Advances in Neural Information Processing Systems*, 25.

Kumar, V., Singh, R., & Dua, Y. (2021). Morphologically dilated convolutional neural network for hyperspectral image classification. *Signal Processing Image Communication*, *101*, 116549. doi:10.1016/j.image.2021.116549

Lanzi, A. M., Ellison, J. M., & Cohen, M. L. (2021). The "Counseling+" Roles of the Speech-Language Pathologist Serving Older Adults With Mild Cognitive Impairment and Dementia From Alzheimer's Disease. *Perspectives of the ASHA Special Interest Groups*, *6*(5), 987–1002. doi:10.1044/2021_PERSP-20-00295 PMID:35647292

Lesoil, C., Bombois, S., Guinebretiere, O., Houot, M., Bahrami, M., Levy, M., Genthon, R., Bozon, F., Jean-Marie, H., Epelbaum, S., Foulon, P., Villain, N., & Dubois, B. (2023). Validation study of "Santé-Cerveau", a digital tool for early cognitive changes identification. *Alzheimer's Research & Therapy*, *15*(1), 70. doi:10.118613195-023-01204-x PMID:37013590

Li, Y., Guo, J., & Yang, P. (2022). Developing an Image-Based Deep Learning Framework for Automatic Scoring of the Pentagon Drawing Test. *Journal of Alzheimer's Disease*, *85*(1), 129–139. doi:10.3233/JAD-210714 PMID:34776440

Martínez-Nicolás, I., Llorente, T. E., Martínez-Sánchez, F., & Meilán, J. J. G. (2021). Ten Years of Research on Automatic Voice and Speech Analysis of People With Alzheimer's Disease and Mild Cognitive Impairment: A Systematic Review Article. *Frontiers in Psychology*, *12*, 620251. doi:10.3389/fpsyg.2021.620251 PMID:33833713

Mezzi, R., Yahyaoui, A., Krir, M. W., Boulila, W., & Koubaa, A. (2022). Mental Health Intent Recognition for Arabic-Speaking Patients Using the Mini International Neuropsychiatric Interview (MINI) and BERT Model. *Sensors (Basel)*, *22*(3), 3. doi:10.339022030846 PMID:35161594

Mini-Mental State Exam (MMSE) Test for Alzheimer's / Dementia. (n.d.). Dementia Care Central. https://www.dementiacarecentral.com/mini-mental-state-exam/

Narasimhan, R., G., M., & McGlade, C. (2021). Current State of Non-wearable Sensor Technologies for Monitoring Activity Patterns to Detect Symptoms of Mild Cognitive Impairment to Alzheimer's Disease. *International Journal of Alzheimer's Disease*. doi:10.1155/2021/2679398

Orouskhani, M., Zhu, C., Rostamian, S., Shomal Zadeh, F., Shafiei, M., & Orouskhani, Y. (2022). Alzheimer's disease detection from structural MRI using conditional deep triplet network. *Neuroscience Informatics (Online)*, *2*(4), 100066. doi:10.1016/j.neuri.2022.100066

Qiao, H., Chen, L., & Zhu, F. (2022). Ranking convolutional neural network for Alzheimer's disease mini-mental state examination prediction at multiple time-points. *Computer Methods and Programs in Biomedicine, 213*, 106503. doi:10.1016/j.cmpb.2021.106503 PMID:34798407

Saleem, T. J., Zahra, S. R., Wu, F., Alwakeel, A., Alwakeel, M., Jeribi, F., & Hijji, M. (2022). Deep Learning-Based Diagnosis of Alzheimer's Disease. *Journal of Personalized Medicine, 12*(5), 5. Advance online publication. doi:10.3390/jpm12050815 PMID:35629237

Sato, K., Niimi, Y., Mano, T., Iwata, A., & Iwatsubo, T. (2022). Automated Evaluation of Conventional Clock-Drawing Test Using Deep Neural Network: Potential as a Mass Screening Tool to Detect Individuals With Cognitive Decline. *Frontiers in Neurology, 13*, 896403. doi:10.3389/fneur.2022.896403 PMID:35592474

Sharma, T., Nair, R., & Gomathi, S. (2022). Breast Cancer Image Classification using Transfer Learning and Convolutional Neural Network. *International Journal of Modern Research, 2*(1), 1.

Souillard-Mandar, W., Penney, D., Schaible, B., Pascual-Leone, A., Au, R., & Davis, R. (2021). DCTclock: Clinically-Interpretable and Automated Artificial Intelligence Analysis of Drawing Behavior for Capturing Cognition. *Frontiers in Digital Health, 3*, 750661. doi:10.3389/fdgth.2021.750661 PMID:34723243

Tahami Monfared, A. A., Byrnes, M. J., White, L. A., & Zhang, Q. (2022). Alzheimer's Disease: Epidemiology and Clinical Progression. *Neurology and Therapy, 11*(2), 553–569. doi:10.100740120-022-00338-8 PMID:35286590

Tasaki S. Kim N. Truty T. Zhang A. Buchman A. S. Lamar M. Bennett D. A. (2023). Interpretable deep learning approach for extracting cognitive features from hand-drawn images of intersecting pentagons in older adults. doi:10.1101/2023.04.18.537358

Tian X. Liu J. Kuang H. Sheng Y. Wang J. Initiative T. A. D. N. (2022). MRI-based Multi-task Decoupling Learning for Alzheimer's Disease Detection and MMSE Score Prediction: A Multi-site Validation. https://arxiv.org/abs/2204.01708

Wang, J., Yang, J., Zhang, H., Lu, H., Skreta, M., Husić, M., Arbabi, A., Sultanum, N., & Brudno, M. (2022). PhenoPad: Building AI enabled note-taking interfaces for patient encounters. *NPJ Digital Medicine, 5*(1), 1. doi:10.103841746-021-00555-9 PMID:35087180

Yamada, Y., Shinkawa, K., Nemoto, M., Nemoto, K., & Arai, T. (2023). A mobile application using automatic speech analysis for classifying Alzheimer's disease and mild cognitive impairment. *Computer Speech & Language, 81*, 101514. doi:10.1016/j.csl.2023.101514

Zhou, Y., Li, Z., Ma, Y., Yu, C., Chen, Y., Ding, J., Yu, J., Zhou, R., Wang, X., Liu, T., Guo, X., Fan, T., & Shi, C. (2022). The Effect of Propofol versus Sevoflurane on Postoperative Delirium in Parkinson's Disease Patients Undergoing Deep Brain Stimulation Surgery: An Observational Study. *Brain Sciences, 12*(6), 6. doi:10.3390/brainsci12060689 PMID:35741575

Compilation of References

Aazam, M., & Huh, E. N. (2014). Fog computing and smart gateway based communication for cloud of things. In *Proceedings of the 2nd IEEE International Conference on Future Internet of Things and Cloud (FiCloud' 14)*, (pp. 464–470). IEEE. 10.1109/FiCloud.2014.83

Abdulhadi, N., & Al-Mousa, A. (2021). Diabetes detection using machine learning classification methods. In 2021 International Conference on Information Technology (ICIT), (pp. 350–354). IEEE. 10.1109/ICIT52682.2021.9491788

Achenbach, P., Hippich, M., Zapardiel-Gonzalo, J., Karges, B., Holl, R. W., Petrera, A., Bonifacio, E., & Ziegler, A.-G. (2022). A classification and regression tree analysis identifies subgroups of childhood type 1 diabetes. *EBioMedicine*, 82, 104118. doi:10.1016/j.ebiom.2022.104118 PMID:35803018

Adam, E., Mutanga, O., Odindi, J., & Abdel-Rahman, E. M. (2014). Land-use/cover classification in a heterogeneous coastal landscape using RapidEye imagery: Evaluating the performance of random forest and support vector machines classifiers. *International Journal of Remote Sensing*, 35(10), 3440–3458. doi:10.1080/01431161.2014.903435

ADI - Dementia statistics. (n.d.). Alzheimer's Disease International. https://www.alzint.org/about/dementia-facts-figures/dementia-statistics/

Agievich, V. (2014). *Mathematical model and multi-criteria analysis of designing large-scale enterprise roadmap*. IGI Global.

Ahammad, S. H., Rajesh, V., Hanumatsai, N., Venumadhav, A., Sasank, N. S. S., Gupta, K. B., & Inithiyaz, S. (2019). MRI image training and finding acute spine injury with the help of hemorrhagic and non hemorrhagic rope wounds method. *Indian Journal of Public Health Research & Development*, 10(7), 404. doi:10.5958/0976-5506.2019.01603.6

Ahammad, S. H., Rajesh, V., Indumathi, U., & Charan, A. S. (2019). Identification of cervical spondylosis disease on spinal cord mri image using convolutional neural network-long short-term memory (Cnn-lstm) technique. *Journal of International Pharmaceutical Research*, 46, 109–124.

Ahammad, S. H., Rajesh, V., Neetha, A., Sai Jeesmitha, B., & Srikanth, A. (2019). Automatic segmentation of spinal cord diffusion MR images for disease location finding. *Indonesian Journal of Electrical Engineering and Computer Science*, 15(3), 1313–1321. doi:10.11591/ijeecs.v15.i3.pp1313-1321

Ahammad, S. H., Rajesh, V., & Rahman, M. Z. U. (2019). Fast and accurate feature extraction-based segmentation framework for spinal cord injury severity classification. *IEEE Access : Practical Innovations, Open Solutions*, 7, 46092–46103. doi:10.1109/ACCESS.2019.2909583

Ahammad, S. H., Rajesh, V., Rahman, M. Z. U., & Lay-Ekuakille, A. (2020). A hybrid CNN-based segmentation and boosting classifier for real time sensor spinal cord injury data. *IEEE Sensors Journal*, 20(17), 10092–10101. doi:10.1109/JSEN.2020.2992879

Ahammad, S. H., Rajesh, V., Venkatesh, K. N., Nagaraju, P., Rao, P. R., & Inthiyaz, S. (2019). Liver segmentation using abdominal CT scanning to detect liver disease area. *International Journal of Emerging Trends in Engineering Research*, 7(11), 664–669. doi:10.30534/ijeter/2019/417112019

Ahammad, S. K., & Rajesh, V. (2018). Image processing based segmentation techniques for spinal cord in MRI. *Indian Journal of Public Health Research & Development*, 9(6), 317. doi:10.5958/0976-5506.2018.00571.5

Ahan, S., Polat, K., Kodaz, H., & Gne, S. (2005). The medical applications of attribute weighted artificial immune system (awais): Diagnosis of heart and diabetes diseases. *Lecture Notes in Computer Science*, 456468.

Ahmad, M. O., & Siddiqui, S. T. (2022). The Internet of Things for Healthcare: Benefits, Applications, Challenges, Use Cases and Future Directions. In *Advances in Data and Information Sciences* (pp. 527–537). Springer. doi:10.1007/978-981-16-5689-7_46

Ahmed, S. T., Kumar, V. V., & Kim, J. (2023). AITel: eHealth Augmented Intelligence based Telemedicine Resource Recommendation Framework for IoT devices in Smart cities. *IEEE Internet of Things Journal*, 1, 1. Advance online publication. doi:10.1109/JIOT.2023.3243784

Alex, D. S., Mahesh, T. R., Kumar, V. V., Aluvalu, R., Maheswari, V. U., & Shitharth, S. (2022). Cervical Cancer Diagnosis Using Intelligent Living Behavior of Artificial Jellyfish Optimized With Artificial Neural Network. *IEEE Access : Practical Innovations, Open Solutions*, 10, 126957–126968. doi:10.1109/ACCESS.2022.3221451

Ali, Z., Hossain, M. S., Muhammad, G., & Sangaiah, A. K. (2018). An intelligent healthcare system for detection and classification to discriminate vocal fold disorders. *Future Generation Computer Systems*, 85, 19–28. doi:10.1016/j.future.2018.02.021

AlJahdali, H., Albatli, A., Garraghan, P., Townend, P., Lau, L., & Xu, J. (2014, April). Multi-tenancy in cloud computing. In *2014 IEEE 8th international symposium on service oriented system engineering* (pp. 344-351). IEEE. 10.1109/SOSE.2014.50

Aljahdali, H., Townend, P., & Xu, J. (2013, March). Enhancing multi-tenancy security in the cloud IaaS model over public deployment. In *2013 IEEE seventh international symposium on service-oriented system engineering* (pp. 385-390). IEEE. 10.1109/SOSE.2013.50

Allah, L. & Shimshoni, I. (2012). k Nearest Neighbor using Ensemble Clustering. In Data Warehousing and Knowledge Discovery. Springer Nature Switzerland AG.

Almahmouda, M., Alzu'bib, D., & Yaseen, Q. (2021). "ReDroidDet: Android Malware Detection Based on Recurrent Neural Network", Science Direct, *The 2nd International Workshop on Data-Driven Security (DDSW 2021)*, Warsaw, Poland. *Procedia Computer Science*, 184, 841–846. doi:10.1016/j.procs.2021.03.105

Alsaadi, E., & Tubaishat, A. (2015). Internet of things: Features, challenges, and vulnerabilities. *International Journal of Advanced Computer Science and Information Technology*, 4(1), 1–13.

Alshari, E. A., & Gawali, B. W. (2021). Development of classification system for LULC using remote sensing and GIS. *Global Transitions Proceedings*, 2(1), 8–17. doi:10.1016/j.gltp.2021.01.002

Altay, E. &. (2005). Stock market forecasting: Artificial neural networks and linear regression comparison in an emerging market *Journal of Financial Management and Analysis*.

Althelaya, K. A., E.-S.-M. E.-A. (Apr. 2018). Evaluation ofbidirectional LSTM for short-and longterm stock market prediction. *inProc. 9th Int. Conf. Inf. Commun. Syst. (ICICS)*. IEEE.

Amani, M., Ghorbanian, A., Ahmadi, S. A., Kakooei, M., Moghimi, A., Mirmazloumi, S. M., Moghaddam, S. H. A., Mahdavi, S., Ghahremanloo, M., Parsian, S., Wu, Q., & Brisco, B. (2020). Google earth engine cloud computing platform for remote sensing big data applications: A comprehensive review. *IEEE Journal of Selected Topics in Applied Earth Observations and Remote Sensing, 13*, 5326–5350. doi:10.1109/JSTARS.2020.3021052

Anandhavalli, M. S. K. (2009). *Optimized association rule mining using genetic algorithm.* Advances in Information Mining.

Anand, R., Singh, J., Pandey, D., Pandey, B. K., Nassa, V. K., & Pramanik, S. (2022). Modern Technique for Interactive Communication in LEACH-Based Ad Hoc Wireless Sensor Network. In M. M. Ghonge, S. Pramanik, & A. D. Potgantwar (Eds.), *Software Defined Networking for Ad Hoc Networks.* Springer. doi:10.1007/978-3-030-91149-2_3

Andersen, T. B. (2018). Intraday trading variance in the E-Mini S&P 500 futures market. *Social Science Research Network.*

Andrew, G. (2017). *MobileNets: Efficient Convolutional Neural Networks for Mobile Vision Applications.* Cornell University. https://arxiv.org/abs/1704.04861

Arathi, S., & Johnson, R. F. (2021). Predicting the number of new cases of COVID-19 in India using Survival Analysis and LSTM. *2021 Fifth International Conference on I-SMAC (IoT in Social, Mobile, Analytics and Cloud) (I-SMAC),* (pp. 1-4). IEEE. 10.1109/I-SMAC52330.2021.9640899

Archip, N., Erard, P. J., Egmont-Petersen, M., Haefliger, J. M., & Germond, J. F. (2002). A knowledge-based approach to automatic detection of the spinal cord in CT images. *IEEE Transactions on Medical Imaging, 21*(12), 1504–1516. doi:10.1109/TMI.2002.806578 PMID:12588034

Arlt, S. (2013). Non-Alzheimer's disease—Related memory impairment and dementia. *Dialogues in Clinical Neuroscience, 15*(4), 465–473. doi:10.31887/DCNS.2013.15.4arlt PMID:24459413

Arun Kumar, K., Rajalakshmi, R., & Shashikala, H. K. (2022). Gestational Diabetes Detection Using Machine Learning Algorithm: Research Challenges of Big Data and Data Mining. *International Journal of Intelligent Systems And Applications In Engineering, 10*(2s), 260–263.

Ashokkumar, P., & Don, S. (2019). Link-based clustering algorithm for clustering web documents. *Journal of Testing and Evaluation, 47*(6), 20180497. doi:10.1520/JTE20180497

Ashour, A. S., Nour, M. K. A., Polat, K., Guo, Y., Alsaggaf, W., & El-Attar, A. (2020). A novel framework of two successive feature selection levels using weight-based procedure for voice-loss detection in parkinsons disease. *IEEE Access : Practical Innovations, Open Solutions, 8*, 76193–76203. doi:10.1109/ACCESS.2020.2989032

Atzori, L., Iera, A., & Morabito, G. (2011). IoT: Giving a social structure to the internet of things. *IEEE Communications Letters, 15*(11), 1193–1195. doi:10.1109/LCOMM.2011.090911.111340

Ayad, A., Farag, H. E., Youssef, A., & El-Saadany, E. F. (2018). Detection of false data injection attacks in smart grids using recurrent neural networks. In 2018 IEEE Power & Energy Society Innovative Smart Grid Technologies Conference (ISGT). IEEE.

Baader, F., Calvanese, D., McGuinness, D., Nardi, D., & Patel-Schneider, P. (Eds.). (2002). *The Description Logic Handbook.* Cambridge University Press.

Babu, M. V., & Sreedevi, M. (2021). *A Comprehensive Study on Enhanced Clustering Technique of Association Rules over Transactional Datasets.* 2021 Fifth International Conference on I-SMAC (IoT in Social, Mobile, Analytics and Cloud) (I-SMAC), Palladam, India. 10.1109/I-SMAC52330.2021.9640681

Babu, M. V., & Sreedevi, M. (2022). Performance Analysis on Advances in Frequent Pattern Growth Algorithm. *2022 International Conference on Advances in Computing, Communication and Applied Informatics (ACCAI)*, Chennai, India. 10.1109/ACCAI53970.2022.9752650

Badawi, E., & Seddig, Y. (2016). Design and Implementation of ISRASAT1 Cube Satellite Structure. *Third International African CubeSat Workshop*, Cape Peninsula University of Technology, Cape Town.

Bala, R., Gill, B., Smith, D., Wright, D., & Ji, K. (2021). *Magic Quadrant for Cloud Infrastructure and Platform Services.* Gartner Inc. https://www.gartner.com/doc/reprints?id=1-271SYZF2&ct=210802&st=sb

Bandara, R., Fernando, M., & Akter, S. (2020). Addressing privacy predicaments in the digital marketplace: A power-relations perspective. *International Journal of Consumer Studies*, *44*(5), 423–434. doi:10.1111/ijcs.12576

Bansal, R., Jenipher, B., Nisha, V., Pramanik, S., Roy, S., & Gupta, A. (2022). Big Data Architecture for Network Security, in Cyber Security and Network Security. Wiley.

Bansal, R., Obaid, A. J., Gupta, A., Singh, R., & Pramanik, S. (2021). Impact of Big Data on Digital Transformation in 5G Era. *2nd International Conference on Physics and Applied Sciences (ICPAS 2021).* IEEE. 10.1088/1742-6596/1963/1/012170

Bao, W., Yue, J., & Rao, Y. (2017, July). A deep learning framework for financial timeseries using stacked autoencoders and long-short term memory. *PLoS One*, *12*(7), e0180944. doi:10.1371/journal.pone.0180944 PMID:28708865

Barentsz, J., Takahashi, S., Oyen, W., Mus, R., De Mulder, P., Reznek, R., Oudkerk, M., & Mali, W. (2006). Commonly used imaging techniques for diagnosis and staging. *Journal of Clinical Oncology*, *24*(20), 3234–3244. doi:10.1200/JCO.2006.06.5946 PMID:16829647

Barnaghi, P., Presser, M., & Moessner, K. (2010). Publishing Linked Sensor Data. In *Proceedings of the 3rd International Workshop on Semantic Sensor Networks*. IEEE.

Barnett, A. (2001). Safety in numbers may not be enough. *News Scientist.* https://www.newscientist.com/article/mg16922764-000-safety-in-numbers-may-not-be-enough/

Basodi, S., Tan, S., Song, W., & Pan, Y. (2020). Data integrity attack detection in smart grid: A deep learning approach. *International Journal of Security and Networks*, *15*(1), 15–24. doi:10.1504/IJSN.2020.106506

Berners-Lee, T. (2000). *Weaving the Web: The Original Design and Ultimate Design of the World Wide Web by its inventor.* Harper Business.

Bethel, D. (1997). *Optimisation of still image compression techniques* [Ph.D. Thesis]. Bath University.

Bethencourt, J., Sahai, A., & Waters, B. (2007, May). Ciphertext-policy attribute-based encryption. In 2007 IEEE symposium on security and privacy (SP'07) (pp. 321-334). IEEE. doi:10.1109/SP.2007.11

Bharadwaj, S. P., Subramanian, S., Manda, S., Ray, T. A. N. I. Y. A., Mukherjee, P. R. A. B. I. R., & Rao, I. R. (2003). Bamboo livelihood development planning, monitoring and analysis through GIS and remote sensing. *Journal of Bamboo and Rattan*, *2*(4), 453–461. doi:10.1163/156915903322700476

Bhargavi, P., & Jyothi, S. (2009). Applying naive bayes data mining technique for classification of agricultural land soils. *International journal of computer science and network security, 9*(8), 117-122.

Bhattacharya, A., Ghosal, A., Obaid, A. J., Krit, S., Shukla, V. K., Mandal, K., & Pramanik, S. (2021). Unsupervised Summarization Approach with Computational Statistics of Microblog Data. In D. Samanta, R. R. Althar, S. Pramanik, & S. Dutta (Eds.), *Methodologies and Applications of Computational Statistics for Machine Learning* (pp. 23–37). IGI Global. doi:10.4018/978-1-7998-7701-1.ch002

Binaco, R., Calzaretto, N., Epifano, J., McGuire, S., Umer, M., Emrani, S., Wasserman, V., Libon, D. J., & Polikar, R. (2020). Machine Learning Analysis of Digital Clock Drawing Test Performance for Differential Classification of Mild Cognitive Impairment Subtypes Versus Alzheimer's Disease. *Journal of the International Neuropsychological Society*, *26*(7), 690–700. doi:10.1017/S1355617720000144 PMID:32200771

Boghey, R., & Singh, S. (2013). Sequential Pattern Mining: A Survey on Approaches. *2013 International Conference on Communication Systems and Network Technologies*, (pp. 670-674). IEEE. 10.1109/CSNT.2013.142

Bonomi, F., Milito, R., Natarajan, P., & Zhu, J. (2014). Fog computing: a platform for internet of things and analytics. In Big Data and Internet of Things: A Road Map for Smart Environments. Springer.

Bonomi, F., Milito, R., Zhu, J., & Addepalli, S. (2012). Fog computing and its role in the internet of things. In *Proceedings of the 1st ACM MCC Workshop on Mobile Cloud Computing*, (pp. 13–16). ACM. 10.1145/2342509.2342513

Bordel Sánchez, B., Alcarria, R., Sánchez de Rivera, D., & Robles, T. (2018). Process execution in CyberPhysical Systems using cloud and Cyber-Physical Internet services. *The Journal of Supercomputing*, *74*(8), 4127–4169. doi:10.100711227-018-2416-4

Bourke, J., Castleden, C. M., Stephen, R., & Dennis, M. (1995). A comparison of clock and pentagon drawing in Alzheimer's disease. *International Journal of Geriatric Psychiatry*, *10*(8), 703–705. doi:10.1002/gps.930100811

Broy, M., Cengarle, M. V., & Geisberger, E. (2012). Cyber-Physical Systems: Imminent Challenges. In *Large-Scale Complex IT Syst. Dev., Operat. and Manag*. Research Gate.

Buettner, R., Bilo, M., Bay, N., & Zubac, T. (2020). A Systematic Literature Review of Medical Image Analysis Using Deep Learning. *2020 IEEE Symposium on Industrial Electronics & Applications (ISIEA)*, (pp. 1-4). IEEE. 10.1109/ISIEA49364.2020.9188131

Burger, W., Burge, M. J., Burge, M. J., & Burge, M. J. (2009). *Principles of digital image processing* (Vol. 111). Springer.

Buyya, R., Vecchiola, C., & Selvi, S. T. (2013). *Mastering cloud computing: foundations and applications programming*. Newnes.

Caliskan, A., Yuksel, M., Badem, H., & Basturk, A. (2018). Performance improvement of deep neural network classifiers by a simple training strategy. *Engineering Applications of Artificial Intelligence*, *67*, 1423. doi:10.1016/j.engappai.2017.09.002

Campbell, S., Greenwood, M., Prior, S., Shearer, T., Walkem, K., Young, S., Bywaters, D., & Walker, K. (2020). Purposive sampling: Complex or simple? Research case examples. *Journal of Research in Nursing*, *25*(8), 652–661. doi:10.1177/1744987120927206 PMID:34394687

Campomanes, F., Pada, A. V., & Silapan, J. (2016). *Mangrove classification using support vector machines and random forest algorithm: a comparative study*.

Cardoso, J., Sheth, A., Miller, J., Arnold, J., & Kochut, K. (2004). Quality of service for workflows and web service processes. *Journal of Web Semantics*, *1*(3), 281–308. doi:10.1016/j.websem.2004.03.001

Çarkacı, N. & Sogukpına, I. (2016). Frequency-based metamorphic malware detection. *IEEE 2016 24th Signal Processing and Communication Application Conference (SIU)*. IEEE. doi:10.1109/SIU.2016.7495767

Ceballos, G., Ehrlich, P. R., Barnosky, A. D., García, A., Pringle, R. M., & Palmer, T. M. (2015). Accelerated modern human-induced species losses: Entering the sixth mass extinction. *Science Advances*, *1*(5), 1–5. doi:10.1126ciadv.1400253 PMID:26601195

Cecato, J. F. (2016). Pentagon Drawing Test: Some data from Alzheimer's disease, Paraphrenia and Obsessive compulsive disorder in elderly patients. *Perspectivas En Psicología: Revista de Psicología y Ciencias Afines, 13*(2), 21–26.

Chaitanya Reddy, P., Chandra, R. M. S., Vadiraj, P., Ayyappa Reddy, M., Mahesh, T. R., & Sindhu Madhuri, G. (2021). Detection of Plant Leaf-based Diseases Using Machine Learning Approach. *2021 IEEE International Conference on Computation System and Information Technology for Sustainable Solutions (CSITSS)*, (pp. 1-4). IEEE. 10.1109/CSITSS54238.2021.9683020

Chalmers, C., Fergus, P., Wich, S., & Montanez, A. (2019). *Conservation AI: Live Stream Analysis for the Detection of Endangered Species Using Convolutional Neural Networks and Drone Technology*. Academic Press.

Charles (2017). *Hosting and Cloud Software Delivery modelled in Archimate*. Agile Enterprise Architecture. https://agileea.com/2017/04/hosting-and-cloud-software-delivery-modelled-in-archimate/

Charles Leek, E., Leonardis, A., & Heinke, D. (2022). Deep neural networks and image classification in biological vision. *Vision Research, 197*, 108058. doi:10.1016/j.visres.2022.108058 PMID:35487146

Chaudhari, A. (2021). Smart Accident Detection and Alert System. Academic Press.

Chaudhary, B. S., Saroha, G. P., & Yadav, M. (2008). Human induced land use/land cover changes in northern part of Gurgaon district, Haryana, India: Natural resources census concept. *Journal of Human Ecology (Delhi, India), 23*(3), 243–252. doi:10.1080/09709274.2008.11906077

Che, R. P. (2009). Textual analysis of stock market prediction using breaking financial news. *The AZF in text system" ACM Trans. Inf.*

Cheng, H., Xue, L., Wang, P., Zeng, P., & Yu, H. (2017). Ontology-based web service integration for flexible manufacturing systems. In *15th Int. Conf. on Ind. Inf.*, (pp. 351–356). IEEE. 10.1109/INDIN.2017.8104797

Chen, L., Qiao, H., & Zhu, F. (2022). Alzheimer's Disease Diagnosis With Brain Structural MRI Using Multiview-Slice Attention and 3D Convolution Neural Network. *Frontiers in Aging Neuroscience, 14*, 871706. doi:10.3389/fnagi.2022.871706 PMID:35557839

Chen, P. Y., Yang, S., McCann, J. A., Lin, J., & Yang, X. (2015). Detection of false data injection attacks in smart-grid system. *IEEE Communications Magazine, 53*(2), 206–213. doi:10.1109/MCOM.2015.7045410

Chen, Y., Jin, B., Yu, D., & Chen, J. (2018). Malware Variants Detection Using Behavior Destructive Features. *2018 IEEE Symposium on Privacy-Aware Computing (PAC)*, (pp. 121-122). IEEE. 10.1109/PAC.2018.00020

Chollet, F. (2017). Xception: Deep Learning with Depth wise Separable Convolutions. *IEEE Conference on Computer Vision and Pattern Recognition (CVPR)*. IEEE. 10.48550/arXiv.1610.02357

Choudhary, S., Narayan, V., Faiz, M., & Pramanik, S. (2022). Fuzzy Approach-Based Stable Energy-Efficient AODV Routing Protocol in Mobile Ad hoc Networks. In M. M. Ghonge, S. Pramanik, & A. D. Potgantwar (Eds.), *Software Defined Networking for Ad Hoc Networks*. Springer. doi:10.1007/978-3-030-91149-2_6

Choudhary, S., & Sharma, A. (2020). Malware Detection & Classification using Machine Learning. *2020 International Conference on Emerging Trends in Communication, Control and Computing (ICONC3)*, (pp. 1-4). IEEE. 10.1109/ICONC345789.2020.9117547

Choudhry, R. G. K. (2008). A hybrid machine learning system for stock market forecasting. *World Academy of Science, Engineering and Technology*, 315–318.

Ciortea, A., Mayer, S., & Michahelles, F. (2018). Repurposing Manufacturing Lines on the Fly with Multi-agent Systems for the Web of Things. In *Proc. of the 17th Int. Conf. on Autonomous Agents and Multi-Agent Systems,* (pp. 813–822). Int. Found. for Autonomous Agents and Multiagent Systems / ACM.

CITES. (n.d.). History of CITES listing of sharks (Elasmobranchii). *Cites.* https://www.cites.org/eng/prog/shark/history.php

Cloud Computing Patterns. (2022). *Private Cloud.* Cloud Computing Patterns. https://www.cloudcomputingpatterns.org/private_cloud/

Colitti, W., Steenhaut, K., Caro, N. De., (2011). *Integrating Wireless Sensor Networks with the Web.* Extending the Internet to Low power and Lossy Networks (IP+SN).

Colucci, S., Di Noia, T., Pinto, A., Ruta, M., Ragone, A., & Tinelli, E. (2007). A Nonmonotonic Approach to Semantic Matchmaking and Request Refinement in E-Marketplaces. *International Journal of Electronic Commerce, 12*(2), 127–154. doi:10.2753/JEC1086-4415120205

Cory, A., Henson, J., Pschorr, K., Sheth, A. P., & Thirunarayan, K. (2009). SemSOS: Semantic sensor Observation Service. In *Proceedings of the International Symposium on Collaborative Technologies and Systems.* IEEE.

Coscia, M., & Rios, V. (2012). Knowing where and how criminal organizations operate using web content. *Proceedings of the 21st international conference on information and knowledge management* (pp.1412-1421). ACM. 10.1145/2396761.2398446

Counsell, C., Giuntoli, C., Khan, Q. I., Maple-Grødem, J., & Macleod, A. D. (2022). The incidence, baseline predictors, and outcomes of dementia in an incident cohort of Parkinson's disease and controls. *Journal of Neurology, 269*(8), 4288–4298. doi:10.100700415-022-11058-2 PMID:35307754

Courbis, C., & Finkelstein, A. (2005). Weaving Aspects into Web Service Orchestrations. In *Proceeding of International Conference of Web Services (ICWS '05).* IEEE. 10.1109/ICWS.2005.129

Creamer, S. a. (2007). *Automated trading with boosting and expert weighting.* Quant.

D'Angelo, G., Ficco, M., & Palmieri, F. (2020). Malware detection in mobile environments based on Autoencoders and API-images. *Journal of Parallel and Distributed Computing, 137,* 26–33. doi:10.1016/j.jpdc.2019.11.001

Daellenbach, H., & McNickle, D. (2012). *Management Science. Decision-making through systems thinking* (2nd ed.). Plagrave Macmillian.

Dalsania, A. K., Fastiggi, M. J., Kahlam, A., Shah, R., Patel, K., Shiau, S., Rokicki, S., & DallaPiazza, M. (2022). The Relationship Between Social Determinants of Health and Racial Disparities in COVID-19 Mortality. *Journal of Racial and Ethnic Health Disparities, 9*(1), 288–295. doi:10.100740615-020-00952-y PMID:33403652

Das, S., & Konar, A. (2009). Automatic image pixel clustering with an improved differential evolution. *Applied Soft Computing, 9*(1), 226–236. doi:10.1016/j.asoc.2007.12.008

Das, S., & Namasudra, S. (2022). A Novel Hybrid Encryption Method to Secure Healthcare Data in IoT-enabled Healthcare Infrastructure. *Computers & Electrical Engineering, 101,* 107991. doi:10.1016/j.compeleceng.2022.107991

De Virgilio, R., Di Sciascio, E., Ruta, M., Scioscia, F., & Torlone, R. (2011). Semantic-based rfid data management. In *Unique Radio Innovation for the 21st Century* (pp. 111–141). Springer. doi:10.1007/978-3-642-03462-6_6

Demeau, E., Vargas, M., & Jeffrey, K. (2019). Wildlife trafficking on the internet: A virtual market similar to drug trafficking? *Criminality Magazine, 61*(2), 101–112.

Deshmukh, Dubal, TR, & Chauhan. (2012). Data Security Analysis And Security Extension For Smart Cards Using Java Card. *International Journal of Advanced Information Technology, 2*(2).

Di Minin, E., Fink, C., Tenkanen, H., & Hiippala, T. (2018). Machine learning for tracking illegal wildlife trade on social media. *Nature Ecology & Evolution, 2*(3), 406–407. doi:10.103841559-018-0466-x PMID:29335570

Di Minin, E., Tenkanen, H., & Toivonen, T. (2015b). Prospects and challenges for social media data in conservation science. *Frontiers in Environmental Science, 3*, 63. doi:10.3389/fenvs.2015.00063

Digital Innovation Junction. (2020). Cloud Innovative Model. *Digital Innovation Junction.* https://www.digitalinnovationjunction.com/cloud-innovative-model/

Ding, W. M., Ghansah, B., & Wu, Y. Y. (2016). Research on the virtualization technology in cloud computing environment. In *International journal of engineering research in Africa* (Vol. 21, pp. 191–196). Trans Tech Publications Ltd.

Djenouri, Y., Drias, H., & Habbas, Z. (2014). Bees swarm optimisation using multiple strategies for association rule mining. *International Journal of Bio-inspired Computation, 6*(4), 239–249. doi:10.1504/IJBIC.2014.064990

Dubey, S, Vijay, S., & Pratibha. (2018). A Review of Image Segmentation using Clustering Methods. *International Journal of Applied Engineering Research, Research India Publications, 13*(5).

Eid, E., & Handal, R. (2017). Illegal hunting in Jordan: Using social media to assess impacts on wildlife. *Oryx.* doi:10.1017/S0030605316001629

Eini, SEiny, S. (2013). Image Segmentation using Gaussian Mixture Adaptive Fuzzy C-mean Clustering. *International Journal of Computer Science and Network Security, 13*(10), 114–118.

Eisavi, V., Homayouni, S., Yazdi, A. M., & Alimohammadi, A. (2015). Land cover mapping based on random forest classification of multitemporal spectral and thermal images. *Environmental Monitoring and Assessment, 187*(5), 1–14. doi:10.100710661-015-4489-3 PMID:25910718

Elayan, O. N., & Mustafa, A. M. (2021). Android Malware Detection Using Deep Learning. *Procedia Computer Science, 184*, 847–852. doi:10.1016/j.procs.2021.03.106

Elhariri, E., El-Bendary, N., & Taie, S. A. (2020). Using hybrid filter-wrapper feature selection with multi-objective improved-salp optimization for crack severity recognition. *IEEE Access : Practical Innovations, Open Solutions, 8*, 84290–84315. doi:10.1109/ACCESS.2020.2991968

Elmoataz, A. & Chahir, Y. (2005). Skin-color detection using fuzzy clustering. *Proceedings in ISCCSP.*

Erhan, D. B. Y. (2010). Why does unsupervised pre-training help deep learning. *Journal of Machine Learning Research.*

Esmalifalak, M., Liu, L., Nguyen, N., Zheng, R., & Han, Z. (2014). Detecting stealthy false data injection using machine learning in smart grid. *IEEE Systems Journal, 11*(3), 1644–1652. doi:10.1109/JSYST.2014.2341597

Farraj, A., Hammad, E., & Kundur, D. (2017). On the impact of cyber attacks on data integrity in storage-based transient stability control. *IEEE Transactions on Industrial Informatics, 13*(6), 3322–3333. doi:10.1109/TII.2017.2720679

Fathi, S., Ahmadi, M., & Dehnad, A. (2022). Early diagnosis of Alzheimer's disease based on deep learning: A systematic review. *Computers in Biology and Medicine, 146*, 105634. doi:10.1016/j.compbiomed.2022.105634 PMID:35605488

Ferreira, C. A., Gama, J., & Costa, V. S. (2008). RUSE-WARMR: Rule Selection for Classifier Induction in Multi-relational Data-Sets. *20th IEEE International Conference on Tools with Artificial Intelligence,* (pp. 379-386). IEEE. 10.1109/ICTAI.2008.73

FGCV. (2019). *CVPR 2019 Fine-Grained Visual Categorization*. iWildCam - FGVC6. kaggle.com/c/iwildcam-2019-fgvc6

Fischer, T., & Krauss, C. (2018). Deep learning with long short-term memory networks for financial market predictions. *European Journal of Operational Research*, *270*(2), 654–669. doi:10.1016/j.ejor.2017.11.054

Fradet, L., Arnoux, P. J., Ranjeva, J. P., Petit, Y., & Callot, V. (2014). Morphometrics of the entire human spinal cord and spinal canal measured from in vivo high-resolution anatomical magnetic resonance imaging. *Spine*, *39*(4), E262–E269. doi:10.1097/BRS.0000000000000125 PMID:24253776

Frehill, P., Chambers, D., & Rotariu, C. (2007, August). Using zigbee to integrate medical devices. In *2007 29th Annual International Conference of the IEEE Engineering in Medicine and Biology Society* (pp. 6717-6720). IEEE. 10.1109/IEMBS.2007.4353902

Friedl, M. A., & Brodley, C. E. (1997). Decision tree classification of land cover from remotely sensed data. *Remote Sensing of Environment*, *61*(3), 399–409. doi:10.1016/S0034-4257(97)00049-7

Gattim, N. K., Pallerla, S. R., Bojja, P., Reddy, T. P. K., Chowdary, V. N., Dhiraj, V., & Ahammad, S. H. (2019). Plant leaf disease detection using SVM technique. *International Journal of Emerging Trends in Engineering Research*, *7*(11), 634–637. doi:10.30534/ijeter/2019/367112019

Gautam, K., & Singhai, R. (2018). Color Image Segmentation Using Particle Swarm Optimization in Lab Color Space. *International Journal of Engineering Development and Research*, *6*(1), 373-377.

Ge, L., Yu, W., Moulema, P., Xu, G., Griffith, D., & Golmie, N. (2017). Detecting Data Integrity Attacks in Smart Grid. *Security and Privacy in Cyber-Physical Systems: Foundations, Principles and Applications*, 281-303.

Geeks for Geeks. (n.d.). *Image Classification using Google's Teachable Machine*. GeeksforGeeks. https://www.geeksforgeeks.org/image-classification-using-googles-teachable-machine/

Ghosh, P., & Mahesh, T. R. (2016). A privacy preserving mutual authentication protocol for RFID based automated toll collection system. *2016 International Conference on ICT in Business Industry & Government (ICTBIG)*, 1-5, 10.1109/ICTBIG.2016.7892668

Giani, A., Bitar, E., Garcia, M., McQueen, M., Khargonekar, P., & Poolla, K. (2013). Smart grid data integrity attacks. *IEEE Transactions on Smart Grid*, *4*(3), 1244–1253. doi:10.1109/TSG.2013.2245155

Gislason, P. O., Benediktsson, J. A., & Sveinsson, J. R. (2006). Random forests for land cover classification. *Pattern Recognition Letters*, *27*(4), 294–300. doi:10.1016/j.patrec.2005.08.011

Goel, N., Yadav, A., & Singh, B. M. (2016). *Medical image processing: A review. Second International Innovative Applications of Computational Intelligence on Power, Energy and Controls with their Impact on Humanity*. CIPECH. doi:10.1109/CIPECH.2016.7918737

Google. (2022a). *Cloud for financial services*. Google. https://cloud.google.com/solutions/financial-services

Google. (2022b). *Where should I run my stuff? Choosing a Google Cloud compute option*. Google Cloud. https://cloud.google.com/blog/topics/developers-practitioners/where-should-i-run-my-stuff-choosing-google-cloud-compute-option

Goralski, W. (2017). *The illustrated network: how TCP/IP works in a modern network*. Morgan Kaufmann.

Gorelick, N., Hancher, M., Dixon, M., Ilyushchenko, S., Thau, D., & Moore, R. (2017). Google Earth Engine: Planetary-scale geospatial analysis for everyone. *Remote Sensing of Environment*, *202*, 18–27. doi:10.1016/j.rse.2017.06.031

Goswami, J., Tajo, L., & Sarma, K. K. (2010). Bamboo resources mapping using satellite technology. *Current Science*, 650–653.

Government of Australia. (2004). *October 2, 2004: A Single Day Snapshot of the Trade in Great White Shark (Carcharadon carcharias).* CITES. https://cites.org/common/cop/13/inf/E13i51.pdf

Gowramma, G. S., Mahesh, T. R., & Gowda, G. (2017). An automatic system for IVF data classification by utilizing multilayer perceptron algorithm. *ICCTEST, 2017*(2), 667–672. doi:10.21647/ICCTEST/2017/49043

Gravina, R., Alinia, P., Ghasemzadeh, H., & Fortino, G. (2017). Multi-sensor fusion in body sensor networks: State-of-the-art and research challenges. *Information Fusion, 35*, 68–80. doi:10.1016/j.inffus.2016.09.005

Green, J. (2020). *Google Cloud GCPAIE: Hyper-Accessible AI & Machine Learning.* Towards Data Science.

Gubbi, J., Buyya, R., Marusic, S., & Palaniswami, M. (2013). Internet of Things (IoT): A vision, architectural elements, and future directions. *Future Generation Computer Systems, 29*(7), 1645–1660. doi:10.1016/j.future.2013.01.010

Gunasekaran, K., Kumar, V. V., Kaladevi, A. C., Mahesh, T. R., Bhat, C. R., & Venkatesan, K. (2023). Smart Decision-Making and Communication Strategy in Industrial Internet of Things. *IEEE Access : Practical Innovations, Open Solutions, 11*, 28222–28235. doi:10.1109/ACCESS.2023.3258407

Gupta, I. (2019). *CS 425 / ECE 428 Distributed Systems-Introduction to Cloud Computing.* IG.

Gupta, A., Verma, A., & Pramanik, S. (2022). Advanced Security System in Video Surveillance for COVID-19. In *An Interdisciplinary Approach to Modern Network Security, S. Pramanik, A. Sharma, S. Bhatia and D. N. Le.* CRC Press. doi:10.1201/9781003147176-8

Gupta, A., Verma, A., & Pramanik, S. (2022). Security Aspects in Advanced Image Processing Techniques for COVID-19. In S. Pramanik, A. Sharma, S. Bhatia, & D. N. Le (Eds.), *An Interdisciplinary Approach to Modern Network Security.* CRC Press.

Haas, T. C., & Ferreira, S. M. (2015). Federated databases and actionable intelligence: Using social networks analysis to disrupt transnational wildlife trafficking criminal networks. *Security Informatics, 4*(2), 2. doi:10.118613388-015-0018-8

Hamdaqa, M., & Tahvildari, L. (2012). Cloud computing uncovered: A research landscape. *Advances in Computers, 86*, 41–85. doi:10.1016/B978-0-12-396535-6.00002-8

Han, J., Pei, J., & Yan, X.-F. (2004). From sequential pattern mining to structured pattern mining: A pattern-growth approach. *Journal of Computer Science and Technology, 19*(3), 257–279. doi:10.1007/BF02944897

Hao, J., Piechocki, R. J., Kaleshi, D., Chin, W. H., & Fan, Z. (2015). Sparse malicious false data injection attacks and defense mechanisms in smart grids. *IEEE Transactions on Industrial Informatics, 11*(5), 1–12. doi:10.1109/TII.2015.2475695

Haq, A. U., Zhang, D., Peng, H., & Rahman, S. U. (2019). Combining multiple feature-ranking techniques and clustering of variables for feature selection. *IEEE Access : Practical Innovations, Open Solutions, 7*, 151482–151492. doi:10.1109/ACCESS.2019.2947701

Hassan, R. & Ema, R., & Islam, T. (2017). Color Image Segmentation using Automated K-Means Clustering with RGB and HSV Color Spaces. *Global Journal of Computer Science and Technology: F Graphics & Vision, 17*(2).

Hayes, D., Cappa, F., & Cardon, J. (2018). A Framework for More Effective Dark Web Marketplace Investigations. *Information, 9*(8), 186. https://doi.org/10.3390/info9080186

Hazarika, R. A., Maji, A. K., Kandar, D., Jasinska, E., Krejci, P., Leonowicz, Z., & Jasinski, M. (2023). An Approach for Classification of Alzheimer's Disease Using Deep Neural Network and Brain Magnetic Resonance Imaging (MRI). *Electronics (Basel), 12*(3), 3. doi:10.3390/electronics12030676

Hazra, A., Adhikari, M., Amgoth, T., & Srirama, S. N. (2021, November). A Comprehensive Survey on Interoperability for IIoT: Taxonomy, Standards, and Future Directions. *ACM Computing Surveys*, *55*(1), 1–35. doi:10.1145/3485130

Hegland, M. (2007). *The Apriori Algorithm*. CMA, Australian National University.

HeK.ZhangX.RenS.SunJ. (2015). Deep Residual Learning for Image Recognition https://arxiv.org/abs/1512.03385

Hernandez-Castro, J., & Roberts, D. (2015). Automatic detection of potentially illegal online sales of elephant ivory via data mining. *PeerJ. Computer Science*, *0*(0), 1–11. doi:10.7717/peerj-cs.10

Hettiarachchi, R., & Peters, J. F. (2016). *Vorono I Region-Based Adaptive Unsupervised Color Image Segmentation*. Research Gate.

He, Y., Mendis, G. J., & Wei, J. (2017). Real-time detection of false data injection attacks in smart grid: A deep learning-based intelligent mechanism. *IEEE Transactions on Smart Grid*, *8*(5), 2505–2516. doi:10.1109/TSG.2017.2703842

Hoops, S., Nazem, S., Siderowf, A. D., Duda, J. E., Xie, S. X., Stern, M. B., & Weintraub, D. (2009). Validity of the MoCA and MMSE in the detection of MCI and dementia in Parkinson disease. *Neurology*, *73*(21), 1738–1745. doi:10.1212/WNL.0b013e3181c34b47 PMID:19933974

Ho, S. Y.-C., Chien, T.-W., Lin, M.-L., & Tsai, K.-T. (2023). An app for predicting patient dementia classes using convolutional neural networks (CNN) and artificial neural networks (ANN): Comparison of prediction accuracy in Microsoft Excel. *Medicine*, *102*(4), e32670. doi:10.1097/MD.0000000000032670 PMID:36705387

Hosiaisluoma, E. (2021). *ArchiMate Cookbook-Patterns & Examples*. Hosiaisluoma.

Huang, G., Liu, Z., van der Maaten, L., & Weinberger, K. (n.d.). *Densely Connected Convolutional Networks*. https://arxiv.org/abs/1608.06993

Ian, H. (2017). *Witten, EibeFrank,Christopher J. Pal, Data Mining Practical Machine Learning Tools and Techniques* (4th ed.). Willey publishers.

IEEE. (2010). *Survey: Wildlife Trade and Related Criminal Activities Over the Internet*. IEEE.

Ikonomakis, N., Plataniotis, K. N., & Venetsanopoulos, A. N. (2000). Color image segmentation for multimedia applications. *Journal of Intelligent & Robotic Systems*, *28*(1/2), 5–20. doi:10.1023/A:1008163913937

Inthiyaz, S., Prasad, M. V. D., Lakshmi, R. U. S., Sai, N. S., Kumar, P. P., & Ahammad, S. H. (2019). Agriculture based plant leaf health assessment tool: A deep learning perspective. *International Journal of Emerging Trends in Engineering Research*, *7*(11), 690–694. doi:10.30534/ijeter/2019/457112019

Introduction—Free IP Geolocation by geoPlugin. (n.d.). Geoplugin. https://www.geoplugin.com/introduction

Iodice, F., Cassano, V., & Rossini, P. M. (2021). Direct and indirect neurological, cognitive, and behavioral effects of COVID-19 on the healthy elderly, mild-cognitive-impairment, and Alzheimer's disease populations. *Neurological Sciences*, *42*(2), 455–465. doi:10.100710072-020-04902-8 PMID:33409824

Ionita, A. D. (Ed.). (2012). *Migrating Legacy Applications: Challenges in Service Oriented Architecture and Cloud Computing Environments: Challenges in Service Oriented Architecture and Cloud Computing Environments*. IGI Global.

Iqbal, S., & Zulkernine, M. (2018). SpyDroid: A Framework for Employing Multiple Real-Time Malware Detectors on Android. *2018 13th International Conference on Malicious and Unwanted Software (MALWARE)*, (pp. 1-8). IEEE. 10.1109/MALWARE.2018.8659365

Jahn, H. (2013). Memory loss in Alzheimer's disease. *Dialogues in Clinical Neuroscience*, *15*(4), 445–454. doi:10.31887/DCNS.2013.15.4/hjahn PMID:24459411

Jakl, A., Schoffer, L., Husinsky, M., & Wagner, M. (2018), Augmented Reality for Industry 4.0: Architecture and User Experience. In *Proceeding of the 11ᵗʰ Forum Media Technology, CER-WS*, (pp. 38-42). ACM.

Jammalamadaka, S. Q. (2019). Predicting a stock portfolio with multivariate Bayesian structural time series model: do news or emotions matter. *Int. J. Artif. Intell.*

Jandl, C., Nurgazina, J., Schoffer, L., Reichl, C., Wagner, M., & Moser, T. (2019). SensiTrack – A Privacy by Design Concept for Industrial IoT Applications. In *Proceeding of the 24th IEEE International Conference on Emerging Technologies and Factory Automation*, (pp. 1782-1789). IEEE. 10.1109/ETFA.2019.8869186

Jansen, W. A. (2011, January). Cloud hooks: Security and privacy issues in cloud computing. In *2011 44th Hawaii International Conference on System Sciences* (pp. 1-10). IEEE.

Jansen, L. J., & Di Gregorio, A. (2003). Land-use data collection using the "land cover classification system": Results from a case study in Kenya. *Land Use Policy, 20*(2), 131–148. doi:10.1016/S0264-8377(02)00081-9

Javeed, A., Moraes, A. L., Berglund, J., Ali, A., Anderberg, P., & Ali, L. (2023). Predicting Dementia Risk Factors Based on Feature Selection and Neural Networks. *Computers, Materials & Continua, 75*(2), 2491–2508. doi:10.32604/cmc.2023.033783

Jayasingh, R., Kumar, J., Telagathoti, D. B., Sagayam, K. M., & Pramanik, S. (2022). Speckle noise removal by SORAMA segmentation in Digital Image Processing to facilitate precise robotic surgery. *International Journal of Reliable and Quality E-Healthcare, 11*(1), 1–19. Advance online publication. doi:10.4018/IJRQEH.295083

Jeschke, S., Brecher, C., Meisen, T., Ozdemir, D., & Eschert, T. (2017). Industrial Internet of Things and Cyber Manufacturing Systems. In Industrial Internet of Things. Springer.

Jha, K. K., Jha, R., Jha, A. K., Hassan, M. A. M., Yadav, S. K., & Mahesh, T. (2021). A Brief Comparison On Machine Learning Algorithms Based On Various Applications: A Comprehensive Survey. *2021 IEEE International Conference on Computation System and Information Technology for Sustainable Solutions (CSITSS)*, (pp. 1-5). 10.1109/CSITSS54238.2021.9683524

Jhala, Y. V. & Sadhu, A. (2017). *Field Guide for Aging Tigers*. BMC Zoology.

Jia, J., Xu, J., Liu, J., Wang, Y., Wang, Y., Cao, Y., Guo, Q., Qu, Q., Wei, C., Wei, W., Zhang, J., & Yu, E. (2021). Comprehensive Management of Daily Living Activities, behavioral and Psychological Symptoms, and Cognitive Function in Patients with Alzheimer's Disease: A Chinese Consensus on the Comprehensive Management of Alzheimer's Disease. *Neuroscience Bulletin, 37*(7), 1025–1038. doi:10.100712264-021-00701-z PMID:34050523

Joe Abinas, J., Chandolu, H. V. K., Nagabushanam, P., Radha, S., & Krishna, V. M. (2021), Analysis of diabetes patients using classification algorithms. In 2021 10th IEEE International Conference on Communication Systems and Network Technologies (CSNT), (pp. 810–814). IEEE. 10.1109/CSNT51715.2021.9509642

Jonkers, H., Band, I., & Quartel, D. (2012a). *ArchiSurance Case Study*. The Open Group.

Juyal, P., Kulshrestha, C., Sharma, S., & Ghanshala, T. (2020). Common bamboo species identification using machine learning and deep learning algorithms. [IJITEE]. *International Journal of Innovative Technology and Exploring Engineering, 9*(4), 3012–3017. doi:10.35940/ijitee.D1609.029420

K.aushik, D., Garg, M., Annu, Gupta, A. & Pramanik, S. (2021). Application of Machine Learning and Deep Learning in Cyber security: An Innovative Approach. In M. Ghonge, S. Pramanik, R. Mangrulkar and D. N. Le (eds.) *Cybersecurity and Digital Forensics: Challenges and Future Trends*. Wiley.

Kamal, M., Jamaluddin, I., Parela, A., & Farda, N. M. (2019). Comparison of Google Earth Engine (GEE)-based machine learning classifiers for mangrove mapping. In *Proceedings of the 40th Asian Conference Remote Sensing*, (pp. 1-8). ACRS.

Kanade, S., & Manza, R. (2019). A Comprehensive Study on Multi Tenancy in SAAS Applications. *International Journal of Computer Applications*, *181*(44), 25–27. doi:10.5120/ijca2019918531

Kang, W. X., Yang, Q. Q., & Liang, R. P. (2009, March). The comparative research on image segmentation algorithms. In *2009 First international workshop on education technology and computer science* (*Vol. 2*, pp. 703-707). IEEE. 10.1109/ETCS.2009.417

Kang, Y., Na, D.-L., & Hahn, S. (1997). A validity study on the Korean Mini-Mental State Examination (K-MMSE) in dementia patients. *Journal of the Korean Neurological Association*, 300–308.

Kannadasan, K., Edla, D. R., & Kuppili, V. (2019). Type 2 diabetes data classification using stacked autoencoders in deep neural networks. *Clinical Epidemiology and Global Health*, *7*(4), 530–535. doi:10.1016/j.cegh.2018.12.004

Karakostas, B. (2013). A DNS architecture for the Internet of things: A case study in transport logistics. *Procedia Computer Science*, *19*, 594–601. doi:10.1016/j.procs.2013.06.079

Kara, Y. A. B. (2018). Predicting direction of stock price index movement using artificial neural networks and support vector machines: The sample of the Istanbul Stock Exchange. *Expert Systems with Applications*.

Karimipour, H., Dehghantanha, A., Parizi, R. M., Choo, K. K. R., & Leung, H. (2019). A deep and scalable unsupervised machine learning system for cyber-attack detection in large-scale smart grids. *IEEE Access : Practical Innovations, Open Solutions*, *7*, 80778–80788. doi:10.1109/ACCESS.2019.2920326

Karthick Raghunath K. M, V. Vinoth Kumar, V.Muthukumaran, krishna kant singh, Mahesh T R, Akansha Singh, Raghunath, K., Kumar, V., Muthukumaran, V., Sing, K., Mahesh, T. R., & Singh, A., J. Detection And Classification Of Cyber Attacks Using Xgboost Regression And Inception V4. Journal of Web Engineering, *RIVER PUBLISHERS*, *21*(4). doi:10.13052/jwe1540-9589.21413,2022

Karthick Raghunath, K. M., Koti, M. S., Sivakami, R., Vinoth Kumar, V., NagaJyothi, G., & Muthukumaran, V. (2022). Utilization of IoT-assisted computational strategies in wireless sensor networks for smart infrastructure management. *International Journal of System Assurance Engineering and Management*, 1-7.

Karthy, G., Surya Kumar, M., & Gudipadu Bhargav, K. (2021). Medication Alerts and Supervisory of Health Using IOT. *2021 Second International Conference on Electronics and Sustainable Communication Systems (ICESC)*, 4-6.

Karunarathne, S. M., Saxena, N., & Khan, M. K. (2021). Security and privacy in IoT smart healthcare. *IEEE Internet Computing*, *25*(4), 37–48. doi:10.1109/MIC.2021.3051675

Katasonov, A., Kaykova, O., Khriyenko, O., Nikitin, S., & Terziyan, V. (2008). Smart Semantic Middleware for the Internet of Things. In *Proceedings of the 5th International Conference of Informatics in Control, Automation and Robotics*, (pp. 11-15). IEEE.

Kayaer, K. & Yldrm, T. (2003). *Medical diagnosis on pima indian diabetes using general regression neural networks*.

Kearney, H., Yiannakas, M. C., Abdel-Aziz, K., Wheeler-Kingshott, C. A., Altmann, D. R., Ciccarelli, O., & Miller, D. H. (2014). Improved MRI quantification of spinal cord atrophy in multiple sclerosis. *Journal of Magnetic Resonance Imaging*, *39*(3), 617–623. doi:10.1002/jmri.24194 PMID:23633384

Ker, J., Wang, L., Rao, J., & Lim, T. (2019). Deep Learning Applications in Medical Image Analysis. *IEEE Access: Practical Innovations, Open Solutions*, *6*, 9375–9389. doi:10.1109/ACCESS.2017.2788044

Keskinock, P., & Tayur, S. (2001). Quantitive analysis of Internet-enabled supply chain. *Interfaces*, *31*(2), 70–89. doi:10.1287/inte.31.2.70.10626

Kestila, A., Tikka, T., Peitso, P., Kestila, A., Tikka, T., Peitso, P., Rantanen, J., Nasil, A., Nordling, K., Saari, H., Vainio, R., Janhunen, P., Praks, J., & Hallikainen, M. (2013). Aalto-1 nanosatellite – technical description and mission objectives. *Geoscientific Instrumentation, Methods and Data Systems*, *2*(1), 121–130. doi:10.5194/gi-2-121-2013

Khalfay, N. S. (2017). Stock Prediction using Machine Learning a Review Paper. *Int. J. Comput. Appl.*, 975–8887.

Khan, Z., Ni, J., Fan, X., & Shi, P. (2017). An improved k-means clustering algorithm based on an adaptive initial parameter estimation procedure for image segmentation. *International Journal of Innovative Computing, Information and Control*, *13*(5), 1509.

Khanna, K., Panigrahi, B. K., & Joshi, A. (2016). Data integrity attack in smart grid: Optimised attack to gain momentary economic profit. *IET Generation, Transmission & Distribution*, *10*(16), 4032–4039. doi:10.1049/iet-gtd.2016.0350

Khan, R., Khan, S. U., Zaheer, R., & Khan, S. (2012). Future internet: the internet of things architecture, possible applications and key challenges. In *Proceedings of the 10th International Conference on Frontiers of Information Technology (FIT '12)*, (pp. 257–260). IEEE. 10.1109/FIT.2012.53

Khan, S., & Mohiuddin, K. (2018). Evaluating the parameters of ArcGIS and QGIS for GIS Applications. *Int. J. Adv. Res. Sci. Eng*, *7*, 582–594.

Kolanovic, M. a. (2017). Big data and AI strategies: Machine learning and alternative data approach to investing. *J.P. Morgan Global Quantitative & Derivatives Strategy Report*.

Kotsiantis, S. (2006). DimitrisKanellopoulos,Association Rules Mining: A Recent Overview. *GESTS International Transactions on Computer Science and Engineering*, *32*(1), 71–82.

Koudelia, N. (2011). *Acceptance test-driven development*. [Master Thesis, Uuniversity of Jyväskylä].

Krishnasamy, K., & Stoner, S. (2016). *Trading Faces: A Rapid Assessment on the use of Facebook to Trade Wildlife in Peninsular Malaysia*. Traffic Facts. http://www.trafficj.org/publication/16_Trading_Faces.pdf

Krizhevsky A, Sutskever I, & Hinton, G.E. (2012). ImageNet classification with deep convolutional neural networks. *Advances in Neural Information Processing Systems*, *1*, 1097–1105.

Krizhevsky, A., Sutskever, I., & Hinton, G. E. (2012). Imagenet classification with deep convolutional neural networks. *Advances in Neural Information Processing Systems*, *25*.

Kruk, M. E., Gage, A. D., Arsenault, C., Jordan, K., Leslie, H. H., Roder-DeWan, S., Adeyi, O., Barker, P., Daelmans, B., Doubova, S. V., English, M., García-Elorrio, E., Guanais, F., Gureje, O., Hirschhorn, L. R., Jiang, L., Kelley, E., Lemango, E. T., Liljestrand, J., & Pate, M. (2018). High-quality health systems in the Sustainable Development Goals era: Time for a revolution. *The Lancet. Global Health*, *6*(11), e1196–e1252. doi:10.1016/S2214-109X(18)30386-3 PMID:30196093

Kumar, S. S., & Koti, M. S. (2021, December). Efficient Authentication for Securing Electronic Health Records using Algebraic Structure. In *2021 5th International Conference on Electrical, Electronics, Communication, Computer Technologies and Optimization Techniques (ICEECCOT)* (pp. 366-370). IEEE. 10.1109/ICEECCOT52851.2021.9708050

Kumar, S. S., & Koti, M. S. (2022). Adaptive error approximate data reconciliation technique for healthcare framework. *International Journal of System Assurance Engineering and Management*, 1-11.

Kumar, M. S., Inthiyaz, S., Krishna, P. V., Ravali, C. J., Veenamadhuri, J., Reddy, Y. H., & Ahammad, S. H. (2019). Implementation of most appropriate leakage power techniques in vlsi circuits using nand and nor gate. *International Journal of Innovative Technology and Exploring Engineering*, *8*(7), 797–801.

343

Kumar, M. S., Inthiyaz, S., Vamsi, C. K., Ahammad, S. H., Sai Lakshmi, K., Venu Gopal, P., & Bala Raghavendra, A. (2019). Power optimization using dual sram circuit. *International Journal of Innovative Technology and Exploring Engineering, 8*(8), 1032–1036.

Kumar, S. S., & Sanjay, M. (2018). Improved Quality of Patient Care and Data Security Using Cloud Crypto System in EHR. *International Journal of Advanced Studies of Scientific Research, 3*(10). Amru, M., Mahesh, A. V. N., & Ramesh, P. (2020, December). IoT-based Health Monitoring System with Medicine Remainder using Raspberry Pi. []. IOP Publishing.]. *IOP Conference Series. Materials Science and Engineering, 981*(4), 042081.

Kumar, V., Singh, R., & Dua, Y. (2021). Morphologically dilated convolutional neural network for hyperspectral image classification. *Signal Processing Image Communication, 101,* 116549. doi:10.1016/j.image.2021.116549

Kunhuang, H. &. (2006). The application of neural networks to forecast fuzzy time series. *Physical A: Statistical Mechanics and Its Applications.*

Kuramochi, M. & Karypis, G. (2004). An Efficient Algorithm for Discovering Frequent Subgraphs. *IEEE Transactions On Knowledge And Data Engineering, 16*(9).

Lanzi, A. M., Ellison, J. M., & Cohen, M. L. (2021). The "Counseling+" Roles of the Speech-Language Pathologist Serving Older Adults With Mild Cognitive Impairment and Dementia From Alzheimer's Disease. *Perspectives of the ASHA Special Interest Groups, 6*(5), 987–1002. doi:10.1044/2021_PERSP-20-00295 PMID:35647292

Lasi, H., Fettke, P., Kemper, H.-G., Feld, T., & Hoffmann, M. (2014). Industry 4.0. BISE, 6(4):239–242. Lastra, J. L. M. and Delamer, I. M. (2006). Semantic Web Services in Factory Automation: Fundamental Insights and Research Roadmap. *IEEE Transactions on Industrial Informatics, 2*(1), 1–11.

Latif, J., Xiao, C., Imran, A., & Tu, S. (2019). Medical Imaging using Machine Learning and Deep Learning Algorithms: A Review. *2nd International Conference on Computing, Mathematics and Engineering Technologies (iCoMET),* (pp. 1-5). IEEE. 10.1109/ICOMET.2019.8673502

Lazarescu, M. T. (2013). Design of a WSN platform for long-term environmental monitoring for IoT applications. *IEEE Journal on Emerging and Selected Topics in Circuits and Systems, 3*(1), 45–54. doi:10.1109/JETCAS.2013.2243032

LeadingEdge. (2022). Advantages of Cloud Computing. *LeadingEdge.* https://www.leadingedgetech.co.uk/it-services/it-consultancy-services/cloud-computing/advantages-of-cloud-computing/

Lee, B. K., & Pattee, J. (2019). Implications for Hardware Acceleration of Malware Detection. *2019 IEEE 30th International Conference on Application-specific Systems, Architectures, and Processors (ASAP),* (pp. 138-138). IEEE. 10.1109/ASAP.2019.00-14

Lee, H. L., & Billington, C. (1992). Managing supply chain inventories: Pitfalls and opportunities. *Sloan Management Review, 33*(3), 65–77.

Lee, J., Kao, H.-A., & Yang, S. (2014). Service Innovation and Smart Analytics for Industry 4.0 and Big Data Environment. *Procedia CIRP, 16,* 3–8. doi:10.1016/j.procir.2014.02.001

Lefort, L., Henson, C., Taylor, K., Barnaghi, P., Compton, M., Corcho, O., Garcia-Castro, R., Graybeal, J., Herzog, A., Janowicz, K. (2005). *Semantic Sensor Network XG Final Report.* W3C Incubator Group Report. https://www.w3.org/2005/Incubator/ssn/XGR-ssn/

Lesoil, C., Bombois, S., Guinebretiere, O., Houot, M., Bahrami, M., Levy, M., Genthon, R., Bozon, F., Jean-Marie, H., Epelbaum, S., Foulon, P., Villain, N., & Dubois, B. (2023). Validation study of "Santé-Cerveau", a digital tool for early cognitive changes identification. *Alzheimer's Research & Therapy, 15*(1), 70. doi:10.118613195-023-01204-x PMID:37013590

Li, J., Post, M., Wright, T., & Lee, R. (2013). Design of Attitude Control Systems for Cubesat-class Nanosatellite. *Journal of Control Science and Engineering*, *1*, 1–12. doi:10.1155/2013/657182

Li, L., & Horrocks, I. (2004). A software framework for matchmaking based on semantic web technology. *International Journal of Electronic Commerce*, *8*(4), 39–60. doi:10.1080/10864415.2004.11044307

Lim, L. S., Bui, T. D. V., Lau, Z., Tissera, M. S. C., Soon, J. J., Lew, J. M., Aung, H., Ye, C., Low., K. S., Goh, S. T., & Chen, S. S. (2015). *Development and design challenges in VELOX-I nanosatellite*. International Conference on Space Science and Communication (IconSpace), Malaysia. 10.1109/IconSpace.2015.7283826

Li, S., Yılmaz, Y., & Wang, X. (2014). Quickest detection of false data injection attack in wide-area smart grids. *IEEE Transactions on Smart Grid*, *6*(6), 2725–2735. doi:10.1109/TSG.2014.2374577

Litjens, G., Kooi, T., Bejnordi, B. E., Setio, A. A. A., Ciompi, F., Ghafoorian, M., van der Laak, J. A. W. M., van Ginneken, B., & Sánchez, C. I. (2017). Geert Litjens, Thijs Kooi, Babak Ehteshami Bejnordi, Arnaud Arindra Adiyoso Setio & Francesco Ciompi. (2017). A survey on deep learning in medical image analysis. *Medical Image Analysis*, *42*, 60–88. doi:10.1016/j.media.2017.07.005

Li, Y., Guo, J., & Yang, P. (2022). Developing an Image-Based Deep Learning Framework for Automatic Scoring of the Pentagon Drawing Test. *Journal of Alzheimer's Disease*, *85*(1), 129–139. doi:10.3233/JAD-210714 PMID:34776440

Lobov, A., Lopez, F. U., Herrera, V. V., Puttonen, J., & Lastra, J. L. M. (2008). Semantic Web Services framework for manufacturing industries. In *Int. Conf. on Rob. and Biomim.*, (pp. 2104–2108). IEEE.

Lu, T., & Hou, S. (2018). A Two-Layered Malware Detection Model Based on Permission for Android. *IEEE International Conference on Comp.* IEEE. 10.1109/CCET.2018.8542215

Maass, W., Filler, A. (2006). Towards an infrastructure for semantically annotated physical products. *INFORMATIK 2006–Informatik für Menschen–Band 2, Beiträge der 36*. Jahrestagung der Gesellschaft für Informatik eV (GI).

Mabu, S. O. M., Obayashi, M., & Kuremoto, T. (2015). Ensemble learning of rule-based evolutionary algorithm using multi-layer perceptron for supporting decisions in stock trading problem. *Applied Soft Computing*, *36*, 357–367. doi:10.1016/j.asoc.2015.07.020

Madakam, S., Lake, V., Lake, V., & Lake, V. (2015). Internet of Things (IoT): A literature review. *Journal of Computer and Communications*, *3*(05), 164–173. doi:10.4236/jcc.2015.35021

Madankar, A., & Agrawal, A. (2021). IoT based Advance Pill Reminder System for Distinct Patients. *2021 Fifth International Conference on I-SMAC (IoT in Social, Mobile, Analytics and Cloud) (I-SMAC)*, 11-13.

Mahesh, T. R., Dhilip Kumar, V., & Vinoth Kumar, V. (2022). AdaBoost Ensemble Methods Using K-Fold Cross Validation for Survivability with the Early Detection of Heart Disease. Computational Intelligence and Neuroscience.

Mahesh, T. R., Dhilip Kumar, V., & Vinoth Kumar, V. (2022). AdaBoost Ensemble Methods Using K-Fold Cross Validation for Survivability with the Early Detection of Heart Disease. Computational Intelligence and Neuroscience. doi:10.1155/2022/9005278,2022

Mahesh, T. R., Kumar, D., Vinoth Kumar, V., Asghar, J., Mekcha Bazezew, B., Natarajan, R., & Vivek, V. (2022). Early predictive model for breast cancer classification using blended ensemble learning. *Int J Syst Assur Eng Manag.* . doi:10.1007/s13198-022-01696-0,2022

Mahesh, T. R., Kumar, D., Vinoth Kumar, V., Asghar, J., Mekcha Bazezew, B., Natarajan, R., & Vivek, V., (2022). Blended Ensemble Learning Prediction Model for Strengthening Diagnosis and Treatment of Chronic Diabetes Disease. *Computational Intelligence and Neuroscience.* , 2022 doi:10.1155/2022/4451792

Mahesh, T. R., Vivek, V., Kumar, V. V., Natarajan, R., Sathya, S., & Kanimozhi, S. (2022). A Comparative Performance Analysis of Machine Learning Approaches for the Early Prediction of Diabetes Disease. 2022 International Conference on Advances in Computing, Communication and Applied Informatics (ACCAI), (pp. 1-6). IEEE. 10.1109/ACCAI53970.2022.9752543

Mahesh, T. R., Vivek, V., Saravanan, C., & Vinay Kumar, K. (2022) Data Analytics: The Challenges and the Latest Trends to Flourish in the Post-COVID-19. In: Dua M., Jain A.K., Yadav A., Kumar N., Siarry P. (eds) *Proceedings of the International Conference on Paradigms of Communication, Computing and Data Sciences. Algorithms for Intelligent Systems*. Springer, Singapore. 10.1007/978-981-16-5747-4_43

Mahesh, Vinoth Kumar, Muthukumaran, Shashikala, Swapna, & Guluwadi. (2022). Performance Analysis of XGBoost Ensemble Methods for Survivability with the Classification of Breast Cancer. *Journal of Sensors*. doi:10.1155/2022/4649510

Mahesh, S., Mahesh, T. R., & Vinayababu, M. (2010). Using Data Mining Techniques For Detecting Terror-Related Activities On The Web. *Journal of Theoretical and Applied Information Technology*, 16.

Mahesh, T. R., Kumar, V. V., & Lim, S. J. (2023). UsCoTc: Improved Collaborative Filtering (CFL) recommendation methodology using user confidence, time context with impact factors for performance enhancement. *PLoS One*, *18*(3), e0282904. doi:10.1371/journal.pone.0282904 PMID:36921014

Mahesh, T. R., Prabhanjan, S., & Vinayababu, M. (2010). Noise Reduction By Using Fuzzy Image Filtering. *Journal of Theoretical and Applied Information Technology*, 15.

Mahon, B. (2004). *The Man Who Changed Everything: The Life of James Clerk Maxwell*. John Wiley & Sons Ltd.

Maithili, K., Vinothkumar, V., & Latha, P. (2018). Analyzing the Security Mechanisms to Prevent Unauthorized Access in Cloud and Network Security. *Journal of Computational and Theoretical Nanoscience*, *15*(6), 2059–2063. doi:10.1166/jctn.2018.7407

Maktoubian, J., & Ansari, K. (2019). An IoT architecture for preventive maintenance of medical devices in healthcare organizations. *Health and Technology*, *9*(3), 233–243. doi:10.100712553-018-00286-0

Marcek, D. (2014). Forecasting high frequency data: An ARMA-soft RBF networkmodel for time series. *Applied Mechanics and Materials*, *596*, 160–163. doi:10.4028/www.scientific.net/AMM.596.160

Markley, F. L. (2002). Fast Quaternion Attitude Estimation from Two Vector Measurements. *Journal of Guidance, Control, and Dynamics*, *25*(2), 411–414. doi:10.2514/2.4897

Marrella, A. (2018). *Automated Planning for Business Process Management*.

Martínez-Nicolás, I., Llorente, T. E., Martínez-Sánchez, F., & Meilán, J. J. G. (2021). Ten Years of Research on Automatic Voice and Speech Analysis of People With Alzheimer's Disease and Mild Cognitive Impairment: A Systematic Review Article. *Frontiers in Psychology*, *12*, 620251. doi:10.3389/fpsyg.2021.620251 PMID:33833713

Mashal, I., Alsaryrah, O., Chung, T. Y., Yang, C. Z., Kuo, W. H., & Agrawal, D. P. (2015). Choices for interaction with things on Internet and underlying issues. *Ad Hoc Networks*, *28*, 68–90. doi:10.1016/j.adhoc.2014.12.006

Masoud, N. M. (2017). The impact of stock market performance upon economic growth. *International Journal of Economics and Financial Issue*, (pp. 788–798).

Matthew, W., Smith, Sara Seager., Christopher, M., Pong, Matthew, W, Knutson. David W. Miller. (2011). The Exo planet sat mission to detect transiting exoplanets with a cubesat space telescope. *AIAA/USU Conference on Small Satellite*, USA.

McClintock, M. (2020). *The Top 3 Cloud BPM Solutions-Exploring the Workflow Providers Who Think Cloud First.* ProcessMaker. https://www.processmaker.com/blog/top-3-cloud-based-bpm-solutions/

Mehtab, S. S. (December 2019). A robust predictive model for stock price prediction using deep learning and natural language processing. In: *Proceedings of the 7th International Conference on Business Analytics and Intelligence*, Bangalore, India. 10.2139srn.3502624

Mell, P., & Grance, T. (2011). *NIST SP 800-145, The NIST definition of cloud computing. Nat. Inst. Standards Technol.* Tech. Rep.

Meng, X.-H., Huang, Y.-X., Rao, D.-P., Zhang, Q., & Liu, Q. (2013). Comparison of three data mining models for predicting diabetes or prediabetes by risk factors. *The Kaohsiung Journal of Medical Sciences*, 29(2), 9399. doi:10.1016/j.kjms.2012.08.016 PMID:23347811

Mezzi, R., Yahyaoui, A., Krir, M. W., Boulila, W., & Koubaa, A. (2022). Mental Health Intent Recognition for Arabic-Speaking Patients Using the Mini International Neuropsychiatric Interview (MINI) and BERT Model. *Sensors (Basel)*, 22(3), 3. doi:10.339022030846 PMID:35161594

Mhetre, M., & Kumar, L. M. (2021). MedicalEmergency System. *2021 International Conference on Communication information and Computing Technology (ICCICT)*, 25-27.

Ming, D., Zhou, T., Wang, M., & Tan, T. (2016). Land cover classification using random forest with genetic algorithm-based parameter optimization. *Journal of Applied Remote Sensing*, 10(3), 035021. doi:10.1117/1.JRS.10.035021

Mini-Mental State Exam (MMSE) Test for Alzheimer's / Dementia. (n.d.). Dementia Care Central. https://www.dementiacarecentral.com/mini-mental-state-exam/

Minin, E., Fink, C., Hiippala, T., & Tenkanen, H. (2018). *A framework for investigating illegal wildlife trade on social media with machine learning.* NIH.

Minor, M., Montani, S., & Recio-García, J. A. (2014). Process-oriented Case-based Reasoning. *Information Systems*, 40, 103–105. doi:10.1016/j.is.2013.06.004

Mirghani, M., Abobaker, H., Adel, E., & Saeed, A. (2015). Orbit Design of Cube Satellite, *The 10th Scientific Conference of National Center for Research*, Khartoum.

Mirghani, M., TagElsir, A., & Saeed Kajo, A. (2015). Hardware selection for attitude determination and control subsystem of 1U cube satellite. *IEEE International Conference Computing, Control, Networking, Electronics and Embedded Systems Engineering (ICCNEEE).* IEEE.

Miyachi, C. (2018). What is "Cloud"? It is time to update the NIST definition?. *IEEE Cloud computing, 5*(03), 6-11.

Mnih, V. K. K., Kavukcuoglu, K., Silver, D., Rusu, A. A., Veness, J., Bellemare, M. G., Graves, A., Riedmiller, M., Fidjeland, A. K., Ostrovski, G., Petersen, S., Beattie, C., Sadik, A., Antonoglou, I., King, H., Kumaran, D., Wierstra, D., Legg, S., & Hassabis, D. (2015). Human-level control through deep reinforcement learning. *Nature, 518*(7540), 529–533. doi:10.1038/nature14236 PMID:25719670

Moghaddam, S. H., & Abbaspour, M. (2014). Sensitivity analysis of static features for Android malware detection. *2014 22nd Iranian Conference on Electrical Engineering (ICEE)*, (pp. 920-924). IEEE. 10.1109/IranianCEE.2014.6999667

Mokashi, B., Bhat, V. S., & Pujari, J. D. S. (2022). Efficient Hybrid Blind Watermarking in DWT-DCT-SVD with Dual Biometric Features for Images. Contrast Media & Molecular Imaging. doi:10.1155/2022/2918126,2022

Monostori, L. (2014). Cyber-physical Production Systems: Roots, Expectations and R&D Challenges. *Procedia CIRP*, *17*, 9–13. doi:10.1016/j.procir.2014.03.115

Montenegro, G., Kushalnagar, N., Hui, J., & Culler, D. (2007). Transmission of IPv6 packets over IEEE 802.15.4 networks. Internet proposed standard RFC. IEEE.

Moses, J. C., Adibi, S., Shariful Islam, S. M., Wickramasinghe, N., & Nguyen, L. (2021, July). Application of smartphone technologies in disease monitoring: A systematic review. []. MDPI.]. *Health Care*, *9*(7), 889. PMID:34356267

Motaharul Islam, Ridwan, Mary, Siam, Mumu, & Rana. (2020). Design and Implementation of a Smart Bike Accident Detection System. *IEEE Region 10 Symposium (TENSYMP)*.

Mrak, M. (2003). Picture Quality Measures in Image Compression Systems. *EUROCON*, *1*, 233–236.

Müller, G. (2018). Workflow Modeling Assistance by Casebased Reasoning. Springer Fachmedien, Wiesbaden. .

Murkute, A., & Sarode, T. (2015). Forecasting market price of stock using artificial neural network. *International Journal of Computer Applications*, *124*(12), 11–15. doi:10.5120/ijca2015905681

Murphy, T., Kanaber, J., & Koehler, C. (2011). PEZ: expanding CubeSat capabilities through innovative mechanism design. *AIAA/USU Conference on Small Satellite, SSC11-XII-5*, USU.

Muthukumaran, V., Arun, M., Kumar, S. S., Kumta, S. D., Kavitha, M. A., & Vijayaraghavan, R. (2021, July). Secure efficient signature for internet of things over near-ring. []. IOP Publishing.]. *Journal of Physics: Conference Series*, *1964*(2), 022015. doi:10.1088/1742-6596/1964/2/022015

Myla, S., Marella, S. T., Goud, A. S., Ahammad, S. H., Kumar, G. N. S., & Inthiyaz, S. (2019). Design decision taking system for student career selection for accurate academic system. *International Journal of Scientific and Technology Research*, *8*(9), 2199–2206.

Nagageetha, M., Mamilla, S. K., & Hasane Ahammad, S. (2017). Performance analysis of feedback based error control coding algorithm for video transmission on wireless multimedia networks. *Journal of Advanced Research in Dynamical and Control Systems*, *9*(Special Issue 14), 626-660.

Nagarajan, S. M., Deverajan, G. G., Chatterjee, P., Alnumay, W., & Muthukumaran, V. (2022). Integration of IoT based routing process for food supply chain management in sustainable smart cities. *Sustainable Cities and Society*, *76*, 103448. doi:10.1016/j.scs.2021.103448

Nagarajan, S. M., Muthukumaran, V., Vinoth Kumar, V., Beschi, I. S., & Magesh, S. (2021). *Fine Tuning Smart Manufacturing Enterprise Systems: A Perspective of Internet of Things-Based Service-Oriented Architecture, Handbook of Research on Innovations and Applications of AI, IoT, and Cognitive Technologies, IGI Publication, September 2018, USA*. IGI Global Publication. doi:10.4018/978-1-7998-6870-5.ch006

Napoleon, D., Shameena, A., & Santhoshi, R. (2013). Color image segmentation using OTUS method and color space. *International Journal of Computer Applications*.

Narasimhan, R., G., M., & McGlade, C. (2021). Current State of Non-wearable Sensor Technologies for Monitoring Activity Patterns to Detect Symptoms of Mild Cognitive Impairment to Alzheimer's Disease. *International Journal of Alzheimer's Disease*. doi:10.1155/2021/2679398

Narayana, V. V., Ahammad, S. H., Chandu, B. V., Rupesh, G., Naidu, G. A., & Gopal, G. P. (2019). Estimation of quality and intelligibility of a speech signal with varying forms of additive noise. *International Journal of Emerging Trends in Engineering Research*, *7*(11), 430–433. doi:10.30534/ijeter/2019/057112019

NatureServe. (2019). *Comprehensive Study of World's Reptiles: More Than One in Five Reptile Species are Threatened with Extinction.* IUCN.

Nida, M., Zaitoun, Musbah, & Aqel. (2015). Survey on Image Segmentation Techniques. *Procedia Computer Science, 65*, 797 – 806.

Nigussie, A. a. (2017). J. Water Resour. Planning Manage. *Monthly water consumptionprediction using season algorithm and wavelet transform_based model.*

Ning, H., & Wang, Z. (2011). Future internet of things architecture: Like mankind neural system or social organization framework? *IEEE Communications Letters, 15*(4), 461–463. doi:10.1109/LCOMM.2011.022411.110120

Noor, A., Rafiqul I., Kha, Z., & Hasan, M. (2013). Comparative Study of Skin Color based Segmentation Techniques. *International Journal of Applied Information Systems, 5*(10).

Norouzzadeh, M.S., Nguyen, A., Kosmala, M., Swanson, A., Palmer, M., Packer, C., & Clune, J. (2018). Automatically identifying, counting, and describing wild animals in camera-trap images with deep learning. *Proceedings of the National Academy of Sciences of the United States of America.* National Academy. . doi:10.1073/pnas.1719367115

Obthong, M. T. (2020). *A survey on machine learning for stock price prediction: algorithms and techniques.* In: *Proceedings of the 2nd International Conference on Finance, Economics, Management and IT Business, FEMIB 2020*, Prague, Czech Republic. 10.5220/0009340700630071

Ocker, F., Kovalenko, I., Barton, K., & Tilbury, D., and VogelHeuser, B. (2019). A Framework for Automatic Initialization of Multi-Agent Production Systems Using Semantic Web Technologies. *IEEE Robotics and Automation Letters, 4*(4), 4330–4337.

OMG. (2022). *DECISION MODEL AND NOTATION (DMN).* OMG. https://www.omg.org/dmn/

Ormsby, T., Napoleon, E., Burke, R., Groessl, C., & Bowden, L. (2010). *Getting to know ArcGIS desktop.* Esri Press.

Orouskhani, M., Zhu, C., Rostamian, S., Shomal Zadeh, F., Shafiei, M., & Orouskhani, Y. (2022). Alzheimer's disease detection from structural MRI using conditional deep triplet network. *Neuroscience Informatics (Online), 2*(4), 100066. doi:10.1016/j.neuri.2022.100066

Oscar Z., Au, C., Zou, R., Yu, W., & Tian, J. (2010). An adaptive unsupervised approach toward pixel clustering and color image segmentation. *Pattern Recognition, 43*, 1889–1906.

P. Liang, H.-D. Y.-S.-Y.-Z. (Apr. 2018). Transferlearning for aluminium extrusion electricity consumption anomaly detectionvia deep neural network. *Int. J. Comput. Integr. Manu.*

Pal, K. (2018). A Big Data Framework for Decision Making in Supply Chain. IGI Global.

Pal, K. (2020). Information Sharing for Manufacturing Supply Chain Management Based on Blockchain Technology. In I. Williams (Ed.), Cross-Industry Use of Blockchain Technology and Opportunities for the Future. IGI Global. doi:10.4018/978-1-7998-3632-2.ch001

Pal, K., & Ul-Haque, A. (2000). *Internet of Things and Blockchain Technology in Apparel Manufacturing Supply Chain Data Management.* In 11th International Conference on Ambient Systems, Networks and Technologies (ANT-2020), Procedia Computer Science, Warsaw, Poland.

Palanivinayagam, A., & Nagarajan, S. (2020). An optimized iterative clustering framework for recognizing speech. *International Journal of Speech Technology, 23*(4), 767–777. doi:10.100710772-020-09728-5

Pal, K. (2017). Supply Chain Coordination Based on Web Services. In H. K. Chan, N. Subramanian, & M. D. Abdulrahman (Eds.), *Supply Chain Management in the Big Data Era* (pp. 137–171). IGI Global Publication. doi:10.4018/978-1-5225-0956-1.ch009

Pal, K., & Karakostas, B. (2014). A Multi Agent-Based Service Framework for Supply Chain Management, In the proceeding of International Conference on Ambient Systems, Networks and Technology. *Procedia Computer Science, 32,* 53–60. doi:10.1016/j.procs.2014.05.397

Pandey, B. K., Pandey, D., Wairya, S., Agarwal, G., Dadeech, P., Dogiwal, S. R., & Pramanik, S. (2022). Application of Integrated Steganography and Image Compressing Techniques for Confidential Information Transmission. In Cyber Security and Network Security. Wiley. doi:10.1002/9781119812555.ch8

Pandey, P. C., Koutsias, N., Petropoulos, G. P., Srivastava, P. K., & Ben Dor, E. (2021). Land use/land cover in view of earth observation: Data sources, input dimensions, and classifiers—a review of the state of the art. *Geocarto International, 36*(9), 957–988. doi:10.1080/10106049.2019.1629647

Panwar, P. & Gulati, N. (2013). Genetic Algorithms For Image Segmentation Using Active Contours. *Journal of Global Research in Computer Science, 4*(1), 34-37.

Park, H., Kwon, E., & Byon, S. (2021). Emergency Call Fusion Analysis System for Disaster Response. *2021 International Conference on Information and Communication Technology Convergence (ICTC),* 20-22. 10.1109/ICTC52510.2021.9621071

Park, T. Y., Chae, B. G., Jung, H. M., & Oh, H. U. (2014). Conceptual design of electrical power subsystem for cube satellite with permanent magnet attitude stabilization method. *Journal of Aerospace System Engineering, 8,* 42–47.

Patel J, S. S. (2015). Predicting stock market index using fusion of machine learning techniques. *Expert Systems with Applications: An International Journal,* 2162--2172.

Patel, P., Ranabahu, A. H., & Sheth, A. P. (2009). *Service level agreement in cloud computing.* Wright State University.

Pattee, J., & Lee, B. K. (2020). Design Alternatives for Performance Monitoring Counter based Malware Detection. *2020 IEEE 39th International Performance Computing and Communications Conference (IPCCC),* (pp. 1-2). IEEE. 10.1109/IPCCC50635.2020.9391559

Patzelt, F. a. (2017). Universal scaling and nonlinearity of aggregate price impact in financial markets. *Physical Review, 97*(1), 012304. PMID:29448465

Pavel, F. (2011). Grid Database—Management, OGSA and Integration. Academy of Economic Studies Romania Database Systems Journal, 2(2).

Pei-Chann Chang, C.-Y. F.-L. (2011). *Trend discovery in financial time series data using a case based fuzzy decision tree.* Elsevier Science Direct.

Pektaş, A., & Acarman, T. (2020). Learning to detect Android malware via opcode sequences. *Neurocomputing, 396,* 599–608. doi:10.1016/j.neucom.2018.09.102

Peltier, J. W., Schibmwsky, J. A., & Schuhz, D. E. (2002). Interactive Psychographics:Cross-Selling in the Banking Industry". *Journal of Advertising Research, 4*(2), 7–22. doi:10.2501/JAR-42-2-7-22

Pena-opez, I. (2005). *Internet Report 2005.* The Internet of Things.

Peng, Z., Zhong, J., Wee, W., & Lee, J. H. (2006, January). Automated vertebra detection and segmentation from the whole spine MR images. In *2005 IEEE Engineering in Medicine and Biology 27th Annual Conference* (pp. 2527-2530). IEEE.

Peterson, S. (2011). Why it Worked: Critical Success Factors of a Financial Reform Project in Africa. *Faculty Research Working Paper Series.* Harvard Kennedy School.

Pickrell, J. (2006). Introduction: Endangered Species. *News Scientist.* https://www.newscientist.com/article/dn9961-introduction-endangered-species/

Pietruszewski, A. N., & David, A. (2013). Prox-1 Attitude Determination and Control. Center for Space Systems, 10, 25-36.

Pinaki, G., & Mahesh, T. R. (2015). Smart city: Concept and challenges. *International Journal on Advances in Engineering Technology and Science, 1,* 1.

Polat, K., & Gne, S. (2007). An expert system approach based on principal component analysis and adaptive neuro-fuzzy inference system to diagnosis of diabetes disease. *Digital Signal Processing, 17*(4), 702710. doi:10.1016/j.dsp.2006.09.005

Popper, N. (2017). AlphaBay, Biggest Online Drug Bazaar, Goes Dark, and Questions Swirl N Popper. *The New York Times.*

Porshnev, I. R. (2013). Machine Learning in Prediction of Stock Market Indicators Based on Historical Data and Data from Twitter Sentiment Analysis. *IEEE 13th International Conference on Data Mining Workshops.* IEEE.

Porshnev, A. R. (2013). *Machine learning in prediction of stock market indicators based on historical data and data from Twitter sentiment analysis.* In *Proceedings of the IEEE International Conference on Data Mining Workshops,* Dallas, TX, USA. 10.1109/ICDMW.2013.111

Pradhan, D., Sahu, P. K., Goje, N. S., Myo, H., Ghonge, M. M., Rajeswari, R., & Pramanik, S. (2022). Security, Privacy, Risk, and Safety Toward 5G Green Network (5G-GN). In Cyber Security and Network Security. Wiley.

Pradhan, R., Ghose, M. K., & Jeyaram, A. (2010). Land cover classification of remotely sensed satellite data using bayesian and hybrid classifier. *International Journal of Computer Applications, 7*(11), 1–4. doi:10.5120/1295-1783

Pramanik, S. (2022). An Effective Secured Privacy-Protecting Data Aggregation Method in IoT. In M. O. Odhiambo, W. Mwashita, & I. G. I. Global (Eds.), *Achieving Full Realization and Mitigating the Challenges of the Internet of Things.* doi:10.4018/978-1-7998-9312-7.ch008

Pramanik, S. (2022). Carpooling Solutions using Machine Learning Tools. In *Handbook of Research on Evolving Designs and Innovation in ICT and Intelligent Systems for Real-World Applications, K. K. Sarma, N. Saikia and M. Sharma.* IGI Global. doi:10.4018/978-1-7998-9795-8.ch002

Pramanik, S., & Bandyopadhyay, S. (2022). Analysis of Big Data. In J. Wang (Ed.), *Encyclopedia of Data Science and Machine Learning.* IGI Global. doi:10.4018/978-1-7998-9220-5.ch006

Pramanik, S., Galety, M. G., Samanta, D., & Joseph, N. P. (2022). Data Mining Approaches for Decision Support Systems. *3rd International Conference on Emerging Technologies in Data Mining and Information Security.*

Pronk, T., Hirst, R. J., & Wiers, R. W. (2022). *Can we measure individual differences in cognitive measures reliably via smartphones? A comparison of the flanker effect across device types and samples.* Behav Res. doi:10.375813428-022-01885-6

Puttonen, J., Lobov, A., & Lastra, J. L. M. (2013). Semantics-Based Composition of Factory Automation Processes Encapsulated by Web Services. *IEEE Transactions on Industrial Informatics, 9*(4), 2349–2359. doi:10.1109/TII.2012.2220554

Puttonen, J., Lobov, A., Soto, M. A. C., & Lastra, J. L. M. (2010). A Semantic Web Services-based approach for production systems control. *Advanced Engineering Informatics, 24*(3), 285–299. doi:10.1016/j.aei.2010.05.012

Qiao, H., Chen, L., & Zhu, F. (2022). Ranking convolutional neural network for Alzheimer's disease mini-mental state examination prediction at multiple time-points. *Computer Methods and Programs in Biomedicine*, *213*, 106503. doi:10.1016/j.cmpb.2021.106503 PMID:34798407

Qin, Z., Denker, G., Giannelli, C., Bellavista, P., & Venkatasubramanian, N. (2014, May). A software defined networking architecture for the internet-of-things. In 2014 IEEE network operations and management symposium (NOMS) (pp. 1-9). IEEE. doi:10.1109/NOMS.2014.6838365

Rahman, A., Chakraborty, C., Anwar, A., Karim, M. R., Islam, M. J., Kundu, D., Rahman, Z., & Band, S. S. (2022). SDN–IoT empowered intelligent framework for industry 4.0 applications during COVID-19 pandemic. *Cluster Computing*, *25*(4), 2351–2368. doi:10.100710586-021-03367-4 PMID:34341656

Raj Kumar, A., Kumar, G. N. S., Chithanoori, J. K., Mallik, K. S. K., Srinivas, P., & Hasane Ahammad, S. (2019). Design and analysis of a heavy vehicle chassis by using E-glass epoxy & S-2 glass materials. *International Journal of Recent Technology and Engineering*, *7*(6), 903–905.

Rajani Shree, M., & Shambhavi, B. R. (2022). POS Tagger Model for South Indian Language Using a Deep Learning Approach. In A. Kumar & S. Mozar (Eds.), *ICCCE 2021. Lecture Notes in Electrical Engineering* (Vol. 828). Springer. doi:10.1007/978-981-16-7985-8_16

Rajendran, G. B., Kumarasamy, U. M., Zarro, C., Divakarachari, P. B., & Ullo, S. L. (2020). Land-use and land-cover classification using a human group-based particle swarm optimization algorithm with an LSTM Classifier on hybrid pre-processing remote-sensing images. *Remote Sensing (Basel)*, *12*(24), 4135. doi:10.3390/rs12244135

Rajesh, V., Saikumar, K., & Ahammad, S. K. H. (2019). A telemedicine technology for cardiovascular patients diagnosis feature using knn-mpm algorithm. *Journal of International Pharmaceutical Research*, *46*, 72–77.

Ramakrishna, M. T., Venkatesan, V. K., Bhardwaj, R., Bhatia, S., Rahmani, M. K. I., Lashari, S. A., & Alabdali, A. M. (2023). HCoF: Hybrid Collaborative Filtering Using Social and Semantic Suggestions for Friend Recommendation. *Electronics (Basel)*, *12*(6), 1365. doi:10.3390/electronics12061365

Ramakrishna, M. T., Venkatesan, V. K., Izonin, I., Havryliuk, M., & Bhat, C. R. (2023). Homogeneous Adaboost Ensemble Machine Learning Algorithms with Reduced Entropy on Balanced Data. *Entropy (Basel, Switzerland)*, *25*(2), 245. doi:10.3390/e25020245 PMID:36832611

Ramani, RBalasubramanian, L. (2015, June). Retinal blood vessel segmentation employing image processing and data mining techniques for computerized retinal image analysis. *BBE*, *85*, 1–17.

Rani, P., & Bhardwaj, R. (2016). An Approach of Colour Based Image Segmentation Technique for Differentiate Objects using MATLAB Simulation. *International Journal of Advanced Research in Computer and Communication Engineering*, *5*(7), 553-556.

Rao, D., F. D. (2015). Qualitative Stock Market Predicting with Common Knowledge Based Nature Language Processing: A Unified View and Procedure. *7th International Conference on Intelligent Human-Machine Systems and Cybernetics*. IEEE. 10.1109/IHMSC.2015.114

Rashid, A., & Chaturvedi, A. (2019). Cloud computing characteristics and services: A brief review. *International Journal on Computer Science and Engineering*, *7*(2), 421–426.

Rawat, D. B., & Bajracharya, C. (2015). Detection of false data injection attacks in smart grid communication systems. *IEEE Signal Processing Letters*, *22*(10), 1652–1656. doi:10.1109/LSP.2015.2421935

Rawat, V., Joshi, S., Gupta, S., Singh, D. P., & Singh, N. (2022). Machine learning algorithms for early diagnosis of diabetes mellitus: A comparative study. *Materials Today: Proceedings*, *56*, 502–506. doi:10.1016/j.matpr.2022.02.172

Reddy, A. P. C., Kumar, M. S., Krishna, B. M., Inthiyaz, S., & Ahammad, S. H. (2019). Physical unclonable function based design for customized digital logic circuit. *International Journal of Advanced Science and Technology*, *28*(8), 206–221.

RedmonJ.DivvalaS.GirshickR.AliF. Y. O. L. O. (n.d.). Unified, Real-Time Object Detection. https://arxiv.org/abs/1506.02640

Ren, S., He, K., Girshick, R., & Sun, J. (n.d.). *Faster R-CNN: Towards Real-Time Object Detection with Region Proposal Networks*. https://arxiv.org/abs/1506.01497

Richardson, Ch. (2014). *Pattern: Microservices architecture*. Microservices. https://microservices.io/patterns/microservices.html

Rishi, Yede, Kunal, & Bansode. (2020). Automatic Messaging System for Vehicle Tracking and Accident Detection. *2020 International Conference on Electronics and Sustainable Communication Systems (ICESC)*, 2-4.

Roberts, D. & Alfino, S. (2019). *Code word usage in the online ivory trade across four European Union member states*. University of Kent. https://kar.kent.ac.uk/67136/3/Alfino_%252526_Roberts_ivory_code_words_Oryx_revision.pdf

Roberts, D., & Hernandez-Castro, J. (2017). Bycatch and illegal wildlife trade on the dark web. *Oryx*, *51*(3), 393–394. doi:10.1017/S0030605317000679

Rodriguez-Galiano, V. F., Ghimire, B., Rogan, J., Chica-Olmo, M., & Rigol-Sanchez, J. P. (2012). An assessment of the effectiveness of a random forest classifier for land-cover classification. *ISPRS journal of photogrammetry and remote sensing, 67*, 93-104.

Roopashree, S., Anitha, J., Mahesh, T. R., & Vinoth Kumar, V. (2022). An IoT based authentication system for therapeutic herbs measured by local descriptors using machine learning approach. *Measurement, 200.* . doi:10.1016/j.measurement.2022.111484

Rountree, D., & Castrillo, I. (2013). *The basics of cloud computing: Understanding the fundamentals of cloud computing in theory and practice*. Newnes.

Rozi, M. F., Novitasari, D. C., & Intan, P. K. (2018). Brain disease classification using different wavelet analysis for support vector machine (svm). *Proceedings of the International Conference on Mathematics and Islam*. Scite Press. 10.5220/0008523704600465

Russomanno, D. J., Kothari, C. R., & Thomas, O. A. (2005). Building a Sensor Ontology: A Practical Approach Leveraging ISO and OGC Models. In *the 2005 International Conference on Artificial Intelligence*, (pp. 637-643). Research Gate.

Ruta, M., Colucci, S., Scioscia, F., Di Sciascio, E., & Donini, F. M. (2011). Finding commonalities in RFID semantic streams. *Procedia Computer Science*, *5*, 857–864. doi:10.1016/j.procs.2011.07.118

Ruud, J. G. Van Sloun, Regev Cohen & Yonina C. Eldar. (2019). *Deep learning in Ultrasound Imaging*. arXiv: 1907.02994v2.

Sadeg, S., Hamdad, L., Benatchba, K., & Habbas, Z. (2015). BSO-FS: bee swarm optimization for feature selection in classification. In International Work-Conference on Artificial Neural Networks (pp. 387-399). Springer, Cham, Palanivinayagam. doi:10.1007/978-3-319-19258-1_33

Said, O. (2013). *Development of an Innovative Internet of Things Security System, 10*(6), 155–161.

Said, O., & Masud, M. (2013). Towards internet of things: Survey and future vision. *International Journal of Computer Networks*, *5*(1), 1–17.

Saikumar, K., Rajesh, V., Ramya, N., Ahammad, S. H., & Kumar, G. N. S. (2019). A deep learning process for spine and heart segmentation using pixel-based convolutional networks. *Journal of International Pharmaceutical Research*, *46*(1), 278–282.

Sai, M. P. D., Sayadi, H., Makrani, H. M., & Nowzari, C. (2019). "Lightweight Node-level Malware Detection and Network-level Malware Confinement in IoT Networks", *2019 Design* [DATE]. *Automation & Test in Europe Conference & Exhibition*, *2019*, 776–781. doi:10.23919/DATE.2019.8715057

Sakthivel, K., Nallusamy, R., & Kavitha, C. (2014). Color Image Segmentation Using SVM Pixel Classification Image. *World Academy of Science, Engineering and Technology International Journal of Computer, Electrical, Automation, Control and Information Engineering*, *8*(10), 1924–1930.

Sakuldee, RUdomhunsakul, S. (2007). Objective Performance of Compressed Image Quality Assessments. *PWASET*, *26*, 434–443.

Saleem, T. J., Zahra, S. R., Wu, F., Alwakeel, A., Alwakeel, M., Jeribi, F., & Hijji, M. (2022). Deep Learning-Based Diagnosis of Alzheimer's Disease. *Journal of Personalized Medicine*, *12*(5), 5. Advance online publication. doi:10.3390/jpm12050815 PMID:35629237

Sanjab, A., & Saad, W. (2016). Data injection attacks on smart grids with multiple adversaries: A game-theoretic perspective. *IEEE Transactions on Smart Grid*, *7*(4), 2038–2049. doi:10.1109/TSG.2016.2550218

Sarkar, I., Adhikari, M., Kumar, N., & Kumar, S. (2021). Dynamic task placement for deadline-aware IoT applications in federated for networks. *IEEE Internet of Things Journal*, *1*, 2021.

Sarkar, T. K., Mailloux, R. J., Oliner, A. A., Salazar-Palma, M., & Sengupta, D. L. (2006). *History of Wireless*. John Wiley & Sons Inc. doi:10.1002/0471783021

Sarveshvar, M. R., Gogoi, A., Chaubey, A. K., Rohit, S., & Mahesh, T. R. (2021, December). Performance of different machine learning techniques for the prediction of heart diseases. In *2021 International Conference on Forensics, Analytics, Big Data, Security (FABS)* (Vol. 1, pp. 1-4). IEEE. 10.1109/FABS52071.2021.9702566

Sato, K., Niimi, Y., Mano, T., Iwata, A., & Iwatsubo, T. (2022). Automated Evaluation of Conventional Clock-Drawing Test Using Deep Neural Network: Potential as a Mass Screening Tool to Detect Individuals With Cognitive Decline. *Frontiers in Neurology*, *13*, 896403. doi:10.3389/fneur.2022.896403 PMID:35592474

Saxton, W. O., Pitt, T., & Horner, M. (1979). Digital image processing: The Semper system. *Ultramicroscopy*, *4*(3), 343–353. doi:10.1016/S0304-3991(79)80044-3

Scammell, L., & Bo, A. (2016). Online supply of medicines to illicit drug markets: situation and responses. In European Monitoring Centre for Drugs and Drug Addiction (Ed.), The internet and drug markets (Vol. 21). Luxembourg: Publications Office of the European Union.

Schneider, M., Hippchen, B., Abeck, S., Jacoby, M., & Herzog, R. (2018). Enabling IoT platform interoperability using a systematic development approach by example, In *Proceedings of the Global Internet of Things Summit (GIoTS'18)*, (pp. 1-6). IEEE. 10.1109/GIOTS.2018.8534549

Schulman, J. L. S. (2015). Trust region policy optimization. *International conference on machine learning*, (pp. 1889–1897). IEEE.

Seiger, R., Huber, S., & Schlegel, T. (2018). Toward an execution system for self-healing workflows in cyber-physical systems. *Software & Systems Modeling*, *17*(2), 551–572. doi:10.100710270-016-0551-z

Selvin, S. V. (2017). Stock price prediction using LSTM, RNN, and CNN-sliding window model. In. *Proceedings of the IEEE International Conference on Advances in Computing, Communications, and Information,* (pp. 1643–1647). IEEE. 10.1109/ICACCI.2017.8126078

Sharma, K., Mahesh, T. R., & Bhuvana, J. (2021). Big Data Technology for Developing Learning Resources. *Journal of Physics: Conference Series, 1979*(May), 012019. doi:10.1088/1742-6596/1979/1/012019

Sharma, T., Nair, R., & Gomathi, S. (2022). Breast Cancer Image Classification using Transfer Learning and Convolutional Neural Network. *International Journal of Modern Research, 2*(1), 1.

Sharma, V. K. (2019). Time series with sentiment analysis for stock price prediction. *In: Proceedings of the IEEE International Conference on Intelligent Communication and Computational Techniques (ICCT).* IEEE. 10.1109/ICCT46177.2019.8969060

Shashikala, H. K., & Madhuri, G. S. (2021). Image Pre-processing Techniques for X-Ray Medical Images: A Survey. *International Journal of Creative Research Thoughts, 9*(1).

Shashikala, H. K., Madhumala, R. B., Keerthana, C., Priyanka, S., & Meghana, R. (2022). Smart Reminder SOS & Emergency Detection Device. *IEEE International Conference on Distributed Computing and Electrical Circuits and Electronics (ICDCECE).* 10.1109/ICDCECE53908.2022.9793171

Shashikala, H. K., Mahesh, T. R., Vivek, V., Sindhu, M. G., Saravanan, C., & Baig, T. Z. (2021). Early detection of spondylosis using point-based image processing techniques. *Proceedings of the 2021 International Conference on Recent Trends on Electronics, Information, Communication & Technology (RTEICT),* 655–659. 10.1109/RTEICT52294.2021.9573604

Shen, W., Wang, J., & Han, J. (2014). Sequential Pattern Mining. In C. Aggarwal & J. Han (Eds.), *Frequent Pattern Mining.* Springer., doi:10.1007/978-3-319-07821-2_11

shibata K, O. Y. (1997). Reinforcement learning when visual sensory signals are directly given as inputs. *International conference on neural networks,* (pp. 1716–1720). IEEE.

Shrestha, P., Singh, A., Garg, R., Sarraf, I., Mahesh, T. R., & Sindhu Madhuri, G. "Early Stage Detection of Scoliosis Using Machine Learning Algorithms," *2021 International Conference on Forensics, Analytics, Big Data, Security (FABS),* 2021, pp. 1-4, 10.1109/FABS52071.2021.9702699

Sindhu Madhuri, G., & Shashikala, H. K. (2022). Analysis of Medical Images using Image Registration Feature-based Segmentation Techniques. *2nd International Conference on Technological Advancements in Computational Sciences (ICTACS).* 10.1109/ICTACS56270.2022.9987895

Sindhu, M. G., & Shashikala, H. K. (2021). Image Processing Techniques for detecting Extra Growth of Teeth in Medical Images. *Solid State Technology, 64*(2).

Singh, R., & Kaur, L. (2021). Magnetic Resonance Image Denoising using Patchwise Convolutional Neural Networks, *8th International Conference on Computing for Sustainable Global Development (INDIACom),* (pp. 652-657). IEEE. doi: 10.1109/INDIACom51348.2021.00115

Sinha, M., Chacko, E., Makhija, P., & Pramanik, S. (2021). Energy Efficient Smart Cities with Green IoT. In C. Chakrabarty (Ed.), *Green Technological Innovation for Sustainable Smart Societies: Post Pandemic Era.* Springer. doi:10.1007/978-3-030-73295-0_16

SirignanoJ. C. R. (2018). Universal features of price formation in financial markets: perspectives from deep learning. Ssrn, doi:10.2139/ssrn.3141294

Sitthi, A., Nagai, M., Dailey, M., & Ninsawat, S. (2016). Exploring land use and land cover of geotagged social-sensing images using naive bayes classifier. *Sustainability (Basel)*, *8*(9), 921. doi:10.3390u8090921

Sivarasa, A., & Jerew, O. D. (2020). Deep Learning For Minimally Invasive Computer Assisted Surgery. *5th International Conference on Innovative Technologies in Intelligent Systems and Industrial Applications (CITISIA)*, (pp. 1-5). IEEE. 10.1109/CITISIA50690.2020.9371813

Sollund, R. (2016). Wildlife Trafficking in a Globalized World: An Example of Motivations and Modus Operandi from a Norwegian Case Study. In F. M. Angelici (Ed.), *Problematic Wildlife: A crossdisciplinary Approach*. Springer International Publishing. doi:10.1007/978-3-319-22246-2_25

Song, S., Lee, S. Y., Kim, H. R., & Chang, Y. K. (2017). KAUSAT-5 development and verification based on 3U Cube-Sat standard platform. *Journal of the Korean Society for Aeronautical & Space Sciences*, *45*(8), 686–696. doi:10.5139/JKSAS.2017.45.8.686

Souillard-Mandar, W., Penney, D., Schaible, B., Pascual-Leone, A., Au, R., & Davis, R. (2021). DCTclock: Clinically-Interpretable and Automated Artificial Intelligence Analysis of Drawing Behavior for Capturing Cognition. *Frontiers in Digital Health*, *3*, 750661. doi:10.3389/fdgth.2021.750661 PMID:34723243

Srikant, R., & Agrawal, R. (1996). Mining sequential patterns: Generalizations and performance improvements. In *Proc. 5th Int. Conf. Extending Database Technology*. Springer-Verlag.

Srinivasa Reddy, K., Suneela, B., Inthiyaz, S., Kumar, G. N. S., & Mallikarjuna Reddy, A. (2019). Texture filtration module under stabilization via random forest optimization methodology. *International Journal of Advanced Trends in Computer Science and Engineering*, *8*(3), 458–469. doi:10.30534/ijatcsc/2019/20832019

Srivastava, H. (2017). *What Is K-Fold Cross Validation? - Magoosh Data Science Blog*. Magoosh Data Science Blog.

Stojmenovic, I., & Wen, S. (2014). The fog computing paradigm: scenarios and security issues. In *Proceedings of the Federated Conference on Computer Science and Information Systems (FedCSIS' 14)*, (pp. 1–8). IEEE. 10.15439/2014F503

Stroman, P. W., Wheeler-Kingshott, C., Bacon, M., Schwab, J. M., Bosma, R., Brooks, J., Cadotte, D., Carlstedt, T., Ciccarelli, O., Cohen-Adad, J., Curt, A., Evangelou, N., Fehlings, M. G., Filippi, M., Kelley, B. J., Kollias, S., Mackay, A., Porro, C. A., Smith, S., & Tracey, I. (2014). The current state-of-the-art of spinal cord imaging: Methods. *NeuroImage*, *84*, 1070–1081. doi:10.1016/j.neuroimage.2013.04.124 PMID:23685159

Sullivan, D. (2020). *Official Google Professional Cloud Architect-Study Guide*. John Wiley & Sons, Inc.

Swaminathan, J. M. (2000). *Supply chain management*. International Encyclopedia of the Social and Behavioural Sciences, Elsevier Sciences.

T. R. Mahesh, V. Vinoth Kumar, V. Muthukumaran, H. K. Shashikala, B. Swapna, Suresh Guluwadi, "Performance Analysis of XGBoost Ensemble Methods for Survivability with the Classification of Breast Cancer", Journal of Sensors, vol. 2022, Article ID 4649510, 8 pages,. . doi:10.1155/2022/4649510,2022

Taati, A., Sarmadian, F., Mousavi, A., Pour, C. T. H., & Shahir, A. H. E. (2015). Land use classification using support vector machine and maximum likelihood algorithms by Landsat 5 TM images. [WJST]. *Walailak Journal of Science and Technology*, *12*(8), 681–687.

Tahami Monfared, A. A., Byrnes, M. J., White, L. A., & Zhang, Q. (2022). Alzheimer's Disease: Epidemiology and Clinical Progression. *Neurology and Therapy*, *11*(2), 553–569. doi:10.100740120-022-00338-8 PMID:35286590

Taheri, R., Ghahramani, M., Javidan, R., Shojafar, M., Pooranian, Z., & Conti, M. (2020). Similarity-based Android malware detection using Hamming distance of static binary features. *Future Generation Computer Systems, 105*, 230–247. doi:10.1016/j.future.2019.11.034

Tanabe, H., Masuzaki, H., & Shimabukuro, M. (2021). Novel strategies for glycaemic control and preventing diabetic complications applying the clustering-based classification of adult-onset diabetes mellitus: A perspective. *Diabetes Research and Clinical Practice, 180*, 109067. doi:10.1016/j.diabres.2021.109067 PMID:34563587

Taneja, A., Ranjan, P., & Ujjlayan, A. (2015). *A Performance Study of Image Segmentation Techniques, (ICRITO – 2015)*. IEEE.

TasakiS.KimN.TrutyT.ZhangA.BuchmanA. S.LamarM.BennettD. A. (2023). Interpretable deep learning approach for extracting cognitive features from hand-drawn images of intersecting pentagons in older adults. doi:10.1101/2023.04.18.537358

The Open Group. (2011a). *Architecture Development Method.* The Open Group. https://pubs.opengroup.org/architecture/togaf9-doc/arch/chap05.html

The Open Group. (2011b). *TOGAF 9.1*. The Open Group. https://www.opengroup.org/subjectareas/enterprise/togaf.

The Open Group. (2021a). *The Open Group Cloud Ecosystem Reference Model – Using the Cloud Ecosystem Reference Model with the TOGAF Standard (Informative)*. The Open Group. http://www.opengroup.org/cloud/cloud_ecosystem_rm/p5.htm

The Open Group. (2021b). *Cloud Computing for Business*. The Open Group. http://www.opengroup.org/cloud/cloud_for_business/index.htm

Thejas, G. S., Garg, R., Iyengar, S. S., Sunitha, N. R., Badrinath, P., & Chennupati, S. (2021). Metric and accuracy ranked feature inclusion: Hybrids of filter and wrapper feature selection approaches. *IEEE Access : Practical Innovations, Open Solutions, 9*, 128687–128701. doi:10.1109/ACCESS.2021.3112169

Tian, L., Han, L., & Yue, J. (2016). Research on Image Segmentation based on Clustering Algorithm. *International Journal of Signal Processing, Image Processing and Pattern Recognition, 9*(2), 1-12.

TianX.LiuJ.KuangH.ShengY.WangJ.InitiativeT. A. D. N. (2022). MRI-based Multi-task Decoupling Learning for Alzheimer's Disease Detection and MMSE Score Prediction: A Multi-site Validation. https://arxiv.org/abs/2204.01708

Tigga, N. P., & Garg, S. (2020). Prediction of type 2 diabetes using machine learning classification methods [International Conference on Computational Intelligence and Data Science.]. *Procedia Computer Science, 167*, 706–716. doi:10.1016/j.procs.2020.03.336

Togaf-Modeling. (2020). *Application communication diagrams*. Togaf-Modeling.org. https://www.togaf-modeling.org/models/application-architecture/application-communication-diagrams.html

Trad, A. (2022a). Business Transformation Projects: The Integration of Cloud Business Platforms (ICBP). *SCF International Conference on "ontemporary Issues in Social Sciences*. SCF.

Trad, A. (2022c). *Enterprise Transformation Projects-Cloud Transformation Concept–Holistic Security Integration (CTC-HSI)*. IGI Global. doi:10.37394/23205.2022.21.41

Trad, A., & Kalpić, D. (2017). *An Intelligent Neural Networks Micro Artefact Patterns' Based Enterprise Architecture Model*. IGI-Global.

Trad, A., & Kalpić, D. (2019a). *The Business Transformation Framework and Enterprise Architecture Framework for Managers in Business Innovation-Knowledge and Intelligence Driven Development (KIDD)*. Encyclopedia. IGI-Global.

Trad, A., & Kalpić, D. (2020a). *Using Applied Mathematical Models for Business Transformation. IGI Complete Author Book*. IGI Global. doi:10.4018/978-1-7998-1009-4

TroyeeSharmisthaSaha, Bin Hassan, Anjum, & IshfakTahmid. (2020). loT Based Medical Assistant for Efficient Monitoring of Patients in Response to COVID-19. *2020 2nd International Conference on Advanced Information and Communication Technology (ICAICT),* 28-29.

Tsai, C. F., W. S. (2009). Stock price forecasting by hybrid machine learning techniques[. *Proceedings of the International MultiConference of Engineers and Computer Scientists,* (755). IEEE.

Tsamados, A., Aggarwal, N., Cowls, J., Morley, J., Roberts, H., Taddeo, M., & Floridi, L. (2022). The ethics of algorithms: Key problems and solutions. *AI & Society,* *37*(1), 215–230. doi:10.100700146-021-01154-8

Tsou, M. (2017). Research challenges and opportunities in mapping social media and big data. *Cartography and Geographic Information Science,* *42*(sup1), 70–74. doi:10.1080/15230406.2015.1059251

UN. (2019). *Nature Decline Unprecented Report. Sustainable Development.* https://www.un.org/sustainabledevelopment/blog/2019/05/nature-decline-unprecedented-report/

United Nations. (2018). *Nature's Dangerous Decline 'Unprecedented' Species Extinction Rates 'Accelerating': A Framework for More Effective Dark Web Marketplace Investigations.* MDPI. https://www.mdpi.com/2078-2489/9/8/186

Usmani, M., S. H. (2016). Stock Market Prediction Using Machine Learning Techniques. *3rd International Conference On Computer And Information Sciences (ICCOINS).* IEEE. 10.1109/ICCOINS.2016.7783235

van Sloun, R. J. G., Solomon, O., Eldar, Y. C., Wijkstra, H., & Mischi, M. (2017). Sparsity-driven super-resolution in clinical contrast-enhanced ultrasound. *IEEE International Ultrasonic Symposium (IUS),* (pp. 1-4). IEEE. 10.1109/ULTSYM.2017.8092945

Van Uhm, D.P. (2018). The social construction of the value of wildlife: A green cultural criminological perspective. *Theoritical Criminology, 22*(3), 384-401.

Varelas, G., Voutsakist, E., Raftopoulout, P., Petrakis, E. G. M., & Milios, E. (2005). Semantic Similarity methods in WordNet and their application to information retrieval on the Web. In *Proceedings of the 7th annual ACM international workshop on web information and data management.* ACM. 10.1145/1097047.1097051

Venkatesan, V.K., Izonin, I., Periyasamy, J., Indirajithu, A., Batyuk, A., & Ramakrishna, M.T. (2022). Incorporation of Energy Efficient Computational Strategies for Clustering and Routing in Heterogeneous Networks of Smart City. *Energies, 15,* 7524. . doi:10.3390/en15207524,2022

Venkatesan, V. K., Izonin, I., Periyasamy, J., Indirajithu, A., Batyuk, A., & Ramakrishna, M. T. (2022). Incorporation of Energy Efficient Computational Strategies for Clustering and Routing in Heterogeneous Networks of Smart City. [MDPI AG]. *Energies, 15*(20), 7524. doi:10.3390/en15207524

Venkatesan, V. K., Ramakrishna, M. T., Batyuk, A., Barna, A., & Havrysh, B. (2023). High-Performance Artificial Intelligence Recommendation of Quality Research Papers Using Effective Collaborative Approach. *Systems, 11*(2), 81. doi:10.3390ystems11020081

Venkatesan, V. K., Ramakrishna, M. T., Izonin, I., Tkachenko, R., & Havryliuk, M. (2023). Efficient Data Preprocessing with Ensemble Machine Learning Technique for the Early Detection of Chronic Kidney Disease. *Applied Sciences (Basel, Switzerland), 13*(5), 2885. doi:10.3390/app13052885

Vermesan, O., Friess, P., & Guillemin, P. (2011). Internet of things strategic research roadmap in Internet of Things. *Global Technological and Societal Trends, 1,* 9–52.

Vijaykumar, G., Gantala, A., Gade, M. S. L., Anjaneyulu, P., & Ahammad, S. H. (2017). Microcontroller based heartbeat monitoring and display on PC. *Journal of Advanced Research in Dynamical and Control Systems*, 9(4), 250–260.

Vivekananda, G. N., Swathi, R., & Sujith, A. V. L. N. (2021). Multi-temporal image analysis for LULC classification and change detection. *European journal of remote sensing, 54*(sup2), 189-199.

Wang, D., Guan, X., Liu, T., Gu, Y., Shen, C., & Xu, Z. (2014). Extended distributed state estimation: A detection method against tolerable false data injection attacks in smart grids. *Energies*, 7(3), 1517–1538. doi:10.3390/en7031517

Wang, J. H. R., Hou, R., Wang, C., & Shen, L. (2016). Improved v-support vector regression model based on variable selection and brain storm optimization for stock price forecasting. *Applied Soft Computing*, 49, 164–178. doi:10.1016/j.asoc.2016.07.024

Wang, J., Yang, J., Zhang, H., Lu, H., Skreta, M., Husić, M., Arbabi, A., Sultanum, N., & Brudno, M. (2022). PhenoPad: Building AI enabled note-taking interfaces for patient encounters. *NPJ Digital Medicine*, 5(1), 1. doi:10.103841746-021-00555-9 PMID:35087180

Wang, P., Zhang, J. X., Jia, W. J., & Lin, Z. J. (2008, June). A study on decision tree classification method of land use/land cover-Taking tree counties in Hebei Province as an example. In *2008 International Workshop on Earth Observation and Remote Sensing Applications* (pp. 1-5). IEEE. 10.1109/EORSA.2008.4620331

Wang, Q., & Shi, Y. (2019). Machine Learning in Medical Imaging. *IEEE Journal of Biomedical and Health Informatics*, 23(4), 1361–1362. doi:10.1109/JBHI.2019.2920801 PMID:30908957

Wang, Y. Q., & Liu, X. (2015). Improved support vector clustering algorithm for color image segmentation. *Engineering Review*, 35(2), 121–129.

Wang, Y., Amin, M. M., Fu, J., & Moussa, H. B. (2017). A novel data analytical approach for false data injection cyber-physical attack mitigation in smart grids. *IEEE Access : Practical Innovations, Open Solutions*, 5, 26022–26033. doi:10.1109/ACCESS.2017.2769099

Wang, Y., & Wang, C. (2017). High Resolution Remote Sensing Image Segmentation Based On Multi-Features Fusion. *Engineering Review*, 37(3), 289–297.

Wang, Y., & Wu, G. (2014, June). Data mining base noise diagnosis and fuzzy filter design for image processing. *Computers & Electrical Engineering*. doi:10.1016/j.compeleceng.2014.06.010

Wardhani, Anggraini, Anggraini, Hakiem, Shofi, & Rosyadi. (2021). Medicine Box Reminder for Patients with Chronic Disease with IoT-Based Database Monitoring. *2021 9th International Conference on Cyber and IT Service Management (CITSM)*, 22-23.

Wei, J., & Mendis, G. J. A deep learning-based cyber-physical strategy to mitigate false data injection attack in smart grids. In *2016 Joint Workshop on Cyber-Physical Security and Resilience in Smart Grids (CPSR-SG)* (pp. 1-6). IEEE, 2016 10.1109/CPSRSG.2016.7684102

Wei, L., Gao, D., & Luo, C. (2018). False data injection attacks detection with deep belief networks in smart grid. In *2018 Chinese Automation Congress (CAC)* (pp. 2621-2625). IEEE. 10.1109/CAC.2018.8623514

Weyrich, M., & Ebert, C. (2016). Reference architectures for the internet of things. *IEEE Software*, 33(1), 112–116. doi:10.1109/MS.2016.20

Wikipedia. (2022a). *Cloud computing*. The Wikipedia. https://en.wikipedia.org/wiki/Cloud_computing .

Woskowski, C. (2014, September). A pragmatic approach towards safe and secure medical device integration. In *International Conference on Computer Safety, Reliability, and Security* (pp. 342-353). Springer, Cham. 10.1007/978-3-319-10506-2_23

Wu, M., Lu, T. J., Ling, F. Y., Sun, J., & Du, H. Y. (2010) Research on the architecture of internet of things. In *Proceedings of the 3rd International Conference on Advanced Computer Theory and Engineering (ICACTE' 10)*. IEEE.

Wymann, B. E. E. (July 2019). Torcs. *the open racing car simulator*. TORCS. http://torcs.sourceforge.net

Xiao, Y., Wang, J. (2015). Moving Target: tracking online sales of illegal wildlife products in China. *TRAFFIC Briefing Paper*. TRAFFIC..

Xiao, J. R., Gama, B. A., & Gillespie, J. W. Jr. (2007). Progressive damage and delamination in plain weave S-2 glass/SC-15 composites under quasi-static punch-shear loading. *Composite Structures*, 78(2), 182–196. doi:10.1016/j.compstruct.2005.09.001

Xiao, Y. X. (2014). *A multiscale modeling approach incorporating ARIMA and ANNs for financial market volatility forecasting*. J. Syst. Sci. doi:10.100711424-014-3305-4

Xin, Y., Kong, L., Liu, Z., Chen, Y., Li, Y., Zhu, H., Gao, M., Hou, H., & Wang, C. (2018). Machine learning and deep learning methods for cybersecurity. *IEEE Access : Practical Innovations, Open Solutions*, 6, 35365–35381. doi:10.1109/ACCESS.2018.2836950

XuMay, L., Guan, J., & Xiao, Y. (2016). *Wildlife Cybercrime In China*. E-commerce and social media monitoring. (TRAFFIC)

Yamada, Y., Shinkawa, K., Nemoto, M., Nemoto, K., & Arai, T. (2023). A mobile application using automatic speech analysis for classifying Alzheimer's disease and mild cognitive impairment. *Computer Speech & Language*, 81, 101514. doi:10.1016/j.csl.2023.101514

Yamashita, R., Nishio, M., Do, R. K. G., & Togashi, K. (2018). Convolutional neural networks: An overview and application in radiology. *Insights Into Imaging*, 9(4), 611–629. doi:10.100713244-018-0639-9 PMID:29934920

Yan, X., & Han, J. (2002). gSpan: graph-based substructure pattern mining. 2002 IEEE International Conference on Data Mining, (pp. 721-724). IEEE. 10.1109/ICDM.2002.1184038

Yang., W. (July 2009.). *Granule Based Knowledge Representation for Intra and Inter Transaction Association Mining*. Queensland University of Technology.

Yang, C., Wu, G., Ding, K., Shi, T., Li, Q., & Wang, J. (2017). Improving land use/land cover classification by integrating pixel unmixing and decision tree methods. *Remote Sensing (Basel)*, 9(12), 1222. doi:10.3390/rs9121222

Yazgana, P. & Osman, A. (2016). A Literature Survey on Association Rule Mining Algorithms. *Southeast Europe Journal of Soft Computing*. doi:10.21533/scjournal.v5i1.102

Ylimäki, T. (2006). Potential critical success factors for EA. *Journal of Enterprise Architecture*, 2(4), 29–40.

Yoo, P. D., M. H. (2005). Machine Learning Techniques and Use of Event Information for Stock Market Prediction: A Survey and Evaluation. *International Conference on Computational Intelligence for Modelling*, (pp. 835–841). IEEE. 10.1109/CIMCA.2005.1631572

Yoshioka, N., Honiden, S., & Fnkelstein, A. (2004). Security Patterns: A Method for Constructing Secure and Efficient Inter-Company Coordination Systems. In *Proceedings of Enterprise Distributed Object Computing Conference 2004 (EDOC'04)*, (pp. 84–97). IEEE. 10.1109/EDOC.2004.1342507

Young, E. (2003). Biodiversity wipeout facing South East Asia. *News Scientist.* https://www.newscientist.com/article/dn3973-biodiversity-wipeout-facing-south-east-asia/

Young, Q., Burt, R., Watson, M., & Zollinger, L. (2009). *PEARL CubeSat bus building toward operational missions.* Small Satellites Conference from AIAA/Utah State University.

Yu, H., Joshi, P. K., Das, K. K., Chauniyal, D. D., Melick, D. R., Yang, X. U. E. F. E. I., & Xu, J. (2007). Land use/cover change and environmental vulnerability analysis in Birahi Ganga sub-watershed of the Garhwal Himalaya, India. *Tropical Ecology*, *48*(2), 241.

Zanaty, E. A. (2012). Determining the number of clusters for Kernelized fuzzy c-means algorithms for automatic medical image segmentation. *Egyptian Informatics Journal*, *13*(1), 39–58. doi:10.1016/j.eij.2012.01.004

Zeynettin, A., Alfiia, G., Assaf, H., Daniel, R., & Bradley, E. (2017). Deep Learning for Brain MRI Segmentation: State of the Art and Future Directions. *Journal of Digital Imaging*, *30*(4), 449–459. doi:10.100710278-017-9983-4 PMID:28577131

Zhao Z, Voros S, Weng Y & Chang F Li R. (2017). Tracking-by-detection of surgical instruments in minimally invasive surgery via the convolutional neural network deep learning-based method. *Comput Assist Surg (Abingdon), 22.* . doi:10.1080/24699322.2017.1378777

Zhao, J., & Kumar, V. V. (2021). *Handbook of Research on Innovations and Applications of AI, IoT, and Cognitive Technologies.* IGI Global Publication. doi:10.4018/978-1-7998-6870-5

Zhou, P., Li, P., Zhao, S., & Wu, X. (2021). Feature interaction for streaming feature selection. *IEEE Transactions on Neural Networks and Learning Systems*, *32*(10), 4691–4702. doi:10.1109/TNNLS.2020.3025922 PMID:33021946

Zhou, Y., Li, Z., Ma, Y., Yu, C., Chen, Y., Ding, J., Yu, J., Zhou, R., Wang, X., Liu, T., Guo, X., Fan, T., & Shi, C. (2022). The Effect of Propofol versus Sevoflurane on Postoperative Delirium in Parkinson's Disease Patients Undergoing Deep Brain Stimulation Surgery: An Observational Study. *Brain Sciences*, *12*(6), 6. doi:10.3390/brainsci12060689 PMID:35741575

Zinovev, D.,, Duo, Y.,, Raicu, D.,, & Furst, J., G, S., & Armato, G. (2011). Consensus Versus Disagreement in Imaging Research: A Case Study Using the LIDC Database. *Journal of Digital Imaging*, 423–436. PMID:22193755

Zook, M., Barocas, S., boyd, Crawford, K., Keller, E., Gangadharan, S. P., Goodman, A., Hollander, R., Koenig, B. A., Metcalf, J., Narayanan, A., Nelson, A., & Pasquale, F. (2017). Ten simple rules for responsible big data research. *PLoS Computational Biology*, *13*(3), e1005399. doi:10.1371/journal.pcbi.1005399 PMID:28358831

Zubair, A. O. (2006). Change detection in land use and Land cover using remote sensing data and GIS (A case study of Ilorin and its environs in Kwara State). Department of Geography, University of Ibadan.

About the Contributors

Jingyuan Zhao is a research fellow at University of Toronto, Canada. She is a also professor at Beijing Union University (China). She obtained her PhD in Management Science and Engineering from University of Science and Technology of China (China) and completed a postdoctoral program in Management of Technology from University of Quebec at Montreal (Canada). Dr. Zhao's expertise is on management of technology innovation, technology strategy, regional innovation systems and global innovation networks, knowledge management, management information systems, and science and technology policy.

V. Vinoth Kumar is an Associate Professor in the Department of Computer Science and Engineering in MVJ College of Engineering, Bangalore, India. He is a highly qualified individual with around 8 years of rich expertise in teaching, entrepreneurship, and research and development with specialization in computer science engineering subjects. He has been a part of various seminars, paper presentations, research paper reviews, and conferences as a convener and a session chair, a guest editor in journals and has co-authored several books and papers in national, international journals and conferences. He is a professional society member for ISTE, IACIST and IAENG. He has published more than 15 articles in National and International journals, 10 articles in conference proceedings and one article in book chapter. He has filed Indian patent in IoT Applications. His Research interest includes Mobile Adhoc Networking and IoT.

* * *

Anandapriya B. is working as an Associate Professor & Head, Dept of BCA, Patrician College of arts and Science, Chennai, Tamil Nadu, Also Holding the position of Academic Affairs Coordinator, IQAC Convener and SPOC - SWAYAM -NPTEL, More than 22 Years of Experience in College Level teaching .Published articles in Journals and Conferences, Published 2 Text Books Python Programming and IoT and Its Applications.

Megha Gupta Chaudhary is serving as an Assistant Professor in Department of Physics, SRM Institute of Science and Technology, Modinagar, Ghaziabad. She completed her post graduate in physics from IITR, Roorkee followed by M.Tech in VLSI. She obtained her Ph.D. Degree from Gurukula Kangri University, Haridwar. She has 17 years of experience in teaching and research. Her research area includes Atmospheric Physics, Materials, Nanomaterials, Chip designing, Ancient Indian Science. She has many national and international journal publications and patents, 3 book publications to her credit. At present, four research scholars are working under her guidance. She is associated with many national/international academic associations.

V. Geetha obtained her B.Sc. & M.Sc. in Computer Science from Madras University, Tamil Nadu. and Ph.D. in Computer Science with specialization in Internet of Things (IoT) from Galgotias University, U.P., She has 8 Years of teaching experience from reputed institutions in Bangalore. She attended many workshops on "Research Writing skills". She is currently working as Assistant Professor in REVA University, Bangalore. Her area of interest in Computer Networks, Internet Security and the latest disruptive technologies brought her to narrow down her research to IoT Security.

Ankur Gupta has received the B.Tech and M.Tech in Computer Science and Engineering from Ganga Institute of Technology and Management, Kablana affiliated with Maharshi Dayanand University, Rohtak in 2015 and 2017. He is an Assistant Professor in the Department of Computer Science and Engineering at Vaish College of Engineering, Rohtak, and has been working there since January 2019. He has many publications in various reputed national/ international conferences, journals, and online book chapter contributions (Indexed by Scopus, ESCI, ACM, DBLP, etc). He is doing research in the field of cloud computing, data security & machine learning. His research work in M.Tech was based on biometric security in cloud computing.

G Maria Jones is an Assistant Professor, Department of Computer Science and Engineering Under School of Computing at Sathyabama Institute of Science and Technology, Chennai, Tamil Nadu. She has completed her Ph.D in 2022 at Anna University, Chennai. She has published seven research articles in international and also she published six book chapters and one patent. She is an active reviewer for many international journals. Her Area of interest includes Mobile Forensics, Malware Analysis and Mathematical Modelling.

Amandeep Singh K. has completed B.E in Computer Science Engineering in Saveetha School of Engineering, M.Tech Computer Science Engineering in SRM University and pursuing PhD in the domain of Machine Learning in the Department of Computer Science and Engineering of ABET accredited Dr. M.G.R. Educational and Research Institute, Deemed to be University with Graded Autonomous Status, Chennai, India. He also published six papers in International journals, applied for the funded proposal to government funding Agencies.

Sree Vijaya Lakshmi Kothapalli, M.Tech,(Ph.D), LMISTE, is working as an Assistant Professor in the Department of Computer Science and Engineering, Velagapudi Ramakrishna Siddhartha Engineering College, Vijayawada since March 2010 and worked as a Programmer for 15 years in the same Department and College from 1995 to 2010. Pursuing Ph.D. from JNTUK, Kakinada. Awarded a Certificate of Merit from DOEACC Society (Department of Electronics Government of India and Computer Society of India) on 31st July 2002. Number of Publications: 18.

S. Satheesh Kumar received the MCA Post Graduate degree from the Anna University and currently pursuing Ph.D in Visvesvaraya Technological University, Karnataka, India. Currently working as an Assistant Professor & Coordinator in Department of Computer Science, School of Applied Sciences, REVA University with 12 years of teaching experience. He is the author or coauthor of many papers in international refereed journals, Book chapters and many conference contributions. He has given several invited talks at various institutions. His research interests cover several aspects across Network security, Data Mining, Data Security and mainly Internet of Things (IoT). He is the reviewer for many reputed journals

Rajani Shree M. is pursuing her Ph.D. under Visvesvaraya Technological University, Belagavi, Karnataka, India. She is working as an Assistant Professor for the Department of CSE, BNM Institute of Technology, Bengaluru. Her research domain is "Natural Language Processing". She has 6 International conferences, 3 National conferences publications and 2 Scopus indexed International Journals. She is a life member of Indian Society of Technical Education. She has 22 years of teaching experience. The subjects taught are C, C++, Java, Microprocessor 8085, 8086, Unix System Programming, Network Management System, Operating System, Interactive Web Application Development, Information Security, Software Engineering, etc.

Vinaya M. is a Research Scholar under the esteemed guidance of Dr.MooramreddySreedevi, in the Department of Computer Science, Sri Venkateswara University, Tirupati, Andhra Pradesh. I have completed MCA from Osmania University in 2001 and M.Tech (CSE) from JNTU, Hyderabad in 2013. I am qualified; in APSET, I have attended 12 Workshops and FDPs Sponsored by AICTE and SERB DST. I have published 20 research papers in UGC reputed journals and participated in 10 International Conferences. My area of interest is Data Mining. I am a Professional Member in L.M.I.S.T.E., M.I.A.C.S.I.T., M.I.A.E.N.G., M.C.S.T.A., etc

Natasha Renchi Mathew secured MBBS from Sri Ramachandra Institute of Higher Education and Research, Chennai, Tamil Nadu. She loved working with and uniting people and was the student member of the International Student Support Cell of her Institute. She was a member of the Organizing Committee of the National Medical Conference-Optimus. She also spent her time volunteering for MedHope, a social initiative run by interns and medical professionals of SRIHER with the aim of providing relief to Pediatric cancer survivors from poor socio economic backgrounds. She participated in several medical conferences such as Connaisance Medical conference held in JIPMER Pondicherry, India. She presented the poster - "Detection and Treatment of Epilepsy" at Innovation Bazaar 2018, a program for Innovative ideas in Health sciences sponsored by the Indian Council of Medical Research.

Sreedevi Mooramreddy is working as an Associate Professor, in the Department of Computer Science, Sri Venkateswara University, Tirupati, Andhra Pradesh since 2007. She published 92 research papers in UGC reputed journals, participated in 64 International Conferences and 42 national Conferences. She acted as resource person for different universities. She acted as Deputy Warden for Women for 4 years and acted as an EC Member and Lady Representative for 2 years in SVUniversity Teachers Association SV University Tirupati. She is acting as BOS member for UG-Computer Science of Bangalore University in Bengaluru, Karnataka, since 2018

Ramaraj Muniappan is an Assistant Professor Department of Computer Science Rathinam College of Arts and Science Coimbatore-21

S. Nagini, Professor and in CSE, VNRVJIET, Hyderabad, has total teaching experience of 21 years. Her specialized area of research is Data Mining.

Rahul V. Nair is a medical professional currently employed as a medical officer (Grade A) in the Accident and Emergency Department at Royal Oman Police Hospital, Oman. He has 13+ years of experience in medical field. Holding a basic medical degree from Rajeev Gandhi University of Health Sciences, Bangalore, India, he conducted a research project on the relationship between Vitamin C and Blood Pressure during his undergraduate studies, earning him Indian Council of Medical Research (ICMR) student grant award in 2007. Dr Rahul worked as co-investigator in several research projects funded by The Research Council (TRC), Oman. He published many research articles in International Journals and Conferences. His research interests include Neurosciences, Biomedical engineering, Bioinformatics and Robotics surgery.

Sravani Nalluri received the master's degree in computer science and engineering, in 2015.she is currently working as an Assistant Professor with the Department of CSE, VNRVJIET, Hyderabad, India. her areas of interest are Machine Learning and deep learning

V. R. Niveditha completed her B.E in Computer Science Engineering in PB college of Engineering, M.Tech Information Security and Cyber forensics and pursuing doctoral research in the domain of Mobile Security in the Department of Computer Science and Engineering of Dr. M.G.R. Educational and Research Institute, Deemed to be University with Graded Autonomous Status, Chennai, India. She published six articles in the National conferences, 26 papers in refereed International Indexed journals, including ESCI, WoS, SCOPUS, Compendex (Elsevier Engineering Index) to her credit, published 7 Patents and 8 books with ISBN. She has submitted several funded proposals to Government funding Agencies

Rajasekar P. is an Assistant Professor at the Department of Computer Science and Engineering Under the School of Computing at Sathyabama Institute of Science and Technology, Chennai, Tamil Nadu. He received her B.E. degree in the Department of Computer Science and Engineering at Anna University, India, in 2014. An M.E. degree in the Department of Computer Science and Engineering at Anna University, India, in 2016 and a Ph.D. in the Department of Computer Science and Engineering at Anna University, CEG Campus in 2022, Chennai, Tamil Nadu, India. He has published a survey paper on IEEE International Conference, National Conference Proceedings, Reputed SCI Indexed Journal, and Patent. He has organized various Workshops and seminars. He is a reviewer for various Journals. He is a member of a Professional ACM chapter. His current area of research interest includes emotion Distributed systems, Cloud computing, Fog computing, and Operating Systems.

Sherimon P. C. is a faculty member at the Faculty of Computer Studies at the Arab Open University (AOU) in Oman, where he has been teaching, conducting research, and serving in administrative roles. He holds a Ph.D. in Computer Applications from Manonmaniam Sundaranar University, Tirunelveli, Tamilnadu, India. In recognition of his research contributions, Dr. Sherimon has received several awards, including the first National Research award from The Research Council (TRC) of the Government of Oman, making him the first Indian national to receive this award. He also received the Group Research Award from the Arab Open University in 2015, the Best Researcher Award in 2022, and the Research Excellence award in February 2020. Dr. Sherimon has published over 75 research papers in indexed journals such as Springer, Elsevier, and ACM, and has presented papers at various International conferences in countries including the USA, UK, Russia, China, Malaysia, India, Kuwait, Jordan, Dubai, Ajman, and Oman. He has also delivered keynote addresses at various conferences and served as the Chairman and Scientific committee member of various conferences. Dr. Sherimon also serves as a reviewer for The Research Council (TRC), Oman, and other International journals and is the Principal Investigator of many research projects funded by The Research Council of Oman and other funding agencies.

Kamalendu Pal is with the Department of Computer Science, School of Science and Technology, City, University of London. Kamalendu received his BSc (Hons) degree in Physics from Calcutta University, India, Postgraduate Diploma in Computer Science from Pune, India, MSc degree in Software Systems Technology from the University of Sheffield, Postgraduate Diploma in Artificial Intelligence from Kingston University, MPhil degree in Computer Science from the University College London, and MBA degree from the University of Hull, United Kingdom. He has published over hundred international research articles (including book chapters) widely in the scientific community with research papers in the ACM SIGMIS Database, Expert Systems with Applications, Decision Support Systems, and conferences. His research interests include knowledge-based systems, decision support systems, teaching and learning practice, blockchain technology, software engineering, service-oriented computing, sensor network simulation, and supply chain management. He is on the editorial board of an international computer science journal and is a member of the British Computer Society, the Institution of Engineering and Technology, and the IEEE Computer Society.

Santhiya Parivallal is an Assistant Professor, Department of Computer Science and Engineering Under School of Computing at Sathyabama Institute of Science and Technology, Chennai, Tamil Nadu. She received her B.E. degree in Department of Computer Science and Engineering at Anna University, India, at 2015. The M.E. degree in Department of Computer Science and Engineering at Anna University, India, at 2017 and currently pursuing the Ph.D in Department of Computer Science and Engineering at Anna University, CEG Campus, Chennai, Tamil Nadu, India. She has published a survey paper on IEEE International Conference, National Conference Proceedings, Reputed SCI Indexed Journal and Patent. She has organized various Workshops and seminars. She is the reviewer for various Journals. She is a member of a Professional ACM-Women's chapter. Her current area of research interest includes on emotion recognition, signal processing, machine learning, deep learning, electroencephalogram signals and cognitive computing.

Sabyasachi Pramanik is a Professional IEEE member. He obtained a PhD in Computer Science and Engineering from Sri Satya Sai University of Technology and Medical Sciences, Bhopal, India. Presently, he is an Associate Professor, Department of Computer Science and Engineering, Haldia Institute of Technology, India. He has many publications in various reputed international conferences, journals, and online book chapter contributions (Indexed by SCIE, Scopus, ESCI, etc). He is doing research in the field of Artificial Intelligence, Data Privacy, Cybersecurity, Network Security, and Machine Learning. He is also serving as the editorial board member of many international journals. He is a reviewer of journal articles from IEEE, Springer, Elsevier, Inderscience, IET, and IGI Global. He has reviewed many conference papers, has been a keynote speaker, session chair and has been a technical program committee member in many international conferences. He has authored a book on Wireless Sensor Network. He has edited 8 books from IGI Global, CRC Press, Springer and Wiley Publications.

Rajalakshmi R. is working at Arignar Anna College (Arts & Science) Krishnagiri Assist. Professor & Head Department of Computer Science 15 years experienced

C. Prasanna Ranjith is a Teaching Faculty in the department of IT at University of Technology and Applied Sciences-Shinas, Oman since October 2011. During this period, he has served as Quality Assurance Coordinator of IT Department from January 2012 to September 2013 ensuring best practices in teaching and learning. Now being the Chairperson of Department Research Committee from September 2016, he holds the responsibility of planning and implementing various Workshops, Seminars and Conferences towards professional Research and development. Obtained Ph.D. in Computer Science from Bharathidasan University, Trichy, India. His research interests center on improving the performance of routing algorithms in networked computer systems and in Ad Hoc Networks, mainly through the application of Genetic Algorithm.

Reepu is currently working as an Assistant Professor at Chandigarh University.

Sujitha S. is currently Assist Professor in Dr M. G. R Educational and Research Institute, Chennai.

Justus Selwyn is working as a Professor in the Department of Computer Science, John Brown University, AR, USA. He has a Ph.D. in computer science from Chennai, India. Specializing in software engineering and knowledge engineering, Dr. Selwyn has taught at the university level undergraduate and graduate students and project lead at Infosys, Syntel India Ltd., for over 22 years, and has supervised Ph.D. scholars. With hands-on experience in software design and development, he has done several consultancies and research projects in his areas of expertise, which are published in reputed international journals and conferences. He has served as session chairs in several International Conferences, in the US and India, and is serving as Chief Editor in a few International Journals. He has also travelled to Germany, Israel, Singapore and Malaysia as part of his research works, presentations and publications. Presently Dr. Selwyn is working on a funded project in the areas of Artificial Intelligence and Knowledge Visualization.

Khalid Shaikh is a Senior Diabetologist and Specialist Physician in Internal Medicine with keen interest in research and real-world practice in the field of diabetes and Internal Medicine. Practicing since 1989 after completing MBBS, he went on to do Post graduate diploma in Endocrine from University of South Wales UK and a Masters in Diabetes from Cardiff University UK. He has achieved more than 33 years of clinical practice, with over 20 publications in international journals, besides being an external reviewer in developing guidelines on insulin therapy in diabetes for the East African Diabetes Study Group. He is also on editorial board and reviewer for many National and International journals like Diabetes Therapy with Springer and Indian Journal of Endocrine and Metabolism. And a co-editor of "Safe Feasting and Fasting" a monthly newsletter by the South Asian Federation of Endocrine Societies (SAFES) - dedicated to fasting and diabetes in different religion including intermittent fasting.

Vinu Sherimon has been a faculty member at the University of Technology and Applied Sciences, Muscat, Sultanate of Oman since 2004, teaching in the College of Computing and Information Sciences. She holds a Ph.D. in Computer Science from Manonmaniam Sundaranar University, Tirunelveli, Tamilnadu, India. Over the years, she has completed more than 15 research projects funded by The Research

Council (TRC), Oman, and has published several book chapters and peer-reviewed journal articles in various international journals, including Springer, Elsevier, and ACM. Additionally, she has presented research papers at numerous International Conferences and published papers in several conference proceedings. Dr. Vinu is also a reviewer for The Research Council (TRC), Oman, and other international journals. In recognition of her work, a research paper that she co-authored won the first National Research award in Oman in 2014. Her research interests are centered around semantic web, pervasive computing, ontology, big data, blockchain, and data mining.

Somula Ramasubbareddy received the master's degree in computer science and engineering, in 2015, and the Ph.D. degree in computer science and engineering from the VIT University, Vellore, Tamilnadu, India, in 2019.He is currently working as an Assistant Professor with the Department of IT, VNRVJIET, Hyderabad, India. His areas of interest are mobile cloud computing and big data analytics, Machine Learning.

Manik Soni received the bachelors degree in computer science and engineering, in 2021 from VN-RVJIET. His areas of interest are Machine Learning and bib data.

G. Sreeram is a Professor in the Department of Computer Science and Engineering, 14 Years Experience, Expertised in the areas of Blockchain, Cloud Computing, Networks, Security

Antoine Trad is a holder of a Dr degree in computer sciences degree and a Dr degree in business administration (DBA). Actually, I am a professor and a researcher at IBISTM in Europe and the Middle East. My research field's title is: Transformation Projects' Impacts, AI based Mathematical Models and Enterprise Architecture; mainly intended for Managers and Architects in Business Innovation and Transformation Projects. My works are leading in mentioned fields in front of global corporations, which can be verified using google scholar; and I have published more than 300 articles in the mentioned fields. In my research project I work on inspecting AI and enterprise architecture solutions in business and digital transformation projects; in parallel to my academic activities I work as a consultant in transformation and enterprise architecture projects. The Framework that I have developed is a leader in transformation projects' related topics.

Muthukumaran V. was born in Vellore, Tamilnadu, India, in 1988. He received the B.Sc. degree in Mathematics from the Thiruvalluvar University Serkkadu, Vellore, India, in 2009, and the M. Sc. degrees in Mathematics from the Thiruvalluvar University Serkkadu, Vellore, India, in 2012. The M. Phil. Mathematics from the Thiruvalluvar University Serkkadu, Vellore, India, in 2014 and Ph.D. degrees in Mathematics from the School of Advanced Sciences, Vellore Institute of Technology, Vellore in 2019. He has 4 years of teaching experience and 8 years of research experience, and he has published various research papers in high-quality journals Springer, Elsevier, IGI Global, Emerald, River, etc. At present, he has a working Assistant Professor in the Department of Mathematics, REVA University Bangalore, India. His current research interests include Algebraic cryptography, Fuzzy Image Processing, Machine learning, and Data mining. His current research interests include Fuzzy Algebra, Fuzzy Image Processing, Data Mining, and Cryptography. Dr. V. Muthukumaran is a Fellow of the International Association for Cryptologic Research (IACR), India; He is a Life Member of the IEEE. He has published more than 50 research articles and 8 book chapters in peer-reviewed international journals. He has published 10

IPR patents in algebraic with IoT applications. He also presented 25 papers presented at national and international conferences. He has also been a reviewer of several international journals including, Journal of Intelligent Manufacturing (Springer), International Journal of Intelligent Computing and Cybernetics, International Journal of e-Collaboration (IJeC), International Journal of Pervasive Computing and Communications (IJPCC), International Journal of System of Assurance Engineering(IJSA), International Journal Speech Technology (IJST)-Springer, Journal of Reliable Intelligent Environments (JRIE), International Journal of Information Technology and Web Engineering (IJITWE).

Poonam Yadav has done Master's Degree in computer Science and engineering from University of Mumbai, India, and Bachelor's Degree in computer engineering with Distinction from Ch. Shivaji University, India. With experience of 10 years in academic and industry, she worked as assistant professor in reputed educational institutes and as Test Engineer in Software Industry in Netherlands Europe. Currently she is working as Assistant Professor in Reva University. During her tenure in teaching she was responsible for teaching, paper setting, conducting live practical for different subject and valuation process, and in software industry she worked on testing e-games and different gaming devices and systems against the standards established by relevant gaming jurisdictions worldwide.

Index

Recommended Reference Books

IGI Global's reference books are available in three unique pricing formats:
Print Only, E-Book Only, or Print + E-Book.

Order direct through IGI Global's Online Bookstore at
www.igi-global.com or through your preferred provider.

Biomedical and Business Applications Using Artificial Neural Networks and Machine Learning

ISBN: 9781799884552
EISBN: 9781799884576
© 2022; 394 pp.
List Price: US$ 270

Advances in Deep Learning Applications for Smart Cities

ISBN: 9781799897101
EISBN: 9781799897125
© 2022; 335 pp.
List Price: US$ 250

3D Modeling Using Autodesk 3ds Max With Rendering View

ISBN: 9781668441398
EISBN: 9781668441411
© 2022; 291 pp.
List Price: US$ 270

Glocal Policy and Strategies for Blockchain

ISBN: 9781668441534
EISBN: 9781668441558
© 2023; 335 pp.
List Price: US$ 270

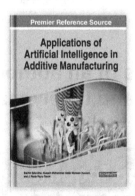

Applications of Artificial Intelligence in Additive Manufacturing

ISBN: 9781799885160
EISBN: 9781799885184
© 2022; 240 pp.
List Price: US$ 270

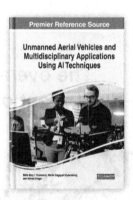

Unmanned Aerial Vehicles and Multidisciplinary Applications Using AI Techniques

ISBN: 9781799887638
EISBN: 9781799887652
© 2022; 306 pp.
List Price: US$ 270

Do you want to stay current on the latest research trends, product announcements, news, and special offers?
Join IGI Global's mailing list to receive customized recommendations, exclusive discounts, and more.
Sign up at: **www.igi-global.com/newsletters.**

Publisher of Timely, Peer-Reviewed Inclusive Research Since 1988

IGI Global
PUBLISHER of TIMELY KNOWLEDGE

www.igi-global.com   Sign up at www.igi-global.com/newsletters   facebook.com/igiglobal   twitter.com/igiglobal   linkedin.com/igiglobal

Ensure Quality Research is Introduced
to the Academic Community

Become an Evaluator
for IGI Global Authored
Book Projects

Premier Reference Source

Tax Audit and Taxation
in the Paradigm of
Sustainable Development

Premier Reference Source

Controlling Epidemics
With Mathematical and
Machine Learning Models

Premier Reference Source

School-Museum
Relationships and
Teaching Social Sciences
in Formal Education

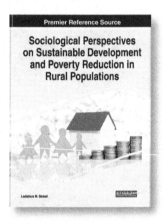

Premier Reference Source

Sociological Perspectives
on Sustainable Development
and Poverty Reduction in
Rural Populations

The overall success of an authored book project is
dependent on quality and timely manuscript evaluations.

Applications and Inquiries may be sent to:
development@igi-global.com

Applicants must have a doctorate (or equivalent degree) as well as publishing, research, and reviewing experience. Authored Book Evaluators are appointed for one-year terms and are expected to complete at least three evaluations per term. Upon successful completion of this term, evaluators can be considered for an additional term.

If you have a colleague that may be interested in this opportunity,
we encourage you to share this information with them.

Easily Identify, Acquire, and Utilize Published Peer-Reviewed Findings in Support of Your Current Research

IGI Global OnDemand

Purchase Individual IGI Global OnDemand Book Chapters and Journal Articles

For More Information:

www.igi-global.com/e-resources/ondemand/

Browse through 150,000+ Articles and Chapters!

Find specific research related to your current studies and projects that have been contributed by international researchers from prestigious institutions, including:

- Accurate and Advanced Search

- Affordably Acquire Research

- Instantly Access Your Content

- Benefit from the InfoSci Platform Features

*"It really provides **an excellent entry into the research literature of the field**. It presents a manageable number of **highly relevant sources** on topics of interest to a wide range of researchers. The sources are **scholarly, but also accessible** to 'practitioners'."*

- Ms. Lisa Stimatz, MLS, University of North Carolina at Chapel Hill, USA

Interested in Additional Savings?

Subscribe to

IGI Global OnDemand *Plus*

Learn More

Acquire content from over 128,000+ research-focused book chapters and 33,000+ scholarly journal articles for as low as US$ 5 per article/chapter (original retail price for an article/chapter: US$ 37.50).

7,300+ E-BOOKS.
ADVANCED RESEARCH.
INCLUSIVE & AFFORDABLE.

IGI Global e-Book Collection

- **Flexible Purchasing Options** (Perpetual, Subscription, EBA, etc.)
- Multi-Year Agreements with **No Price Increases** Guaranteed
- **No Additional Charge** for Multi-User Licensing
- No Maintenance, Hosting, or Archiving Fees
- Continually Enhanced & Innovated **Accessibility Compliance Features** (WCAG)

Handbook of Research on Digital Transformation, Industry Use Cases, and the Impact of Disruptive Technologies
ISBN: 9781799877127
EISBN: 9781799077141

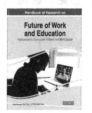

Handbook of Research on New Investigations in Artificial Life, AI, and Machine Learning
ISBN: 9781799886860
EISBN: 9781799886877

Handbook of Research on Future of Work and Education
ISBN: 9781799882756
EISBN: 9781799882770

Research Anthology on Physical and Intellectual Disabilities in an Inclusive Society (4 Vols.)
ISBN: 9781668435427
EISBN: 9781668435434

Innovative Economic, Social, and Environmental Practices for Progressing Future Sustainability
ISBN: 9781799895909
EISBN: 9781799895923

Applied Guide for Event Study Research in Supply Chain Management
ISBN: 9781799889694
EISBN: 9781799889717

Mental Health and Wellness in Healthcare Workers
ISBN: 9781799888130
EISBN: 9781799888147

Clean Technologies and Sustainable Development in Civil Engineering
ISBN: 9781799898108
EISBN: 9781799898122

Request More Information, or Recommend the IGI Global e-Book Collection to Your Institution's Librarian

For More Information or to Request a Free Trial, Contact IGI Global's e-Collections Team: eresources@igi-global.com | 1-866-342-6657 ext. 100 | 717-533-8845 ext. 100

Are You Ready to
Publish Your Research

PUBLISHER of TIMELY KNOWLEDGE

IGI Global offers book authorship and editorship opportunities across 11 subject areas, including business, computer science, education, science and engineering, social sciences, and more!

Benefits of Publishing with IGI Global:

- Free one-on-one editorial and promotional support.

- Expedited publishing timelines that can take your book from start to finish in less than one (1) year.

- Choose from a variety of formats, including Edited and Authored References, Handbooks of Research, Encyclopedias, and Research Insights.

- Utilize IGI Global's eEditorial Discovery® submission system in support of conducting the submission and double-blind peer review process.

- IGI Global maintains a strict adherence to ethical practices due in part to our full membership with the Committee on Publication Ethics (COPE).

- Indexing potential in prestigious indices such as Scopus®, Web of Science™, PsycINFO®, and ERIC – Education Resources Information Center.

- Ability to connect your ORCID iD to your IGI Global publications.

- Earn honorariums and royalties on your full book publications as well as complimentary content and exclusive discounts.

Join Your Colleagues from Prestigious Institutions, Including:

Learn More at: www.igi-global.com/publish

or Contact IGI Global's Aquisitions Team at: acquisition@igi-global.com

Individual Article & Chapter Downloads
US$ 29.50/each

Easily Identify, Acquire, and Utilize Published Peer-Reviewed Findings in Support of Your Current Research

- Browse Over *170,000+ Articles & Chapters*

- *Accurate & Advanced* Search

- Affordably Acquire *International Research*

- *Instantly Access* Your Content

- Benefit from the *InfoSci® Platform Features*

THE UNIVERSITY
of NORTH CAROLINA
at CHAPEL HILL

It really provides **an excellent entry into the research literature of the field.** *It presents a manageable number of* **highly relevant sources** *on topics of interest to a wide range of researchers. The sources are* **scholarly, but also accessible** *to 'practitioners'.*

- Ms. Lisa Stimatz, MLS, University of North Carolina at Chapel Hill, USA

Interested in Additional Savings?

Subscribe to

IGI Global OnDemand *Plus*

Learn More

Acquire content from over 137,000+ research-focused book chapters and 33,000+ scholarly journal articles for as low as US$ 5 per article/chapter (original retail price for an article/chapter: US$ 29.50).

IGI Global Proudly Partners with

Editorial Services

Providing you with High-Quality, Affordable, and Expeditious
Editorial Support from Manuscript Development to Publication

Copy Editing & Proofreading

Perfect your research paper before publication.
Our expert editors will correct faulty spelling,
grammar, punctuation, and word usage.

Scientific & Scholarly Editing

Increase your chances of being published. Our
expert editors will aid in strengthening the quality
of your research before submission.

Figure, Table, Chart & Equation Conversions

Enhance the visual elements of your research. Let
our professional designers produce or correct your
figures before final submission.

Journal Recommendation

Save time and money when you rely on our
expert journal selectors to provide you with a
comprehensive journal recommendation report.

Order now to receive an automatic
10% Academic Discount on all your editorial needs.

Scan the QR Code to Learn More

Upload Your Manuscript, Select Your Desired Editorial Service, and Receive a Free Instant Quote

Email: **customerservice@econtentpro.com**

econtentpro.com